P9-CKG-749

IRELAND'S CIVIL WAR

"Ireland's civil war, though lasting less than ten months, was bitter, bloody and destructive. It cost the country thirty million pounds, left in the wake devastated towns, ruined railways, razed mansions, divided families—and long memories of cruelty, duplicity and betrayal. The difficulties of writing about Ireland, in any way, are enormous. An outsider is accused of being superficial, an Irishman of bias, or of pandering to foreigners. Australian Mr. Younger's well-documented and carefully researched book may offend some widely held beliefs, but it cannot be accused of bias or of superficiality."

Bill Kelly, Sunday Mirror

"A shining tribute to Mr. Younger's industry, care and detachment . . . He vividly describes many of the incidents here and there through the country and thereby assembles an accurate picture of the war."

Joseph Keating, Irish Independent

CALTON YOUNGER

Ireland's
Civil War

FONTANA/Collins

First published by Frederick Muller Ltd 1968
First issued in Fontana Books 1970
Third impression, with revisions, April 1979

Copyright © Calton Younger 1968, 1979

Made and printed in Great Britain by
William Collins Sons & Co Ltd, Glasgow

CONDITIONS OF SALE
This book is sold subject to the condition that
it shall not, by way of trade or otherwise, be lent,
re-sold, hired out or otherwise circulated without
the publisher's prior consent in any form of
binding or cover other than that in which it is
published and without a similar condition
including this condition being imposed on the
subsequent purchaser

FOR DEE

CONTENTS

ILLUSTRATIONS

Eamon de Valera with members of the Irish Delegation in London in July 1921 (*Illustrated London News*)

Irish sympathisers outside 10 Downing Street during the Conference (*Central Press*)

Arthur Griffith, Art O'Brien and Michael Collins arrive at 10 Downing Street to begin Treaty negotiations (*Central Press*)

Lloyd George, Lord Birkenhead and Winston Churchill, British representatives at the Treaty talks (*Central Press*)

Sir Austen Chamberlain, Lord Privy Seal (*Illustrated London News*)

Sir Hamar Greenwood, Chief Secretary for Ireland (*Illustrated London News*)

Erskine Childers, Secretary to the Irish Delegation (*Illustrated London News*)

Collins addressing a gathering at College Green, Dublin, in March 1922 (*Illustrated London News*)

Ratification of the Anglo-Irish Treaty at the Mansion House Dublin (*Illustrated London News*)

Countess Markievicz addressing a Republican Party meeting at Cork in early 1922 (*Illustrated London News*)

De Valera reviewing an I.R.A. contingent at Six Mile Bridge, Co. Clare, in December 1921 (*Central Press*)

Collins and General Mulcahy heading the procession at the funeral of Arthur Griffith (*Illustrated London News*)

Rory O'Connor, who led the seizure of the Four Courts (*Illustrated London News*)

General Emmet Dalton, whose artillery was largely responsible for the surrender of O'Connor's garrison (*Central Press*)

Heavy damage was sustained by the Four Courts during the battle, the dome being shattered by a violent explosion (*Independent Newspapers*)

The Strand Barracks, Limerick, after capture by the National Army (*Illustrated London News*)

Election posters at Ennis, Co. Clare, 1923. (*Central Press*)

AUTHOR'S NOTE

When I was a small boy, I read a story about Ireland's Civil War in an annual—*The Purple Book for Boys*, I think. The heroes, young Republican soldiers on the run in the mountains, had to fight for their lives against an overwhelming force of villainous "Staters". My sympathies were strongly engaged and still lingered when I began this book.

If, in middle age, I plump for law and order and respect for majority rule, I haven't lost my feeling for those young men who could not bring themselves to relinquish, at any cost, the ideal of an Irish Republic for which they had fought mighty Britain to a stalemate. To prevent its eclipse they fought old comrades, even brothers, who, no less concerned for the ideal, had accepted the Anglo-Irish Treaty of December, 1921, in the belief that with the British gone and with peace in the land the Republic, first declared in 1916, would re-emerge.

Sometimes I have wondered at my temerity as an outsider in undertaking a study of Irish history. The Irish writer is steeped in the history of his country, is sensitive to its atmosphere and familiar with its contours, but perhaps to the distant eye the perspective is clearer. Irish friends have instructed me in their traditions and guided me through their lovely land. Patiently they have led me through the complex maze of circumstance that led to civil war. They have helped me to awareness of an atmosphere electric with history and to understanding of the Irish temperament.

They will all challenge some of my ideas and no doubt we shall argue them through many a bottle of good Irish whiskey into the misty hours of the Irish morning. But I hope I have not hurt any of them, nor aggravated residual bitterness. I should like them to think that they have helped towards a work that has some value.

Nomenclature has been a problem. The terms, "Irregulars" and "Staters", used by the adversaries to describe each other, still give offence to some. Except when quoting, I have used the names they preferred for themselves. I have been sparing in the use of ranks, which are rather confusing and were of little significance to most I.R.A. men. Promotions were swift and there were rather a lot of generals. The story is told that when Timothy Healy, first Governor-General of the Irish Free State, was asked by a lady guest at a reception why there were so many generals, he answered, "And why not? Sure, some of their mothers were generals, too."

The Irish remember their heroes by familiar names, not by high-sounding ranks. British General Sir Nevil Macready was indignant when Tom Barry insisted that he be addressed as "Commandant-General". Few Irish would even have known his rank. Those who went on to a career in the regular Army are referred to, of course, in the text and in my acknowledgements, by the ranks they held at retirement.

It is difficult to know how to thank all the people who have helped me. Some lent me treasured documents, photographs, letters and even dispatches scribbled during the fighting. These were invaluable. I should emphasise that opinions expressed are my own. I should like to thank those who provided material but asked to remain anonymous and those who declined to help for their invariable courtesy.

In Ireland, Jim McGarry was my guide and mentor, and he and his wife made me one of the family at their home in Dublin. My first real interest in Irish history stemmed from Larry Slattery, ardent Republican from Tipperary, close friend since our prisoner of war days in Germany. He has encouraged me from beginning to end and kept a kindly, critical and sometimes rueful eye on my efforts. Both he and Jim McGarry obtained material on my behalf.

I am especially grateful to General Sean McEoin, Sean Hendrick of Cork and Frank Carty, all of whom were patient and charming when, more eager than knowledgeable, I sought their help in the beginning. Emmet Dalton, who now lives near London, Dermott MacManus whose home is in Harrogate, General Michael Brennan and Colonels Tommy Ryan, Tony Lawlor and Patrick Paul have all gone to endless trouble to assist me. Dan Breen was splendid. Tom O'Reilly, secretary of the Four Courts Garrison Association, helped me through a difficult patch. Professor Michael Hayes, Patrick McGilligan and that lively writer, Peadar O'Donnell, from their different angles lighted the political picture for me.

John L. O'Sullivan very kindly asked me to join him and

other members of the Kilmichael Memorial Committee after a meeting at Dunmanway, Co. Cork. All made me most welcome and several I was able to meet again. Among them Tom Barry and Neilis O'Driscoll were most helpful. I should like also to record my appreciation of Tom Hales and of John O'Connell of Mallow, both of whom are now dead.

I remember with gratitude the hospitality of Dinny Cronin at lovely Gouganebarra, where Sean Hendrick allowed me to interrupt his fishing holiday, and the warmth of Mrs Jerry Ryan of Clogheen upon whom I called without warning.

Others to whom I owe much are Mrs MacSweeney of Cork, daughter of the redoubtable Joseph O'Sullivan, Patrick O'Connor, T.D., Miss Nora O'Sullivan, Vincent Byrne, Frank O'Friel, Maurice Twomey, Joe Dolan, Mike Stack, Joe McGuinness, James Dwyer of Clonmel, Jack Byrne of Limerick, Jim Doyle, David Moran and Tommy Doyle. Michael Sadleir of Holycross, Thurles, Thady Davern of Donohill, Willie Dwyer and Denis Tuohy of Annacarty and the late Miss Josie Ryan of Grange, Donohill, contributed much and I am grateful.

I wish to thank, too, Mr J. Stewart and his staff at the Belfast Public Libraries, and members of the staffs of the National Library in Dublin, the British Museum Reading Room and Newspaper Library and the Public Record Office in London, all of whom made research a pleasure. Also GAEL LINN for showings of their two contemporary newsreels.

Between them Mrs Lucy Reid and Mrs Margaret Mahon typed the several drafts of this book, patiently accepting time after time the scrapping of meticulously typed chapters and often picking up threads that I had lost. I could not have coped without them.

C.Y.

NOTE FOR THE THIRD IMPRESSION

It has been necessary to up-date the last page or two of the epilogue, otherwise the text remains unaltered. In the revision I have borrowed a little from my own *A State of Disunion* (Fontana, 1972) without, however, attempting an analysis of the situation in Northern Ireland as I did in that work.

11

Some of those whose help I acknowledged in my original "Note" are now dead and I remember them gratefully. I was affected especially by the premature death of Larry Slattery, my wartime friend, and by the passing of Dermott MacManus whose scholarly company was always rewarding. I can now acknowledge, as I could not do in his lifetime, the invaluable criticism and guidance I had from General Richard Mulcahy when I was writing both *Ireland's Civil War* and *A State of Disunion*. General Mulcahy's remarkable collection of papers now belongs to a trust headed by his son, Dr Risteard Mulcahy, and is housed at the National University in Dublin.

October, 1978   C.Y.

ONE

From St Patrick's Hall in Dunmanway on a summer Saturday in 1965 came a group of men, elderly for the most part. They wore their Sunday suits and in their eyes shone the stars of old memories. It was not difficult to picture them in the breeches and gaiters and trench coats they once had worn. There was vigour in their years and the spiritual toughness, which had seen them through turbulent days, was evident in the mould of their faces.

They had met, these men, as the Kilmichael Memorial Committee, to consider how best to furnish a landmark for posterity, to ensure that Michael McCarthy and Jim O'Sullivan and Pat Deasy would never be forgotten.

Before November 28th, 1920, the Auxiliaries, the force which the British Government hoped would put paid to revolution in Ireland, had rampaged the countryside with never a check. Terror was their business and practised exponents of terror they were. Tough, ex-officer adventurers, misleadingly called "cadets", they were braver, more refined than the ruffianly Black and Tan motley, but crueller and just as treacherous. And with fear in their hearts the people had come to think of them as invincible. Where were the valiant Volunteers? Hidden safely away in the lonely valleys or sticking to their lasts in the town no doubt, drilling in secluded fields perhaps, to and froing, up and down, and never raising a gun to stop the shooting and looting, the beatings and burnings with the innocent never knowing when their turn would come.

Then Tom Barry set up his ambush, not in a place he would have chosen, but one dictated by circumstances, a little to the south of Kilmichael on the road to Gleann. It is treacherous, eerie country, where heather grows sparsely in the bogland and the only cover is provided by outcrops of gaunt rock. Barry's plan was brilliantly conceived and his column, only one or two two of whom had fired a shot in anger, matched with courage his inspiration.

Eighteen Auxiliaries in two lorries died that day. Some need not have died but their own treachery recoiled upon them.

13

Crying surrender, they fired again when some of the column showed themselves. Barry was merciless then and his men did not let up until every one of the enemy was dead. And when the morale of his own men showed signs of cracking, he drilled them in the light of the burning lorries until discipline gripped again. Three men he had lost, two of them because of the surrender trick. And one of these was Pat Deasy, sixteen year old brother of the redoubtable Liam. Pat should never have been there at all, for he was ill, and only at the last moment and by subterfuge, had managed to join the column.

It is fitting that Tom Barry, youthful seeming still, should have been among those men who issued from the Committee meeting that day in Dunmanway. Tom Hales, within a few months of his death, was there, too, large and reticent, and John L. O'Sullivan, large and jovial, and Neilis O'Driscoll. And there were others. At the time of Kilmichael they were comrades and theirs was a single purpose. But then came the Truce and the Treaty and, though the purpose remained unshaken in the minds of them all, they pursued paths tragically at variance to achieve it. They fought each other in the way they had learned to fight together. When at last the guns were put away and the ditches were emptied of waiting killers and men no longer hunted each other in the streets of Dublin, in the glens of the countryside or in the caves of Kerry, when the damage had been assessed and the lives of some of Ireland's finest young men had been counted, memories remained of the unforgivable and bitterness was rooted deep.

The men of the Kilmichael Memorial Committee had put bitterness away and gone back to the days of truth. Not long before, Tom Barry had unveiled the memorial to Michael Collins at his birthplace of Sam's Cross in West Cork, and soon afterwards a committee in Dublin arranged for a Mass for the repose of the soul of Cathal Brugha, who died as their enemy and yet was always their friend. And, each year, more and more people make the pilgrimage to Beal na mBlath and there in the bleak valley where Collins fell to the guns of an ambush, remember their lost leader.

Perhaps the greatest achievement of Michael Collins was to die young. What Ireland lost by his death can never be reckoned; it may be that he had already lived his finest days. What she gained was an immortal hero. For the hero who

14

lives sheds his aura; his moment has passed and he is seen to be as ordinary men. But he who dies young is ever young in memory and ever a hero. It is upon the loom of Collins's memory and the memory of all those other hero-patriots who died in their dynamic youth, that Irishmen are weaving the pattern of enduring national unity.

The Irish did not put their guns away when the Truce was signed in case they should need them again. Now there would be endless talk, endless negotiations, and God only knew what the outcome would be. England was not to be trusted; she had deceived them often enough. Crafty Lloyd George might well have hidden in his sleeve an ace that did not belong to the accepted pack. If the talking failed to produce results then the fighting would begin again. The Black and Tans would be back, and the "Auxies", to kill the innocent and burn their homes, to bayonet to death helpless men who were "attempting to escape" and to raze to the ground any village that happened to be in the vicinity of an ambush or a mined road. There would be cheerful English soldiers too, not sure what it was all about, hating the action they had to take against people who spoke, if reluctantly at times, the same tongue as they, and much more prettily.

And the English were not at all sure that the recalcitrant Irish under the prickly de Valera would accept a reasonable solution. The Irish did not put their guns away but at least the English would know in future who was using them. For flushed with their success, which was less than they believed but more than they could ever have hoped for, the legendary young guerrilla fighters, elusive and anonymous until now, emerged from their hiding places, their unsuspected homes, their mundane jobs, and paraded proudly in Dublin. De Valera took the salute in O'Connell Street (Sackville Street as it was then) and English agents prompted by Irish hirelings made lists of names. Gay young patriots junketed round the countryside in hare-brained cars, swinging their guns and setting the hearts of young girls throbbing in their fervent breasts. These boys were heroes. They knew it and made the best of it. Other youths, less enthusiastic when the guns were going off, grabbed weapons to wear as badges and sought a share of reflected glory. The people did not begrudge youth

15

its moment. Many of them, in sheltering the young men of the Irish Republican Army, harbouring them when they were on the run, providing bases for their exploits, travelling with risky dispatches, had been just as heroic as the fighters. Now they were overjoyed that there was peace and they did not wish ever to yield it again. That the offer of a truce had come from the British Cabinet was an indication that England would make concessions—concessions sufficient, they would hope, to enable guns to be put away for all time.

Not all the young men lived for the hedonistic day. Some with careers sadly interrupted bethought themselves of the future, often enough a future with a girl who had bravely waited and, perhaps as a member of *Cumann na mBan* (Irish Women's Organisation), had played a part as hazardous as theirs. And many, preoccupied still with ideals and concerned as to how the Truce would end, continued to train, to practise with their guns, to teach new recruits to use them. But the tension was gone; the tempo had declined; it would be difficult to start again. Michael Collins himself believed that if the fighting began anew the I.R.A. would last no more than a fortnight. The Truce period was long, too long. It was July 8th, 1921, when Sir Nevil Macready, the British C.-in-C., with his automatic bulky in his pocket, strode through cheering Irish crowds into the Mansion House to treat with the Irish leaders; July 11th when the Truce came into force; and it was the night of December 6th when the Treaty that was to sunder the new Ireland and set a gun between friends finally was signed.

In that period of Truce, the twilight of one war and the dawn of another, signs of a crack appeared, signs reflected in the bitter argument among the Irish plenipotentiaries at their London headquarters in Hans Place before, having won a great deal but not quite enough, they finally capitulated to Lloyd George's consummate mixture of cajolery, statesmanlike generosity, sincere but insufficiently grounded promises, plain trickery and the ultimate theatrical threat of "immediate and terrible war".

Though all five members of the delegation signed the Treaty, the hearts of Robert Barton and Gavan Duffy were not in it, Barton's so little that he later repudiated his part, claiming duress. Only Arthur Griffith was absolutely sure that he was doing the right thing and Griffith, as Macready had already noted, was not a man to be swerved from what be believed to be a right course. Michael Collins signed because he saw that the English would concede no more, but that Ireland would be rid of them. If the Irish did not get the Republic they had fought for at least they had won freedom and the Republic would come one day. But grimly he predicted that he would not live to see it. Duggan, the remaining delegate, agreed with Griffith and Collins. Fanatically, Erskine Childers, secretary to the Delegation, fought for rejection. English bred, he never won Irish hearts.

The rift was to be reflected in the Cabinet, in the Dail, in the secret conclaves of the Irish Republican Brotherhood, and in the Irish Republican Army. It should have been foreseen perhaps from the moment when the men of the 1916 Easter Rebellion signed their proclamation of a Republic, not only because civil war tends to follow revolution almost as surely as puberty follows infancy, but because the various strains of opinion had been apparent even then. Revolutions overturn regimes; they do not immediately replace them. Moderates and extremists, realists and idealists unite in common purpose; once they have achieved it they diverge once more. And yet, the Irish Civil War ought to have been fought with words on the floor of the Dail and it could have been. If it had to take place at all, then it should have been on the issue of partition, but it was not upon that issue, or not ostensibly upon that issue. Tragically, no one seemed able to stop the drift towards internecine battle which began during the Truce and was accelerated by the signing of the Treaty. While I.R.A. leaders struggled to reach agreement among themselves, comrades dear to each other began to ignore one another in the streets.

As the British moved out of the posts they had held, local I.R.A. groups took over. Some were in favour of the Treaty, others bitterly opposed to it; all knew very well that the posts they occupied would probably become strongholds against their own countrymen.

Beggar's Bush was the first of the Dublin barracks to be handed over by the British. There was a moving touch of ceremony as the I.R.A., matching the British in smartness, marched triumphantly in. When, a year later, British H.Q., Parkgate, was transferred, there was an amusing moment which Professor Michael Hayes, former Speaker of the Dail, vividly remembers. Under General Richard Mulcahy, Minister for Defence and Commander-in-Chief of the Free State Army, the Dublin Guards marched proudly to take over. Parkgate was the last barracks to be vacated by the British. Outside the gate a British sergeant-major tramped restlessly a few paces one way, a few the other. With the contempt that sergeant-majors have for all living creatures other than their peers, he ignored the presence of the eager, excited crowd. When the Guards arrived the custodian of the gate looked carefully at his watch.

"You're three minutes late," he admonished.

"Blast ye to hell," retorted Sean O'Murthuile before Mulcahy could reply, "you've been here for seven hundred years and three minutes more won't do any harm."

Three minutes was a large concession for an Irishman to make, but it is unlikely that the sergeant-major appreciated that. Even less would he have understood the allusion to the British occupation of all those centuries. He might have said, "We've been in Yorkshire a bloody sight longer than that, but *they* don't want us to get out." Joseph Chamberlain, indeed, had once said much the same thing in the House of Commons. Acutely aware of their own nationality, the British have only with reluctance recognised the sovereign aspirations of other people. In frustrating them they have strewn martyrs all the way through history. Recently the leader of a newly independent African state said, very simply, that it was only "humanness" for people to wish to govern themselves, and whether or not they were capable of doing so in the opinion of others was irrelevant. In Ireland's case there was no question of the fitness of the people to govern. After all, they had sent a large contingent of members to Westminster for years, and, from the Renunciation Act of 1783 until the egregious Act of Union was purchased with titles, hard cash and Pitt's unfulfilled promise of Catholic emancipation in 1800, Ireland had had a Parliament of her own, with Dublin as a roaringly resplendent capital. True, the set-up was corrupt and in the hands of the "ascendancy", and surrounding the gay lights blazing for the young bloods were purlieus dark with poverty. True the Irish were scarcely better represented immediately after the Union than they had been before, but time was to throw up some splendid leaders. If John Bull had treated Cathleen ni Houlihan with consideration when he took her to wife, all might have been well. But he was domineering and stupid and an occasional kindness when he was in a good humour was not enough to evoke the loyalty he took as his right. Too spirited to be cowed for long, she soon cried for a separation, and little wonder.

Wise old Gladstone sought to give her a measure of freedom but was thwarted. Twice, in 1886 and 1892, his Home Rule Bills were thrown out, the first by the Commons, the second by the Lords. Some freedom to run her own life then might well have saved the annulment that, in the end, Cathleen ni Houlihan was to compel upon her obtuse spouse.

Revolutions never spring from suppressed peoples. Only when the pressure is eased do they find their voices, throw up barricades and look for weapons. In Ireland the pressure had been eased, especially by the Conservatives with their "Kill Home Rule with kindness"[1] policy of the first years of the new century and, in particular, the land reforms put through by that enlightened Chief Secretary for Ireland, George Wyndham. At the same time, Tom Clarke returned from sixteen years in English jails and breathed new vitality into the Irish Republican Brotherhood, which had been formed first in 1856 as part of the Fenian organisation begun in America by Irish patriots in exile after the rising of 1848. After years of inertia it was in the process of being resuscitated, ironically perhaps, in the North by McCullough, Bulmer Hobson and Sean MacDermott. MacDermott, transferring to Dublin, revived the Brotherhood there but it was Clarke with his great reputation who gave it real momentum again. The Brotherhood was a physical force movement in direct descent from Wolfe Tone's United Irishmen who had rebelled in 1798. *Sinn Fein*, "Ourselves" founded in 1905 by Arthur Griffith, was not. This, a fusion of Griffith's own *Cumann na nGaedheal*, then eight years old and another separatist organisation, the Dungannon Clubs—under cover of which MacDermott and his friends had worked for a time—inevitably was caught in the tide of revolutionary violence. Its name was to become the symbol of

1 Like so many aphorisms this was lifted out of context. The original comment, from Gerald Balfour, was that it was not possible to kill Home Rule with kindness but that he, as Chief Secretary, would try to ameliorate the lot of the people.

the physical force movement in Ireland, but in the beginning it gave political shape to the fervent but inchoate separatist ideal.

The ideal had sprung, as such ideals frequently do, from a resurgence of indigenous culture. In 1893 the Gaelic League came into being to revive the dying Gaelic language and drew into its quick spread poets and dramatists, among them Yeats, Synge and Lady Gregory. The rediscovery of the language by the intellectuals, a growing awareness of history, never buried very deep in the Irish mind, the patriotic blaze of poetry evoked pride in all that was Irish and threw into clear relief the alien irritant that prevented the natural expression of it. Concomitantly the Gaelic Athletic Association, born at Thurles in 1884, worked to popularise Irish native games and to exclude foreign importations. The athletes and the aesthetes both aimed at reviving a truly Irish spirit. But national culture can flourish only in a national political setting and the idealism of the poets and the exuberance of the hurley players soon overspilled into the political field where Sinn Fein was waiting to channel the flow and the Irish Republican Brotherhood to power-pump it to its destination. But workers were needed in the field too. They were soon to appear. On November 25th, 1913, Eoin MacNeill, a mainstay of the Gaelic League, proposed to a vast meeting in the Rotunda in Dublin the formation of a force of volunteers "to secure and maintain the rights and liberties common to all the people of Ireland". The majority of the young Irishmen who welcomed the idea so enthusiastically, among them future leaders like Eamon de Valera, did not know—nor did MacNeill himself know—that behind MacNeill was the potent Irish Republican Brotherhood. And they did not care that the meeting was held without the knowledge of Redmond, leader of the Irish Nationalists at Westminster, who, adroitly but perfectly legitimately, had bought the Home Rule Bill of 1912 from the Liberals with the votes of his party.

The Irish Volunteers were not the first force of this kind in the country. In the North the Ulster Volunteers were already in existence, pledged to maintain the Union and to defeat, at whatever cost, Home Rule for Ireland. The Liberal Government had countenanced the militant Ulster Volunteers who were commanded nominally by Sir George Richardson, a retired general, but were, in essence, the striking arm of Sir

Edward Carson and his loyal lieutenant, James Craig. Supporting them was no less a person than Bonar Law, leader of the Conservative Party, who could "imagine no length of resistance to which Ulster will go in which I shall not be ready to support them", a minatory utterance which not only bespoke the ferocity the Irish question engendered in the political arena of the day but postulated that treason was excusable if a view were strongly enough held. The lesson was noted by those who held strong views in the South, but when the leaders of the Easter Rising were tried, and Roger Casement prosecuted, the length of *their* resistance found few supporters at Westminster.

Belated and half-hearted though it was, the third Home Rule Bill went close to satisfying the national aspirations of the majority of the Irish at the time. Many simple country folk scarcely knew what Home Rule was, but they were, all unknowingly, on the threshold of political education, and from their sons came many of the fighting leaders of the revolution a few short years later. Of those who were already politically aware, a majority of the whole country wanted Home Rule for Ireland, for the whole of Ireland. Ireland was an entity and the idea of partitioning it had entered no one's head. Those who opposed Home Rule, the Unionists of both North and South, opposed it for the whole country. Even in the four counties of Derry, Down, Antrim and Armagh, where alone there was a definite majority in favour of continuance of the Union, there was no thought of separation. No one took very seriously an amendment to the Bill moved by T. G. R. Agar-Roberts to exclude these four of the nine Ulster Counties from its operation.

So long as the House of Lords had enjoyed the power to veto Commons Bills, Home Rule for Ireland was a pipe-dream. The peers from the backwoods would flock to Westminster and crush such a bill like a cockroach. But the Parliament Act of 1911 opened the way to Redmond to push Asquith, who needed the 86 Irish votes to stay in power, into introducing a Home Rule Bill. The Parliament Act provided new machinery to resolve deadlocks between the two Houses. The Lords could reject a bill twice, but once it had passed through the Commons a third time, the peers were impotent.

Asquith's Bill, introduced in the summer of 1912, passed through the Commons for a third time in May, 1914. It required only Royal assent and would become law if Ireland, and perhaps England herself, did not dissolve in civil war first over this very issue. The fact was that England had lost her chance in 1906 when the Liberals were returned to Westminster with a massive majority. Though pledged to give Ireland some form of self-government, they drew back for fear of the Conservatives of England, many with a stake in Irish soil, and the Protestants of Ulster, a breed of people as obstinate as any on earth. Instead, they poured money into the country in the hope that benevolence would be accepted as a substitute for self-government. It was not. Canny country people invented famine after famine to qualify for a share of the largesse, but the money brought no loyalty, for was it not the will of God that inspired the rich to help the poor? And for the Irish who looked further than the satisfaction of primary needs nothing would do but the elimination of Dublin Castle, a monstrous administrative jellyfish that splurged over the whole of Ireland and controlled every aspect of Irish life.

The Home Rule Bill, though pleasing enough to the majority, had come too late as things turned out. Even before it passed the Commons, Carson had organised his private army and had obtained the signatures of 200,000 to his Ulster Covenant. Some of the signatories, recalling the mystique of boyhood games, signed with their own blood. Carson, big, powerful, fullblooded, persuasive barrister and penetrating orator, won the admiration of the southern Irish. He had been born in the South himself. They liked the way he exuberantly defied the Imperial Parliament, of which he was a member, with every prospect of success. He underlined the point, which had been almost overlooked, that if anything was to be won from Britain a little well organised violence was the way to do it. The one regret of the southern Irish was that so tenacious a fighter was not on their side. But they learned from him and the Irish Volunteers followed the Ulster Volunteers into existence like the second of twins.

Taking advantage of a loophole in the law, the Ulster Volunteers were openly drilling under arms. Asquith's Liberal Government certainly did not approve, but took no active steps against them. But they moved swiftly when the Irish

Volunteer movement rapidly caught on, not least in Ulster, and only a week after its inception proclaimed the importation of arms into Ireland. Like small boys enjoying forbidden cigarettes, both sets of volunteers went in for gun-running. It was easier for the northerners, for they had both money and the under-the-counter approval of many officials. On April 24th, 1914, officialdom slept through the hullabaloo of the landing of a huge cargo of rifles and ammunition at Larne. Lacking the money and the organisation, the Irish Volunteers managed to slip in only occasional small parcels of weapons until a committee in London under the chairmanship of Mrs Alice Stopford Green solved the problem for them. In July, Erskine Childers, his American wife who was to play an influential but enigmatic part in Irish affairs, and Mary Spring Rice, daughter of Lord Monteagle, landed a consignment of arms at Howth. Another lot was put ashore at Kilcoole. The arms had been dramatically transhipped from the Hamburg tug *Gladiator* to the *Asgard* and the *Kelpie* off the Belgian coast.

There was an ugly incident as police and soldiers tried to stop the Volunteers marching with their newly landed guns. At Bachelor's Walk in Dublin crowds stoned the British soldiers, who opened fire, killing three civilians and wounding more than thirty. Only the previous day armed Ulster Volunteers had paraded through Belfast while authority looked the other way.

It was little wonder that Padraic Pearse and his friends were sceptical of the Home Rule Bill ever reaching the Statute Book. They could see little possibility of any coercion of the stubborn Orangemen by the British Government, who could not even rely on their own army. Carson had already warned that many officers would resign their commissions if ordered to move against Ulster. In March, 1914, Brigadier Hubert Gough and 57 other officers proved Carson's point when they stated their intention to accept dismissal rather than obey any order to march against Ulster. There was misunderstanding at the root of the incident which has become known, not very appropriately, as the Curragh Mutiny, and a great deal more in bringing it to a conclusion. In London Gough was given written assurances that satisfied him but upset the Cabinet. Some distinguished resignations followed but did

23

not include that of Sir Henry Wilson who had played an egregious part. The wily Wilson was using all his astuteness to frustrate Home Rule. He moved as smoothly through the labyrinthine paths of intrigue as a snake through a rabbit warren. He was to play a significant though hardly a chosen role in the story of the Irish Civil War.

Meanwhile, Churchill had lost patience with the Orangemen. Booming warnings in phrases of sonorous rhythm, he went so far as to try to frighten them with a show of battleships. At Westminster feelings were held by hair-triggers and bitterness cut so deep that parliamentary opponents were not on speaking terms. As the wrangling went endlessly on, the Irish separatists became thoroughly disillusioned. There seemed no way out of the impassse. Ulster Protestants simply refused to be ruled by Dublin Catholics. In England's fertile ground of compromise the scarcely heeded idea of partition put forward by Agar-Robartes was beginning to take root.

Even Carson was becoming convinced that partition might be the only solution, but he wanted it permanent; the six years' grace that Asquith was prepared to concede was just "a stay of execution" in his eyes. He also insisted upon six, not four, counties being excluded. Cavan, Donegal and Monaghan of the nine counties of the province he was prepared to let go. Overwhelmingly Catholic and Nationalist, they could well upset calculations if the question of a plebiscite covering the whole of the province were raised. The Protestant minority in the South opposed both Home Rule and partition, having no desire to be governed by a Catholic Parliament without even the consolation of support from their co-religionists in the North.

No one was more conscious of impending disaster in the situation than King George V, whose affection for Ireland was undoubted. "The Government is drifting and taking me with it," he complained, and several times he remonstrated with Asquith for not keeping him properly informed, urging repeatedly that the issue should not be made a bone of party contention. But, of course, it was; it is difficult to assess how much of the trouble in Ireland was due, not to genuine disagreement on principles, but to party manoeuvre. Certainly Conservative opposition to Home Rule was dictated as much by the prospect of toppling the Liberal Government as it was by their natural affinity with the Unionists who were, of course, their own sort of people.

By the end of June, 1914, it was agreed that the Home Rule Bill finally should go through, accompanied by an Amending Bill which should provide for either four or six of the Ulster counties to be excluded from the operation of the Bill—without a specified time limit. On which side of the boundary Fermanagh and Tyrone were to go was still undecided. In July a conference, urged by the King for several months, was held at Buckingham Palace. Attended by Asquith and Lloyd George for the Government, Bonar Law and Lord Lansdowne for the Opposition, Carson and Craig for Ulster and Redmond and Dillon for the Irish Nationalists, it ended in predictable failure, in spite of the King's own interviews with individual delegates.

The Amending Bill was never debated, for the international situation transcended all else in the last days of July. Instead, with the outbreak of World War I, the Government of Ireland Bill was quickly passed with a simultaneous Bill postponing its operation for the duration, and postponing, too, consideration of the Ulster puzzle. Dutifully, the King signed the Bill on September 17th.

England turned to face formidable Germany and her leap to the defence of little Belgium was a welcome indication to many Irishmen that she was not as oblivious to the rights of small nations as they might have supposed. Irishmen from North and South alike flocked to the colours, which must have been something of a shock to the Kaiser who, counting on England's preoccupation with troublesome Ireland, believed he could with impunity tear up the famous "scrap of paper".

Carson's volunteers, who had been ready to fight Britain to remain united with her, went to France as a division, with their own officers and colours, but Kitchener, indulging in as tactless a form of discrimination as could have been conceived at that time, refused to allow the same honour to the southern Irish whose services, nevertheless, he was eager to secure. Nor did he approve Redmond's offer of the Volunteers, in which the old Nationalist had wangled a 50% interest, as a Home Guard for Ireland in order to release British garrison troops for service elsewhere.

Not all the Volunteers were ready to follow Redmond's

25

lead and fly to the aid of the foster mother country. At first, Redmond's entry into Volunteer affairs had been welcomed as providing a link between the political and military sections of the Nationalist movement, but even before his enthusiastic espousal of England's cause, there had been disillusionment with him. Pearse and the Irish Republican Brotherhood, as other Irish leaders before them, were anxious to take advantage of England's embroilment in Europe. In September the Volunteers split on the issue and were reconstituted under Pearse. Insurrection had already been decided upon.

To call Pearse and his comrades a minority is not quite the truth. They were leaders whose potential followers had not yet realised that they wanted to follow. The people wanted change, release from the ubiquitous Dublin Castle and the right to govern themselves, but majorities invariably want change to be gradual, want to keep grasping familiar props with one hand while they reach for the unfamiliar with the other. Tradesmen and shopkeepers like to see new customers on their thresholds before they relinquish their old ones. So the majority of the Irish still believed in Redmond's nationalism, not seeing that this was outmoded, that Home Rule was obsolescent before it was even implemented, that new young leaders were breaking new ground and seeing ahead of them, far away as yet, and beyond innumerable barriers, a promised land.

The Easter Rising of 1916 was not a matter of impatience, of reluctance to wait until the end of the war for Home Rule. In 1912 even Pearse had thought the Bill acceptable, but the desire for independence had mounted, outstripping the laborious passage of the Bill. Its provisions of a bi-cameral Parliament in Dublin with little more power than a County Council no longer went far enough, but it might have been tolerated as a stepping stone to complete independence had the threatened amendment on partition not cracked the stone in two. Even as it stood, Pearse and his friends were sure that England would leave the legislation to moulder rather than engage in fresh struggles with the intransigent Orangemen.

TWO

The Rising was a travesty of what it might have been but, perhaps because it was a travesty, triumph flowed from it. Skilled professional revolutionaries would never have won the hearts of the people, and, without their faith, their conviction, there could have been no effective fight for freedom in the subsequent years. It was the ardour, the dedication, the heroism of the young rebels in the face of inevitable disaster, and finally the cold, professional savagery with which they were met, that won them their day. For the people saw at last that all the complexities of past years were meaningless, that the issue was as clear and as substantial as Waterford glass. That was the real consequence of the Rising.

It was in Tom Clarke's little tobacconist's shop in Parnell Street, Dublin, that the plan for revolution was born and nurtured, there too that Padraic Pearse was inducted into the Irish Republican Brotherhood. Thought by some too moderate, he was to become a member of the Brotherhood's Supreme Council and of the Military Council which planned the Rising. He was also to become the Commander-in-Chief.

Clarke, prematurely old after fifteen years' imprisonment in England and with his steel spectacles and soup strainer moustache, hadn't the mien of a revolutionary, but there was an unquenchable fire within him, and he saw in Pearse a smouldering power which marked him out for leadership. Pearse belongs to the St Joans and the Gandhis of this world, with the great martyrs. One cannot imagine that he could ever have become a political leader in an untrammelled land. His life revolved on the plinth of death, but that great end had to be made to serve a great purpose. Intensely interested in the Irish language, in 1895, at the age of sixteen, he joined the Gaelic League. Gradually he became immersed in the problem of Ireland's freedom until, in 1913, he was accepted into the I.R.B. Schoolmaster and poet, self-contained to the point of aloofness, he yet had a quality which lit fervour in those around him.

As Director of Organisation of the Volunteers, Pearse was

27

the connecting link with the Irish Republican Brotherhood, of whose concealed power the average Volunteer was unaware and the nominal heads, MacNeill, Chief of Staff, and Bulmer Hobson, Secretary, were unenlightened. A peculiar predilection for plural control was, except for the period of the war of independence, to plague Irish progress for years to come. Pearse had already been designated as Commander-in-Chief by the Military Council of the I.R.B., whose members were Pearse himself, Clarke, Joseph Plunkett, Sean MacDermott, Eamonn Ceannt and Tom MacDonagh, but MacNeill had no idea that his word was not law in the Volunteer movement. Through its organisation of circles within circles, the local circles contained within district circles, and the district within county, each with its own centre, the influence of the I.R.B. permeated the whole Volunteer structure. So the real power was in the hands of Pearse but, because it was a hidden power, the command of MacNeill also carried force. In this anomalous situation were the seeds of failure.

MacNeill had no idea of using the Volunteers for insurrection. He intended them to raise their guns only if England attempted to introduce conscription in Ireland or took some other action that would be inimical to his country's interests. The scholarly MacNeill conferred a certain respectability on the movement and, perhaps for this reason, the English authorities did not take too seriously the marching and drilling of the Volunteers in many parts of the country for a full twelve months before the Rising. Often, Volunteers did land in court having become involved in affrays which usually arose from the hostility of the general population, an aspect which must have blunted English sensitivity to danger. Only a month before the Rising, a crowd marched through Tullamore waving Union Jacks and shouting "Down with the Sinn Feiners", following the arrest of four Volunteers. Several young men suspected of Sinn Fein sympathies were roughly handled on the fringes of the procession.

So the reports which flowed into Dublin Castle from the Royal Irish Constabulary smoothed away English apprehension and no one bothered very much about the poetry of Pearse or James Connolly's militant prose in the *Workers Republic.* Amusedly sceptical of the Irish blatherskite, George

Bernard Shaw, the English were not prone to take the nostalgic incendiarism of Irish writing very seriously. Much better that they got their grievances off their chests and on to paper. Yet, if Pearse's poetry was disdainfully passed over, it is surprising that a little more attention wasn't paid to his pamphleteering, a traditional political weapon in England. Pearse was striking dangerous blows to the core of English political philosophy when he wrote:

"The right to the control of the material resources of a nation does not reside in any individual or in any class of individuals; it resides in the whole people and can be lawfully exercised only by those to whom it is delegated by the whole people, and in the manner in which the whole people ordains."

But then, nearer home, the English had never taken Keir Hardie very seriously either. In England, as in Ireland, property belonged, as of right, to the privileged. Keir Hardie, the one-time miner, would have been more in sympathy perhaps with James Connolly than with the intellectual Pearse. For Connolly, too, had come up the hard way. Born in Ulster, in 1870, he spent his early years in Glasgow. From the age of eleven he was forced to work and there grew in him a loathing of the industrial system upon which British imperialism was based. Love of Ireland was strong in him and he left Glasgow, where he was a Corporation dustman, and settled in Dublin with his wife and two children in 1896. He was by now a fervent socialist. Well versed from boyhood in the aims of the Fenians, he was also an ardent Republican. In Connolly's opinion, the way to republicanism in Ireland was through socialism, and vice versa, and he founded the Irish Republican Socialist Party which would in time, he hoped, tumble the existing institutions one by one until, with all its props gone, the Monarchy itself would crumble. Opposition to his ideas was formidable and finally, in 1903, poverty forced him to emigrate to the United States.

In 1910, he returned to his native Ulster where he became Chief Organiser of the new Transport and General Workers' Union. Not only did he unite the Belfast workers, Catholics and Protestants, into a militant body no longer prepared to endure without protest the despotism of the employers, but he began *Labour in Irish History*, a vast opus in which his ideas for Irish freedom were put explicitly. But it is doubtful if this work meant any more to the English authorities of the time than Karl Marx's *Das Kapital*.

When fiery Jim Larkin departed for America in 1914, Connolly took his place at the head of the Transport and General Workers' Union in Dublin and took over the Irish Citizen Army, which had been formed to protect workers' strike meetings after Dublin Metropolitan Police, causing injury and death, had broken up meetings during the big transport strike of 1913-14. In Connolly's hands the Irish Citizen Army, though numerically small, became potent enough for Connolly to prepare to begin an insurrection himself. His approach differed radically from that of Pearse whose ethereal ideas of self-immolation had no appeal for the earthy Connolly. The new Republic was not to be built on some sacrificial altar but was to be won, then and there, by force of arms.

When it seemed that Connolly was on the point of throwing his little Citizen Army against the gate of Dublin Castle—he even carried out a daylight rehearsal—the Supreme Council of the I.R.B. feared that he would wreck their own careful plans to rise on Easter Sunday, 1916. In January, Connolly was invited to meet Pearse, Plunkett and MacDonagh; as a result, he pledged the support of the Irish Citizen Army and was himself co-opted to the Military Council. It was not difficult to reconcile the two sets of aims for they had the common premises of a Republic, and equality and justice for all its citizens. Nevertheless, there were subtle conflicts of ideals, unimportant at the time, which were to manifest themselves in days to come. And neither Pearse's aims nor Connolly's coincided with those of Arthur Griffith, though he, too, the advocate of non-violence, was beginning to wonder whether anything could be achieved without the use of physical force.

All resented the occupation of their country by an alien and oppressive power, and all were prepared to find their friends where they could. They had no particular sympathy for Germany, but neither had they anything against her. In England's view a transaction with Germany was treasonable as, in the Second World War, the co-operation of the French Resistance with England was treachery in German eyes. Most Irish people of the time would have supported the British view, especially the families of the thousands of young Irishmen who were fighting in France. Those thousands were fighting for Irish freedom in their own way; they also believed that "England's difficulty was Ireland's opportunity". But they saw it as an opportunity to prove by valour their country's right to freedom, and they believed that as Britain was fighting for the right of small nations to exist, their own claim would be recognised. It was not, and thousands of disillusioned Irish soldiers were to swell the ranks of the Volunteers. They no longer thought of the Easter Rising as a stab in the back and they saw Roger Casement not as a man guilty of treason but as one who had been less blind than they.

Casement had been a distinguished, if eccentric, member of the British Consular Service. He dressed like a scarecrow, but a contemporary said of him: "No man I know has ever been more sincere on behalf of any cause he has taken up." Much was made of his acceptance of a knighthood in justifying the accusation of treason against him. But there was no paradox. Several million Irish people were prepared to accept Britain's rule for long, patient years on the promise of a modicum of freedom. When promises remained unfulfilled, they changed their minds. Casement, like Pearse, changed his earlier than most. It was ironical that Sir Edward Carson should have become Attorney-General when, as late as June, 1914, he had declared at a public meeting in Belfast:

"They reproach me with having Mausers. I can only say that I always intended to have them, and I tell the Government, with all their fleet and their other preparations, that I am going to have more Mausers."

The outbreak of war probably saved Carson from taking up arms against England and precipitated him into the Cabinet, as it impelled Casement to act against England and landed him in the dock.

Casement retired from the Consular Service to Ireland in 1913 and was soon active in the Volunteer movement, of which he was the first treasurer. He had been interested in Sinn Fein for some years but Griffith's idea of a dual monarchy did not involve any denial of allegiance to the King. Casement became a separatist about the time of his retirement and later he was a Howth conspirator.

It was in America, whence he had gone to raise funds for

31

the Volunteers, that he was caught up in a plan conceived by *Clan na Gael*, led by John Devoy and Judge Cohalan, which was more Irish than the Irish, yet even more fervently American as de Valera found to his cost a few years later. Clan na Gael was separatist through and through, with close ties with the I.R.B. In October, 1914, Casement made a devious way to Germany and stayed until just before the Easter Rising. He achieved very little. Given the run of the prison camps he was unable to induce more than a few Irish prisoners to join his Irish Brigade. The Germans fobbed him off with vague assurances of future Irish freedom and the half promise of some ancient guns and continued to deal with Devoy, and also with Sean T. O'Kelly and Dr. P. McCartan who had travelled to the United States, through the German Ambassador in Washington. Casement, it seems, was not taken very seriously. Room 40 OB., the Admiralty Intelligence Section, picked up and decoded most of the cables sent.

First Joseph Plunkett of the I.R.B. Military Council and later Robert Monteith arrived in Germany to negotiate over Casement's head, and Casement himself, when he finally set out for Ireland, was so unconvinced of German support and of the usefulness of the cargo of 20,000 obsolete Russian rifles which Monteith had arranged that he intended to have the Rising called off.

It almost was—without Casement's assistance. Plans for the Rising, not merely in Dublin but in various parts of the country, and especially in Cork, had gone ahead without MacNeill's knowledge. The scheme was as subtle as it was surreptitious. Carefully worded advertisements had ensured that 10,000 Volunteers would be ready for Easter Sunday, and Plunkett having heard something of a round-up of Sinn Fein and Volunteer leaders, produced a detailed plan of the operation which, passed off as genuine and known as the "Castle Document", aroused the indignation of the Volunteers, and even MacNeill was prepared to fight. But at last MacNeill got wind of the plot and, incensed at the deception, countermanded the order. Later, when he had been informed by Pearse of the expected arrival at Fenit of the *Aud* with a consignment of arms, he decided to resign and allow Pearse and his friends to go ahead. But already he had sent J. J. O'Connell to command the Volunteers in Cork where Tomas MacCurtain and Terence MacSwiney, the two ill-fated Lord Mayors of Cork city, normally were in charge.

By the time a fresh go-ahead order was received in Cork, news had already reached that city that the *Aud* plan had gone awry. Somehow, the arrival date had been bungled. At first, the *Aud* was to arrive in Tralee Bay on April 20th, then it was decided that April 23rd should be the day. Germany was not informed and the *Aud* left too soon. She had no radio and could not be informed of the change. She arrived on April 20th as originally planned but, by another oversight, the local Volunteers under Austin Stack had not been told that she would arrive early after all. They saw her but took no notice of her signals. On the same day Casement, Monteith and another man, Bailey, brought by submarine into Tralee Bay, went ashore in difficult conditions in a dinghy.

Monteith and Bailey went in search of the Kerry Volunteers, leaving Casement, who was exhausted. They were able to get a message to Stack, but Stack delayed, and when finally the Volunteers went to collect Casement, the boat had been found and reported to the R.I.C. at Ardfert. Casement had been discovered hiding in an old rath, or round fortress tower, and arrested. He gave his name as Richard Morton. Stack naïvely went to the R.I.C. in Tralee to make what he hoped were discreet inquiries and was promptly arrested himself. Incredibly, no effort was made by the Volunteers to rescue Casement on the way to Tralee barracks, or from the barracks themselves, or when he left under escort for Dublin. At no time was his guard formidable but the young Kerry Volunteers were inexperienced and probably bewildered by the strange events.

Meanwhile the *Aud* was intercepted by a British vessel and at the first opportunity her commander, Captain Spindler, scuttled her. MacNeill learned of the loss on the morning of Saturday, April 22nd. In spite of his earlier resignation, he sent out more couriers with messages, which he signed as Chief of Staff, cancelling Volunteer activity on Easter Sunday for the second time. For good measure, he had his countermanding order inserted in the newspapers. Nothing could now be done to begin the Insurrection on Easter Sunday but it was decided to go ahead on Easter Monday.

The Cork men went on with their mobilisation as planned, although they were astonished that there was no cancellation in view of the loss of the *Aud* cargo which, in any case, was mainly intended for them. At the last minute, MacNeill's countermanding order arrived and MacSwiney and Mac-Curtain decided to carry on for the day and to dismiss the men that evening. In the event, drenching rain persuaded them to end the march early. They were themselves still in the country when Pearse's message that the Rising would now take place on Easter Monday reached Cork. In their absence nothing was done. Elsewhere, the reasons for the confusion in Cork were not appreciated and there was some bitterness towards the Corkmen. Afterwards, in Frongoch internment camp, a man named O'Riordan, angered by accusations that Cork had failed to play its part, answered tellingly, in the presence of Richard Mulcahy, Dick Fitzgerald and others: "Casement's ghost won't haunt Corkmen, but Casement's ghost haunts Kerry."

In Belfast jail the Kerry men themselves ostracised their leader, Austin Stack, for failing to attempt Casement's rescue.

The Rising began in Dublin on the morning of Easter Monday and a splendid chance of capturing the infamous Castle was lost. The Volunteers could not know how ill-guarded it was and did not realise that, had they pushed home their attack, England would have been humiliated beyond their dreams; the mockery which they endured from their fellow-countrymen would surely have been turned against the British. As it was, an unarmed policeman named O'Brien was killed when he could have been captured; a life would have been spared and the alarm would not have been raised. The attacking party contented themselves with keeping a watch on the gates.

The G.P.O. in O'Connell Street had been decided upon as Pearse's headquarters, and it was from the portico that he read the brave and beautifully worded proclamation of the Irish Republic:

POBLACHT NA H EIREANN
The Provisional Government
of the Irish Republic
To the people of Ireland

IRISHMEN AND IRISHWOMEN: In the name of God and of

the dead generations from which she receives her old traditions of nationhood, Ireland, through us, summons her children to her flag and strikes for her freedom.

Having organised and trained her manhood through her secret revolutionary organisation, the Irish Republican Brotherhood, and through her open military organisations, the Irish Volunteers and the Irish Citizen Army, having patiently perfected her discipline, having waited for the right moment to reveal itself, she now seizes that moment, and supported by her exiled children in America and by gallant Allies in Europe, but relying in the first on her own strength, she strikes in full confidence of victory.

We declare the right of the people of Ireland to the ownership of Ireland, and to the unfettered control of Irish destinies, to be sovereign and indefeasible. The long usurpation of that right by a foreign people and Government has not extinguished the right, nor can it ever be extinguished except by the destruction of the Irish people. In every generation the Irish people have asserted their right to national freedom and sovereignty; six times during the last 300 years they have asserted it in arms. Standing on that fundamental right and again asserting it in arms in the face of the world, we hereby proclaim the Irish Republic as a Sovereign Independent State, and we pledge our lives and the lives of our comrades-in-arms to the cause of its freedom, of its welfare, and of its exaltation among the nations.

The Irish Republic is entitled to, and hereby claims, the allegiance of every Irishman and Irishwoman. The Republic guarantees religious and civil liberty, equal rights and equal opportunities to all its citizens, and declares its resolve to pursue the happiness and prosperity of the whole nation and of all its parts, cherishing all the children of the nation equally, and oblivious of the differences carefully fostered by an alien government, which have divided a minority from the majority in the past.

Until our arms have brought the opportune moment for the establishment of a permanent National Government, representative of the whole people of Ireland and elected by the suffrage of all her men and women, the Provisional Government, hereby constituted, will administer the civil and military affairs of the Republic in trust for the people.

We place the cause of the Irish Republic under the protection of the Most High God, whose blessing we invoke on our arms, and we pray that no one who serves that cause will dishonour it by cowardice, inhumanity or rapine. In this supreme hour the Irish nation must, by its valour and discipline and by the readiness of its children to sacrifice themselves for the common good, prove itself worthy of the august destiny to which it is called.

Signed on behalf of the Provisional Government

Thomas J. Clarke	Thomas MacDonagh
Sean MacDiarmada	Eamonn Ceannt
P. H. Pearse	Joseph Plunkett
James Connolly	

Pearse's poetry and ideals stamped the document but Connolly's basic convictions glinted in it, too, like the unexpected flashes of colour in an opal. Sturdy ideas lay beneath the emotional appeal in the name of God and of Ireland's dead generations. The Proclamation was ingeniously thought out and is far more comprehensive than its first impact suggests. The signatories knew very well that their Provisional Government would be short-lived but they signed, not as members of the Provisional Government which, in fact, they were, but simply on its behalf. It was a secret government within the Irish Republican Brotherhood, a government which would act as trustees until the people were in a position to elect a permanent National Government, and so long as there was an I.R.B. it could contain within it a provisional republican government. There was, therefore, an opportunity to maintain continuity, and it was not lost when the signatories themselves were to be counted among the dead generations.

A warning that partition could not be countenanced was sounded clearly and with it assurance was given that the Protestant minority would enjoy the same rights and privileges as the Catholic majority. And, in the declaration of "the right of the people of Ireland to the ownership of Ireland" there is, apart from the paramount assertion of national sovereignty, a hint of the possibility of Connolly's socialist republic. Though Tom Clarke as the doyen of the movement was given the honour of signing first, Pearse as President of the Supreme Council was the first President of the Irish Republic. Each of the signatories had been appointed to a specific position in his Cabinet.

As Pearse read the Proclamation the crowd listened with astonishment, amusement, indignation or indifference—as crowds do listen to those whom they look upon as exhibitionists or cranks.

Pearse's men and Connolly's Citizen Army took over the Post Office, moved in bedding from a nearby hotel and began to set up barricades, while trimly uniformed girls of the Cumann na mBan organised kitchens and dressing stations. Other units seized buildings elsewhere in Dublin. At St. Stephen's Green the flamboyantly uniformed Countess Markievicz (nee Constance Gore-Booth) was second-in-command to Michael Mallin. About a score of girls were with her. Eamonn Ceannt, with Cathal Brugha as his No. 2, took possession of the South Union building. Another signatory, Thomas MacDonagh, occupied Jacob's biscuit factory, Eamon de Valera, Boland's Mill and Edward Daly the Four Courts, the Irish courts of justice on the banks of the Liffey. In the Post Office, on Pearse's staff, was the young Michael Collins, until recently a clerk in London. Numerous small posts were established to cover specific roads and bridges.

The insurgents planned to isolate the centre of Dublin but they were inexperienced and some of the buildings were ill-chosen for the purpose. The Post Office itself, allowing little freedom of action, was a bad choice. Moreover, they had made the fatal mistake of not seizing the Dublin telephone exchange, which operated merrily through the Rising; and although the telegraph office was in their hands, an ingenious Post Office engineer devised an alternative route, so that the British, though taken unawares by the insurrection, were soon able to take counter measures. Had the Rising been widespread, the British would have been hard put to it to deal with it. But MacNeill's countermanding orders had saved them. In Dublin the rebels still hoped that the whole country would rise, but there were only a few isolated incidents and virtually the whole of the tragedy was played out in the capital; a strange and tragic city in that week. It should be emphasised that the men who took up arms against England did not consider themselves rebels but freedom-fighters. The authority they were trying to overturn was a usurping authority and the fact that it had

37

existed for centuries gave it neither moral nor legal standing. Their allegiance was to their own newly constituted Republic. It was a view which George Bernard Shaw trenchantly supported.

Throughout Easter Monday more Volunteers found their way into Dublin and swelled the garrisons which, however, remained pitifully small. Arthur Griffith, though he disapproved the Rising, and still thought uneasily about violence of any kind, felt that he should throw in his lot with the Volunteers but, fortunately for Ireland, they sent him away. That day, even as the Post Office was being secured, a troop of Lancers was caught between fires from the Four Courts and Church Street bridge. Four were killed and the others went plunging through back streets until their commander rallied them and led the main body to safety. Later, five members of the Dublin Veterans Corps were killed when their company was ambushed by one of de Valera's outposts. It seemed a fine victory at the moment and a captured pennant was hoisted triumphantly.

The Viceroy, Lord Wimborne, warned "all His Majesty's subjects that the sternest measures are being and will be taken for the prompt suppression of the existing disturbances and the restoration of order". But the British made no real move until Tuesday as coolly they established their own posts. Skilfully they picked the holes in the Irish cordon and drove through them like a chef dissecting a chicken. They established a line, from west to east along the Liffey, and began to bring up artillery. Already, with the police keeping out of trouble, people from the slums, and some who had less reason to be opportunist, were indulging in an orgy of looting in O'Connell Street and its environs. Sometimes the Volunteers fired shots over their heads, and Mrs Tony Lawlor remembers watching from the window of her home in O'Connell Street a ragged woman drop her armful of loot and fall on her knees in prayer each time a shot came near her; then she would gather it all up again until the next bullet whined past.

Many people ignored the flights of bullets, most of which were aimlessly in search of a target, and went nonchalantly or fatalistically about their business, or sought vantage points to witness the spectacular show as they might have watched a fireworks display. One man who went his way undeterred was

Francis Sheehy-Skeffington, one of those great characters that Ireland produces from time to time, a man bulging with goodness but full of eccentricity, good humour and an understanding of human frailties. With voice and pen "Skeffy" fought for the underdog, any sort of underdog. In sympathy with Sinn Fein ideals, as he was with the suffragette movement—there were startling parallels between the two groups struggling for their respective freedoms—he was no believer in violence, and he was endeavouring to organise public action against looters when he was arrested by a section of the Royal Irish Rifles on Portobello bridge.

He came into the hands of Captain Bowen-Colthurst that same evening and was taken by him as a hostage on a weird rampage in the course of which Bowen-Colthurst arrested two journalists in a public house and shot dead in the street a boy of seventeen who was on his way home from church. Next day, Bowen-Colthurst, having spent the night in distorted prayer, ordered a firing squad and executed Sheehy-Skeffington and the two journalists, Patrick McIntyre and Thomas Dickson, a cripple. Later, with unspeakable callousness, he personally fatally wounded Richard O'Carroll, who was a Volunteer and a Dublin City councillor, and executed, by shooting through the back of the neck, a boy whom he made kneel on the pavement. The man was unbalanced but what was unforgivable was that, although the military authorities knew of his crazy crusade, nothing was done to halt it until Major Sir Francis Vane took matters into his own hands and had him confined.

On Wednesday British artillery opened up and shells began to fall in the city from the Liffey, where the gunboat *Helga* had been stationed. But that day, too, British reinforcements marching in from Dun Laoghaire ran into a trap set by de Valera at Mount Street Bridge. De Valera had been able to spare no more than twelve men, but those men, under Lieutenant Michael Malone, in a five-hour battle during which they drove back attack after attack, accounted for some 250 killed and wounded, nearly half the British casualties of the entire Rising. Malone died fighting with calm heroism. But already Sean Heuston's garrison of twenty men in the Mendicity Institution, an outpost of the Four Courts, had been cut off and, after two days of fierce and obstinate defence, had had to surrender. But Daly soon compensated himself for the loss of this post. His men captured twenty-four Dublin Metropolitan policemen hiding in the Bridewell police station, and they also took the Linenhall police barracks. Daly could not afford men to garrison the barracks and, to prevent their use by the British, he burned them, an action which was to set a pattern for future troubled days.

The fighting was vicious, but in the G.P.O. still the garrison sang their songs whilst, in the streets, Dubliners in their thousands stood or sat in the sunshine to watch, heedless of the risk from wayward bullets fired by rooftop snipers. Most wanted the British to bring about a speedy return to normality; few imagined that before long they too would be involved, gladly, in the fight begun that Easter. Already youthful enthusiasts were sneaking away from law-abiding homes and a young medical student named Ernest O'Malley, who on Easter Monday was prepared to help defend Trinity College against the rebels, by Thursday had established his own rebel outpost with a friend. They shared an old Mauser rifle and on two nights tried their hands at sniping. O'Malley was to break away from his Unionist background and throw his poet's soul and the steel of him into the struggle for freedom.

Incendiary shells set the heart of the city ablaze. It was now Thursday. From Abbey Street the fire spread to O'Connell Street, and, as the shops were ravaged one after another, the depredations of the looters ceased to have much significance. Machine-guns lashed the streets and Volunteers in the outposts along O'Connell Street had to tunnel from one building to another to keep ahead of the flames. In the Post Office across the road the heat from the furnace first baked and then threatened to incinerate the garrison. Among the many wounded tended fervently by the girls of Cumann na mBan was James Connolly, twice hit by snipers when, courageously but rather foolishly, he left the building to inspect the neighbouring posts.

The South Dublin Union building was heavily attacked and Cathal Brugha was terribly wounded by a bomb and then by bullets. There was a lull in the fighting and Ceannt, dispirited, had had enough. But then the voice of Brugha was heard. He was singing *God Save Ireland* and challenging the British to attack as he lay, his rifle still gripped in his aggressive hands.

Inspired, the garrison rallied and once more manned the barricades.

But now the end was near. Dublin was a shambles. The dead still lay in the streets; through the smoke from the raging fires armoured cars prowled, machine-guns clamoured and shells burst in gouts of rubble.

The Volunteers had taken up defensive positions from the outset and, in effect, challenged the British to winkle them out. In the beginning they had had a little elbow room and excursions such as the Mount Street ambush had been possible, but now the garrisons were pinned down in their posts as British firepower inexorably increased. Only the Four Courts garrison under Edward Daly was able to maintain a series of outposts which gave flexibility to their operations.

At last the heat in the Post Office became intolerable and as fire swept through the upper floors, Pearse, after consulting with Connolly, assembled the garrison and issued instructions for the evacuation of the building. He hoped that they might hang on until the evening, but the heroism of those men who were fighting the flames while machine-gun bullets picked off first one and then another was not enough. The British, at a safe distance behind the barricades, did not attack but waited for the fire to smoke out the rebels; in their turn, they were waiting tensely for a do-or-die onslaught.

The wounded, except for Connolly who refused to leave, and the women, apart from two nurses and Connolly's secretary, made a painful way through holes battered in the walls of adjoining buildings and over rooftops until they reached the Coliseum Theatre in Henry Street. With them were Father Flanagan and a prisoner, a British Army doctor named Captain Mahony who had not forgotten the Hippocratic Oath during his enforced stay in the Post Office.

An hour after they had gone, at about seven o'clock that Friday evening, the fire burst volcanically through the entire building. Explosives were hurriedly moved and fifteen prisoners were released, only to run into machine-gun fire from their friends. One man was killed, another seriously wounded. The first party of fighting men left, led by The O'Rahilly, one of the original committee of the Volunteers, their task to set up a new headquarters. Quietly they went westward along Henry

Street, through their own barricade, then northward up Moore Street. As they dashed from doorway to doorway they came under devastating fire from a barricade at the end of Moore Street. O'Rahilly fell, but drew his body together and set out again, firing as he went, much more exposed now as if he sought to draw the deadly *mistral* of bullets upon himself. His men followed bravely and fell to the blast. Hit again, The O'Rahilly stumbled into Sackville Lane and gathered up the last crumbs of life to write a note, no more than a line, to his wife.

The smoke-laden dusk was deepening and the main body of Pearse's garrison were assembling to leave the Post Office, beaten and exhausted but strangely triumphant, and still they sang *The Soldiers' Song*, their voices sounding above the harsh crepitation of flames. Realising that The O'Rahilly's party had run into trouble, a group led by John MacLoughlin, a lad of sixteen who throughout the Rising had behaved with heroism and shrewd initiative far beyond his years, and Michael Collins who was ten years older, raced into Moore Street, but they were too late.

More men ran from the Post Office, but the shriving fire of machine-guns in Moore Street held them back. They took refuge in the nearest buildings. Finally, Pearse and Connolly, the three remaining girls and a small escort made their slow way to the corner of Moore Street and Henry Place. Behind them a tower of flame stood like a monument above the still-born body of the Irish Republic. But the ideal lived, shattered like the body of Connolly, whom they carried on a litter through the smoke-filled street.

That night, the leaders made the boy MacLoughlin a commandant and left to him the ordering of the men, but in the morning the great burden of responsibility was shouldered again. Orders were given to the men to begin tunnelling from house to house down Moore Street, towards the British barricades at Great Britain Street from which had come the fire that decimated O'Rahilly's party. But this seemed likely to end in disaster and MacLoughlin suggested that they try to link up with the Four Courts where Daly, with his string of outposts, was still holding out, though his garrisons were now enduring the most ferocious British assault of the Rising and some had already been overrun. General Sir John Maxwell had arrived on the Friday to take over command of the British forces from Major-General Friend and used armoured cars and borrowed rebel tactics of tunnelling from house to house. The attack was bound to succeed. Civilians who remained in the area received scant consideration from the British soldiers whose belief that the Rising was a treacherous stab in the back had inflamed their tempers. Some were caught in the fierce exchanges of shots and some were put to death without any justification whatsoever. It was because of the danger to civilians that Pearse, who at first agreed to MacLoughlin's plan, decided to abandon it.

At 12.45 p.m. on Saturday, young Elizabeth O'Farrell, carrying a Red Cross flag, walked stonily towards the British barricade. General Lowe, who had commanded the actual operation against the Irish insurgents was summoned and Miss O'Farrell was sent back to tell Pearse that only unconditional surrender was acceptable. Twice more, as Pearse fought for terms for his men, Miss O'Farrell made her tense journey. But the British would not relent and Pearse himself reported to the barricade, handed up his sword and was taken to Maxwell. He signed the document of surrender at 3.45 p.m. on April 29th, 1916. The text was:

"In order to prevent the further slaughter of Dublin citizens, and in the hope of saving the lives of our followers now surrounded and hopelessly outnumbered, the members of the Provisional Government present at Headquarters have agreed to an unconditional surrender and the Commandants of the various districts in the City and Country will order their commands to lay down arms."

Connolly, now also in custody—in the hospital at Dublin Castle—added his signature. In O'Connell Street, in front of the Gresham Hotel, the men from the Post Office tossed down their arms. Nurse O'Farrell went the rounds of the other posts with the pathetic instrument of surrender in her hands. The Four Courts had fallen at last; elsewhere the garrisons were still holding out. Several commandants, de Valera among them, were reluctant to give in, were even suspicious of the surrender document, but in the end all did so. As the men marched towards captivity or the firing squad, they were reviled by most of the onlooking Dubliners. Only a few brave hearts cried out in their defence and to one jeering group de Valera made his bitter remark: "If only you'd come out with knives and forks." He had forgotten that the rebels were men ahead of their time, that leaders of revolutionary movements, of new movements, whether in politics, art, fashion, architecture or anything else, must wait in patience until time and events prove them to be right or wrong and decide whether the momentum they have generated will gain force or die.

From Swords, Co. Dublin, Richard Mulcahy came as an emissary to General Lowe. The irony of his situation was felt acutely by Mulcahy, for Thomas Ashe, whose second-in-command he was, had won the only victory of the Rising. It was a victory which showed what might have been won had MacNeill not sent out his counter-instructions, and it was, furthermore, a victory won by tactics which were to be remembered and remembered again.

Ashe and Mulcahy had raised quite a strong force, and on the Wednesday they set out to attack the radio station at Skerries about sixteen miles north of Dublin. They gave up the idea when they saw British gunboats in the harbour, but two days later they put a fresh plan into operation, first making an assault on the R.I.C. barracks at Ashbourne, just across the county border in Meath, and then ambushing a strong party of reinforcements, who surrendered after a five-hour shooting match. The R.I.C. men lost eight killed and twice as many wounded. Ashe was to make a short, vivid mark on the pages of Irish history, Mulcahy, twenty-nine at this time, a longer, more significant and more controversial mark. Born at Waterford, and educated by the Christian Brothers there and in Thurles, like Collins he had joined the postal service. For long an active member of the Gaelic league (he is still a loving student of the Irish language), he had joined the Volunteers at the inception of the movement and Ashbourne was the first of a series of exploits as hair-raising perhaps as those of Collins.

In Enniscorthy, Co. Wexford, too, the Volunteers had "come out", inspired by news of the happenings in Dublin. They assembled in the early hours of Thursday, ran up the Republican flag, patrolled the streets, sealed roads into the town, seized the station, tore up some railway track and cut telephone and telegraph wires, none of which endeared them to the townspeople. In the evening they exchangd shots with two constables who had taken refuge in the Bank of Ireland, and stormed, but failed to take, the R.I.C. barracks. However, they did take possession of Enniscorthy Castle, the home of the Roche family whom they evicted.

On the Saturday, the day of the surrender in Dublin, a party of Enniscorthy rebels travelled to nearby Ferns in motor cars and seized the post office and the police barracks. The men went happily to Mass in Enniscorthy on Sunday, but later in the day they learned from District Inspector McGovern and Father Kehoe, who came by car under a white flag from Arklow, that the Rising in Dublin was over. They refused to believe it, and only after Captains Etchingham and Doyle had been taken under military escort to see Pearse in Dublin did they capitulate.

Liam Mellows, regarded by Connolly as the most promising of the younger leaders, led an uprising in County Galway. Deported to England, he had escaped by exchanging identities with his brother, who had crossed for the purpose, and had returned to Ireland disguised as a priest. Again, the Volunteers fought valorously and even succeeded in capturing Athenry, twelve miles east of Galway, before they were surrounded and compelled to surrender.

The last, short, tragic chapter of the drama, almost an epilogue, was played out, on the Tuesday following Pearse's surrender, at Bawnard House in East Cork where four brothers, Thomas, David, Richard and William Kent, all active Volunteers, resisted the efforts of a squad of armed police to arrest them in their own home. Even after military reinforcements arrived they kept fighting until they were out of ammunition. Richard was fatally wounded when he tried to escape and David also was wounded. One constable was killed. Thomas Kent, who was hanged in Cork a week later, is numbered among "the sixteen" of Easter week.

And so the insurrection ended. "A terrible beauty was born," wrote Yeats who, searching his conscience, also wondered, "What words of mine sent out certain men the English shot?"

It is unlikely that they did, but after the Rising he contributed imperishable poetry to the spate of song and verse that flowed from it, and it may well be that posterity will know more of the spirit of the Easter Rising from Yeats than from all the songs and stories of shot and shell.

THREE

Padraic Pearse, that strange fusion of melancholy and purity, was ready, eager perhaps, to die. What was needed to fire the courage of the people, to slough off their apathy, to throw a single gleaming star into the dark heavens to guide them, was a blood sacrifice. In his lovely poem *The Rose Tree* Yeats caught the feeling exactly:

> *"O words are lightly spoken,"*
> *Said Pearse to Connolly,*
> *"Maybe a breath of politic words*
> *Has withered our Rose Tree;*
> *Or maybe but a wind that blows*
> *Across the bitter sea."*
>
> *"It needs to be but watered,"*
> *James Connolly replied,*
> *"To make the green come out again*
> *And spread on every side,*
> *And shake the blossom from the bud*
> *To be the garden's pride."*
>
> *"But where can we draw water,"*
> *said Pearse to Connolly,*
> *"When all the wells are parched away?*
> *O plain as plain can be*
> *There's nothing but our own red blood*
> *Can make a right Rose Tree."*[1]

Pearse hoped that his own life would be enough, though all

[1] In *Insurrection Fires at Eastertide* (Mercier Press, 1966) compiled by Professor O'Doubhghaill the poem is given with extra quotation marks in the final stanza which put the last three lines into Connolly's mouth rather than Pearse's.

seven signatories of the Proclamation knew that they were liable to receive the death sentence.

The life of Pearse was not enough. Thirteen more lives were demanded in retribution. The half-spent body of Connolly was propped in a chair to receive the ordained volley. The other five signatories also were executed, but Tom Clarke had seen to it that his young widow was primed with such information as would enable the I.R.B., into which he had infused new life and new spirit, to survive and to recover in the hands of a new generation. Six leaders of the scattered garrisons were court martialled and shot, and so was Pearse's brother William, largely it seems because of the relationship. De Valera's death sentence was commuted in deference to his American nationality, that of Countess Markievicz—to her great chagrin—because of her sex.

Maxwell, who confirmed all the sentences, may have realised, but probably did not, that his policy of wholesale executions was to present that brave, impassioned, improvised little army with the only victory it could have achieved. To deny that victory it would have been necessary to treat the Volunteers and their leaders as well-intentioned but misguided cranks, to laugh off their efforts, and to send them home or, at most, to jail. In this case they would have won little public sympathy—for a time. But England would have had to act swiftly nonetheless, for the work would have gone on, the movement attracted more and more young people, and even their elders become impatient for something better than the Home Rule offer over which England had dithered for so long.

But a policy of heaping ridicule on the rebels was just not possible. Too many lives had been lost and too much damage done, and the English people, who at that time were so screamingly sensitive to espionage and treachery promoted by the Germans that any dear old lady with a cranky streak was likely to be suspected as a spy, were genuinely shocked that the Irish had had any truck with the enemy. But G. B. Shaw, protesting against the executions, maintained that "an Irishman resorting to arms to achieve the independence of his country is doing only what Englishmen will do if it be their misfortune to be invaded and conquered by the Germans in the course of the present war." In his view an Irishman was as much entitled to seek German assistance as England to seek

47

Russia's. And sagely he pointed out: "The fact that he knows that his enemies will not respect his rights if they catch him, and that he must therefore fight with a rope round his neck, increases his risk, but adds in the same measure to his glory in the eyes of his compatriots and of the disinterested admirers of patriotism throughout the world."[2]

Pearse and his friends had won because they had all but forced England into the position of having to resort to the death penalty, which was precisely what they wanted.

Perhaps Maxwell bears a too-heavy burden of blame. Asquith's Cabinet gave him "plenary powers under martial law over the whole country",[3] and at a time when shell-shocked boys in France were being shot for cowardice it was hardly to be expected that a military mind of the day would have dictated measures any less drastic in the Dublin situation. His cardinal blunder was in dragging out the courts martial and executions over a period of ten days. The Cabinet knew what course he would pursue. They had agreed at this time, even before the Rising ended, "that if civil proceedings could be resorted to and carried through as promptly as those by court-martial, in the case of R. Casement that course should be adopted."[4] They failed to see—though Dillon gave them warning enough—the reaction that would follow. England was at fault, not so much because she was ruthless in circumstances which could be argued to justify ruthlessness, but because she lacked foresight and did not sufficiently examine the circumstances. She dealt violently with the symptoms of trouble without seeking—until too late—the causes.

England had possessed Ireland for centuries, had exploited her, patronised her, policed her and planted in her a privileged class. To the English the ordinary people of Ireland were endearing comics or faithful servants, with a sprinkling of trouble makers, and the whole lot could talk the hind leg off a donkey. Ireland was an eccentric but intrinsic part of Britain. The majority of her people, whether from apathy, ignorance, loyalty, affection or fear, supported the Crown, and thousands of them were dying for it. An insurrection in the middle of a desperate war was too much to stomach. But a competent

[2] In a letter to the *Daily News* of 10th May, 1916.
[3] P.M.'s report to King George P of Cabinet meeting of 27/4/16.
[4] Ibid.

government with its finger on the pulse of the people ought to have seen beyond this superficial reading.

Perhaps it is only in retrospect that one can see that Irish fealty was thin ice which had been recklessly walked over for a long time. Beneath it flowed unseen the real faith of the Irish in themselves, and it needed but that one hammer blow from Maxwell to smash the ice. Most of it melted quickly; a few Unionist splinters of loyalty to England remained floating on the surface.

The Prime Minister, Mr Asquith, arrived in Dublin on May 12th. Early that morning the last two executions, those of Connolly and MacDermott, had been carried out. Six days earlier, with Maxwell in attendance, the Cabinet had agreed "to leave to his discretion the dealing with particular cases, subject to a general instruction that, death should not be inflicted except upon ringleaders and proved murderers, and that it is desirable to bring the executions to a close as soon as possible".[5]

Asquith spent six days in Ireland and from talking to prisoners and reading the court-martial speeches of the leaders, he began to understand their motives. On May 25th, he reported to the House of Commons that the existing machinery of government in Ireland had broken down and that he had already asked Lloyd George to begin negotiations with both the Nationalist and Ulster Unionist leaders, so that the Home Rule Act could be taken down from its war-time shelf, dusted and put into operation. This was tantamount to an admission that the Rising was justified or, at least, that the grievance which had led to it was a genuine one and that consequently the execution of the leaders had been hasty.

The people of Dublin, and especially the Irish press, incensed by the destruction, had denounced the revolutionaries at first, had clamoured for Maxwell to exercise a retributive hand, but the mood changed. Maxwell's calculated mercilessness caused revulsion, an emotional swing of sympathy towards the underdog. Asquith's quick concession gave frail emotionalism the backing of reason. People saw that the Volunteers had won more in a week than the Irish Parliamentary Party had gained in years of political struggle. The cause of the politicians was not helped by their attitude to

5 P.M.'s report to the King of Cabinet meeting 6/5/16.

the Rising. In the Commons, siding with Carson who wanted "to put down those rebels for ever more", Dillon called for punishment "swift and stern", and Redmond spoke of "treason to the cause of Home Rule" and of "a German invasion of Ireland". Redmond, however, did plead with the Government "not to show undue hardship or severity to the great mass of those who are implicated and on whose shoulders lies a guilt far different from that which lies on the instigators and promoters of the outbreak . . ."

Within a few days, both Carson and Redmond were advocating clemency. Perhaps Carson remembered that he had sailed with the same wind but in a different vessel, that, but for German ambition, he might easily have ended by leading his own surrendered Volunteers from the post office in Belfast as Pearse had done in Dublin. Perhaps he saw that the whole flow of events in Dublin had stemmed from the intransigence and belligerence of those he had led.

In the United States of America many sections of public opinion, particularly Irish-American, were angrily critical of the British handling of the Rising but President Wilson resisted pressure to intervene, unwilling to add the Irish problem to his worries. But due note of influential American opinion was taken in England where there was no wish to antagonise America which, largely because of political questions centring on the Irish-American vote, was maintaining a starchy neutrality in the war, and a cable from the American Cardinal Gibbons may well have been responsible for de Valera's reprieve and perhaps others. In Ireland certainly it was believed that English firing squads put their guns in the rack only because of their awareness of American resentment.

The Catholic Hierarchy in Ireland had never been friends of the Fenians, nor sympathetic towards revolutionary ideals. Their power was great in the land and they reacted automatically to any threat to it. The incredible thing was that so many young Irishmen risked the promised wrath of God for the sake of freedom in their own land in their own lifetime. This needed courage, but they were helped by the nationalistic ardour of some parish priests, and when Maxwell called upon the Bishop of Limerick to discipline some of his disputatious priests, Dr O'Dwyer was stung to reply, in an open letter to the press on May 17th, "You took good care that no plea for
50

mercy should interpose on behalf of the poor young fellows who surrendered to you in Dublin." And he expressed his belief that Maxwell's action had "outraged the conscience of the country." Some consciences which had been trying to suppress instinctive indignation because they were not sure of God's view in the matter were stripped of inhibition by the Bishop's lead. His words meant a great deal, too, to the young Volunteers who were now British prisoners and in some of whose minds there lurked behind the dazzling blaze of freedom's ideal a chilling shadow of uncertainty.

The Bowen-Colthurst episode and the blood-letting by British troops in King Street remained to be dealt with and honest measures would have won back for England some of her lost ground. But when it was seen that, like a slovenly maid, Maxwell was busily sweeping the dirt under the mat, disillusionment grew among those whose loyalty was still swinging on precarious hinges. Asquith himself had sense enough to force the Bowen-Colthurst issue into the open and this unhappy lunatic went to Broadmoor. The King Street incidents could not be so easily explained away and, although Maxwell was compelled to admit that "some unfortunate incidents, which we should regret now, may have occurred", he brushed them off as inevitable in the circumstances and, despite an elaborate inquiry, the culprits were never made to answer for their crimes.

The various factors all weighed heavily with the thinking Irish people. In any country it is the middle classes, with most to lose, who most resist violent change and tend to remain loyal to the established order. When convinced that change is necessary, they will spare no effort to bring it about, but they are wary of extremes, anxious to see order restored the moment the sense of rightness and of justice is no longer offended. The Irish middle classes were true to pattern. Their ideals meant much to them, and without their support the Irish revolution would have failed, but the time was to come when they saw no virtue in standing with a smoking gun on a slag-heap of corpses and rubble and declaiming triumphantly that ideals alone survived.

Asquith's turnabout on the possibility of introducing Home Rule despite the War came to nothing. The stumbling block of Ulster, shelved with the Act, reappeared with it, formidable as ever. Lloyd George met Redmond and Carson and a paper described as "Headings of Agreement" was produced which embodied concession on either side. Twenty-six counties would be ruled from Dublin while six of the nine Ulster counties would recognise Belfast as their capital. Though Lloyd George had supported Home Rule for a quarter of a century, Redmond was never sure of him. Lloyd George offered his own political existence as security, vowing to resign if the Cabinet did not uphold an agreed settlement.

Wittingly or not, he gave Redmond the impression that partition would be temporary and Carson a private promise that it would be a permanent arrangement. The Cabinet decided that "Sir E. Carson's claim for the definitive exclusion of Ulster could not be resisted."[6] Redmond, finding that he had been duped, withdrew his own support. Lloyd George discovered that his country needed him and put his pledge to resign in cold storage until 1921. Carson complacently pocketed his promise of permanent partition and the British Government won a wintry smile from America for the attempt to promote a solution. Redmond was left once more with failure on his hands and Southern Ireland, now ruled under martial law by Maxwell, was more than ever disenchanted with the Irish Parliamentary Party.

Maxwell saw now that there had been some justification for the Rising and that it was Carson who had wound up the spring. He could make little of the Government's vacillating policy, and urged a civil administration which would adopt a programme of social reform. Gradually a civil administration did take over again but it was the same broken-down old horse which went back between the shafts. Following representations from Redmond, the Cabinet decided to give Maxwell another command—one which would "show that the Government fully appreciated his services."[7] In November he left Ireland.

On August 3rd, Sir Roger Casement was hanged. Under English Law he was unquestionably guilty, but English Law lost something of its lustre when F. E. Smith, the Attorney-General, an avowed opponent of Irish nationalism, was permitted to lead for the prosecution, though he did the job

6 P.M.'s report to the King of Cabinet meeting of 19/7/16.
7 P.M.'s report to the King of Cabinet meeting of 18/10/16.

fairly enough, even suggesting that the defence plead insanity on the strength of the notorious "black diaries" which had just come to light, a proposal that Serjeant Sullivan rejected with contempt. In a speech from the dock Casement achieved a grandeur which made the diaries, in all probability a secret fanfaronade of fantasy, seem trivial. A medical report on the diaries, ordered by the Cabinet, declared that Casement was abnormal but not certifiably insane.[8]

The Archbishop of Canterbury and other men of stature urged that sentence of death be commuted to life imprisonment, but the Cabinet decided unanimously to hang Casement, and so missed yet another chance of conciliating the affronted spirit of the Irish. Their reasons were set out in a statement to be shown by the British Ambassador to Senator Lodge and other interested Americans,[9] and it was hoped that the moral Irish would not number Casement among their martyr-heroes. But not an Irishman to this day has counted any less than sixteen heroes of the Rising at Easter.

Casement was not long in his grave in Pentonville Prison before plans to extend conscription to Ireland were mooted. Redmond fought this grimly and he fought, too, for the release of the two thousand men arrested after the Rising. Some had been no more than passers-by in the streets. They were being released gradually but it was a slow process. He was vehemently opposed to conscription and he was certain that thousands of people in Ireland would be prepared to give their lives to prevent it. The continued incarceration of the men of the Rising he thought harsh and unnecessary. He also knew that what the Government had created, in Frongoch internment camp especially, was a breeding-ground for revolution. At this point, the fortunes of the Irish Parliamentary Party might well have been restored if Redmond's pleas had been successful, and England would have been saved a great deal of trouble.

In December, 1916, Asquith was pushed out of office and Lloyd George became Prime Minister. One of his first actions was to release the last six hundred men interned in Frongoch, both as a move towards reconciliation and because, being no fool, he recognised the explosive potential of the place. The

8 P.M.'s report to the King of Cabinet meeting of 14/7/16.
9 P.M.'s report of Cabinet meeting of 2/8/16.

move was too late anyway for by then youngsters who had gone into the Rising with a strong and simple faith but with little idea of the complex issues involved, little understanding of Pearse's philosophy or Connolly's theories or the doctrine of Sinn Fein, were now educated and dedicated revolutionaries. Michael Collins had emerged as a leader, and he had already the nucleus of the network of loyal and ruthless men, bound by ties of imperishable affection, which was to prove the most effective single element in the destruction of British power in Ireland.

Collins was a strange, attractive mixture of a man. Like so many of the Irishmen who were to become leaders in the struggle for freedom, he had an innate sense of scholarship, and throughout his short life, filled to overflowing as it was, he always found some time to get down to his books. He was boisterous, athletic, emotional and quick tempered; he had generosity and immense charm, the ability to deal with big issues on a broad scale and, at the same time, to cover the smallest detail. He had a filing cabinet of a memory, a warmth that won him many friends and a confidence in himself which, allied with impatience of those who were less efficient, earned him some enmity. Above all, he had a vein of supreme ruthlessness rarely found in a man of such warm blood, ruthlessness which seemed casual rather than calculated and yet was an essential part of him.

In Frongoch he had time to assess the events of Easter Week and the leaders. Writing to his friend, Kevin O'Brien in London, he said that the Rising "had the air of a Greek tragedy about it", and that it " was bungled terribly, costing many a good life".[10] Nor did he think it was "an appropriate time for the issue of memoranda couched in polite phrases". It was a sensible appraisal, indicative not only of Collins's essential realism but of his intolerance of anything which smacked of inefficiency, however well-intentioned the aim. He was not unsympathetic towards the concept of the blood sacrifice but he would have demanded a richer flow of English blood first.

As Collins made his mark at Frongoch, so at Dartmoor and at Lewes did de Valera's quality of leadership assert itself. As the only surviving commandant of the Rising, he had a

[10] Quoted by Rex Taylor in *Michael Collins*.

good start and every stringy inch of him had an ambient authority which seems to come naturally to teachers of mathematics and which quickly earned the respect of his prisoner compatriots. In spite of this, he was to prove himself a strangely hesitant man; he was like a powerful motor with a spluttering cylinder.

The Frongoch men returned to find themselves heroes and their dead leaders all but deified, their pictures everywhere on display, their once unheeded writings passing from hand to hand. And the returning men of the Rising knew then that the bullets fired in the yard of Kilmainham jail on those ghastly May mornings had rebounded from the hearts of their leaders. They had won.

Somehow the name of Sinn Fein had become attached to the Volunteers, but it was a misnomer for Sinn Fein was still a non-violent political group. If its doctrines were something of a mystery, its name was a convenient, and appropriate, label for the nationalist movement that was now superseding the moderate Redmond's party, but many who had an appreciation of Griffith's theories were not at all happy to be tagged "Sinn Feiners".

Griffith had been ready to wait years before his party gained any real political power, but in February, 1917, Count Plunkett, whose son Joseph had been one of the martyred sixteen, won Roscommon for Sinn Fein in a by-election, easily defeating the Parliamentary Party candidate. In accordance with the Sinn Fein pledge, Count Plunkett declined to take his seat in the House of Commons.

On April 4th, 1917, America entered the War and England breathed more easily. Lloyd George was anxious to scrub his Irish doorstep, partly to reassure America's influential Irish population but also to remove, if he could, the stains of Easter blood. He was jolted when, early in May, another Sinn Fein candidate, Joseph McGuinness, won Longford, especially as the man was a prisoner in Lewes jail throughout the campaign. Absence in English jails was soon to become a notable qualification for election. McGuinness's was a narrow victory but the more significant for its having been won in an area where Redmond's party enjoyed strong support.

If the spread of Sinn Fein power was to be checked, Lloyd George had to move quickly, and in May he offered Redmond immediate Home Rule. The six counties would not be included in its operation for a period of five years, after which the destiny of North East Ulster would be decided. Mindful perhaps of the promise of a permanent division given to Carson, Redmond turned down the offer but accepted an alternative suggestion of a great Convention of representatives from every Irish walk of life. There would be places for Sinn Fein but the hope of Lloyd George and of Redmond was that it would be overwhelmed by the great mass of less extreme representatives from the Church and associated organisations, from trade and commerce, education, local government, trade unions and, of course, other political groups. It would not be fair to suggest that the Convention was "packed" with the object of crushing Sinn Fein. There was genuine desire to give all sections the opportunity to express an opinion but it was confidently believed that, while it was no longer doubted that the people wanted Home Rule and wanted it quickly, the Republican ideal, to which Sinn Fein was now definitely committed, did not attract the bulk of the people. And it was hoped that Sinn Fein would recognise that they were an extremist minority, and that if they had any reverence for democratic government they would accept what the majority wanted, or what it was believed they wanted, self government with allegiance to the Crown. To generate goodwill Lloyd George released the men who were serving sentences in English prisons.

They came home to a fantastic welcome and it was de Valera who was singled out for special adulation. The austere commandant of Boland's Mill made it clear at once that Easter week had been but a beginning. The Provisional Government of the Republic of Ireland, risen from the flames of the Post Office, where its first edict had been read, addressed to the American President and Congress a declaration of its intention to establish the right, which was the right of all small nations, to independence.

From the start the Irish Convention was bedevilled by its ambiguous *raison d'être*, the innumerable conflicts of interests and the deliberate absence of Sinn Fein, the Irish Labour Party and other groups. The meetings dragged on for months and achieved little except to keep America in a benevolent mood. Nevertheless, it was of the utmost importance for

Lloyd George and his Cabinet. On February 13th, 1918, the Prime Minister gave his colleagues an account of his meetings with different sections of the Convention.[11] He gathered that "the Unionists were divided into two quite distinct groups, one composed mainly of Southern Unionists and the other of the Ulster Party's representatives. The Nationalists were divided into at least three groups. Mr. Redmond did not agree with Mr. Devlin, nor Mr. Devlin with Mr. Murphy. Outside the Convention stood the Sinn Feiners who, though not represented in the Convention, had indirect influence upon the more extreme section of the Nationalists."

He told the Cabinet that Belfast Labour men "were all in favour of a settlement" but Carson had told him that they "did not accurately represent the views of the Protestant workmen in Belfast." Some members of the Cabinet, however, doubted Carson's assessment. Lord Southborough said forthrightly that "Labour questions were apt to be pushed aside in the minds of the Belfast workmen by the old feeling for Protestant and racial ascendancy." Southborough also explained that there had been in the Convention "something approaching a general acceptance of the principle of a Dublin Parliament" provided that Ulster's interests were safeguarded, but then there had been a division of opinion on the question of Customs revenue.

The Chief Secretary for Ireland, Mr Duke, pointed out that if the Convention failed the Government would be compelled to rule Ireland by force, and added prophetically that "matters would drift into a state of affairs which could hardly be controlled".

The Cabinet agreed with Professor W. G. Adams, who attended the meeting, that an all-Ireland Parliament was the only basis for a satisfactory solution, and Lloyd George proposed to inform representatives of the Convention that afternoon that during the war a settlement was only possible that provided for "one Parliament for the whole of Ireland, sitting in Dublin" and for Great Britain to retain control of Customs and Police. It is noteworthy that, long after the partition of the country had first been mooted, and so soon after the offer of Home Rule with the six counties of the North-east excluded, the English Prime Minister and his

11 War Cabinet minute 311(5) of 13/2/18.

Cabinet should now have come down firmly on the side of a united Ireland. If they could achieve this, much of the steam would be let out of the Sinn Fein boiler.

The British Government did not underrate Sinn Fein's potential but they were convinced that they were still in time to prevent the spread of anti-British heresy, and so they staked all on the success of the Convention.

Of infinitely greater significance in Ireland's history, as things turned out, was Sinn Fein's own Convention or *Ard-Fheis*, which was held at the Mansion House in October 1917. Eamon de Valera who, a month after his return from England, had become yet another absentee member of the House of Commons, having won East Clare in a by-election, was elected President of Sinn Fein on October 26th. There is little doubt but that Arthur Griffith would have kept the leadership had he chosen to do so, but after a long meeting with de Valera, who gave him certain assurances, he came away declaring that this was the young man he had been looking for to take over, and he stood down. So, too, did Count Plunkett, who was also a candidate.

Griffith had now accepted that independence would not be won without physical force, and he knew that the character of Sinn Fein inevitably would change as, in association with the Volunteers, it became part of the physical force movement. It seemed to him that a man of de Valera's proved fighting calibre and political acumen was better fitted to lead the party than a reluctant convert from a long-held faith in passive resistance. On October 27th, de Valera was elected President of the Volunteers and a General Headquarters staff was appointed by the National Executive of the movement, of which Cathal Brugha was Chairman.

There was no solid block of single-minded opinion in either Sinn Fein or the Volunteer movement, separate but intermixed now as companies are conjoined by interlocking directorships. Some, even then, would have been content with Griffith's original dual monarchy demand; those connected with trade and commerce could see obvious advantages in this. Others adhered to Connolly's vision of a socialist republic, but no man with his qualities of leadership, had emerged to take his place. For some the Republican ideal was the beginning and end of everything; others had not thought beyond freeing themselves from English rule. Even de Valera, at that time and for some time to come, would have been satisfied with a status equal to that of Canada or Australia, and had England been both magnanimous enough and imaginative enough to offer them what she had to concede in 1921, there would have been no revolutionary war in Ireland.

The differences of opinion which did exist at the Sinn Fein Ard-Fheis of October, 1917, would one day reappear, but they seemed of little moment in the face of the overwhelming aim to establish the right of the Irish to rule Ireland. An independent Irish Republic was the kind of umbrella beneath which all kinds of national aspirations could shelter and just such an umbrella was provided by the formula adopted at the Ard-Fheis:

> "Sinn Fein aims at securing the international recognition of Ireland as an independent Irish Republic. Having achieved that status the Irish people may by referendum freely choose their own form of Government."

This was typical of formulas devised to give a common aim to people of divergent views and it was capable of more than one interpretation. It is when the common aim is won that the several interpretations appear to cause trouble.

Beneath the overt stratum of the Irish independence movement the Irish Republican Brotherhood had begun to reorganise and rebuild its energies. Its secrets were in the hands of Mrs Kathleen Clarke, put there in his wisdom by her husband, who knew very well that after the Rising the Supreme Council would no longer exist. It was to Mrs Clarke that Michael Collins and his close friend, Harry Boland, hurried on their return to Ireland. With the help of Thomas Ashe, victor at Ashbourne during the Rising, Diarmuid Lynch, Con Collins and others, they set about reorganising the Brotherhood. Ashe became President of a caretaker Supreme Council and Collins, who had also become Secretary of the Irish National Aid Association, a fund hitherto administered by Mrs Clarke to help the dependants of Volunteers either killed in the Rising or imprisoned after it, was able through his work to make innumerable contacts. By the autumn a new constitution had been worked out and Sean McGarry became the new President with Collins as Secretary and Lynch as Treasurer. The writ of the new I.R.B. was to run wide but there were notable absentees from the organisation. De Valera, once an uneasy member, decided to keep out because of the Catholic Church's disapproval of secret organisations.

There were, therefore, three organisations working to the same end. All three were linked, from the leaders to the most humble members, but there was in the situation a schismatic potential. It was difficult for the recognised leaders who were not members of the Brotherhood to know the extent of influence and power in the hands of their colleagues who were, and at this time the I.R.B. still held that their own secret President was the unnamed President of the Republic. Not everywhere was the I.R.B. potent. "In Clare," says General Michael Brennan, "they were the conspirator type and didn't want to fight at all. Our fellows wanted to get out in the open and fight. They just pushed the old I.R.B. men aside." Brennan, who retired in 1940 as Chief of Staff of the Irish National Army, was early a member of the Volunteers and at the time of the Rising was already serving a jail sentence for making seditious speeches.

The British were disturbed by the total failure of the Irish to learn their lesson, to realise that this was no time for the old order to change and yield place to new. Frantically they tried to curb the activities of the Sinn Fein and Volunteer dissidents, activities which were no longer repugnant to the general populace. Men who made speeches to exacerbate the clamour for independence were clapped into jail. Among them was Thomas Ashe, arrested in August, 1917, and sentenced to twelve months' imprisonment with hard labour. In Mountjoy jail Ashe, with Austin Stack, went on hunger strike. He was forcibly fed for a week, collapsed and was allowed to lie unattended on the stone floor of his cell. Ashe died as a result of his treatment and his funeral, following a lying-in-state, was made an occasion for a demonstration, the more impressive because of the solemn silence of the vast crowds, of the resurgent spirit of nationalism. Although the Volunteers wore uniforms and a guard fired volleys over Ashe's Glasnevin grave, the Castle authorities took no action—wisely, because
60

this time the Dublin crowds might easily have "come out with knives and forks".

Perhaps for humanitarian, but more probably for politic, reasons, the English Government now employed the "Cat and Mouse" Act, introduced originally to prevent suffragettes from hunger-striking to death. Under this simple but effective measure, hunger strikers were released from prison when their weakness threatened to become an embarrassment and were re-arrested when they had regained their strength. There was something singularly appropriate about the use of this device, for between the struggle of the Irish for independence and that of the suffragettes for emancipation, there were sharp parallels. The basic similarity was that rank injustice affected a large number of people, that the majority condoned it and, far from setting out to achieve their rights, were disapproving of the militant minority who took violent action until, angered by the ruthless punitive measures taken by the authorities against those who made the protest on behalf of them all, the majority at last threw their weight on the side of justice. Half a century later, the Irish have their Republic but the women of England do not yet enjoy equality, though without the Pankhursts they might still exist under conditions of Victorian subjugation. So might the Irish have done without their revolutionary leaders of that era.

Duke told the Cabinet in February[12] that there was a conspiracy among Sinn Fein prisoners to go on hunger strike. Irish prison doctors, he explained, would not take the responsibility for forcible feeding and he thought that, although the Church pronounced that deliberate starving was wrong, there might be deaths. He believed the Government should be ready "to accept the responsibility of such consequences." He was also concerned about the outbreak of serious trouble in some western counties involving conflicts with the police. The Cabinet gave him covering authority to proclaim Sinn Fein a dangerous association in some areas and sanctioned the arrest, and deportation if necessary, of any Sinn Fein leaders "whose speech or action was dangerous to the public interest."

Considering that Great Britain's fate was in the balance in France, the Cabinet dealt with remarkable equanimity with the needling reports of the deterioration of the Irish situation.

[12] W.C. min. 351 (13) of 21/2/18.

On February 25th, they approved the internment of likely trouble makers to reduce unrest, but the next day the Home Secretary explained that, as the Sinn Fein leaders were British subjects, "it was necessary to prove legally hostile association". Solemnly he gave it as his opinion that "it was more than doubtful whether connection with the Dublin rebellion of 1916 could still be regarded as hostile association."[13]

Three days later, the Cabinet were still concerned with the problem, the more so since the Prime Minister had received a Memorial from forty per cent of the Convention who thought that lawlessness in the country was prejudicing proper consideration of the Prime Minister's offer, contained in a letter to Sir Horace Plunkett, Chairman of the Convention, to introduce a Home Rule Bill in terms of the Convention's report. In this precarious setting a measure to apply conscription in Ireland seemed as out of place as a hatchet in a basket of eggs. Asquith had seen justification for conscription only in the context of general approval, but the Irish had made it plain enough that no such approval existed in Ireland.

But the decision to extend the call-up to Ireland was hammered out of agonised discussion in the Cabinet room, and the Home Rule Bill promised with it was not intended to coat an unpalatable pill but was insisted upon as a prior requisite by Lloyd George, in fulfilment of his pledge. In spite of warnings from Lord French and Sir Henry Wilson that every day's delay was dangerous as Britain reeled on the brink of military ruin, the decision on the conscription bill, which, it must be remembered, was primarily to extend the Government's powers in Great Britain itself, was actually deferred by the Cabinet until the Report of the Convention was received.

Lord French, then C.-in-C., Home Forces, told the Cabinet on March 25th[14] that with " a slight augmentation of the existing troops", conscription could be enforced in Ireland. The recruits, he suggested, should be drafted to English and Scottish units rather than to Irish ones where the present volunteers would not regard conscripts with any favour. It was pointed out to French that this was hardly the way to encourage Irish unity and that it would "shatter any hope of the Convention being a success."

13 W.C. min. 353 (3) of 25/2/18 and 354 (8) of 26/2/18.
14 W.C. min. 372 (13) of 25/3/18.

The Cabinet were looking ahead to putting an army in the field in 1919, and the prospect seemed bleak. They decided to raise the age limit to 50 or 55, to call up ministers of religion, many of whom were "of excellent physique", and to send conscientious objectors to serve in non-combatant units—which involved revoking a pledge given by Asquith early in the war. A suggestion to call up boys of 17 was ultimately rejected because it was thought the public would not stand for it.

On the following day, Sir Bryan Mahon and General Byrne, respectively General Officer Commanding in Chief, Irish Command, and head of the Royal Irish Constabulary, together with the Chief Secretary, discussed the conscription issue with Lloyd George. Between them Mahon and Byrne drafted a memorandum[15] in which they said: "Conscription can be enforced but with the greatest difficulty. It will be bitterly opposed by the united Nationalists and the clergy." They thought it the worst possible time, anticipated strikes and bloodshed, "for the first fortnight at least", and hardship for the civilian population. Several more brigades would be required to maintain order. There would have to be some kind of military control in the country, all known leaders would have to be got out of the way at once, and "everyone, irrespective of who he is, arrested on first sign of giving trouble."

They admitted the measures were drastic but, they concluded, "the situation is serious, or it would not be considered necessary to have conscription at this inopportune time."

Lloyd George informed his Cabinet that Duke had grave doubts about conscription, Byrne thought it a mistake, and Mahon favoured it on the whole though he knew it meant trouble.[16] The Prime Minister himself was reluctant to introduce conscription before the Report of the Convention was received; on the other hand, if Ireland remained exempted while drastic measures were applied in England, the Government would have to reckon with bitter resentment at home.

By ruthlessly combing through the reserved occupations, raising the age to 50 and reducing the minimum to 17 for home-based troops, possibly 550,000 men could be raised in Britain. It was thought that 150,000 could be raised in Ireland.

15 W.C. min. 374 (12) Appendix, of 27/3/18.
16 W.C. min. 374 (12) of 27/3/18.

"Such numbers were based on the assumption that the situation was thoroughly bad and that the nation was bound to make a supreme effort."[17]

Bad the situation certainly was. On March 21st Ludendorff had begun his mighty offensive and British casualties were enormous. Those 150,000 fresh men in Ireland were tempting indeed to the war-weary Government. Concerning them there appeared to Lloyd George to be two alternatives:

"(a) Ireland could be told, 'Come and fight, and without any loss of time we will give you Home Rule on the basis of the Convention Report.' That is to say, beginning by saying that their nationality was recognised, and the right of self-determination given them, but that they must fight for the Empire.

"(b) We should say to Ireland, 'Are you prepared to fight for this country in this emergency?' Ireland might reply, 'We will fight if you will give us self-government.' On the other hand, if Ireland said, 'No, under no conditions will we fight,' then it would be hopeless to invite Parliament to take its thoughts away from the War in order to carry through a Home Rule measure."[18]

Duke was sceptical. "We might almost as well recruit Germans," he said, and prophesied that the result would be the loss of Ireland. His suggestion was to maintain the nine Irish regiments by a process similar to the Militia Ballot. Mahon and Byrne thought this was not a bad idea for "only a proportion of men would be taken . . . those that remained would be so glad to have escaped that they would not make trouble." Then Byrne had second thoughts. "The efficient Sinn Fein organisation would probably be utilised to develop conscientious objection and passive resistance on a large scale." Churchill was "rather attracted by Mr. Duke's suggestion because it recognised nationality and he would be inclined to support it if it meant "that from 70,000 to 80,000 men would be forthcoming with the goodwill of the rest of the population", a cheerful if rather out-of-touch view.

Generally the Ministers were agreed that the recommendations of the Convention should be implemented but Lloyd George emphasised that it would be impossible to carry a Home Rule measure in Parliament "unless compulsory military

17 W.C. min. 375 (2) of 27/3/18.   18 W.C. min. 375 (2) of 27/3/18.

8

service or its equivalent were applied in Ireland." Balfour thought that "it would not do to give the aspect of a bargain to the transaction" but that "the effect of a bargain" could be obtained by introducing the Bills simultaneously. Earlier, Balfour had recorded his objection to the policy of the Government. In his opinion, "the only possible way out of the difficulty was to divide Ireland."[19]

On March 28th, though the Cabinet had decided to draft the Military Service Bill, they called in Sir Edward Carson and the Lord Chief Justice of Ireland, Sir James Campbell, to hear their views on the thorny issue[20]. Campbell thought the opportunity to impose conscription had been lost two years earlier, immediately after the Rising. A new class had since grown up, "the late backbone of the Irish disaffection, namely farmers and their sons," had given way to people "who were more or less educated and had ideas of their own." He was convinced that the cost of conscription would be "enormous bloodshed." The agricultural population in Ulster would be against compulsory service and "practically the whole of the clergy, from the Archbishop downwards, would take the field against the British Government."

Carson, too, was "forced to the conclusion, with much regret" that conscription was inadvisable. But, he added, if men could not be got in Great Britain without enforcing conscription in Ireland, "the question became a very different one." This lawyer's viewpoint could not have helped the Government very much.

Duke insisted that conscription should be treated as secondary, "dependent on the acceptance of the Convention". From his own knowledge of Ireland, "it was not impossible," he said, "to carry out in that country measures that were demonstrably just."

Over and over, in their dilemma, the Ministers thrashed out their arguments. There was the growing power of Sinn Fein to be reckoned with, and the possibility of the Convention's breaking up if conscription were applied. Some military advice was that Irish conscripts might shoot their officers, other that British military discipline would make soldiers of them. Public opinion at home was a vital factor but the attitude of the United States and of the Dominions had also to be taken

[19] W.C. min. 351 (12) of 24/2/18. [20] W.C. min. 376 (5) of 28/3/18.

into account. The British people would not take kindly to Home Rule legislation if the Irish were to be exempted from conscription while British fathers of fifty years and sons of seventeen were rooted out.

The Prime Minister insisted that they were pledged to Home Rule in terms of his letter to Plunkett and the logical order "would be first to pass Home Rule, so removing a wrong, or an imaginary wrong, to the people of Ireland, and then to bring in conscription." It was possible, perhaps, to make provision in the Bill for power to extend conscription by Order in Council, a power which would not be used until the Report of the Convention had been accepted by the Government. Despite protests from Sir Henry Wilson and Lord French, it was decided not to summon Parliament on April 2nd as planned, but a week later when, it was hoped, the Report would have been received. Amid the gloom the only light that broke into the Cabinet room that day was news that the Americans were to hasten the dispatch of troops.

By the end of the month, the fact that the British War Cabinet were considering conscription for Ireland was the talk of Dublin, a circumstance which Mahon, enjoined to strict silence on the subject by the Cabinet, reported wryly in a letter to French. At the same time he stated that opposition might be less than expected because the German advance had swung Irish sympathy, not so much towards the British, as towards their fellow Catholics, the French, and the moment might be opportune for the introduction of a Home Rule Bill. He advised that, as soon as conscription had been decided upon, Cardinal Logue should be informed, for if he and the Hierarchy "denounced futile resistance which might lead to bloodshed, opposition would be diminished."[21] The Cabinet decided not to confide in Cardinal Logue for the moment,

21 W.C. min. 377 (9) of 29/3/18.

FOUR

Although the need for men in France was stringent, Britain had to keep back some troops, mainly belonging to Cyclists Divisions, in case reinforcements were required in Ireland. But they were relatively few, and had the 1916 rebels waited until Easter, 1918, the outcome of the Rising might have been very different. The Government saw the danger, and when the first draft of the Military Service Bill was considered, Duke warned that instant rebellion was inevitable if Clause 4, which provided for immediate conscription in Ireland on the same terms as were to apply in Britain, were allowed to stand. He urged the adoption of the alternative clause drafted which gave power to enforce conscription of the Irish by Order in Council. He insisted, however, on the retention of Sub-section 2 of the alternative clause. This was a fascinating piece of humour:

"If any male British subject in Ireland who has attained the age of eighteen years takes part in any manner, at any time after the passing of this Act, in any military exercises, movements, or drill promoted by or conducted in connection with any such organisation or body formed for or having as one of its objects the practice of such exercises, movements, or drill, he shall as from the prescribed day be deemed to have been duly enlisted in His Majesty's regular forces for general service with the colours or in the reserve and to have been forthwith transferred to the reserve, and the provisions of the Act shall, subject to such necessary modifications and adaptations as may be prescribed, apply to him in like manner as if he had been a man to whom Sub-section 1 of Section one of this act applies."[1]

Those who came under this sub-section were to be treated in exactly the same way as British males between the ages of 18 and 50, to whom the Act would apply immediately. As Duke pointed out, it would mean that "it would be possible to enlist at once some thousands of Volunteers who had some military knowledge and who had arms and leaders, and that

[1] Cabinet paper GT 4124.

once this opposition was removed, the party which would be most strongly antagonistic to compulsory service in Ireland would disappear."[2] Ruefully he admitted that the Government was quite unable to control the activities of the Volunteers. It was an ingenious idea to draft de Valera and Collins, Brugha, Mulcahy, Boland and all their men, and to send them with their elected officers and their illicit arms to France, so, with one stroke, reinforcing England's threadbare army and removing from Ireland the main opposition to conscription.

The alternative was adopted but Lloyd George was adamant that a Home Rule Bill must be introduced also, otherwise "it would be stated, and rightly so, that the pledges given on this subject had not been redeemed". Government supporters, the whole of the Labour Party, the American people and he, himself, would not accept one measure without the other.

Brushing aside Bonar Law's objection that if there were not substantial agreement in the Convention, the pledge that Ulster would not be coerced might be difficult to sustain, the Prime Minister stated his intention to carry through a bill based on the Convention's recommendations if possible, and, if not, then based on the original letter to Sir Horace Plunkett. Only in the event of Irish Members of all sections opposing the Home Rule Bill in the House of Commons would Lloyd George concede conscription without Home Rule. Barnes went further and declined to be party to the application of conscription in Ireland unless Home Rule went through.[3]

On April 6th, the Prime Minister sombrely reported to the Cabinet that great numbers of men had been lost in France and that hundreds of thousands more would be needed. He had now received the Report of the Convention, but his determination of the day before not to introduce one measure without the other had wilted. The calamitous situation in France had impelled him to come to a decision that legislation should be passed providing for conscription in Ireland. There would be trouble, perhaps bloodshed, he acknowledged, but this he now believed had to be accepted.

He then stated the considerations which had weighed with him.

"Even if Home Rule were carried tomorrow, the army and navy would be under the control of the Imperial Parliament.

[2] W.C. min. 383 (16) of 5/4/18.   [3] W.C. min. 383 (17) of 5/5/18.

The claim has never been put forward by any Irish party that the army and navy and the defence of the Realm are local matters. In the second place, I do not believe it possible in this country to tear industry about, to break up single businesses, to take fathers of forty-five and upwards from their homes to fight the battles of a Catholic nationality on the Continent without deep resentment at the spectacle of sturdy young Catholics in Ireland spending their time in increasing the difficulties of this country by drilling and by compelling us to keep troops in Ireland. I do not know any grounds of justice or equity on which conscription could not be applied to Ireland."

The Government had shown indulgence to Ireland, "wise and reasonable indulgence", he thought, in the hope that she would become "reconciled to her Imperial association". But they could not "go to the House of Commons and ask our people to make sacrifices, sacrifices which the Irish in America are making, and leave the Irish at home out. I think we ought to accord to Ireland the same rights as Irishmen are enjoying in America."

Whether Home Rule should be brought in during war-time was another question, but it had to be remembered that when it was shelved no one had thought that the war would drag on for four years. Now the Convention, which the Government had sponsored, had agreed to a Report by a majority of 44 to 29, which Lloyd George considered a remarkable result. In the minority were Catholic Bishops, Ulstermen and Sinn Fein; those in favour included moderate Nationalists, Southern Unionists and Anglican Bishops. With dubious optimism, Lloyd George reported that, had the Sinn Fein demand for control of Customs been met, Sinn Fein and the Catholic Bishops would have joined the majority.

"But they would have found some other grievance then," interjected a sceptical Churchill.

Unabashed, the Prime Minister continued, with even less well grounded hope, that the Ulstermen, though they had not committed themselves definitely, would come round to the majority viewpoint if they were given satisfactory safeguards.

Summing up, Lloyd George stated that provision would be made in the Military Service Bill for conscription to apply to Ireland by Order In Council, and that it would apply as soon as Home Rule had been carried in Parliament. It would be a mistake not to take the necessary powers until after the Home Rule Bill was through as the Irish might resist Home Rule. "We must not give them that incentive," he said. And, with less of his earlier forthrightness, he declined also to undertake categorically to postpone the application of conscription until the Home Rule Bill was through. Here was the usual Lloyd George loophole; having stated his intention, he reserved the right to change his mind. It would take time to put conscription into force, he explained; they would have to improvise a register with the aid of the police. In the meantime, borrowed American troops would fill the gaps in the British Army, then British drafts would have to be drawn upon. Clearly, it was in his mind that, from then, only Ireland would remain as a source of manpower. His colleagues took up the argument, and the debate in the Cabinet that day is revealing.

Lord Curzon: We must stand or fall by both (measures).

Mr Bonar Law: How would you justify to the House of Commons delaying conscription? You can say, as the Prime Minister has just said, that time is required for machinery, but it must be made plain that the two Bills are not contingent.

Lord Robert Cecil: You will have to say the postponement is in connection with Home Rule.

The Prime Minister: I would say it will take time, and that time we mean to use to put through the Home Rule Bill.

Lord Robert Cecil: You will have to indicate that both will have to be worked together.

Lord Milner: It is our intention to proceed with conscription even if the Home Rule Bill is generally opposed.

Dr Addison: We can say, "You are getting the right of self-government, you must do your share to defend your liberties."

Mr Bonar Law: Suppose we start with trying to force both Bills through, and then find that Members of all kinds are opposed to the Home Rule Bill, how can you possibly carry it through?

Answering, the Prime Minister said it was "absurd to decide what we can do before the crisis arises."

Mr Churchill: The two measures should be regarded as independent, and be simultaneously introduced. I do not see the advantage of delaying the application of the Military Service

Act to Ireland. The dual policy should be loyally followed. I would press forward on the two roads. There is a great deal to be said against any delay in action once conscription is announced.

Mr G. N. Barnes: You have in the Bill a clause which would deal with the Sinn Feiners who are now drilling. That can be applied at once. I cannot assent to apply conscription willy-nilly without any guarantee of Home Rule. I shall have to reserve the right to reconsider the position later.

Lord Robert Cecil: I do not know what the Cabinet's scheme of Home Rule is. Many of my Unionist colleagues are in the same position. I am anxious to get conscription through in Ireland, and am prepared to pay a high price to get men in this emergency.

The Prime Minister: I can only say, in a general way, that our scheme will proceed on the lines of the Cabinet letter, with safeguards for Ulster in the shape of an Ulster Committee.

Mr Bonar Law: You do not ask your colleagues to commit themselves today to the form of the Home Rule Bill.

The Prime Minister: That would be hardly fair.

Mr Herbert Fisher: Has not the Government given a pledge to proceed if there was substantial agreement at the Convention?

The Prime Minister: I do not think you can say that 44 to 29 is substantial agreement. We are now going on the other line: that, failing substantial agreement, the Government will produce a Bill, and in that Bill we must make provision for Ulster.

Mr Bonar Law: It is absurd to ask Ministers to commit themselves now.

Mr Churchill: That is a hard saying. The enforcing of conscription on Ireland is a rupturing of political associations and involves a complete new orientation of antagonisms, and therefore it is folly not to see how grave that decision is. I could not agree to that unless our Unionist friends come with us on the other measure, which profoundly affects opinion here, in Ireland, and in the United States. It is hard that we should commit ourselves to conscription unless we can count on cordial agreement among our Unionist colleagues that they will go forward in support of Home Rule with equal energy. Dr Addison concurred.

The Prime Minister: That is the policy of the Government. The Cabinet have agreed to a definite plan.

Mr Bonar Law: But the letter gives no definite plan.

The Prime Minister: Unless we follow the lines of the Cabinet letter and the Cabinet agreement, then I cannot put forward conscription for Ireland on Tuesday.

Mr Bonar Law: It depends upon the form in which the principles of the letter are put in the Bill.

Lord Curzon: We have accepted the broad principles of the letter, and our colleagues are entitled to see the letter.

Mr Bonar Law: It must depend on whether the Bill carries out the principles of the letter.

The Prime Minister: That is a different matter.

Lord Milner: I am prepared to accept such a Home Rule Bill as conforms generally to the proposals put forward in the Prime Minister's letter to the Convention. It is very hard for us to support such a Bill if Ulster opposes it, but I am prepared to do that and to put forward every effort in support of the Home Rule Bill but I am not prepared to abandon conscription even if we completely fail with the Home Rule Bill.

Mr Barnes: Why not put both in one basket? I am voting for conscription because I am thereby hoping to get Home Rule. If not, I shall have to reconsider my position.

Lord Robert Cecil: If I vote for Home Rule it is because I hope thereby to get conscription.

Mr Barnes: If we fail we can go to the country.

The Prime Minister: We could not do that. The Government can go if we fail.

Lord Derby: We must stake our existence on passing both Bills.

Mr Herbert Fisher: Are you definitely satisfied that there is a military advantage in applying conscription to Ireland? I feel absolutely with you as to the bad effect on English public opinion of continuing to exempt Ireland; but we should look at it as a cold military proposition. English public opinion is sound. Our artisans will do their duty. You have to decide whether it is worth your while to enforce conscription in Ireland and thereby perhaps obtain disaffected elements for your army.

Lord Derby: They will be distributed through the army.

The Prime Minister: That is the one consideration that chiefly worried me. Is it worth while in a military sense? You will get 50,000 at any rate, at a minimum, who will fight. These five divisions will be made up of excellent material, of young men up to twenty-five, at a time when we are taking old men.

Mr Churchill: I have not met one soldier in France who does not think we shall get good fighting material from Ireland. I think the decision of the War Cabinet is a battlefield decision but a wise one.[4]

The new Military Service Bill was introduced in the House of Commons on April 10th. On the same day a telegram from Duke warned the Government that de Valera was urging on the Sinn Fein executive that it would suit their policy if conscription came, for they could then take systematic and violent opposition to its enforcement. According to the Chief Secretary, de Valera was advocating a policy of the stoppage of all transport work and the shooting of the recruiting authorities whether Army or Royal Irish Constabulary.[5]

In the Commons the Bill was vehemently opposed by the Irish Parliamentary Party, led by Dillon since the death of the brokenhearted John Redmond in March, and in protest they marched out of the House. There were misgivings still in the Cabinet.[6] Barnes said he had "always understood that the policy of the War Cabinet was, firstly, to stand or fall by the two Bills", and "secondly, that military service was only to be applied in Ireland after an interval during which a measure of Home Rule could be passed." He was particularly concerned that the Home Secretary's speech had been "in favour of compulsory military service pure and simple."

Lloyd George answered that in his own speech, he believed, he had made the position clear, but he had thought it inadvisable to make too many references to Home Rule. But Barnes "could not forget the evidence which had been given before the War Cabinet by responsible men to the effect that conscription without Home Rule was out of the question." The Cabinet decided that the Home Rule Bill should be immediately prepared. Their thoughts turned now to the possibility of enlisting volunteers in Ireland "to meet the critical situation." Any approach to the Nationalist Party by the War Cabinet would be useless, but representations by the Labour Party might possibly produce results.

This was optimistic for, two days after their indignant

4 W.C. min. 385 of 6/4/18.   5 W.C. min. 388 (6) of 10/4/18.
6 W.C. min. 389 (9) of 11/4/18.

departure from the House, Dillon and Devlin appeared at an anti-conscription meeting at the Mansion House in Dublin on the same platform as de Valera and Griffith. From that meeting emanated a statement that the Bill was tantamount to a declaration of war on Ireland and that any attempt to implement it would be resisted. The Catholic Hierarchy, in general still suspicious of revolutionary activity, denounced conscription "against the will of the Irish people and in defiance of the protests of its leaders" as "an oppressive and inhuman law". In Belfast, too, there were protest meetings.

The Chief Secretary for Ireland warned the Cabinet that the Nationalist M.P.'s would probably abandon Westminster after the Third Reading of the Conscription Bill and "make common cause with the Sinn Feiners".[7] Duke was more percipient than most of his colleagues but even he did not see that, in driving the Nationalist leaders into the arms of Sinn Fein, the Government was causing their supporters to transfer their allegiance to Sinn Fein. Better, they thought, to vote for the party whom their leaders had now admitted to be right rather than vote for the right at second hand. From Duke's letter the Cabinet also learned that a meeting was to be held in Dublin "to make preparations for the establishment of a revolutionary Provisional Government."

Lloyd George said tenaciously that the Government would stand or fall by the Bill and they were determined to enforce it, but he recalled once more that they were "definitely pledged to introduce and to enact a Home Rule Bill for Ireland." It was agreed that in the event of a rising in Ireland the 15,000 troops then in Ireland would be quite inadequate and that Lord French should hasten to Dublin to consult with Mahon and Byrne and to come back with a plan of action in case the military had to be used to enforce conscription. They were to indicate the number of reinforcements required and to offer suggestions "as to whence these could be obtained". In the meantime "preliminary dispositions should be made at once in order to protect important strategical and tactical points."[8]

On the question of Home Rule, "while it was agreed that the two proposals could not be linked together, and that even the Nationalist Members of Parliament understood that there

7 Cabinet paper GT 4218.   8 Ibid.

was no question of a bargain . . . a statement on this subject should be made on the Third Reading of the Bill." Lloyd George was also recklessly ready to stake his Government's existence on passing a Home Rule Bill and putting it into operation at once. So the life of the Government was twice put at risk.

It was left to Long, Secretary of State for the Colonies, to draft the Bill. He was to base his proposals on the Report of the Convention as far as possible and to make sure that they would be adjudged fair by British and American opinion.[9]

The British Government was still seeking a way to get the dangerous Sinn Fein leaders out of harm's way so that conscription would be applied without too much trouble. Sir George Cave, Home Secretary, now suggested that Section 14B of the Defence of the Realm Regulations should be amended so that they could be interned without proof of "hostile associations". The Easter Rising was a thing of the past and "at the present moment," said Cave, "it was doubtful whether connection with the enemy could be proved in the case of most of the Sinn Fein leaders." Barnes objected. Such an amendment could only "inflame public opinion there." Lloyd George answered drily that "according to his information the opinion of the people in Ireland was already as inflamed as it was possible to be." He supported the amendment.[10]

Rumours that de Valera had been discovered to be in communication with the enemy were mentioned in the Cabinet room but it had to be conceded that there was nothing in them. French, reporting by letter to the Cabinet that the signs were that conscription would be met by passive rather than active resistance did not mention de Valera, but he recommended that speeches and actions which incited active opposition should be stopped.[11]

French's confidence that conscription could be enforced despite opposition evidently persuaded Lloyd George that the Field-Marshal should replace Lord Wimborne as Lord Lieutenant. He had already told Lloyd George that he "was prepared to take every step possible to put a stop to any German intrigues." Before taking up his duties he attended a Cabinet meeting and declared his intention to issue a proclama-

9 W.C. min. 392 (13) of 16/4/18. 10 W.C. min. 395 (13) of 19/4/18.
11 W.C. min. 398/9 of 24/4/18.

tion and to arrest "those against whom evidence of intriguing was produced." He returned to Ireland with greater powers than his predecessors had enjoyed. Except that he was to refer to the War Cabinet on matters of policy, he was given a free hand. He was to deal promptly with seditious speeches but reminded that "to hold a meeting to organise resistance to a prospective law was not treason".[12] Privately Lloyd George told him that he wanted the onus of shooting first to be on the rebels.

Two days later Long, Secretary of State for the Colonies, was asked to accept sole responsibility for Irish affairs, referring only the most vital matters to the War Cabinet. His condition that it must be "clearly understood that most drastic steps should be taken to stamp out pro-German intrigues" was accepted.[13]

The drastic steps were soon taken. French took up his appointment on May 11th. On May 15th the Cabinet approved the terms of French's proclamation, having at their previous meeting vetoed them, and on the night of the 17th there were wholesale arrests. Collins had got wind of the move but, in spite of his warning, Griffith, de Valera, Sean McGarry, Count Plunkett and many other prominent Sinn Fein personalities were dispatched to English jails. Among them were several women, the celebrated Maud Gonne, Countess Markievicz and Tom Clarke's irrepressible widow. Collins, Cathal Brugha and some others evaded arrest.

It was only after the Home Secretary had made his pernicketty discovery that they would have to prove "hostile association" if they were to get the stormy petrels out of Ireland that "German intrigues" became a topic of discussion in the Cabinet room. Nevertheless, Cabinet documents show that some Ministers at least were genuinely apprehensive of the existence of a German plot to inspire and assist another rising.

Even the placable Barnes agreed with the arrests but he considered that "public opinion would not be satisfied until the evidence in the possession of the Government had been submitted to Judges." It was pointed out to him that "where evidence of conspiracy existed, any conspirator could, under the Defence of the Realm Regulations, be kept a prisoner

[12] W.C. min. 407/5 of 8/5/18.   [13] W.C. min. 408/11 of 10/5/18.

76

without trial." He did have the right to appeal to a Special Committee; the evidence against him would then be laid before Judges.[14]

The Cabinet, in the Prime Minister's absence in Paris, passed for publication a statement about the arrests, but Lloyd George telephoned that he wished "to insert in the statement in regard to the Irish arrests some words which would connect with the German designs in Ireland persons who had been detained, other than de Valera." De Valera's speeches, quoted in the statement, "identified him with the German Sinn Fein plans", but "no speeches were quoted or evidence produced in the statement with respect to the other persons detained".[15] As there were no readily available advisers from the Irish Office, the Cabinet decided to let the statement stand. It was an anaemic document, but convincing enough in its recollections of the 1916 commerce with Germany to give an appearance of verisimilitude to the allegations of recent transactions. There was some stronger evidence which could not be published[16] at the time for it would have been of assistance to Germany:

Within a few weeks of the 1916 Rising, the failure of which they blamed largely on Casement, the American Irish were again in negotiation with Germany. By September they were requesting arms and an expeditionary force and urging the advantages of western Ireland for submarine bases and Ireland itself as a base for zeppelins.

Three months later, Zimmermann offered the Fenians two consignments, each of 30,000 rifles, 10 machine-guns and 6 million rounds of ammunition, for landing in Galway and Tralee between 21st and 25th February, 1917, or, alternatively, between the same dates in March. But the Germans were adamant that they would not land troops and the offer was declined.

Liam Mellows and Dr Max von Ricklinghausen, a German subject, were arrested in New York by the U.S. Secret Service in October, 1917. Mellows had a false passport in the name of Patrick Donnelly. Dr Patrick McCartan, envoy of the Provisional Government of Ireland in the United States, was also detained as, it was alleged, he was setting out for Germany via

14 W.C. min. 416 (1) 23/5/18.   15 W.C. min. 417 (1) 24/5/18.
16 Cabinet paper CP 2392 of 31/12/20.

Stockholm to work out plans for a new rebellion. Both he and Mellows were charged with possessing fraudulent passports. Both were leading members of Sinn Fein, so that the British Government's suspicion of a link with Germany was not altogether misplaced.

British code-breakers intercepted message after message passing between Germany and the Irish-Americans and some consignments of arms which were in fact dispatched from Germany never reached Ireland. America's entry into the war in April temporarily broke the line of communication with Germany but it was soon re-established by way of South America and Madrid. In August, Germany again offered arms to help Sinn Fein but refused to send troops, and early in 1918 the British Government learned that arms were to be landed on the west coast of Ireland.

James Rouane, described as a local Sinn Fein leader, was arrested in County Mayo with German pamphlets in his possession and other Sinn Feiners were alleged to be conveying messages to U Boats off the west coast, and also off Kerry, using fishing boat skippers as intermediaries. This kind of information was probably no more than hearsay, but to the worried British Ministers trivial incidents and snippets of rumour added up to an alarming answer.

On April 16th, 1918, a U Boat was sighted in Dublin Bay and during the same night Robert and James Cotter, one of whom was de Valera's brother-in-law, were intercepted in a small sailing boat. It could not be proved that they were in communication with the submarine and they were convicted only of contravening Admiralty Regulations. On the west coast "one of Casement's men", a Connaught Ranger named Dowling, landed from a German submarine and was arrested.

The Government were satisfied "that a design existed on the part of Germany, in combination with the Sinn Fein extremists and Irish revolutionaries in America, to land arms in Ireland and bring about another Irish Insurrection and thus divert British troops from the front in France." German aims were to follow up the anticipated success of their great offensive by further embarrassing the British in Ireland. British Intelligence agents, who had earlier warned the authorities to expect Dowling, now reported that on April 26th, at Cuxhaven, rifles and machine-guns had been transferred from closed railway cars to large submarines. "These consignments did not arrive in Ireland," Ministers were informed.

"The continued efficacy of the Irish movement is for us a guarantee of peace," said the German *Kolnische Zeitung*, while the Sinn Feiners themselves, according to the British view, "had been led to believe that another revolution would bring the case of Ireland before the Peace Conference and that independence would then be secured." This was, indeed, the gist of de Valera's speeches. As early as 1916 he had told the Volunteers that the Allies could not win the war. Ireland should stake her claim at the Peace Conference—but she should have an army behind her.

Sinn Fein also looked to the possibility of help from the Russian socialists and when de Valera was arrested a copy of a lengthy statement in French, presented by the Friends of Irish Freedom in America to an international socialist conference at Stockholm, was found in his attaché case. This was simply a history of Sinn Fein together with a report of the Ard-Fheis of the previous October. Also in the dispatch case, and in de Valera's own handwriting, were a draft statement of Ireland's case for submission to the Peace Conference, a list of towns on the five main roads from Dublin—into which some significance was read—and a long, thoughtful and authoritative plan for the Ireland of the future. This dealt particularly with the defence of the country. Envisaging a striking force of flying artillery, cyclists, machine-gunners and snipers, the document described in detail measures for recruitment—including conscription up to the age of 40, the training of officers and N.C.O.'s and the formation of divisional areas. It provided against attack from the sea and even suggested ways of employing retired servicemen.

Nothing in any of the documents found even hinted at a liaison with Germany and, in spite of the arrest of the Sinn Fein leaders, the intrigues continued with unabated, if ineffectual, enthusiasm. But at least many of the most dangerous opponents of conscription were out of the way.

The intervention of the Catholic Hierarchy in the conscription issue also had incensed Lloyd George and it was agreed by the Cabinet that the British Representative at the Vatican was to be notified of "any cases that might come to light of the improper interference of the Irish priesthood in secular affairs

79

and, more particularly, the recent promises of absolution to persons engaged in resistance to the Military Service Act".[17] On May 6th he received a deputation of Belfast Trades Unionists "to whom he had pointed out that it was impossible to enforce conscription in Ireland without some reasonable measure of Home Rule. He had also shown them how the supremacy of Parliament had been challenged by the action of the Catholic Hierarchy and how important it was that they should render him every assistance in their power in order to defeat this challenge which had been thrown down."[18]

To play on religious susceptibilities in this way was as dangerous as it was underhand.

Stubbornly Lord French insisted that conscription could be enforced and a plan was prepared, but Duke thought the proposals would only "hasten preparations to resist conscription."[19] Already a 24-hour general strike had been provoked, farmers were threatening to plough up their crops and seventeen King's Counsel and two Sergeants-at-Law had announced their approval of the Hierarchy's opposition to conscription.

By May 15th, two days before the arrest of the Sinn Fein leaders, the British Cabinet was swinging to the idea of campaigning for volunteers in Ireland. Long had introduced a new element into the Home Rule argument.[20] He had come to the conclusion that intransigents of all points of view could be reconciled "if a beginning could be made with the establishment of a Federal system for the UK", that "it would be very difficult for Irishmen to oppose measures which it was intended to make applicable to each of the four parts of the United Kingdom."

Lloyd George agreed that "if Ireland was to appear as much an integral part of the UK as England, Scotland and Wales, it would go a long way to meet objections to being treated differently from the UK." The Welsh wizard added piquantly that greater progress would have been made in Wales if she had enjoyed Home Rule. Another supporter of the Federal idea was Austen Chamberlain; he thought the Home Rule Bill could be the first instalment. But Barnes was all for sticking to the framework of the Convention Report and General Smuts, who was present on this occasion, thought

[17] W.C. min. 405 (14) of 6/5/18.   [18] Ibid.
[19] W.C. min. 397/6 of 23/4/18.   [20] W.C. min. 397/7 of 23/4/18.
80

that any other course would lay the British Government open to a charge of breach of faith and "force the Nationalists to reject any other treatment of the problem less favourable to their point of view".

Reiterating that he had been against any consideration of the Home Rule problem during wartime, Balfour said it had now become a war measure in which the Dominions and the United States were vitally interested. But the question of federation had received "very imperfect consideration" and, like Barnes, he plumped for a Convention Bill. Long remarked that opinion in Ulster was hardening and that the only hope of a united Ireland lay in a federal scheme.

Until Home Rule had been dealt with there could be no conscription, insisted Lloyd George. But, by "challenging the right of the Imperial Parliament to impose upon them an Act which they dislike", the Irish Nationalists were throwing out "a challenge to the unity of the Kingdom". The situation should be made "as favourable as possible for the Cabinet to engage upon such a conflict", for them to be able to say: "These domestic issues we hand over to you, but conscription we mean to enforce." He likened the issue to that which had divided the northern and southern states of America and expressed his belief that when the dust had settled the Irish would settle too.

There seemed no prospect of an early Home Rule Bill and, as Chamberlain put it, there was "strong reason to appeal for voluntary recruits at the present time as the Government has precluded itself by its pledges from putting conscription into force for the present, and therefore the present time should be used to the best advantage."[21] At the end of May the Government decided to issue a proclamation calling for volunteers. No anticipated figure was to be stated for, if the figure were put too high, in Long's view, the people of Ireland would consider that too much was being asked of them whereas, if it were set too low, Lloyd George thought they "would create the impression that the Government was not in earnest in the policy of compulsory military service." So it was decided that "the adjective 'adequate' should be used" and it was left to the Irish to work out what was "adequate".

In effect, both Home Rule and Conscription had been

21 W.C. min. 412/18 of 15/5/18.

deferred indefinitely and some Ministers were anxious to know how the Government was to explain its backtracking to both Houses of Parliament.[22] Long remarked drily, "It was understood to be part of the dual policy that, if they failed to pass the Home Rule Bill the Government would resign."

At once Lloyd George corrected him. The Government would resign only if, after conscription in Ireland were enforced, a Home Rule Bill were defeated in Parliament. In any case, the position had been much affected by the discovery of "a grave Sinn Fein conspiracy" involving the leaders of Irish opinion, men like de Valera and Arthur Griffith, whose programme had been "timed to coincide with a great German offensive which would menace the existence of the British Army", and by the challenge of the Roman Catholic Church "on an issue which hitherto has always been assumed to rest solely in the sphere of the Imperial Government." He thought that, two months earlier, a Home Rule Bill would have been welcomed by Liberals and tolerated by many Unionists, but not now.

Some of Lloyd George's colleagues remained unconvinced by his devious logic. Barnes thought the production of a Home Rule Bill would improve relations with the Irish; Lord Hewart anticipated a charge of insincerity; and Long put the Unionist case that "one of the most serious defects of British policy in Ireland was that the Irish were kept in suspense as to what that policy really was."

A month or so later, Long predicted that if municipal elections were held in Ireland Sinn Fein would capture 90% of the seats outside Ulster and "would do the same in regard to Parliamentary seats". So strong was their support now that even Mr Dillon would probably be beaten in County Mayo, considered one of the safest Nationalist seats.[23]

Conscription was to be reconsidered in October and during the Parliamentary recess some Home Rule plan could be worked out. Again, the sage Long warned that if the six counties were excluded it would be "the worst settlement of all". Lloyd George engaged in some characteristic double talk which some of the Cabinet must have found hard to swallow. "The British Government certainly were not going to surrender to the challenge of the Roman Catholic Church on the con-

[22] W.C. min. 433/2 of 19/6/18.   [23] W.C. min. 453/7 29/7/18.

scription issue," he announced, his Welsh non-conformist hackles still rising, and then he stated that he did not agree that "the questions of the application of the Military Service Acts and the introduction of a measure of Home Rule stood together." In his speech in the Commons on April 9th, he had said that each question would be considered on its merits. But, he maintained, the policy announced in April still stood. "There could be no greater mistake than to introduce a Bill which both sides would repudiate." He apologised that he had not had time even to look at the draft Bill already prepared by Long—his time was "now taken up with the gigantic task of dealing with the problem created by the German offensive on the Western front."

After all the months of argument within the Cabinet and dissension in Ireland, Lloyd George shelved the whole problem, labelling it for future reference, "We will and we won't."

The attempt to step up voluntary enlistment was hardly successful. Ineptitude, vacillation and what appeared to be a total indifference to Irish sensibilities had lost the British Government the support of people who, until now, despite the revulsion inspired by Maxwell, had been ready to wait for self-government while Britain fought for her own life-blood. Again, England's sin was clumsiness rather than wickedness.

Sinn Fein, after losing three by-elections, began to capture seats again. The old firm of the Irish Parliamentary Party was finally bankrupt. Their last implacable stand against conscription was no more than an effort to save something from the crash for their shareholders. Now the new firm was taking over. Invoking the Defence of the Realm Act, known ribaldly as "Dora", Lord French was trying to suppress Sinn Fein, the Volunteers, the Cumann na mBan and even the Gaelic League. Assemblies and processions in public places were prohibited. But they still went on. There were hundreds of arrests and innumerable raids on private houses, but in some parts of the country R.I.C. men would ask where a meeting was to be held and make sure that their duty led them in the opposite direction.

Quietly, but with growing determination, the Volunteers went on training and drilling, building up their strength to something like 100,000 men, though there were arms for only a small proportion. Like the British they saw that a clash was now almost inevitable and they were schooling themselves to deal ruthlessly with any opposition, English or Irish. Collins, Adjutant-General and Director of Organisation, Cathal Brugha, Chief of Staff, and Richard Mulcahy, deputy Chief of Staff, with skilled and energetic helpers, reorganised the whole Volunteer movement and, at the same time, Collins was constructing his devastating secret service network which was to reach in time into the heart of Dublin Castle and even into high places in England.

The end of the war in Europe brought an end to the ill-timed conscription plan which had done as much as, perhaps more than, the Easter Rising to unite Irishmen against the suzerain power of England. It also brought the General Election of December, 1918, an election in which the English, in retributive mood, concerned themselves with the fate of the Kaiser, and gave scarcely a thought to what was happening in "John Bull's other Island". If they recked little now of the Irish problem, they were to be rudely shocked, for Sinn Fein won 73 of 105 seats in the 32 counties. The Unionists gained eight seats, bringing their total to 26, while the Nationalists were practically crushed out of existence, holding only six of their pre-election 68 seats. Sinn Fein's success did not represent the huge majority of votes it suggests but it certainly reflected the mighty swing of public opinion in the thirty months since the Rising. It was widely acclaimed by the jubilant Sinn Feiners as a whole-hearted vote for a Republic, since this was a clearly stated objective of the Sinn Fein manifesto, and this verdict of the people was the gauntlet to be flung down by ardent Republicans when the time came that Irish plenipotentiaries settled for less. It was then that the ambiguity in the Ard-Fheis declaration transcended the apparent unanimity in which it was concocted. That statement, it will be remembered, laid down that first "the international recognition of Ireland as an independent Irish Republic" should be secured, and that then "the Irish people may by referendum freely choose their own form of Government". Sinn Fein had won the right to go ahead and seek to achieve the first objective but, as yet anyway, their share of the vote did not reflect the simple majority in the country which, in a referendum, would have been necessary to establish, as the form of government chosen by the people, a Republic.

FIVE

Two Irish policemen were shot dead at Soloheadbeg, on January 21st, 1919. On the same day the newly elected Sinn Fein members of the British House of Commons met in the Mansion House, with a detachment of the Dublin Metropolitan Police obligingly acting as sentries, and instituted the first *Dail Eireann*, or Irish Assembly. The two events were in no way connected but those who participated in them were all to be drawn inseparably together in the days to come.

The name of Soloheadbeg still brings a blush to the cheeks of some Irishmen. One distinguished public man once described it to me as "not much more than a piece of brigandage". Dan Breen, who was there, is unrepentant. He was one of the eight men of the South Tipperary Brigade of what was soon to be widely known as the Irish Republican Army who lay in ambush for five days waiting for a cart of gelignite being transported from Tipperary town to Soloheadbeg quarry. They wanted the gelignite for the manufacture of hand grenades. The ambushers did not know how many guards there would be but they expected about ten. Even with the advantage of surprise, they themselves would suffer casualties, they believed.

In the event, the cart was guarded by two unwary constables, MacDonnell and O'Connell. MacDonnell, who had seen thirty years service with the Royal Irish Constabulary, had a large family, and both he and O'Connell were popular enough in the district. With them were two employees of the South Tipperary County Council, Godfrey and Flynn. All four were startled out of their wits when a shout of "Hands up" rang out from behind the hedge. It was something quite new in their experience. They glimpsed masked faces and gleaming revolver barrels, made some attempt to level their carbines, then were shot down by Sean Treacy, second-in-command of the South Tipperary Brigade. The other members of the ambush party had orders not to fire unless told to do so by either Seamus Robinson, their commanding officer, or Treacy. Dan Breen was the Brigade Quartermaster.

Treacy, Breen and Sean Hogan dumped the gelignite which, in the next few days, was several times transferred by brave men who ventured into the network of police and army searchers. Then Tom Carew and his brother Dan, who had not been involved in the ambush, drove the explosives away in one of two carts in which they were carrying timber and buried them on the family farm at Golden Garden. On the way they were halted by police, but Tom Carew bluffed his way through. Later, perhaps putting two and two together, the authorities ransacked the farm and only just missed finding the gelignite, but they sent Tom Carew to jail for three months anyway and after that he was advised by Michael Collins to "go on the run".

The Soloheadbeg ambush was the first of hundreds of incidents which were to be put under the general heading of "outrage", the usual classification for the activities of men fighting for the independence of their country. The word is understandable for such men must operate of necessity outside the law of those who govern them, and must, because invariably they are facing a larger and better equipped power, resort to stealth and to terror to achieve their aims. Since both sides believe themselves to be in the right, what is terrorism to one is heroism to the other.

At the time, even the Irish were more inclined to label Soloheadbeg "terrorism". They had not seen yet that this was the only effective method of fighting for independence, were not even certain that it would be necessary to fight at all. Moreover, the victims had seemed to stand little chance and, too, they were Irish. Even Volunteer Headquarters in Dublin was disapproving. It has been asked frequently whether the gelignite could have been seized without loss of life. Dan Breen's answer is forthright:

"Soloheadbeg was calculated by Treacy and myself. The gelignite was only incidental. We were surprised that there were only two of them—we'd hoped we could take on ten. We knew that we'd get it in the neck from everyone." He confesses that his reaction was "very sharp, very sorrowful", but he and Treacy believed that it was necessary to light the fuse if ever anything was to be achieved.

Sean Treacy and Dan Breen epitomised what was soon to be called "the Irish gunman", but neither was a callous nor a brutal man. Breen had then, and has now, a horror of taking life however insignificant. They were the first to steel themselves to kill, to acquire the kind of mentality that men must acquire to win freedom. This is an act of will, not an instinct. Von Stauffenberg needed it to plant the bomb he hoped would kill Hitler; men in resistance movements all over Europe needed it, and acquired it, during the Second World War.

It is not often that a country produces a generation of men and women fanatical enough and ruthless enough to carry through a revolution, a generation of poets and propagandists and political idealists, dedicated fighting leaders, brave men to follow them and a civilian population ready to shelter, feed and protect them. Ireland had produced her visionaries, her ardent revolutionaries before, brave coteries of men who fought for their hopeless causes while the ignorant gaped and those who understood stayed in their unheroic homes. In the soft sunshine of the early morning the gallows cast long, long shadows across the land.

Of that incredible generation that won Ireland her independence one of the most remarkable men is Dan Breen. Politically he was of no great significance, and he was not a great military leader. He was the fighter *par excellence*, an individualist whose exploits fired the imaginations of the young and were the despair of his enemies. Until Sean Treacy's death, he and Dan Breen formed a close-knit partnership. Breen always walked in front because Treacy was short-sighted, and he maintains that Treacy would never have been trapped as he was if he had been with him. Often he has wished that they had been killed together. Several times Breen ought to have died from fearful wounds but a splendid physique and a granite will ensured his survival.

A heavily built man, he moves now with difficulty but his mind is far-ranging and mobile. His schooldays ended when he was twelve, but like so many Irishmen he has a bent for scholarship and he has built on this throughout his life with the instinctive patience and persistence of a spider engineering its web. He has travelled a great deal, knew seamy New York in prohibition days and saw Paris in the rarefied company of Joyce. In all sorts of places, with all kinds of people, he has searched out experience and knowledge.

His friend Treacy, like Pearse, Liam Lynch and Cathal Brugha, had an ascetic quality. They were men driven by the silent power of a high voltage electric current. Breen differed from Treacy as Connolly from Pearse. He is almost spiky with honesty and a sense of justice smoulders in him like a fierce, damped-down forge.

"The thing that always hurt me," he explains, "was not the killing, not the war, but the taking from us of our culture and the genocide of the starvation in '47. But I was willing to forget it at any time in the common interest if they would treat us as equals.

"But we couldn't get them to see that we as a free people here, and they as a free people there, could be a combination, an accord, a commonwealth—call it what you like—which was to everyone's advantage. We have something in Ireland to give the world, a certain civilisation. Among the old people, practically illiterate though a lot of them were, and especially among our women, there was a culture and a courtesy that I've never seen anywhere else in the world. Some of it exists still."

That was what Dan Breen fought for and he was not willing to compromise. "Concessions are only for slaves," he says sharply.

While the men of the South Tipperary Brigade were taking the law into their own hands at Soloheadbeg, in Dublin the elected representatives of the Irish people were, in a much more literal sense, doing exactly the same thing. Asserting that English rule in Ireland was, and always had been, "based upon fraud and force and maintained by military occupation against the declared will of the people", the Dail, having already approved a provisional constitution, confirmed the Proclamation read by Pearse on the steps of the G.P.O. in 1916. The new Declaration of Independence ratified the establishment of the Irish Republic, pledged *Dail Eireann* and the people "to make this declaration effective by every means at our command", and demanded "the evacuation of our country by the British Garrison". The insistence at this stage upon the establishment of a republic was later regretted by many Irishmen, who saw that it placed a constraint upon negotiations, and left no room for manoeuvre. Whether at this time de Valera, could he have been present, would have drawn so hard an edge, is doubtful.

Declaring in the words of Pearse, who was specifically referred to as "our first President", that "the nation's sovereignty extends not only to all men and women of the nation, but to all its material possessions, the nation's soil and all its resources", the Dail accepted a democratic programme designed to ensure that the nation's soil and resources did become the property of the nation and were equitably distributed. On the second day of the assembly a provisional government was appointed with Cathal Brugha as its acting President in the absence of de Valera in Lincoln Prison. It was clear that the office was not that of President of the Republic but of Dail Eireann only. Apparently the claim of the Irish Republican Brotherhood that their own President was also President of the Republic was not being challenged. At the same time the Supreme Council, which General Sean McEoin has described as " a predecessor of the many patriot underground governments which functioned and received recognition during the recent war", now handed over to the democratically elected Dail Eireann all other executive offices and functions.

With the audacious help of Collins and Harry Boland, de Valera, Sean Milroy and Sean McGarry broke goal on February 3rd.

For several weeks, Shortt, who had succeeded Duke as Chief Secretary for Ireland and was now Home Secretary, and Barnes had been urging the release of Sinn Fein prisoners held in England. French had vigorously opposed it, but suddenly, on February 4th, he sent the Chief Secretary no less than three telegrams urging the release of the men the same night.[1] The Cabinet were also informed that the Governor of Reading jail was finding it impossible to control Sinn Fein prisoners in his charge. There were, moreover, signs that they would resort to a hunger strike. Churchill was not prepared to accept that the Government should make decisions to save the face of the prison authorities. He wanted the same firmness as had been shown the suffragettes and saw no need to court public favour in Ireland where, in his view, there was less danger of any trouble than anywhere else in the world. MacPherson, now Chief Secretary, agreed that the men should

[1] W.C. min. 526/3 of 4/2/19.

no longer be held, without trial, under the Defence of the Realm Act Regulations and pointed out that the prisoners were now all M.P.'s "and consequently could claim privilege if they chose." Bewildered by French's *volte face* the Cabinet decided to ask him to explain it.

French continued to press for the release of the men and by next day the Government were wondering whether it would be taken as a sign of weakness if they relented.[2] It seemed to them that there was little between Sinn Fein and Bolshevism and, boomed Churchill, "There never was a time when it was more necessary to take every possible precaution for the public security." Curzon, recalling the release of prisoners taken during the Rising to create a good atmosphere for the Convention, did not want the mistake repeated. Others, too, expressed opposition or doubt and it was agreed that Bonar Law would see French and explain that the release of the Irish revolutionaries was not going to help when it came to dealing with trouble makers in England, where unemployment, industrial unrest and communist activities were creating an atmosphere in which ideas for radical social change and the overturn of the Establishment could take root. It was public security in England as much as in Ireland which bothered Churchill.

Not until March 4th did the Government finally decide on the gradual release of Sinn Fein prisoners interned in England.[3] The Home Secretary proposed "to give Bowen-Colthurst unconditional release at the same time." The man wanted to emigrate to British Columbia and Shortt thought "permission for him to do this might conveniently be given. At present he was confined to Great Britain." This was the man who ran amok during the Easter Rising. He had been released from Broadmoor some time previously. The Irish were always sceptical of the British Government's handling of Bowen-Colthurst's case and suspected another "whitewashing job".

De Valera, who had been hidden in Manchester and Liverpool since his escape, had decided to journey to the United States, believing that he could best serve Ireland by drumming up both money and moral support across the Atlantic. It was one of those odd decisions which were to become almost habitual with de Valera and which were to cause consternation

[2] W.C. min. 527/2 of 5/2/19.   [3] W.C. min. 541/4 of 4/3/19.

among his friends. Cathal Brugha, who travelled to Liverpool expressly to dissuade him, prevailed upon him to break his journey in Ireland but could not turn him from his purpose.

It was assumed that the amnesty applied also to him and at the end of March, de Valera returned quietly to Dublin. A great meeting and procession to welcome him, arranged by the Sinn Fein Executive, were seen by the Irish Government[4] as a "fresh overt act of defiance" and were proclaimed on the telegraphed instructions of the British Cabinet.

On April 1st he was elected President of the Dail and his chosen Ministers began to set up their departments and to corrode the powers of Dublin Castle. Brugha became Minister of Defence with Mulcahy as his Chief of Staff. A fiercely effective move was de Valera's resolution, passed by the Dail on April 10th, that the men of the Royal Irish Constabulary should be ostracised. Their history he saw as "a continuity of brutal treason against their own people." It was true that the R.I.C., always quasi-military in character, were the agents of Dublin Castle, that their reports were the prime source of information about the activities of those engaged in the independence movement. But the movement was only now achieving respectability and their function as informants had not earned the R.I.C. general disapproval in the past. It was difficult for old stalwarts of the Constabulary to adjust to this new concept that their duties amounted to treason. Apart from their allegiance to Dublin Castle, which they took for granted, the R.I.C. served the community well and were generally well-liked within it. Communications were poor and in their own areas, operating from barracks which were never designed as military fortresses, they succeeded well enough in keeping law and order.

Now they became the objects of obloquy, and sometimes violence, for which very often there was no justification or provocation. Some were scared into resignation and some, accepting the new creed of independence, happily donned the uniform of the I.R.A. Most went on doing their duty as they saw it, looking ahead to their pensions, avoiding trouble when they could and facing it often bravely and

4 The Irish Government was the British Administration centred upon Dublin Castle under the Lord Lieutenant and Chief Secretary for Ireland.

resolutely when they could not, and enduring the hurt and loneliness of ostracism by neighbours many of whom did not believe in it themselves but lacked the courage to swim against the tide.

On May 13th, a sergeant and a constable were killed at Knocklong. Since Soloheadbeg, seventeen-year-old Sean Hogan had been on the run with Sean Treacy and Dan Breen. They could have been spirited away from Ireland and I.R.A. Headquarters, indeed, had seen this as the solution to the dilemma imposed by Soloheadbeg. To have run away would have been to deny the purpose of their act and they chose instead to endure the privations of hunted men. Only the doors of their stoutest-hearted supporters were open to them. Early on Monday, May 12th, Hogan had been captured by police at the home of friends. At first the police thought they had made a routine arrest of an armed man but then Hogan's identity was realised. Guarded by four policemen, he left Thurles by train for Cork. At Knocklong Breen, Treacy, Seamus Robinson and several others of their comrades carried out an audacious rescue. They had planned it hurriedly but carefully and were greatly helped by the Intelligence work of several Cumann na mBan girls, Brigid Meagher, Mai Maloney, Brigid O'Keeffe and Bridget Fitzpatrick, all of whom were as brave as they were resourceful. Miss Fitzpatrick actually put her name on a warning telegram and was soon suspected and interrogated. She claimed simply that someone else had used her name.

The policemen were shot dead in a desperate struggle in the train. Treacy and Sergeant Wallace wrestled frenziedly, each striving to gain possession of the sergeant's revolver. Neal O'Brien intervened and Wallace managed to fire a shot which pierced Treacy's throat before Treacy grabbed his gun and mortally wounded him. Hogan was led from the train and Treacy staggered out. Two other Volunteers were slightly wounded. On the platform Dan Breen was shot through the lung by Constable Reilly, who had crawled unnoticed from the train with a carbine. The fourth member of Hogan's escort had decamped at the first whiff of danger.

Two doctors, brought clandestinely to a friend's home, attended to Dan Breen but had no hope of his surviving. Yet, within a few hours he was raced away by car, through the vengeful cordon of military and police, into west Limerick. With him was Sean Treacy who had been fortunate that the bullet which ploughed through his neck did not kill him. The chase grew hotter, and they pushed on into Kerry then back to County Limerick. In Clare they were looked after by the Brennan brothers, themselves marked men. Their stay could not be prolonged and they moved back into Tipperary, where they were passed from friend to friend until, tiring of the lack of action, they cycled to Dublin and persuaded Collins to agree to use their services, and those of Hogan and Seamus Robinson, in the capital.

Although Hogan's rescuers were branded butchers by priest and press, ordinary people were beginning to take a different view of the exploits of Treacy and Breen. If there had been a doubt about fair play at Soloheadbeg, there was none at Knocklong. The people admired the audacity and courage of the men in rescuing their comrade in such incredible circumstances and rejoiced that a seventeen-year-old Irish boy had been saved from the British gallows. They began to see that "the boys" were not going round murdering policemen for fun but were urged by a fierce determination to free their country. General opinion was reflected by the verdict of the jury at the inquest on Hogan's dead guards. Refusing to bring in a verdict of murder, the jurors condemned the arrest of "respectable persons" and, in a logical Irish way, "blamed the Government for exposing the police to danger." For good measure they "demanded self-determination for Ireland".

In September, a Fermoy jury took the same line when a party of Volunteers under Liam Lynch ambushed a squad of King's Shropshire Light Infantry on their way to church, seized their arms and escaped in cars. One soldier was killed and his friends, enraged by the jury's verdict, took the law into their own hands and wrecked the homes of the stubborn jurymen. This kind of reprisal, unauthorised at first but later receiving the blessing of the British Government, was soon to become an accepted pattern of what was to develop into a horrifying war.

Primarily it was a war between the British Secret Service and the Collins network in Dublin, a war of harassment and reprisal in the country and a war of propaganda. Britain, hopeful of some remission of her enormous war debt to

America and anxious for American participation in the League of Nations, could not afford to lose American sympathy. With the support of the strong Irish-American element across the Atlantic, the Irish were more than willing to blacken Britain's name. It was one of their strongest weapons, for if Britain went too far she would find herself having to mollify America. But the Irish desired also the goodwill of the proud, democratic English people who, they were sure, could not possibly support the tyrannical excesses of their Government.

"I considered that our fight was only half physical, the other half was propaganda," says General Michael Brennan, who was thinking, not in terms of political advertisement, but simply of investing the I.R.A. with a good name. Once, when he billeted his men in a mansion belonging to a prominent Unionist, he confined them to the hall and asked the butler to keep a note of the food consumed. Later he wrote to the owner asking for a statement of any damage and a bill for the food. The owner replied that there had been no damage, that he would not accept payment for food and, indeed, he now had an entirely different viewpoint about the I.R.A.

Britain did the greatest disservice to herself when, in 1920, she brought the Black and Tans into Ireland and gave them licence to subdue the Irish by terrorism, when her statesmen got up in the House of Commons and uttered demonstrable lies, when she resorted to every kind of fake photograph and mendacious explanation to cover up the tracks of torturers and murderers who wore the King's uniform. It was little wonder that, however gentle the man who wore it, as a symbol the Crown was anathema to the Irish.

When he landed in New York in June, 1919, Eamon de Valera knew exactly the value of what he could accomplish in America. To the Americans he was President of the Irish Republic. They were not the ones to bother with subtle distinctions and "President of the Dail" meant little to them. Britain had no one to counter de Valera's triumphal progress, no way of arresting the dollars—ten million of them—that flowed to subscribe to the Irish National Loan. In Ireland the loan was floated by Collins, as Minister of Finance, and somehow he found the time to sit at a table in the street personally signing bonds. Old newsreels show him, his hair blowing in the wind, laughing with his "customers" as if he had not a care in the world. He had many. Says Dan Breen: "There was no burden too big to put on Mick's shoulders and there was no job too small for him to do and there was no person too small for him to see."

By December 1919 Lloyd George was in no doubt that the Irish question mark had become very large and very black. In an Orange Day speech Carson had again threatened to bring out the Ulster Volunteers if there were any attempt to take away "one jot or tittle of your rights as British citizens". That made things very difficult for the Prime Minister, who needed Unionist support to keep his coalition Government in office.

Until they had arms, money and a government of their own the Irish in the South had been no very serious threat. The Volunteers' determined drilling merely took the steam out of them and spates of eloquence from seditious platforms accomplished little but to put their speakers in jail. While detectives of G. Division of the Dublin Metropolitan Police had the unseen upper hand in the capital and faithful men of the I.R.C. had been penning ponderous but knowledgeable reports from all over the country, Dublin Castle had seemed to have the country firmly in its constrictive grasp.

Now the Irish had their own Parliament and, although it had been proscribed in September, it was working secretly and effectively to supplant the British Administration and Judiciary. In America and in Ireland large sums of money had been raised for the Dail's clandestine coffers and de Valera was winning many friends and influencing many people across the Atlantic. The shooting war had begun; there had been skirmishes in Tipperary, Limerick, Clare and elsewhere. During 1919, eighteen R.I.C. men had lost their lives, and they included G. Division men carefully picked off by the dedicated gunmen of Collins's "Squad" led by Patrick Daly. And, in a few short months, from repugnance after Soloheadbeg the temper of the Irish people had progressed almost to dismay when an attempt on the life of the Lord Lieutenant, Lord French, failed.

This occurred on December 19th, an earlier ambush planned by Collins having been cancelled when French's programme was altered. Paddy Daly headed a party of eleven men, including Dan Breen, Sean Treacy, Seamus Robinson,

95

and Sean Hogan from Tipperary, and Martin Savage, Tom Keogh, Vincent Byrne, Tom Kilcoyne, Joe Leonard and Mick MacDonnell from Dublin units. A bomb was thrown too soon and the official convoy speeding from Ashtown station accelerated when the explosion was heard. The ambush party opened fire, concentrating on the second car, but French was travelling in the first. There was answering fire. Martin Savage bled to death at the roadside and Dan Breen was wounded in the leg. The driver of the second car and a constable were wounded, but the symbol of the Crown in Ireland had gone untouched. But, although the attempt had failed, the fact that it had been mounted at all shook the British Government. It was clear that the I.R.A. now had enough arms to set up small but deadly and widespread ambushes and the merciless will to use them.

Of a series of brilliant raids for arms carried out by the I.R.A., a particularly audacious one was the boarding and disarming of a British naval sloop in Bantry Bay by men of the local battalion of the 3rd Cork Brigade led by Maurice Donegan. A fine haul of weapons and ammunition cost not a drop of blood. The booty was stowed in the belfry of the church, where it remained for some months until needed.

An adversary with leadership, money and arms was to be reckoned with, and Lloyd George decided to make a twin-pronged attack, using as his weapons bribery of the Irish and corruption of the Crown Forces. He failed in the first, succeeded only too well in the second.

On December 22nd, only three days after the attack on Lord French, Lloyd George introduced the Better Government of Ireland Bill in the House of Commons. Again, Britain offered too little, too late. The Bill provided for the setting up of two parliaments, one for the intransigent six counties in the north-east and one for the twenty-six counties. The Bill, known ever since as the Partition Bill, was a stark admission of failure to find a solution to the Orange problem. The division of the country had been mooted before, but this Bill, however well intentioned, blatantly set Britain's seal on dismemberment. Irishmen will have it that it was simply another example of Britain's traditional policy to divide and rule. It was not that. Lloyd George was only too anxious to settle the trouble in Ireland. Partition was not intended to weaken; it was simply the only compromise that offered. Both Irish Governments were to nominate members to a joint Council of Ireland and in this way the British Government hoped to provide a bridge which the two sections of the Irish community could cross if they wished.

Two years earlier the proposal almost certainly would have been blessed by the great bulk of the Irish people, North and South, and it is doubtful indeed if the fierier Volunteers would have made much headway towards their ideal of a Republic. Now that the Dail was already in existence and in control of an army, with money to finance it and weapons to put in its hands, the climate of public opinion in Ireland had changed. The British offer meant about as much as the loan of a snow plough when winter has sped. Now, the people who once would have been glad of it wanted to make their own preparations for the snow to come. Under the Bill, Britain was to be responsible for the armed forces, foreign affairs, customs and excise and much else. Ireland was left with a glorified brand of local government and it was not enough. One cannot blame the Irish and yet it can be asked fairly whether, with such a beginning, they might not have obtained, within relatively few years, something better than the Treaty of December, 1921, might, indeed, have secured the united Ireland which remains today on amorphous horizons.

SIX

Recruited by advertisement, the men who were to become known as Black and Tans were, Winston Churchill claimed, carefully selected from "a great press of applicants". Praise be to God the British were kind enough not to send their larrikins, was to be the burden of Irish prayers in the next months. Determined that the Irish were not to be allowed to fight a romantic war for freedom but should be presented to the world as malcontents and murderers, the British Government set out to keep "law and order" by police action, bringing in the military only to help the police when things got out of hand. For ten shillings per day and all found, the "carefully selected" men became temporary constables of the R.I.C. As there were not enough R.I.C. uniforms to go round, the temporary constables had to make do with an ensemble of khaki and dark green, with black belts, which put some inspired wit in mind of a famous pack of hounds, the Black and Tans. Given perfunctory police training, they appeared in Ireland late in March 1920, and at about the same time General Sir Nevil Macready was appointed Commander-in-Chief of the British Forces in Ireland. He was Chief Commissioner of the Metropolitan Police, and would have preferred to remain so, especially as he disliked Ireland anyway. But to please his old chief, French, he accepted the command. Because of earlier police experience in trouble spots it was thought that he would be a good man to co-ordinate police and military activities.

Lloyd George was bent on showing the Irish that if they could be ruthless, Britain could be more so, and he wanted to be sure that there were no faint-hearts among his Empire crusaders. A short, sharp shock or two should settle the revolutionaries while the Irish people, he thought, would quickly see the virtues of "better government" in Ireland. To give the Prime Minister his due, he had much else to think about; Versailles, India, the Middle East all made their demands on his time and energies. By putting Ireland in safe, none-too-sensitive hands, he thought to gain a breathing space for himself. It is improbable that he ever imagined the trouble building up into a war the labelling of which as "police action" was only a fiction.

Macpherson was replaced as Chief Secretary for Ireland by Sir Hamar Greenwood, a Welsh-Canadian, who began by declaring his love for Cathleen ni Houlihan but had a strange way of showing it. Sir John Anderson was the effective Under-Secretary with James MacMahon, as joint holder of the office, remaining as something of a sop to the Irish Catholics. Their assistant was Alfred Cope who had had an exciting and spectacular career as a detective in H.M. Customs and Excise. He was to play a major, and not unworthy, part in events to come.

The Black and Tans, together with the regular R.I.C. and the Dublin Metropolitan Police, were placed under the command of Major-General Tudor. Sir Joseph Byrne who, as Inspector-General of the R.I.C., had strenuously advised the

Cabinet against conscription, and was certainly not the man to organise a campaign of terror, disappeared from the scene. A sinister appointment was that of Colonel Ormonde Winter, whose orders were to develop a secret service, which was designed to destroy the Collins network and, in the end, was itself largely enmeshed. Between them the two undercover bodies were to be responsible for many of the most savage killings of the struggle, with each side feeding its propaganda machine with lurid accounts of the other's crimes.

One of Collins's purposes was, having first warned them, to eliminate the detectives of G. Division of the Dublin Metropolitan Police. These men knew the Dublin scene from long acquaintance with it. They could recognise most of the Irish leaders and their associates, and it was they who first schemed to break up the Collins Intelligence web. But they suffered the disadvantage of being equally well known to the men they hunted, and first one and then another was shot down by Collins's Squad. One or two of these were paying for identifying leaders of the Easter Rebellion. From some Collins went in no danger—they had signed up with him and stayed in their jobs to become some of his most valuable agents.

In January, 1920, Assistant Commissioner Redmond sprang a trap and very nearly caught Collins in it. His office was raided but he escaped through a skylight after passing himself off as a clerk when he encountered the detectives in the passage. A few days later the Squad stalked Redmond in a Dublin street and wounded him fatally. He was the fifth G. Division casualty. The most squalid killing was that of an Irish Civil Servant named Alan Bell who was unfortunate enough to have been given the task of tracing National Loan funds deposited in Irish banks in the names of various trustees. He had already nosed out and seized some funds and his activities menaced the perilous finances of Sinn Fein. Quietly he was taken off a tram in broad daylight and shot in the gutter. No one moved to help him. The British held that this was murder and a nasty one at that. On the Irish side it was regarded as the judicial execution of an enemy of the State ordered by the legal Government and carried out mercilessly and messily only because the State was unlawfully occupied by an aggressor. The Crown forces at least had the proper facilities for their judicial executions.

A few days earlier, on March 19th, Tomas MacCurtain, Lord Mayor of Cork, was shot dead in his own home, and in front of his wife, by a gang with blackened faces. Shortly after his death soldiers arriving to arrest him were surprised to find that they had been forestalled. This, too, was murder, said Sir Hamar Greenwood, and, tongue in cheek, he accused MacCurtain's own colleagues of the crime.

MacCurtain had been blamed by some at one time for the mix up which had prevented the Cork Volunteers from joining in the Easter Rising. But the facts had long been known and even against Eoin MacNeill whose countermanding orders had been responsible for the confusion, there was little malice. The jury, hand picked by the police, brought in a formidable verdict of wilful murder against Lloyd George, Sir Hamar Greenwood and Lord French as well as District Inspector Swanzy of the R.I.C. and men under his command. They might have been thought prejudiced, but they were right. District Inspector Swanzy had organised the raid with the intention of killing MacCurtain. The Irish Government, that is to say the British Government in Ireland, might not have ordered the murder but were certainly accessories after the fact and brazenly shielded the killers.

A Volunteer since 1914, MacCurtain was Commandant of Cork No. 1 Brigade at his death. Membership of the Gaelic League had evoked in him, as in so many of his contemporaries, a passion for freedom and had led him into both the political and physical force wings of the movement. Shocked by his callous death, the people of Cork assembled in tearful thousands as the body was carried to the City Hall to lie in state. The procession took three hours to reach its destination.

Some months after MacCurtain's death, G.H.Q. sent out instructions for the formation of flying columns based on plans he had put forward. Guerrilla warfare had been evolving haphazardly and MacCurtain saw the need for small, disciplined units which would move swiftly through the countryside, strike and steal away. Groups should replace one another in turn, for in this way all available arms could be kept constantly in use, and men could absent themselves for short periods from their normal way of life until suspicion gathered too darkly and they had to go on the run. His activities as an I.R.A. leader in Cork were enough to land him in a British jail but it is difficult to understand why he should have been assassinated. Perhaps Swanzy and the Cork R.I.C. were acting on their own initiative but this is unlikely. And if he acted under orders these apparently did not emanate from the same source as those received by the Army—unless the Army move to arrest MacCurtain was meant to give credence to the tale that he was shot by his own men.

Probably MacCurtain's death was intended to intimidate the new local authorities, was a warning that the British did not mean to lose their close control of local government in Ireland, always a cardinal factor in their administration of the country. MacCurtain had been Lord Mayor of Cork only since the election of January 20th when, to the consternation of Dublin Castle, Sinn Fein won control of all twelve cities and boroughs in Ireland save Belfast, and of the majority of local councils. It was by no means a clean sweep; opposition parties won a good proportion of seats; but it was an emphatic confirmation of the General Election verdict. And much more.

The Local Government Act of 1898 had given the Irish a say in local affairs in the hope that their grumbling would cease. And, as expected, duly elected councillors argued happily while officials of the Local Government Board, some of them able, understanding men, got on with the work. Councillors whose pet projects received official blessing and the necessary finance wore an air of pride among the electors and saw that contracts were helpfully placed. The scheme worked well enough and, for everyone's satisfaction, a proper genuflection had been made in the direction of democracy. The measure of 1898 had been meant as a safety valve and the British had never thought that the sluices would be opened wide to drain their authority away and leave their officials flapping in the Custom House in Dublin like stranded fish.

The youthful Sinn Fein councils cleaned out the old ruts, time-worn grooves of graft and indolence. They remembered the precepts of Pearse and of Connolly which had been grained into the constitution of the Dail and they began to plan for the good of the people. Hopefully the Local Government Board sent its inspectors to see the books. They were received politely and shown nothing. Returns were demanded but none were sent. Rates were collected by the Sinn Fein local authorities and spent with wisdom. The whole object of Sinn Fein

101

was to show that Ireland could govern itself and was governing itself, that the parallel British functions were superfluous. W. T. Cosgrave, a veteran of 1916 and an experienced member of the Dublin Corporation, was Minister of Local Government. With the young, ill-starred Kevin O'Higgins as his assistant, he was one of the most effective of the Dail heads of department.

Of the courts established by Sinn Fein Professor Michael Hayes remarks that "they were good in some places, bad in others". The conduct of some of them was so notably fair that even Unionists and others who were bitterly opposed to Sinn Fein soon resorted to them and even applauded them. Many ordinary courts were powerless because they had no police support. The Royal Irish Constabulary were either chasing the I.R.A. all over the countryside, often in response to thoroughly misleading information, or they were penned up in their barracks by I.R.A. sharpshooters, so they had little time for their normal duties. To fill the need the Volunteers provided their own police force. If their methods were not always orthodox, they were usually effective. Cattle driving and land grabbing still flourished in some parts of the country and old feuds were pursued, often with violence and sometimes within the I.R.A. itself. Heaven may be the goal of most Irishmen, but many are willing to try the good Lord very hard on the way. But on the whole there was less rather than more crime and those who sought to use the I.R.A. as a shield for their misdeeds were speedily dealt with.

"The Republic had only one sanction really, and that was death," says Hayes. "The only real force they had was that of the Volunteers and there was no way of enforcing punishment except death—or deportation in some cases. That is why they usually released prisoners." On mere suspicion many Irishmen were cruelly done to death. Their bodies were found on roadways and in ditches and were invariably labelled "Spies and informers beware." The I.R.A. has always maintained that it acted in this ruthless way only when there was near-certainty of treachery, but the label was one which could disguise the private vendetta and which was used time and again by the Black and Tans to cover their own excesses.

But for all the flaws in the system of clandestine government, the Dail, with its control of local government, its courts and its police was governing more effectively than was the Irish Government centred upon Dublin Castle. Arthur Griffith had always held that the way to independence was to establish a rival administration which would win the confidence of the people. Once this had been done England's institutions in Ireland were bound to atrophy and expire of their own flabby inanition. A long memorandum prepared by Griffith while he was in jail was the basis for the whole of the new administration. He had always believed that physical force was not necessary to achieve this condition and, as late as February, 1920, he had taken the Albert Hall in London for a political protest meeting, but even he had had to admit finally that Britain yielded nothing except at gunpoint.

Anticipating trouble in Dublin to celebrate the Rising in April, the British were ready for almost anything but what did happen. Income tax offices all over the country were burned and the records destroyed, another blow to the British administration. Two hundred police barracks, evacuated because they were too vulnerable to attack from the I.R.A., also were destroyed, so that they could not be reoccupied by the R.I.C. Burning police barracks was to become something of an obsession, persisting into the Civil War.

Burning empty buildings was easy, if wasteful. Assaults on occupied barracks were more profitable. In Clare, Cork, Limerick, Tipperary and elsewhere the I.R.A. attacked the R.I.C. in their barracks, capturing and burning the buildings, seizing arms and ammunition. Michael Brennan, Sean Forde, Ernie O'Malley, Dinny Lacey and Sean Treacy led daring raids. Some of the buildings were never built to withstand a siege and presented little difficulty. Garrisons of others yielded quickly. But in many cases the fighting was long and brave. Kilmallock, well protected except that its roof was open to attack from a neighbouring hotel, was the scene of a battle which lasted from midnight until 7 a.m. The R.I.C. garrison refused to surrender and even when fire drove them finally from their barracks they held out in an adjacent building until the I.R.A. attackers dared stay no longer. There were several dead.

Incendiary bombs and petrol often won the day for the I.R.A. They attacked the roofs of the barracks, frequently climbing exposed ladders to reach them. At Rear Cross,

Sergeant O'Sullivan was shot down as he stood at the doorway of his blazing barracks fighting back with a courage that won the admiration of his opponents.

Several garrisons surrendered only when they were in danger of being incinerated and were careful to leave their arms behind. But I.R.A. men rushed into the flames to secure the all-important rifles. Ernie O'Malley was felled by a burning beam as he was carrying a box of ammunition from the inferno of Drangan barracks. Captured R.I.C. men were invariably freed, usually with a warning to get out of their uniforms.

Arvagh barracks, on the border of Counties Cavan and Longford, gave Sean McEoin little trouble. "I told them I had the whole gable mined and warned them to get back from the wall. Then I threw an old grenade into the archway and they surrendered. Wasn't that better than killing them?"

At Ballymahon, after the garrison surrendered, McEoin saw "an old constable, stubble on face, who hadn't had time to put his boots on when the attack started. I told him to go back for his boots. 'Oh, sir,' says he, 'I wouldn't go back in there for anything,'" McEoin sent the old man back to his lodgings. Sergeant Hambledon who, with Sergeant Martin, had been in charge of the barracks, used to tell against himself the story of what happened afterwards. Martin and he had explained to the District Inspector, who arrived shortly after the attack, that his men had fired their last round before surrendering. Then they had broken their rifles. The two sergeants gave such an heroic account that they felt sure of promotion before long.

"Then," Hambledon would relate, "that old so and so who Sean McEoin sent back landed in and the D.I. roared, 'Where were you?'

" 'I were at home where the dacent man put me.'

" 'What do you know about this?'

" 'Nothing, sir. Only that we must all be grateful to Sergeant Martin for surrendering when he did. And if he'd had to break the rifles we'd all be killed.' " In fact, McEoin and his men had seized not only the garrison's arms but weapons from miles around which had been handed in for safe keeping.

Easter brought other problems for the British which, also, were not so easily settled as the outbursts of violence which had been expected in Dublin. All the national organisations
104

had been declared illegal, among them the women's organisation, Cumann ne mBan, and the Gaelic League as well as the Volunteers and Sinn Fein. The jails were full. In Mountjoy nearly one hundred prisoners produced that awkward weapon, the hunger strike. Their object was to compel the British to acknowledge that Ireland's freedom-fighters were soldiers, not felons, and to treat them therefore as prisoners of war—or else release them. Crowds gathered outside in an atmosphere that was electric with emotion, their minds ablaze with pictures of the imagined scene inside.

The British Government refused to give way. These men had been detained to protect society from unlawful violence. It would be futile to arrest them if they could simply secure their release by moral blackmail. Then the Irish Labour Party, led by Thomas Farren and Thomas Johnson, called for a general strike in support of the prisoners. After two days the Viceroy released all detainees against whom no charges had been brought and the general strike was called off. But the British Government was adamant in its policy to treat the dissidents as civilians breaking the law. More and more "police" were recruited and military garrisons also were strengthened.

On April 28th, Black and Tans rampaged Limerick on a drunken spree. This was their first "outing" but their conduct was little more than the kind of hooliganism which seems to afflict large groups of men, from soldiers to football supporters, when they visit someone else's country. It was not long before the Black and Tans made their début on constabulary duties but their conduct went from bad to worse. They were not the dregs of English jails, as Irishmen have so often alleged, but bored, unsettled, often workless ex-soldiers, young men whose ordinary pity and honour had been dried up by their long and merciless ordeal in the trenches. Perhaps they were incapable of spiritual rehabilitation, perhaps just not so lucky as the vast majority of their contemporaries, or perhaps they were of the ilk who had dispensed torture and death to countless young conscientious objectors in those terrible years. Their methods at least were to prove the same.

Soon, as they went their bruising rounds of towns and villages, battering at frightened doors in the night, arrests of young Irishmen who were, or might have been. Volunteers
105

became more numerous. But, even before their advent, their regular R.I.C. colleagues and the British forces had kept the jails brimming. So far, there had been no executions. These were to come. But if the I.R.A. gained one advantage by fighting out of uniform, their adversaries were able to counter it by arresting suspects and holding them behind bars. There did not seem to be much the Irish could do about that, but then Liam Lynch, Commandant of Cork No. 2 Brigade, began to think of quality rather than quantity. In Cork jail were men, among them Lynch's very good friend, Michael Fitzgerald, who had been arrested following the ambush in Fermoy. Lynch was worried about them, as he was about the small but steady dribbling of good men into the hands of British jailers.

He conceived the idea of capturing one or two British officers of senior rank. Local Intelligence officers were asked to look out for opportunities and on June 26th Lynch, with Sean Moylan, Paddy Clancy and George Power, stalked Brigadier-General Lucas and two colonels, Danford and Tyrrell, who were enjoying some fishing near Fermoy. The three officers were duly captured and transported from the Fermoy area in two cars. Travelling in the second car, Lucas and Danford, having plotted together in Arabic, suddenly attacked Lynch and Clancy. A fierce struggle developed and the car crashed into a ditch. The fight continued on the ground until Lynch had overpowered Lucas and shattered Danford's jaw with a bullet. Full of fight and courage, Danford, who had been getting the better of Clancy had ignored Lynch's warning to surrender. When the first car containing Power, Moylan and Colonel Tyrrell turned back and reached the scene, Lynch released Tyrrell to look after Danford and contented himself with holding Lucas. His coup boosted I.R.A. morale and humiliated the English. Angrily Lucas's troops raided Fermoy, causing considerable damage and one death.

"I was asked to take Lucas over from the Cork fellows for a couple of days," recalls Michael Brennan, then Commandant of East Clare Brigade. "Then he was to be handed over to the fellows in Limerick. They brought him across the Shannon and just dumped him on me. I had the damned fellow for nearly a month. Funds were low and it was ruinous."

The I.R.A. men treated their prisoner with casual respect and did their best to keep him in the manner to which he was
106

accustomed. Lucas enjoyed his whiskey and it was this item particularly that Brennan found expensive. He had to keep Lucas on the move because troops, and even aeroplanes, were searching for him, and this meant that valuable men were needed to guard him. It was not only to Brennan that the General was an embarrassment. One hostess almost died of fright when she heard who was to be a guest in her house. What did a general eat, she wanted to know. The good lady rose to the occasion and Lucas certainly had no complaints about the way he was looked after. But life as a closely guarded prisoner was tedious and Brennan was sympathetic.

"We had him for about ten days in a house near the Shannon, a famous fishing district. Castleconnell was just across the river. Lucas was always looking longingly at the river. I had some local fellows from across the river—the Limerick side—helping out with guard duties. One of them, Sean Carroll, said to me, 'Would the General like to go fishing one night?' I said, 'I'm sure he would.' Sean thought for a minute, then he added, 'The only thing is, it's stroke-hauling. He mightn't like that.'"

Brennan asked Lucas if he would like to go fishing with Sean and had an enthusiastic answer, but when he mentioned stroke-hauling, the General jibbed. "Oh, my God, no!" he exclaimed. Brennan left it at that. He did not know what stroke-hauling was but guessed it was illegal. Next day the temptation was too much for Lucas, who seemed less concerned about fishing by illegal methods than being caught at it. Assured by Sean Carroll that there was no risk, he agreed to go.

"That night they went down to the river," Brennan continues. "There was a very rapid current but these fellows were skilled boatmen and were able to keep the boat stationary while Lucas made cast after cast. But he was apprehensive all the time in case the bailiffs appeared. Sean kept reassuring him and all went well."

On the following day, Lucas said to Brennan, "I can't understand how Sean was so certain that there'd be no trouble. The bailiffs are always local fellows and they know all the tricks."

Brennan could not explain it so he asked Sean Carroll. The answer, to Lucas's amusement, was simply that Sean was the head bailiff.

After five weeks in captivity, Lucas escaped on the road. It was a brave effort, for he did not realise that his captors would not try very hard to stop him. His capture had been a notable moral victory.

The Black and Tans, exhorted by Dublin Castle, set out to make Ireland a "hell for rebels to live in". Their misdeeds have been catalogued over and over again and, less tediously if more tendentiously, woven into countless Irish songs. Using stealth and surprise, the only tactics with any possibility of success, the Irish fighters dealt out shrewd and relentless death to the invader. The forces of the Crown struck back with ever less pity or scruple. Terror was met with terror. Atrocity was piled on atrocity in a ghastly game of tit for tat that seemed as if it could have no end. Who began it did not matter any more. Each blow was an answer to the one before, and a prelude to the next. The British Government condoned the tactics of its servants and protected them with the starkest lies while raising pious hands in horror as they reported the outrages of their adversaries. As always, the bitter truth was that neither side had much to be proud of.

At Listowel, on June 19th, Lieutenant-Colonel Smyth, appointed R.I.C. Commissioner for Munster, told his men that "Sinn Fein has had all the sport up to the present and we are going to have the sport now." They were to use ambush tactics, too, and anyone approaching with hands in pockets or seeming suspicious in any way was to be shot down. "The more you shoot the better I will like it, and I assure you no policeman will get into trouble for shooting any man." Among his listeners were some Irish policemen, who had already expressed reluctance to be transferred to smaller and more dangerous posts. They were unimpressed by Smyth's pep-talk and several resigned. The I.R.A. did not think much of it either and, following Smyth's own precepts, they shot him in a club in Cork.

In twelve months, by the end of June, nearly eighty policemen and soldiers had been killed, but there were many parts of Ireland where life ran on much as it always had. English visitors enjoyed quiet holidays and the hospitality of their Irish hosts never faltered. At the races the bookies took the money of I.R.A. men and Black and Tans with impartiality. A church offered less protection and, one July Sunday, at Bandon in West Cork, an R.I.C. sergeant was shot dead in the
108

church porch as he was about to attend mass. He was described by Tom Barry in *Guerilla Days in Ireland* as "the most dangerous member of the British forces in West Cork", and perhaps he was, but his death in sacred precincts affronted the consciences of many religious Irish folk, I.R.A. men among them. The Bishop of Cork pronounced an "Interdict" on the culprits. Dr Cohalan was not very popular among the Volunteers, for he had made a number of scorching utterances concerning their activities. Some, at one time, even contemplated hanging him.

Violence was censured again and again by the Irish Hierarchy. "Callous and deliberate murder" was how the Bishop of Ross described the killing of four policemen at Timoleague in April, and, later, Dr Cohalan decreed that anyone killing from an ambush was a murderer and would be excommunicated.

To many of the Volunteers the Bishops were reactionary, afraid that their own power would disappear in the maelstrom. It was ironical that riots were sparked in the North by religious rivalry. Religion provided inflammable material for a rabble-rousing torch but religious differences had never been the core of opposition to Home Rule by a majority in six counties of Ireland. "Home Rule is Rome rule," had been an incandescent slogan but, like so many catch-cries, it did not state the problem but distorted it. It meant as much as the slogan YANKS GO HOME which has plastered the walls of so many European cities since the Second World War.

The Ulster Unionists were a minority in the whole of Ireland who were afraid of losing privilege and power. All privileged minorities, wherever they may be, react at any threat to their security and, having the power, they use it to protect themselves. Carson had used that power brilliantly so that not only the demands of the majority of people of Ireland had been denied, but the will of the House of Commons had been stultified too. When he could not stave off Home Rule for the whole country, he endeavoured to protect his kind by forcing the hiving off of part of it, as large a part as would preserve a majority. For the sake of that majority he had had to concede three of Ulster's nine counties, then he entrenched himself behind the bulwark of majority rule. Weakly, the British Government allowed itself to be pressurised, before World

109

War 1 by the threat of violence and, after it, by the threat to its own uncomfortably coalescing tissues.

Sinn Fein and Catholicism were never synonymous but Sinn Fein and Irish Nationalism were, and it was nationalism that was the danger. The control of Belfast industry was not to fall into the hands of the rural South, which was already tainted by socialist theories. Those who had money and position meant to keep it. Like the big land owners in the South, they stemmed not from the native soil but from England and Scotland. Their forbears had seized privilege, had had wit enough to build on it and they had established an ascendancy, *the* Ascendancy. There were among Unionists sane, sympathetic and sensible men, ready to advance with the times in a steady, sophisticated way, willing to make concessions, though naturally unwilling to strip themselves of all they owned. And, genuinely, they wished to retain their British birthright. It was not easy for these men, but just as the moderate people of the South had been pushed by the extremes of British imperialism to support Sinn Fein even though they did not always approve of their methods, so the moderate Unionists were impelled by the violence of Sinn Fein into the aggressive camp of the Orange Lodges. There was, and still is, in the north-east of Ireland a virulent brand of Presbyterianism which, allied to the Empire drum thumping of Unionism, engendered an antagonism to Sinn Fein and the Roman Catholic Church which went further than the enmity the South bore towards England.

It was nothing new for Catholics to suffer at Protestant hands on Orangeman's Day and, following riots in Derry in the last week in June, when Catholics were attacked without provocation, Belfast was tense on July 12th, 1920. Leaders, clergy among them, of both political parties and religious persuasions were able to contain violence, but Sir Edward Carson fulminated against Sinn Fein, which he alleged used both the Roman Catholic Church and Labour to mask its true identity. "We have been handed down great traditions and great privileges, and in our Orange Order we have undertaken to preserve those and to hand them on to our children, and we must proclaim today clearly that, come what will, and be the consequences what they may, we in Ulster will tolerate no Sinn Fein—no Sinn Fein organisation, no Sinn Fein methods."

His words turned the flame a little higher and the pot boiled over a few days later. Resentful of the way that predominantly Catholic workers from the South had infiltrated into shipyard employment during the First World War, Protestant workers in South Yard tried to oust the interlopers, first by demanding an undertaking from each man that he did not belong to Sinn Fein, and then by violence. Catholic workers were beaten with iron bars, sledge hammers, anything that came to hand, and pitched into the river. They were even pursued to their homes, some of which were burned down. The motive for the attack was primarily economic, but the fact was that Protestants beat up Catholics. Word flew quickly and for the next few days Belfast was hell. Protestant mobs killed, burned and looted. Catholics, many of them Sinn Feiners, hit back. The military were called in and were soon in conflict with crowds from both sides. A Roman Catholic church was attacked and a convent set on fire. Eighteen people died in Belfast in four days. Rioting broke out in other towns. Eventually the trouble simmered down but there were spasms from time to time during the coming months.

The pattern was usually the same. Protestant mobs rampaged through Catholic areas and there were reprisals, which were stepped up as the I.R.A. strengthened its forces in the North. Dramatically, but not unjustifiably, the Catholics labelled the campaign a "pogrom" and the word is enough to rouse the indignation of any Irish Catholic today. With clumsy good intentions the authorities formed the Ulster Special Constabulary whose members, part-timers, were Protestant civilians. It looked as if officialdom was sanctioning violence against Catholics and the "Specials" enjoyed a place in the affections of the Southern Irish beside that of the Black and Tans. But they endured for much longer and their place in Irish history is probably even more significant.

In the second half of 1920, however, the Black and Tans dominated the Irish scene. They were joined in August by the Auxiliaries, a force of about 1,500 men, raised at Churchill's suggestion from among ex-officers of the British Forces and placed under the command of Brigadier-General F. P. Crozier. The "Auxies", as they came to be called, were distinguished from the Black and Tans by their Tam O'Shanters. Ruthless as the "Tans", they carried out some of the most notorious outrages of those outrageous days. Yet there is a warmer gleam

111

in the eye of an old I.R.A. man when he recalls the "Auxies", for they were brave, tough soldiers and the Irish recognised them as such, despising the specious label of auxiliary policemen.

The British Army, as distinct from the quasi-policemen, the Black and Tan mercenaries, behaved on the whole with admirable restraint. Against them the Irish have few complaints. An exception was the Essex Regiment. Major A. E. Percival of this regiment was described as "easily the most viciously anti-Irish of all serving British officers" by Tom Barry, who made an abortive attempt to shoot him in Bandon and, more than twenty years later, sent him an ironical telegram when as Lt.-General Percival, he surrendered Singapore to the Japanese.

It was the Essex Regiment which tortured Tom Hales, O.C., and Pat Harte, Quartermaster, of the West Cork Brigade. Hales was one of four brothers, all of whom served in the I.R.A. Harte became insane as a result of his sufferings and died in a mental hospital some years later. Tom Hales died in 1966, a stocky, straight man with silver hair and a hat with the brim turned down over bright blue eyes, a man who said little but watched smilingly about him. He told his English torturers nothing and was sent to Pentonville. On the way he managed to send an account of his experiences to Michael Collins who wrote to Arthur Griffith that "a really good case should be made of this statement." He thought that the Propaganda Department should make the most of it and "particularly, the treatment meted out by us to Brigadier-General Lucas should be contrasted with the treatment meted out by them to Brigadier-General Hales." At Headquarters no propaganda opportunity was lost but the men on the spot thought more of revenge and Tom Barry harassed the Essex Regiment at every turn.

Barry was to become one of the hardest and most brilliant of the guerrilla war leaders. He had served under Allenby in the British Army and began his I.R.A. career in 1919 as an Intelligence officer at Bandon. A born fighter, he went to war for the hell of it, but he began to ask questions when he read of the Easter Rising, and when he joined the I.R.A. he knew what he was fighting for. But he still enjoyed the hell of it.

Men like Barry began to make names for themselves and in
112

Ireland they will be remembered with the illustrious train of Irish heroes of a thousand years.

In essence, a tribal system like Scotland's clanship still existed in rural Ireland. It was strongest in the west. Family attachments and rivalries counted a great deal in the election of leaders and the quality of leadership varied greatly. In some areas there was little action because there were few arms and little opportunity, or sometimes little initiative, to obtain more. Pleas went to Dublin from other areas for more arms and Collins, who was Adjutant-General as well as Minister of Finance and Director of Intelligence, and who seemed to find time for everything, often stingingly suggested in reply that they should first make some use of those they had. General Headquarters had to accept as leaders the men who came to the top in their own areas and, except in a few instances, such as the secondment of Ernie O'Malley to Tipperary, leaders were not transferable.

In these circumstances a concerted war effort was difficult to achieve. Quietly Richard Mulcahy worked in his role of Chief of Staff to create order and method. A very active and much wanted man, he lived from one hairsbreadth escape to another, his exploits rivalling those of Collins. But his staffwork was not always appreciated and one leader in the south grumbled that they had started the war with hurleys but would probably finish it with fountain pens. The real cohesive force was the growing unison of the people. It is true that in some areas fear of the I.R.A. engendered close-mouthed co-operation, but this was exceptional. Over most of the country it was the terror tactics of the Black and Tans, the Auxiliaries and of many of the regular R.I.C. which inspired ordinary people to leave the sidelines and to participate, often with great heroism, in unshackling Ireland.

Their enthusiasm may not have been everywhere at white heat, but the men of the I.R.A. never lacked a bed or a meal, whatever the risk of giving it to them. Their Intelligence system was almost unbeatable because half of the people were their agents. Telephone operators, typists, domestics, shop-keepers, publicans and, in Dublin, even prostitutes, collected information and passed it on. Dockers and railway men refused to carry British equipment and sometimes even British coffins.

113

Throughout August, 1920, the Volunteers took an Oath of allegiance to the Irish Republic and its Government, Dail Eireann. Approved by the Dail in August, 1919, and subsequently by a majority of the I.R.A., this was a logical step which gave the Dail formal control of the Army. But many Volunteers were dubious about removing control from their own Executive and one day they were to restore it.

The Irish campaign of harassment went on. Roads were trenched or mined, trees were felled and convoys ambushed, though the I.R.A. were careful not to interfere with fair-days or to inconvenience local people. Snipers went about their insidious business. Barracks were captured and burned. Arms were stolen and stored. Because of all this Irish homes were burned, shops and public houses looted, innocent people were killed. At Tuam in Galway, two constables were shot dead in ambush. In retaliation Black and Tans went on a drunken bender, looting and burning. Creameries were destroyed in the south to punish the civilian population and to make it more difficult for the I.R.A. to get food. In Templemore, Co. Tipperary, the market hall was burned down.

Sir Henry Wilson was astonished that Lloyd George "seemed to be satisfied that a counter-murder association was the best answer to Sinn Fein murders." It was "a crude idea of statesmanship," he said, and prophesied that the Prime Minister would have "a rude awakening." Wilson's own answer would have been the more conventional one of throwing in much stronger military forces, though rather less conventionally he did once advocate the shooting of Sinn Fein leaders by roster.

SEVEN

The same quirky humorist who had hit upon the title of the Better Government of Ireland Bill probably was responsible for that of the Restoration of Order in Ireland Bill, which Sir Hamar Greenwood introduced in the House of Commons on August 2nd, 1920, and which became law the following month. It was noted by the Irish with sardonic laughter.

The new measure provided for the trial of "civilians" by court martial and for the imprisonment of Sinn Feiners on suspicion. It empowered the authorities to impose curfews and to restrict the movement of traffic, even to prohibit fairs. Instead of coroners' inquests there were to be military courts of inquiry.

The Act was typical of the Coalition Government's process of double-think. In maintaining that the I.R.A. were merely a subversive civilian minority, outlaws who were not entitled to treatment as prisoners of war, and at the same time arraigning them in secret before a military court, or holding military inquiries over their dead bodies, the British Government tried to have it both ways. They got rid of the exasperating verdicts of Irish juries according to whom Volunteers were always wilfully murdered and members of the Crown Forces never, but they still claimed that a majority of the Irish people opposed the I.R.A., and they still blandly maintained the fiction that the law was kept by policemen and not by soldiers.

The courts of inquiry found that members of the Crown Forces who had come to a violent end invariably had been murdered, while they themselves rarely killed anyone except in the course of duty. The number of I.R.A. men shot "while attempting to escape" increased suddenly, but it often happened, strangely enough, that when a court of inquiry recorded that a Volunteer met a nice clean death, perhaps brought down by one bullet as he attempted a cavalier escape by the barred window of a room full of interrogators, his body with all the scars of the torture chamber was, either callously or naïvely, handed over to his relatives.

Sometimes the various authorities did not co-operate very well, as when soldiers were on their way to arrest MacCurtain unaware that the R.I.C. had shot him. When MacCurtain's successor, Terence MacSwiney, was arrested in a raid on Cork City Hall on August 12th, it was the military who acted first. It happened that a meeting of the staff of Cork No. 1 Brigade was in progress that night. Some I.R.B. officers also were meeting and a Dail Eireann court was hearing a case in which an English insurance company was plaintiff. The raid caused a great deal of confusion and many arrests were made. In the end, only twelve men were held, later being transported to

Cork jail. The prisoners included Sean O'Hegarty, Mac-Swiney's Vice O/C, most of the staff of Cork No. 1 Brigade, and Liam Lynch, O/C Cork No. 2 Brigade. Had the R.I.C. made the arrests there would have been a dearth of good officers in the Cork area, but the British Army accepted the ingenious cover stories of all but MacSwiney, who was hardly in the position to offer one, and let them go.

MacSwiney was sentenced to two years' penal servitude for possessing seditious documents. Doubtless he was in possession of quite a number, but those produced in evidence against him had been found tucked away in various obscure crevices after the raid took place. So Liam Lynch went free to plague the British from the hills and MacSwiney went to Brixton where he was to achieve the most devastating single-handed stroke of the Anglo-Irish War.

In Cork jail several prisoners who had not been brought to trial had begun a hunger strike the day before MacSwiney's arrest. They included Michael Fitzgerald, Liam Lynch's close friend, who had been arrested almost a year before, following the church parade ambush at Fermoy. MacSwiney, too, went on hunger strike. Fitzgerald died on October 17th, after an ordeal of sixty-seven days, and Joseph Murphy endured another eight days. On the day of Murphy's death, October 25th, Terence MasSwiney died in Brixton.

The hunger strikers in Cork had made their protest with the same fortitude as MacSwiney made his, but it was the marathon in Brixton which caught the attention of the world. Shaken by the wave of sympathy from press and public, the Cabinet almost gave in.[1] Balfour said that "in logic, the case against release is indisputable", that to give in meant "paralysis of the law". In the end, Macready's views were sought before the Cabinet decided to stand firm.

Though the imagination insists upon placing his deathbed in a prison cell, MacSwiney's last weeks were spent in a hospital ward. He was allowed visits from friends and nursed with gentleness. Food was always beside him, but weak from tuberculosis, he was in no condition to be fed forcibly. These were things which drove the sting of his hunger even deeper, which demanded even more effort in steeling his will. For this was essentially a battle between the will of the Government,

[1] Cabinet conclusion 49A 20 of 25/8/20.

which had power and majesty behind it, and that of a man who had only his faith. That faith he expressed in a letter, which he dictated three weeks before his death, to his fellow hunger strikers in Cork jail:

"Comrades, if we twelve go in glorious succession to the grave, the name of Ireland will flash in a tongue of flame through the world, and be a sign of hope for all time to every people struggling to be free. Let that thought inspire us and let our dying prayer be an exhortation to each other and to our people that everyone be prepared to sacrifice everything, and God will at last redeem our country."

MacSwiney had won just as the men of 1916 had won: he had driven the British Government into a position where they had the choice of relenting and thus showing weakness or of allowing him to become a martyr, so demonstrating their usual heartlessness. But there was no "glorious succession" of twelve deaths. The Dail Cabinet, who had allowed MacSwiney to die because they were no more ready to give way than the British, stepped in at last. Griffith thought they had done enough. The strike was called off.

In that strange era MacSwiney's body was allowed to lie in state in the Roman Catholic Southwark Cathedral, where it was seen by thousands of people. Thousands more lined the route when the funeral procession, headed by men of the I.R.A., trailed to Euston Station where MacSwiney's body was entrained. The Government insisted that the coffin be taken to Cork direct to avoid the inevitable scenes in Dublin.

The profound influence of his death can be gauged perhaps from a minor episode of local government politics in London almost twelve months later. The Poplar Council in East London was resisting uniform contributions to the London County Council, claiming that these bore upon them much more severely than upon an affluent borough like Westminster. An Alderman swore that councillors upon whom a writ of attachment had been served "would be glad to go to Brixton prison, a place honoured by the martyrdom of Terence MacSwiney . . ."

During the long decline of MacSwiney, misery and death had been the lot of Ireland. When an R.I.C. inspector was killed near Balbriggan in County Dublin, 150 Black and Tans from the Gormanstown depot swept into the town like starving locusts into a cornfield. They looted and drank, wrecked and burned, leaving behind them two murdered townsmen and the blackened walls and gabled ends of houses.

In the same week Mallow, Lahinch, Ennistymon and Trim were sacked. One night Michael Brennan stood on a hilltop in Clare watching fire after fire leap brutally from the darkness below. He counted thirty-six homes blazing.

The I.R.A. were quick to retaliate by burning the homes of Loyalists, the big homes of the Ascendancy. Until now, unless they were suspected of passing information to the British, the Loyalists had been mostly unmolested. They were not all disliked. Many had contributed a great deal to Ireland's good. Many, indeed, like the ordinary people of England, were aghast at the behaviour of the "Tans" and contrasted their eternal drunkenness with the deliberate abstemiousness of the I.R.A. The Tans dragged men behind lorries, cut out tongues and murdered even children.

Their activities could scarcely be held secret but in England Ministers made speeches in which they lied, contradicted themselves, denied the policy of reprisals then sought to justify it. Sir Hamar Greenwood, especially, tailored his utterances to the occasion. Sometimes the men on the spot had "seen red" in circumstances of extreme provocation but, as often as not, the provocation had occurred months before. Reprisals were at first "unauthorised", regrettable but understandable, then "authorised", regrettable but necessary.

"There is no such thing as reprisals, but they have done a great deal of good,"[2] was Lord Hugh Cecil's pithy comment on the explainings-away. English newspapers, too, were not to be muzzled. *The Times*, once opposed to concessions for Ireland, had become acid in its strictures on the Government. The *Daily News* correspondent, Hugh Martin, was hurting so much by his revelations of the truth that Black and Tans made an attempt on his life. In the *Manchester Guardian*[3] C. P. Scott wrote:

"Englishmen are at bottom resolved to do justice to Ireland. Still more they are resolved in the process to keep their hands decently clean and their reputation in the world unsullied. This is where Mr. George is failing us."

[2] Quoted by Frank Pakenham in *Peace by Ordeal*.
[3] *Manchester Guardian* October 11th, 1920.
118

The influential Scott, a personal friend of Lloyd George, was unrelentingly hostile to his policy.

In Dublin the war was even more sordid. Men hunted each other through the streets. Spies and informers betrayed one side or the other. Households were roused in the night and their very beds were searched. Sometimes innocent men were bundled off in lorries and sometimes equally innocent babies squirmed as they lay on a quickly hidden gun. And as the British became increasingly ruthless feeling against them grew. Even Irishmen who had brilliant records in the British Army and had once been proud of them now made a disillusioned way into the I.R.A.

Dermott MacManus, for example, had had an upbringing which was traditionally British. Born into a well-to-do family in Mayo, he had been educated at Westminster and Sandhurst. He had been a gay young subaltern in the London of 1910. Blown up at Gallipoli, he had been eventually invalided out of the Inniskilling Fusiliers and entered Trinity College. Disgusted with the new British attitude, he wrote to Michael Collins. Perhaps a letter was intercepted for suspicion quickly fell on him and he was arrested in his flat.

"I was thrown into the most amazing dungeon under the old tower in the Castle," recalls MacManus. Nothing incriminating was found on his person or, as he discovered when he was released after interrogation, in his flat. The one thing the searchers missed was a note concerning methods of interrogation in the Castle which he had been writing when the raiders arrived and slipped into a history notebook on the table. He had obtained this information in rather a curious way.

"There was a little fellow at Trinity who was very gullible. Friends in pubs used to pull his leg. One day, they told him Mick Collins wanted a Sinn Fein Ambassador to Belfast. Would he be prepared to take on the job? He agreed with delight and a few days later was given a paper purporting to carry Collins's signature making the appointment. He would get further orders later.

"A few days afterwards in the 'Sod of Turf', a tea place, he was searched in the course of a raid.

"'Have you got a gun on you?'

"'Not here,' he said bravely. They grabbed him, went to his flat where they found his ambassadorial credentials and

119

thought he must be one of the most important men in the I.R.A. At the Castle he fell into the hands of two interrogators, a barrister and Captain King who was an ex-Connaught Ranger. Their methods were completely contrasting; King was harsh and brutal, the barrister soft and persuasive. The barrister apparently enjoyed himself, for he found that the little fellow could be made to agree to anything put into his head."

They let him go.

Shortly afterwards, MacManus was introduced into the I.R.A. by his friend Cathal Brugha. He was still a Monarchist at heart and he did not agree with some of the methods of Brugha and Collins. Me made it clear that he would not participate in anything he thought wrong and went to work with Ginger O'Connell on Brugha's personal staff in the office on the quays from which he ran his ecclesiastical candle-maker's business. It was not long before MacManus was on the run.

Sean Treacy and Dan Breen had been on the run since Soloheadbeg, almost two years. On October 12th, 1920, they were trapped in the house of Professor Carolan in Drumcondra. The raid was led by Major G. O. S. Smyth whose brother had been shot in the club in Cork. Breen and Treacy shot their way out, killing Smyth and another officer. Breen was wounded, Treacy stayed to cover his retreat and the two men were separated, each believing the other dead. The British admitted the loss of the two officers but, years later, Dan Breen was told by a man who had gone to the house with an ambulance that several more bodies were found. Professor Carolan was fatally wounded and it was stated that his death was accidental but he lived long enough to explain that he had been put face to a wall and shot through the back of the neck. His statement was published in Dublin newspapers and was never denied.

Both Breen and Treacy managed to reach friendly hands and were reunited in an old stable where Breen, in great pain, was hidden. He was smuggled at last into the Mater Hospital where he was in constant danger of being discovered. The whole Dublin I.R.A. organisation was buzzing with plans to rescue him if the need arose. Their nervous activity and the ferocity of raids on houses where it was thought information about Breen, Treacy, and their Tipperary friends, Robinson and Lacey, might be picked up, or tricked or battered out of someone, led to clashes. Gunfire echoed in several areas of the city until its culmination on 14th October when Sean Treacy was trapped in Talbot Street as he tried to leave the Republican Outfitters, one of the I.R.A's principal meeting places, where he had gone to meet Peadar Clancy.

Treacy, anxious about Breen and inclined to be reckless, had been trying to shake off shadows all day. Now they had caught up with him, bringing an armoured car and two lorry loads of Auxiliaries. He tried to get away on a bicycle but was knocked down, and Intelligence men closed in on him. As people raced to see what was happening, a gun battle broke out. Treacy killed two, possibly three, of his adversaries and fell dead himself as panicky machine-gun fire burst from the armoured car killing a messenger boy and another lad who was passing on a bicycle.

The British could be generous to a valorous foe and they were so to Sean Treacy. The girl who identified his body saw that it had been impeccably laid out, and a soldier on guard gave her a lock of Treacy's hair. He was buried at Kilfeacle in Tipperary and Volunteers, including several on the run, escorted the coffin. There were one or two incidents as the five-mile long procession passed detachments of the British Army, but little real interference, and at one point British soldiers saluted. Dan Breen still suffers from the effects of his wounds and he does not find it easy to travel. But each year on the anniversary of Sean Treacy's death, he visits his grave at Kilfeacle.

On November 1st, 1920, the day that Terence MacSwiney was buried in Cork, the British threw yet another flaming torch into the dry tinder of Irish emotions. At Mountjoy Prison that morning Kevin Barry, a medical student aged eighteen, was hanged. A few weeks previously, on the day that Balbriggan was wrecked, Barry was one of a party of Volunteers who ambushed a British rations party drawing bread from a Dublin bakery and killed six soldiers.

Barry, the only one caught, was tortured, refused to give any information about his companions and was sentenced to death by hanging. Here again was an example of the British determination to treat the activities of the I.R.A. as crimes by civilians, though Barry will be remembered always in Ireland as one of their finest young soldiers.

"Why not shoot me like a soldier
Do not hang me like a dog,
For I fought to free old Ireland,
On that bright September morn"

runs the ballad of Kevin Barry.

Even in England efforts were made to save Barry from the gallows, a last minute appeal from Joseph Devlin was rejected by the Cabinet,[4] and the barbaric ritual was gone through. Outside the prison hundreds of Irish men and women knelt in prayer, their tears falling upon their rosaries, a black acre of mourning.

In the annals of England Kevin Barry died the death of a felon. Had he been spared that day he would have been re-leased with his comrades of the Irish Republican Army twelve months later. He was at the time of his death a "gunman". It was a term made famous by O'Casey in his plays and by O'Flaherty in *The Informer*. It did not apply so much to the flying columns, the men who fought on the roads and in the hills, as to those who killed at short range with parabellum or Mauser, sometimes, like Barry, in fair fight, sometimes in silence and without warning. Had Kevin Barry lived he might today be a distinguished man of medicine. For the generation of fiery young revolutionaries is today the older generation of the country. It is not a generation of reformed rakes but of men in the professions or in trade, shop keepers and craftsmen, who happen to have fought for their country in their youth. Gradually their numbers are being whittled down. They are like the older generation of every country.

A typical member of this generation is Vincent Byrne. One would associate him with nothing more lethal than the garden shears with which he keeps his hedge as trim, and his home as reticent, as he is himself. But in 1920 he was a member of the Squad which liquidated to order men whom Collins, invari-ably with good reasons, designated dangerous to Ireland.

4 Cabinet conclusion 59/20 App. VIII (2).

Byrne's career in Ireland's volunteer army began in 1915 when he was a slip of a boy serving an apprenticeship as a cabinet maker. In the Easter Rising he fought in Jacob's Factory and at the surrender he was dropped from a window into the street by a Franciscan father. He got home safely but someone must have informed against him for a detachment of British soldiers called to arrest him. The sergeant in charge, "the nicest man you ever met in your life", had a son of Byrne's age and did not like having to arrest the Dublin boy.

"Would you like some steak and onions?" he asked gruffly.

"I would," said Byrne.

The fatherly sergeant fed him well then regretfully handed him over to Richmond Barracks where he was detained for a week, during which his captors tried to channel his aggressive spirit into British khaki.

"No," said Vinny Byrne, aged 14. "I want to fight for Ireland."

So they gave him his wish, though they did not see the Irish putting up a fight again. With some other boys he was marched out of the gates and left to find his own way home. Four years later, Vinny Byrne became a gunman because, as a soldier in a resistance army he believed being a gunman was simply his duty.

Byrne was "out on Bloody Sunday", the occasion that provoked more horror in England than almost any other incident in the war with the Irish. In a carefully planned operation eleven British Intelligence officers were shot dead by men of the Dublin Brigade and the Squad on that Sunday morning. November 21st, 1920. Some were routed out of their beds and shot down as they stood. Two Auxiliaries died in an attempt to capture the raiders and an army officer, mistaken for another man, also died. And in the afternoon of that ghastly day the Black and Tans enjoyed their revenge. They went to Croke Park, apparently to look for men with arms, and turned their own guns on a football match crowd—and the players on the field. Fourteen people were killed, several of them children; over sixty were wounded. In official communiqués much was made of the "murder" of the Intelligence officers but the Croke Park incident was glossed over.

Both sides made much of their own tragedy at the time, but

only the Irish have remembered it. Well they might, for Croke Park was a senseless and bloody massacre of innocent people, and only the fact that a few horrified British officers intervened at crucial moments lessened a little the stain on Britain's honour. The British officers who were assassinated were brave men, experienced and tough, who knew the danger they ran and knew that it grew as they tightened their remorseless net about the amateur but deadly Intelligence system of the Irish. They were a specially chosen group dedicated to smashing the Collins network and given an entirely free hand as to how they did it.

Collins was warned of their coming and it was not long before the two undercover groups were fighting a deadly battle of wits. In Cork, Limerick and elsewhere the British gunmen had struck first. The Irish could not afford to allow this to happen in Dublin. As the weeks went by, the adversaries built up their dossiers. Agents and counter-agents set traps or betrayed them. A business man named Lynch was done to death in his Dublin hotel room, his British killers having apparently mistaken him for Liam Lynch. The British used paid Irish informers. Liam Tobin, Deputy Director of Intelligence, and his assistant, Tom Cullen, were trapped in a raid but talked their way to freedom. Frank Thornton, another Collins man, was actually released after ten days in detention. Collins himself had a number of narrow escapes. In his turn he had agents in Dublin Castle, who lived on the very margins of safety and served him well. The "Cairo gang", as the new British Intelligence ring was called, worked independently of the Castle and it was more difficult for Collins to get information about their movements. But gradually the pattern of their activities was pieced together and the dossiers submitted to Cathal Brugha, Minister of Defence.

Twenty of the dossiers Brugha put aside. The cases were unproven. No English civilian in Ireland who was not with certainty involved in activities harmful to the I.R.A. had suffered at their hands and Brugha, for all his passionate hatred of Britain, did not intend that any should, though he was quite prepared to blow up the House of Commons. The Cabinet accepted his recommendations and on November 17th Dick McKee, Commandant of the Dublin Brigade, and his deputy, Peadar Clancy, were instructed by Collins to make
124

arrangements for the informal executions of the "particular ones" as he designated them in his order.

Almost by chance, McKee and Clancy were betrayed that night, and at 2 o'clock on Sunday morning they were taken by raiding Auxiliaries with so little warning that they only just managed to destroy documents which would have given away the whole plan for liquidating the "particular ones". But destroy them they did and the plan was carried through. Of the I.R.A. men the only casualty was Frank Teeling, wounded and captured by Auxiliaries, and saved from a bullet through the head by General Crozier, their commanding officer.

In *Ireland for Ever* Crozier, who was to become disillusioned with the Government's methods which condoned if they did not actually license murder, writes scathingly of "the solemn pomp and circumstance which accompanied the cavalcade of death through the streets of London when coffins on gun carriages draped with the Union Jack, containing the remains of murdered officers and ex-officers, were solemnly paraded before the populace, followed by Ministers of the Crown and attended by the King's representatives and guards of 'honour' ". There was a service at Westminster Abbey and, for the Roman Catholics, Requiem Mass at Westminster Cathedral.

The British public, steeped in the creed of good sportsmanship, was gulled into believing that these men were uniformed officers engaged in normal military duties who had not been given a chance to die in honest combat but had been foully murdered. There is no denying that they were killed with cold cruelty. Wives witnessed their husbands' deaths, no-one's feelings were spared, and scarcely a word uttered was grained with humanity. But these were men of the same stamp as the more experienced of their killers, brave and pitiless men for whom murder was a military operation.

"We had to learn to kill in cold blood and we got used to it," Joe Dolan, another member of the Squad, said almost laconically when he talked to me about the assassination, less than two years later, of Sir Henry Wilson, the man who had brought into being the decimated Cairo gang.

But not all of the young men of the Dublin Brigade who

were in action that morning were "used to it". It was one thing to set out to destroy dangerous Intelligence agents, quite another to shoot down defenceless men in the intimacy of their bedrooms, and of those who were scheduled for execution that morning several survived because bullets flew wildly from shaking guns.

It was not easy to learn to kill in cold blood and one day the lesson had to be unlearned.

"You had to keep great control of yourself not to become a killer," Dan Breen told me. "Even for years afterwards I wouldn't trust myself in a crowd for fear I'd lose my temper."

The final act on that gothic Sunday was the killing in Dublin Castle of Peadar Clancy and Dick McKee, who had organised the plan for the morning, and of Conor Clune, a young man from Clare who had no connection with the Volunteers but who had been arrested on suspicion, apparently because his hand shook when he was questioned. The Castle authorities explained that they were shot while trying to escape from a room which, in the ludicrously unconvincing photographs published to support the story, is shown with windows barred and sandbagged. Irish accounts of British atrocities were naturally heightened, but the report of a doctor who examined the bodies, and found that the three men had been shot through the head at close range and that McKee and Clancy had been beaten up, rings true. Collins arranged the medical examination and also the funerals of the two I.R.A. men, and risked his own life to attend a Requiem Mass in the Pro-Cathedral.

A week after Bloody Sunday, when the Auxiliary Division had its first casualties, Tom Barry laid his ambush at Kilmichael near Macroom in which sixteen Auxies were killed outright, one was fatally wounded and one died in a bog.

Neither Kilmichael nor Bloody Sunday had deterred the British Cabinet from pursuing secret negotiations for peace already in train. In the House of Commons and in speeches in various parts of the country Ministers were passionate in denouncing I.R.A. tactics and in defending the actions of the Crown Forces, but out of the limelight they spoke with a detachment bred perhaps of their orderings of life and death during World War I on a scale beyond imagination except in the form of statistics.

126

After Bloody Sunday Churchill earned an indignant line in Sir Henry Wilson's diary when he "insinuated that the murdered officers were careless and ought to have taken precautions". Lord Riddell, another indefatigable diarist, who was with Lloyd George when the news of the killings was telephoned to him, recorded that the Prime Minister was "much concerned and from time to time very busy on the telephone, but meanwhile he read the book he was reading when the news came as if nothing had happened".

Less phlegmatically, the Cabinet arranged to take precautions for their own protection and the security of both Houses of Parliament and Government buildings.[5]

It suited the Government to make political capital out of the Irish "murder gangs", but their own policy put them in danger of losing it. They had winked at, even encouraged, ruthless retaliation but the Black and Tans had gone too far. The Cabinet met on November 10th, before Bloody Sunday to consider a memorandum from Churchill in which he cited "strong representations" by the military authorities for a system of reprisals regulated by senior officers.

"It is thought by many that such a policy would be less discreditable and more effective than what is now going on," wrote Churchill. He had complaints that "besides clumsy and indiscriminate destruction, actual looting and thieving as well as drunkenness and gross disorder are occurring."

He could not "feel it right to punish the troops when, goaded in the most brutal manner and finding no redress, they take action on their own account." He did not consider the Government attitude on reprisals could be maintained much longer.

The Attorney-General's opinion was that "anything in the nature of authorised reprisals could not be carried out without legislation". It was decided that the moment for this step was not opportune and that the Chief Secretary "should do all in his power to prevent houses and creameries being burned by the R.I.C. and the troops as reprisals".[6]

Convinced that Britain had the upper hand at last, had "murder by the throat" as he put it publicly, Lloyd George had sounded Arthur Griffith on proposals put forward by

[5] Cabinet conclusion 66/20 App. I of 25/11/20.
[6] Cabinet conclusion 59A of 10/11/20.

General Cockerill in a letter to *The Times*. The suggestions, which might easily have been the blueprint for what ultimately came to pass, attracted Griffith who had been acting President of the Dail since de Valera's departure for America eighteen months earlier. On November 26th, Griffith was arrested and Collins assumed effective control of the Dail. A few days later the Roman Catholic Archbishop of Perth, Australia, Dr Clune, at the request of Lloyd George, took peace proposals to Griffith in Mountjoy Prison.

On December 4th, the Archbishop saw Collins and agreed with him upon a formula which Collins put to him in a letter.

"If it is understood that the acts of violence (attacks, counter attacks, reprisals, arrests, pursuits) are called off on both sides, we are agreeable to issue the necessary instructions on our side, it being understood that the entire Dail shall be free to meet, and that its peaceful activities be not interfered with."

Several Irishmen then took a private hand in trying to secure peace. One of these was Father Michael O'Flanagan, a fiery priest disciplined by his Bishop for political activities in 1918. He was a vice-president of Sinn Fein. It was now an empty title, for O'Flanagan had no place in the Dail Cabinet, and Lloyd George was not sure whether or not his telegram came from Sinn Fein.[7] In the House of Commons he announced the proclamation of martial law in Cork and Tipperary—a direct result of the Kilmichael ambush—and he insisted that the Irish must surrender their arms before any truce could be considered. He knew perfectly well that this was an impossible condition and he made any proposition even less attractive by stating that a "safe conduct" would be granted to some members of the Dail but not to others. He had already told Dr Clune that Collins and Mulcahy would not be acceptable members of the Dail and advised that they disappear for a time. Reading to the House the telegram he had received from Father O'Flanagan and also a message from six Galway County Councillors, Lloyd George adduced these as indications that the Irish nut was almost cracked. It was Greenwood who had advised his Cabinet colleagues to stand firm. They had at first favoured an amnesty so that all members of the Dail could meet—provided that a motion to "cease the murder campaign" was proposed. They thought

[7] Cabinet conclusion 66/20 (2) of 6/12/20.

128

5

there was little prospect of capturing the wanted men, "so little would be lost".[8]

Lord French declared martial law in the South on December 10th. Two days later, following an ambush in which one of their men was killed, Auxiliaries and Black and Tans exploded into Cork and burned as much of the city as they could. Hundreds of gallons of petrol were taken from military depots with the connivance of the guards, poured into buildings, mainly in Patrick Street, and set alight with Verey pistols. As the drunken stampede ignited building after building, the frenzied joy of the incendiarists sounded with the roar of the flames while they pillaged insensately and even cut the hoses of fire brigades sent to the rescue. Some of the fever caught up soldiers and civilians, who joined in the plundering and danced in the fire-lit street. But there were others, civilians and soldiers and even Black and Tans, who were appalled by the madness to destroy and fought the fires and the incendiarists too.

So there was just a tang of truth in Sir Hamar Greenwood's claim in the House of Commons that the Crown Forces had "saved Cork from destruction." But Sir Hamar blamed the disaster on the Irish themselves, implying that the I.R.A. had tried in this way to bring non-supporters to heel. Damage totalled about £3 million and the City Hall and the fine Carnegie Library as well as a considerable part of the shopping area were destroyed.

Both in England and in Ireland an independent inquiry was demanded but Lloyd George would agree only to a military inquiry. This was presided over by General Strickland who, as General Officer Commanding Cork, had hardly shone in dealing with the emergency, and it closed before people who asked to give evidence, or to be represented, knew that it had opened. Though Lloyd George had promised to publish the report, he did not do so "in the public interest". At a special Cabinet meeting, attended also by General Strickland, Tudor, Macready and Boyd, and by Sir John Anderson,[9] it was decided that "the effect of publishing the report if Parliament was sitting would be disastrous to the Government's whole policy in Ireland". Tudor felt that the report, which put most of the

8 Cabinet conclusion 66/20 (2) of 6/12/20.
9 Cabinet conclusion 79A of 27/12/20.

blame on one company of Auxiliaries, reflected on him, but Strickland soothed him.

Macready said he had "made it clear that he would break any officer who was mixed up in reprisals"—for the Army's sake, not Ireland's. With "no code to work under", the police had a more difficult job, he thought. Nevertheless, Lloyd George hoped that Tudor "will realise the importance of preventing such incidents as will add to the difficulties of the Government."

Meanwhile, the Auxiliaries were strutting about Dublin, wearing burnt corks on their braggart caps. Later, their Government agreed to pay substantial compensation for their wild night.

In spite of his exhibition of belligerence in the Commons, Lloyd George was still trying to make peace with the Irish. On the night that his Black and Tans were sacking Cork, his emissary, Archbishop Clune, was interviewing Arthur Griffith and Eoin MacNeill in Mountjoy. At a further meeting the next morning, December 13th, the Archbishop was accompanied by Dr Fogarty, Bishop of Killaloe, whom Auxiliaries had tried to murder a few days earlier. Griffith reported to Collins, in a note smuggled from the prison, "Lloyd George is nebulous in his proposals. He apparently wants peace but is afraid of his militarists." Dr Clune was sure that Lloyd George would insist upon a surrender of arms, apparently as a sop to the "military element"—but Griffith told him this would not be a truce but a surrender.

Answering Griffith's letter, Collins said there seemed no point in taking the matter any further. "We have clearly demonstrated our willingness to have peace on honourable terms. Lloyd George insists upon capitulation." On December 14th, the Archbishop brought Griffith a proposal he had just received from Lloyd George through Sir John Anderson. The Prime Minister offered a truce of one month. This had been urgently recommended by the Castle after the Archbishop's talk with Griffith and MacNeill. Arms were to be surrendered and, in the martial law area, uniforms. Sinn Fein was to order the cessation of all violence and "so-called" reprisals would stop automatically. Sinn Fein deputies could assemble except for a "specified list". "Ask your fellows to lie low for a month or so," was the tenor of the message, the Archbishop explained. He thought Lloyd George was anxious for peace and felt that the Cork burnings had strengthened his hand against die-hard opponents in England. The Dail Cabinet, however, were not prepared to accept any proposals unless the Dail could meet freely.

Collins was very suspicious of the English Prime Minister and was not prepared to let him "dissociate himself from his public actions". He believed Lloyd George was pretending a willingness to co-operate, using his die-hards as an excuse for his tough line in public and trying with under-the-counter offers of peace to tempt any Irish leaders who might be weakening to break away from the others.

On December 15th, Griffith sent a peace formula to Collins for his approval and that of the Cabinet. This did not insist explicitly upon the rights of the Dail to meet freely but put it that both sides should eschew violence "with the object of creating an atmosphere favourable to the meeting together of the representatives of the Irish people, with a view to bringing about a permanent peace". Brugha and Stack agreed with Collins that the proposal was reasonable. Throughout, Griffith and Collins favoured peace so long as it could be got on honourable terms and Griffith believed that Lloyd George, too, was in favour but had to smooth the feathers of the powerful military clique. Collins was much less certain of the British Minister's eagerness for peace.

Dr Clune had named Collins as "the only one with whom effective business could be done", but the Cabinet was reluctant to deal openly with the "organiser of murder". On the surrender of arms condition there was deadlock. Encouraged by reports that Sinn Fein was cracking and "rapidly being discredited in Ireland", the Cabinet thought of postponing any further approach until an election under the Government of Ireland Act could be held. Against this, Lloyd George warned, were "two great risks", the possibility of American intervention and the danger of friction between the military and police forces.[10]

He elaborated on these at the meeting with the Generals.[11] The burning of Cork and the murder of Canon Magner "were the kind of incidents that drove a country like the

[10] Cabinet conclusion 77/20 (6) of 24/12/20.
[11] Cabinet conclusion 79A of 29/12/20.

United States to do something beyond discretion." He wanted to know whether Tudor and Strickland could keep their men in control "if there was a chance of patching up some kind of truce", adding that he thought there was a lot of drunkenness. Tudor admitted this, but deprecated any suggestion of friction between soldiers and police.

When Macready said he would not object to a truce without surrender of arms, if it were politically expedient, the Prime Minister remarked wryly that Michael Collins had said he couldn't get his men to surrender arms even if he tried. The general opinion of the meeting was that any truce would be a sign of weakness and would allow a dispirited Sinn Fein to reorganise.

Would there be any intimidation if the election were held in February or March? Lloyd George asked. The answer was terse:

"A general boycott at the point of the pistol, on the word of Michael Collins."

"If Michael Collins can stop three million people using their vote, it doesn't say much for the success of the policy His Majesty's Government is now pursuing," declared the Prime Minister.

The Generals thought four months would be enough to "break the terror". Next day the Cabinet acceded to Macready's request to extend the martial law area to Kilkenny, Clare, Waterford and Wexford.[12]

On Christmas Eve, Collins and his friends had a gay dinner party at the Gresham Hotel and bluffed their way through a raid by Castle agents. The same day, de Valera reappeared in Ireland, the British Cabinet, who knew of his movements, having decided to allow him to land unhindered.[13]

They were not keen on political arrests at this time and Lloyd George carpeted General Boyd for arresting Arthur Griffith without authority. Boyd had thought it advisable to arrest several leaders after Bloody Sunday because angry regimental officers were in the mood to commit murder.[14]

It was a good defence, for the Cabinet were already alarmed by murder incidents. When the Auxiliary who murdered Canon

[12] Cabinet conclusion 81/20 (1) of 30/12/20.
[13] Cabinet conclusion 74/20 (1) of 20/12/20.
[14] Cabinet conclusion 79A of 29/12/20.
132

Magner was found unfit to plead, they felt this was "peculiarly unfortunate in view of the fact that the murderer of Mr Sheehy-Skeffington had also been declared insane", and ordered a further medical examination to put the matter beyond doubt.[15]

Despite his long absence in America, the whole Irish independence movement was solidly behind de Valera. The British had a tender regard for his safety. Although it was "difficult for forces of the Crown to apprehend other important Sinn Feiners who were resorting to him", and there was "always the possibility that he might be accidentally shot in raids if opposition were met", the Cabinet confirmed that he should remain "free from arrest unless and until the Irish Government were in a position to bring some new, definite criminal charge against him." The Crown Forces, however, could arrest accused persons at meetings "irrespective of whether Mr de Valera was present or not".[16]

EIGHT

One of de Valera's first decisions was to send Collins to America. In a characteristically long letter he set out what he expected of his Minister of Finance in his new appointment. It was the letter of a leader kicking a man upstairs and giving him details of some useful bits of plumbing he could carry out there. Collins declined to go and it is surprising that de Valera ever thought he would. Nor is it easy to see why, with success in the balance, he should have wanted to remove one of the most effective weights on Ireland's end of the scale.

Collins had become the powerhouse of the revolution. Never resting, he never allowed anyone else to rest either. He controlled the resources of the fugitive Government and had killed to keep them safe. He kept the books meticulously. His Intelligence ring and ruthlessly used killers were the lynch pin of the war effort. Directives from his own pen streamed across the country co-relating effort in almost every field. Slackness and inertia, the failure to put weapons to good use,

[15] Cabinet conclusion 81/20 (3) of 30/12/20.
[16] Cabinet conclusion 2/21 (2) of 14/1/21.

produced harsh rebukes. He arranged the import of arms by the "Irish Mail", as his smuggling organisation was called, and saw to their distribution. Nothing escaped his attention and nothing slipped his memory. Every minute of the day he was hunted, yet he cycled openly about the city, his well-dressed ordinariness his only disguise, went to the theatre and met his friends and contacts in pubs. Legends grew about his innumerable escapes. But he calculated risks and whenever it was practicable Squad men lurked with chameleon instincts in his vicinity. The aura of the romantic hero gathered about him and he was widely regarded as *the* Irish leader. The British thought him their most dangerous adversary, but newspaper publicity did not fool the British Government or their Castle functionaries into underrating other leaders and their lives were as hazardous as his. Cathal Brugha, working in his office with unremitting intensity, and Richard Mulcahy, tirelessly ordering the variegated fragments of the I.R.A. throughout the country, were men whose capture would have sent the top hats of Downing Street spinning in the air.

But if Collins had been the driving power behind the revolution, de Valera, quite rightly, believed that the inspiration should now derive from him. Unlike his contemporaries, unlike the people themselves, he had not been gradually inured to the horror of the struggle and he was appalled by the burden borne by the people. He agreed that Irish soldiers were entitled to use the stone walls of the countryside as the English used armoured vehicles, but he thought the sacking of a village, sometimes the murder and ill-treatment of innocent people, too high a price for a handful of dead Black and Tans.

He favoured an "easing-off" of military operations and a stepping-up of political activity. Lloyd George's peace feelers suggested that Britain was under strain and it seemed to him a propitious time to attempt to outplay the British Prime Minister before Ireland cracked first. He wanted a more conventional campaign, with fewer operations mounted on a larger scale, and an end to the gutter feuding of the Collins network and their counterparts in Dublin Castle, in which he saw little military significance. Collins's tactics did not belong to de Valera's ethical code. Like Sir Henry Wilson in England, he was ruthlessly committed to a cause but critical of the methods adopted by his side to further it.

It semed to many of his friends that he still had a 1916 mentality and did not appreciate that the I.R.A. strategy had developed from experience and the need to conserve limited resources, that guerrilla warfare could be carried on indefinitely.

"Our tactics were to hit hard then get away," says Dan Breen. "If we succeeded in smashing them in twenty minutes or half an hour, well and good, if not we cut our losses and got out because they could always bring up reinforcements. In guerrilla warfare it isn't a question of arms. Unlimited arms would have wrecked us. I was never in favour of too many men in the field at a time. That would have meant heavy losses and no guerrilla army can afford heavy losses."

De Valera was not convinced that the towns and villages could endure the strain of an interminable guerrilla war. And, as always, his mind ranged ahead. He did not want Ireland to be in the eyes of the world the nation that won its freedom with revolvers in dark streets rather than by courage and ideals of its soldiers.

Closer to home, in the six counties of the North a hostile majority had to be won over if Ireland was to remain an undivided land. The 300,000 Unionists in the South would be needed in the new Ireland. They were, for the most part, people who had clung to the land of their antecedents but who had pride, too, in the land of their birth and who had much to offer if they were willing to stay, abandoning old loyalties and looking to the future of their native Ireland.

It may have seemed desirable to de Valera to detach Collins from the Dublin imbroglio and at the same time to ease tensions which he had quickly discerned in the Cabinet. Cathal Brugha and Austin Stack were both simmering with resentment towards Collins who, supremely confident of his own ability, often dealt with matters rightly theirs. He was like an elegant "poacher" on the tennis court, brilliantly intercepting shots which should have been left to his partner. As Director of Intelligence Collins was subordinate to Brugha as Minister of Defence, but it was Collins who attracted the publicity and the glamour. He did not seek it but Brugha was sceptical. His bitter prejudice almost certainly did not stem from affronted vanity, for though a difficult man, Brugha was an obsessed patriot. What riled him was that any one man was exalted

135

above his fellows in the fight for freedom. Ill health and strain had embittered Stack, Minister for Home Affairs, who was greatly offended when Collins, half in jest, baited him. Once Collins told him that his Department was "just a bloody joke".

De Valera quickly abandoned the idea of sending Collins to America, nor did he press at once for any change of direction in the Irish war effort. At a meeting of the Dail on January 25th, 1921, attended by twenty-four Deputies, the remainder being in prison or on the run in the country, his ideas had no support. He went more slowly, carefully sounding the opinions not only of the Chief of Staff, Mulcahy, and other Headquarters men, but also of those like Ernie O'Malley who was appointed to command the 2nd Southern Division. Existing brigades were now to be regrouped in divisional areas. O'Malley, one of the most resolute fighting men, had held a roving commission until he had been captured. After three months in Kilmainham jail under an assumed identity which prolonged torture had not impressed him to forgo, he had escaped with Simon Donnelly and Frank Teeling, the man taken on Bloody Sunday. Teeling had been due for hanging.

The war now entered its final and most bitter phase. In the martial law area the British had after all instituted "official" reprisals. Houses of suspected Sinn Fein sympathisers were burned under supervision. There was no cessation of "unofficial" reprisals either, but in the vicious circle of retaliation each side was capable of matching the other.

In Dublin the British sought to get the better of Collins and his network by bringing in new forces of plain-clothes men and augmenting their crew of spies. Hostages, sometimes prisoners, sometimes well-known residents, were carried in lorries to deter I.R.A. attacks. Netting protected the vehicles from grenades. Streets were suddenly sealed with barbed wire and every man caught in the trap was rigorously searched. But many of their moves were forestalled by advance information from Collins's agents in the Castle and by forming, within the Dublin Brigade, an Active Service Unit on the lines of the Squad. Most of the Volunteers in Dublin and in the country were still unpaid part-time men but the fifty members of the Active Service Unit were full-time and drawing pay.

Consequent on the Cabinet's agreement, martial law had been extended to Clare in the west, Wexford in the east and to Waterford and Kilkenny, so that it applied in a belt right across the south of the country. In Cork several Volunteers were executed by firing squad, others were hanged in Dublin.

On March 7th the Mayor of Limerick and a former Mayor were shot dead in the presence of their wives. In the House of Commons Sir Hamar Greenwood, with cheerful mendacity, blamed the crime on the I.R.A.

The previous month, General Crozier's resignation from his command of the Auxiliaries had been widely publicised. The outspoken commander, who had once trained Carson's Ulster Volunteers, had taken issue with his superiors following the reinstatement of nineteen of twenty-six Auxiliary "cadets" dismissed by him for a roughneck looting expedition in Trim. He had other complaints about sham courts-martial and Government condonation of them but the Cabinet were more concerned than Crozier knew. They had decided not to set up another tribunal to inquire into the Cork burning, but Lloyd George pressed Tudor to dismiss seven men of the reprehensible K Company who were awaiting court-martial. He could not go into the House and admit they were still wearing the King's uniform. He wanted "to be able to say that it is very difficult to get evidence in Ireland, that the atmosphere is one in which no one is willing to give anybody away" —on either side—but that those suspected of indiscipline had been dealt with. Colonel Latimer commanding K Company he wanted suspended.[1]

The excitable Crozier may have been moved partly by personal grievance, but his revelations were a shock to the British people. Official reprisals were even more repugnant to them than the malefactions of the Black and Tans, which could be passed off—and usually were—as loss of control in the face of stiff provocation. Neither could British taxpayers have been pleased with the cost of containing the Irish aspirations to independence. The figure was £20 million per annum.[2]

On both sides of the Irish Sea, churchmen inveighed against the awfulness of the struggle. "What Devil's doctrine has

[1] Cabinet conclusion 7/21 (3) of 14/2/21.
[2] Cabinet Paper CP 2829 of 13/4/21.

gripped your minds?" asked the Bishop of Kilmore in a pastoral letter. Dr Cohalan, the outspoken Bishop of Cork, offered as little comfort to the I.R.A. as he did to the Black and Tans. In Dublin, Cardinal Logue exerted all his influence to contain the beastliness, and perhaps he succeeded a little. But there the struggle had taken on the aspects of gangster warfare. One especially revolting incident was the murder of two young men—not even Volunteers—by Captain King and some Auxiliaries at Drumcondra. They were found beaten and shot, with buckets over their heads. De Valera's efforts to woo the Hierarchy met with little success. He set out to show them that the I.R.A. was the properly constituted army of a properly constituted state, but they remained unconvinced that the methods by which it was sought to achieve independence were deserving of the approbation either of God or man. The less sophisticated approach of Sean McEoin, the famous "Blacksmith of Ballinalee", proved more effective.

"I went to my Bishop after he had condemned us in Longford from the pulpit. And I said, 'My Lord, why do you do this when these are the facts?' and I went on to explain the proper constitution of the Irish Republican Government.

"'How was I to know that?' he said. 'Nobody knows anything in this country. As a loyal son of the Church you should have told me this long ago.'

"'I told my parish priest, my Lord, I had discharged my duty.'

"Now he gave me his blessing. Later I asked my parish priest why he hadn't explained it all to the Bishop.

"'He's a conscientious sort of man,' answered Father Markey. 'What he doesn't know won't trouble him.'

"Later, the Bishop took an unrepentant Father Markey to task and asked the curate what he knew about it all.

"'Nothing, my Lord. It happened at the other end of the parish.'"

McEoin was then leader of the Longford column and very much a "wanted man". Old newsreels show him as a tough, dynamic young officer with large shoulders, a rakishly worn cap and a cheeky grin. No one was more dedicated to the Irish cause than he, or knew better exactly what he was fighting for. The conviction which so impressed his Bishop derived not only from the simple faith of a countryman but

138

from study and an intelligent appraisal of events in Ireland over a long period. Like Collins, he had a romantic quality but he had also a magnanimity which distinguished him from most of the other Irish leaders. He could think out an engagement as brilliantly as Tom Barry but he never allowed his hatred of the British regime to intrude on his essential humanity. He never forgot that English soldiers and Irish policemen, and even English auxiliary policemen, under their uniforms and braggart masks were human beings like himself.

"McEoin's behaviour brought a glimmer of decency into a dark and sordid era," says Emmet Dalton, who was at the time the I.R.A.'s Assistant Director of Training and was himself cast in the heroic mould. Dalton had fought through the First World War, reached the rank of major and won the Military Cross. He had become one of Collins's most valuable aides.

McEoin's exploits had long been recognised in the Midlands and by the Headquarters staff, but he became a national hero early in November 1920, when Granard was fired and looted and the glow of the flames could be seen from Ballinalee. Anticipating an attack on Ballinalee, McEoin deployed his men so that each of the four roads into the village was covered. Once the direction of the attack was known, he could bring them all in. Eleven lorries of Black and Tans entered the village by the road from Granard late on the night of November 3rd. Having first investigated McEoin's home and forge, the Black and Tans pulled up in a compact body in the north end of the village. McEoin attacked, and fighting went on through the night hours. At one point there was a cease fire and the Black and Tans asked McEoin for his surrender terms. When he answered that he would accept only unconditional surrender, they elected to fight on. At five o'clock next morning they withdrew in great disorder, leaving an indescribable scene. Loot from Granard, military equipment, revolvers and thousands of rounds of ammunition lay in a morass of blood.

Reprisals were inevitable but the British bided their time. Again there was fighting in Ballinalee and a number of houses in the district were burned down. Counter reprisals were authorised by the Dail Cabinet. McEoin planned retaliation by burning a number of Loyalists' houses in the area, including

139

the home of James Mackay Wilson, brother of Sir Henry, Chief of the Imperial General Staff. Then the young Irish commandant had a better idea. He called on James Mackay Wilson and advised him to write to his brother informing him that if his forces burned down another house in County Longford, the Wilson home, "Currygranne", would be burned down, and Wilson with it. Though James M. Wilson doubted that his brother would heed such warning, there were no more burnings.

McEoin also visited the Rev H. J. Johnston, Rector of Ballinalee, who was, he knew, associated with the Ulster Volunteers and acting as Chaplain to the British forces occupying Ballinalee. He explained to him that Father Markey, a local parish priest, had been sentenced to death by the British though his connection with the I.R.A. was adventitious and not of his choosing. He told Johnston to tell the British that if any harm befell Father Markey he would suffer the same fate. Both clerics survived and McEoin likes to remember that for many years they signed his nomination papers for Dail Eireann.

On January 9th, 1921, District Inspector McGrath led a party of Black and Tans to capture McEoin in a cottage near Ballinalee where he had his headquarters. To draw their fire from the cottage, where there were women and children, McEoin came out into the open to fight a lone battle. This move, characteristic both of his courage and his concern for the safety of others, had an unexpected outcome, perhaps because of its very audacity. Blazing his way through his attackers, McEoin escaped, but McGrath was fatally wounded.

On February 2nd, at Clonfin near Ballinalee, McEoin with eighteen men attacked a motor patrol of some twenty men, most of them Auxiliaries. The battle lasted an hour and then the Auxiliaries, who had fought courageously, surrendered. They had lost three men killed and twelve wounded. McEoin arranged for medical attention for the wounded men and freed the survivors, who undertook to remain neutral for the rest of that day and, when twelve lorries of reinforcements arrived, observed their undertaking. In the new battle, which lasted two hours, the British had many casualties; McEoin had one man slightly wounded.

When returning to Longford after a visit to Dublin in early

March, McEoin was captured at Mullingar. Desperately wounded when he tried to escape, he was beaten up then taken first to the R.I.C. barracks and later to the military barracks in Mullingar and, next day, removed to King George V Hospital (now St Bricin's) in Dublin. There, in the political wing where he was confined, he met General Sir Nevil Macready who, in his *Annals of an Active Life*, records that "he seemed a more cheery individual than most of his fellows". He added that McEoin and Michael Collins were the only Irishmen he met who had a sense of humour.

The first of his several meetings with Macready was on the morning that McEoin was to undergo an operation. To the nurse who tucked him in tightly McEoin vigorously protested that he needed room to wiggle his toes. She would not relent; there was to be an inspection, she explained. The daughter of an old friend of McEoin's, she soon was wheedled into telling him who the visitor was. McEoin was ready for him.

Arriving at the foot of McEoin's bed, Macready looked at the card.

"Well, McEoin, I suppose you're feeling sorry for yourself now."

"Who are you?" demanded McEoin.

"That doesn't matter."

"It does matter. I don't talk to people I don't know."

Macready gave his name and McEoin gave an elaborate whistle.

"You mean you're the big boss himself?"

"Well," answered Macready, "I could be so described."

"Dammit, you have a good job if you mind it."

Macready laughed, got himself a chair and sat down.

Again he pressed McEoin to admit that he was sorry for himself, hoping perhaps to point out the error of his ways.

"Of course, I'm sorry for myself. Very sorry. Time is so short and I'm realising all the things I could have done and should have done and didn't do. I'm damned sorry. I could have done ten times as much."

Macready gave up. He knew that there was little hope now for the young Irishman. When he had recovered from his wounds he would be court-martialled for the "murder" of District Inspector McGrath and, in due course, he would be hanged. It was unlikely, even if certain ambiguous negotia-

141

tions crystallised into a truce, that McEoin could be saved from the gallows.

Even in the British Cabinet the question of a truce was being discussed. At a meeting on March 24th[3] the Cabinet decided that after the Easter adjournment they would consider whether to announce a truce to be effective during the elections, which were to implement the Government of Ireland Act—become law in the previous December—or whether to offer a truce for negotiations prior to the elections.

The Cabinet was under pressure and very much on the defensive. On March 21st the Lord Chancellor, the Earl of Birkenhead, had received a distinguished deputation headed by the Archbishop of Canterbury.[4] Birkenhead explained that the campaign in Ireland was "in the hands of very desperate men who know their minds quite plainly". Their object, which he described as "notorious", was "the establishment of an Irish Republic in complete independence of the British Empire." To achieve their object they used the method of murder but claimed in justification that they were engaged in a war. But, he said, they were "hardly sticking to the rules." On the other hand, if any of His Majesty's Forces took the law into his own hands there was a yell. "What's more, a fairly successful yell," he added.

The Auxiliaries were former officers "of unblemished record" recruited at a time when the Sinn Fein courts were "openly and most audaciously usurping the functions alike of civil and criminal jurisdiction", and when "vast areas of the country were not protected by the police or anyone else." The result was that the morale of the R.I.C. was up, the Sinn Fein courts had been put down and police protection was back.

There had been outrages under extreme provocation "but no force in the world—and I throw in the Metropolitan Police—would have gone through such cruel trials and risks without complaint."

The Archbishop wanted to know more about the murderers, whether they were crooks or fanatics, indigenous or imported.

"They are certainly indigenous; rumours of imported bravos have never been confirmed," said the Lord Chancellor. Some were in it for money, but the great majority "by fanatical and

[3] Cabinet conclusion 15/21 (1) of 24/3/21. [4] Cabinet Paper CP 2807.

mistaken patriotism and by the halo of romance which has always rested on the head of the young Irish rebel."

A truce was "perfectly possible", he said, and he thought Dail Eireann the most likely possibility for negotiation. But the rebels would have to surrender their arms. It was their refusal to do so which had aborted the negotiations in the previous December.

Birkenhead's view of the surrender of arms was not shared by Edwin Montagu, Secretary of State for India, who saw a truce as a "stand to arms".[5] There should be no amnesty nor demand for the surrender of arms. Such demands appertained to peace not truce. He insisted that some offer should be made so that the Government of Ireland Act could be discussed "with the object of making it more acceptable to the Irish."

Another Cabinet colleague, Dr Addison, thought that "no offer of a truce would be worth making unless it were frank and generous in its terms and unaccompanied by harassing or ambiguous restrictions".[6] He was convinced that the people of Ireland, though they hated murder and atrocity, were becoming increasingly hostile and that a national antagonism on the part of the whole Irish people was building up which was more significant than the outrages. The Government "had proved its sincerity in seeking to give effect to the Government of Ireland Act and in its firmness in repressing crime", but a truce would certainly strengthen the allegiance of the Government's supporters "who entertain serious misgivings as to the wisdom of the methods that we are pursuing in Ireland." He advocated a truce first, then negotiation with Sinn Fein, and suggested that an offer of fiscal autonomy might be sufficient inducement for Sinn Fein to agree to work the Act.

On April 21st, Lord Derby went unofficially to see de Valera. He reported straight to Lloyd George that his visit had been unavailing. Earlier in the month, Lloyd George had entertained ideas of himself meeting Michael Collins who, he thought, was the effective head in Ireland. But, he said, it was "a strong order to see a man who has given orders to shoot down innocent, unoffending policemen".[7] He thought it would take another twelve months to quell the trouble in

[5] Cabinet Paper CP 2840 of 14/4/21.
[6] Cabinet Paper CP 2829 of 13/4/21.
[7] *Intimate Diary of the Peace Conference and After*: Lord Riddell.

Ireland but he doubted if the British people would allow it to go on for so long. The Irish problem, in Lloyd George's eyes, was analogous to the American Civil War and he believed that history would vindicate his policy just as it had proved Abraham Lincoln right.

In Dublin Castle, too, the impression existed that de Valera was now second to Collins. In a report dated April 14th[8] it was said that Collins had modified his attitude on the question of meeting Sir James Craig, who had taken over the driving-seat in Belfast from Carson, and was willing to talk about the interests of Ireland with any representative Irishman. When Craig came to Dublin a fortnight after Lord Derby's visit, it was to meet de Valera. He was taken by car to a secret rendezvous in Clontarf. Emmet Dalton, who sat beside him, advised Craig to pass him off as his secretary if they were stopped. If there were trouble Craig would be "first to go". Dalton admired his courage. Collins was taking no chances but de Valera was not "wanted" by the British. They would have to negotiate with someone and, unlike Collins, de Valera had no blood on his hands. The meeting achieved little and there was doubt afterwards as to who had taken the initiative in arranging it. It seems to have been one of Cope's ploys. Cope was extremely anxious for peace in Ireland and was often thought in British Government circles to be pushing the Irish viewpoint just a little too hard.

In official British eyes Ireland now comprised the six counties of Northern Ireland, and the twenty-six counties of Southern Ireland. Elections for the two new Parliaments and for the representatives of each country at Westminster were scheduled for May. The North had agreed to work the Act, for although it imposed upon them an unwanted Home Rule it did seem to secure them from the danger of Dublin's dominion. There was no possibility of co-operation from the South who saw the Act only as the implementation of Britain's partition plan, as a giving way to the threat of violence which Carson had uttered before the First World War, and which subtly he had maintained ever since with the help of Sir James Craig.

Divide and Rule, the Irish saw with increasing bitterness was being applied once more, and in the usual cavalier way.

8 Cabinet Paper CP 2838.

And yet, clumsy and tactless though they were, the British Government genuinely believed they were taking a practical step towards peace, even though in the end they had made no offer of an election truce. They knew the Republican Irish did not want their Southern Parliament, but somehow the struggle would be brought to an end and the Irish would see that their demand of a Republic was impossible, that they were being given a measure of independence and that, hey presto, the machinery for it already existed. As for dividing Ireland, that was up to the Irish. The provision for a Council of Ireland pointed the way to a welding of the break, and the British Government underlined their meaning, not only by appointing a Lord Lieutenant for the whole of the country, but by their choice as the first holder of the office of Lord FitzAlan, a Roman Catholic.

It was a well-meaning but naïve move, the Irish reaction to which was capsuled in a story current at the time that when Cardinal Logue was asked whether the appointment would please the Hierarchy he had answered they would be as gratified as they would be by the appointment of a Catholic hangman. Not so easily was the persecution of Catholics in the North to be glossed over. Now it seemed that they were to be cut off altogether, with the ricketty bridge of the Council of Ireland as the only concession to unity. And no one was willing to put a foot on that.

Measures were taken by the Dail to reinforce the Belfast Boycott which had been introduced in August 1920 as a protest against the indignities suffered by Catholic workmen, especially in the Belfast shipyards. The Protestant businessmen of Belfast owed much of their affluence to the 26-county market, and it was intended they should see that religious discrimination was not good for secular profit.

The boycott had been partially effective, but it also hit the shopkeepers of the South and they had continued to order goods from Belfast. But the Dail was determined that there should be no ready market for goods made across the unwanted and unrecognised border. An I.R.A. "Boycott Patrol", formed early in 1921, soon had results. Trains were raided and contraband freight confiscated; Belfast goods found in Dublin shops were destroyed. That the measures were successful was admitted by the Castle Government in reports to London.

145

The I.R.A. had taken the fight to England too. Signal boxes were blown up, telephone wires cut and buildings burned. Brugha, who initiated these activities, also had it in mind to assassinate British Cabinet Ministers. The Cabinet were already preoccupied with industrial strife in the country. Mines had been flooded and the miners were refusing to allow them to be pumped out. A Special Defence Force had been raised, the men enlisting for ninety days, to protect volunteers whose task was to get the water out of the mines, and Ministers feared that not only miners, but Sinn Feiners too, were joining the force in order to decamp with arms.[9]

The fight went on, the background of peace moves as insubstantial and unremarked as the cigarette haze hovering above a championship ringside. Early in April, Roscarbery Barracks were stormed and taken by Volunteers of Cork No. 3 Brigade. Only a fortnight before, the same brigade under Tom Barry, had engaged a much larger British force at Crossbarry and broken it with heavy casualties. The British admitted thirty-nine dead of this force, which ironically was part of an encircling movement designed to trap Barry and his elusive column.

But the Volunteers also were losing valuable men. Between April 28th and May 16th no less than six were executed in Cork. In several instances the I.R.A. men tried to save their friends by threatening to shoot hostages, and in some areas English officers captured were executed.

District Inspector Potter was captured in Tipperary and, although he was generally well-liked, the I.R.A. tried to bargain his life for that of Thomas Traynor who was under sentence of death in Mountjoy. But Traynor was hanged on April 25th and Potter died two days later. In a last letter to his wife Potter wrote charitably of his executioners but the British blew up ten farmhouses in the area as a reprisal. In 1966, Dan Breen was visited by Commander Gilbert Potter, son of the man he had helped to kill. Breen told me that Commander Potter and Traynor's son had served together in the Second World War, a nice story but an old man's fancy, it appears.

Three officers captured by Ernie O'Malley in the Clonmel area were shot against a wall outside a church. They had declined O'Malley's offer to fetch them a clergyman of their

[9] Cabinet conclusion 19/21 (5) of 12/4/21.

146

own religion but were grateful that he allowed them to write home, sealing their own letters. As they marched through the early morning fields, the stoic condemned and the jittery firing squad, one of the prisoners remarked nostalgically, "Stiff banks those for hunting."

"There's not much hunting now," said O'Malley.[10]

Mrs Lindsay, a brave old lady from Coachford, Co. Cork, died before a firing squad when the British went ahead with the execution of five Volunteers captured as a result of information she had given.

On May 28th, Major Compton-Smith died gallantly when survivors from a group of Volunteers who surrendered after an hour's hard fighting with Black and Tans at Clonmult were shot in Cork jail. In both cases Dublin Headquarters heard of the proposed executions too late to intervene. In the case of Major Compton-Smith a dispatch was sent to Collins asking whether the officer, who was greatly respected by the I.R.A., might be released.

Postponement of the Irish election had been considered and rejected by the Cabinet. It was also decided that, in spite of the memoranda of Montagu and Addison, no initiative to promote a truce in Ireland should be taken until advice from police and military leaders had been sought.[11] By May 12th, it was considered that "the opportunity to declare a cessation of military activity for the period of the Elections had passed" and that the Irish policy should be pursued.[12] In the meantime, American proposals for American relief in Ireland were "emphatically rejected on the ground that there is not the smallest need for relief in Ireland".[13] The proposals were evidence of the way the wind of American sympathy was blowing but British public opinion too was disconcerting. Lloyd George advocated a propaganda campaign which would emphasise the powers conferred by the Government of Ireland Act and would show that not only was Sinn Fein stubbornly refusing to accept these powers but they were murdering civilians simply because they were Protestants or ex-servicemen.

Thinking people in England had been well enough informed

10 *On Another Man's Wound* by Ernie O'Malley.
11 Cabinet conclusion 27/21 (2) of 21/4/21.
12 Cabinet conclusion 39/21 (2) of 12/5/21.
13 Cabinet conclusion 36/21 (4) of 10/5/21.

147

by their own responsible journalists to see this as no more than opportunist hyperbole. The case of Sean McEoin, for one, would give the lie to it. McEoin was to be tried for murder as soon as he was well enough and there was little doubt of his fate. He had fought single handed eleven men and killed one. That was his crime and even the victim's mother could not bring herself to see it as murder.

McEoin's capture grieved Michael Collins who conceived plan after plan to rescue him. A scheme to recover him from the hospital was frustrated by McEoin's transfer to the hospital block in Mountjoy Prison. A file and soap were smuggled to him and McEoin succeeded in cutting through the bars and refixing them with soap. But the work pushed his temperature up dangerously, and as the British wanted to make sure he died on the gallows and not comfortably in bed, they moved him to a less dank cell upstairs.

On May 14th, an ingenious plan to seize him in Mountjoy prison was put into execution. In a stolen armoured car Emmet Dalton, posing as a British officer in the uniform he once had worn, with Joe Leonard in his second uniform, and Pat McCrea, Tom Keogh, Bill Stapleton and Paddy McCaffrey disguised as Tommies, drove into the yard of the prison. Dalton, authoritatively waving a forged document requiring the delivery of McEoin to him, had no trouble in getting past the guard. Dalton and Leonard went to the Governor's office where they expected to find McEoin who, on one pretext or another, had managed three mornings running to arrange an interview with the Governor. There was no McEoin this morning, for an unlooked-for inspection of the prison had thwarted him. With the Governor were the deputy Governor and the prison medical officer, Dr Hackett. Dalton presented his document but the Governor decided to confirm the order with Dublin Castle. Dalton and Leonard moved quickly, held up the three officers and were tying them up when there was trouble at the gate, a shot from the sentry on the roof and an answering shot from Keogh which tumbled the sentry from his perch. There was nothing left now but to run for it and the invaders got clean away. Their exploit earned the admiration even of the British but McEoin remained in Mountjoy and, a month later, was court martialled and sentenced to be hanged. Evidence of his chivalrous conduct given by three of the

148

Auxiliaries who had survived the Clonfin ambush and a plea for mercy from the relatives of McGrath did not weigh with his judges. McEoin heard the sentence with the dignity of a countryman.

"I said from the dock that I was an officer of the Irish Army carrying out my duties in accordance with the usages of war, that I was acting under an elected Government, that if they still would not treat me as a prisoner of war, then at least they could send my body home."

While he awaited his trial, Sean McEoin was elected to the Dail.

Dail Eireann had decided to use the British election machinery as a cheap and convenient way of electing the Second Dail, which would be a larger assembly since the Government of Ireland Act provided for a lower house in Southern Ireland of 128 members, as well as representation by 33 members in Westminster. The British Government had no illusions. They knew that Sinn Fein, though many of their candidates were in prison or on the run, would win overwhelmingly and that the elected members would neither take their seats in the Southern Parliament nor send representatives to Westminster. No doubt Westminster was not altogether sorry to think that the recalcitrant Irish would stay at home. In a way, it is strange that after the 1918 election Sinn Fein's 73 elected members of Parliament preferred to constitute themselves a clandestine Parliament and fight a bloody war when they could have brought mayhem to the House of Commons. De Valera, Griffith, Collins, Brugha, Countess Markievicz and their merry band might well have reduced the British legislature to impotence. But to have taken their seats would have been to concede the right of the British Government to govern Ireland, and so the Irish chose to fight for their freedom the hard way. Nor did they intend now to participate in a parliament created by an Act passed by the British Parliament.

At the election, which took place on May 24th, 1921, Sinn Fein candidates were returned unopposed in every constituency save the Unionist stronghold of Trinity College which elected four members. That there was the traditional intimidation of Irish elections is undeniable. Opinion was not quite so unanimous that there was no desire to nominate any other candidates, but opposition to Sinn Fein at this time

149

would have been foolhardy. This was a pity, because the artificial unanimity obscured the truth, which was that British policy had so alienated the great mass of the Irish people, even many who earlier would have opposed Sinn Fein, and the ardour of the young men of the I.R.A. had won such admiration, that only a sorry minority of opponents could possibly have been elected. If the I.R.A. were sometimes inexcusably pitiless, as when they shot up and killed four members of a mixed tennis party in Galway, their ruthlessness detracted little from their cause. When Black and Tans thought nothing of killing men by dragging them behind lorries it was easy to condone retaliation. Black does not notice on black. Heroic episodes like the attempted rescue of McEoin, on the other hand, stood out like white splashes, and it was little wonder that so many young I.R.A. officers were elected to the Dail.

Collins, Griffith and de Valera also won seats in the election for the Northern Parliament which was held, five days earlier, on May 19th. Altogether, Sinn Fein won six of the 52 seats. Again, the new border was ignored. So far as Sinn Fein was concerned, the elections in both North and South were for Dail Eireann. Neither they nor the six Nationalists led by Devlin took their seats at the time, though the Nationalists did so later. Craig was comfortably placed with 40 Unionists in Belfast.

The day set for the opening of the Southern Parliament was June 28th. If less than half the elected members attended, this Parliament would be dissolved in accordance with the Government of Ireland Act, and it was the British Cabinet's intention in that even to impose Crown Colony Government, and to extend the martial law area from July 12th. Further conversations between Craig and de Valera were thought likely and the Cabinet agreed that Lloyd George should first brief Craig "to avoid the risk of placing the British Government in the invidious position of possibly having to reject joint proposals made by the leaders of the two parts of Ireland".[14]

On May 25th, the day following the election, the British Cabinet decided on the points which Craig was to keep in mind.[15] The Irish were to have no separate armed services; Irish harbours and creeks were to remain in British control;

[14] Cabinet conclusion 41/21 (3) 24/5/21.
[15] Cabinet conclusion 42/21 (2) of 25/5/21.

Ireland was to contribute towards defence and towards the cost of the First World War—on the grounds that Irish opinion had favoured the war; and there was to be no Customs duty on U.K. goods. On the last point Winston Churchill, Edwin Montagu and H. A. L. Fisher recorded dissent.

The same day, the I.R.A. took a fierce swipe at British administration when they burned the Custom House, headquarters of the British Civil Service in Ireland and one of Dublin's finest buildings. De Valera rated the destruction of the British records, and the chaos which inevitably would follow, of more importance than the preservation of this historic landmark. Led by Tom Ennis under the overall command of Oscar Traynor the Volunteers succeeded in their purpose. But five lost their lives and eighty were taken prisoner, losses that the I.R.A. could ill afford.

The British Cabinet, also, were worried about manpower. Until the industrial unrest in England was ended, military reinforcements, which would be necessary in the event of martial law being extended to all twenty-six counties, could not be spared. The Cabinet realised that an effort must be made to secure peace in Ireland before the almost inevitable dissolution of the Southern Parliament compelled them to take drastic measures. Macready was notified "that reprisals, which already have practically ceased outside the Martial Law area, must also cease within that area, and that aggressive action must in every case be based on strictly military grounds defined by military orders."

On June 22nd, King Geoge V opened the Parliament of Northern Ireland and gave the British Government the opportunity they needed. From the beginning the King had been at odds with the Government's handling of the Irish problem. He hated reprisals and wanted to know where the policy was going to lead Ireland—and England too. Innocent people were being punished no less severely than guilty, he contended, and gave it as his opinion that the Black and Tans should be disbanded and that the police should come under military command.

Afraid that, by agreeing to open the Northern Parliament, he might affront his unhappy subjects in the South, he gladly accepted the suggestion of Field-Marshal Smuts that he should

151

offer a message of peace to the whole country. He asked Smuts and Lord Stamfordham, his secretary, to draft a speech which then was submitted to the Cabinet, Sir Edward Grigg undertook the final draft.

Ignoring the fears of his courtiers, King George V and his imperturbable Queen braved the streets of Belfast in an open carriage. Lloyd George had intended to be present also but was ill. Lord Londonderry was chosen by the King as Minister in attendance and the Chief Secretary for Ireland represented the British Cabinet.

The King spoke for the British people, as well as for himself, when he appealed to all Irishmen "to pause, to stretch out the hand of forbearance and conciliation, to forgive and forget, and to join in making for the land they love a new era of peace, contentment and goodwill." The King's concern for his people was deeply felt but, as the traditionalist Monarch of an imperialist power, he would have held as stubbornly as his Ministers the view that his subjects were in rebellion. He deplored the methods of his Government, acknowledged the grievances of Ireland, but never could have imagined it as other than British. So his address struck no real responsive chord in the South where it was seen as yet another peace ploy of Lloyd George's. The British Prime Minister was persistent and devious but the Irish remained suspicious. Nevertheless, they sensed that the British Cabinet were anxious to conclude the struggle and they determined to show no weakness.

De Valera was arrested on June 23rd and, somewhat to his chagrin, at once released. The following day Lloyd George reminded his Cabinet of the King's appeal for reconciliation and suggested implementing it with an invitation to Craig and de Valera to try to reach agreement with His Majesty's representatives.[16] There was some evidence, he said, that de Valera would accept something less than a Republic, that he might waive the right to have Irish armed forces, accept free trade and forgo the right to impose tariffs hostile to Great Britain. The Cabinet were in favour of an attempt for peace but Churchill still thought Lloyd George too exacting. He was prepared to go on supporting a policy of coercion

[16] Cabinet conclusion 53/21 of 24/6/21.

"so long as the vital strategic interests of this country are threatened", but he did not consider continued coercion justifiable "if peace could be secured by the grant of fiscal autonomy." Lloyd George read the draft of the letter he proposed to send to de Valera and to publish. The Cabinet toned it down, cutting in particular "all reference to the cessation of hostilities as a condition precedent to conversations."

Making a final appeal "in the spirit of the King's words", Lloyd George invited de Valera, and any colleagues he should choose, to meet him and Sir James Craig in London. He expressed "a fervent desire to end the ruinous conflict which has for centuries divided Ireland, and embittered the relations of the peoples of these two islands . . ."

Collins evidently had little faith in the offer, for on June 27th he sent de Valera a carefully thought out plan to nullify British administration in Ireland. Citing parallels in the American War of Independence, he advocated legislation by the Dail to make it illegal for anybody to "administer or dispense English Law in this country", or "to collect taxes in the name of the Foreign Government." He wanted to sever every English connection except perhaps the Post Office and the Board of Education.

Uncompromising, too, was de Valera's immediate answer to Lloyd George's invitation:

"We most earnestly desire to help in bringing about a lasting peace between the peoples of these two islands, but see no avenue by which it can be reached if you deny Ireland's essential unity, and set aside the principle of national self-determination." After meeting the Earl of Middleton and other Unionist leaders de Valera accepted Lloyd George's invitation. Craig had already accepted and for that reason declined to take part in a preliminary discussion with the President of the Dail. Perhaps, too, he did not like de Valera's description of him as a "representative of the political minority in this country".

On June 30th, Arthur Griffith, Professor MacNeill, E. J. Duggan and Michael Staines were released from prison. The following day Robert Barton was freed from jail in England. The British Cabinet had already suspended executions.

In Dublin the change of tempo was quickly remarked and

153

delighted crowds cheered Macready to his meeting with the Irish leaders at the Mansion House on July 8th. It was agreed that a truce should come into force at noon on Monday, July 11th. And until that moment the I.R.A., dubious still about halting their effort, persisted in the fight. In a Cork town, where the local I.R.A. had made a remarkably small contribution to the war an old R.I.C. sergeant was shot dead as he dug his garden. Someone was unwilling to let the war die without a notch on his gun. The deed won little applause. It was a dark exclamation mark at the end of a disagreeable passage of history.

As a postscript, one could perhaps add a Cabinet minute which not only conveys the scale of the struggle but highlights the ambivalence and the naïveté of the British Government of the day. On March 24th, 1921, they authorised Macready to use aeroplanes against Sinn Fein. The Cabinet Secretary recorded that "considerable stress was laid on the great risk of death and injury to innocent people owing to the extreme difficulty of distinguishing innocent from guilty from an aeroplane, summoned possibly from a distance by telephone and necessarily proceeding at a high speed and operating at a considerable height."[17]

It is strange to think that Winston Churchill was to lead Great Britain into the age of the atomic bomb.

NINE

Mr de Valera, with Griffith, Barton, Stack, Childers and Count Plunkett to support him and to represent the various sections of Irish opinion, went to London on July 14th to try to reach agreement with Lloyd George. But the little Welshman, who in the beginning tried in a good-humoured but rather patronising way to impress de Valera with the might of the Empire as represented by the sprawling red blotches on a wall map of the world, ended by being thoroughly exasperated. He was impatient of the Irish President's

[17] Cabinet conclusion 15/21 (2) of 24/3/21.

labyrinthine logic and of his obsession with the malignity of Cromwell, to which he constantly reverted.

In spite of this Lloyd George was able to tell his Cabinet that the Irish leader had "an agreeable personality".[1] De Valera had asked about "such matters as the entry of South Ireland into the Empire, swearing allegiance, the form of the oath, the name of the new state and so forth." He wanted a Republic but Lloyd George had told him it was impossible. Both Craig and de Valera were anxious for a settlement but afraid of their respective supporters, the Prime Minister believed. Ulster was the real difficulty; under no circumstances would Northern Ireland agree to a single Parliament which would enable the South "to pack the fiscal administration with Sinn Feiners and Roman Catholics."

Lloyd George had pointed out to de Valera that if he insisted on a single Parliament the South might well find itself "in the same position to the North as Great Britain now occupied towards Southern Ireland." To Lloyd George's warning that this might result in civil war and lead to trouble throughout the Empire, de Valera answered that "Southern Ireland would never allow itself to be implicated in civil war" —a statement which, a year later, his opponents would have delighted to fling at him.

Declaring that the proposals Lloyd George put to him conceded something but also took much away, de Valera concluded that he must consult his Cabinet. The proposals were now drawn up formally by Lloyd George, Austen Chamberlain and Balfour and submitted to the Cabinet. Some thought the word "pact" should be used rather than "treaty", which was "a precedent fraught with danger, involving recognition of an existing Irish Republic and which might prove impossible to resist in the case of India." The fear that concessions to Ireland would add momentum to the independence movement in India was always sharp in the hearts of Cabinet Ministers and was responsible in a large measure for the stubborn and ruthless policy in Ireland.

However, Lloyd George insisted that the word "treaty" was essential to Sinn Fein and Hewart, the new Attorney-General pronounced that there was no vital difference between "treaty" and "pact".

[1] Cabinet conclusion 60/21 (1) of 20/7/21.

An advance on the ill-fated Home Rule Bill of 1912, the Cabinet's proposals offered dominion status with certain limitations. Ireland was to make her harbours available to the Royal Navy and contribute to imperial defence. Britain was to have the right of recruitment for her armed forces. The Irish were to shoulder a share of the National Debt and there were to be no protective tariffs. Lloyd George, faced with the task of placating Northern Ireland as well as Southern, had made no mention of including the tug-of-war counties and de Valera saw that, by implication at least, partition was assumed.

There is no doubt that the Prime Minister was eager to settle the Irish problem. De Valera and Craig believed he was trying to play off one against the other, but nothing would have suited him better than that they should get together. His own political future would then have been much more secure. As it was, his Liberal colleagues in the Cabinet were not unsympathetic to the Irish cause but the Conservative-Unionist element smelled concession in the air and he knew that they would not tolerate his yielding too far.

He had warned de Valera that if the Truce had to be terminated "the struggle would bear an entirely different character".[2] The reduction of overseas commitments had produced a big concentration of troops in England. "As it is immaterial whether they are quartered in Great Britain or Ireland they will be sent to the latter country, where a great military concentration will take place with a view to the suppression of the rebellion and the restoration of order."

This threat did not impress de Valera, who probably knew more about the real state of Britain's forces than Lloyd George supposed. In fact, the Prime Minister was asked to avoid a sudden rupture of the Truce if negotiations seemed to be breaking down. Time would be needed to recall the many garrisons troops and police who were on leave in Ireland.

The Dail Cabinet agreed with de Valera that the proposals he had brought back were not nearly good enough. Cathal Brugha and Austin Stack were all for having no further truck with England, but for the majority this was too drastic and de Valera's reply, dated August 10th, 1921, was delivered to the Lord Privy Seal the following day.

[2] Cabinet conclusion 60/21 (1) of 20/7/21.

The bearers, Robert Barton, Joseph McGrath and Art O'Brien, the Dail representative in London, raised the question of publication. Chamberlain said that he would transmit the contents of the note to Lloyd George in Paris immediately and agreed to simultaneous publication in London and Dublin.[3]

It was a long letter in which Irish aspirations and convictions were made clear with a dogged insistence which was as much a plea to reason and to generosity as it was a declaration of rights and a reiteration of grievance.

"The Irish people's belief is that the national destiny can best be realised in political detachment, free from imperialistic entanglements which they feel will involve enterprises out of harmony with the national character, prove destructive of their ideals and be fruitful only of ruinous wars, crushing burdens, social discontent and general unrest and happiness. Like the small states of Europe they are prepared to hazard their independence on the basis of moral right, confident that as they would threaten no nation or people they would in turn be free from aggression themselves."

The British Dominions enjoyed freedom because of "the immense distances which separate them from Britain and have made interference by her impracticable", he maintained. He was patently convinced that Britain would never keep her meddling hands off Ireland and he put it tactfully that "true friendship with England, which military coercion has frustrated for centuries, can be obtained most readily now through amicable but absolute separation."

He had an alternative to Dominion status:

"A certain treaty of free association with the British Commonwealth group, as with a partial league of nations, we would have been ready to recommend, and as a Government to negotiate and take responsibility for, had we an assurance that the entry of the nation as a whole into such association would secure for it the allegiance of the present dissenting minority, to meet whose sentiment alone this step could be contemplated."

De Valera's idea of "external association", as it came to be called, was to be the plinth on which he set his flag for a long time to come. To Lloyd George it meant simply Ireland's

[3] Cabinet Paper CP 3212 of 11/8/21.

secession from her allegiance to the King and in his reply a few days later he said flatly that it was a point "upon which no British Government can compromise".

To the Irish leaders any form of association with the British Empire was a concession to the Unionists, particularly in the North but also in the South, and it was offered solely to avert partition.

"We cannot admit the right of the British Government to mutilate our country, either in its own interest or at the call of any section of our own population," wrote de Valera, firmly and correctly putting the Unionist majority in the six counties in their place. Unfortunately, the rights of majorities were not always to weigh quite so heavily in his mind.

To enable their proposals to be put to the Dail, the British Cabinet agreed on August 8th, two days before de Valera's answer, that it was proper to grant an amnesty to thirty-seven members of the Dail who were held in prison.

Macready grumbled in his weekly report[4] that, earlier, Griffith and others had been released without reference to him, and he understood that the Castle authorities had known for a week that the release of the Dail members was contemplated. "It might have been useful had I been also informed," he added dryly.

"For some inscrutable reason," writes Macready[5], "McKeown alone was debarred from this amnesty by the authorities in London."

Collins insisted that if Sean McEoin (McKeown is the old form of his name) were not released there should be no meeting of the Dail and de Valera agreed. The Cabinet were reluctant. Lloyd George, absent in Paris, communicated through his Private Secretary his opinion that "no risk should be taken of jeopardising settlement over this case".[6] Austen Chamberlain, the Lord Privy Seal, telegraphed the Prime Minister that he had "got together" Worthington-Evans (Secretary for War), Greenwood (Chief Secretary for Ireland) and the Attorney-General, Sir Gordon Hewart, to consider McKeown's case. They were reluctant to reverse the Cabinet's original decision but the Attorney-General had observed

4 Cabinet Paper CP 3219 of 9/8/21.
5 *Annals of an Active Life* by Sir Nevil Macready.
6 Cabinet Paper CP 3204 (Exchange of telegrams 7-8/8/21).

that they had "swallowed camel of negotiations with instigators and procurers and must not wreck settlement by straining at gnat of one more release." Worthington-Evans agreed but wanted to be satisfied that Lloyd George would not "be blackmailed into further surrender, especially as regards internees." With a fine disregard for the tax-payer's money, Chamberlain went on: "At this point when I was about to express my view a further message sent in following telegram was received from Macready and this is decisive for all of us."

In the telegram referred to, Macready gave his personal opinion that "if Government can recede with dignity from position taken up and release McKeown it would be well to do so." He thought, anyway, that McEoin's crime did not compare with those of Collins, de Valera and Brugha. Finally, he made what was probably the decisive political point: "If hostilities do recommence we must be in a position in which the onus must be entirely on Sinn Fein." He was thinking, perhaps, of another Soloheadbeg.

The Second Dail was convened in the Mansion House on August 16th, able for the first time to meet in the open. The old Ministry gave an account of its administration as a clandestine Government, then the proposals made by Lloyd George to de Valera and rejected by the Cabinet on August 10th were put before the assembly, which unanimously confirmed their rejection. On August 26th the Ministry resigned. Eamon de Valera was elected President. In the First Dail he had held the slightly more ambiguous title of Prime Minister, or *Priomh-Aire*. It fell to the lot of Sean McEoin to propose him for the Presidency of the Republic of Ireland. Until this date, within the Irish Republican Brotherhood at least, and to many outside it, the President of the Supreme Council was still, as he had been in Pearse's time, President of the Republic. Now the Brotherhood was relinquishing to the Dail, as it had earlier ceded all other political offices, that of Head of State. McEoin nominated de Valera on the instructions of the man he was in effect succeeding, the President of the Supreme Council of the I.R.B., Michael Collins.

A protracted exchange of letters between Lloyd George and de Valera followed, with the Irish leader trying to manoeuvre Lloyd George into accepting the Republic of which he was now formally President and the wily Welshman refusing to be trapped.

"If a small nation's right to independence is forfeit when a more powerful neighbour courts its territory for the military or other advantages it is supposed to confer, there is an end to liberty," wrote de Valera on August 24th.

Lloyd George claimed in return that his proposals had been made after very careful consideration and "not in any haggling spirit." He and his colleagues had gone "to the very limit of our powers in endeavouring to reconcile British and Irish interests." It was to prove that Lloyd George and his colleagues had gone nowhere near the very limit of their powers, but there is no reason to doubt Lloyd George's sincerity when he wrote that within her shores Ireland would be free "in every aspect of national activity, national expression and national development." He quoted Grattan, Daniel O'Connell and Thomas Davis to prove that the great Irish patriots of the past had "explicitly disowned" the idea of secession from allegiance to the King. This letter Lloyd George gave to Robert Barton and Art O'Brien on August 26th. They asked him what notice would be given if the British Government decided to terminate the Truce. "One week by proclamation," was the answer. However, only a flagrant violation of the Truce would result in its termination; small breaches could be dealt with by liaison.

Multitudinous problems hinged on the issues of peace or a continuation of the struggle. One of these was brought to the notice of the British Government on August 10th by Sir Henry Robinson, Vice President of the Local Government Board in Ireland.[7] Under the Criminal Injuries Ireland Act of 1920, "a person who has obtained a decree against a County Council for compensation for criminal injuries is entitled to claim from the High Court an order attaching the rates payable by any particular ratepayer to the Council in satisfaction of the amount recovered by his decree."

These were known as Garnshee Orders and they had been described by Cosgrave, the Dail's Minister for Local Government, as "an enemy device appealing to selfish individuals designed to divert money from rates from being spent on poor relief and health services and essential services." At the proper

[7] Cabinet Paper CP 3230.

time, Cosgrave promised, those who had a claim to compensation for injury or loss due to the "necessary operations of the National Forces" would get it and the burden would be equitably distributed.

The trouble, Sir Henry explained, was that "at present people have been warned that if they apply for Garnshee Orders, they and their solicitors will be shot", and that local councils were afraid that once the war was over "Garnshee Orders will come down upon them like snowflakes."

Robinson was genuinely concerned for the fate of local government in Ireland and in his opinion the new Sinn Fein councils were neglecting the sick and the destitute. They were hampered, he said, by the difficulty of collecting rates and by their refusal to seek financial assistance from the Local Government Board. Local Sinn Feiners were "so elated at the sway they have established" and had become "so utterly reckless" that, in Robinson's view, de Valera would not find it easy to "bring them into line". Robinson wanted to be sure that if the Government was going to be handed over to the Southern Parliament "as a going concern" the work of the Local Government Board in restoring financial equilibrium would not be hampered by the Dail.

Sir Henry Wilson, Chief of the Imperial General Staff, was not thinking in terms of peace at all. Protesting to the Secretary for War that by the end of the year British battalions in Ireland would be down to "ration strength", he pointed out that it would be "impossible to engage in a really strenuous winter campaign." He urged that 40,000 men should be recruited, men who were already trained soldiers, adding that "if the Government decide to engage in these further hostilities, our best chance of a success is to carry them out with the maximum strength which we can possibly attain."

The I.R.A. also were preparing themselves for a possible renewal of the fray. Their activity was intensifying everywhere, Macready reported.[8] Men "on the run" had returned home but some had drunk heavily and were inclined to "trail their coats". Many had been recalled "partly perhaps because they talked too much but also no doubt to assist in the drive for and training of recruits and conscripted men." Referring to reports that the smuggling of arms had been stepped up,

[8] Cabinet paper CP 3219 of 9/8/21.

Macready commented, "The precautions taken in the English ports are ludicrously inadequate. Unless improved there is no reason why the I.R.A. should not bring in as many rifles as they are able to buy."

Macready was a shrewd observer and he saw that the I.R.A. leaders were concerned in case a long truce weakened the bonds of discipline. He thought that they were afraid they had "given themselves away during the Truce and that they will make and are making efforts to find out all they can about the Crown Forces." Sinn Fein propaganda was "vigorous", he said. "The Crown Forces are still maligned with brilliant disregard of essential facts."

He forecast that the moderates in the Sinn Fein Party would prevail. He was aware already of some division of opinion among the leaders but, oddly, thought that de Valera, Arthur Griffith and Michael Collins were in favour of accepting the British proposals whilst Richard Mulcahy, Austin Stack and Erskine Childers wished to obtain more liberal terms or to fight on.

Other reports[9] suggested that de Valera's difficulty was that the Prime Minister "has offered the Irish what they don't want, and the one thing they do want—unity with Ulster—he had no power to give them." It was thought that even the extremists would see the danger of alienating American sympathy if they resumed the fight. "The whole crux of the matter is Ulster," the report concluded.

In the South the Irish were optimistic about an agreement with the North, but already in Belfast there had been bombing outrages against Catholics and other acts of violence which the Chief Secretary reported were "without apparent provocation and having no assignable motive other than sectarian animosity".

Resuming his correspondence with Lloyd George, de Valera wrote on August 30th. Refraining in a lordly way from commenting "on the fallacious historical references in your last communication", he claimed that the British proposals were based on the notorious Act of Union of 1800.

On September 7th, Lloyd George answered that if de Valera meant that he repudiated all allegiance to the Crown and all membership of the British Commonwealth, any further dis-

[9] Cabinet Paper CP 3261 of 25/8/21.

cussion would serve no useful purpose. He went on, "If your real objection to our proposals is that they offer Ireland less than the liberty which we have described, that objection can be explored at a conference."

Assuming de Valera's agreement that the correspondence had lasted long enough, Lloyd George asked for a definite reply as to whether he was prepared "to enter a Conference to ascertain how the association of Ireland with the community of nations known as the British Empire can best be reconciled with Irish National aspirations." He suggested that a Conference should meet at Inverness on September 20th.

This letter was drafted at a Cabinet meeting in the Town Hall, Inverness,[10] at which the Prime Minister advised his colleagues that he had discussed the situation with the King, "who had expressed anxiety that the Government's reply should not be in the nature of an ultimatum or of a character likely to precipitate hostilities."

The Cabinet were divided as to whether they should insist on a conditional conference on the basis of allegiance to the Crown, or whether de Valera and other Dail representatives should be invited to resume the unconditional conference which had been held with the Prime Minister in July. It was thought that de Valera might not be able to accept conditions publicly because of pressure from extremists both in Ireland and the United States, but that he might well make "vital concessions at the conference table." On the other hand, the Cabinet had to consider whether an unconditional invitation at this point might not lower British prestige in India, another trouble spot, and in Europe as well as in Ireland.

The Secretary of State for India, E. S. Montagu, opposed preliminary conditions. He thought that these would "achieve nothing but the renewal of war." It was one thing to fight on the refusal of Sinn Fein to accept membership of the British Empire but quite another to fight on Sinn Fein's refusal to accept membership as a condition *prior* to negotiations.

So the invitation was sent. De Valera accepted it but could not resist adding: "Our nation has formally declared its independence and recognises itself as a sovereign state."

The Prime Minister declined to accept de Valera's answer with the offending paragraph and tried to persuade the Sinn

10 Cabinet conclusion 74/21 (1) of 7/9/21.

163

Fein couriers, Boland and McGrath, to have it altered. Lloyd George told a Conference of Ministers at Gairloch that one of the Irish emissaries was "an out-and-out extremist" and both had shown "great alarm when it was suggested to them that there would be no conference." In their turn, they recorded that it was Lloyd George who was angry and upset. The two leaders now proceeded to bombard each other with telegrams and Lloyd George was able to report to his Ministers[11] that the Irish leader seemed more amenable. It was possible that his "unwise paragraph about a sovereign and independent state" had put de Valera in an awkward position. If that were so, then Lloyd George was willing to help him save face but if de Valera meant what he said then the matter should be fought out at once.

The Government was in rather a sticky position. If they could "enter a conference without the risk of recognising an Irish Republic, all would be well, and if the Conference failed the Republic would never have been recognised by us". It had to be remembered that "the public has set its heart on a conference" and if there were no conference because Sinn Fein would not accept the Crown as a preliminary condition then "general support might not be given to the Government."

This was a pretty piece of political sophistry.

The Prime Minister thought it best to abandon the Inverness plan and to start afresh in London. The suggestion of a new conference would "be of undoubted assistance to de Valera inasmuch as it would free him from the position he had taken up." Finally, he issued "a fresh invitation to a conference in London on October 11th where we can meet your delegates as spokesmen of the people whom you represent with a view to ascertaining how the association of Ireland with the community of nations known as the British Empire may best be reconciled with Irish National aspirations." The formula, an improvement on that of the earlier invitation, was an ingenious piece of phrasing for it neither agreed with de Valera's contention that Ireland was already a republic, nor denied that it might be. This time, in accepting the invitation, de Valera said simply that they had stated their "respective positions" and

[11] Cabinet conclusion 76/21 App. III, Conference of Ministers of 21/9/21.

that a "conference, not correspondence, is the most practical and hopeful way of an understanding."

If the formula seemed to de Valera not to preclude the possibility of a republic with some form of "external association" with the British Empire, it also cut a lot of ground from under his feet. For the delegates were to go as "spokesmen of the people", a people in some kind of political limbo, to whom no label, republican, colonial or anything else was attached. Probably only the English could have devised a situation so ambiguous; perhaps only the Irish could have accepted it. Or was it that both sides were so anxious for a settlement that, unable to find a basis to begin negotiations, they agreed in the end to do without?

The delegates were chosen by the Cabinet and their appointment confirmed by the Dail. They were to have plenary powers. But, having handed the ball to his team, de Valera tied a string to it. The plenipotentiaries were not to sign any agreement without first referring it to Dublin. But so vigorously was the game played between the Irish and the English teams that the string was jerked out of the President's hands.

The difficulty stemmed from de Valera's anxiety to force England into the position of accepting Ireland as a sovereign state and so he wanted the representatives to be recognised as plenipotentiaries. At the same time he intended to exercise control himself. No wonder the French newspaper *Figaro* derisively defined "plenipotentiary" as "man with full powers but powerless".

Why de Valera did not take the obvious course of going to London himself remains a matter for conjecture. In *The Big Fellow* Frank O'Connor suggests that in declaring a republic and proclaiming independence in the first place, the Irish had given themselves no room for manoeuvre and that, as President of the Irish Republic, it would have been embarrassing for de Valera to have to make the inevitable compromise.

In the Dail the President urged that he was not a "doctrinaire Republican" and he is said to have implored Griffith to get him out of the "strait-jacket of the Republic". These phrases have been produced ever since as evidence that de Valera recognised that Britain would never concede a republic and that the original declaration of a republic was a burden to him. But, in *Peace by Ordeal* Frank Pakenham

165

argues that they have been misconstrued. It is true that, though he had the subtlest of minds, de Valera was never very successful in putting his ideas across.

When he advanced his proposal of external association no one knew what he was driving at. It was an impossible concept in the minds of the British Cabinet. Extremist Republicans saw no virtue in any kind of association with Britain; Collins simply could not see the point of it and even Griffith, though he argued it brilliantly during the negotiations, was unconvinced.

It was suggested by P. S. O'Hegarty[12] that de Valera brewed up his plan as a compromise between dominion status and an isolated republic to reconcile the extremist Cathal Brugha, and that he explained it to Arthur Griffith in these terms. He may have been inspired by Brugha's intransigence to produce the idea, but there was much more depth to it than that. The association with Britain was designed to tempt the Six Counties; it was a carrot for the Ulster donkey. More than that, it offered a measure of security to the middle-class trading people in the main towns of Southern Ireland who had always been moderate in their views and who were anxious for peace so that their normal way of life could be re-established. They had turned against Britain in the first place not because of the Republican ideal but because they believed in an independent Ireland and because of the harshness and clumsiness of the British Government in prevaricating about Home Rule, in dealing with the men of the Easter Rising, in planning to introduce conscription and, finally, in setting loose the Black and Tans.

De Valera was about a quarter of a century ahead of his time. India, a republic associated with the Commonwealth, enjoys today exactly the status that he envisaged for Ireland at that time. Indeed, since World War II the pattern has become firmly established. His distinction between an isolated republic and an associated republic was a subtle one but what he wanted essentially was independence of Great Britain. He was not unduly concerned with the form of government adopted once that had been secured. If the Irish people had wanted a new Irish dynasty he might well have conceded the point.

12 *The Victory of Sinn Fein*, by P. S. O'Hegarty.

The decision not to lead the delegation to parley with Lloyd George's team was implemented only by reason of his own casting vote in the Cabinet. He considered that by remaining in Ireland, remote from the fray, he could more effectively act as a brake if the delegates seemed likely to be carried away in the heat of argument and, further, that his presence was needed to restrain the impatience and bellicosity of Brugha and, to a lesser extent, Stack.

Sean McEoin's own forthright opinion is that "Mr de Valera knew that he personally could not get any more than what he had already been offered by Lloyd George in London. He had begun—and concluded—his negotiations and he knew that if he went he might not even get what he had already brought back. I think he had reasonable ground for that. He thought that Collins with his personality and Griffith with his sagacity might do better—and, indeed, they did."

The chosen team seemed an unlikely one and yet, apart from de Valera himself, it is difficult to see who else should have gone. Men, such as Cosgrave, were to emerge who had the ability, but at the time they had yet to prove themselves. It was inevitable that Arthur Griffith should lead the delegation in de Valera's absence, but he believed in his heart that it was a mission for younger men.

Dan Breen recalls a conversation with Arthur Griffith one night in 1920. Out after the curfew in the Clontarf area, Breen made for a house where he was sure of a welcome. He found Griffith staying there and the two men talked through the night until curfew was over and Breen left. Griffith confessed that the struggle had gone far beyond anything he had ever imagined. The time for negotiation would surely come and when it did then it was the men of Breen's generation who must negotiate. "I'm a King, Lords and Commons man, Dan, and you're a Republican," he said. Breen's answer was that he would not have been under arms in that house that night for less than a republic; he would never have fired a single shot to win a concession. "I understand," said Arthur Griffith, "and my ideas wouldn't suit your age."

Second in command of the delegation was Michael Collins, who resisted the assignment vehemently and only gave in when he was convinced that it was his duty to go. He saw him-

167

self as a soldier rather than as a politician, as an administrator rather than a diplomat. Ruthless when there was need, sometimes riding roughshod over his associates—never with malice but simply because he was intolerant of standards that fell below his own—hugely generous, a spontaneous, emotional, out-giving, explosive man, Collins was to mature and to gain in stature during the next months. Propaganda had made him the epitome of the gunman and Sir Henry Wilson, for one, persisted in regarding him as leader of the "murder gangs". Lloyd George, who had done much to create the image, knew better. Only a man of tremendous fibre could have engineered the Intelligence system which, in essence, had brought his cause to triumph and Lloyd George respected him.

Collins must have had qualms about putting his head, on which there was a price of £10,000 a few months earlier, into the British lion's mouth. He could not imagine that the British would give him a safe-conduct back to Ireland so that he could operate his lethal network again. During the negotiations Collins lived, not at Hans Place with the rest of the delegation, but at Cadogan Square. Collins's men travelled to and fro, men like Liam Tobin, Cullen, Thornton, Joe Dolan and Emmet Dalton. They were always at hand. One of them would sleep in his bedroom. On Collins's instructions, Emmet Dalton purchased a light aircraft from Canada and the machine and its pilot stood by at Croydon throughout the negotiations.

Once, during the negotiations, a member of the Collins entourage who prided himself on his marksmanship visited a shooting gallery in Leicester Square to keep his hand in. His first shots were wide and to the Irishman's disgust a man who had been watching him at once hit the bullseye with a series of shots. The man put down the pistol, addressed the Irish marksman by name and suggested that he needed a little more practice. It was a warning that not all English secret agents died on Bloody Sunday.

The other members of the team, Gavan Duffy, Eamonn Duggan and Robert Barton, cousin to Erskine Childers, were of lighter weight. Barton was Minister of Economic Affairs, the other two were lawyers. As Collins was Minister of Finance and Griffith Minister of Foreign Affairs, the delegation had a balanced and expert look about it but it needed more men of the stature of Griffith and Collins and, above all, it needed
168

de Valera. The secretaries were Childers, John Chartres and Fionan Lynch. It was against Griffith's will that Childers was appointed and as the conference proceeded his distrust of the other man hardened into an almost pathological hatred. The irritant of this enmity was an important factor in the dissension which developed between members of the delegation, and the fact that Childers was in constant communication with his chief and seemed to be a kind of watchdog did not promote harmony.

The British selected their team of negotiators at a meeting of the Cabinet on October 6th[13]. Lloyd George pointed out that the problems were complicated and the conference might be a long one. Obviously he and the Lord Privy Seal, Austen Chamberlain, "cannot sit from day to day for weeks discussing questions of detail". Sub-committees would be necessary and "some questions might with advantage be remitted to individuals." This practical approach the members of the Irish delegation quickly accepted but it was to be held against them by their opponents later that they had allowed the team to be segmented by the adroit English politicians.

Lloyd George, Chamberlain, Birkenhead, Churchill, Worthington-Evans and Greenwood were chosen to handle the British case, and Hewart was to join them when constitutional issues were involved. Only on questions "involving a departure of a fundamental character from the policy already approved" would the full Cabinet be consulted. The Cabinet also decided that while in special cases interned Sinn Feiners might be released, "attempts to secure the release of the whole body of internees at this juncture should be resisted."[14]

Excited London crowds cheered both teams as they appeared at 10 Downing Street to begin the conference on the morning of Tuesday, October 11th. Lloyd George greeted the Irishmen warmly, but led them to their places at the table before introducing them to his team, so obviating the need for handshakes. Three or four months earlier, the English Ministers would have sent Michael Collins to the gallows had they laid hands on him and gladly paid £10,000 to the man who enabled them to do so; now they faced the 31-year-old giant across the conference table and some of them at least

[13] Cabinet conclusion 76/21 (6) of 6/10/21.
[14] Cabinet conclusion 76/21 (8) of 6/10/21.

came to like him. Even Lloyd George was to describe Collins as "one of the most courageous leaders ever produced by a valiant race", while Birkenhead conceived a special admiration and affection for him and, in his turn, earned the esteem of the Irish delegates, for he, hitherto one of their most relentless opponents, displayed as much understanding and humanity as he did ability and wit.

But it was Arthur Griffith, who with his great machine of a mind, profound love of his country and honour which seemed embedded in concrete, commanded the respect of both his colleagues and his opponents. It was upon the sturdy base of Griffith's honour that Lloyd George caused the Treaty to stand and perhaps, after all, he did not build better than he knew, for if Lloyd George owned little honour himself, he was not slow to perceive it in others.

TEN

In the first plenary sessions the delegates explored the spiky fringe of the Irish problem, matters of defence, trade and finance. Lloyd George began by stating that he and his colleagues were bound by certain limitations as no doubt Mr Griffith and his colleagues were. In the background was always the factor of public opinion. He had "no desire to curtail discussion but time might not be on the side of peace." From the outset, Griffith made it plain that the Irish were counting upon "a change in the policy of subordinating Ireland to English interests." Lloyd George assured him that "we seek nothing in the way of military domination of Ireland", but the use of Irish ports and the right to build aerodromes were vital to Britain's security. The virtues of free trade were then spelled out by the British Prime Minister, who emphasised that whereas the Irish market was of little significance to Great Britain, the U.K. market was of the utmost importance to Ireland. Why then did he fear a tariff war? Barton thrust shrewdly.

Griffith said that the Irish did not object to free trade in English goods but must protect themselves against foreign goods sold by English merchants.

The representatives of the two countries used these opening discussions to size up their opponents, to probe their minds, to anticipate the trend of argument and to look for common ground before striking through to the core, the two cores, of the problem—partition and the character of Ireland's future government. Sub-committees were appointed to deal with finance and defence. In a curiously ungenerous way the British Government were determined to fasten upon Ireland a share of the War Debt, as they were determined also to ensure that she was not left out of any wars of the future. Griffith insisted that the Irish wanted to remain neutral if Great Britain were at war with a foreign power, and this at once brought the question of dominion status into the open. The Dominions had never claimed to be neutral but, said Lloyd George, if they didn't approve of a war they were "free to limit assistance in men and money." As for getting into war in the first place, Ireland, like the other Dominions, would be consulted on foreign affairs but the conduct of them would remain the preserve of the British Government. At this point, however, Griffith was not keen to go too deeply into the question of dominion status.

Negotiations might well end in stalemate, and the strategy of the Irish delegation was orientated to ensure that if the Conference did break down it would do so on the issue of partition. The British Cabinet, on the other hand, sensitive to public opinion as they were, had seen that this would be "far less favourable to us than if the break came on the refusal to accept British Sovereignty."[1]

The Ulster question intruded into the conversations at the fourth full session, on Friday, October 14th. Lloyd George played it down. All the Dominions had begun by being divided, he said encouragingly. Union was bound to come, but it would never come if an attempt was made to force it from the first. Collins retorted that this was no true analogy. In this instance "the British have divided an ancient and historic State." Griffith, who had not yet received his instructions from Dublin, extemporised with calculated tediousness. The exasperated Lloyd George confided to Lord Riddell at the weekend that "unfortunately he (Griffith) had no power of ex-

[1] Cabinet conclusion 74/21 (1) of 7/9/21.

pression".[2] While pressing hotly their claim that to sever the north-eastern counties from the rest of Ireland had been an act of political vandalism, the Irish delegates denied any intention of using force against the Ulstermen. They were confident that left to themselves they could come to an agreement with their countrymen. Ulster didn't really want separation, Griffith claimed; only the business interests wanted it. "The Ulster question is a Belfast City question," he said, and so long as they thought England was behind them, they wouldn't co-operate. Unexpectedly, Lloyd George promised his blessing upon their efforts. The British Government were only behind Ulster "in the sense that it could not allow civil war at its doors."

By Monday, Griffith had received his briefing on Ulster. There were two alternatives, both of which cut across the provisions of the 1920 Government of Ireland Act. But then, by consenting to negotiate at all, the British Government had put that Act on the market. Ulster was to be invited to become again a natural part of Ireland with her representatives in a Dublin Parliament and no other. If any part of the Six Counties were to decline the invitation then they could have their Northern Parliament, but it should be subordinate, not to Westminster, but to Dublin. However, Griffith was playing his cards close to his body and he stated only that England should stand aside and allow Dublin to make a "fair proposal" to the North. If no agreement could be reached with the Six Counties, then some arrangement should be made which allowed the people to choose. Some kind of Boundary Commission was mooted and, somewhat mischievously, Lloyd George suggested a plebiscite over the whole of the nine counties of Ulster. This idea was received by Griffith with about as much enthusiasm as Carson had shown for it several years earlier. Griffith produced a map indicating by Poor Law Unions the division of Ulster between Catholics and Protestants. His idea was that the people should vote by parishes. In this way Tyrone and Fermanagh at least, and parts of Down and Derry, could be expected to cross the border. The Irish were determined that the British should undo the damage they had done in imposing partition and the British seemed eager to help—they would approve any persuasion short of

[2] Lord Riddell's *Intimate Diary of the Peace Conference and After*.
172

force by Southern Ireland. Lloyd George said the border was "a compromise reached as the result of negotiations with previous representatives of Southern Ireland", and added blandly, "No compromise is logically defensible."

Griffith reported the exchanges faithfully to de Valera, who remained wary and suspicious of Lloyd George. The Irish President reacted swiftly to an exchange of telegrams between the Pope, who prayed that His Majesty the King would be granted "the great joy and imperishable glory of bringing to an end the age-long dissension", and George V, who joined in the Pope's prayer that the Conference "may achieve a permanent settlement of the troubles in Ireland and may initiate a new era of peace and happiness for my people."

In the King's answer de Valera saw the Machiavellian hand of Lloyd George. At once he dispatched a long telegram to the Pope. With impatient courtesy he thanked the Pope for his paternal regard then went on to express confidence "that the ambiguities in the reply sent in the name of King George will not mislead you, as they may the uninformed, into believing that the troubles are *in* Ireland or that the people of Ireland owe allegiance to the British King."

It is not difficult to see the reason for de Valera's stinging intervention, for here was the Pope almost acknowledging that the struggle for independence was, after all, a rebellion against the English King, and here was England blandly answering that it was indeed a domestic issue. De Valera's message set out at some length the right of Ireland to a separate identity and the nature of her struggle for freedom from a brutal occupying power. But the delegates in London thought he was being rather too prickly in the circumstances and were angered that he had made their delicate mission more exacting.

It came as no surprise to the delegates when Lloyd George protested that de Valera's action, which dealt with "the very issues in controversy", made the task of negotiation almost impossible. There was also the matter of a shipment of arms from Hamburg. The British Government did not want to waste time in conferences which would lead to no result and were only prolonged to allow the Irish Republican Army to be equipped. The Irish representatives rode out the storm, and when the British Prime Minister laboured the political risk to himself and his Government which negotiation with the Irish involved, they were sure that they were in calmer waters. But every move Lloyd George made had been worked out at a meeting of the British representatives beforehand. Now he pressed for an answer to three vital questions. He wanted to know whether Ireland was prepared to belong to the Empire, to swear allegiance to the King and to provide defence facilities.

Griffith cleverly expressed his support of de Valera's message to the Pope without making too much of an issue of it. He was proposing to table Ireland's proposals after the weekend and was optimistic that a solution would be found. In the meantime, it would be helpful to know the British attitude concerning Ulster.

When the British team met on Monday, October 24th, Lloyd George told them that Mr Tim Healy had seen him and Sir Gordon Hewart the previous day and had suggested a Parliament "with Channel Islands powers" for the whole of Ireland which would then negotiate a treaty with England. The British representatives thought that the acceptance of some proposals was first necessary. There was little promise of this in the written proposals which Griffith had now put. The text was adroitly ambiguous. In the preamble the British were exhorted to remember that "Ireland is not a colony or dependency but an ancient and spirited nation." The present British proposal offered no basis for an agreement which would both safeguard the security of Britain's Empire and give Ireland her freedom. The Irish proposition was put simply.

"On the one hand Ireland will consent to adhere for all purposes of agreed concern to the League of Sovereign States associated and known as the British Commonwealth of Nations. On the other hand, Ireland calls upon Great Britain to renounce all claims to authority over Ireland and Irish affairs." Ireland was to be a free state guaranteed by the British Commonwealth, and the League of Nations and the United States of America were to countersign the guarantee.

Succinctly the partition issue was put: "The responsibility for this unnatural and indefensible dismemberment rests with the British Government, but as the fact exists we propose to deal with it in the first instance by meeting the elected representatives of our countrymen in the area and forming an

174

agreement with them safeguarding any lawful interests peculiar to the area. Should we fail to come to an agreement, and we are confident we shall not fail, then freedom of choice must be given to electorates within the area."

The document discreetly omitted the word Republic and it did not refer specifically to the Crown link. Ireland would "adhere" to the Commonwealth "for all purposes of agreed concern." What precisely did that mean? Lloyd George wanted to know. Was Ireland prepared to accept the same status within the Empire as Canada? Griffith fenced cleverly. This was not quite the concept of "association". Lloyd George pinned him down. What was the distinction between association and belonging? Griffith admitted that they would not accept the Crown, though they would recognise the King as head of the Commonwealth with which Ireland would be associated. The British Prime Minister tried to come to grips with what seemed to him a contradiction in terms. Yet the plan was a simple solution. If Lloyd George's offer of dominion status was genuine, then Ireland was prepared to accept obligations similar to those of a dominion, though she owned no obligations to become embroiled in Britain's wars. But she was not prepared to *be* a dominion. The Republican ideal was too precious to be abandoned; the Republic had become Ireland's symbol as the Crown was Britain's. All she asked was the liberty to preserve her own symbol.

"To put it bluntly, will you be British subjects or foreigners? You must be either one or the other," said Lloyd George. Griffith had a plan for reciprocal civil rights. On the neutrality issue it was pointed out to Griffith that if the Irish extended facilities other countries might not regard this as neutrality. Griffith said that he had not considered that and Collins remarked enigmatically that "it would be a compensating point for England." Hewart asked whether, if the Irish were "prepared to render unneutral services, it was not a mistake for them to pin themselves to a meaningless trophy."

"In principle we accept that your safety should be secured," said Griffith.

It did not seem to Lloyd George that the position was too hopeless and he and Chamberlain argued it further with Griffith and Collins at a private meeting, the first of many. This was a surer way of doing business, but Collins and Griffith

175

were to be roundly blamed for allowing what was seen by other members of the Dail Cabinet, and some of their fellow delegates, as a shrewd British manoeuvre.

There were already certain sub-committees, one dealing with the observance of the Truce. Breaches or allegations of breaches often brought an acid note to the negotiations. I.R.A. training and drilling, the importation of arms and, once, a conspiracy to blow up certain installations in England itself were the main British grievances. There were, too, numerous instances of trigger-happy Volunteers attacking English troops. In their turn, the Irish protested about the movements of British troops in Ireland and other signs of preparations for a renewal of hostilities.

Emmet Dalton recalls accompanying Collins to one meeting of the Sub-Committee at which Churchill read with great solemnity a long list of breaches of the Truce by the Irish. Collins scribbled a note to Dalton:

"Have we any answer to these?"

"No," wrote Dalton, and passed the note back. Collins listened for a few more moments then, banging his fist on the table, he exclaimed, "For Christ's sake, come to the point."

Churchill seemed stunned. Dalton was sure his own hair stood on end as he awaited the wrath of the Secretary of State for the Colonies. Before Churchill could collect himself, Collins gave a great shout of laughter and, in spite of himself, Churchill laughed too. All the steam had gone out of his case.

Following the meeting between Lloyd George, Chamberlain and the two Irish leaders, a row blew up in the Irish camp. Griffith had stubbornly resisted all arguments on the Crown link.

"If we came to an agreement on all other points I could recommend some form of association with the Crown," was as far as he would go, and even this, he made it clear, was a concession to Ulster for the sake of the "essential unity" of Ireland. Collins, according to the British records, tried to whittle down Griffith's offer and suggested an oath of allegiance to the Constitution rather than to the Crown.

Lloyd George had summed up the Irish proposals for his own colleagues in a way that the Irish themselves could not have bettered.

176

1. Irish not to be aliens but there is to be common and interchangeable citizenship.

2. They will come into the mechanism of the Empire and take part in the Empire's common council to discuss common purposes e.g. defence of British and Irish coast, though they boggle over joining in a war on behalf of the Dominions.

3. They agree in principle that British Government should occupy their ports for Imperial defence even if the exercise of that right involved war. They do not however accept the Crown. The head of the State would be chosen by them.

If only the British, having comprehended so well, could have given a simple yes. But Lloyd George was confident that in the end the Irish would accept the Crown, but only if Ulster could be brought in. This, he said, was not a denial of autonomy to Ulster. Chamberlain was convinced that the real difficulty would prove to be the Crown.

Recognition of the Crown in any sense had been no part of de Valera's "association" plan and he was alarmed when he received Griffith's report. There would be no question of any allegiance to the King, he wrote warningly. "If war is the alternative, we can only face it."

Angrily the plenipotentiaries protested to de Valera at this interference with their powers to range freely in discussion. In any case, if Ireland was to accept association with the Commonwealth they should have to recognise its head in one way or another. It was John Chartres, one of the Irish secretaries, who, Frank Pakenham tells us,[3] first saw that simply to recognise the King as head of the Commonwealth in no way vitiated the concept of the Republic.

De Valera wrote placating the delegation. There had been a misunderstanding; he had only wanted to keep them in touch with views in Dublin.

Nevertheless, Lloyd George had managed to insert the thin end of a wedge and for the next month he tapped away at it, driving it in barely perceptibly. First, the British decided to explore the Ulster situation and delegated Chamberlain and Hewart to meet two Irish representatives. The secretaries "should endeavour to arrange that the Irish representatives should be Griffith and Collins".

The four met on October 25th, and Chamberlain reported

[3] *Peace by Ordeal*, by Frank Pakenham.

to his colleagues that there had been satisfactory replies on safeguards and autonomy for Ulster. But the Irish were "inexorable that they must not leave homogeneous Catholic areas in Ulster." The offer of autonomy applied, therefore, to a reduced area of some kind. Churchill had told them that the British were not free agents and could not abandon the 1920 Act, but they would do their best to recommend inclusion of the Six Counties in the large Parliament—plus autonomy held from Dublin instead of Westminster.

"This was a new proposal," Griffith reported to de Valera, "and while we did not hold out any hope that it might be a basis we, between ourselves, thought it might be a possible basis."

If the Irish accepted the other proposals, then an approach to Craig was possible, the British considered. If they refused, then the break would not come on Ulster.

The British answered the written proposals of the Irish on October 27th. Ignoring Griffith's idea of "reciprocal citizenship", they reiterated their insistence upon the inclusion of the Crown in the Irish political system. "No man can be a subject of two states," they said, and asserted: "The essence of common citizenship is that all who enjoy it are at peace or at war together in respect of any foreign state. It is not compatible with neutrality in any form." In their reply of October 29th the Irish conceded defence facilities "such as may be agreed to be necessary", and they also put on paper their willingness to recommend acceptance of the Crown as "symbol and accepted head of the combination of signatory states"—meaning the Commonwealth—but only if Ireland herself were "free and undivided".

Lloyd George's reaction to the Irish note was unusual. He sent Tom Jones to explain that he must have "absolute reassurances on fundamentals" before he faced a censure motion in the House of Commons on Monday, October 31st. Jones saw Duggan and read to him the draft of a letter Lloyd George wanted Griffith to send him:

"Dear Prime Minister,

You can appreciate the difficulty of conducting negotiations by means of written documents which, in the event of a breakdown, might be made public and be used by one side against the other. For that reason it is natural that the
178

formal reply which we have sent to you today may seem to be couched in terms of such diplomatic caution as to conceal our genuine desire for peace. We therefore give you this personal assurance that in essence the meaning of our reply is that we are prepared to be free partners in the British Commonwealth, to recognise the golden link of the Crown at its head, and to have unity of control in all matters of the naval defence of these islands. All this to be subject to our securing the unity of Ireland as a condition precedent to or incorporated in whatever Treaty may be made."

The "golden link of the Crown" was a nice touch.

Duggan suggested an interview instead, and telephoned later to say that Griffith and Collins were agreeable.

Jones arranged the meeting for Sunday, October 30th, at Churchill's home. Lloyd George told Griffith and Collins that he would hope to push through a plan to allow a six-county Parliament subordinate to Dublin or, alternatively, though less optimistically, that he would try for a new boundary, or a vote by the Six Counties on the issue of inclusion in the new State. He took the line that he needed the support of the Irish delegates to fight off the die-hards in the Commons. He painted himself as the Irishman's friend. This was not altogether a misrepresentation of himself; much depended upon how the political light caught his prismatic character. At all events, Griffith was able to report to de Valera that Lloyd George and Birkenhead, who had also been present, had indicated that "if they were certain of real goodwill on our side they would take risks and fight."

The vote of censure was steam-rollered by 439 votes to 43 and Lloyd George's next hurdle was, he said, the Unionist Conference at Liverpool on November 17th at which he hoped to move the Craig faction from their stony stand. To help him, Griffith explained to his colleagues, he wanted Griffith to set down on paper the assurances given verbally at the meeting of 30th. Griffith prepared a letter which he proposed to send in his own name. He apparently did not mention that his letter was first drafted at the meeting with Lloyd George at Churchill's. Robert Barton and Gavan Duffy were tenaciously opposed to sending any document that was not signed by all the plenipotentiaries. Moreover, they were concerned that the wording gave too much away. Gavan Duffy argued

179

in a memorandum prepared in matutinal solitude that "the main effect of the letter must be to undermine the stand we have taken." Any concessions made so far had been on the Irish side and he was convinced that Lloyd George had uses for Griffith's letter other than as a shot in his locker for Craig.

Griffith gave way. The letter was amended to preserve the Irish insistence upon recognition of the Crown only as head of the Association of Free States, where Griffith had simply stated that the plenipotentiaries would urge recognition of the Crown and free partnership with the British Commonwealth, the formula in each case to be agreed later. The deliberate ambiguity of the original, Gavan Duffy saw, by its very omissions could be taken to imply much more than was meant. His misgivings were justified.

On the morning of November 2nd, Griffith and Collins delivered the note to Birkenhead, who at once attempted to have them change "free partnership *with* the British Commonwealth" to "free partnership *within* the British Commonwealth." They resisted this stoutly but when, later in the day, they met Birkenhead, Lloyd George and Chamberlain, Griffith accepted "free partnership with the other states associated within the British Commonwealth" as essentially the same as his own phrase. But, closely examined, it is not the same thing at all. It was a clever play with words, which even de Valera failed to spot when the text reached him, but it was the cleverness of a man securing his price by including a spurious coin in the change.

Birkenhead told Griffith and Collins next day, November 3rd, that the British Government now felt that they could tackle Craig and that if Ulster proved difficult the Cabinet would resign rather than renew the war against Sinn Fein on that issue. Lloyd George had a happy knack of tossing his political future into the scales but he invariably contrived to rescue it in time. On this occasion he appears to have been genuine. There is no suggestion of any resignation in the Cabinet records but at Downing Street he told Lord Riddell[4]: "Things look very awkward. Bonar Law has come out as the advocate of Ulster. Whether he thinks he sees his opportunity to become Prime Minister or whether he is solely actuated by a conscientious desire to champion the cause of Ulster, I don't

[4] Lord Riddell's *Intimate Diary of the Peace Conference and After*.

know." Lloyd George was inclined to give Bonar Law the benefit of the doubt. But, he reminded Riddell, "There are no friendships at the top." He went on: "I am not going to continue the Irish war if a settlement is possible. I shall resign and the King will have to send for someone else." His reading of the situation was that the Irish would accept allegiance to the Crown and remain part of the Empire but that they would insist on Tyrone and Fermanagh being ceded to them or, at the least, on a plebiscite, and that they would also require that fiscal, postal and telegraphic arrangements should be "relegated to a Central Parliament to be elected on the basis of population."

"If the matter can be settled on those lines," the Prime Minister declared, "I am not prepared to continue civil war."

It seemed to Griffith that things were going well. The British appeared to accept that settlement of the Ulster problem came first. Either they pushed the North into "essential unity" or the Government would resign. Griffith could not imagine that any new Government would resume the war against Sinn Fein merely because Ulster was recalcitrant. The British had also accepted a Crown and Commonwealth formula which, though not yet precise, did not preclude the Irish proposal of associating with the Commonwealth but not belonging to it. Griffith had played the diplomatic game very shrewdly, but perhaps did not appreciate that he was up against a master craftsman of intrigue, political bargain hunter *par excellence*, the quality of whose wit, ingenuity and experience has rarely been paralleled.

Craig, whom Lloyd George saw twice, on Saturday, November 5th and Monday 7th, refused to be budged. He would have no truck with a Dublin Parliament nor accept adjustment of the border. This was explained to Griffith by Tom Jones, Assistant Secretary to the Cabinet and one of the Conference secretaries, whose role in the negotiations was becoming increasingly important. Like Lloyd George, Jones had worked his way up from a humble Welsh home. A formidable scholar, he had become Professor of Economics at Belfast before forsaking academic life for the Civil Service. Jones remained for many years the confidant of Prime Ministers. Later, as Secretary of the Pilgrim Trust, his qualities of sincerity, sagacity and compassion had a full outlet.

181

Though a genuine friend of Ireland, Jones was yet part of a team bent upon achieving a settlement within the limits of the British political set-up of the day. Advising Griffith that Lloyd George would make one more attempt to sway Craig, failing which he would resign, Jones put to him the likelihood of a Government led by Bonar Law, which would be anything but friendly to Sinn Fein. He brought up again the idea of a Boundary Commission which, in all justice it would seem, inevitably must award Tyrone, Fermanagh and parts of several other counties to the South. Griffith saw the problem as Lloyd George's and was still convinced that little danger to Ireland would stem from a transfer of power in England.

In a letter to Griffith, de Valera sounded a note of warning. There would be a temptation to make concessions in other directions for the sake of keeping up the pressure on Ulster. Jones called again on November 9th and pushed the Boundary Commission a little harder. The purpose of the Commission would be to delimit the six-county area, Griffith explained to de Valera, "so as to give us the districts in which we are a majority." Griffith told Jones that he did not think Ulster would agree. Jones was of the same opinion. The point was that it would be foolish for Lloyd George to resign and allow in the intransigent Bonar Law when it was clear to everyone that Ulster's obduracy was the stumbling block. Now, Jones wanted to know, would Griffith and his team support the proposal? This was going a bit too far, Griffith thought.

"We said it was their proposal, not ours," he reported to his chief, "and we would therefore not be bound by it, but we realise its value as a tactical manoeuvre and if Lloyd George made it we would not queer his position."

Griffith seemed to have reacted with great circumspection. But what he had done, in fact, was to release Lloyd George from his pledge to resign if Ulster baulked at an all-Ireland Parliament and also, by not opposing the "tactical manoeuvre", tacitly to accept the Boundary Commission as a practical alternative.

At a Cabinet meeting on November 10th, Lloyd George's negotiation policy was approved but "emphasis was laid upon the importance of exercising the greatest patience in the conduct of negotiations with the Cabinet of Northern Ireland".[5]

[5] Cabinet conclusion 87/21 of 10/11/21.

A long memorandum, for which Churchill and Chamberlain were largely responsible, was dispatched to Craig, who was in London with his Ulster Cabinet colleagues. It began by recapitulating the history of Irish antipathy to England. The position reached was that "a dominant section of Irishmen have pledged themselves to projects which are, in fact, fatal to the security of Great Britain and therefore to the existence of the Empire itself. Unless their projects are abandoned, Great Britain must make whatever effort may be necessary for the reconquest of Ireland. If statesmanship can find no other alternative this effort can and will be made." The effort would be expensive, involving war on a hitherto unattempted scale. The real need was peace not a "wasted and bloodstained wilderness."

It was believed that Sinn Fein would accept the Crown provided the Northern Parliament became subordinate to Dublin. There would be adequate safeguards, the present powers of Belfast would be undiminished and no revenue due to Ulster would be withheld from her. Ulster was warned:

"It is no answer to say that Southern Ireland is alone to blame for the present position and that these concessions are offered as the reward of rebellion."

Sacrifices would have to be made all round. Ulster was invited to talk but the British Government was clear that they did not intend to waste their opportunity. "For the first time in history a British Government has found itself face to face with a party of physical force and is in a position to make a final settlement with the spokesman of that party."

In a forthright reply Craig expressed surprise that British representatives had allowed any discussion on the Crown. Northern Ireland refused emphatically to belong to an all-Ireland Parliament, or to subordinate their own Parliament to Dublin, and were perturbed that there should be any suggestion of a revision of the area within their jurisdiction.

Craig put a new proposal. The 1920 Act had provided for equal powers for North and South. If the South were now to become a Dominion the North could become one too. Lloyd George had suggested slyly that if Ulster insisted upon remaining subordinate to Westminster, she would have to share the imperial tax burden. Craig as slyly rejoined that if Ulster became a Dominion this would not apply.

183

One day, perhaps an all-Ireland Parliament might be possible, in which case, said Craig, the machinery of the 1920 Act would be sufficient.

Lloyd George's answer on November 14th at once squashed the idea that the Six Counties should constitute a separate dominion. "Such a partition must militate with increasing force against the ultimate unity of Ireland," he replied, adding that "frontiers once established harden into permanence." The border was not acceptable to the majority of the Irish people, "nor could we conscientiously attempt to enforce it. It would be fatal to the purpose of a lasting settlement on which the negotiations from the outset have been steadily directed."

In a visit to Griffith on the afternoon of November 12th, for which Tom Jones paved the way in the morning, Lloyd George had explained the line he intended to take with Craig. Ulster would be offered an all-Ireland Parliament with the right to vote themselves out of it within twelve months. If they exercised this right they must submit to a Boundary Commission. He was determined to have it out with them, to the extent of either dissolving Parliament or pushing through legislation on these lines. Griffith disclaimed any responsibility; the proposals were the British Government's. Lloyd George agreed, but argued that when battle commenced with the die-hards at the Unionist Conference in Liverpool, they would be lost if the Irish delegates repudiated them. Griffith reported to de Valera that he had said he could not guarantee to accept the proposal. "But I would guarantee that while he was fighting the 'Ulster' crowd we would not help them by repudiating him."

In Griffith's mind this was no more than he had already told Tom Jones but Lloyd George either misunderstood him or pretended to. Chamberlain and Birkenhead were to go to Liverpool and Pakenham makes it clear that Lloyd George "had no intention of asking them to embark on an enterprise which, even if ultimate settlement resulted, might smash their political careers, unless he felt sure that he could rely on Griffith not to let him down."[6] But Lloyd George's account of his conversation with Griffith went further and Chamberlain understood from him that Griffith would not now force a

[6] *Peace by Ordeal*, by Frank Pakenham.

184

break on the Ulster issue at any stage of the negotiations. Griffith remained blissfully certain that all he had done was to refrain from embarrassing Lloyd George while Conservative Ministers in his hybrid Cabinet fought for his policy at Liverpool. He even hoped that his co-operation would smooth the way to external association.

Griffith, indeed, casually initialled a note of the proposals which Lloyd George had had drafted. He did not even bother to mention the document to his colleagues. It reiterated, harmlessly enough, that if Ulster declined to belong to an all-Ireland Parliament "it would be necessary to revise the boundary of Northern Ireland", that "this might be done by a Boundary Commission which would be directed to adjust the line both by inclusion and exclusion so as to make the boundary conform as closely as possible to the wishes of the population." How the wishes of the population were to be ascertained was not specified. The phrase was to be preserved, together with its ambiguity, and was in time to have great significance.

At this juncture, however, it was trivial. What mattered was that Griffith, though he believed he was simply standing aside in benevolent neutrality, had assented to a proposed solution of the Ulster problem. Lloyd George had managed to move a long way from the point where he pledged his resignation if he failed to bring Ulster to heel.

Support for a united Ireland came also from the Southern Unionists. Lord Midleton and Mr Andrew Jameson saw Lloyd George on November 15th. They wanted to be sure of protection for their minority and were worried about the armies of both the North and the South. They complained also of breaches of the Truce and the Prime Minister arranged for them to discuss this issue with the Irish plenipotentiaries next day.

Negotiations were advanced a stage further when, on November 16th, the British delivered a rather rough draft of terms they now were disposed to offer the Irish. They embodied the Ulster solution upon which Griffith had half raised his hands in blessing. One or two small concessions were made but, basically, Great Britain's demands were unchanged. But there was a careful absence of any reference to allegiance to the Crown, to oath-taking, even to the Crown itself. Ireland was to "have the status of a self-governing Dominion", and in Irish minds there still seemed to be an opening here for their externally associated Republic. Encouraging too, in spite of the "let-out" clause on Ulster, was the provision of a Parliament for the whole of Ireland.

Cracks were showing in the walls of the Conservative Party and the outcome of the Liverpool Conference was anxiously awaited by Lloyd George and his Ministers. But all was well. The die-hards had their say but the Conference carried an amendment put by Sir Archibald Salvidge, champion of the Orange cause, whose opposition was so feared that Birkenhead made a secret trip to Liverpool to see him. Birkenhead assured him that a settlement which preserved the supremacy of the Crown, kept Ireland within the Empire and safeguarded Ulster's position was within reach. His sincerity impressed Salvidge who, however, had already decided that he should use his influence to help secure a peaceful settlement.

Craig replied to Lloyd George on November 17th claiming that it was dishonest even to talk on a position which was known beforehand to be quite unacceptable to Ulster. His dominion proposal was not merely a counter proposal. The point was: "If you force Ulster to leave the United Kingdom against the wishes of her people, she desires to be left in a position to make her own fiscal and international policy conform as nearly as possible with the policy of the Mother Country, and to retain British traditions, British currency, British ideals, and the British language, and in this way render the disadvantages entailed by her separation from Great Britain as slight as possible."

He ended that he was at Lloyd George's disposal to talk, but next day he went down with influenza and at a Conference of Ministers it was decided merely to wish him well and in the circumstances not to worry him with a lengthy reply. But Craig was worried anyway. On November 20th, he wrote that he wished the correspondence between him and Lloyd George to be published before Parliament assembled in Belfast on 28th. He wanted the public to know that it was not Ulster's fault that no settlement had been reached. Sinn Fein's insistence on a subordinate status for Ulster was impossible. Coming right to the point, he wanted to know "whether Sinn Fein was prepared to give allegiance to the Crown without reservation, which was one of the conditions of your invitation, or whether their consent is still withheld and made dependent on your first having procured the consent of Ulster to an All-Ireland Parliament."

Lloyd George soon had an answer to that sixty-four dollar question. From Dublin de Valera advised his team that they should submit fresh proposals, "as far as possible our final word", and recommended a modified version of the original Draft Treaty A. The drafting of a *Memorandum by the Irish Representatives* led to a heated exchange between Griffith and Childers, who thought that too many concessions had been made. Griffith apologised in the end but his rancour towards the man he thought of as a renegade Englishman was driving deep.

The Memorandum required that legislative and executive authority in Ireland should derive exclusively from the elected representatives of the Irish people. For "purposes of common concern" Ireland would associate itself with the Commonwealth, recognising the Crown "as the symbol and accepted head of the Association." This was the Chartres concept which had not been mentioned in the first set of proposals, Draft Treaty A. The "essential unity" of Ireland was a pre-requisite but the document made no mention of the Boundary Commission. On defence there were definite concessions, but it seemed to Lloyd George that in the weeks of negotiation he had come no nearer to securing full allegiance to the Crown. Ireland must come into the Empire, not hang around like a sulky adolescent son having his meals with the family but sleeping in the garden shed instead of in the fine bedroom which mother proposed to redecorate to her own good taste.

Tom Jones hastened to Hans Place, like an old and influential family retainer, and after some discussion with Griffith and Collins he professed to find phrases in the Irish document which might have been misconstrued. The British dilemma, Griffith wrote to de Valera, was that unless they could be sure that Ireland would come into the Empire they had little hope of any agreement with Craig on the Ulster question.

A meeting was arranged for next day. Pakenham is convinced that this was what Lloyd George had wanted, but the Cabinet records disclose that Lloyd George was prepared to break off negotiations but that the Irish asked for an interview. The answer would seem to be that Jones and Griffith between them held the pieces together.

Before the meeting with the Irish plenipotentiaries on November 23rd there was an embarrassed session at 10 Downing Street to discuss a circular which Colonel Wickham, Divisional Commissioner of Police in Belfast, had issued to Commissioners, County Inspectors and County Commandants. It dealt with the enrolment of "Class C" Specials, a Loyalist defence force to be formed into regular military units. The circular had fallen into Sinn Fein hands and had been published by them, and in the daily press. It emerged that the circular was unauthorised and the proposal illegal. It all stemmed from a conference at the War Office on November 7th when measures to be taken should the Truce come to an end had been discussed. The British Ministers and Macready, Tudor and Lord FitzAlan, who were also present at Downing Street, suspected that Wickham may have been given authority by certain Ulster Ministers and it was decided that Craig should publicly repudiate the document.

The meeting arranged by Tom Jones was attended by Birkenhead, Chamberlain, Lloyd George, Collins, Griffith and Barton.

Lloyd George called the Irish proposals a "complete let down." It was only Griffith's assurance that had got the Government through the vote of no confidence in the Commons and at Liverpool. Without that assurance Lloyd George would have gone to the country. He knew the distrust of the British in Ireland, but there was suspicion on both sides, and the position of the British representatives was just as difficult as that of the Irish team.

Turning to the Irish document, Lloyd George protested that there was no mention of the Ulster proposals.

"If Ulster accepts your proposal we'll accept it," Griffith answered simply. "It is not our proposal but we would accept it." Lloyd George came back to the Crown.

"To say that the King was not King for everything was to say that he was not King." This was not the position in Canada. Collins retorted that Britain put Canada up as an example and then ran away from it, as she had in the matters of trade and defence.

"If you have the Crown in the affairs of Ireland you will
188

interfere because of the propinquity of Ireland," said Griffith, who maintained that as head of the Commonwealth the role of the King would be much more significant.

Lloyd George then quarrelled with the defence facilities clause. The Irish coast must be completely at Britain's disposal. "Nothing else will do." Collins answered that Admiral Beatty had put much more reasonable demands to him. The Irish were willing to give guarantees but "freedom to take every port and harbour was another matter." Griffith thought perhaps there was a misunderstanding. Did Britain demand absolute right in peace and war?

"If you make clear what you want in peacetime, we can agree," he said.

Barton took up the trade question. Would Britain ask the same conditions of France or America as she intended to ask of Ireland? Chamberlain was exasperated by this oblique return to the Crown versus Republic issue and thought it useless to go on. Hastily Barton substituted Canada in his argument. The Prime Minister pointed out that trade questions were of vital concern to Ulster. They were making it difficult for Ulster to enter a united Parliament by consent, "and that is the only way that you will ever get them."

Collins heatedly introduced the matter of the Wickham circular, claiming that the Irish were being fooled. Lloyd George answered that Wickham had had authority from neither the British Government nor General Tudor. "I'll take Tudor's word but someone high up was behind it," Collins said darkly. He referred to the disturbances in Belfast and claimed that the Lord Mayor could end them within twenty-four hours if they wished. Chamberlain said Collins and his friends were not able to secure observance of the Truce in the South. He did not doubt their good faith but they might remember that Craig also had his difficulties.

This was Lloyd George's cue. Disturbances on both sides were imperilling the negotiations. They should get a move on. He suggested that Collins and Griffith meet Birkenhead, as before, to try to clarify the constitutional issues. Collins thought a constitutional lawyer should accompany Griffith, and he mentioned that he himself had prepared a memorandum surveying the position of the Dominions and offering suggestions, which he wanted the British to see. Birkenhead

189

agreed heartily to the idea of a lawyer, but hoped Collins
would come too. He would be very pleased to see the memorandum.

The Prime Minister dampened the atmosphere of amiability
that Birkenhead was trying to engender. He was to see Craig
next day and wanted to be able to put his Government's proposals to both North and South. Griffith said again that the
Irish delegates would agree to the Ulster proposals if Ulster
did, and Lloyd George deemed this satisfactory but insisted
that he "must have a complete agreement as to the Crown
and other fundamentals."

Next day, November 24th, Birkenhead and Sir Gordon
Hewart, England's constitutional experts, met Griffith, Collins,
Gavan Duffy and Chartres.

It was Chartres who made it quite clear that what was
meant by Association was that within Ireland the Crown
should have no significance at all. "Powers which existed in
theory might be of little account in relation to distant Dominions. They would appear much more real to the Irish people,
and in relation to Ireland ought not even in name to exist,"
was how Hewart summed up the Irish argument in an *aide-
memoire* of the same date.

There is little doubt that Griffith would have accepted the
Crown, provided that the Ulster position was satisfactory, but
his orders were to fight for external association and he argued
it with great skill. The Irish proposals he maintained, with
great reasonableness it can be seen now, would "preserve the
honour and interests of both peoples and satisfy the pride
of both."

Notes of the conversation made by Chartres, and approved
by Birkenhead and Hewart at the time, were later disputed by
the British. Quibbles over words, but these quibbles were vital
in the long run. According to Chartres, Hewart said reassuringly that the Irish delegates "must not suppose that the
British Government was contemplating the alternative of war."
And one would have expected this from Hewart. The British
sent a painstaking note to disabuse the Irish of the idea that
Hewart had nonchalantly thrown away Lloyd George's ace.
The British version ran: "The Irish delegates must not suppose that the British Government was contemplating with
equanimity the alternative, which was war." Hewart himself

had thought so little of his throwaway phrase, whatever it was, that he made no mention of any allusion to war in his own *aide-memoire*. So Lloyd George scrabbled back his ace and quietly slid it back into his sleeve where he had one or two other aces filched from the pack.

The meeting ended with the Irish promising to draft a formula expressing "the limited sense in which they were prepared to recognise the Crown", and Birkenhead and Hewart saw Chartres next day, presumably to lend some assistance. In speeches at Leicester and Tunbridge Wells respectively Hewart and Birkenhead gave some idea of the trend of the talks. That they did so was evidently part of the British campaign since their speeches are referred to in the records of the negotiations.

At the weekend the Irish plenipotentiaries returned to Dublin and the memorandum they presented on Monday, November 28th, had the authority of their Cabinet, including the difficult Brugha and Stack. The main points were that the Irish Legislature, Executive and Judiciary were to derive their power solely from the Irish people, that for matters of common concern Ireland would associate herself with the Commonwealth and that in recognition of the King's position as its head an annual sum would be voted to his personal revenue. This contribution to the royal purse had been suggested as something of a red herring by Chartres and the bones of it must have stuck in the gullets of Brugha and Stack.

In a well-argued note attached, Griffith claimed that Ireland was not being offered the same as Canada. The Crown would not be a symbol only "but will continue to possess the real power of repression and veto which Ireland knows." The nearness of Ireland to England meant, the Irish recognised, that they must concede facilities for defence purposes such as were not demanded of distant Dominions. Equally, the British should allow that her propinquity made Ireland vulnerable to interference in her affairs. Griffith had a point. Even during the Second World War, after the Statute of Westminster and the general slackening of the imperial reins between the Wars, decisions which vitally affected the Dominions were taken by the British Cabinet without reference to them.

Griffith's argument was nearly cut away when with Duggan

he met Lloyd George at Chequers. Birkenhead and Sir Robert Horne, Chancellor of the Exchequer, were also present at the talk, which endured from 10 p.m. until midnight on the night of 28th. The British invited the inclusion of any phrase which would satisfy the Irish that in practice the Crown should function exactly as in Canada or the other Dominions. As Griffith admitted in his report to de Valera, the offer had "knocked out my argument." It also represented a genuine British understanding of the Irish objection. Lloyd George also promised to try to modify the Oath, and by next morning he had drafted a new form of Oath which he had based as far as was consonant with British requirements on the United States form. It read:

"I . . . solemnly swear to bear true faith and allegiance to the Constitution of Ireland; to the Community of Nations known as the British Empire and to the King as Head of the State and of the Empire."

Griffith was given further assurances that "the Crown would function both in law and usage as in Canada", and he asked for time to consider the Oath. He suggested that if the Representative of the Crown in Ireland could be elected "it would greatly facilitate things for us." Birkenhead said that an elected Head of State and an elected Prime Minister would be embarrassing. "There is no room for two kings in Brentford," was how he put it. No, the Irish would be consulted, but the Crown Representative would be appointed, not elected. After further discussion on trade and defence initiated by Collins, Lloyd George referred to his interview with Craig on November 24th. He had promised to put the British proposals to him not later than Tuesday, December 6th, and had added: "As to what follows I do not ask you for an answer now and I do not want one. But I would beg you seriously to consider whether it may not be better for you to come into an All-Ireland Parliament than to stay outside it."

Griffith was afraid that if Ulster received the proposals at the same time as he did, the text might leak out in Ulster before the Dail Cabinet had agreed to them. Admitting the difficulty, Lloyd George said Griffith should have them unofficially on Thursday, December 1st. There were many details to be worked out, the treatment of dispossessed officials for one. Birkenhead offered that he and Collins had discussed
192

this, taking judges as an example, and Collins had promised fair treatment.

"Oh yes! There are even more disagreeable people, such as County Inspectors of Police, to be dealt with, but we quite agree that they must be treated fairly," interjected Collins.

Events were moving rapidly now. In an agreed statement to the Ulster Commons on November 29th, Craig said:

"By Tuesday next these negotiations will have broken down or the Prime Minister will send me new proposals for consideration by the Cabinet. In the meantime the rights of Ulster will be in no way sacrificed or compromised."

He emphasised that the Southern Irish had one week to give a definite answer.

On November 30th, the Articles of Agreement were redrafted, largely by the brilliant Lionel Curtis, and delivered to the Irish camp at 10 p.m. by his colleague Tom Jones, who explained that the British representatives would be available the following afternoon if any explanations were needed.

Collins and Griffith did, in fact, meet Lloyd George, asking certain explanations and objecting to some clauses. They countered Lloyd George's Oath with one of their own. It read:

"I . . . do solemnly swear to bear true faith and allegiance to the Constitution of the Irish Free State as by Law established and that I will be faithful to His Majesty King George in acknowledgement of the Association of Ireland in a common citizenship with Great Britain and the group of nations known as the British Commonwealth."

There was a desperate note in the wording, an attempt to come as nearly as possible to British requirements and at the same time to stop short of swearing allegiance to the King. The key was the ambiguous phrase "in acknowledgement of", for the British might interpret this to mean that a member of the Dail taking the Oath was swearing to be faithful to His Majesty King George (though not perhaps to his heirs and successors) in all senses *because* Ireland acknowledged common citizenship with Great Britain and the Commonwealth. But in Irish hearts the words would mean that they would be faithful to the King only in his capacity as Head of the Commonwealth.

It was neat, but Lloyd George's colleagues vetoed it at once.

Nevertheless, the Irish did win some small concessions and even on the following day, Friday, December 2nd, redrafting went on. Jones handed Childers twenty copies of the final draft, complete except for an annex on finance, which was handed to Collins as he boarded the boat train that evening.

By eleven o'clock on Saturday morning the Dail Cabinet had begun a bitter meeting that was to last for seven hours. De Valera, Brugha, Stack and Cosgrave, the stay-at-home Ministers, were joined by Griffith, Collins and Barton. The other delegates, Gavan Duffy and Duggan, and the secretary, Childers, were present for the first part of the meeting and again later in the day. So was Kevin O'Higgins, then Assistant Minister for Finance, who was soon to rise unenviably in the ranks of power.

Griffith was certain that no better bargain could now be struck. He was convinced that to break on the Crown would be to lose Ulster, but de Valera, quite rightly, could not see that Griffith had gained either point. Barton and Gavan Duffy were convinced that Lloyd George was bluffing and Barton, in particular, was sure that England would not resume the war for a quibble about the Oath. Duggan supported Griffith and, in a rather bristly way, so did Collins. Childers was coldly and meticulously opposed to the British Articles. Alluding to the way in which so much of the negotiation had been carried on by Griffith and Collins without the other plenipotentiaries, Brugha sneered that the British Government "had selected its men." But Brugha saw also that the Agreement would "split Ireland from top to bottom", and, conceding this, Griffith offered to return with the document unsigned and simply to put it to the Dail or, if necessary, to the people of Ireland. He did not like the document himself but did not think it dishonourable.

De Valera was anxious for the plenipotentiaries to return to London and get a settlement if they could, but he stubbornly reiterated his doctrine of external association. If there had to be an oath at all, then he suggested something on the lines of:

"I do solemnly swear true faith and allegiance to the Constitution of the Irish Free State to the Treaty of Association, and to recognise the King of Great Britain as Head of the Association."

194

It was, G. B. Shaw said later[7] "obviously very much better, if only as a piece of literature (and it has no other real value), than Mr Lloyd George's." But the English and the Irish went on struggling for a pattern of words which befitted the dignity of the Monarchy on the one hand and upheld the cherished ideal of a Republic on the other.

When the Irish representatives returned to London the day after their Cabinet meeting, the British heard privately of its outcome. They knew who had supported and who opposed the proposals, that the delegation itself was split. But they do not seem to have taken satisfaction from it. According to the Cabinet records, Collins was "fed up" with the dissension and sent Barton and Duffy to see if the Prime Minister could convert them. It seems a strange move on Collins's part, for he had seemed uncertain in his own mind, and it may be that it was de Valera, Brugha and Stack with whom he was really "fed up". From the beginning he had suspected that he was being made a dupe, that he was to be made the "scapegoat" for the inevitable failure to secure the Irish demands in full.

The plenipotentiaries left the Cabinet meeting in Dublin angry, divided and rather confused as to what they were to do next.

For Griffith the negotiations had become an exasperating game of snakes and ladders. His instructions, so far as can be ascertained from the exiguous notes taken by the acting secretary, Colm O'Murchadha, were to refuse the suggested Oath unless it were amended, to refuse to sign the Agreement and to inform the British that it was a matter for the Dail. The break was to come on the Ulster issue.

Griffith and his colleagues bravely began the wearisome argument again. They knew that their arguments would be rejected. Lloyd George was terse. He would have considered rewording the Oath, if that was all, but vital considerations had been rejected. "If that is your last word, your answer means war, as desired by you." However, Britain would wait to receive their proposals next morning.

"I can't understand what is your difficulty in accepting Clauses 1, 2 and 3 of our proposals," said Lloyd George.

"Our difficulty," answered Duffy, "is to come into the Empire, looking at all that has happened in the past." His

7 *Manchester Guardian* 27/12/21.

195

spontaneous words crushed the opportunity Griffiths had been angling for, not very successfully, to force the break on Ulster. The break was to come on the Crown.

"In that case it's war," snapped Lloyd George and the meeting broke up with the Irish promising to send a formal rejection.

Lloyd George did not give up. He was sure that Griffith supported the proposals and that Collins was almost won over. Twice he sent Tom Jones to get Griffith to persuade Collins to see him early next morning, December 5th. Finally, reluctantly, Collins did do. They argued the negotiations through again, even defence and trade. Collins wanted Craig's answer on whether or not the North would come into an all-Ireland Parliament and Lloyd George reminded him that Collins himself had pointed out that the North "would be forced economically to come in" after the Boundary Commission had done its work. The form of the Oath concerned Lloyd George much less than it did Collins. What he wanted was acceptance of dominion status and an oath which did not deny this, whereas Collins did not seem perturbed by the prospect of Ireland's being a Dominion in practice so long as the actual wording of the Oath did not proclaim it.

It was an inconclusive session but Collins left seeming somewhat reassured. Lloyd George, however, was "excited and angry, said the Irish had gone back on everything—allegiance naval securities, in fact all along the line".[8] according to C. P. Scott who saw the Prime Minister for a moment before Lloyd George went to see the King. But the line of communication was not yet frayed through. Some of the Irish plenipotentiaries were to meet the British again that afternoon.

At midday the British Cabinet met and Lloyd George gave a detailed resume of the negotiations and described the position reached.[9] Ireland had been offered "full Dominion status, subject to one or two modifications especially in regard to the Navy, and her position in the Empire would be the same as that of the great self-governing Dominions. In particular there would be no question of any veto by Great Britain upon purely Irish legislation."

A majority of the Irish Cabinet had rejected the terms and

[8] *C. P. Scott of the Manchester Guardian* by J. L. Hammond.
[9] Cabinet conclusion 89/21 (1) of 5/12/21.

submitted counter-proposals from which it was clear that the Irish had no intention of coming within the British Empire for certain specific purposes, or of bearing allegiance to the King. On the other hand, there had been no objection raised to the proposal regarding Ulster. Mr Arthur Griffith and Mr Michael Collins were disappointed by the rejection and Collins appeared to be not unwilling to accept the Dominion clauses. "He would have preferred an immediate decision on Ulster and he would have remitted the question of Ulster safeguards for discussions between representatives of Ulster and the rest of Ireland. Collins had been told that it would be useless to hold a plebiscite on the Agreement unless at least some of the leaders would publicly recommend acceptance.

Ministers were generally of the opinion that some effort should be made to modify the Oath, provided that the wording did not make for differences of interpretation and provided, too, the Irish accepted the first three clauses. It should be pointed out to them that acceptance would involve recognition of the King in Ireland and that, for example, all writs would run in His Majesty's name.

The Attorney-General was asked to look into the publication by *The Times* on December 3rd of the full text of the British proposals—"obviously given by someone in possession of the actual document." It had not been revealed by the Irish representatives, who had been scrupulously honest in this respect throughout the negotiations.

At 3 p.m. Griffith, Collins and Barton met Lloyd George, Chamberlain, Birkenhead and Churchill. The meeting began with Griffith taking up the Collins theme of eliciting an answer from Craig. It might make the position easier.

"But if he refused—?" asked Chamberlain.

"It would not make it worse for us," Griffiths answered, and Collins added. "It might help us even if it was a negative because it would put a stop to what is now happening in the two countries. We should have a Boundary Commission at once."

Asked whether he would accept the vital first three clauses Griffith replied that he would if Ulster were settled as well as the Oath and points on trade and defence. He was speaking for himself only.

"And you, Mr. Collins?" asked Lloyd George. Collins said

197

he would answer only when Craig replied and Lloyd George snapped that he "wished Collins had told him that earlier before the British Representatives had had to face their die-hards."

Griffith repeated that he would accept inclusion in the Empire if Ulster came in and Lloyd George reminded him that he had also accepted the alternative proposal if Ulster contracted out.

"Then in that case," said Griffith, "if you stand by the Boundary Commission, I stand by you." But he did not think it was fair to press his colleagues on this point yet. Collins and Barton, knowing nothing of the document so casually initialled by Griffith on November 12th, were puzzled and Collins persisted in demanding a reply from Craig. But Lloyd George claimed that he had promised to send Craig Sinn Fein's answer that night. The issue now was peace or war. Would the delegation as a whole accept the Ulster solution?

"I thought I'd made the position clear," said Collins. "You have our conditional agreement on the one side. It is just as easy to get Craig's conditional agreement on the other."

Griffith asked that the question be put to Craig: "If Sinn Fein accepts the Government conditions for the creation of the Irish Free State will Ulster accept unity?"

This was no good, Lloyd George said. Griffith had agreed to the alternative proposed, "and now you put a totally different one to us. If you say now that you are not going to accept the preliminary conditions, which to us are fundamental, we are not going to put the rest to Ulster."

Dramatically he produced the initialled document, made at Sir Philip Sassoon's home on November 12th, which Griffith had thought no more than confirmed his promise not to repudiate the British proposal during the Unionist Conference at Liverpool but which, apparently quite genuinely, Lloyd George had believed conveyed a final promise. Now, cannily, he accused Griffith, that man of honour, of going back on his word. It was too much for Griffith.

"I said I would not let you down on that and I won't," he said. It had been a close squeak for Lloyd George, for the document had been delivered to him only after a search of his wardrobe. He had carelessly tucked it away in a pocket until the moment when he realised either its significance as a weapon
198

or the necessity to remind Griffith of a promise he honestly believed he had given. It was probably the latter. Devious though Lloyd George was, it must be remembered that he had told Chamberlain, at the time, of Griffith's agreement not to let him down on this issue. Even so, the astute Lloyd George must have realised the likelihood of a misunderstanding between them. There was certainly no reason why peace or war should have depended upon an answer being dispatched to Craig that night, or why Craig's answer to Griffith's question should not first be sought.

The British representatives retired for a consultation and Birkenhead was asked to "return and find out exactly, without argument, what the Irish delegates wished to secure in respect of the oath and the naval and trade proposals."

When Lloyd George returned to the conference room with his colleagues he said simply, "Let's take the three points, first the Oath." Birkenhead read a draft Oath handed to Lloyd George by Collins that morning and his own alternative. The Oath, as it was incorporated in the Treaty, read:

"I . . . do solemnly swear true faith and allegiance to the Constitution of the Irish Free State as by law established, and that I will be faithful to H.M. King George V, his heirs and successors by law, in virtue of the common citizenship of Ireland with Great Britain and her adherence to and membership of the group of nations forming the British Commonwealth of Nations."

That Oath had, in fact, been passed by the Cabinet at their midday meeting, with the exception that "forming the British Commonwealth of Nations," had replaced "known as the British Commonwealth" in the final text.

The formula was a near relative of the rather desperately worded Oath submitted by Collins and Griffith the previous week. Now "in virtue of" replaced "in acknowledgment of" as the key phrase which might allow Irishmen to believe that their allegiance was not given as subjects of the King but only as a respectful acknowledgment of their position as associates of the Commonwealth.

Defence came up and Churchill was unexpectedly accommodating, conceding points to which he had clung only an hour before. The Irish won more points on trade and the British agreed that Ulster should give her decision, for or against union with the South, within one calendar month of the passing of the Act. There were minor changes. Again the British retired.

"We have gone through this document and met you fairly," said Lloyd George when he returned. "Are you now prepared to stand by this Agreement whichever choice Ulster makes?" Griffith agreed. But his was a lone voice.

Lloyd George exerted pressure: "Is it a bargain between Sinn Fein and the British Government? I have to communicate with Sir James Craig tonight. Here are the alternative letters which I have prepared, one enclosing the Articles of Agreement reached by His Majesty's Government and yourselves, the other telling Sir James Craig that the Sinn Fein representatives refuse allegiance and refuse to come within the Empire, and that I have therefore no proposals to make to him. If I send this letter it is war—and war within three days. Which of the two letters am I to send? That is the question you have to decide."

To this piece of theatre Griffith replied quietly that he understood that the proposals were to be put before Parliament as soon as possible and that steps would be taken to set up the Provisional Government and evacuate British troops as soon as both Parliaments had ratified the Agreement. "On that understanding," he said, "I will call the Dail within a week and do my best to get the Agreement ratified. But this is my personal pledge only." This was not good enough for Lloyd George. He was willing to risk the fate of his Government on the issue and the Irish delegates must decide whether they would all accept the obligation. On their answer, he reminded them, hinged peace or war.

At 7.15 the Irish withdrew. They were to return with their decision at 10 p.m. At 9 p.m. the amended Articles were delivered to Hans Place where a titanic struggle was raging. Collins's mind had snapped to a decision in favour of signing almost as soon as he had left Lloyd George. Childers argued for rejection with deep-grained bitterness, but first Duggan, then Barton and finally Gavan Duffy decided to sign. What overcame them was the thought of plunging their country into renewed war. There was always the possibility that the British Prime Minister was bluffing. In fact he was not. Months later, when it seemed possible that a Republic would be proclaimed in Ireland, he was determined to crush it by armed intervention. Lloyd George's dramatic deadline for notifying Craig was a nonsense. He was not afraid of Craig and, had it suited his own book, would have kept him waiting for years. This was a mere ploy, the object of which was to bundle the Irish through the door once he had got it half open. The negotiations had dragged on too long. The Irish had to be made to run or they would jog along forever. Moreover, it was doubtful if Lloyd George's uneasy Government could survive either failure or prevarication and there were other fearsome obstacles apart from Ireland in the pathway of power. Lloyd George master-minded the long, drawn-out conference with enormous skill and shrewdness but his powerful team contributed much, meeting a score of times during the negotiations to chart their course.

They offered now a political bargain which was practically mean but generous in the context of centuries of misrule and generous coming from men in whose bones the very marrow was steeped in colonialism.

And the Irish accepted it. They forgot their instructions not to sign without consultation with Dublin; they forgot even the telephone and they signed.

At 11.15 p.m. Griffith, Collins and Barton called at 10 Downing Street and discussed the position with Lloyd George, Chamberlain, Birkenhead and Churchill. They suggested minor amendments and Lloyd George asked them whether, if these were accepted, "they would sign as a delegation and recommend the Agreement with their united strength to the Dail."

Griffith agreed.

"Then we accept," said Lloyd George.

At 2.10 a.m. on December 6th, 1921, the Articles of Agreement, newly retyped, were signed and Craig's copy put into the hands of the waiting courier, Mr. Geoffrey Shakespeare, (later Sir Geoffrey) who could not understand then, and never understood afterwards, what all the hurry was about.

The British Cabinet met in a mood of self-congratulation on December 6th, "one of the greatest days in the history of the British Empire",[10] Lloyd George told his colleagues. The settlement "would enormously increase Great Britain's pres-

[10] Cabinet conclusion 90/21 (1) of 6/12/21.

tige in the world and would show that she was still capable of overcoming almost insuperable difficulties". Those difficulties had included the reluctance of the Irish extremists to swear allegiance to the King and to repudiate an Irish Republic.

It is difficult to see how Lloyd George could have imagined that the Irish had repudiated their Republic. Under duress the plenipotentiaries had accepted postponement, no more. In fact, the British were as far from understanding Irish psychology as they had ever been.

"For the first time in the history of Ireland the extremists had accepted a situation in which it was open to Ulster to contract out of a United Ireland." This was the tenor of Lloyd George's self-laudatory assertion to his Cabinet. But he forgot that the situation had been accepted only because he had suggested that once the Boundary Commission had done its work, what remained of the Six Counties would not be a viable entity. Indeed, he told his Cabinet that "it had been represented that a Boundary Commission would possibly give Ulster more than she would lose."

Robert Barton had maintained that the Irish plenipotentiaries could have held out for a less exacting oath of allegiance than they finally accepted. His fellows believed that the British would not relent any further. Yet Lloyd George was able to inform his colleagues that "the terms of the Oath to be taken by members of the Parliament of the Irish Free State are remarkable and are better in many respects than the terms of the Oath of Allegiance ordinarily required in Great Britain." So Barton was right. The British had got the better of the haggling, had not yielded the last two pence of the ultimate price. That may have been a source of satisfaction to Lloyd George but the difference might have been sufficient to prevent a civil war in Ireland. "A just and righteous settlement of the Irish question," he called it, but is any settlement righteous which exacts a surrender on a vital principle beyond that which is necessary?

Lloyd George thanked his Ministers for their support and Lord Curzon replied that the settlement "represented an astonishing victory for the Empire which would have incalculable effects throughout the whole world and in particular would remove a dark cloud which had hung for years over Great Britain's relations with the United States of America."

Beneath the fatty tissue of righteousness the imperial heart of Britain beat strong.

There was a fly in the ointment of success, the Cabinet saw. This was that criticism could be expected, "on the lines that the settlement now effected might equally have been reached some time before."[11]

The answer to that was that "a year ago Sinn Fein would not have entertained, or even agreed to discuss, proposals similar to those which the Irish Representatives had now signed." Conveniently the Cabinet overlooked the fact that they had insisted upon a surrender of arms as a pre-requisite condition a year previously and that the Truce had come about only because they had realised that that condition was impossible. Now they convinced themselves that "the attitude of Sinn Fein was mainly attributable to the rough treatment to which the Irish extremists had been subjected during the last twelve months, and which had brought home to the men in the field the need for some equitable compromise."

Success, in the mind of Lloyd George, had stemmed from the employment of the Black and Tans, and he congratulated Greenwood "on the able and courageous manner in which he had throughout discharged the very difficult and disagreeable duties entrusted to him." He added that "but for the way in which the decisions of the Cabinet had been enforced by the Irish Executive, and particularly by the Chief Secretary, the present settlement would never have come about." Any self-respecting Irishman hearing those words would have torn up the Articles of Agreement which, in response to a request from the Irish representatives, the Cabinet now agreed might be described as a Treaty.[12]

As evidence of British good faith it was agreed by the Cabinet to summon Parliament for the sole purpose of ratifying the Articles of Agreement, for which action an unhappy precedent had been set at the time of the Union. The State opening of Parliament was to be made as impressive as possible with companies from all the Regiments of Guards and massed bands to be stationed in the neighbourhood of the Houses of Parliament.

On December 7th, the Cabinet considered "strong represen-

11 Cabinet conclusion 90/21 (5) of 6/12/21.
12 Cabinet conclusion 90/21 (7) of 6/12/21.

tations" from the Irish delegates for the immediate release of internees.[18] This, rather than an impressive State opening, was likely to secure acceptance of the Treaty by Dail Eireann. Macready, who was present, readily agreed to the release of 4,000 internees. He admitted that conditions in the camps were unsatisfactory, though he blamed the internees themselves for much of the trouble. It was decided to advise the King to act at once as "it would be more difficult for the Irish Parliament to reject the Articles of Agreement if the internees had been released as an act of clemency immediately after the signature of those Articles." The question of convicted Irish prisoners, as distinct from men held without trial, was put back pending the negotiation of a mutual amnesty.

Assuming that Dail Eireann accepted the Treaty, the next problem would be the financing of the Provisional Government. If Crown Colony Government were set up with Sinn Fein leaders nominated as rulers no special financial arrangement would be required, but this would involve the dissolution of the Southern Parliament, which could be carried out only with the assent of Sinn Fein. The alternative was to set up and finance an administration "on an admittedly irregular basis".[14]

A Cabinet sub-committee appointed to examine the problem reported[15] that two matters should be dealt with urgently, "presumably by legislation". An Act of Indemnity would be required to protect "those persons who had been engaged in operating Martial Law in Ireland". That was the first thing. The second stemmed from Article 17 of the Treaty, the establishment of a provisional Government in Ireland. This, the sub-committee thought, could operate only through the machinery of the 1920 Act, "but this would involve the taking of the Oath of Allegiance by Irish Ministers in the usual form, a form to which the Irish delegates had objected". Unless the machinery of the 1920 Act were used, the Irish Government would be bound by the appropriations of the British Parliament, able to collect only such taxes as had been imposed by Westminster and to spend the proceeds only as directed by them. "They would thus lose all popular support in Ireland," concluded the sub-committee with great prescience.

[18] Cabinet conclusion 91/21 (1) of 7/12/21.
[14] Cabinet conclusion 91/21 (5) of 7/12/21.
[15] Cabinet conclusion 92/21 (3) of 12/12/21.

204

There were strong objections to introducing any legislation other than required for the ratification of the Articles of Agreement. The Lord Chancellor arrived at this point and agreed that only the two courses were open—legislation or the Act of 1920. Strict interpretation of Section 72 of the Act would mean that members of the Provisional Government would have to be appointed Privy Councillors and take the Oath.

Here was a pretty pass, but Birkenhead was equal to the occasion. Inspiration led him to the loophole. "It would be possible to hold," he suggested, "that, in view of the ratification of the Articles of Agreement by the British Parliament, Section 72 of the Government of Ireland Act, 1920, must be construed in the light of the Articles of Agreement and the provisions of the Act must be interpreted in conformity with the provisions of that Agreement."

Birkenhead thought that although it would take at least a month to establish the Provisional Government, the spirit of the Agreement would be upheld if discussions on the transfer of powers were to begin at once. And he thought that with the goodwill of the Sinn Fein leaders existing arrangements for the government of Ireland could continue for six weeks. The Cabinet gladly accepted Birkenhead's proposals.

The problem of the Act of Indemnity was trickier. "It was desirable to observe the uniform practice which had prevailed whenever a state of martial law had been abrogated,"[16] not only to protect soldiers and others whose actions in Ireland might, apart from the existence of a state of martial law, land them in civil courts, "but by reason of the necessity from time to time of declaring martial law in different parts of the Empire." Two factors perturbed the Cabinet: Sinn Fein would demand that such an Act of Indemnity should be accompanied by an Act of Amnesty for all prisoners; and, secondly, "the critics of the policy of the Government in Ireland during the last year in its efforts to maintain law and order would undoubtedly oppose the passage of an Act of Indemnity and legislation could not be secured without some expenditure of Parliamentary time." Finally, it was agreed that Lloyd George should inform the Commons, and Curzon the Lords, that an Act of Indemnity would be introduced as soon as possible.

[16] Cabinet conclusion 92/21 (4) 12/12/21.

The saving factor was that although the position of some people remained insecure, the legal vacation prevented their being hauled into the civil courts. Disbandment of the 7,000 Black and Tans would go ahead, with the British Government accepting the responsibility for compensation and pensions. The 6,000 original members of the Royal Irish Constabulary were to be left to the Free State to deal with but they wanted to be disbanded on the same terms as their temporary colleagues.

Meanwhile, the Committee on the State Opening of Parliament had gone thoroughly into the arrangements. They dropped the idea that massed bands should head the King's procession. It was not appropriate for dismounted bands to head a mounted procession and, anyway, they would drown the cheers of the crowd. Instead they should go ahead "and take up a position at the Victoria Tower, where the bands should be able to play in unison."

While the British Cabinet tranquilly sought constitutional loopholes and disposed prancing horses and beating drums, the Dail Cabinet were locked like fighting scorpions in an acrimonious struggle.

ELEVEN

De Valera had received the Treaty with sour disappointment and was incensed by the failure of the plenipotentiaries to consult him before they signed. Was he perhaps piqued that he had had no opportunity to step in at the last minute as "an honest broker"—as one distinguished Irishman put it to me? The plenipotentiaries had achieved far, far more than de Valera himself had managed to prise from Lloyd George, but they had disregarded instructions. On the other hand, de Valera had made it clear that they *were* plenipotentiaries, so that there was some excuse for confusion.

Ireland was not yet committed; the Dail had to approve the action of the plenipotentiaries; Griffith, Collins and their fellows had done nothing irrevocable. Nevertheless, the fact that they had signed the instrument was a powerful lever. Some wanted them arraigned for treason at once. It was
206

Cosgrave who insisted that the Cabinet listen to the defence and it was his vote which, with those of Griffith, Collins and Barton, the Treaty signatories, on December 8th gained a majority for the Treaty within the Cabinet. Brugha and Stack inevitably sided with de Valera whose next and very unusual move was to write a letter to the press in which starkly he revealed the dissession. "The terms of the agreement are in violent conflict with the wishes of the majority of the Nation as expressed freely in successive elections during the last three years," wrote de Valera, adding that he could not recommend acceptance of the Treaty either to Dail Eireann or the country and that the Ministers of Home Affairs (Stack) and Defence (Brugha) supported him. He exhorted the people to face the crisis without bitterness or recrimination, stated reassuringly, "There is a definite constitutional way of resolving our political differences," and concluded, without evident intention of irony, "Let the conduct of the Cabinet in this matter be an example to the whole nation."

News of the Treaty had brought to the majority of the people of Ireland immeasurable joy and relief. With the Truce had come an end to the terror. People slept the night through without fear. There was no thunderous knock on the door, no leaping blaze at the window, no sudden shatter of shots in the night air. The priest no longer called with news of tragedy and words of consolation. Loved ones were coming home. The Treaty seemed to give permanence to their new-found tranquillity. No hardship of the past was regretted, no life lost grudged, but surely, surely the era of sacrifice was done. It was rash of de Valera to claim that the Treaty was in violent conflict with the wishes of the majority. Sinn Fein had carried all before them in the elections of the past three years and it was quite true that Sinn Fein had stood for the Republic and, in that sense, the people had voted for a Republic. But what they wanted above all else was freedom from British misrule and this they had won in a degree they had never imagined possible. The majority were not doctrinaire republicans. Neither, de Valera claimed, was he. Now there was a chance to rebuild Ireland. Ordinary Irish folk did not mind about the King, not enough to relinquish what had been won. Then there were those whose livelihood depended on trade. For them war was ruination and for them, too, the British connection

207

was no bad thing. And there were the realists who wanted to make the most of the freedom won and to allow the Republic to evolve.

For some it was not enough. Some of the more extreme, those men whose ideals would not bend to any wind, seemed to want, not the condition of freedom, but a perennial struggle for freedom. Neither Griffith nor Collins had any affection for England, and of all the Irish leaders Collins was the last who might have been expected to settle for less than a Republic, but they knew that wars that do not end in settlement end in total destruction. In their months of close negotiation with the British delegates they had recognised a genuine desire, which was limited only by certain material concerns, to give Ireland a future of her own. It was not easy for the emotional Collins to unshackle himself from the glorious melancholy of the past, but his huge energy, his vision and the quality of leadership tempered by its contact with sophisticated men of government drove him forward.

He was supported by men like Mulcahy, McEoin, Dalton and Brennan, who had not suddenly become tools of the old enemy, England, but simply made a shrewd appraisal of what had been gained and what could easily be lost. De Valera had taken no part in the negotiations and was guided by his mistrust of Lloyd George. Collins and Griffith knew that they had encountered honesty and even generosity in Birkenhead and Austen Chamberlain, even in Churchill. Lloyd George himself, as can be seen from Cabinet records, was by no means without sympathy for the Irish and certainly did not intend that the Irish Free State should have any less power than the terms of the Treaty conferred. De Valera's fears that Lloyd George rather than King George would stand at Ireland's head were unjustified. The Dail President, too, never really understood what had happened in Ireland or saw at first hand what the people suffered during the worst of the terror. Even in his own constituency the people favoured the Treaty. General Brennan, who was then Chairman of Clare County Council, was able to assure Collins of the Council's support. One Councillor had referred to de Valera's attitude in these words; "It is not that I love Caesar less but that I love Rome more."

De Valera never found it easy to make up his own mind and was greatly influenced by Childers who was knowledgeable, shrewd and afire with Ireland's cause but warped a little by his American wife's hatred of imperialist England and over-fervent in the way of the proselyte. At de Valera's side constantly during the absence of the plenipotentiaries in England, Stack and Brugha had been passionately insistent upon an all-or-nothing end. Cathal Brugha had the fanatic zeal of the true revolutionary, but ultimately government must follow the overthrow of government and Brugha's fibre was too unresilient to accept the relaxation of tension. Stack had wearied through the long struggle and both Brugha and he were prejudiced against Collins. This may or may not have influenced their judgment. Unhappily, in the following months personal friendships and enmities did affect the decisions that men made.

What happened to the Treaty now would rest with the Dail, which was to meet on Wednesday, December 14th. Aghast at the prospect of a schism, de Valera was already working desperately to find the link which would unite the two factions. If it could be put to the British Government that the Treaty as it stood was not acceptable to the Dail but that a slightly modified version would have a favourable reception, then perhaps the British would see the alternative as a reasonable and workable compromise.

At 11.30 a.m. on December 14th, the Speaker, Dr Eoin MacNeill, took the Chair in the Council Chamber of University College Dublin and the Clerk to the Dail, Diarmuid O'Hegarty, called the roll of Deputies; prayers were said by the Rev Dr Browne.

De Valera began the debate by insisting that the Dail consider the Treaty on its merits without allowing "extraneous matters such as what I might call an accidental division of opinion of the Cabinet, or the causes which gave rise to it", to influence them. Differences of opinion he admitted were inevitable. His quarrel with the plenipotentiaries was that they had signed the Treaty without submitting the final text to Dublin. Griffith denied that the delegation had exceeded their instructions and de Valera answered that they had not carried out their instructions. What the plenipotentiaries had done, Collins argued, was simply to sign on the understanding that each signatory would recommend the instrument to the Dail. They had not committed the Dail. In any case he wanted

209

the Treaty to be put side by side with the Cabinet's own final document.

A bitter little argument followed concerning whether or not the credentials given the plenipotentiaries from "the elected Government of the Republic of Ireland" had been presented to, and accepted by, the British—which would have implied recognition of the Republic—and whether, too, Collins was claiming that the authority to "conclude" a Treaty was final and involved no ratification by the Dail. Griffith said shortly that the British Ministers "did not sign the Treaty to bind their nation. They had to go to their Parliament and we to ours for ratification."

Already a great deal of personal spite had been engendered, already the Dail had split into those who were defending and those who were attacking, not only the Treaty, but the men who had signed it. Vituperation and spite, rather than logic and detachment, were to characterise the debate; but beneath the sour skin was genuine fear that much that had been fought for was about to be lost. There were to be long days of talk but no one foresaw them then. After much argument, a private session of the Dail was agreed upon. De Valera suggested that points of difference might be disposed of in an hour, and that next morning the question of ratification should be resolved at a public session.

De Valera must have been confident that the solution he planned to put at the secret session would be joyfully acclaimed by all. His alternative Treaty was essentially a return to the old idea of external association, but painstakingly he had followed the text of the Treaty as far as possible. There was no oath, no provision for a Governor-General; instead he harked back to the formula contained in the memorandum which the plenipotentiaries had presented to the British on November 28th, "that the legislative, executive and judicial authority of Ireland shall be derived solely from the people of Ireland", but "that for purposes of common concern, Ireland shall be associated with the States of the British Commonwealth."

Griffith had argued at that time that Ireland was not, in fact, being offered the same status as Canada, that the Crown would interfere in Irish affairs, and the British had countered by inviting the Irish to include any phrase which they thought
210

necessary to ensure that they were as well-safeguarded as was Canada. That the Irish had cause for apprehension was appreciated and the British had been ready to bar themselves from meddling. But they had made it plain that Ireland should belong to the Empire or the war would go on, and de Valera must have known as well as Griffith that to offer to the British the formula he put forward now, in what was to become known as Document No. 2, was like offering a three-legged donkey instead of the normal quadruped already promised in sale. Griffith's attitude was that the three-legged animal had already been offered and declined and all that remained was to confirm the transaction entered into or to renounce it altogether.

De Valera did not win a majority for his proposal. Some of the deputies were rather puzzled anyway by the animal and could not be sure whether it had three legs or four, one of them a little short. Though Brugha enthusiastically likened his chief to an experienced skipper taking over the helm from incompetent amateurs (who would have been very happy if he had never handed over the helm in the first place), many of those who opposed the Treaty could not see that de Valera's proposal was very different. It seemed to them that Document No. 2 provided for Ireland to be half in and half out of the Empire, whereas they wanted no connection. Those who supported the Treaty could not see that de Valera's document was any more than a quibble. It was a compromise, just as the Treaty was a compromise; it did not provide for a republic and nothing but a republic. Indeed, it weakened the Irish position because it voluntarily surrendered what the plenipotentiaries had surrendered under duress.

Far from disposing of the points of difference in an hour, the private session accomplished nothing in two snarling days. Then the weekend intervened and the Dail resumed in public session on Monday, December 19th.

De Valera insisted that his Document No. 2 was now withdrawn and was not for public discussion. He had put it forward "for a distinct purpose, to see whether we could get a unanimous proposition by this House." Griffith and Collins protested: De Valera had publicly denounced the Treaty yet he was not prepared to let the people see his alternative, his hairsplitting compromise. The President laboured to explain his viewpoint. The document "would cease to be of value" unless it commanded practically unanimous approval.

Moving the motion standing in his name, "that Dail Eireann approves of the Treaty between Great Britain and Ireland, signed in London on December 6th, 1921", Griffith stated that while as far as possible he would respect President de Valera's wish, he was "not going to hide from the Irish people what the alternative is that is proposed."

The task given the plenipotentiaries, Griffith said, was "as hard as was ever placed on the shoulders of men." They had not sought the responsibility but had accepted it when others declined to do so, and they did not shirk the responsibility now. The Treaty was not ideal but it was honourable to Ireland and safeguarded her vital interests.

"And now by that Treaty I am going to stand," he asseverated, "and every man with a scrap of honour who signed it is going to stand. It is for the Irish people—who are our masters, not our servants as some think—it is for the Irish people to say whether it is good enough."

He referred to the effort made outside to represent that some "stood uncompromisingly on the rock of the Republic" but that Collins, "the man who won the war", had "compromised Ireland's rights". In the correspondence prior to negotiations not one demand had been made for the recognition of the Irish Republic. The difference in the Cabinet and in the Dail was between "half recognising the British King and the British Empire and marching in, as one of the speakers put it, with our heads up." It was a quibble, and "so far as my power or voice extends not one young Irishman's life shall be lost on that quibble".

Griffith went on that this was the first Treaty between the Irish and English Governments signed on an equal footing since 1172. It meant the recognition of *Saorstat na hEireann*— the Free State of Ireland. After 700 years British occupation would cease. Ireland would have her own flag, her own army, fiscal control and a voice in the direction of foreign affairs equal to that of the other Dominions. The British had pledged their word before the world; they had ratified the Treaty. As for the Oath, it was one "that any Irishman could take with honour".

If the Irish people were to say, "We have got everything else

212

but the name Republic, and we will fight for it," Griffith would tell them they were fools but he would follow in their ranks. But he did not believe that the Irish people would reject the Treaty. Griffith had always taken as his guide Thomas Davis, a "Young Irelander" who died at an early age in 1845. Davis had said: "Peace with England, alliance with England to some extent, and, under certain circumstances, confederation with England; but an Irish ambition, Irish hopes, strength, virtue, and rewards for the Irish."

Griffith believed that the plenipotentiaries had fulfilled these precepts.

Sean McEoin seconded Griffith. The Irish people wanted "not shadows but substances" and he believed that the Treaty gave substance. "As long as the armed forces of Britain are gone and the armed forces of Ireland remain," he said, "we can develop our own nation in our own way." He believed that the Treaty brought the freedom to do that, the freedom for which they had all been ready to die.

In a long passage of bleak sincerity de Valera refuted Griffith and McEoin. The Treaty would not end the centuries of conflict, he maintained. Because " a war-weary people will take things which are not in accordance with their aspirations", the Treaty party might get a vote from the people now, but the contest would be renewed in time. "I am as anxious as anyone for the material prosperity of Ireland and the Irish people," claimed de Valera, "but I cannot do anything that would make the Irish people hang their heads." The crux of his argument was that they had been elected "to be the guardians of an independent Irish State" and that they could not therefore vote away that independence.

He was supported by Austin Stack, who professed not to be able to understand the Dominion clauses of the Treaty and saw no relevance in them anyway. Whether Ireland was to have the same status as Canada and the other Dominions was beside the point, he said. Naturally those other countries had an affection for England, their mother land. "This country, on the other hand, has not been a child of England's, nor never was." England had come as an invader to Ireland, and therefore Stack stood "for what is Ireland's right, full independence and nothing short of it."

Stack was right. England had come as an invader and she

had imposed a privileged people, the Ascendancy, on Irish lands, just as at a later date she had done in India and elsewhere. Ideally, British statesmen should have recognised this, should have seen that they had no right to dictate that Ireland should have this government or that, that Ireland must belong willy-nilly to the British Empire. Unhappily, in the making of history realities have always counted. They have been softened and modified by the ideal, but they have never coincided with it. Boundaries have always been fashioned by conquest, and throughout the eighteenth and nineteenth centuries nations had contended for possessions and power. Colonialism was not to become a dirty word for another half century. Britain, too, had self-interests to consider, had only just survived a massive contest in Europe and was very conscious that Ireland was a soft under-belly vulnerable to attack. Stack was right, but unrealistic in a way that de Valera. was not. For the Dail President understood Britain's dilemma as well as he understood the simple sentiments of men like Stack, and quibbled about words only because he sought a formula which would not radically change material conditions but which would satisfy both sides that their interests were being met.

Taking up the cudgels on behalf of himself and his colleagues, Collins read the final exchange of telegrams between Lloyd George and de Valera prior to the negotiations, and pointed out that "if we all stood on the recognition of the Irish Republic as a prelude to any conference we could very easily have said so, and there would be no conference." What Collins wanted to emphasise was that "it was the acceptance of the invitation that formed the compromise", that by entering into negotiations at all de Valera had acknowledged that a Republic was out of the question. In Collins's opinion the Treaty "gives us freedom, not the ultimate freedom that all nations desire and develop to, but the freedom to achieve it".

There, in essence, was the argument which was to be called the "stepping-stones to the Republic" thesis.

Collins asserted that he would make the same decision again in the same circumstances, reminding the Dail that the plenipotentiaries had not been "in the position of conquerors dictating terms of peace to a vanquished foe. We had not beaten the enemy out of our country by force of arms." He declared that few people, even supporters of the Treaty, really understood it and appreciated "the immense powers and liberties it secures". If the Dail rejected the Treaty his responsibility was at an end, but he believed that it was up to him to put the position clearly to the nation. As he saw it, England's long occupation of Ireland had not been "a struggle for the ideal of freedom for 750 years symbolised in the name Republic", but a story of "slow, steady economic encroach by England".

Political freedom had been essential to stop this chronic exploitation. "Our aspirations," said Collins, "by whatever term they may be symbolised, had one thing in front all the time, that was to rid the country of the enemy strength." It must have been a shattering blow to the die-hard Republicans to hear no less a person than Michael Collins, the inspirational force of the Revolution, admitting that the Republic was a symbol only, a resistance device. For him the departure of British forces was "the chief proof that our national liberties are established." If the Treaty did not recognise the Republic, at least Great Britain had given Ireland "more recognition than we have got from any other nation". America had not recognised the Republic, Collins reminded the Dail, slyly perhaps recalling that in almost two years in America de Valera had failed to persuade either Republicans or Democrats to recognise the Republic of Ireland.

Collins elaborated on the theme of England's "economic penetration". "Nobody notices, but that is the thing that has destroyed our Gaelic civilisation." This could be stopped and they should be thinking of organising the nation. "Are we never going to stand on our own feet?" he asked. This was a new Collins. As Minister of Finance he had done well and it would seem that he was seeking now to put militancy behind him, to make the most of what had been won and with liberty and control of Ireland's own affairs, including the purse-strings, to build up a new and self-sufficient country in which Gaelic civilisation might revive and thrive. If this could be achieved did it really matter that the country was named the Irish Free State and not the Republic of Ireland? Even that might come once the country was strong, self-reliant and confident. It would seem that the statesman was taking over from the revolutionary.

Collins was bringing his formidable weight to bear in the open chamber of the Dail, but he had already cut an enormous chunk of ground from beneath Republican feet by convincing the Supreme Council of the Irish Republican Brotherhood, of which he was President, that Ireland's future was locked in the Treaty. On December 10th, only four days after the signing of the Treaty and four days before the Dail assembled to debate it, Liam Lynch alone held out against him at a tense meeting of the Supreme Council. Lynch and McEoin almost came to blows. Two days later, division and country centres received a directive from the Supreme Council. It had been decided that the Peace Treaty should be ratified, but members of the organisation who had to take public action as representatives were given freedom of action. This meant that Dail deputies who belonged to the Brotherhood were permitted to vote as they thought fit; all other members—including Liam Lynch, who was not a deputy—were expected to obey the edict.

This was a powerful lever, though not quite as powerful as once it might have been. Many, on both sides, had little time for secret societies and now, with the country on the edge of free, democratic government, saw even less justification for the continued existence of the Brotherhood. De Valera and Brugha had long since left the movement. Soon after the Dail first met, in 1919, and declared Ireland an independent Republic, Dan Breen urged that the revolutionary movement should be entirely open. "But," he says, "the argument put forward by Collins and the other people was that if they allowed the politicians to take over and didn't keep the I.R.B. in control, when negotiations came they would surrender the Republic. 'Well,' I said, 'I don't think the I.R.B. will stand up to it any more than the politicians because as far as I can see all the I.R.B. men are already semi-politicians.'"

Perhaps Breen was right, but then the I.R.B. had been from the beginning a political movement. In the course of time Breen was to become a politician himself, though his heart was not in it.

One other point Collins made in his speech to the Dail, and

216

it was an important one in the light of future events. He asked, "What was the use of talking big phrases about not agreeing to the partition of our country?" and went on, "Surely we recognise that the North-east corner does exist, and surely our intention was that we should take such steps as would sooner or later lead to mutual understanding." The arrangement made under the Treaty was not ideal, he said, "but if our policy is, as has been stated, a policy of non-coercion, then let somebody else get a better way out of it."

Erskine Childers rose and complimented Collins on a "manly, eloquent and worthy" speech. The erstwhile secretary to the delegation then put to the Dail the arguments he had insisted upon so stubbornly at Hans Place. He went at once to what he believed was the heart of the problem, "the question whether Dail Eireann, the national assembly of the people of Ireland, having declared its independence, shall approve of and ratify a Treaty relinquishing deliberately and abandoning that independence". There had never been any question of the plenipotentiaries attempting to secure an isolated republic without any ties elsewhere. They were, indeed, to find some form of association which was acceptable to England and honourable to the Irish nation. But they had, at the last minute, abandoned the proposals which would have required the independence of the country and the exclusion of the English King, and only then allowed of the entry of Ireland into a free and honourable association with Britain. He denied that the Treaty gave true dominion status anyway, shaking his head over the very fact of Ireland's geographical proximity to Great Britain, which had led already to the cession of defence facilities to England and would lead, when England's interests dictated, to endless interference and the limitation of Ireland's freedom and powers. He struck at the emotions of his listeners. Under what title would Ireland hold her position under the Treaty? He answered himself "that the constitution of Ireland and the relation of Ireland to England are going to depend, so far as Ireland is concerned, on the Act of a British Parliament". And, he wanted to know, "What does this assembly think of that?" It was a strange question from a man who had once been a clerk in the House of Commons that he so despised.

"Don't you see every act and deed of the Irish Parliament

is going to be jealously watched from over the water," he cried, "and that every act of legislation done by Ireland will be read in the light of that inflexible condition that Ireland is virtually a protectorate of England, for under this Treaty she is nothing more."

Everything that could have been said had now been said. The old arguments had been spread out with all their frayed edges. Beside them lay the workaday serge of the Treaty, while de Valera's patchwork Document No. 2 was bundled up under the counter. Nothing new was left but, like exasperated cats in a tangle of twine, the deputies worried at the stale phrases in the hope of shaking them into some overlooked permutation for peace.

Kevin O'Higgins put the case with the lucidity which was soon to stamp him as a man of unusual qualities. He reminded the Dail that the British had made last minute concessions, not to be brought back to Dublin for consideration but as the price of signature. The plenipotentiaries had decided that they should sign but the Dail was free, as the House of Commons also was free, to reject the document.

"We would all desire better terms," he said, "and what we have to decide is whether we are going to take our chance of securing them if we repect these." Deputy Childers had taken "a lot of unnecessary time and trouble in explaining how much nicer it would be to get better terms than these. He did not tell us, as an authority on military and naval matters, how we are going to break the British Army and Navy, and get these better terms." (Childers in his time had served in the Honourable Artillery Company, the Royal Navy and the Royal Flying Corps.)

O'Higgins went on that "a sovereign and independent Republic was our claim and our fighting ground". They would have been fools to fight for less than their full rights. "But," he emphasised, "the fact that we were willing to negotiate implied that we had something to give away." He brought up the question of external association, referring to someone's simile of the limpet and the rock. "Ireland would be outside and attached, not inside and absorbed." But he clashed with de Valera, who protested that he was making Cabinet discussion public, when he tried to put it that the choice was not between the Treaty and a sovereign Irish Republic but a much
218

narrower choice between the terms of the Treaty and those which constituted Document No. 2—which de Valera was still not prepared to make public. Cleverly he dealt with the Oath. Allegiance to the Constitution of the Irish Free State was the first thing, then came faith to the King of England. Faith was not quite the same thing as allegiance; it implied mutuality, reciprocity between equals. Childers had waved aside the clause that the relationship with the Crown and Imperial Parliament should be governed by the law, practice and constitutional usage which governed that relationship with Canada. That clause had been expressly included at the invitation of the British to guarantee freedom from British interference. He thought the British had been unstatesmanlike and unwise to compel acceptance of certain clauses by threatening war. "I do the English people the justice of believing that they would gladly have endorsed a more generous measure. I hardly hope that within the terms of the Treaty there lies the fulfilment of Ireland's destiny," he went on, "but I do hope and believe that with the disappearance of old passions and distrusts, fostered by centuries of persecution and desperate resistance, what remains may be won by agreement and by peaceful political evolution."

In that statement was contained, surely, the wisdom and statesmanship, as well as the generosity, which he felt, quite rightly, the British representatives had lacked. But it awoke no response in Deputy Sean MacSwiney who capsuled his objection and that of many others with the words: "I have sworn an oath to the Republic and for that reason I could not vote for the Treaty."

For such men it was like telling a Roman Catholic that his religion is not acceptable and that it would be reasonable if he compromised by becoming a Methodist.

Even Robert Barton got up to say that his oath of allegiance to the Republic was still to him "the most sacred bond on earth". Emotionally he explained, "I broke my oath because I judged that violation to be the lesser of outrages forced upon me, and between which I was compelled to choose." Briefly he recounted the circumstances of Lloyd George's threat of war, uttered "with all the solemnity and the power of conviction that he alone, of all men I met, can impart by word and gesture", of the struggle at Hans Place and the final capitula-

219

tion. Barton stated that he was in honour bound to recommend the Treaty but every broken fibre of him proclaimed his denial of it.

The next day, December 20th, Dr Patrick McCartan charged the Cabinet with failing to provide leadership. The two elements of the Cabinet were separated by a quibble between one compromise and another and were equally guilty of betraying the Republic. "Personally," he said, with a gesture towards the de Valera faction, "I have more respect for Michael Collins and Arthur Griffith than for the quibblers here."

"Let those of you who can conscientiously do as Robert Barton has done boldly—be false to your oath," he challenged. "Let you vote for a bird in the hand," he said and, alluding to de Valera's Document No. 2, went on, "I tell you that the bird in the bush that we have seen is not worth going after, thorny though the bush may be."

Beginning the third day's proceedings, Gavan Duffy added little to what his fellow-plenipotentiary, Barton, had already said, but he did make an attempt to restore a sense of perspective. He deplored the grievous wound the Treaty inflicted upon the dignity of the nation by foisting an English king upon it; on the other hand, there were influential people who were overstating their case in asking deputies to believe that the Irish Army would be commanded by his Majesty's officers. He did not like the Treaty but he saw no rational alternative. It was true that the plenipotentiaries had signed under duress and he reminded the Dail that the alternative was not just the resumption of the war at some time, but immediate war. But the fact of duress did not seem of itself to warrant rejection of the terms.

Last of the plenipotentiaries to speak was Duggan. He found no new ground to cover but he was incisive and cool as he stated that he had not been threatened by Lloyd George but had signed "deliberately with the fullest consciousness of my responsibilities to you who sent me there, to the country, to the movement, and to the dead." He stated that no one could seriously suggest that the plenipotentiaries and their staff had been sent to London to ask the British Government to recognise the Irish Republic. They had gone to compromise.

"Now the President," he went on, "when he gets up and

makes one of his impassioned and eloquent speeches, creates a kind of smoke screen of words, so that it is almost impossible to see out of it into the world of fact." Members had now seen the Cabinet minutes, the alternative oath, Document No. 2 and certain other documents. "You know who compromised, and so do I, and so do the public," he said. They all had. The signatures of the plenipotentiaries had bound the Dail to nothing but some critics of the Treaty "speak as if we had brought home a bag full of sample treaties and that they could choose whichever one they liked". Their choice was to accept the Treaty or reject it and take the consequences.

"I say under the terms of that Treaty that if the Irish people cannot achieve their freedom it is the fault of the Irish people and not of the Treaty," declared Duggan and, emotionally, a few minutes later: "Let us think seriously before we take it up and throw it back in the faces of the dead, and say it is not good enough for us."

For two hours and forty minutes Miss Mary MacSwiney, sister of the self-immolated Lord Mayor of Cork, blasted the Treaty. A teacher, she swore that if a Free State Government were set up under its aegis then she would teach rebellion. The Ministers of the other side could imprison her as one of "their first and most deliberate and irreconcilable rebels". She recalled the Easter Rising and cried passionately: "It was a minority that fought in 1916; it is always a minority that saves the soul of a nation in its hour of need." Labelling Lloyd George "the most unprincipled scoundrel in history," she begged the Dail not to be fooled by him. She rambled and vituperated, sometimes was incoherent, but beneath the ferocious flow of her words ran a quieter and more intense current. Mary MacSwiney believed that she represented that day the grieving womenfolk of Ireland. "I know the women of Ireland," she asserted, "and I know what they will say to the men that want to surrender." Mrs O'Callaghan, widow of the murdered ex-Mayor of Limerick, had spoken more briefly, and perhaps more tellingly, the previous day, but she denied that bitterness influenced her. "No woman in this Dail is going to give her vote merely because she is warped by a deep personal loss." All the women in the Dail opposed the Treaty and most of them had suffered grievously, but Mary MacSwiney did not know the women of Ireland as well as she believed. There

221

were many, particularly members of the Cumman na mBan, who thought as she did and there were no more resolute opponents of the Treaty than these. But vast numbers of women who still had sons and husbands and brothers to lose weighed their lives against a principle which even Michael Collins they knew was ready to concede, and they plumped for peace.

The widow of Thomas Clarke, the woman in whose hands the secrets of the Irish Republican Brotherhood had rested after his execution in 1916, recalled his words to her in the death cell: "Tell the Irish people that I and my comrades believe we have saved the soul of Ireland. We believe she will never lie down again until she has gained absolute freedom." She acclaimed every one of the men who had carried on the fight since. "I have sorrow in my heart now, but I don't despair; I never shall. I still believe in them." She was convinced that they would be brave enough to turn back when they discovered that they had taken the wrong turning.

Her moving words were quickly overlaid by General Mulcahy's analysis of procedures and practicalities. None had been braver than he, but for Mulcahy this was a matter of common sense. "I see no solid spot of ground upon which the Irish people can put its political feet but upon that Treaty," he said, and reminded his hearers that "we have not been able to drive the enemy from anything but from a fairly good-sized police barracks". But Mulcahy, too, allowed nostalgic blades to cut through the dry crust of his reasoning and probe the emotions. Inevitably, throughout the debate, the dead had been invoked to damn or to justify the Treaty: was this brand of freedom worthy of their sacrifices? General Mulcahy asked a different question. Were the Potters of Ireland, the Compton-Smiths of England to go on dying, or were the people of the two countries to seek the amity that politics had denied them?

At the end of the day the Dail adjourned for Christmas, and met again on January 3rd. There was to be no speech-making in the interim, but there was talk in homes and pubs and churches and streets, and many members had agonising changes of heart. One deputy succeeded, after a long argument, in convincing an I.R.A. officer, a friend of his, that he should support the Treaty but himself voted against it a few days later. Press and pulpit propaganda was working steadily towards acceptance of the Treaty and many deputies who opposed it themselves returned to the Dail to vote, as they had discovered their constituents wanted, for it. Had the vote been taken before the recess it is quite possible that de Valera would have carried the day, but the argument drifted along its sterile way. Every deputy was to have his say. All were agreed that Great Britain had sold Ireland a pup. The question was whether it should be put down at once or reared until it could use its teeth against the British.

Few reputations were enhanced and perhaps only Griffith emerged from the long debate with increased stature, though he was waspish at times and once in exasperation allowed his loathing of Childers to break through. Countess Markievicz angered Collins by mockingly suggesting that he might marry Princess Mary and he chose to make an elaborate protest. Piaras Beaslai, one of Collins's several biographers and for five years—except for a spell of imprisonment—editor of *An-t-Oglach*, the I.R.A. newspaper, spoke with admirable lucidity and lack of bitterness. He deplored the absence of a constructive alternative from the opponents of the Treaty. "I have heard much talk of what are called principles, but are really political formulas," he said and quoted from Padraic Colum's play, *The Hand*: "The nation, the nation—do you ever think of the poor Irish nation which is trying to be born?"

As speaker followed speaker, Brian O'Higgins against the Treaty, Ernest Blythe for, Frank Fahy against, George Nicholls for, Donal O'Callaghan against, as bitter asides and interjections piled up, Michael Collins tried to break the log-jam of rhetoric. His words were a little confused but his meaning was clear. To avoid a division and an ever-widening split in the country, he suggested that the opponents of the Treaty abstained from voting. They would be meeting the wishes of the people without compromising their principles. To reject the Treaty was to "absolve the English from their bargain", and in those circumstances neither the Treaty nor any alternative document would be effective. The opposition could have the honour and glory of striking their ideal of the Republic—"and we can have all the shame and disgrace."

"What is the proposition?" asked Countess Markievicz.

"That you allow the Treaty to go through and let the

223

Provisional Government come into existence; and if necessary you can fight the Provisional Government on the Republican question afterwards."

"We will do that if you carry ratification perhaps," put in de Valera.

In the ensuing discussion the President's Document No. 2, which had been rumbling in the belly of the Dail throughout the debate in spite of his attempts to suppress it, belched into the open again. Mr Lorcan Robbins claimed that he had never listened to anything so unreal as the debate. "There are three parties in the Dail," he said. "There are the uncompromising Republicans, the Treaty party, and the Document No. 2 party." The uncompromising Republicans could not support de Valera any more than they could the Treaty party. He protested that, because of the President's veto on discussion of his Document No. 2, deputies had been unable to explain to their constituents what alternative to the Treaty had been suggested.

De Valera at once expressed his willingness to produce the document, but only if he could put it as an amendment to the Treaty, as a substitute for the Treaty Griffith would not have that. There must be a straight vote on the Treaty. Then, said de Valera, Document No. 2 was not to be discussed. It was all a question of tactics. Having failed to gain a majority for his alternative at the private session, de Valera was not going to allow it to be a factor in the Treaty vote. It was his baby and he was not going to risk its going down the drain with the bath water.

The House adjourned without any real consideration of the Collins proposal, but it had impressed some members and nine of them, from both parties, met at the home of Sean T. O'Kelly. With one exception, Liam Mellows, they agreed that to avoid a split the President might advise abstention from voting against the Treaty on the understanding that de Valera should continue as President of the Dail, from which the Provisional Government should derive its powers and to which it should remain responsible. The Army and all other services should be controlled by the Provisional Government.

Looking back, Professor Michael Hayes, one of the participants in the scheme, describes it as "manifestly absurd that we should agree to keep de Valera on as President and work the

224

5

Treaty." But when Hayes walked home that night with Mellows, the sole dissenter, there seemed to be some hope that differences might be settled. Griffith and Collins agreed to the proposal, but de Valera angrily threw it out.

On January 4th, after further argument about his suppression of Document No. 2, de Valera gave formal notice that next day he would move that the document be brought forward as an amendment to the Treaty.

"I suggest that President de Valera should hand that document to the Press as we asked him a fortnight ago," said Griffith dryly.

He was to rise in protest again before the day was out, for when de Valera's proposals were distributed in readiness for his amendment on the morrow, six clauses of the twenty-three clauses of the original Document No. 2 had been dropped. De Valera answered that Griffith was quibbling. He would propose his amendment in his own terms; it would be for the Dail to decide whether they would accept his amendment to Griffith's motion.

The House met at 11.15 a.m. on Thursday, January 5th, but within five minutes adjourned until 3 p.m. to allow the group which had taken up the Collins abstention proposal to complete their discussions. At the resumption complaints came from all sides of the House concerning an article attacking de Valera which had appeared in *Freeman's Journal*, never popular with Sinn Fein. A motion to exclude representatives of that paper from the Dail was finally dropped but de Valera then brought up another matter of privilege, the publication of the text of Document No. 2 as it had been put to the private session in December. At the time he had gathered up the copies but one had been smuggled out. Griffith freely admitted that he had handed the text to *Freeman's Journal* the previous evening. He had, throughout, honoured de Valera's request to keep quiet about Document No. 2, though the President had agreed at the time it was not a confidential document. Griffith had had to speak "as with one hand tied", but when the President had accused him of quibbling over the omission of the six clauses, he had thought it time to let the Irish people see whether he was quibbling or not. De Valera argued mildly that he was putting an amendment to the motion to approve the Treaty, not an amendment to the Treaty itself, though whichever way he chose to describe it, the effect would be the same.

Eoin O'Duffy then rose to report that the self-appointed committee, of which he was a member, had come to a large measure of agreement but that this had not been reflected by the leaders to whom they had reported that morning. This was the "keep de Valera as President but work the Treaty" plan which de Valera had rejected. O'Duffy said that he was not in a position to disclose details, but Dr McCartan and Liam de Roiste were not prepared to let the matter drop so easily. The Speaker put it that by their adjourning that morning to give the committee further time for consideration the Dail had, in effect, made it official.

"No," said de Valera sharply.

But the Speaker ruled that the committee, which O'Duffy said was to meet again that evening, should make a report. It was agreed that the House should adjourn and that the committee be heard at a private session next morning.

But by then the anti-Treaty members had been swayed from their moderate views and would not permit the agreement to be made known to the Dail.

When the public session began in the afternoon of January 6th, President de Valera made a long speech in the course of which he adverted to the circumstances in which, in October 1917, he had become the connecting link between the Sinn Fein organisation and the Volunteers, taking over the leadership of the one from Griffith and of the other from Cathal Brugha. The two men, he said, "differed then as fundamentally as they differ today". For four years he had had the difficult job of keeping a balance between the disparate elements which the two men represented. He had succeeded, until the signing of the Treaty. Again he covered the ground which had led to that point, again he went through the history of Document No. 2. This was not a pet scheme of his own but a policy which accorded with the wishes of the Irish people. He had always been able to examine his own heart "and it told me straight off what the Irish people wanted", he claimed.

The Dail would have to decide between two rival policies. He stood for the Irish Republic, as it was proclaimed in 1916 and constitutionally established by the nation in 1919, and for no policy not consistent with that. If he were re-elected, he would reconstitute his Cabinet, throw out the Treaty and offer the British his alternative. "If there was not a gun in Ireland we would carry out that programme," he vowed.

Then he resigned, including his Cabinet in the resignation, and offered himself for re-election once Griffith had had his say. It was an ingenious red herring. He was ignoring the Treaty motion and challenging Griffith to a straight out vote on personalities. Griffith was not to be caught like that. His motion stood, and until it had been dealt with, the President's proposal was out of order. De Valera's answer was that the Government could resign at any time and there must be an Executive to carry out the work of the House. The Speaker ruled emphatically, "The Dail itself is the authority . . . any other body in the country is subordinate to it." Griffith's motion stood, but a motion to suspend standing orders would be accepted.

Collins pointed out that if the Treaty were rejected de Valera could have a Republican Government in ten minutes. An alternative way of getting a unified Cabinet was for Collins and the other advocates of the Treaty to resign. As it was, the discussion on suspending standing orders meant that he could not comment on Document No. 2 or No. 3, whichever de Valera liked to call it, and he alleged Tammany Hall methods. He accused "three or four bullies" of preventing the House from hearing the report of the *ad hoc* committee. Asked to withdraw the term, Collins replied tersely, "I can withdraw the term but the spoken word cannot be recalled. Is that right, sir?"

The argument about suspending standing orders so that de Valera could put his proposal, or not suspending them so that the Treaty discussion could go on, was flung backwards and forwards until at last Griffith protested that he had listened for days while attacks were made on his honour and he had waited patiently to wind up the discussion. He did not see why, in the middle of the discussion, a vote on the personality of President de Valera should be sprung on them.

At that, de Valera exclaimed with weary theatricality, "I'm sick and tired of politics—so sick that no matter what happens I would go back to private life." He was not a person for political trickery, he said, and he did not want to pull a red herring across. He would be satisfied with a straight vote in the

227

House if it came within forty-eight hours. So the standing orders were not suspended and the Treaty debate went on.

Collins, at whom both Brugha and de Valera had taken swipes, was now assailed by Seamus Robinson, leader of the Soloheadbeg ambush which had sparked off the struggle with England. Setting up questions for Brugha to answer, he asked what positions Collins had had in the Army and whether there was any record of his having fired a shot for Ireland at an enemy of Ireland. The plenipotentiaries in his view were guilty of treason.

On the last day of the debate, Saturday, January 7th, Cathal Brugha took up the attack on Collins and the animosity he had contained for so long spurted viciously. As he reiterated the questions Robinson had asked, he was interrupted by Sean Milroy's indignant, "Is that in order?" and Collins's own careless, "Carry on." Griffith's reference to Collins, early in the debate, as "the man who won the war" had caught a raw edge of Brugha's vanity, but it had affronted him, too, because it implied that other patriots had done less than Michael Collins.

Elaborately Brugha described the working of his Department of Defence to show that Collins had been merely the head of a sub-section under the Chief of Staff who, in turn, was responsible to Brugha. The Headquarters staff, he said, had worked "conscientiously and patriotically for Ireland without seeking any notoriety, with one exception; whether he is responsible or not for the notoriety I am not going to say". The press and the people, he went on, "put him into a position which he never held; he was made a romantic figure, a mystical character such as this person certainly is not; the gentleman I refer to is Mr. Michael Collins—"

"Now we know the reason for the opposition to the Treaty," Dan MacCarthy interjected. Brugha carried on, fenced for a moment with Griffith who exclaimed ironically, "Bravo, Cathal, bravo."

One deputy tried to stop him.

"Too late. Let him carry on now," answered Sean Mc-Garry.

"The damage has been done," added Patrick Brennan, but Collins mildly contradicted him, "No damage is done."

Brugha spoke for a long time, clumsily but colourfully,
228

with unassailable prejudice and a raw honesty which was typical of him and endeared him to many, even to Collins, who forgave him readily. He struggled to explain the difference between the Treaty and de Valera's alternative, for him the difference between a draught of poison and a draught of water, and he ended by appealing to Griffith and the other plenipotentiaries not to vote. This suggestion was Collins's abstention plan in reverse. Griffith had earned great respect when he had stood down from the leadership of Sinn Fein in favour of de Valera, Brugha said, and if he agreed now to follow the course Brugha suggested, his name would live forever in Ireland.

With great dignity Griffith began his closing speech: "I cannot accept the invitation of the Minister of Defence to dishonour my signature and become immortalised in Irish history." He defended Collins in warm, simple words, concluding, "Though I have not now, and never had, an ambition about either political affairs or history, if my name is to go down in history I want it associated with the name of Michael Collins."

Turning to the Treaty, he told the House that he had said at a Cabinet meeting: "If I go to London I can't get a Republic: I will try for a Republic, but I can't bring it back." The plenipotentiaries had been sent "to make some compromise, bargain or arrangement; we made an arrangement; the arrangement we made is not satisfactory to many people. Let them criticise on that point, but do not let them say that we were sent to get one thing and that we got something else."

He recalled de Valera's letter to Lloyd George in which he had written: "We have no conditions to impose, no claim to advance but one—that we are to be free from aggression." Griffith maintained that the Treaty met that claim.

He scored off devout Republicans who, between them, had taken seven separate oaths to the King of England yet insisted that the Treaty oath would stick in their gullets. This was damnable hypocrisy which was going to involve the lives of brave men. He had been told that "this generation might go down, but the next generation might do something or other", and he asked, "Is there to be no living Irish nation? Is the Irish nation to be the dead past or the prophetic future?"

Again he alluded to Document No. 2, and challenged

de Valera to let the people know what it involved—recognition of the King, a payment to the King and association with the Commonwealth. At once de Valera interjected, "There is no oath." But Griffith would not accept this. In the Cabinet room de Valera had drafted an oath, but he had omitted it from Document No. 2. Griffith would not agree that "the people of Ireland should be sacrificed for a formula".

"I do not care whether the King of England or the symbol of the Crown be in Ireland so long as the people of Ireland are free to shape their own destinies."

De Valera uttered a last protest "—that document will rise in judgment against the men who say there's only a shadow of difference—" and Collins cried out, "Let the Irish nation judge us now and for future years."

The vote was taken.

The Speaker: "The result of the poll is sixty-four for approval and fifty-seven against. That is a majority of seven in favour of approval of the Treaty."

At once de Valera stated that he would resign as Chief Executive, but he insisted that all that had happened was that "a certain resolution" had been approved. The Republic could be disestablished only by the Irish people and until they had voted, whatever arrangements were made by the Treaty party, the Dail must remain the supreme Government.

Collins declared that the first duty of them all was public safety and de Valera applauded him. Still unable to believe that the Dail had split down the middle, Collins pleaded for unity, some kind of joint committee, to help them through the period of transition from English rule to Irish government. "So far as I am concerned, this is not a question of politics, nor never has been," he said.

But, bitterly, Mary MacSwiney spurned the offer. Approval of the Treaty was "the grossest act of betrayal that Ireland ever endured," she accused, and warned the Treaty party, "I tell you here there can be no union between the representatives of the Irish Republic and the so-called Free State."

De Valera attempted to have his last word. He spoke of four years "of magnificent discipline in our nation". Then, as he said eloquently, "The world is looking at us now—", tears overcame him.

Cathal Brugha quietly promised that discipline would be kept in the Army, then the long, long debate was at an end.

There was a startling development when, on Monday, January 9th, de Valera announced the resignation of his Cabinet and himself. Collins at once expressed his belief that "no one here in this assembly or in Ireland wants to be in the position of opposing President de Valera." He suggested a committee, perhaps from both sides, to look after public safety, and a Treaty party committee to "do all the dirty work" of taking Ireland over from the English. There would be problems both for the Irish and for the English, and the main thing was to stop talking and get on with the work.

Mrs Clarke then proposed that Eamon de Valera be re-elected President of the Irish Republic and Liam Mellows supported her. Collins thought this would make them a laughing stock. With irony he suggested that "you go on here —remain here talking and watching us doing the work." Mary MacSwiney insisted that "we have to re-assert here today that this is a Republican Government" and that "we must have a symbol of office until the people have disestablished the Republic". It was clear that the President of the Republic could not be a supporter of the Free State, she pointed out.

The curious dichotomy which was to plague the country for the next few months was emerging. De Valera interpreted the vote on the Treaty simply as " a resolution of approval which means that the Government of the Republic is not going actively to interfere with those who are to complete that Treaty". When they had finalised the Treaty they could put it as a definite issue to the people.

Patrick Hogan answered, scathingly, "If you elect the President again on a policy of fighting the Treaty after the resolution that has been passed by this House, let us have no more talk of constitutionalism."

A new debate had sprung up on the issue, with de Valera insisting petulantly, "Go and elect your President and all the rest of it. You have sixty-five. I do not want office at all."

Much of the argument that followed ploughed along the well-worn furrows of the Treaty debate but the point to it all was that many who had voted for the Treaty did not want to vote against de Valera who, until the contentious issue had arisen, had commanded the affection of almost everyone. The great surviving commandant from the Easter Rising had become almost god-like. During the long debate he had sniped and snarled, argued tortuously and indulged in occasional histrionics. For many he had emerged as a rather tattered saint, but for the majority the old love did not die easily.

Griffith saw that if the proposal for de Valera's re-election was carried, it would, in effect, nullify the Treaty vote. He saw it as a political manoeuvre, "put forward to us in a guise that is not straight". He admitted wholeheartedly that no one on his side wanted to vote against de Valera and he believed that the resigning President should not have allowed his name to go forward. There was, in fact, no necessity for him to resign and so create the issue. "We suggested," Griffith reminded the Dail, "that Dail Eireann might continue until the Free State election came into effect."

His argument did not budge de Valera, who claimed that it was constitutional for him to resign. The majority should now elect a new President. It was a challenge. Would Griffith's majority for the Treaty stand with him in a straight fight with de Valera? Stack suggested that as no other candidate had been nominated de Valera was unanimously re-elected. An amendment from Collins was that Griffith should be invited to form a Provisional Government. The motion that de Valera be re-elected President of the Irish Republic was then taken and he very nearly was. Voting was 58 for the motion, 60 against. Generously, Griffith jumped to his feet. He wanted all Ireland to know that the vote was not to be taken "as against President de Valera. It is a vote to help the Treaty, and I want to say now that there is scarcely a man I have ever met in my life that I have more love and respect for than President de Valera. I am thoroughly sorry to see him placed in such a position. We want him with us." De Valera answered as handsomely that he had allowed his name to go forward only because he believed that "we should not scrap our machinery before they take theirs". He added that "the people who are responsible have done the right thing, and therefore I hope that nobody will talk of fratricidal strife. That is all nonsense. We have got a nation that knows how to conduct itself." He

232

was against the Treaty because it was a promise that could not be kept. The opponents of the Treaty would remain a compact body. "We will not interfere with you, except when we find that you are going to do something that will definitely injure the Irish nation."

What he seemed to be saying was that he and his followers would form a constitutional Opposition and Sean McEoin exclaimed, enthusiastically, "My respect for the President is one hundred and fifty per cent higher than it has been before." Momentarily he had forgotten that de Valera was no longer President and a minute later, Griffith said, "I must still and always call him President."

Collins now nominated Griffith to form an Executive and General Mulcahy seconded him, but there was doubt as to how the Government was to function. Who was to establish the Provisional Government and to whom would it be responsible? The Treaty required that the Parliament of Southern Ireland set up by the 1920 Act should assemble to ratify the instrument and appoint a Provisional Government. This meant that the four members from Trinity, who had never taken their seats in the Dail, would join them. The Parliament of Southern Ireland would be summoned but, said Collins, "it will be what I would call Dail Eireann".

The unyielding Mary MacSwiney asserted that the Dail was the Parliament of the Republic of Ireland. If Griffith proposed to form a Provisional Government he could not form it from this Assembly. He should "go now and call the members elected to sit in the Parliament of Southern Ireland and form his Provisional Government from that." Stack, Mellows and other Republicans also made it clear that no co-operation could be expected from them and Sean MacEntee suggested that not Griffith, who was committed absolutely to the Treaty, but some member who would "hold the resources of the Republic in trust for the Republic" should be elected President of the Dail.

Argument continued into the next day. There was doubt as to whether Griffith, if elected, would be President of the Republic—until the establishment of the Free State—or of Dail Eireann only. Griffith said that he would occupy the same position as de Valera had occupied, until the issue was put to the Irish people. This was a fair answer, de Valera thought, but would Griffith assure him that he would not use the office to destroy the Republic. To this Griffith replied that he had already agreed to "keep the Republic in being until such time as the establishment of the Free State is put to the people to decide for or against."

When at last the motion to elect Griffith was put, de Valera led his supporters from the House to the accompaniment of bitter and childish epithets from both sides. The roll was called and Griffith was elected. At once he made known his Cabinet appointments. Collins was to continue as Minister of Finance, Gavan Duffy was to take charge of Foreign Affairs, Duggan of Home Affairs, Cosgrave of Local Government, and Kevin O'Higgins of Economic Affairs. General Mulcahy succeeded Brugha as Minister of Defence.

After an adjournment, de Valera and his party returned and the House listened sympathetically to a deputation of the Irish Labour Party led by Thomas Johnson. Reminding the Dail that Labour had refrained from contesting elections in the past so as not to split the vote, and that Irish workmen had played their full part in the national struggle, Johnson asked them to remember that there was a social problem at home. He estimated that 130,000 people were unemployed.

The resources of the country should be organised to provide a decent life for its people. "You are responsible to see that this problem is dealt with and tackled effectually. If it is not so done the people will rise and sweep you away, as they would sweep any government away that failed to do its duty to the common people," he concluded. Griffith thanked Johnson and stated that a committee would be appointed to meet Labour representatives to try and find a solution to the unemployment problem.

De Valera, though he stopped short of congratulating Griffith on his election, had some cordial words for him and promised him the same respect that Griffith had always accorded him. "On this side of the House," he said, "even amongst those who most bitterly oppose his policy, there is a sympathetic feeling, and the magnitude of the task imposed upon him is realised." He pressed Griffith for some statement of his policy.

In his precise way Erskine Childers demanded details.

Griffith had made "a very general statement of policy," he said, after Griffith had reiterated his position. Griffith, it appeared to him, was to be both Chief Executive Officer of Dail Eireann and Chief of the Provisional Government, a "curious and ambiguous situation," he thought.

He was interrupted, began to speak again, then Griffith, thoroughly nettled, intervened. President de Valera, he said, still using the title now his own, had made a generous statement to which he had replied. "I will not reply to any damned Englishman in this Assembly," he rapped out, thumping the table.

The day, January 10th, ended with much left in the air. It was clear that the Irish Labour Party would have to be reckoned with in future elections; de Valera had made it plain that any move to "disestablish" the Republic would mean trouble: finally, there was the question of allegiance of the Irish Republican Army. The new Minister of Defence assured the Dail that the Army would remain the Army of the Irish Republic.

"I don't think that was a wise thing to say," says General McEoin, "because, while it might have been political wisdom at that moment to ease the situation, it was not a thing that he could do. It was not a Government decision; he was giving it on his own."

Of the Headquarters staff of the I.R.A. the majority favoured the Treaty. They were Mulcahy, Chief of Staff, Eoin O'Duffy, his Deputy, J. J. O'Connell, Assistant Chief of Staff, Gearoid O'Sullivan and Sean MacMahon, Adjutant-General and Quartermaster-General respectively, Emmet Dalton, Director of Training, Diarmuid O'Hegarty, Director of Organisation, and Piaras Beaslai, Director of Publicity, as well as Michael Collins, Director of Intelligence. Against the Treaty were Liam Mellows, Director of Purchases, Rory O'Connor, Director of Engineering, Sean Russell, whose responsibility was munitions, and Seamus O'Donovan, Director of Chemicals. But the anti-Treaty officers had strong support from a number of divisional commandants, among them Liam Lynch, Joe McKelvey, Liam Pilkington and Oscar Traynor, the Dublin Brigade commandant. Following a series of meetings a number of officers wrote to the new Minister of Defence on January 12th calling for an Army Convention, to be held not later than February 5th, at which it was proposed that the Army not only affirm its allegiance to the Republic but appoint its own Executive which would have supreme control. This meant a return to the control which had existed before the I.R.A. accepted Dail control in 1920. Mulcahy naturally turned down the proposal that the Dail, still the elected Government of the Irish Republic, should not control the Irish Republican Army, but on January 18th he presided over a meeting at which he agreed that a Convention should be called within two months and reiterated his assurance that the Army would continue as the army of the Republic.

In the meantime, on January 14th, the Parliament of Southern Ireland, from which the anti-Treaty members of the Dail absented themselves, assembled in the Mansion House, with Liam de Roiste presiding, and elected the Provisional Government. As Arthur Griffith was President of the Dail, he was omitted from the new team, so frustrating Childers's argument that he would be presiding over the Dail and also over a body which was committed to destroying the Dail. Instead, Michael Collins became Chairman of the Provisional Government and, two days later, led his Ministers, Cosgrave, Duggan, O'Higgins, Eoin MacNeill, Patrick Hogan, Fionan Lynch and Joseph McGrath, to Dublin Castle to take over the administration of the country from the English. The surrender of this massive citadel of English power, symbol above all symbols of the subjugation of Ireland, was a momentous day. Many of the Irish Government officials loved Ireland and had the welfare of her people at heart, though their benevolence had been exercised within a system which was essentially a tyranny, paternalistic when it was expedient, ruthless when there was a hint of opposition. For these men it was a day of sadness. Some were bewildered that the British Government should ever have come to such a bargain with rebels.

In his autobiography[1] Sir Henry Robinson, doyen of local government, tells how he found the heads of departments "sitting on one side of the Under-Secretary's room and the Sinn Fein leaders sitting opposite, glowering at each other", while Lord FitzAlan was formally handing over the government to Michael Collins in the Council Chamber. Lord Fitz-

[1] *Memories: Wise and Otherwise* by Sir Henry Robinson Bt., K.C.B.

Alan then left and "avoided meeting his trusty and well-beloved civil servants with a *sauve qui peut*, which was the only advice he would have had to offer them".

The rest of Collins's Administration joined him in the Council room and the heads of department were called in to meet their new chiefs. Robinson was struck by the youth of most of the new Ministers and thought they all looked "pale and anxious". Collins, however, was "cordiality itself, and there was none of the 'top dog' attitude about him at all events". But Robinson appreciated the magnitude of the task before Collins and his team, for normal administration had come to a halt. He was concerned especially for the poor, the sick and the aged, who were suffering because as yet there was no money to finance the new services which would replace the old.

For Collins a new era of great responsibility lay ahead, but it seemed that neither the strain of the past years nor his ordeal in Dail Eireann had vitiated his huge energy. As Chairman of the Provisional Government it was his job to take over the machinery established by the British, often involving ticklish negotiation. As Griffith's Minister of Finance he was still responsible for his Department of the Dail, but he had also to arrange finance for the Provisional Government. Several times he journeyed to London, and before January was out he had reached an agreement with Sir James Craig by which he undertook to end the boycott on Belfast goods in return for Craig's promise to protect the Catholic minority in the Six Counties from persecution. He answered attacks by his opponents and sought to explain the new Ireland both to the people at home and to interested countries abroad. His object now was to make Ireland Gaelic once more.

The tempo of the British evacuation quickened. Beggar's Bush Barracks, the first barracks to be delivered to the Irish, became Army Headquarters and a new Civic Guard was established which would replace the Royal Irish Constabulary, the Dublin Metropolitan Police and the Republican police.

On January 23rd, the British Cabinet approved the Craig-Collins agreement of January 21st[2], then Churchill reported on recent meetings with Collins and other Irish Ministers which had resulted in "Heads of Working Arrangements for imple-

2 Cabinet conclusion 3/22 (3) of 23/1/22.

menting the Treaty"[3]. Churchill said that the Irish wanted a Free State Government and an approved constitution in the shortest possible time.[4] They also wanted an election as soon as fresh registers could be prepared. He put it forward as "worthy of consideration whether without infringing the Treaty it was possible to ratify the Treaty and approve the Constitution of the Free State by means of a One Clause Bill. There were great advantages from the point of view of the Irish Ministers in getting their draft Constitution approved by the Parliament for Southern Ireland, not only because the followers of Mr de Valera abstained from attending that body, but because they could then contend that their Constitution derived its authority from the Treaty and not from a British Act of Parliament." A Cabinet committee was appointed to examine this question, then it was agreed that the House of Commons should be asked to sanction the expenditure of £500,000 to finance the Provisional Government to March 31st. However, it was to be doled out cautiously and "care should be taken to retain a substantial amount in hand."

When, a week later, the Cabinet considered Craig's request for £2,000,000 on account—Ulster was claiming £6,000,000— Churchill proposed[5] "first to settle with the Free State on the basis of each side paying for its own damages and to conclude this settlement in such a way as to debar the Free State from making fresh claims for equal treatment with the Northern Parliament when a settlement was made with the latter." At the same meeting Churchill was authorised to assure the Irish Ministers that if their draft Constitution was ready by the middle of March "every effort would be made to pass it through the British Parliament in one month, but that it was not possible at this stage to forecast the amount of opposition which the Irish Bill would meet in Parliament." The Treaty was not a dead political issue in England either.

A draft General Amnesty prepared by Duggan was accepted in substance but the Cabinet wanted the form of the proclamation materially altered. Duggan also requested the release of Irish prisoners convicted in England and Scotland, certain cases in Ulster and the Connaught Rangers, who had been sentenced for mutiny in the Punjab when they refused to

3 Cabinet Paper CP 3648.   4 Cabinet conclusion 3/22 (4) of 23/1/22.
5 Cabinet conclusion 6/22 (6) of 30/1/22.

obey orders as a protest against the depredations of the Black and Tans. One, James Daly, had been shot, thirteen had been sentenced to penal servitude for life after the commuting of death sentences, and nearly 340 had received varying terms of imprisonment. Churchill agreed with all of Duggan's requests, but there were strong objections from other Ministers to releasing these men under a political amnesty. It was thought that they might be quietly released when the Regiment was disbanded. Subsequently their sentences were reduced.

The pulse of the Craig-Collins agreement soon fluttered to a standstill as Craig made it clear that the North had no intention of joining the South and would fight any unfavourable judgment by the Boundary Commission. There was trouble on the border. Some captured Volunteers in the North were threatened with hanging and early in February raids across the border by Aiken and others resulted in prisoners being taken by the I.R.A. On February 11th, a clash between Ulster Specials, who had wandered across the border at Clones, Co. Monaghan, cost the lives of one I.R.A. officer and four Specials. More prisoners were taken. The British Cabinet were told a few days later that Craig would agree to an exchange of prisoners on condition that the Provisional Government accepted the validity of decisions in Ulster courts and did not again press for the release of prisoners on political grounds.

In all the circumstances the British Government was doing its best to expedite the establishment of the new Irish State. They were patient, even to the extent of suffering without retaliation attacks on their departing troops, and the Irish Ministers visiting London were hard put to it to explain away these breaches. General Emmet Dalton, their Liaison Officer, had a busy time. Republican opposition in Ireland was hardening into something very dangerous.

TWELVE

"To vacate a position is to lose it," says Sean McEoin, "and it was believed on the Treaty side that when it was seen that the British had proved their good faith and really had left the country, then even the most irritated of the anti-Treaty people would accept the situation and there would be no civil war."

But the British were still in possession of posts throughout the country. "They are not gone yet," cried the dissidents and were not convinced that they would ever go. This was one reason why the Provisional Government were insistent upon the British evacuating the country as quickly as possible, thought it meant, inevitably, that the handing over of Government departments, the handing over of power, could not be as smooth as it might have been. The other reason for urging the British to leave was that if trouble started it was likely to be the British who were hit first. Already there had been incidents. If the British hit back it would be the end of the Treaty and the end of freedom so newly and so hardly won. "It was essential," says McEoin, "that before the Government could govern, the British should get right out of the country." The British saw this point of view, saw that their continued presence would spark off either a civil war or the renewal of the old conflict. They did not cynically abandon the country as some writers have suggested, but co-operated with the Provisional Government in expediting the transfer of power.

At first, military posts evacuated by the British were taken over by local I.R.A. brigades, whether their members were predominantly for the Treaty or against it, or whether opinion was divided. The I.R.A. was still supposedly a homogeneous organisation and none of its members so far had accepted that the split would widen beyond the point of reconciliation.

When McEoin took over Longford Barracks much of the stuff on the inventory was missing. He reported the losses to Collins and to Cope and insisted on an early take-over of Athlone Barracks. The longer the British stayed the less would be the quantity of military stores handed over. Not only were they being used in the ordinary way but certain British officers
240

and N.C.O.'s, realising that checking was difficult in the chaotic situation, had set themselves up in under-the-counter business on a large scale. It was arranged that the British should evacuate within a week. "It was holy murder," McEoin says.

On the appointed day, the British colonel commanding the barracks asked McEoin to call on him. It was 11 a.m., an hour before the take-over. The colonel came quickly to the point.

"I'm supposed to hand over these barracks to you at midday but the inventory isn't nearly complete. So I can't do so."

"Do you say that everything that ought to be on the inventory is there, so far as you know?" asked McEoin.

The colonel was sure that there had been no rifling of stores under his control.

"Then I take over at twelve."

"But I hear you're planning to let the public in at twelve," protested the colonel.

"You command the barracks until twelve o'clock. What I do at two minutes past is none of your damn business."

In fact, the British left promptly, but not before they had churlishly hacked down the flagstaff. "We met them coming across Athlone Bridge and they didn't return our 'eyes right'," recalls Colonel A. T. Lawlor. "It was the bitterness of their evacuation which reinforced my convictions." Lawlor's first reaction to the Treaty had been "We can't touch that." He was afraid that "people would become content with an attenuated form of independence and go no further."

McEoin and Collins had convinced him that there was no reasonable alternative to acceptance of the Treaty.

"What are you going to fight with?" Collins asked him, and went on to argue, as he must have argued so often in those critical days, that the Treaty gave them international recognition, their own Government, civil service and national revenue. They had the opportunity to consolidate the State; the people would develop politically; inevitably the Republic would come.

The argument made sense to Lawlor but to many I.R.A. men it seemed that the Republic they had fought for was slipping away from them.

True, the new Minister of Defence, General Mulcahy had promised reassuringly that the I.R.A. would continue to be the Army of the Republic, but once the will of the people had been made clear at an election the future of the Army would be in the melting pot, as would every other department of the emergent state. It was planned, in fact, to create a regular National Army under the command of General J. J. O'Connell. Those members of the Irish Republican Army who did not wish to continue a military career were to return to their civilian occupations, the way that demobbed war-time soldiers usually do. More was read into Mulcahy's words than he had meant, and it was believed by many that if the I.R.A. was to continue as the Army of the Republic, then the Republic somehow was also to continue. Mulcahy had agreed that within two months an Army Convention should be held to thrash out the position, but the I.R.A. as a whole was required to take its orders from G.H.Q. at Beggar's Bush in the meantime.

On the political front, too, prevarication seemed to dominate. Sinn Fein held an Ard-Fheis on February 21st. Although the feeling of the meeting was distinctly anti-Treaty, Collins and de Valera agreed that no vote should be taken, but that the General Election should be postponed for three months. Collins was pleased to avoid a Sinn Fein vote against the Treaty and de Valera was equally satisfied that the inevitable verdict of the people had been deferred.

Many unhappy I.R.A. men were impatient of the postponements, the deferments, the delays and preliminaries of compromise which they had no intention of accepting. For them the heart of the matter was contained in the stubborn, memorable statement of Liam Lynch: "We have declared for an Irish Republic and will not live under any other law."

It was the 2nd Southern Division, under Ernie O'Malley, which first came out into the open, repudiated the Treaty and declared its independence of central authority. In a long discussion with Dermott MacManus soon after the return of the plenipotentiaries from London, O'Malley had decided that it was logical to support the Treaty, but then he had gone back to Tipperary where Seamus Robinson had persuaded him they should accept a republic or nothing. O'Malley's enthusiasm blazed. Once more at the head of the men he knew so well, again in pursuit of the Holy Grail of the Republic, exuberantly he raided the R.I.C. barracks at Clonmel on February 26th. One of his men was admitted on giving the password, promptly
242

held up the duty room and let his friends in. The garrison were hustled into two rooms while the place was ransacked. Guns, ammunition and grenades, brought into Clonmel from evacuated barracks for storage, were loaded on to Crossley tenders and driven away.

Winston Churchill at once protested to Collins because the Provisional Government had failed to prevent the attack on R.I.C. men detained under their protection. He received the laconic answer that "the British Government ought to take more care in the distribution of lethal weapons to unauthorised persons."[1]

Collins was being a little hard on the British who, pressed to get out of the country as quickly as possible, had no way of knowing whether I.R.A. units to whom they were handing over posts were loyal to the Provisional Government or not. They were equally unfriendly to the British. Sent to investigate the Clonmel affair, General Tudor reported that "the capture of arms had put the rebels in relatively a better position than the forces of the Provisional Government, who were complaining of the niggardly distribution of arms to them."[2]

The Mid-Limerick Brigade, which in the usual course of events would have moved in to the posts evacuated by the British in Limerick city, followed the example of the 2nd Southern Division. On February 18th the Brigade Commandant, Liam Forde, renounced G.H.Q. whose aims, he said, were "now unquestionably to subvert the Republic and support the Provisional Government and make possible the establishment of the Irish Free State." His proclamation followed a meeting at the Limerick Town Hall at which Forde turned the issue into a vote of confidence in himself. The British had begun to move out and G.H.Q. saw that Limerick, which commanded the Shannon and held the key to both the south and the west, was likely to pass to a unit which denied their authority. Michael Brennan, then Commandant of the 1st Western Division, was ordered to forestall the dissident Forde by himself taking over posts in Limerick as the British evacuated them. He marched his men in quietly by the railway line and took over about six police barracks from the departing Black and Tans, a move which angered the local I.R.A., who regarded the men from Clare as poachers on their preserve.

[1] Cabinet conclusion 16/22 (1) of 8/3/22.   [2] Ibid.

The Mid-Limerick Brigade was far from unanimous in opposing the Treaty and the Brigade Quartermaster, Captain John Hurley, in an attempt to douse down the hostility towards the interlopers from Clare, began to organise his own pro-Treaty unit to take over the posts. But anti-Treaty men who had moved into Limerick from Cork and Tipperary arrested Hurley, and on March 6th set up posts of their own. Three different forces now shared the possession of Limerick, for some posts were still in British hands. Brennan felt keenly the indignity of the I.R.A. men snarling at each other while the British looked on, but the British took no pleasure in the situation. They were anxious about their own men and all too aware of the frailty of the Treaty. For several days an explosion into civil war seemed imminent.

Efforts by the Mayor of Limerick and others to find a peaceful solution failed, but eventually an acceptable compromise was suggested by Liam Lynch and Oscar Traynor, who were asked by Mulcahy to intervene but were soon to take leading roles in the fight against the Provisional Government. The terms of the agreement were confirmed in writing by General Eoin O'Duffy and both I.R.A. occupying forces withdrew from Limerick, except for a small garrison force responsible to Lynch himself.

Brennan was annoyed that after being ordered into Limerick by G.H.Q. he should now be told to withdraw. He believed it was weakness to leave the city when the dissident element had unequivocally repudiated the authority of G.H.Q. His own position was humiliating and, his resignation in his pocket, he went at once to Dublin to see Collins. "So you're going too!" Collins exploded. "The rats leaving the ship. Well, go on. Clear out! Leave it all to me. You're all the same, you fellows, putting your bloody vanity ahead of the good of the country." Collins went on wrathfully for a full ten minutes, then Brennan acknowledged that his chief was right about his wounded pride and tore up his resignation. But was Collins right? Or was he counting too much on the ultimate loyalties of the Irish Republican Brotherhood. The incident is significant because it shows that Brennan was no more ready for compromise with those who declined to accept the decision of the Dail majority, or to acknowledge the authority of their own

244

headquarters, than were men such as McEoin. It is important because Brennan himself was later thought by the General Staff to be wavering when he entered into negotiations with Lynch, only days after they had themselves allowed Lynch to leave Dublin in the expectation that he would co-operate.

The outburst of ill-feeling in Limerick, an all too recognisable symptom of deep-rooted trouble, jaundiced the already unhealthy relationship with the Six Counties. It is quite possible that a settled and sturdy Government in Dublin which made it plain that bygones were to be bygones would have induced the North to accept the thirty-two county Dominion for which the Treaty provided.

"It was believed that when the Constitution was drafted it would be so liberal and so distinct a guarantee of freedom, not only of the individual but of the collective group, that the opponents of the Treaty would see the value of it and the Six County Parliament also would see the value of it," General McEoin comments.

Nothing could be further from the truth than the suggestion that the British Government divided Ireland as a matter of deliberate policy. Partition was a compromise born of exasperation, the sorry solution of a problem which was rooted in prejudice and nourished by prevarication. A unified, peaceful Ireland would have delighted Lloyd George and his Government, not least the Treasury who had reluctantly agreed to pay £650,000 for the cost of the Special Constabulary alone in the financial year 1921/22 and a further £850,000 for the first six months of the following year, these estimates to be included in a general grant to Ulster "for unemployment and other services, so as to avoid, if possible, raising a controversy in Parliament in regard to this Force."[3]

The Provisional Government were anxious to re-open negotiations with the North but Craig refused while the Clones hostages were still being held. His position was weakened because, once more, a vendetta against Catholics was being pursued in Belfast, and Churchill would have put pressure on him—but for Limerick. "Once this situation was cleared up, however, he would not be disposed to accept a simple refusal from the Northern Government in view of the heavy obligations in regard to troops and Special Constabulary which we

[3] Cabinet conclusion 15/22 (8) of 6/3/22.

were incurring on their behalf."[4] But Churchill insisted also on the Provisional Government's responsibility for the preservation of peace and order.

Churchill's attitude was understandable, but he must have thanked God that he was a politician on the English side of the Irish Sea. In Ireland politicians could not afford uncompromising attitudes. The Dail met on February 28th, 1922, and again on March 1st and March 2nd, and it was quickly made apparent that a bifurcated system of government was not going to work. It had been agreed that the Dail should continue as the Parliament of the Republic but the two sides had different motives. Griffith was willing to keep the Dail alive until the people voted for its abolition, but he intended to allow the Provisional Government to press on in preparation for the establishment of the Free State in terms of the Treaty. The Republicans, under de Valera, were intent upon maintaining the supremacy of the Dail as Ireland's sovereign Parliament in expectation of the early demise of the Provisional Government, with the Free State still in its womb. They were determined that real control should remain with the Dail and when the names of the Ministers not of Cabinet rank were put forward for approval by the Dail some waspish questions were shot from the Republican benches. Griffith's appointment of Ernest Blythe as Minister of Trade passed without demur but new Ministers in charge of domestic departments such as Trade and Education came under fire, especially when they also held the equivalent office in the Provisional Government.

When de Valera asked ingenuously, "What is the relation between the Minister for Education of Dail Eireann and another Minister for Education that we hear spoken of?" Michael Hayes answered coyly, "The relations between the Minister for Education for the Provisional Government and the Minister of Education of Dail Eireann are of an intimate and cordial character." Pressed, he explained more seriously: "The departments of education in this country which had never functioned under Dail Eireann are now at the disposal of the Provisional Government; and Dail Eireann through me, by amicable arrangement with the Provisional Government, operates in these departments. It is only by virtue of the Treaty and the vote of the majority of this House that we can

4 Cabinet conclusion 16/22 (1) of 8/3/22.

now get possession of the machinery of these departments, and which I am myself, in point of fact, using." But de Valera was not satisfied until General Mulcahy compounded the formula that "whatever powers are in the hands of the Minister of Education for the Provisional Government are used by him only in accordance with the policy of the Minister of Education for this Dail," and added that in educational matters the supreme authority was the Dail's Minister.

Joseph McGrath, the new Minister for Labour, had to assure the House that in his department, "Not a single sheet of notepaper has been used but Dail Eireann notepaper," but Patrick Hogan had to defend himself for answering in his capacity of Minister of Agriculture for the Provisional Government a letter addressed to the Dail Minister for Agriculture.

The hub of the matter was that the British Government was financing the Provisional Government; the Dail could not provide the money for any of the departments—although some of the Republican deputies urged that it could be done by raising a further loan in America—so that, practically, it was an empty gesture to acknowledge Dail sovereignty when it was the Provisional Government who controlled the purse. Again, the force of an ideal was transcending practical politics as sometimes it still does in parliaments all over the world.

At the evening session Collins reported on the Dail accounts up to December 31st, 1921, and was sniped at by the unremitting Brugha on questions of detail. When Collins presented the estimates, the question of policing the country blew up and Griffith rose "to bring a whirl of talk down to plain realities". De Valera had suggested a national police force but in January he had refused to consider Griffith's request for a joint committee for public safety. The Dail could not afford to maintain a police force. "The Provisional Government is trying to organise a force which it proposed to work in harmony with the Dail, and what you are trying to do here is to try and obstruct that, while robbery and murder are rampant in the country."

For two more days ill-tempered exchanges were flung across the Assembly, yet gradually workaday business was got through. Questions asked by de Valera's party were elaborate traps baited with contention and ostentatiously they were

247

avoided. The ritual of question time was scrupulously observed but the niceties did not conceal the propaganda of either side. Tension mounted when Griffith disagreed with the wording of Mary MacSwiney's motion to ratify the Ard-Fheis agreement to postpone any election for three months. The motion was just another device to delay the election further, the Treaty party claimed. De Valera settled the question by including in the motion the relevant clause of the Agreement.

A motion was passed requiring births, deaths and marriages to be registered in Irish and English for twelve months from July 1st, 1922, and from then in Irish only. An amount of £2000, additional to £2000 voted in December, was voted towards the cost of *Aonach Tailteann*, a revival of the ancient games of Tara, an eight-day programme scheduled to begin on August 6th. The Dail also set up a commission to examine abuses in connection with the manufacture and sale of intoxicating liquor. There were areas, it seemed, in which agreement could be obtained, but somehow it did not seem very likely that combative spirits could be worked out in an eight-day revival of the ancient games of Tara.

Limerick still looked insecure and, improvising on the British theme of "gunboat diplomacy", the Provisional Government decided to send down an armoured car. It was the only one in the country outside British hands and it was a proud new toy. "The British handed it over and they lent with it two delightful and charming Black and Tans," recalls Dermott MacManus.

With Staff-Captain Bill Stapleton in charge, the armoured car with its assorted crew made its way to Limerick by way of Templemore, where the huge military barracks were occupied by a unit under Commandant Leahy who was thought to be "safe". The visitors, Black and Tans included, drank some merry pints that night and had no suspicion that they would be any less welcome when they called on their way back three days later. Leahy seized the armoured car and arrested and disarmed its crew. The two Black and Tans were not released with the others but were detained for two days before they were sent back to Dublin.

Lambasting the Provisional Government for utilising the services of the hated Black and Tans, although these happened
248

to be congenial specimens of the breed, Leahy made the most of his propaganda opportunity. That he had very cheerfully entertained them a few days before he had arrested them he did not mention.

It was a typical enough case at a time when if a man put his hand in his pocket there was no knowing whether he would produce a revolver or money to buy a drink. Friends were still friends but the ties of old memories were under strain.

Since their repudiation of Headquarters in February, the Second Southern Division had been increasingly belligerent. Cut off from Headquarters, they had to find some way of financing themselves, and Seamus Robinson and Dinny Lacey had chosen to do so by imposing a system of levies.

Tommy Ryan, who had fought with Lacey and Robinson in the 3rd Tipperary Brigade, resented this. His father having died, Ryan had returned to the family farm, where he was needed. Like every Volunteer he had been disappointed in the Treaty, but he was convinced that if the British were to come back guerrilla warfare would go on for ten years, and he thought that enough had been asked of the people. He did not like to see them now under pressure to finance the breakaway I.R.A. and his decision to support the Treaty was reinforced.

Robinson and Lacey were determined that no man in their command would throw in his lot with the Treaty forces. Apart from the importance of maintaining unity, they foresaw that men so familiar with the countryside would be dangerous in the event of civil war, and they sent word to Ryan asking him to see them in Thurles. He refused to go and a party was sent to fetch him. When he defied them, Robinson and Lacey waited until he turned up in Clonmel one day. There he was surrounded and taken to the two leaders with whom he had a long discussion. They were courteous and frank and advised him finally to think about the position.

"Then, it came about," says Ryan, "that there was a meeting of Brigade and Battalion staffs and any officer who was thinking of going over to the Free State was put out and replaced. I found that I had quite a number of people with me. As I was fairly prominent in my own area, they looked to me for a lead. About fifty of them turned up to a meeting at Cashel and a majority of them accepted the Treaty.

249

"That night, Robinson and Lacey interviewed a lot of my followers and talked them into going anti-Treaty again."

Ryan was one of three officers elected at the meeting to travel to G.H.Q. in Dublin to assure them of the loyalty of South Tipperary flying columns, but at the appointed time he found himself alone. Lacey and Robinson had been heroes in Tipperary since the beginning of the Anglo-Irish War and a direct appeal from them swayed many young men into the anti-Treaty ranks. As yet, except for those who had disowned Headquarters, the I.R.A. still held together, but it was obvious that the rift would soon be complete.

One man who could have done much to bring reason to the forefront and damp down fiery emotions was Eamon de Valera. His influence was enormous and he had lost little of the long-standing loyalty of the I.R.A., the Dail, and the people too. In the Dail he had insisted that a constitutional solution must be found. It appeared that he was prepared to battle exclusively in the political arena when on March 15th the formation of *Cumann na Poblachta*, or the League of the Republic, was announced over his signature as President. Its members were the substantial minority who had opposed the Treaty in the Dail and it contained the germ of a constitutional opposition party.

But, only the next day, in Dungarven, County Waterford, he made the first of a series of inflammatory speeches:

"If you don't fight today, you will have to fight tomorrow; and I say, when you are in a good fighting position, then fight on." And at Killarney he warned: "In order to achieve freedom, if our Volunteers continue, and I hope they will continue until the goal is reached, if we continue on that movement which was begun when the Volunteers were started, and we suppose this Treaty is ratified by your votes, then these men, in order to achieve freedom, will have to march over the dead bodies of their own brothers. They will have to wade through Irish blood." Though de Valera denied any intention to incite and claimed he had been misrepresented, it is impossible, even making the inevitable allowances for the ambiguity and tortuousness of his phrasing, to believe that these words were meant to convey other than what they plainly said. His speeches were made, often enough, with large numbers of I.R.A. men present, many of them armed. They were made at
250

a time when the men were already divided among themselves and in several instances had given way to violence. Only a few days before, shots had been fired around the platform from which Michael Collins was speaking in Cork. Moreover, in a subsequent, and one presumes carefully thought out, statement to the press de Valera held that "there are rights which a minority may justly uphold, even by arms, against a majority."

And about the same time that de Valera was playing on the emotions and susceptibilities of young soldiers who were already in a highly excitable state, a decision was made by the Cabinet which came as a shock to the less militant opponents of the Treaty who had stuck to their conviction that, so long as the Army could be held together, somehow everything would come right in the end. So much hope had centred on the Army Convention, sanctioned by the Cabinet on February 27th and scheduled for March 26th. Pro- and anti-Treaty elements had met and agreed upon the basis of representation and had arranged to meet again on March 15th to prepare the agenda. Clusters of officers hobnobbed and hunched together in tense but amicable endeavour to come up with a new idea, a magic formula to reunite them. They were as sincere and as irreconcilable as religious leaders seeking an ecumenical approach to God. The leaders remained on friendly terms and, in spite of the clash of opinion, the recalcitrance of O'Malley, Robinson and others, the near-explosion in Limerick and sporadic bloody incidents, the main body of the I.R.A. still recognised G.H.Q., under whose aegis the Convention was to be held.

Then, on March 15th, the committee of officers working on the agenda received word that the Cabinet had proscribed the Convention. The Limerick alarm had shown that danger was nearer the surface than the Cabinet had realised, that, if the majority of the I.R.A. was not only against the Treaty but ready to blast it by gunfire, the people would have no option but to accept the verdict of those who had guns in their hands. Bluntly, the Cabinet published the reasons for its prohibition. The Minister of Defence, General Mulcahy, had had to admit that he could not guarantee that "if this Convention was held there would not be set up a body regarding itself as a military government not responsible to the people". He had "given up

251

hope" of even having put to the Convention a resolution "disclaiming any intention of setting up a military government as opposed to any government elected by the people" and agreeing, instead, to examine proposals, after a general election for "associating the I.R.A. with whatever Irish Government was then in authority."

This offended the more moderate Republicans, for they were not disposed towards military government and, unlike Mulcahy, had not given up hope that an arrangement between the I.R.A. and the Government could be worked out. Griffith had no doubt that the Army intended to detach itself from the control of Dail Eireann, which in theory at least was still the Republican Parliament and the elected Government of the people.

Given their opportunity to vote in a general election, they could throw out Griffith, and with him the Treaty and the foetus of the Irish Free State, and declare for a Republic and defiance of Great Britain. But Griffith was insistent that any Government elected by the people of Ireland must have control of the Army.

He maintained, and he carried his Cabinet with him that his Government was entitled, like any other government, to deny its army the right to hold a political meeting. It was an arguable point of view, for the I.R.A. was a revolutionary army, which had created both the climate and the means for an Irish Parliament to exist, and had provided most of its members. The Dail had been as much a weapon of the I.R.A. as the I.R.A. had been an instrument of the Dail. Griffith reasoned that the I.R.A., having pledged its allegiance to Dail Eireann, had no right to question the validity of its decisions. His opponents asserted that if the Dail extinguished itself they were released from any allegiance to it, or to any succeeding assembly which did not embody the ideal of the Republic.

Griffith had been willing to concede the right of the I.R.A. to hold their Convention, though it was in essence a political meeting, so long as he did not foresee an outcome which was inimical to the new State, or which ignored the wishes of the people. When he did foresee such an outcome, he acted.

Other members of the Cabinet who, unlike Griffith, belonged to the I.R.A., were perhaps less adamant than he, and Mulcahy, with his Chief of Staff, General Eoin O'Duffy, went out of his way to attend a meeting of the 1st Southern Division, presided over by Liam Lynch, at Mallow. Lynch did not despair of establishing a proper relationship between Government and Army but he made it plain that the Convention would be held, though to save the Government's face it could be postponed. The meeting insisted also that further recruitment to the Civic Guards, the force designed to replace both the Royal Irish Constabulary and the Dublin Metropolitan Police, but which was regarded by the anti-Treaty I.R.A. as a paramilitary arm of the Provisional Government, must stop. On March 15th, the Chief Secretary for Ireland informed the British Cabinet that the disbandment of the R.I.C. had been delayed at the request of Michael Collins[5]. Differences between the Provisional Government and the British Cabinet concerning the treatment of former R.I.C. members may explain Collins's request, but it is more likely that he was trying to meet the objections of his hostile friends.

Griffith was not in sympathy with Collins's desperate efforts to preserve army unity. He saw very well that trouble was brewing, and he believed that the sooner it came to the boil the sooner the gas could be turned off from under the pot. There is irony in this, for Collins as much as any man had been responsible for compelling Sinn Fein to accept the I.R.B.'s doctrine of physical force in 1919 when Griffith would have preferred to proceed by non-violent means.

A summons to attend the Convention in spite of the prohibition, which was seen as a broken agreement, went out, and Mulcahy countered it in a formal way by writing as Minister of Defence to his Chief of Staff, General Eoin O'Duffy. The letter, dated March 23rd, stated that the calling of a "sectional Convention" against G.H.Q. instructions, though it disrupted the past solidarity of the I.R.A., should not be allowed to destroy their spirit of brotherhood. But it went on to declare that any member who attended the Convention would be regarded as having severed his connection with the I.R.A. Commanding officers were to suspend offenders and report on each case, but were to take the "greatest pains" to avoid antagonising them.

Rory O'Connor claimed that the Army's decision to go ahead with the Convention meant, in effect, their repudiation

[5] Cabinet conclusion 18/22 (3) of 15/3/22.

of the Dail. "If a government goes wrong it must take the consequences," he said. But O'Connor's attitude was much more extreme than that of men like Liam Lynch who was still trying to devise a formula to link Army and Government.

It can never be known what would have been the outcome of the Convention of March 26th had all gradations of I.R.A. opinion, from die-hard Republicans to something approaching approval of the Treaty, been represented.

The Resolution passed by those present was that the Irish Republican Army should reaffirm its allegiance to the Irish Republic, and that its supreme control should rest with an Executive appointed by the Convention as it had before the Oath of allegiance to the Dail. Two days later, the Executive, a temporary body of sixteen, announced that the authority of the Minister of Defence and of the Chief of Staff would no longer be accepted.

Maintaining that the I.R.A. was the country's only legal army, the Executive ordered all regular members to report to their units, an order which, presumably, did not exempt Mulcahy and Collins, and demanded that recruiting for a Provisional Government force and for the Civic Guards should end. Though it has been said often enough that there was no intention to set up a military government, the instruction to the Provisional Government to cease recruitment certainly constituted interference with the civil authority. Someone had to run the country and that is what the dichotomous Government was trying, and in the circumstances not ineffectively, to do. Nor can the resolution that "if the Executive considered fit they could suppress the election"—on the grounds that the register was out of date and defective—be regarded as anything other than an attempt to impose their own will on the people.

McEoin has no doubt about the purpose of the Executive. "Although they called it an Executive to govern the Army, it really was an Executive to supplant both the Dail and the Provisional Government and it was, to all intents and purposes, a government they formed."

For the time being at least, the Executive were anxious that the proceedings of the Convention and their own identity should not be made public. But General Headquarters of the Provisional Government forces had obtained an account of what had transpired and gave it, together with the names of the sixteen, to the press. Censorship by sledgehammer was the Executive's answer to that move. Only the *Freemans Journal* published the complete report and on the night of March 30th a squad of raiders arrived in cars at the office of the offending newspaper. At gunpoint the staff were herded into the front office and held there. Other raiders took sledgehammers "borrowed" from the Great Southern and Western Railway and wrecked as much machinery as they could. All sixteen linotype machines were smashed. Fires were started in some rooms but were soon doused by the fire brigade after the wrecking party had gone. All but one of the raiders had behaved throughout with exemplary courtesy to the staff, other newspapers reported.

McEoin spent two days in Dublin discussing with Collins and Mulcahy the implications of the Army Convention. These were soon made evident to him on his return to Athlone. During his absence Lawlor was in command of the Midland Division headquartered at Athlone. Patrick Morrissey, the local brigadier, who had been a delegate of the Convention, stalked truculently into Lawlor's office, refrained from saluting and stood, legs wide apart, with a revolver stuck prominently in his belt.

"We've decided to stand by the Republic," Morrissey shot out.

"We're all standing by the Republic."

"*You're* not," Morrissey accused.

Lawlor stood up and told Morrissey to get the men on parade. He wanted to talk to them. Morrissey obeyed and Lawlor addressed the troops. "I blackguarded them, told them they were the worst looking crowd I'd ever seen and that if they were going to fight for a Republic none of them was likely to accomplish very much," he recalls.

Lawlor began to drill the troops, an unexpected move which enabled him to regain control. Finally, he ordered them to stack arms and gave them a five-minute respite. When he called them on parade again he made sure that they were well away from the stack of weapons. Carrying a gun in each hand, he threatened to shoot if his orders were challenged. He didn't dare *not* shoot, he told them candidly, for he would be unable to exercise any further control over them. The guns were

255

stored safely in the armoury. Realising they had been tricked, the angry men tried to recover their arms. There was near pandemonium when McEoin arrived back from Dublin. Lawlor, with two sergeants, Danby and Ingram, was standing between the armoury and the mob.

McEoin ordered the men to fall in by companies and, holding that "they were in mutiny", was ready to shoot any man who disobeyed. He called the Brigade to order, then marched across to Patrick Morrissey who had taken up his post in front.

McEoin asked Morrissey if he was prepared to obey orders from the Government. No, said Morrissey, he was not, but he would accept any order from McEoin.

"But I've got no authority to give any orders except Government orders," answered McEoin.

Morrissey stubbornly reiterated his statement, which was not the paradox it sounded. He was simply following the line taken by the Convention. Owing his allegiance to the Executive, he was ready to obey McEoin as his superior officer but not as the mouthpiece of a Government which he did not accept. This was the epitome of the "split". For McEoin, always logical, the line was more sharply drawn than it was for some officers on the side of the Treaty. On this issue he was more decisive than Collins, more even than Mulcahy who had performed verbal acrobatics in declaring that the Army would continue to be the Army of the Irish Republic. Like Griffith, McEoin saw that in no democratic, or even totalitarian, state could an army exist as an independent entity with an independent policy. The whole crux of the matter was that Southern Ireland had two governments and was trying to run the two in harness, hoping by this means to retain the loyalties of both sets of adherents.

Unable to move Morrissey from his point of view, McEoin ripped the Sam Browne from the shoulder of his Brigade Commandant, then, swinging him round, had him pushed through the gate. He did the same with those other officers of the Brigade Staff who took the same line. "That was not in any code that I know," McEoin admits, "but it was an effective method of dealing with the situation."

He then addressed the troops, reminding them that in the Battle of Athlone the officers had lost the day in spite of the
256

valiant efforts of Sergeant Custume and his men. It seemed, he said, that the officers were going to lose Athlone again. "But you can hold it," he rasped, "by obeying the orders." Then, probing their Irish hearts, "in honour of those N.C.O.s and men of the past", he renamed the barracks Custume Barracks.

McEoin next issued a proclamation by which he refused to accept liability for any debts incurred after Saturday other than for legitimate purchases made through the Divisional quartermaster, Commandant Looney. It was a practical precaution, for the departed officers mobilised their own supporters within a few days and seized a number of buildings round the square in Athlone. Holding the centre of the town, they were a threat to the whole of the West, and McEoin acted quickly. Gambling on the loyalty of the troops, on men who only two days previously had tried to break into the armoury, he put arms in their hands, surrounded the dissidents and compelled them to evacuate. No shots were fired but, in McEoin's opinion, the Civil War had already started.

Foreseeing trouble on a big scale in the near future, McEoin was anxious to consolidate the position of the pro-Treaty forces under his command. In his area he held the Upper and Lower Military Barracks in Longford, Athlone and Carrick-on-Shannon. Anti-Treaty forces under Liam Pilkington were in control of Boyle and, in McEoin's view, were a threat to Carrick.

In the first days of April, he called his officers to a council of war at the Bush Hotel, Carrick-on-Shannon. At this meeting, which was attended by General Eoin O'Duffy who was in the area, a plan to take Boyle was put forward by Commandant Martin Fallon and accepted.

Fallon was given the arms he needed and with twenty men he surprised the anti-Treaty garrison and captured Boyle without a shot being fired. Among his prisoners were officers of the Divisional Staff of what were now the Executive Forces. He lodged them in the cells prior to transferring them to Athlone in accordance with McEoin's instructions. The captive officers complained bitterly of this treatment and persuaded Fallon to place them under open arrest, the course they claimed they would have followed had the positions been reversed. A few hours later, Boyle was back in the hands of the Executive Forces and Fallon and his men were in the cells.

When they were released they made their shamefaced way back to Athlone to report to McEoin, who promptly suspended Fallon for failing to obey orders. Fallon pleaded for another chance and McEoin, always willing to forgive a good man for one mistake, but not more than one, relented.

General O'Duffy assembled all the officers in McEoin's command and addressed them at Custume Barracks. He was rather given to making pompous little homilies to meetings of this kind. At the end of his address he introduced Tommy Ryan— as a man from a Tipperary flying column who had resisted the pressure of those leaders of the 2nd Southern Division who had been first to flout the authority of G.H.Q. Ryan knew O'Duffy well and had got in touch with him when the South Tipperary men who had earlier plumped for the Treaty were over-persuaded by Lacey and Seamus Robinson. O'Duffy had suggested that he meet him in Athlone. After a long talk, Ryan offered to return to Tipperary and to make a further attempt to recruit support.

This time he was more successful. Many men who had been wavering had now made up their minds one way or the other. The Army Convention had left them with a clear choice between the Executive and the National Army Staff. Ryan enrolled many men in the National Army and sent most of them to Dublin or Kilkenny. In south Tipperary he became a centre of resistance, raiding dugouts and seizing arms. Soon he heard that Lacey and Robinson were about to have him arrested for "recruiting Irish Black and Tans" and he decided to return to Athlone. He mustered about one hundred men and instructed them to report to him in ones and twos at Cahir railway station.

"I interviewed the station master and told him of my intention to commandeer the first train from Waterford. He was most friendly. Anyway, we held up the Waterford to Dublin train, took it over and took it as far as Portarlington where we got off."

Eventually they reached Athlone where McEoin was suspicious of the influx. He was afraid that they had come to reinforce an anti-Treaty group recently arrived from north Tipperary.

The movement of men up and down the country was

confusing and the Irish capacity for accepting paradox was tested to the limit. McEoin's contention that civil war had already broken out was justified by the sporadic but insistent outbreaks of violence all over the country, and the momentum was gathering velocity. And yet, on one issue, not only was there mutual agreement, but the two sides were co-operating on a level approaching fantasy.

In spite of the agreement between Collins and Craig in January, the religious feud in the Six Counties, and especially in Belfast, had flared into a diabolical blaze. There was, no doubt, provocation on both sides. Two I.R.A. divisions belonged entirely within the Six Counties area and three other divisions operated in territory straddling the border. In constituting their divisions for the whole of the thirty-two counties, the I.R.A. simply ignored what was to them an artificial boundary created by an Act of the British Parliament. Some 8,000 men of the I.R.A. lived and worked within the Six Counties area and, in the border counties especially, the truncation of the North-East was a more excoriating issue than that of the Oath which had split the I.R.A. in most of the Twenty-six Counties. The activities of the I.R.A. in the North were certainly an irritant, but the virulence of the campaign of murder and arson against Catholics in Belfast stemmed from deep wells of fanaticism, fear and hatred. Retaliation was often fierce, and soon it was impossible to identify the participants in the macabre carnival. It is not to be thought that the majority of the Protestant North were other than horrified by it all; the responsibility belonged to the extremist minority. But partisanship blinds, and while the majorities both north and south of the border deplored the terror, each blamed the extremists of the other side.

In January, Craig had promised that he would try to arrange the return of 9,000 Catholic workmen who had been driven from their jobs in factories and shipyards. Collins, in his turn, had agreed to persuade his side to drop the Belfast Boycott. He had kept his word but he did not believe that Craig had even tried to keep his, for not one of the 9,000 had been allowed back to his old job.

Indignation in the South reached a high pitch and Collins, sceptical now of Craig's ability to control the situation, turned the Treaty on its face and co-operated with Liam Lynch in formulating and implementing a policy for the North. The holding of the Convention of March 26th, in defiance of the Cabinet edict, did not swerve him. Only a few days previously, a family of five, the MacMahons, was wiped out by men in uniform, evidently Specials. In reprisal a Protestant family named Donnelly was murderously attacked by a bomb and gunfire. The mother and her baby were killed, the father and two other children terribly injured.

The *Manchester Guardian* called it "a competition in murder" and saw it as a product of Carson's contempt for law since 1913.[6]

Special legislation introduced by Craig brought in flogging or death for men caught in possession of firearms or explosives but, in its strictures on unlawful drilling and the wearing of unauthorised uniforms, it seemed to be aimed at the I.R.A. rather than at Orange extremists, and the appointment as military adviser of Sir Henry Wilson, late Chief of the Imperial General Staff, did little to endear either Craig or Wilson to the South. Craig's fear was of civil war on a North-South axis. Inevitably Britain would have been drawn into such a struggle, and it would have been welcomed by the Republicans as a means of healing the breach in the I.R.A. and of disposing of the Treaty at the same time. For entirely different reasons, the extremists in the North hoped for the same thing; they believed it would end any chance of a Republic in the Twenty-six Counties.

Collins was neither prepared to yield the Treaty nor to stand by while Catholics in the North were murdered. In trying to have it both ways he drove the vessel of the Provisional Government perilously near the rocks. Northern divisions of the I.R.A. were strengthened. Experienced officers, notably Sean Lehane, were sent from Lynch's anti-Treaty First Southern Division to Donegal where, strangely, the majority of posts taken over from the British were in the hands of pro-Treaty elements of the I.R.A. On the other side of the country Commandant Frank Aiken had managed not to commit his Fourth Northern Division to either section of the broken I.R.A. His sympathies were with the Executive Forces but he continued to take his orders from what was now National

Army Headquarters at Beggar's Bush. Aiken's area took in Armagh and South Down across the border and North Louth. His headquarters were at Dundalk.

Arms and equipment for the North were sent mostly from Liam Lynch's area, but Collins lent himself to an incredible transaction: the exchange of rifles provided to the Provisional Government by the British for weapons obtained from other sources by Cork brigades. This was to prevent the British from identifying as their own any weapons which chanced to fall into their hands. Collins believed always in two-fisted action and the fact that he was secretly helping to initiate military action in the North did not prevent him from attempting simultaneously to alleviate the plight of co-religionists by political action. It did not concern him that there was a contradiction between his covert and overt actions, or that he was deceiving Craig and the British Government on the one hand and Arthur Griffith on the other, that he was upholding the Treaty on one count and disregarding it on another. To reach an end that he believed in utterly he set two courses in train and the only thing that mattered to him was that one of them worked.

On March 28th, in the Belfast Parliament, Craig answered Collins's charges that he had failed to keep their January pact by accusing him of keeping him in the dark "about the agreement with Lloyd George that large territories were involved in the Boundary Commission and not merely the boundary line". In fact, Collins had startled him at their January meeting by showing him on a map the territory which Lloyd George had led him to believe would be ceded to the Southern Government. With his usual dazzling ambiguity, Lloyd George had managed to convince both men that the Boundary Commission would inevitably favour their cause. Craig blamed all the disorders on the South and claimed that the high level of unemployment in the Six Counties prevented the return of Nationalists who had lost their jobs. They were only 9,000 in 60,000.

Two days later, on March 30th, Craig and Lord Londonderry met Collins, Griffith and Duggan at the Colonial Office in London and reached a second agreement which was countersigned by the British. "Peace is today declared . . ." the document began optimistically; that same night a Catholic

261

youth was murdered in Belfast and a patrol of Specials was ambushed by the I.R.A. The new agreement provided for the cessation of I.R.A. activities in the Six Counties and for the reorganisation of the Belfast police. In mixed districts half the police were to be Roman Catholic—"How this was to be sorted out, I don't know," says McEoin. "It is surprising that Craig agreed but he did and it certainly showed the extent of the goodwill which was between North and South and that Craig recognised that partition shouldn't be permanent."

Craig also agreed to make a further attempt to get the expelled Belfast workers back and the British Government tried to help on this point by promising a special grant of £500,000 for unemployment relief. The following day, the Irish Treaty Bill received the Royal Assent. The proposal to ratify the Treaty and to approve the Constitution of the Free State by means of a "one clause Bill" had had to be dropped. Churchill expressed his confidence that the Provisional Government would do its utmost to carry out the terms of the Treaty but warned that they were faced with powerful and unscrupulous enemies". From April 1st the Irish Exchequer came into being to which all future revenue collected in the country would go. All powers were now officially transferred to the Provisional Government. Outstanding problems, such as the Constitution and the Boundary Commission, would be settled in terms of the Treaty.

At Dundalk, on April 2nd, de Valera denied the right of the Provisional Government to govern. The only government was that which derived its right from the Irish people and not from the British Government. But he continued to fight shy of testing the will of the Irish people. He derided the new Craig-Collins agreement. It was, he said, "already a scrap of paper". He spoke with some authority. The Republicans had repudiated the pact and it did not seem that the Belfast extremists were taking it very seriously for, on the previous night, four members of a Catholic family were killed and two wounded following the death of a policeman earlier in the evening. The same night, in West Meath, a goods train was held up and Belfast goods were destroyed. On the following day, a man was shot dead and two children were injured by a bomb.

In spite of these incidents, the Agreement could easily have led to better things and the I.R.A. had to take its full share of responsibility for keeping the fire burning. As McEoin points out regretfully, "Such a rapport as that doesn't exist even today. The Six Counties had a point in believing we couldn't or wouldn't keep agreements."

McEoin was somewhat embarrassed at this time when fifteen Ulster policemen taken prisoner during a raid on Belcoo Barracks, Fermanagh, on March 28th were brought into his area. The intention was to hold them as hostages against the return of the I.R.A. men captured across the border. Following his second agreement with Craig, Collins was, for the moment at least, anxious not to offend the Northerner and when he visited Athlone was determined to find the prisoners and have them returned.

"I gave the jailers instructions to tell the prisoners they must not open their mouths whomever they saw or whatever they heard," recalls McEoin.

Collins made a meticulous inspection but found no trace of the prisoners, which was not surprising as Tony Lawlor was moving them from place to place throughout the day. Finally, as Collins leant tiredly against a shed door, he heard cries of "Mr Collins, Mr Collins."

"They were shouting like hell," says McEoin. "He asked who they were and I told him not to mind them, to come on, but they persisted and he had them released."

Collins himself soon lost faith in the Agreement and became more and more suspicious that the British were inciting disorder for their own purposes or, perhaps, that they were in league with Craig to ensure that partition was permanent. He was not even sure that a civil war in the South would not also suit Britain's book, allowing her to reimpose suzerainty on the grounds that the Irish had shown themselves incapable of self-government. His misgivings were reinforced by a strange incident at Cork.

British observers in the Cork area were intrigued by the large number of lorries commandeered by the Republicans but they did not believe there was any reason for British concern. Altogether some eighty vehicles were requisitioned as part of a plan to hijack the 700 ton *Upnor* which was scheduled to sail from Haulbowline Island with a cargo of naval small arms and ammunition. Sean O'Hegarty and Michael Murphy, getting wind of the shipment early in March, schemed to intercept the vessel at sea.

On March 31st, *Upnor* sailed, by which time the alertness of the Republicans had been blunted a little. The launch which was to have pursued *Upnor* was elsewhere. Improvising brilliantly, they seized the tug *Warrior* at the Deepwater Quay and routed her skipper out of a pub. Without him the venture was impossible. He sailed in disgruntled bewilderment with an enthusiastic if inexperienced crew of I.R.A. men. With a stolen ensign fluttering they bluffed *Upnor*'s master to stop, and so innocent did they seem, that two escort vessels steamed unconcernedly on. A boarding party ran *Upnor* into Ballycotton Bay, about ten miles east of the entrance to Cork harbour. There the lorries were waiting. A barge towed by *Upnor* yielded only office furniture but *Upnor* herself carried a large number of rifles, revolvers and machine-guns as well as ammunition and hand grenades. The I.R.A. had just got clear with their loot when a British destroyer put in.

"The reason for the commandeering of a large number of lorries is now explained," reported Macready[7] whose information concerning the "daring outrage" was that Tom Barry, "a dangerous Republican extremist", had commanded the enterprise on land while Captain Collins of the Cork Harbour Board had been in charge of the *Warrior*.

An ironical footnote to the *Upnor* episode is a letter Collins wrote to Churchill on March 28th[8] expressing his satisfaction that Churchill had prevailed on the Cabinet to keep Haulbowline Dockyard open after March 31st. He hoped that the Admiralty would send a vessel for repairs at an early date. This was, no doubt, an expression of Collins's concern about the unemployment problem.

The British should by now have learned something of Irish ingenuity but the *Upnor* incident showed that they had not. But Collins's suspicion that Britain had deliberately left the vessel invitingly vulnerable was unfounded. The one thing that the British Government did not want was trouble in Ireland; they wanted the Irish to stop arguing about the Treaty and to set up the British Dominion of the Irish Free State. There is no

[7] Cabinet Paper CP 3933 of 1/4/22. [8] Cabinet Paper CP 3913.

264

indication at the Cabinet meeting of April 5th, but Macready's report had been circulated and it was but one item in a rapidly deteriorating situation.

On the British side concern was felt over the disappearance of three British officers and a private at Macroom, Co. Cork. It was to prove that they had been kidnapped and murdered but Macready was satisfied that neither element of the I.R.A. was responsible. The crime was evidently the work of a gang who tried to pass off acts of brigandage as outrages by the I.R.A., but Macready believed that the Republican garrison of Macroom could have been more helpful, that they must have known something of what had happened.

Macready's view[9] was that the South was so strongly Republican that Collins and his followers would win no support when the election was held. There would be no civil war, he believed, because the Provisional Government had no army to speak of, and so the Republicans would have no-one to fight.

THIRTEEN

The drums of the Republic were beating louder and the British Government had visions of the proscribed flag being run up gaily on Irish rooftops. But this could never be allowed, Lloyd George explained indignantly to his Cabinet. "A point might come when it would be necessary to tell Mr Collins that if he was unable to deal with the situation the British Government would have to do so."[1] Approval was grunted from wing-collared throats, and it was pointed out that if the Provisional Government had found reliable replacements before insisting on the withdrawal of the British forces, there would be less trouble now.

"One of the main difficulties of the situation," as Churchill explained to his colleagues, "arose from the fact that Mr Arthur Griffith and Mr Michael Collins considered it vital and indispensable to the success of the policy of the Treaty to avoid striking the first blow against the Republicans, or

9 Ibid.   1 Cabinet conclusion 23/22 of 5/4/22.

any preparatory steps which might be regarded as provocative. Any British military or police support at the present stage would prove disastrous to the Provisional Government."

It has been argued that Lloyd George's threat of "immediate and terrible war" as the Irish plenipotentiaries stood on the brink of the Treaty was bluff. This is unlikely in view of the British Government's attitude in April, 1922, as set down in a memorandum by Churchill.[2] "There is no reason to doubt the good faith of the Provisional Government nor the goodwill of the Treaty party who support them in the Dail. There is every reason to believe that the great mass of people in Ireland would gladly vote for the Treaty and the Free State. On the other hand, the Irish Republican Army, which we have not recognised, but to which we have been forced to hand over a number of barracks (on the assurance that it would obey the Provisional Government) now appears to be largely unreliable, and the Provisional Government appears to be incapable of withstanding the extremists."

In short, there was likely to be an attempt to throw over the Provisional Government before any elections took place and to set up an Irish Republican Government. Such a government should not be recognised or parleyed with—"the mere fact of its being brought into being would constitute a state of war between it and the British Empire." His Majesty's Government would not be prepared to add to or detract from the provisions of the Treaty.

In the event of a coup d'état in Dublin, the British General Officer Commanding-in-Chief was to proclaim martial law at once, attack the Republican Government and seize the dissidents—"irrespective of the view taken by the Provisional Government". The existing garrison was thought to be adequate but could be speedily reinforced. Two destroyers were ordered into the river at Dublin as an urgent precaution.

If the attempt to set up a Republican Government were made outside the capital, the Provisional Government would be called upon "to take effective steps to wage war upon the Republican forces". It was envisaged that from all elements in the country favourable to the Treaty an army could be raised to attack the Republicans. The North might be very willing to assist but it was "doubtful if the Provisional Govern-

[2] Ibid.

ment would consent to fight alongside the North for the Treaty." Doubtful was hardly the word.

There was always the possibility that a coup "might not be met by an effective protest" and Churchill pointed out in his memorandum that "if the whole of the twenty-six counties quietly accepted the Republic and no serious attempt were made to resist it . . . there would not then be a civil war between the Treaty Party and the Republicans, but only a Republic in which the people of the whole country will have acquiesced, and in all probability civil war between Northern Ireland and the Southern Republic."

The proposals to deal with such an eventuality were different indeed from the days of the Black and Tans: "Dublin and possibly certain other ports should be held. Flying columns should attack the centres of the Republican Government wherever set up but, speaking broadly, there should be no permanent occupation of towns in Southern Ireland. For the protection of Ulster the British Army should also hold the best military line in the North irrespective of the Ulster boundary."

Aerodromes would be established and, in order that foreign powers did not seize the opportunity to acquire markets the British would want again later, there would be an economic blockade. It was laid down that "the juridical conditions of a conflict between the British Government and an Irish Republic would be, broadly speaking, those between the Union and the Confederate States, that is, there would be military recognition for persons in uniform. They would not be treated as rebels if they belonged to the armed forces of the Republic, but there would be no recognition on our part capable of admitting their rights to recognition by other nations."

Here was a change indeed. The British Government were willing to concede now that members of the I.R.A. were soldiers rather than terrorists and traitors but the situation was to remain essentially a domestic one. In the new set-up, the British Cabinet considered that the Provisional Government had taken over all direct responsibilities for the welfare of the people of Southern Ireland and that this would be an advantage. At the same time, there were some 300,000 Unionists "whose position might at any time become very grave" and who were likely to create a refugee problem.

The Viceroy, Lord FitzAlan, was summoned to the Cabinet meeting on April 10th. Learning that he had been withdrawn from Dublin for his own safety, he protested that it was not fair to the leaders of the Provisional Government for him to be absent from his post, but it was made clear to him that while his personal safety was his own lookout, "any untoward incident, such as seizure by enemies of the Free State, would place His Majesty's Government in a very difficult position."

At this meeting Churchill told the Cabinet[3] that the next ten days in Ireland would be critical and they should soon know "whether the leaders of the Free State were prepared to fight or to endure without resistance the insults now being offered them." He was of the opinion, however, that Collins's attitude was stiffening.

But Collins had by no means reached the end of his patience with his recalcitrant friends, and when, on April 14th, they seized a number of buildings in Dublin, among them the Four Courts, the Kildare Street Club and the Ballast Office, he made no move to put them out. The seizure of the great law buildings was a brazen challenge to the Government and it was not taken up. The occupation was not a revolt against the Government but a declaration that there was no Government. Rule by military junta was now perilously close, and in interviews with the press Rory O'Connor did not deny it. As McEoin said, the Executive had, to all intents and purposes, formed a government. But they made no effort to rule in any positive way. What they were setting out to do was to prevent the Dail Government and its interwoven Provisional Government from ruling either. Apart from the fact that the Four Courts with its self-contained buildings and courtyards was an ideal headquarters, the Executive sought also to disrupt the courts, which continued to function as they had under British rule. Dail courts had operated very effectively in competition with the British courts during the recent war and the Executive tried the same tactics against the Dail. In country areas, as well as in Dublin, there was incessant harassment of the existing courts. The Lord Chief Justice of Ireland, Sir Thomas Moloney, defeated this objective in the capital by simply transferring his courts elsewhere.

The National Army was still very small and most pro-Treaty

[3] Cabinet conclusion 24/22 (1) of 10/4/22.

officers who did not seek an army career had returned to their jobs. Some were available as a Volunteer Reserve and many, as they saw the drift of events, joined the Army. It would not have been easy for Collins to throw O'Connor's men out of the Four Courts, especially if there was resistance, and Collins did not attempt it. Griffith, well aware of Collins's sentimental attachment to many of his adversaries, was not convinced that lack of strength was the main factor in withholding, but he did take the point that it was better not to strike the first blow. Collins was still optimistic about the possibilities of repairing the split Army. If he could achieve this a political settlement would follow more readily. As yet de Valera had not committed himself to the course Rory O'Connor was pursuing, and while he remained strictly a political adversary as leader of the Cumann na Poblachta, or Republican Party, which he had founded earlier in the year, there was hope of containing the quarrel in the political arena, in spite of an assertion to the press that the Executive Forces would be justified in using their strength to save the nation from the consequences of the Treaty.

On the same day that O'Connor relinquished his offices in Suffolk Street for more spacious rooms in the Four Courts, de Valera went from his quite separate offices at the same address to confer with leaders of the Provisional Government.

When the Dail reassembled on April 26th, having adjourned on March 2nd, Griffith explained how, at the invitation of the Archbishop of Dublin, he and Collins had met de Valera and Brugha "with the object of securing a peaceful election". He reported, "There is, so far, no result." The meetings ended, in fact, three days later without any agreement.

The plain fact was that de Valera and his adherents did not want an election which they knew they could not win. They were an admitted minority claiming rights "which a minority may justly uphold, even by arms, against a majority." A peaceful election campaign seemed a remote possibility indeed.

If it could be prevented, even Arthur Griffith was not to be allowed to put his point of view to the people of Ireland. That point of view he had put clearly and convincingly in the almost interminable Dail debate on the Treaty. "Ireland for the Irish people" was the principle he had stood on all his life. "If I can get that with a Republic I will have a Republic," he said in the dying moment of the depressing marethon, "if I can get that with a monarchy I will have a monarchy. I will not sacrifice my country for a form of government." He wanted the people to know "that it is their right to see that this Treaty is carried into operation, when they get, for the first time in seven centuries, a chance to live their lives in their own country and take their place amongst the nations of Europe."

On Easter Sunday, April 16th, Griffith was to address a meeting in Sligo, but Liam Pilkington had proclaimed all meetings in the area following the stormy meeting Collins had had in Castlebar a fortnight earlier, when guns were produced and shots fired by both sides and Collins could not make himself heard as he pleaded: "If Mr de Valera and his friends will not join with us, if they will not co-operate in the work to be done, can they not accept the policy of live and let live?" To a warning telegram from the Mayor of Sligo, Griffith replied that he would not be deterred by any threat of interference with free speech. He would keep to his programme.

On Good Friday the Mayor called an extraordinary meeting of the Corporation at which Brigadier-General Seamus Devins of the anti-Treaty forces, a Councillor, stated that the terms of the proclamation would be "carried out to the last man". A motion was passed urging all citizens "to avoid any public demonstration" and warning of the likely consequences if the exhortation were ignored. In other words, they were advised not to attend Griffith's meeting.

Republican troops from the whole area made for Sligo and, from Friday until Tuesday, the city was almost in a state of siege. Numerous buildings were occupied including the Courthouse, Town Hall, Post Office, Hibernian Bank, Ulster Bank and Victoria Hotel. Nos. 1 & 2 R.I.C. barracks were already in their possession. Commandeered cabs and lorries hissed around wet streets but the Republican soldiers, most of them in civilian clothes, were too tense to heed the fine penetrating drizzle. Indeed, the streets were thronged with watchful, excited people.

Potent, too, was the arrival on the Friday morning of a strong party of National troops from Athlone who took possession of the county jail. They seemed formidable, with a business-like armoured car as part of their equipment. The actual seizure of the jail was carried out by two men, Lawlor and Ned Cooney, who climbed over a wall topped with broken glass and dropped into the Governor's carefully tended rose garden. The noise they made roused the Governor's household and the two young men, with pleasurable embarrassment, had to allay the fears of the Governor's eleven very presentable daughters, who had risen in alarm from their beds, before they could accomplish their purpose.

More Republicans made their way into the town towards nightfall and quartered themselves at Mrs Ramsay's Hotel in Bridge Street, and on the following day they were strongly reinforced from the Tobercurry area. Republicans commandeered a train at Dromahaire and rolled comfortably into the town to seize many more buildings. The market was held as usual on Saturday, but prices were unusually erratic, and it was hard for a man to keep his mind on a shrewd bargain when he needed to be glancing over his shoulder each minute in case he missed the latest excitement.

That day Arthur Griffith travelled from Dublin by train as far as Carrick-on-Shannon. At Longford he was met by a guard of honour and an enthusiastic crowd. Speaking from the train, he assured them that he was "determined to vindicate the right of the people to elect that form of government which they wished to have."

Sean McEoin joined Griffith and his companions, Sean Milroy and Darrell Figgis, at Longford. He, too, was to speak at the meeting. McEoin had recently been promoted to Major-General and appointed G.O.C., Western Command, an appointment he accepted reluctantly. He was a man of action and didn't want to be tied down by administrative work. He would accept the command, he told Collins, only if he were given a legal officer and a quartermaster. Collins quickly produced a dozen lawyers with Treaty sympathies and McEoin chose John Hearne, who afterwards reached ambassadorial rank. Hearns was rushed down to O'Callaghans', the military outfitters where he exchanged his natty lawyer's dress for an army uniform. He emerged with a Sam Browne belt that creaked its newness and a smart holster. Having been issued with a large revolver, he took his place in McEoin's car to travel to Athlone. As they set off, Hearne suddenly realised that McEoin had no escort and asked rather anxiously where

271

it was. McEoin laughed. "Haven't I got you?" he said and, pointing to the revolver added, "and *that*."

It was as G.O.C. Western Command that McEoin accompanied Griffith to Sligo, but he was not in uniform. On Sunday morning, McEoin coolly walked round Sligo checking the positions held by Pilkington's forces, who were taking turns to go to Mass. There was fitful sunshine that morning, which augured well for the meeting, McEoin thought. He could sense the tension in the town.

"I was able to draft a plan that would bottle them properly," he recalls. At 11 a.m., Lieutenant-General "Ginger" O'Connell, then Deputy Chief of Staff, arrived from Dublin with forty men in three lorries. They had travelled overnight with one short stop at Carrick-on-Shannon. O'Connell was unaware that the Imperial Hotel and Mrs Ramsay's Hotel where he planned to billet his men were already occupied by the Republicans. Half of his party went across the river to the Imperial; O'Connell himself knocked at Mrs Ramsay's Hotel. A moment later, his men, who had climbed from the lorries, shouted a warning that he was "covered" from an upstairs window. A shot gun was fired, probably to warn O'Connell off, but the charge came closer than that says McEoin: "Ginger had a green leather coat on him and I swear the back was cut into a fringe of thongs."

At once O'Connell's men opened fire, then they found themselves within range of the Imperial Hotel across the river. Firing went on in both directions for about fifteen minutes when O'Connell, by hard shouting, finally got his men to desist. Meanwhile, a number of his men who had gone to the Imperial had been allowed in, then made prisoner.

Leaving a patrol to watch Mrs Ramsay's, O'Connell went to find McEoin, who assumed that his senior officer would now take over responsibility. O'Connell explained the situation. "I won't touch it at all," he told McEoin. "Here, I take my orders from you."

Back in uniform, McEoin took a small force to the Imperial, dashed in and saved O'Connell's men and their equipment. He also took some prisoners. At this point, Seamus Devins presented himself under a flag of truce.

"Isn't it possible to make peace somehow?" he asked.

"Quite easy," snapped McEoin.

"Well, what's your idea?"

"First vacate the post office and then restore all the telephone lines to Dublin."

"Oh, we won't do that," replied Devins, laughing.

"Then no peace."

"But there'll be bloodshed," warned Devins.

"Buckets of it," snorted McEoin, adding slyly, "It'll be the first time Sligo has seen any."

Ignoring the thrust, for Sligo had not been noted for any belligerent activity during the war against England, Devins said disgustedly, "You're a savage, aren't you?"

"Yes, I am. I'm defending the right of the Irish people and the right of the Parliament of this country to govern."

The two men parted.

It was almost time for the meeting. "The Bellman had already gone round telling the people about it and they came in their hundreds," recalls McEoin. "Then we went ahead in accordance with my plan."

At 3.25 that Easter Sunday afternoon the National Forces travelled in their tenders from the jail to the home of Alderman Hanley, where they collected the President, and then on to the meeting. Leading the procession was the armoured car, upon which stood the aggressive figure of McEoin, one hand resting on the turret, the other holding a gun. Ginger O'Connell was on the footboard. The procession attracted cheering crowds of Sligo people, who followed it to the town centre. The armoured car was positioned with its guns trained on the post office, and troops were placed strategically. O'Connell took up a position in John Street, Colonel-Commandant Lawlor guarded the tender from which Griffith was to speak, and Commandant McCabe patrolled with a large revolver. McEoin moved around the various posts until Griffith was to speak, then, with a gun in each hand, he took up a position in a window overlooking the meeting like a fiery Irish Vulcan. From his window he made a speech in support of Griffith who maintained in his earthy way the right of the people to reject the Treaty if they wished. He advised them not to reject it, but promised that if they did he would follow them.

273

There was no trouble; the anti-Treaty men were effectively contained in their posts, unable even to communicate between themselves. Griffith was dispatched safely back to Dublin.

Collins, too, was finding political life turbulent, but neither did he lack protectors. At a meeting in the Square at Dungarvan, Co. Waterford, he was being introduced by the chairman when the lorry on which he and his party were ensconced began to move off down the street. His redoubtable henchman, Joe Dolan, at once smashed the back window of the cabin, thrust a gun inside and threatened to blow the driver's head off. The lorry stopped suddenly and the driver leapt out and began to run. Dolan "just put a shot over his head for luck."

Abandoning the lorry, Collins spoke from the balcony of the hotel. Scathingly he recalled a time when nine Black and Tans had spent a whole day in Dungarvan and not a shot had been fired.

When he visited Killarney on April 22nd, his train was delayed as his opponents had closed the railway gates for miles. McEoin, who was to address the meeting with Collins, Sean Milroy, Patrick O'Keefe and Fionan Lynch, went up on the footplate and ordered the driver to burst through the gates. They were met at Killarney station by Brigadier John Joe Rice with about fifty men. Rice proclaimed the meeting. "He was very excited," says McEoin, "and he stepped up with a parabellum, stuck it in Collins's side and told him he could go no further, to back the train and go away. I noticed the safety catch was on. I threw my left hand over and caught the parabellum. At the same time, I rammed my revolver into his side." Rice conceded the point and marched his men away, but he was not beaten yet.

Collins's party lunched with Dr Bill O'Sullivan (later a Senator), and during the meal Joe Dolan approached McEoin and whispered that Rice had his men drawn up in two lines across the street with bayonets fixed. McEoin rose and left the house with Dolan. Unchallenged, they walked up to Rice who was standing with his parabellum drawn.

"Now," says McEoin, "I stuck my revolver into him and ordered him to call his men off or I'd put the contents through him. 'And for every one that you put that way, I'll put one this way,' Joe Dolan told him!" Rice took the hint and marched his men away for the second time. The meeting was a success, though the platform had been burned and Collins had to speak from a brake.

Next morning the Collins entourage went on to Tralee, where they learned that Humphrey Murphy had proclaimed their meeting. News of the Killarney incident had already reached Tralee. Collins's party was augmented by Commandant Dinny Galvin who had been sent with twenty men to lend support. Murphy, less truculent than Rice and anxious to avoid a clash, went to see McEoin at about midday. "He said there would be bloodshed. I said there would. But we were going to uphold the right of free speech whatever the consequences," McEoin explains. The right of free speech is always most staunchly advocated by those who wish to exercise it and McEoin saw no irony in the fact that a few years earlier he had been wont to break up the meetings of Redmond's followers, just as men like Murphy and Rice had also done. But human rights are like prismatic mirrors and shine according to the angle from which the light of conviction falls. As for free speech, surely it means the right to prevent an opponent from being heard as much as it means the right to speak unhindered.

Murphy wondered whether there was not some way out for them both but McEoin was adamant. Only by calling off the proclamation could Murphy achieve peace that day. Asking McEoin to make his position a little easier, Murphy suggested that they should both issue orders confining their troops to barracks. McEoin agreed to this course and the orders went out, to apply from 1 p.m. Collins enjoyed a meeting free from interruption.

That night there was a celebratory banquet. After two hectic days, McEoin was weary, and when Galvin came in and told him that ten of his men had been disarmed by some of Murphy's troops, he told him in some irritation to go out and disarm ten of their opponents. When McEoin later retired to his room he found Galvin there. The room was full of men and rifles. They were the prisoners McEoin had told him to take, Galvin explained. McEoin was short with him. "I didn't tell you to take prisoners—I told you to take rifles." At that point Murphy arrived, demanding the release of his men, and McEoin bridled. He ordered Murphy out and Murphy challenged him.

"I grabbed hold of him," McEoin remembers wryly. "He was at a disadvantage and I knocked him on to my bed. That shook him—he was a fairly weighty man. Then I whipped him up, ran him through the door and shoved him down the stairs. I was vexed with myself, vexed with Galvin, vexed with everyone, and here was someone I could take it out on. Unfortunately, I jumped on him at the bottom of the stairs and I was giving him a few pucks when Collins caught me by the collar, hauled me up, slammed me into a little room near the foot of the stairs and locked the door."

There were bars at the window and McEoin had to stay there. He had cooled a little but was still fuming when Collins opened the door twenty minutes later and insisted that he come and shake hands with Murphy. McEoin did so unwillingly. Collins then told McEoin that Murphy had not really understood the Treaty and what was involved. Now that he did, he intended to see Sean O'Hegarty of Cork, Dan Breen and several others with the object of drawing up some kind of agreement. "And that was the genesis of the Army Document that was read to the Dail," McEoin concludes.

A number of prominent officers of both sides met in conference several times and on May 1st the "Army Document", based on a draft by O'Hegarty, was signed by Collins, Mulcahy, O'Duffy, Gearoid O'Sullivan and Sean Boylan for the pro-Treaty side and by Breen, Murphy, O'Hegarty, O'Donoghue and Tom Hales for those who opposed the Treaty. This historic document, grounded on common sense and tolerance read:

"We, the undersigned officers of the I.R.A., realising the gravity of the present situation in Ireland, and appreciating the fact that if the present drift is maintained a conflict of comrades is inevitable, declare that this would be the greatest calamity in Irish history, and would leave Ireland broken for generations.

"To avert this catastrophe we believe that a closing of the ranks all round is necessary.

"We suggest to all leaders, Army and political, and all

citizens and soldiers of Ireland the advisability of a unification of forces on the basis of the acceptance and utilisation of our present national position in the best interests of Ireland, and we require that nothing shall be done that would prejudice our position or dissipate our strength.

"We feel that on this basis alone can the situation best be faced, viz.:

(1) The acceptance of the fact—admitted by all sides—that the majority of the people of Ireland are willing to accept the Treaty.

(2) An agreed election with a view to

(3) Forming a Government which will have the confidence of the whole country.

(4) Army unification on above basis.

Dan Breen	Tom Hales
H. Murphy	S. O'Hegarty
F. O'Donoghue	Sean Boylan
R. J. Mulcahy	Owen O'Duffy
Gearoid O'Sullivan	Miceal O'Coileain."

In a stern pronouncement on April 26th the Roman Catholic Hierarchy in Ireland had pressed for a meeting of leaders to seek a peaceful solution and the Army Document, though it owed little if anything to the intervention of the Bishops, reflected the same concern. But the I.R.A. leaders were inspired less by the exhortations of the Church than by bitter personal loss. When on Monday night, April 24th, Brigadier-General Adamson was waylaid in Athlone, and shot dead though he had his hands up, the anti-Treaty garrison in the Royal Hotel, under Commandant Fitzpatrick, marked their repudiation of the deed by surrendering to McEoin, who had returned that day from Killarney. They were taken as prisoners to Custume Barracks but later released.

Though they allowed that "every Irishman is entitled to his own opinion, subject, of course, to truth and responsibility to God", the Bishops themselves thought, predictably, that "the best and wisest course for Ireland is to accept the Treaty and make the most of the freedom it undoubtedly brings us". But the issue was one for settlement by a constitutional election, and they deplored the "unconstitutional policy of certain leaders who think themselves entitled to force their views upon the nation, not by reason but by firearms". They adjured "the young men connected with this military revolt" to remember: "When they shoot their brothers on the opposite side they are murderers."

They pleaded with the leaders to meet "and, if they cannot agree on the main issue, to agree upon two things at all events, and publish their agreement authoritatively to the world—that the use of the revolver must cease and the elections, the national expression of self-determination, be allowed to be held, free from all violence."

From Rory O'Connor in the Four Courts came a sour repudiation of the Document. He deplored attempts by "individual soldiers" to strike bargains with the other side and reminded them that the Executive was now the sole Army authority. But it was an authority on a shoe-string budget. Neither the Republican I.R.A., nor the Dail itself, had money enough to fight a war, but the new Provisional Government was being financed by the British Treasury. The Executive leaders in the Four Courts took steps to remedy the lack of funds. On the grounds that bills for provisions purchased by garrisons of former British posts who happened to be anti-Treaty had not been met by the Provisional Government, they decided to help themselves from the deposits of the official bank, the Bank of Ireland. On May 1st, the same day that the Army Document was signed, branches of the Bank all over Ireland were raided and a total of £250,000 was appropriated. In most instances the raids were carried out with solemn courtesy and receipts were issued.

In Dublin the bank guard was commanded by Lieutenant Vinny Byrne who had taken over from the British garrison. When "the split" came Byrne, formerly of the Squad, followed his old chief, Michael Collins. "I believe he was honest to God in what he did," says Byrne, and cogently he sums up the situation from the point of view of the ordinary I.R.A. man: "When the Treaty was accepted everyone was happy about it, but after a few days politics entered into it. The old Volunteers split and for a while you didn't know who was your friend and who your enemy. I maintain I'm as good a Republican as the man who fought against the Treaty. The only oath of allegiance I ever took was to the Republic." He was prepared to follow Collins across his "stepping-stones"
278

to the Republic, but some of his friends in the Bank guard were among those who wanted to reach it in one jump.

"We had a sergeant of the guard who was a personal friend of mine and the corporal was a friend of mine too, but he was one of the men who were anti-Treaty." Here again was that phenomenon of the times, the garrison of divided loyalties.

"I remember a certain gentleman came down and he spoke to the corporal I mentioned out in the back yard of the bank. Afterwards, this lad said to me he thought he'd chuck it in. He wasn't satisfied. I told him, 'If you're going to do anything I'd do it honourably. I'd come up and hand in my uniform and retire.' Anyway, it all passed off and then, one morning, I'd just had a shave and was putting on my tunic when the Sergeant of the Guard came into me with a note. It was headed Four Courts Garrison, Dublin, and ran briefly: 'If you and your men are ready to move out of the Bank of Ireland, do so immediately—lorry outside.' The messenger had given it to the wrong man.

" 'All right,' says I, and threw on my Sam Browne belt and rushed down the stairs. There were eighteen or twenty men in the main guardroom. The rifles were all on the left-hand side. Standing in the doorway with my .45 in my hand, I said, 'I believe you're planning on leaving. All right. You either drop at my feet or I drop at yours. Now, lads, go for your guns.' Not one man moved." In view of Byrne's reputation as a Squad man the lack of response to his invitation was hardly surprising.

"There was a bank guard marching up and down the colonnade and I told him to ring Beggar's Bush Barracks and tell them the guard had mutinied. In next to no time an armoured car arrived, with G.H.Q. staff and everyone else. Ginger O'Connell was among them. Anyway, a new guard was sent to take over and the men I had disarmed were taken in a lorry to Marlborough Mall, Glasnevin. Some of the fellows were taken back in the Army again later.

"When I looked out at the hullabaloo I saw Oscar Traynor, Rory O'Connor and a few of them all out in the street waiting for the fellows to bring the stuff, but they had their wait for nothing."

Shortly afterwards, Byrne was promoted "in the field" to the rank of captain.

At about this time the Four Courts garrison acquired an armoured car, which they christened *Mutineer*. It was the vehicle which Leahy had impounded at Templemore in March. Leahy had no intention of using the armoured car, but when the National Army made an attempt to recover it, he decided to get rid of it.

The attempt was led by Commandant-General Dermott MacManus, who had followed Dalton as Director of Training. With thirty men, including ten military policemen and the same two Black and Tans who had driven the car to Limerick, MacManus set off for Templemore. One of his three armoured cars broke down and had to be left in safe hands on the way.

"Before we got into Templemore," says MacManus, "I stopped at a farmhouse and pinched a long ladder hung outside it and when we got there we went to the local doctor, knocked him up, and we found they were pretty strong there. They had well over a hundred men in the barracks and machine-guns and everything, and we also found that the armoured car was at the back, in a shed. So I brought my men round to the back. They were wilting and I had to drive some of them on with my revolver. It was no good doing a proper attack. So I put the ladder up at the back. I took the belts off the military police and threaded them through each other to make a rope, fastened it to the top rung, hung it down inside and climbed down with the two Black and Tans. We found a shed with the armoured car and forced open the door. By this time the garrison were getting up in their various rooms and looking at us with amazement, and we ran it out.

"We saw they had built a sandbag wall across inside the main gates so we could not crash out, so we removed some of the innards of the car, then we climbed back."

MacManus lined his troops up in front of the barracks and Leahy came out to talk to him. They knew each other but Leahy remembered MacManus as Burke, a name he had used in earlier days. MacManus continues:

"I said, 'Well you've pinched our armoured car,' and he answered, 'Yes. We're just keeping it. We are not joining either side. We don't want it to be used on our Irishmen.' I told him, 'Look here, it belongs to us,' but he said not. I suggested that he'd have a bit of a job getting the car out and he agreed that they couldn't start it. 'I damn well know you can't,' I said. We walked up and down for three quarters of an hour arguing as to whether he would give me the car to fit the parts or whether I should give him the parts to fit the car."

In the end, MacManus returned to Dublin with the parts, but three days later one of the Beggar's Bush staff officers decided he was on the wrong side and decamped to Templemore, taking the parts with him. The armoured car was driven to Dublin and handed over to Rory O'Connor.

There might, perhaps, have been a lesson in this strange, bloodless encounter, but others were less moderate than Leahy and MacManus.

FOURTEEN

Mass in the parish church of Annacarty on Sunday, April 30th, 1922, was followed by the wedding of pretty Miss Elizabeth Stapleton to Paddy English. As the service ended, soon after midday, a horse clattered up the road to the old R.I.C. barracks which had been occupied the previous day by pro-Treaty forces under Colonel Tom Carew. Since the formal take-over from the British the barracks had stood empty, but with trouble in the air, the Provisional Government supporters had decided to establish a post in them.

The barracks dominated Annacarty, then a village of two pubs, Sadleir's and Bradshaw's, two shops, a post office, a school and a handful of houses of which one was the residence of the schoolmaster, Michael Slattery. Six miles north of Tipperary town, Annacarty was a sleepy Irish village where, for some strange reason, the British had elected to build barracks which had all the properties of a fortress. Sited at the summit of a hill, the building had fat stone walls, a flat roof with a parapet, a corner tower and tiny windows. In the parapet were firing slits. Perhaps the British had an inkling of what was to come in later years, but at the time the barracks were erected Tipperary was a peaceful place.

During the Anglo-Irish war the Annacarty R.I.C. barracks resisted all attacks by the I.R.A., who succeeded, nevertheless, in penning the Black and Tan garrison within them for much of the time. One of the most notorious of the Tans was a loud and colourful character known as "Big Bill" Robinson who swaggered his way about with a revolver on either hip and a rifle slung across his shoulder. Robinson's rowdy exploits had an extrovert viciousness which, in an odd way, almost endeared him to the locals rather as sufferers tend to laugh at a backache. It says much for the Irish capacity to forgive that, forty years later, an old lady remarked of him, "Sure, there must have been some good in the poor misguided boy's heart."

Robinson was not the only character in the area; from Annacarty and the neighbouring parish of Donohill came such I.R.A. stalwarts as Dan Breen, Sean Treacy, Tom and Dan Carew and Dinny Lacey. The sound of Irish guns became as familiar as rattling milk churns in Annacarty, but no one dreamed then that those guns would one day be used by Irishmen against Irishmen.

When, following the Treaty, the English commander of the garrison handed over the barracks to Tom Carew, schoolmaster Slattery, whose pupil Carew had been and whose friend he now was, gave the children a holiday. The boys were marched up the hill by the eldest of them, Andrew Breen, to salute the new flag. It was a very moving moment in the life of Larry Slattery, son of the schoolmaster. Then the controversy began and, as elsewhere, the I.R.A. divided.

No sooner had Carew moved into the barracks than his cousin, Dinny Lacey, and Michael Sheehan prepared to put them out again. The same night Republican troops moved into Annacarty and surrounded the bullet-scarred fortress. Michael Slattery's house, where so often I.R.A. men had foregathered, was taken over by anti-Treaty troops who began to make preparations for an attack on the barracks. The family were ordered out and took refuge with neighbours. Several other families were also compelled to leave their homes. Michael Slattery was upset, not so much because of the inconvenience to himself and his family, but because it appalled him that these young men, many of whom had sat together in his classroom, were threatening to kill each other.

The situation was tragic almost beyond meaning, and the schoolmaster wanted no part in it.

On Sunday morning, Dan Breen and Jerry Ryan arrived separately, each hoping to relieve the tension, but Lacey was determined to clear out the barracks one way or the other.

"Dan, will you get those boys out of my house?" Michael Slattery asked, and shortly was able to take his family home again.

Anti-Treaty men continued to arrive in Annacarty. The air seemed explosive; the people waited with grim expectancy; Miss Elizabeth Stapleton decided to go ahead with her wedding.

From the church the bride and her groom came smiling and at that moment Tom Carew sauntered out of the barracks to take a dispatch from the rider of the horse, John Jo Lysaght of Dundrum. Rifles crackled like a burning cornfield and Carew fell seriously wounded in the hip. For Paddy English that fusillade of shots fired by men who were his friends, almost as if his emergence from the church had been the signal, must have sounded a grim bridal tune. Quietly, anxiously, the congregation scattered to their homes.

Ironically, staying with the Slattery family and unable now to leave Annacarty was a Mr Watson from Waterford who had come to arrange the installation of a stained glass window in the church. It was to be a memorial to Dan Carew who had been shot down in Harcourt Street, Dublin in 1920.

The besieged defenders in the barracks were as well placed to repel attack as the Black and Tans had been, but being under constant fire, were unable to bring in further supplies of food and water. They had not expected an attack and were ill-provisioned, so the Republicans hoped to compel their surrender. The garrison numbered about twenty men sharing fourteen rifles. Annacarty boasts more Ryans than any other parish in Tipperary and there were no less than three in the barracks while two more of the doughty breed, Paddy Ryan (Masters) and Jimmy Ryan (Patsy), set up their own strongpoint in Sadleir's and held out against the anti-Treaty men until late on the Sunday evening when they had to retreat to Bradshaw's across the road. During the night they made their way up the hill to rejoin their friends in the barracks.

During that night, too, Tom Carew had grown weaker and

on Monday morning a temporary cease-fire was arranged so that his sister could take him by car to the hospital in Tipperary. By the end of that day the garrison had no food or water left, two men, Lieutenant James Ryan and Volunteer Patrick Dwyer, had minor wounds and it did not seem that they could go on much longer. They had no hope of reinforcements, for not only were the Republicans several hundred strong and positioned over a wide area, but roads were blocked and rails had been torn up and thrown into hedges at Lisduff, at Goold's Cross and at points on the line from Clonmel to Thurles. It was a novel situation and at Thurles crowds gathered on the station platform, mouth-organs made music and the young people danced.

By now the people of Annacarty had decided to carry on their lives as always. Let the boys fight it out, since fight it out they would, and let God guide the bullets away from innocent folks. So the women shopped and the cows were driven in from the fields for milking, and Michael Slattery's daughter took the milk can and went to collect the family milk. Her brother Larry and his friends hung round to watch the battle and wondered which set of their heroes they wanted to win. They idolised them all. It was not easy for small boys to resolve, so confusing was the issue; and it was not easy for their parents. The truth was they did not want harm to come to any of the boys. What if Bill Burke were to die in the barracks, or his brother Jack to fall outside them? Would the other ever forgive himself, would he even know whether or not he had fired the fatal shot? That was what civil war meant.

But no one was killed at Annacarty, and no civilian or animal even hurt. At ten o'clock on Tuesday morning, the pro-Treaty men surrendered. As prisoners they were marched out, Simon Breen, Bill Corcoran, Bill Burke, all the Ryans, and several more. White-faced and despondent, they were taken to Clonmel by their captors, among whom were Bryan Shanahan, Mick Sadleir from Rathkenny, and Sean Hayes. A few days later they were allowed to go home. The barracks they had defended so sturdily was a burnt-out shell, destroyed so that Provisional Government forces could not reoccupy it. Even the lead roof had melted in the blaze. The stubborn husk still stands and the birds fly through its blank windows and doors.

On the same day that the two divisions of the I.R.A. collided in Annacarty, a train of powder to trouble began to fizzle in historic Kilkenny. The city was controlled by National Forces under Commandant J. T. Prout who, however, had tolerated the occupation of two barracks, in John Street and Parliament Street, by the anti-Treaty members of the I.R.A. His one condition was that their garrisons carried out police duties only, and that they wore a suitable badge to identify them. And, indeed, in Kilkenny as elsewhere, the Republican police were of inestimable service to the community at this time.

On Tuesday, April 25th, the Republican leader, Ruth, and a number of his men took possession of Kilkenny Prison, to which, three days later, they brought forty casks of rum and whiskey seized from a bonded store. Prout foresaw some heady problems, and on Saturday morning presented Ruth with an ultimatum. In the evening, the Republicans departed, muttering their resentment which, since they had to abandon the casks, wasn't surprising. Kilkenny people went to bed that night wondering what would happen. There had been some startling shots in the night, both on the Tuesday and Wednesday preceding. Several bullets had been fired at Parliament Street barracks, the Republican headquarters, on the Tuesday, and the garrison had replied with rifles and machine-guns. Next day, Prout had called on Ruth, who exonerated Prout's men and blamed third parties for trying to cause bad blood. Republicans on Wednesday night mistook one of Prout's men for a man they had been told would pass through Kilkenny on his way to join the Belfast "Specials", and when they tried to arrest him he fired several revolver shots to facilitate an escape.

Sunday in Kilkenny was quiet and a rather relieved populace went about their business next day. But that night, Monday, May 1st, armed men from Waterford, Tipperary and Kilkenny County bustled into the town like tacks hopping on to a magnet. Assisted by the local Republican group, they seized about a dozen buildings, among them the Round Tower and belfry of St Canice's Cathedral, Kilkenny Castle, the workhouse, City Hall, the Working Men's Club, the Imperial Hotel and other carefully selected buildings of seeming strategical significance. Commandeered lorries were loaded with requisitioned provisions, bedding and sacks for use as sandbags, while apprehensive, outraged citizens bent whispering heads in speculative clusters.

The National Forces had the military barracks, the prison and the Bank of Ireland and the clash between the two forces of taut young men seemed imminent. Of the two bridges across the Nore River, Green's Bridge was under the surveillance of the Republicans and had been barricaded, and Prout's men occupied positions on both sides of John's Bridge.

At the respectable hour of eleven on Tuesday morning, when breakfasts had been digested, Prout's men marched from the military barracks towards Green's Bridge. They opened fire on John Lucey's home, which the Republicans had occupied, and in a short time Mr Lucey's house was scarcely habitable; the garrison had surrendered and, crossing the bridge, the National forces had dislodged the squatters from O'Rourke's stores on the other side.

Action developed very quickly now. Firing, none of it very lethal except by accident, broke out all over the city. During the Tan war there had never been anything so noisy in Kilkenny, and as rifles crackled venomously and armoured cars rumbled threateningly round the streets, the people were silent with stupefaction. Snipers on rooftops were a menace to every living creature, especially birds, and shops began to close and people to seek shelter.

St Canice's Tower, quite separate from the Cathedral itself, was next under attack. There, too, the surrender came quickly. After that there was calm until three o'clock, when the garrison of Wilsdon's grocery shop, which overlooked the Dublin Road, came under fire from the nearby railway bridge. The attack was kept up for twenty minutes, during which considerable damage was done to Mr Wilsdon's premises and stock. Bags of flour, used to erect barricades were perforated. Finally, National troops stormed the premises and captured the floury defenders.

A bomb thrown from an unsuspected house landed on John Street bridge and chipped off a chunk of parapet; no one was hurt but the few intrepid citizens who had been watching the action from the bridge moved nervously away.

After another lull, heavy firing began again about 6.30 p.m. The City Hall was evacuated and the John Street barracks surrounded and surrendered. Evacuees from the City Hall reinforced the Imperial Hotel garrison. There was a fierce, hourlong engagement here in which an armoured car positioned on the Parade and National Army snipers on the roof of the Bank of Ireland took part. After a large section of the garrison had sneaked out the back way and gone to join their comrades in the Castle, the remainder surrendered.

During the afternoon 200 troops from Beggar's Bush arrived by train, and an armoured car roared in with Tom Ennis, Tom Flood, Joe Leonard and David Moran aboard, having covered the distance from Dublin in a time that would have startled its designers. Moran's friend, Tommy Doyle, was on the roof of the Bank of Ireland from where, to finish off the day, shots were exchanged with the Republicans in the Castle for ninety minutes.

Moran and Doyle enjoy that kind of affinity which belongs to friendships sustained from schooldays. In conversation they are as one person, never interrupting nor usuring the other, but each taking up the thread of a tale at exactly the right moment. Until their meeting at Kilkenny they had not seen each other for some time.

Imprisoned by the British in 1920, Doyle had been released early in 1922 and soon afterwards joined the National Army in Kilkenny. Moran had been a radio operator at sea for eighteen months and was snapped up by the Second Southern Division when he volunteered for the I.R.A. in 1920. As well as training signallers he spent much of the Anglo-Irish war perched on the breezy tops of telephone poles, where he was extremely vulnerable to passing Black and Tans, listening to telephone conversations members of the I.R.A. were never meant to hear. In March 1922, he enlisted in the National Army at Beggar's Bush and was assigned to the Dublin Brigade. After a stint on outpost duty at the Bank of Ireland, under Vinny Byrne, he was transferred as a lieutenant to the Tipperary 4th Battalion formed in Kilkenny.

Moran idolised Joe Leonard, one of the heroes of the

McEoin rescue attempt, and it was Leonard who, next day, took Kilkenny Castle, a mighty edifice built in the thirteenth century but twice restored. The ancestral home of Lord Ossory, it had four great towers with walls twelve feet thick, each tower an almost impregnable citadel in itself. The Republicans had taken the Castle rather more easily than they were prepared to relinquish it. Gaining entry by a ruse, they were considerably quiet and Lord and Lady Ossory knew nothing of the take-over until the following morning. Then they declined to move to a place of safety, believing no doubt that there were few safer places in the vicinity. They acknowledged later that they had been treated most chivalrously by their uninvited guests.

Prout, too, had a sense of the occasion and instructed his troops to watch where they were firing. There was no need to damage the treasures of the Castle's renowned picture gallery.

Early on Wednesday morning a party of four National Army soldiers succeeded in smashing holes in the entrance gate. They called hopefully upon the garrison to surrender. Instead some vigorous firing wounded two of the party, Fennelly and Kennedy, and the National troops resorted to constant rifle and machine-gun fire. Bullets smashed through windows and many family treasures were ruined, but the picture gallery remained almost unscathed. At about six in the evening another attempt to rush the Castle failed, three men being wounded, but two hours later Leonard's armoured car was brought up. Leonard, a heroic figure, rakishly capped, crept up to the Castle with a gun in either hand, fired some shots to attract attention and yelled up threateningly to the defenders, fewer now for many of them had made off quietly from the rear of the building. Leonard warned the garrison that if they did not surrender, the armoured car would blow the Castle to bits. So the defenders capitulated at last, not, one imagines, because they overrated the fire-power of the armoured car, but because the other side were playing the game too seriously.

Many Republicans at this time were prepared to carry their intransigence as far as, but not beyond, the point of bloodshed, still hoping that their erstwhile friends would come to appreciate their point of view and tear up the Treaty. When they found their protest unavailing, they contented themselves
288

Top Eamon de Valera, seated, centre, with members of the Irish Delegation in London in July 1921. On his left is Arthur Griffith and immediately behind him Lord Mayor O'Neill. On the latter's right is Count Plunkett and, partly hidden, Erskine Childers

Bottom Irish sympathizers outside 10 Downing Street during the Conference

Top   Arthur Griffith, Art O'Brien and Michael Collins arrive at
10 Downing Street to begin Treaty negotiations

Bottom left   Sir Austen Chamberlain, Lord Privy Seal

Right   Sir Hamar Greenwood, Chief Secretary for Ireland

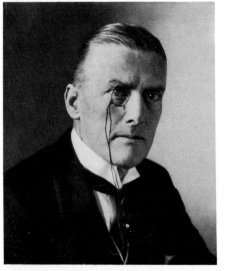

Top Lloyd George, Lord Birkenhead and Winston Churchill, British representatives at the Treaty talks

Bottom right Erskine Childers, Secretary to the Irish Delegation

Top   Collins addressing a gathering at College Green, Dublin, in March 1922

Bottom   Ratification of the Anglo-Irish Treaty at the Mansion House, Dublin

Top Countess Markievicz addressing a Republican Party meeting at Cork in early 1922

Bottom De Valera reviewing an I.R.A. contingent at Six Mile Bridge, Co. Clare, in December 1921

Top Collins and General Mulcahy heading the procession at the funeral of Arthur Griffith

Bottom left Rory O'Connor, who led the seizure of the Four Courts

Right General Emmet Dalton, whose artillery was largely responsible for the surrender of O'Connor's garrison

Heavy damage was sustained by the Four Courts during the battle, the dome being shattered by a violent explosion

Top The Strand Barracks, Limerick, after capture by the National Army

Bottom Election posters at Ennis, Co. Clare, 1923

with having made it. Prout, too, was loath to shed blood, and was delighted with the outcome of the struggle. He had taken a hundred prisoners altogether and, apart from one poor girl whose knee had been shattered by a ricochet, there were no civilian casualties. An enormous number of bullets had caused much damage but there had been surprisingly little blood.

Nevertheless, the Provisional Government, faced with the task of running an election and of building up an administration in the meantime, could not afford a long, drawn-out nuisance campaign. And Republican bullets, whether they were fired with lethal intent or not, certainly hindered government. The man who fires a shot over an opponent's head may be good-humoured about it, but the opponent cannot afford to be. Either he heeds the warning or he takes a chance and fights back.

Even on the Wednesday when Kilkenny Castle was attacked and captured, efforts for peace were being made in the Dail itself. A deputation of five of the signatories of the Army Document was received and Sean O'Hegarty was given the rare distinction of addressing the House, though not a member. Following his moving plea, a committee of ten was elected to try to hammer out a settlement. Among them was Liam Mellows from the Four Courts and Mrs Clarke, widow of the 1916 hero.

The following day, Thursday, May 4th, Major-General Gearoid O'Sullivan, T.D.,[1] with Commandant Dan Breen, Commandant Sean Moylan, T.D. and Commandant Breslane arrived in Kilkenny. They were visited at the Imperial Hotel by Prout, the Mayor of Kilkenny and the local anti-Treaty organiser. Breen and O'Sullivan had signed the Army Document of May 1st, and all were concerned to secure peace. For them the struggle in Kilkenny, though it could easily have been worse, was disheartening. On the day of their visit National troops, with an armoured car in support, went from Kilkenny to Gowran, about seven miles to the east of the city, and there, after twenty minutes of fighting ejected Republicans from the R.I.C. barracks and the courthouse and took twelve prisoners.

Later in the day Moylan and O' Sullivan returned to Dublin to participate in yet another endeavour to find the elusive

1 *Teachtaire an Dail*, Dail Deputy.

formula that would weld the broken Army together again. A joint committee comprising Collins, Mulcahy, O'Duffy, McEoin, O'Sullivan and Diarmuid O'Hegarty on the one hand, Lynch, Rory O'Connor, Mellows, Robinson and Moylan on the other, decided on a four-day truce, and on May 8th this was extended indefinitely. They agreed to release all prisoners held and the Executive Forces were to give up buildings they had occupied in Dublin—except the Four Courts. For some reason Collins did not press for evacuation of the Four Courts. Perhaps he was content that Rory O'Connor had joined those who were trying "to strike bargains with the other side". However, he did resist a demand that the Four Courts garrison should be paid and provisioned. Without food or funds the garrison continued to make local raids and the truce almost crumbled.

After several meetings the Dail Committee failed to find a formula, were persuaded to meet again and came near but not quite to an agreement. The formula they had in mind was that a panel of candidates from both sides should go forward for election and that a coalition government should follow. But although they were agreed on the frame they could not agree on the picture within it. The pro-Treaty side wished naturally to put the Treaty to the people; the others wanted no issue to be put at all, a blank canvas in fact.

In a letter to the Minister of Defence, General Mulcahy, dated May 9th, 1922, Colonel Maurice Moore, brother of the novelist George Moore, expressed doubts which were in the minds of many other thoughtful Irishmen. He said:

"If by an agreed election is meant an election in which both parties agree that the same Deputies be returned to the Dail, the difficulty will be only postponed and made permanent. You will have a new Dail just as hostile, only with a long life before it, and an army lying low ready to take any advantage that circumstances may bring about.

"Moreover, political parties have no right to impose such a rule on the people, it is really an anti-democratic manoeuvre, and even more degrading than the imposition of a military despotism and the prevention of elections."

In the same letter Moore drew Mulcahy's attention to another danger to the Provisional Government. The Republicans were, he claimed, "making a bid for support through an agrarian movement". Protestant families were being driven from their homes and their land was being seized. Said Moore, "Cathal Brugha at a meeting of the officers of Sinn Fein, and in the presence of Mr de Valera, who did not disapprove, proposed to treat the Southern Protestants as the Catholics were being treated in Belfast." The dispossession of Protestants in the west of Ireland was claimed to be a reprisal policy but Moore held that this was merely an excuse. The real reason, he alleged, was not because these people were Protestants but because they were landholders.

He cited the case of a family near Castlebar who were given only a few minutes to pack. "The cattle were driven to the market and sold, though the purchasers refused to take them over when they heard to whom they belonged." Moore interviewed Commandant-General Kilroy who had given the orders for the seizure and Kilroy stated that he had received his instructions from the Four Courts. As a favour to Moore, Kilroy obtained permission for the daughter of the family, who was about to be married, to recover her trousseau. Moore stated that he had written to Liam Mellows reminding him that the Volunteers and the Irish Republican Army had been founded to achieve an ideal, the rights and liberties common to all the people of Ireland, but Mellows had not replied.

"The people of the west have no anti-Protestant feeling, but they have a very strong desire to take the land, and that is being utilised to raise an agrarian agitation, to popularise the anti-Treaty party," Moore summed up pithily. He enclosed a copy of a letter which he had received from the parish priest of Balla, Co. Mayo, which explained in part why the Republicans were in control of the area. Pro-Treaty groups in his parish had sent notification of their adherence to Headquarters and received no reply.

"This is woeful indifference and neglect," wrote Father Reidy. "Here we have Carrowkeel, Ballyglass, Clogher, Belcarra and two Mayo Abbey sections in a suspense which is calculated to provoke indignation, and not a hand of welcome stretched out." He exhorted Colonel Moore to "waken up these Beggar's Bush Generals".

In a postscript, he added, "I have now to go to the post

office to see my letters are not captured and then follow them to the station to see them started to Dublin. How far they get I can't say; surely something should be done to help us."

In a voice sombre with disillusionment, Winston Churchill, Secretary of State for the Colonies, explained the simmering situation in Ireland to his colleagues.[2] "In signing the Irish Treaty we thought we were dealing with the plenipotentiaries of the Irish people," he began, and in these words were contained the essence of the British attitude. A war had been fought, a Treaty negotiated, both sides driving as hard a bargain as they could. Whatever concessions had been made should now have been accepted philosophically.

It was an understandable attitude for a great power which had fought innumerable wars and signed dozens of Treaties, gaining one point, conceding another, accepting this clause, amending that, always pinning down the black and white. But, in retrospect, it is not easy to understand how the British Government was so insensitive to the Irish dilemma. "Even when serious opposition to the Treaty developed in the Dail," Churchill went on, "we hoped that an immediate vote of the Irish people would be taken which would result in a substantial majority for the acceptance of the Treaty." He had every reason to expect such a majority and, on the Irish side, the circumstances being what they were, that majority ought to have been allowed to express itself. What was wrong were the circumstances.

Churchill, Chamberlain, Lloyd George, every member of Britain's team of negotiators and every member of the Cabinet knew well that not one of the Irish plenipotentiaries, not a single member of the Dail and only a small minority of Loyalists among the Irish people considered that Ireland had been given her just due. The majority which undoubtedly would vote for the Treaty would not be approving the creation of a new British dominion but simply intimating that they could stomach no more war.

Churchill went on to give a devastatingly accurate diagnosis of the Irish quarrel but failed to see that it only needed an act of generosity, indeed less of generosity than of justice, to eliminate the cause of it. He saw only what the well-worn

[2] Cabinet conclusion 27/22 (3) of 16/5/22.

292

blinkers of imperialism allowed him to see. Time was to remove those blinkers and to reveal to a new generation of Britons vistas of their colonial past that their forbears never permitted themselves to see.

It must be remembered, however, that in the political ambience of the day the Treaty did represent larger generosity than could ever have been expected, especially as it is apparent that from the beginning the British Government just did not comprehend the Irish demand for freedom any more than many parents, even today, cannot see why their children desire to leave their comfortable home for the independence of baked beans in musty bed-sitters. And it must be remembered, too, that a great majority of the Irish had a naïve understanding of the vocabulary of revolution. To Churchill the idea of an "agreed election," with de Valera taking, say, 40 seats and the Provisional Government 80, was naïvety itself. He had written to Collins, he told the Cabinet, "pointing out that such an election would be received with world wide ridicule and reprobation".

Scathingly he pinpointed the Irish weakness. "The Ministers of the Provisional Government live far too much in the narrow circle of their own associates and late associates, and they think only of placating the obscure terrorists who spring up one after another all over Ireland." He accused them of having "hardly given due thought to the essential measure of going to the Irish people for their opinion of the Treaty".

They had given in to de Valera who knew that an election would be fatal to his position. They had "rather adopted the role of a passive sufferer under the tyranny of the extremist party". With Kilkenny in mind no doubt, he said there really was little difference between them "and there is general reluctance to kill one another."

He explained that, when the truce had seemed to be breaking down a week earlier, Collins had sent him a request for 10,000 additional rifles as well as guns, mortars and other equipment. The Provisional Government intended to deal with the rebels outside Dublin in places like Drogheda and Castlebar but Churchill thought they should first deal resolutely with the Dublin situation. He was afraid that the Four Courts garrison might begin to kidnap and assassinate British officers "with the object of compelling the intervention of the British Army".

If further arms were issued to Southern Ireland more would have to be given to Ulster "so as to keep them well ahead". He remarked also that recruiting in the Free State Army was open only to members of the Irish Republican Army, although the Free State Army was "in theory an anti-republican body." This was a curious statement to make in the confines of the Cabinet room where no one surely believed that the Provisional Government, or their National Army, considered themselves anti-republican. Lord FitzAlan, Lord Lieutenant of Ireland, took up the remark a moment later, they were Republicans in sentiment he pointed out. Birkenhead was becoming anxious about the Constitution. He emphasised the complexity of drafting a Constitution which would accurately interpret the terms of the Treaty. There would not be much time to study it if the election in Ireland was to be held on June 16th. FitzAlan expected an attempt to rush the Government into accepting something not in accord with the Treaty.

Typically Churchill now darted to the defence of his difficult Irish friends whose lives, he said, were in danger. He was "anxious not to put upon them more than they could bear".

Chamberlain wanted British troops withdrawn from Dublin out of harm's way. A Republic would quickly be proclaimed, Churchill rejoined. "If Ireland fell into a state of anarchy, we should have to re-establish a pale again round Dublin prior to reconquest."

If Churchill saw an agreed election as a storm on the horizon, to the Dail it came as the first glint of a dawn. They asked Collins and de Valera to see if they could make the idea workable. For three days they argued it out and on May 20th the Collins-de Valera Pact emerged like sickly sunshine through fog.

Under the pact there was to be a National Coalition Panel for the third Dail. All candidates would carry the Sinn Fein label and the number from each of the parties, pro-Treaty and anti-Treaty, would represent their existing strength in the Dail. The subsequent Government would comprise an elected President, a Minister of Defence who would represent the Army and nine other ministers, five from the majority party and four from the minority. The arrangement was made on the grounds that "the national position requires the entrusting of the government of the country into the joint hands of
294

those who have been the strength of the national situation during the last few years, without prejudice to their present respective positions." Only one chink of democracy remained, the provision that "every and any interest is free to go up and contest the election equally with the Sinn Fein panel."

"You have given them everything," exclaimed a shocked Griffith, but he agreed in the end, packed his customary loyal arguments into his bag and set off with Collins to convince the British Government that what had been done was necessary even if it were in breach of the Treaty.

On May 30th, Churchill explained the dilemma to the Cabinet.[8] The pact was "an arrangement full of disaster. It prevented an expression of opinion on the Treaty; it gave the Provisional Government no further representation of strength or authority from the Irish people; it left the Government in its present weak and helpless position; it ruptured Article 17 of the Treaty." Article 17 required every member of the Provisional Government to have signified in writing his or her acceptance of the Treaty. Obviously the four anti-Treaty Ministers would hardly do that. If they became members of the Provisional Government then there would be a breach of the Treaty.

Griffith and Collins had explained to him that under any other conditions a free election would not have been possible. Collins had said that "whereas there were fanatical Republicans who were pure in motive though violent in method, behind them had gathered all the desperate elements of the population who pursued rapine for private gain. They could not be distinguished from the others and over all of them was the glamour of the Republic." Thus were the sentiments of Collins put in the Churchillian nutshell.

Not without some appreciation of the Irish problem, Churchill put it that "the idea was to try and get a non-party Government so as to secure tranquillity in Ireland and at a later date stage a proper election on the main issue. The June election would not be one in which the Irish people could be regarded as arming the Parliament to carry out the Treaty."

Churchill was not losing sight of the requirements of the Treaty. He was apprehensive that the four Republican

8 Cabinet conclusion 30/22 (3) of 30/5/22.

Ministers who would take office under the Collins-de Valera Pact might resort to subterfuge in the matter of the Oath, to avoid both a breach of the Treaty and any departure from their principles. He was also concerned that the Provisional Government had pledged to de Valera and to the Sinn Fein Ard-Fheis of May 23rd ten days clear to consider the Constitution, which did not leave the British Government very much time, especially as it was, Churchill said, "a negation of the Treaty", though Collins and Griffith had assured him that this was not intended.

"The distance between their Constitution and the Treaty is almost as great as when the Prime Minister began his negotiations with Mr de Valera," said Churchill. And, indeed, the Constitution might just as well have been drafted in terms of de Valera's Document Number Two. Here, in Churchill's mind, was the snare in the Collins-de Valera Pact. If there were a substantial majority for the Treaty in the Dail following the June election there should be no difficulty in pushing through the Constitution. But, with a large body of Republicans being returned by means of the agreed Panel, the likelihood was a further interminable debate in the Dail, anarchy in the South and continued unrest in the North.

"The Constitution adjusted to our view might prove insuperable to them when they return to Ireland," said Churchill but Lloyd George's diagnosis was much more telling. "If they made their Constitution conform to our view de Valera would not be able to accept it and the Pact would be broken. On the other hand, if the Constitution were not made to conform to the Treaty, then we should be confronted with a larger issue of the Republic versus the Empire."

Lloyd George saw that the hub of the Collins-de Valera Pact was the Republican Constitution which the Provisional Government were putting forward, and that so long as Collins and Griffith were prepared to stand by it, and argue for it, the Pact would hold together, the Irish would be united once more and the Dail itself would have become, after all, a unanimous body of opposition to the Treaty.

The strain of their thankless leadership was telling on both Collins and Griffith. Collins's emotions were strung tight and he was given at this time to uncharacteristic bouts of moroseness. Griffith, too, was inclined to be tetchy. Lloyd George reported that Collins had said to him several times that he "was willing to give Ireland back to us as a present", and Chamberlain said Collins and Griffith had "remarked to the Prime Minister that he and de Valera should share the government of Ireland between them, as much as to say that one was as impossible as the other." From these exasperated remarks it can be surmised that neither Griffith nor Collins was happy about the concessions which de Valera had wrung from them.

Churchill maintained that the Collins-de Valera Pact had put paid to any chance of an agreement between the two parts of Ireland. Since the Provisional Government had "joined hands with avowed Republicans", it was hardly surprising that the North had "gone back to its extreme and violent position." Craig certainly was disillusioned. There had been endless difficulties on small points since his Agreement with Collins of March 31st, but on the large issue, "while he could not stand for unity, Craig would resign rather than stand in its way." If Collins had taken strong steps and turned the Irregulars out of their Dublin strongholds, the whole situation in Belfast would have improved, Churchill insisted. Collins claimed that the opposite was true, and in a meeting lasting one and a half hours with Lloyd George and Chamberlain, he and Griffith had talked of little else but "the extermination of the Catholics" in the North-east.

Lloyd George told his Cabinet that 80 Catholics had been killed and 188 wounded since December 6th, 1921, "considerable figures, but they do not justify Mr Collins's description". There had also been 72 Protestant murders. He had pointed out to Collins that 37 murders had occurred in the South and Collins had put these down to anger provoked by Belfast, adding that unless something were done the whole of Ireland would get out of hand.

"I quoted to him Lord Randolph Churchill's remark to Mr Gladstone, 'You call yourselves a Government, whom do you govern?' and added, 'You have handed over the Government of Ireland to an Englishman, to Erskine Childers.'"

The Irish leaders had argued then that the Belfast murders were committed by "Specials" in English pay. Great Britain had "handed over law and order to Sir James Craig" and was therefore responsible. They thought Britain should proclaim

297

martial law in Ulster, declaring that there would be great confidence in British officers. "This was a most extraordinary suggestion," said Lloyd George, "but it was one to which Mr Griffith came back repeatedly."

There were 48,000 Specials who were in fact an army. Craig maintained that they were more useful than an army but Worthington-Evans remarked that they were not under military discipline. Griffith had emphasised to Lloyd George that they were not trained policemen. He "might as well go and arm the East End." Lloyd George thought the Fascisti in Italy "a more exact analogy" and supported Collins's claim for an impartial investigation.

Chamberlain had asked Collins: "Supposing we were to give you this investigation, would you be prepared to disavow the I.R.A. in the Six Counties, to tell them and all persons affiliated to them that they were bound to obey the Northern Government pending the results of the Boundary Commission?" To this Collins had replied that he was "not prepared to hold up the hands of the Ulster Government while Catholics were being murdered."

In Worthington-Evans's opinion, Collins's reply "indicated that he was behind the 2½ divisions of the I.R.A. who are causing so much trouble in the North." To which Lloyd George replied that Collins had said, "I cannot leave these people unprotected with 48,000 Specials out against them."

Churchill was against an inquiry into the Belfast murders. "The temper in this country is high and rising," he said, "and the Government will be told that they have been cheated by the South and that when loyal Ulstermen defend themselves we propose an inquiry. The public will ask, 'What about an inquiry in the South?'"

In a significant reply Lloyd George pointed out that the South was a Dominion, the North was not; significant because here was the Prime Minister reminding his Cabinet of the extent of the power and freedom conferred by dominion status. The Irish had feared interference in their internal affairs; now Lloyd George was emphasising in his own Cabinet that they could not foist an inquiry on to the South.

What did concern him profoundly was how the trouble, when it came, was to be explained to the public. Collins, he
298

thought, was "manoeuvring us into a position where our case is weak". Collins had challenged on Ulster. The first murders had been of members of the Catholic minority. "No one had been punished, we had made no inquiry, we had armed 48,000 Protestants. It would be a bad case." It had to be remembered that the Empire was Protestant and Catholic. So was America.

It was important to carry the Dominions and America with Great Britain, so a breach should be avoided where the case against Britain was a strong one.

"If we broke on the issue of 'Republic versus Monarchy' we could count on solid support, but if we broke on Ulster we should get into the same area of doubtful responsibility as in the case of Reprisals."

It was interesting that the Prime Minister should consider his Black and Tan tactics as within an area of doubtful responsibility, and he underlined this sentiment very firmly. "Democratic communities are sentimental communities," he went on, "and that is why a policy of repression cannot be carried through."

They should eliminate the Ulster issue and leave a clean issue of "Republic versus British Empire". Lloyd George could see that the situation which now existed was similar to that which had obtained during the Treaty negotiations. Just as the Irish would have been better placed than the British if the negotiations had been broken off on the Ulster question, so they would gain sympathy now if the Treaty were to fall on the horns of the same dilemma.

Lloyd George favoured a judicial inquiry, during which neither side would wish to create evidence against itself. For a time anyway the outrages should stop and there would be time for the other issue to develop.

"We must be careful not to put Ulster in the dock and call the South as a witness," warned the Lord President of the Council, the Earl of Balfour.

Austen Chamberlain answered that the strength of the case for an inquiry was that the Specials were definitely charged with murder and were in the British Government's pay.

Still against any inquiry, Churchill suggested instead martial law in a particular area of Belfast.

"And the border too?" asked Lloyd George.

299

"You have not enough troops for that," replied Churchill. "The border trouble starts in Belfast . . ."

It was decided to send for Sir James Craig and to put to him the proposal for a judicial inquiry into the disturbances in Ulster.

Churchill outlined the speech he would make to the House of Commons next day.[4] He would not indicate the differences which had arisen on the Constitution as these might well be sorted out, but he would state the absolute objection to Ministers who declined to take the Oath and, while explaining the reasons for the Collins-de Valera Pact, he would "show the vice of the agreement". He proposed to say that Ulster was being given ships and arms but that responsibility for their use remained with the British Government.

Lloyd George was emphatic that Churchill should not give the impression that the trouble was in Ulster. He could not "carry on a war with a divided country." The Prime Minister did not choose his words well—he meant that he could not resume the war against the South in the event of their refusing to conform to the Treaty if public opinion at home was divided. Another proof, if proof were needed, that his threat of war in forcing a settlement in December was no bluff.

When Churchill made his speech on May 31st, Griffith and Collins were present in the Strangers' Gallery. In the morning they had assured Churchill that Provisional Government Forces had not been responsible for clashes on the border in the Belleek-Pettigo area which, General Macready explained, was a "triangle cut off from the rest of Fermanagh by narrow strips of Free State territory and only approached without causing 'an international incident' across Lower Lough Erne."[5]

The I.R.A. had entered Belleek, which was wholly in Ulster, and had fired at Specials in Pettigo which was divided by the border. Reinforcements of Specials had crossed Lower Lough Erne and there had been skirmishes in the triangle. On May 30th a military reconnaissance party with two armoured cars were fired on in Pettigo from across the border. "It was estimated that about fifty men and a badly handled machine-gun took part in the firing," Macready reported. There had been sniping, too, in Armagh and Tyrone.

[4] Cabinet conclusion 30/22 (4) of 30/5/22.   [5] Cabinet paper CP 4022.

Collins's denial that his men played any part in these incidents placated Churchill, and the Cabinet met on June 1st to consider the much more serious problem of the draft Constitution which, Lloyd George claimed, was "purely republican in character and but thinly veiled", complying with the Treaty neither in substance nor in form.[6] Mr Kennedy K.C. and Hewart, now Lord Chief Justice of England, had met on May 30th and 31st to try to work out satisfactory amendments of the document submitted by the Irish, but Hewart had come back "with a somewhat dismal story of their attitude in this respect."

In the draft Constitution, Lloyd George explained, "the position of the representative of the Crown was reduced to that of a sort of Commissioner". He admitted that "the position of the Crown is not easy to define even in Great Britain, but it is a fact, and a greater potential force, if I might employ such a term, than any other in the every-day arrangements for the government of the country."

Then, the Irish claimed the right to make their own Treaties, a right extended to no other Dominion, though since the war it had been agreed that the Dominions should be consulted on matters of foreign policy which concerned them.

The third objection to the Irish document was its exclusion of the Judicial Committee of the Privy Council in favour of the Irish Supreme Court as the final Court of Appeal. This was a very important matter, Lloyd George said, as "questions would arise between Southern Ireland and Ulster and between the Government and the minorities, and so forth, just as they did in Canada in regard to the position of the French".

The Oath was omitted altogether from the draft Constitution, and there was also the problem of the four Republican Ministers who were to take office under the Collins-de Valera Pact. Were they to take the Oath or not? If not it would be a breach of the Treaty.

A sixth and final query, though admittedly less serious, was that the position of Ulster was not recognised.

The Irish leaders had "emphatically declared that they did adhere to the Treaty", but the fact was that the Constitution was not based on monarchical principle. The King was not

[6] Cabinet conclusion 31/22 (1) of 1/6/22.

part of the Legislature; he would not appoint Ministers nor summon or dissolve Parliament.

Copies of the document had not been circulated to the Cabinet, Chamberlain explained, because the need for secrecy was paramount. The Irish leaders would have been in an impossible position "if it had leaked out that they had come over with one Constitution and gone back to Ireland with another."

Chamberlain's own astute explanation of the attitude of Griffith and Collins was that when they had learned of the British objections to their draft Constitution "they had realised that the gap between the two parties was too large to be bridged", that "they must either quarrel with de Valera or with the British Government". The Prime Minister pointed out that the Irish view was that their position was made impossible by the pogrom against Roman Catholics in Ulster, to which Churchill rejoined that "a very serious case could be made on the other side." Sinn Fein in Ulster, with I.R.A. support, was making government impossible there. He was sure himself that the Irish representatives were "drifting about, refusing to face up to either side".

Sir Alfred Mond could not see how Griffith and Collins could ever hope to work with de Valera yet carry out the Treaty, and he wondered "what would happen if an ultimatum were given to the Irish with the result that the Provisional Government resigned." In this event, thought H. A. L. Fisher, the British Government would be free to take any appropriate action in their own time but, he asked, "Why should they take an action in other parts of Ireland before they had restored order in the North, where they had assumed certain responsibilities?"

Tartly, Chamberlain demanded why Fisher put Ulster in the dock and ignored Southern Ireland. He thought that if the Irish would not conform to the Treaty, the British Government should resume their freedom. In Churchill's opinion the most efficacious way of dealing with the situation was to require the Constitution to be redrafted at once. There might still be "a chance of their coming to heel". The point was that Great Britain should be told definitely whether the Irish intended to adhere to the Treaty.

Balfour put the Ulster view that the outrages in Belfast were due not only to old religious animosities but to a deliberate attempt to break up the whole Treaty policy. He did not know which side was to be believed, "but it is vital that everything possible should be done to put ourselves right with the world and to show that we are doing all that we can to put a stop to the murder of Catholics and the counter-assassination of Protestants." There was doubt as to whether the moral position of the British Government was fully realised in America and the Dominions, Lloyd George interpolated.

A meeting of the British signatories of the Treaty with Lord Balfour added, was arranged for that afternoon to draft an answer to the Irish representatives. The Irish meanwhile had drafted their observations on the British Government's criticisms in a long memorandum containing some spectacular passages.[7] They made one very pertinent point in these words:

"The great body of law, institutions and forms called the 'English Common Law', which has sprung from and so grown to fulness with the genius and character of the English people as to be part of their living fibre, is not in Ireland a common law at all. It is an alien structure imposed by statute, an exotic from which a cutting has been artificially fostered in Ireland but which has not taken root or become acclimatised in any sense."

After the Treaty, English statesmen had made glowing speeches about the Irish, free from British interference, creating a constitution to govern themselves in their own way, "with full play for Irish traditions and Irish thought to give colour and lend vitality to the framing and building up of institutions which the Irish people could honour as their own."

This had been appreciated by the draftsmen of the Treaty for they had not insisted upon the form and ceremonial of English Common Law. "The substance was granted without the ceremonial meaningless in Ireland and liable to be misunderstood." This was the basis for much of the support for the Treaty and it would be impossible to say now that "the substance of Irish free government could not be consummated without the imposition of formality and ceremonial, alien, not understood or appreciated and sure to be interpreted in a sinister sense because [it was] stated to be purely formal and yet insisted on."

[7] Conference on Ireland SF (b) 60 App. I.

Summing up, the Irish said that their Constitution had been framed to suit their special needs, that they could not agree that they were bound to mould their Constitution into the forms of English Common Law and that the Treaty itself recognised this. The Dominions had a different history and tradition but it was within their competence also to adopt a form of Constitution removed from the English pattern. The Constitution which had been presented, they contended, was one which the Dominion of Canada "could not be debarred from adopting." That, of course, was not quite what the British had in mind when they used the Canadian Constitution as their tailor's dummy.

The English reply drafted by the Treaty signatories and Balfour was handed to the Irish leaders at 6 p.m. the same day, June 1st, with the request that they meet the British team half an hour later. Naturally the Irish protested at this short shrift and it was agreed that they should see Lloyd George informally and hand in their formal reply the following afternoon, Collins told Lloyd George that the British Government were behaving like Shylocks in "demanding the fulfilment of the letter of the bond".[8] But both Griffith and Collins had said that they stood by the Treaty and were within the Empire, "an admission which did not agree with their draft Constitution," Lloyd George told his Cabinet. The Prime Minister said that Collins had stressed that there was strong feeling against appeals to the Judicial Committee of the Privy Council. Three of the judges had "publicly taken up a very hostile attitude to the Irish Free State" and Lloyd George admitted that the conduct of these three, Carson, Summer and Cave, "had placed His Majesty's Government in a very awkward and indefensible position." He had told Collins that such men should stand aside "should questions affecting controversy in which they had taken part come before them", but he was concerned that these judges might already have vitiated confidence in the Judicial Committee in other parts of the Commonwealth.

Collins had repeatedly raised the Ulster issue and Britain's responsibility for it which arose from her paying half the cost of the Specials. He had pressed for an impartial inquiry. Lloyd George had told him the Specials were being employed "as

8 Cabinet conclusion 32/22 (1) of 2/6/22.

substitutes for troops which were not available" and then he had spoken in the most solemn terms to the Irish leaders: "If, through their impatience or folly, they threw away an opportunity which had never been given to any of the great Irishmen of the past . . . their names would be execrated for generations to come by their own countrymen." And again Lloyd George had appealed to Griffith's honour, reminding him of the reputation for good faith enjoyed by Irish leaders of the past.

In Lloyd George's opinion Griffith understood that they would have to choose between de Valera and the Treaty, but Collins "still appeared to think he could carry the others along with him."

The Prime Minister expected Griffith's reply later in the day and anticipated difficulties in the matters of the Oath, appeals to the Privy Council and the position of Republican members of the forthcoming Coalition Government.

Britain could not possibly give way on the last point, exclaimed Churchill, but he thought that before denouncing the election "it would be better to wait until we knew the composition of the elected Parliament and the method of its election." With a fine disregard of the many hortatory utterances of His Majesty's Ministers calculated to open the eyes of the Irish to the splendours of their new freedom, he added:

"The more the fear of renewed warfare is present in the minds of the electors, the more likely are they to get to the polls and support the Treaty."

But Balfour thought it would be tragic "if in days to come Irishmen asserted that the Constitution of their country had been adopted by a Parliament which did not truly represent Ireland." And when Churchill suggested that it might be necessary after the June election to tell the Irish the election was not a proper basis for further legislation by the Imperial Parliament, and that therefore ratification would be postponed until their next Parliament had been elected on adult suffrage, Balfour retorted that Britain would be blamed for failing to give notice of this, "having known all the time that the June election was not a *bona fide* expression of Irish public opinion."

The Prime Minister observed tartly that Britain could hardly be blamed for Irish cowardice at the polling booth. In any

305

case, according to the Collins-de Valera Pact any and every national interest was free to run its own candidates.

Chamberlain cut through the argument with the icy comment that "the only people whom the Provisional Government consulted and tried to conciliate were the Republicans. In the meantime murder and looting went on." He added, "We have done all we can to implement our side of the bargain. It is time the Irish leaders did the same and gave us, and that very soon, a Constitution in conformity with the Treaty."

Everything hinged on the Irish answers to the questions put to them. If unsatisfactory there would be a break with Great Britain. On the other hand, if they were satisfactory there would be a break with de Valera. There was now little time to put an amended Constitution to the Irish electorate and he thought that an agreed communiqué which put the "clear and comprehensible" questions and answers would suffice. Birkenhead thought this would be a most unfortunate platform for the supporters of the Treaty, for "it would stress the special points in which we were interested and those only." No new concessions were involved, Churchill countered.

Churchill agreed that at least there should be a compromise on the Privy Council requirement. The Irish should know that the three Law Lords mentioned should have nothing to do with appeals from Ireland.

Birkenhead went further. He had glanced at the amendments proposed by the British and thought they should be modified. A much more moderate instrument should suffice. Surprisingly, Lloyd George supported him. "It had to be remembered," he said, "that the 'Crown' has too often in Ireland represented repression."

On June 2nd the fears of Lloyd George and his Cabinet were set at rest by Griffith's categorical answers to the questions put to him. Griffith began by declaring that the draft Constitution was prepared by a Committee appointed by the Provisional Government whose only instructions had been to work within the Treaty. All members of the Committee were supporters of the Treaty and they had acted "upon their own interpretation of the Treaty, approaching it with minds biased in its favour."

What they had produced was a document very much in line with the "association only" concept which the plenipotentiaries
306

had had to yield, a Constitution which was in essence a Republican Constitution. There was sufficient ambiguity in the terms of the Treaty to enable Griffith to claim quite sincerely that the draft Constitution complied with them and to prompt Collins's remark that Great Britain was behaving as Shylock in requiring the letter of the bond. But both Griffith and Collins realised that they could not get away with it and knew that in accepting amendment they were removing the lynch pin of the Collins-de Valera Pact. It is doubtful if Griffith shed many tears over that.

Forthrightly, Griffith acknowledged that the Free State "shall be, not merely associated with, but a member of and within the Community of Nations known as the British Empire and on the basis of common citizenship as explicitly provided by the Treaty."

On the Crown he believed the "area of difference" to be small. He went on that in all matters in which the Crown is "constitutionally effective"—he defined these as "matters arising out of the relationship of the Community of Nations"— the Crown would be "beyond question" the same as in Canada and the other Dominions. Legislation on matters not concerned with internal government of the Irish Free State should be reserved for the King's assent in person. "The King's Representative would be bound to distinguish such legislation when presented to him for the Royal Assent", and he would also "be bound to signify the King's assent to Bills duly passed which are concerned with purely Irish internal affairs."

The Treaty making power of the Irish Free State would be the same as that of Canada and Griffith added that " we should be glad to have it pointed out in what respect we are supposed to have exceeded that position".

The Privy Council question Griffith said raised "a matter of no small delicacy in Ireland". He cited utterances of several leading Dominion statesmen which suggested that appeal to the Judicial Committee of the Privy Council might well be generally abolished in the near future. Apart from this, Ireland was in a special position in that certain judges had used their position for party political purposes hostile to the Irish people and by doing so had aroused indignation and antipathy to the Tribunal as a whole. The Irish representatives had not thought "that this appeal was a necessary incident of the

307

Treaty position" and, indeed, he was not sure from Lloyd George's letter whether he thought so either. He wanted to know "whether it is regarded as in any way vital, or in what form you may consider that it is to be insisted upon".

As for the Oath, if the British were not satisfied that it was sufficiently incorporated by the fact that the Constitution would accept the Treaty as law, then it would be expressly set forth in the Constitution.

To the sixth question posed by Lloyd George, "Will all members of the Irish Provisional Government be required to sign the declaration under Article 17 of the Treaty?" Griffith said he was "entitled to an affirmative answer".

He concluded by expressing willingness to insert such amendments as would reconcile the terms of the Constitution with those of the Treaty.

Lloyd George read the letter to the Cabinet[9] and it was agreed that while further elucidation of the Crown and Privy Council issues would be necessary there was "nothing to warrant breaking off the negotiations at the present stage". Griffith, who was to return to Dublin that Friday night but would return on Monday if required, was to be told "personally and privately" that on the whole the reply had made a good impression.

The Constitution crisis seemed to have passed but things were hotting up on the border. A detachment of the Lincolnshire Regiment were fired at as they landed in the Belleek-Pettigo triangle on June 3rd and came under fire again next day. More British troops including a section of a Howitzer battery moved into Pettigo from the east the same day and hostile bullets crossed the border in such profusion that four shells from the Howitzers were fired into a wood to the west of the village. Later, Colonel Wyatt met Commandant Michael O'Farrell who wore Free State uniform and was named by Macready as the man who had started the rumpus. O'Farrell was given half an hour to get out but when there was further firing he was taken prisoner. The area was then cleared by the British who took altogether fifteen prisoners.

On the following day Cope telegraphed Churchill[10] that the Provisional Government had received information that British artillery was to be used against barracks on the Free State side

9 Cabinet conclusion 33/22 (1) of 2/6/22.   10 Cabinet Paper CP 4017.

308

of the border. The Provisional Government protested that this would jeopardise steps they were taking to restore order. In a second telegram sent a few minutes after the first, Cope stated that Belleek was the rumoured target and that Collins feared "a repetition of Pettigo at Belleek might easily be disastrous". Collins had said that "he relies on you to give directions to our troops to take no further action pending Griffith's meeting with you when the situation can be freely discussed."

Churchill telegraphed on June 6th a truculent answer[11] direct to Collins. He reminded Collins that the previous Wednesday, May 31st, he had invited him to explain whether armed forces which had invaded Belleek and Pettigo had acted on the authority of the Provisional Government.

"You told us that these forces were not your forces and that you disclaimed any responsibility for them and that you repudiated their action. I announced this to Parliament in your presence the same afternoon." He went on accusingly, "It is with surprise that I read in the Communiqué issued from G.H.Q., Beggar's Bush that there were 'no other Irish troops' than our troops', i.e. Free State Troops, 'in the district then or now,' and I shall be glad if you will explain the discrepancy".

Following Collins's assurance Churchill had ordered the occupation of the area by British troops and, he said, "I have to give you warning on behalf of His Majesty's Government that if British troops entering or holding Belleek are fired at either from Belleek fort or adjoining Free State territory the military authorities have full discretion either to bombard or to occupy the fort or any other points from which fire is brought to bear on the British Forces. It must not be supposed that any part of the border can be kept in a continued state of disorder and alarm either by raids or by fire directed from your territory."

With the occupation of Belleek, he stated, the present occupations were at an end. It was up to Collins to see that there was no need for them to be resumed.

Fire from Belleek Fort was, in fact, directed at British troops, but the garrison retired when the British replied with Howitzers. The same guns also scattered some belligerent in-
11 Ibid.

309

fantry, equipped with machine-guns, to the north-west of Belleek. Local residents reported that about 200 Republicans had been gathered in the area. They had seen no Free State men among them. A few days later, Macready reported that the leaders of North and South had agreed that the Belleek-Pettigo area was to be a neutral zone under the control of British troops reinforced by unarmed police from both sides. The situation was now easier.

In Belfast the tension remained high. A soldier of the Somerset Light Infantry shot two Protestant civilians who were sniping at Catholics. Later, angry Protestants set upon a four-man patrol from the same regiment. Two of the soldiers were wounded and the others, attempting to help them, were brutally beaten. All four rifles were stolen.

There was an outcry when the Mater Hospital was "attacked". Shots in the vicinity excited police at the nearby jail, and imagining that an assault was being launched against them they began heavy firing with rifles and machine-guns. Both the Hospital and Victoria Barracks, where British troops were quartered, were hit. It was very difficult for anyone to know just what was happening in Belfast. Macready said dryly that the newspapers of both North and South "give an entirely distorted or biased view of nearly every incident which takes place".

Collins looked on the actions of the clandestine I.R.A. Forces in the North as protection of the Catholic minority and saw in Craig's apparent inability to control the situation a deliberate attempt to promote war between North and South so that the British should be brought in and, in the end, would preserve the integrity of the Six Counties. Craig's appointment of the detested Sir Henry Wilson, lately retired as Chief of the Imperial General Staff, as his military adviser had driven suspicion irrevocably into Collins's soul. Craig's own dilemma was explained to the British Cabinet by Lord Balfour[12] after he had talked with Craig and Lord Londonderry on June 2nd. "The whole of the rebellion organisation of the South which had been engaged in resisting the British Forces, having nothing further to do in the South, had immigrated to the North where they were concentrating all their machinery and were making the utmost trouble." The

[12] Cabinet conclusion 32/22 (I) of 2/6/22.

I.R.A.'s activity was "deliberately aimed at destroying Ulster—they were part of a great conspiracy for exacerbating the secular feeling between the Roman Catholics and Protestants."

Balfour had warned Craig that if the Treaty broke down, "we should have behind us a united country at home, supported by the public opinion of the Dominions and of the United States of America. This would not be easy if the South had any ground for contending that the Belfast outrages were part of a movement to persecute Roman Catholics."

Craig had agreed to a British inquiry provided it was left to him to invite it. The Ulster Government wanted to put it that "in view of the false reports in regard to what had happened there they would be glad if an impartial body could be sent over to investigate and report." He assured Balfour that order would be restored but he was critical of the parsimony of the Chancellor of the Exchequer. Their Parliament had been foisted on to them by the British Government and it should be treated more generously. Craig was against any application of martial law and Chamberlain murmured sympathetically that the Ulster Government would see this as "tantamount to a declaration of bankruptcy in the power of their Government." Churchill thought they would co-operate if martial law was deemed necessary but Balfour doubted "whether the British Government could maintain order any better than the Ulster Government even if they did declare martial law."

In the South the Provisional Government seemed as helpless to restore order as Craig was in the North. Murder and arson were rife. In Dublin there had been midnight battles as early as April 19th. On O'Connell Bridge and along the quays rifle and machine-gun fire had been opened and armoured cars had had to protect the telephone exchange in Crown Alley, which was under fire. There were bomb explosions, chases in open cars, and General Dalton was fired at from a doorway in one of the innumerable sniping incidents. The Labour Party called a general strike for April 24th as a protest against militarism and, congratulating them, Lord Mayor O'Neill urged, "Send these young men in both armies home."

On June 14th, Mr F. J. R. Hendy, father of one of the British officers kidnapped and murdered at Macroom wrote to *The Times* blaming the British Government for abdicating too soon in Ireland. He supported the Treaty as "the only policy which could be anything but the initiation of a new cycle of horror", but he wanted to know why it had been necessary "to begin handing over almost before the ink was dry". The British Cabinet took note of the letter and so, no doubt, did some of the Irish leaders. Once the election, due on June 16th, established their right to govern they were determined to do so.

Macready reported that the general public in Ireland was anxious to see whether the Collins-de Valera Pact could work without infringing the Treaty but there was not a great deal of interest in nominations for the election. When so much had already been arranged this was not surprising. Panel candidates were addressing crowds all over the country but Labour, Farmers' and Independent Candidates were contenting themselves with election addresses. In some constituencies candidates were intimidated and withdrew from contests against panel candidates but elsewhere Republicans recalled their debt to the Labour Party, who had refrained from contesting seats against Sinn Fein in 1918. An Irish election without some intimidation was hardly imaginable but there was less violence than might have been expected. Two days before the election, on Wednesday, June 14th, in a speech at Cork Collins blew a hole in the agreement with de Valera.

"You are facing an election here on Friday, and I am not hampered now by being on a platform where there are coalitionists, and I can make a straight appeal to you to vote for the candidates you think best of, whom the electors of Cork think will carry on best in the future the work that they want carried on."

His words did not deny the letter of the pact which allowed that "every and any interest is free to go up and contest the election equally with the National-Sinn Fein Panel", but they were an invitation to oust Republican candidates on the panel. On the same day he repudiated in the press an advertisement which had appeared over his name and that of de Valera on June 12th. This began: "The English are furious with the Collins-de Valera Pact because the English fear Irish unity". It urged that only by voting for the Sinn Fein panel could unity be achieved, warning: "You won't get it by voting for a Dail of warring sections and interests."

Collins knew that the Pact would never work within the Constitution which the Provisional Government had now accepted. Once the British had insisted upon driving home every nail of the Treaty there was no possibility of a coalition government.

The Constitution was not published until the morning of the election, not because it had been deliberately delayed as the Republicans alleged, but because the Provisional Government's stratagem of giving the British little time to consider the draft Constitution backfired. The British Government had declined to be stampeded from their position and it was not until the day before the election that negotiations on the Constitution ended.

Although, quite understandably, the Republicans made much of the belated publication of the Constitution, the real issue of the election was whether the Treaty was acceptable or not to the people of Ireland. In terms even more black and white it was a matter of war or peace.

The results of the election were not announced until June 24th, by which time events were in train which were to detonate the explosive ill-feeling in the country and make impossible the assembly of the new Parliament on June 30th. But there was no doubting the wishes of the people. The pro-Treaty panel candidates won 58 of the 128 seats; seventeen of their candidates were returned unopposed; seven were defeated. Only 35 seats were won by anti-Treaty panel candidates, sixteen of whom were elected unopposed and twenty-two defeated. Dan Breen was put up by both panels, but though he had tried since his return from America to reconcile the disputatious factions, fundamentally he was against the Treaty. Four members for Dublin University were elected unopposed, Labour won seventeen seats, and Farmers and Independents each seven.

Both sides were prepared to admit that the vote was a vote for peace but whereas Griffith's party regarded the result as a clear mandate for the Treaty, the Republican Party held that, the panel candidates of the two parties having won a majority overall, the outcome ought to be a coalition government in accordance with the Collins-de Valera Pact. The figures are interesting; pro-Treaty panel candidates gained 239,193 votes of a total of 620,283 votes cast; anti-Treaty panel candidates—counting Dan Breen in this group—polled 133,864

313

votes; and Labour, Independents and Farmers won between them 247,226 votes. It was plain that the pro-Treaty Party was the strongest, but they did not have an overall majority; it was equally clear that the great majority did not want to throw out the Treaty. But the most significant vote of all, perhaps, was that of 247,226 people who did not want either of the main parties. This surely was a protest vote, the vote of people tired of the long wrangling who wanted to rebuild Ireland and put the past behind them.

They were not to be allowed to do so.

In the booking hall of Liverpool Street station, in London, there is a memorial to railwaymen killed in the First World War and, beside it, a bust of Field-Marshal Sir Henry Wilson who unveiled the memorial on Thursday, June 22nd, 1922, and was assassinated as he reached his house after the ceremony. His killers, Commandant Reginald Dunne and Volunteer Joseph Sullivan of the I.R.A.'s London battalion, had been at Liverpool Street too, but they had had no opportunity to shoot and had taken a taxi to Eaton Place to await their quarry. As their bullets hit him, Wilson, in full uniform, sank to his front step and made the last, pathetic, martial gesture of trying to draw his sword.

It was a cowardly, inexcusable attack, and yet there was a rich quality of heroism in Dunne and Sullivan. Ironically, Sullivan had lost a leg while serving with the British Army in France and it was his lack of mobility which made certain his capture and that of Reginald Dunne, who never thought for a moment of leaving him. To understand their attitude, one has to go back to Bloody Sunday and the cold-blooded killing of the "particular ones". Wilson's death was perhaps the last act of Bloody Sunday, for he, too, was a "particular one". Collins had been minded to kill him months before. He is supposed to have given Dunne orders during the Treaty negotiations and forgotten to cancel them, a rather improbable omission for a man with a mind like a filing cabinet. Dan Breen asserts that, on Collins's instructions, he "went to London to try to get Wilson and Lloyd George after the Treaty was signed." Breen was then on his way to America. "I just couldn't get them," he says. There seems little doubt that Collins briefed Dunne only a fortnight before the assassination. His reasons remain obscure, but he was obsessed with

314

the sufferings of his fellow Catholics in the North and saw Wilson as the instigator of the whole persecution campaign. Each day the bitterness in the North was scored deeper and it may have seemed to Collins that the opportunity for a united, Gaelic Ireland, a dream he cherished far beyond that of a Republic, was receding, that if only he could remove the rotten core of hatred the taint would dissolve. It is possible, however, that the decision was taken by the Supreme Council of the I.R.B. rather than by Collins alone.

That Collins had ordered Wilson's death never occurred to the British Government nor, indeed, to Arthur Griffith, who was appalled by the act.

A conference of Ministers was hastily convened at Downing Street as soon as news of the Field-Marshal's death was received. The galleries of the House of Commons were closed and police protection for Ministers, which had been withdrawn when it was believed the Irish problem no longer held menace, was reinstated. Even as the Ministers assembled at 5 p.m. details of the assassination were coming in.[13] The Home Secretary reported that about thirty dangerous Irishmen were under observation in London, mainly members of the Irish Self Determination League, and the Cabinet authorised police searches of all their homes. An immediate order to confine troops to barracks was telephoned to Dublin. Police chief, Colonel Carter, arrived and produced for the inspection of Ministers the guns used by Dunne and Sullivan, as well as documents found on Dunne, a printed scheme for the organisation of the I.R.A. and a letter from W.R. (signed Liam) from prison.

There was no doubt in the minds of Ministers at that time that the Four Courts garrison were to blame for the killing. It was decided to send at once for Macready, and Churchill withdrew to draft a letter to Collins as Chairman of the Provisional Government embodying the points raised in discussion. Signed by Lloyd George, the letter read:

"Dear Mr. Collins,
    I am desired by His Majesty's Government to inform you that documents have been found upon the murderers of Sir Henry Wilson which clearly connect the assassins with
[13] Cabinet conclusion 36/22 App. III of 22/6/22.

315

the Irish Republican Army, and which further reveal the existence of a definite conspiracy against the peace and order of this country. Other information has reached His Majesty's Government showing that active preparations are on foot among the irregular elements of the I.R.A. to resume attacks upon the lives and property of British subjects both in England and in Ulster. The ambiguous position of the Irish Republican Army can no longer be ignored by the British Government. Still less can Mr Rory O'Connor be permitted to remain with his followers and his arsenal in open rebellion in the heart of Dublin in possession of the Courts of Justice, organising and sending out from this centre enterprises of murder not only in the area of your Government but also in the six Northern Counties and in Great Britain. His Majesty's Government cannot consent to a continuance of this state of things, and they feel entitled to ask you formally to bring it to an end forthwith. Assistance has on various occasions been given to Dominions of the Empire in cases where their authority was challenged by rebellion on their soil; and His Majesty's Government are prepared to place at your disposal the necessary pieces of artillery which may be required, or otherwise to assist you as may be arranged. I am to inform you that they regard the continued toleration of this rebellious defiance of principles of the Treaty as incompatible with its faithful execution. They feel that now you are supported by the declared will of the Irish people in favour of the Treaty, they have a right to expect that the necessary action will be taken by your Government without delay."

Churchill followed this up in a speech to the Commons in which he warned that, "if through weakness, want of courage, or some other less creditable reason" the occupation of the Four Courts was not brought to an end, the British Government would regard the Treaty "as having been formally violated".

Preoccupied with plans to rescue Dunne and Sullivan, Collins snapped that Churchill could do his own dirty work. Several men were sent to London to reconnoitre, among them Tom Cullen and Joe Dolan. There seemed little they could do. Dolan remains convinced that a prison van conveying the accused men could have been ambushed by bomb and that either they would have been rescued or at the worst spared the indignities of the scaffold, but events in Dublin moved too swiftly and no would-be rescuers, either Collins men or members of the Executive Forces, were able to return to London.

On Monday, June 26th, the day of Churchill's dark utterance in the House of Commons, Leo Henderson, the Four Courts Garrison's Director of the Belfast Boycott, led a raid on Ferguson's garage in Lower Baggot Street. The object was to commandeer transport for the North and they had no reason to suppose that Provisional Government troops would move to stop them. Action in the North was the one remaining link in the riven I.R.A. This time the National Army was ordered to break up the raid. They did so and made a prisoner of Henderson.

For some time the commandeering of vehicles, not only in the capital but throughout the country, had been rousing a great deal of resentment. Even the British Army had had vehicles stolen and taken into the Four Courts. The Provisional Government had been widely criticised for taking no action now that the people's vote had strengthened their position. They could risk losing it by failing to govern. It was not merely a matter of cars, or of the food the Four Courts Garrison seized to sustain itself, but the whole problem of setting about restoring order. The kernel of that problem was the possession of a great public building by a garrison who refused to acknowledge either the Headquarters of the National Army or the Provisional Government and swore that they would not live under "any other law" than that of the Irish Republic. Provisional Government action at Ferguson's garage was a notice to quit.

Far from quitting, the Four Courts Garrison the same night nipped out and kidnapped General J. J. O'Connell, Deputy Chief of Staff of the National Army, better known simply as "Ginger" O'Connell.

At a meeting presided over by Arthur Griffith and attended by all the military and political leaders of the Provisional Government and National Army the decision was made to clear the recalcitrant garrison from the Four Courts.

It has always been contended by the Republicans that the

Provisional Government bowed to the wrath of the British Government following the assassination of Sir Henry Wilson. On the other side it was maintained that it was the kidnapping of Ginger O'Connell that precipitated action. Both factors played a part, but the situation was more complex.

As Griffith saw the position, the angry eruptions throughout the country would persist so long as the Executive Forces held as their headquarters a large public building in Dublin, particularly a building which throughout its life had been the spinal column of the English judicial system in Ireland—except for that brief, astonishing occupation by Irish forces at Easter, 1916, Griffith had advocated from the date of the seizure of the building action against those who held it though they had no right to be there. But he could not persuade Collins and other leaders of the I.R.A. that they had no hope of coming to terms with their old comrades. Moreover, they had the sound argument that militarily the Provisional Government was not strong enough. Now that he had agreed the Constitution with England and won an election, Griffith wanted to get on and govern. He believed that only by making it plain that the Provisional Government had the will to do this, and the military strength, and was not going to be sidetracked by the arguments of the Treaty debate now hardening into dogma, could unrest in the country be ended. Then only could the new Ireland come into its own and stop making a fool of itself in the eyes of the world.

The dignity and honour of his country meant much to him and it did not please him to see England apprehensive that the document he had signed was about to be torn up, that the people who had claimed the right and the ability to govern themselves were capable only of anarchy, that a country which had signed an honourable peace treaty should still fire on departing English soldiers and send assassins to the English capital. War had justified these things, but now they brought dishonour. England had been neither generous nor unjust and if Griffith had nothing to be grateful for he did not feel entitled to cavil either.

On Griffith's mind the reaction of the British Government to Wilson's assassination worked powerfully, but only to swell the flow of his own indignation, to reinforce his own determination. Not Britain's wrath but the occasion for it moved him. The kidnapping of O'Connell played into his hands, enabled him to spring the trap at last. His military men, though convinced of the soundness of the political argument for implementing the Treaty, needed something to spark their anger, to overcome their reluctance to open fire on their friends. Even now the decision to issue an ultimatum was not taken unanimously, but it was taken and several distinguished men who were present that day are emphatic that threats from the British Government scarcely entered into the discussion and then worked against, rather than for, the decision taken. Resentment against the British was not the prerogative of the Executive Forces.

FIFTEEN

Of the men drinking in Barrys' Hotel on the evening of Tuesday, June 27th, 1922, only Tommy Ryan carried a revolver, and he had no intention of using it. He had decided to have done with fighting, to have done with Ireland, and to begin a new life in Australia. In Athlone, appointed a staff-captain, he had been training troops under Sean McEoin. Then he had seen stores "diverted" and reported it to McEoin, who asked him to become quartermaster. Ryan declined. He did not see himself in an administrative post; if there was to be fighting he wanted to be in it. Nothing happened, so he travelled to Dublin to make arrangements to emigrate. It was not unusual at this time for men to come and go almost as they pleased. One man who joined the National Army and did not like the life went back to his farm after a week and no one noticed his going. Some reported only on pay-days.

The others in Barrys' Hotel were officers and men from the garrison of the Four Courts. During their occupation of the great building the Executive Forces had gone in and out unhindered, the leaders often to meet their opposite numbers of the Provisional Government Forces at the Plaza Hotel, 6 Gardiner Row, where they argued unavailably for hours. Men off duty were given leave passes signed by the Barrack Adjutant, Sean Lemass, who also affixed to them the seal of the Lord Chief Justice of Ireland.

Ryan knew all the men in Barrys' that night and they gave him a friendly welcome. As they drank, they ribbed him about his gun. Their own weapons they had left in the Four Courts. At about ten o'clock a messenger brought word that they were wanted at the Four Courts and they rushed out of the hotel. Ryan made to finish his drink. The National Army Assistant Quartermaster-General who had seen him with the Republicans advised him to get out and report at once to Portobello Barracks.

"I'm not getting out for anyone while I have this," answered Ryan, slapping his revolver. The officer returned to Portobello Barracks and reported to Gearoid O'Sullivan, the Adjutant-General, that he had seen Ryan drinking with men from the Four Courts. Ryan was ordered by telephone to report to the barracks by 10.30, failing which he would be considered an Irregular.

"I'm not coming," said Ryan, and hung up.

He stayed in Barrys' Hotel, drinking meditatively, until midnight. There was no one else in the hotel. Finally he made up his mind and strolled to Portobello Barracks. Paddy Daly, the Officer Commanding, welcomed him, and so did Joe Leonard, another old acquaintance. Ryan had drinks with his friends and a row with the man who had reported him, then he went to bed.

That same night Liam Lynch visited the Four Courts and stayed talking until after midnight. No man had worked harder than he to restore unity in the I.R.A. He was resolutely opposed to the Treaty and disillusioned by the collapse of the Collins-de Valera Pact with its promise of a coalition government, but he would not support any extreme action which would make the repair of the rupture impossible.

Of all the leaders of the time Lynch was probably in the most difficult position. All had conflicting loyalties; all were anxious for the unity of the I.R.A. to be preserved and had to weigh the importance of that unity against their conviction of what was right for Ireland. The idea of mortal struggle between friends appalled every one of them. But Lynch had another loyalty in the balance, a secret and magnetic allegiance to the Irish Republican Brotherhood. Only the strong subterranean influence of the I.R.B. had generated rebellion and revolution. This hidden influence, the power it conferred

320

upon its leaders and the sense of tradition it engendered cannot be over-estimated.

As a member of its Supreme Council, Lynch was a kind of invisible god. He was bound to the Brotherhood by an oath as potent as his oath to the Republic and by a rare quality of cohesion and sympathy among men which sprang as much from loyalty to the dead leaders as from affection between themselves.

His connection with the I.R.B., more than anything else perhaps, explains his reluctance to throw in his lot with the more militant Republicans and his tenacious refusal to accept defeat once he had burnt his boats. Though he still counselled moderation—"I am not thinking of war, I am thinking of peace," he said in a message to the militants—Lynch's sympathies were very much with the men in the Four Courts. The gaps between them did not seem so great. When he left them that night, though he had agreed to resume as Chief of Staff, he little thought that within hours he would have put hesitation aside, or that he, and the leaders of the Four Courts garrison too, were destined to die for their cause.

When the Provisional Government and National Army leaders made the decision to rout the Republicans from the Four Courts they thought at first to starve out the garrison; but they knew that somehow the Republicans would get food and that this course, in any case, would mean a swing of public sympathy towards the besieged men. General Dalton, the Director of Military Operations, urged the use of artillery. "It was my belief at the time," he says, "that the use of these guns would have a very demoralising effect upon a garrison unused to artillery fire, but I realised that their employment as a destructive agent on the Four Courts buildings would be quite insignificant." Dalton was talking from deeply imprinted experience. General Macready, evidently unaware of the British Government's offer of "the necessary pieces of artillery which may be required", declined to sanction the handing over of big guns and Sir Alfred Cope had to refer the request to Churchill, who, of course, agreed.

Tony Lawlor, an airman during the Great War, had been training men in gun drill and loading on an old 15-pounder horse artillery piece left by the British in Athlone. With his men he was summoned from Athlone by General O'Duffy.

At Beggar's Bush Dalton explained the position to him. Lawlor had no misgivings about helping in the attack on the Four Courts, though as a one-time member of the 6th Dublin Brigade he knew that he would be opposing many old friends. The murder of Adamson had dispelled any lingering doubts he had about the Treaty and, as he saw it, "there was now a danger of losing everything."

Emmet Dalton, who had been Chief Liaison Officer for Ireland during the Truce and the Treaty negotiations, now was the sole authority for the taking over of all British equipment, arms, ammunition and vehicles, and his was the responsibility for taking delivery of the four 18-pounder guns promised by Churchill.

He took Lawlor, Captain (later General) Peadar MacMahon and some troops by a roundabout route, by Kilmainham, to the far gate of Phoenix Park where, at dead of night, the guns were handed over by resentful British artillerymen and towed away. Ten shells for each gun were issued, not the high explosive shells that Dalton had asked for, but shrapnell shells, which were much less effective.

Tommy Ryan was shaken awake by the officer with whom he had quarrelled. The man was in conciliatory mood now. He explained that there was to be an attack on the Four Courts, unless the Executive Forces surrendered, and that he and about ten others would have nothing to do with it. Would Ryan join them?

"Damn it all! You were reporting me a couple of hours ago," said Ryan disgustedly. An hour later, forty men who had joined the National Army but, when it came to the point, were not willing to shoot at old friends, were arrested. Many more would have joined them had it not been for the indignation roused by the kidnapping of the popular Ginger O'Connell.

In charge of the guard at the gates of the Four Courts was Tom O'Reilly, usually known as "Skinner", As a boy he had played a man's part in the Easter Rising of 1916. Later, he had been on Collins's staff—"not on the gun end", as he puts it. Trying to elude some British soldiers one day in Grafton Street, he was clubbed down with the butt of a revolver, taken to the Castle and, after three weeks there, sent to Arbour Hill where he was imprisoned until after the Treaty had been signed. Back with Collins as a staff-lieutenant at Beggar's Bush, he refused the oath of allegiance required of members of the National Army and made his way to the Plaza Hotel. He went into the Four Courts. Tom O'Reilly was one of the few men close to Collins who was not impelled by the magnetism of the "Big Fellow" to support the Treaty.

Soon after Liam Lynch had left the Four Courts, O'Reilly was chatting at the gate to some old friends who were now on the opposite side. Among them, he remembers, were Ben Byrne and George Ashe. A motor cyclist raced up to the gate, handed O'Reilly a dispatch and waited for the reply. In his hand O'Reilly held the fuse that was to fire the Civil War. It was the ultimatum, signed on behalf of the Provisional Government by General Tom Ennis, requiring the surrender of the Four Courts by 4 a.m. on Wednesday June 28th, 1922. Already it was after midnight.

"I went up to the Central Hall under the dome and gave the note to Rory O'Connor. He went into a huddle with Liam Mellows and some of the others and then told me to go back to the gate and tell the dispatch rider there was no reply."

Provisional Government troops were already in position. Lancia cars had been drawn up across the gates to prevent the Executive Forces from using their armoured car *Mutineer*, the Rolls-Royce Whippet which MacManus had tried to recover from Templemore. Later, the car was to be re-named by the National Army *Ex-Mutineer*.

Tommy Ryan had not had time to be issued with a uniform. He had no appointment and joined in the attack on the Four Courts as a private. Armed with a Thompson submachine-gun and a parabellum, he went into a house overlooking the improvised citadel and climbed to the top flat. There, an old woman and a girl, who had been roused by the sounds of activity outside, were making tea. They poured Ryan a cup and smilingly the girl prepared eggs on toast for him. At 4.29 a.m. two of the borrowed field guns opened fire on the Four Courts from Winetavern Street. The shells barely scratched the stone. Ryan put down his tea and went to the window.

"There were three or four lads running round the parapet of the dome and I started shooting." A moment later Ryan became probably the first casualty of the action when the old

323

lady smashed her teapot over his head. As he was wearing no uniform, she had mistaken him for a Republican.

Another supernumerary was Commandant-General Dermott MacManus who, in May, had succeeded Major-General Dalton as Director of Training.

I went round with a company that got into houses on the Phoenix Park side of the Four Courts," he says. "I went into a house and turned out the people. They were frightened I must say. Very soon I was in a room with three or four men, and just across the narrow street was this huge building with all the windows sandbagged. I thought it was time we did something and, without realising that there were people covering me there, I took a rifle from one of the men, smashed a window and fired what I believe was the first shot of the battle. It hit a sandbag. A second later, five shots hit the wall behind me. We weren't so rash after that."

Lancia cars were brought up to screen the 18-pounders and the gun crews from lively machine-gun fire.

"Bullets hopped off the cobblestones, flying in all directions," says Lawlor, "and some of our men were scared." Dalton beckoned Lawlor to follow him into the middle of the road. They lit cigarettes, talked quietly for a time, then sauntered back. Lawlor felt that this was rather a hazardous way of inspiring the men, but Dalton was quite unconcerned. He departed then, leaving Lawlor in charge.

At 5.15 a.m. a man in the Four Courts was wounded and at the same hour, according to *War News* which published a diary sent out by Father Albert, one of the two priests with the garrison, General Daly, who was in overall charge of the attack, sent a message: "When will you come out with your hands up?" Rory O'Connor replied, "When you come for me."

At first the big guns were fired only at five-minute intervals, partly to conserve the few shells handed over by the British but also because it was thought that the Republicans would soon decide that their opposition had gone far enough. At 12.30 p.m., reported Father Albert, "the fire was so heavy and so deafening that it was almost impossible for the priest who was hearing confessions to carry out his duties. The firing was carried on furiously for seven and a half hours. We have been heartened by the girls of Cumann na mBan and nurses

324

and doctors who are here unselfishly giving their services to the wounded."

When he was told, as he drove into Dublin that Wednesday morning, that the Four Courts was under attack, de Valera could not believe it. Collins arrived in the city in an emotionally-charged mood. To the last he had been reluctant to take action in spite of his message to Churchill early in May that the Provisional Government intended[1] to fight. Arthur Griffith, who would have acted long before, watched the bombardment from a roof-top, and perhaps the blows to his heart of the reverberating guns contributed to his death six weeks later.

Republican propaganda exploded as thunderously as the National Army artillery which, the Republicans claimed, was being directed by British officers. In truth, it was only their own old friends, Emmet Dalton and Tony Lawlor, and their scratch crew of gunners, all of whom simply aimed along the bore of the gun, which was as much as Dalton himself knew about firing big guns.

"We're fighting the same enemy. They have only a different uniform," remarked a lad in the Four Courts and the theme was echoed again and again in Republican propaganda. "The enemy is the old enemy, England, using new weapons lent her, to their shame, by traitors to the Republic." Even de Valera, in an interview for *War News*, alleged that Collins had broken his election pact with him "at the bidding of the English".

The propaganda was not ineffectual: Churchill reported to the British Cabinet on June 30th that "the prolongation of the operations by the Free State troops against the Four Courts, coupled with the suggestion that had been put about that the Free State Government was acting at the behest of the British Government, had to some extent reacted adversely on public opinion", and he exhorted Cabinet colleagues who might be making speeches "to dwell on the fact that they should avoid any suggestion that the Free State Government was acting on British inspiration, and to lay stress on the fact that they have undertaken the task on their own initiative."

He also informed the Cabinet that 10,000 rifles as well as field guns and "other requirements" had been furnished at the request of the Provisional Government and that although

[1] Cabinet conclusion 27 (22), 3, of 16/5/22.

325

at one time ammunition had run short there were now ample supplies.[2]

Lawlor moved his guns to Bridgefoot Street near the ancient Brazen Head Inn, and the shells began to chunk small pieces out of the Four Courts. Completed near the end of the eighteenth century at a cost of £200,000, the Four Courts was one of Dublin's priceless legacies from the Georgian era. The waters of the Liffey reflected the nobility of its 450-yard frontage and the great Corinthian portico of six columns. The Central Hall under the dome gave access to the four courts—of Chancery, King's Bench, Common Pleas and Exchequer. Twenty-four columns supported the dome.

As the bombardment went on, Dalton received a summons from General Sir Nevil Macready who, surrounded by his officers, was standing on the steps of his headquarters, the Royal Hospital, to receive him. Indignation glinted from every brass button of his uniform. When, just as Dalton arrived, a shell from an 18-pounder exploded in the saddling paddock, Dalton had an inkling of what was coming.

"He said they'd given me the guns on the assurance that they wouldn't be used against the British, but the place was being shelled," Dalton recalls.

"I couldn't make this out at all but I said I'd go back and check up. I found Ignatius O'Neill, a great character from County Clare, with his gun canted up as he tried to hit a sniper in the dome of the Four Courts. He was using an 18-pounder like a rifle and the shells were going right through the dome and landing on the Royal Hospital."

Macready, when he heard the story, was not amused.

From the roof of the dome, on Keegan's corner side, Tom O'Reilly and Bill Gannon tried to pick off the crew of the 18-pounder stationed at Wood Quay, whilst targets themselves for snipers on surrounding roof-tops. "They gave us a bad time at that corner," recalls O'Reilly, "but we stuck it out as best we could."

This could have been said of the whole garrison, which comprised five sections totalling something over two hundred men. "The boys are glorious," Rory O'Connor wrote in a message to *War News*, "and will fight for the Republic to the end. How long will our misguided former comrades outside

2 Cabinet conclusion 36/22 (1) of 30/6/22.

attack those who stand for Ireland alone?" In that last plain-tive, exasperated question was genuine bewilderment. Within it was contained the very essence of the tragedy, for the "mis-guided former comrades" also stood for Ireland alone.

On both sides there was an awareness of the tragedy, yet each was so convinced of the merit of its argument, and so exasperated by the obtuseness of the other, that there could be no giving way. Had the affection between those men been less there might have been more generosity, but a man is never more offended than by those dearest to him. Emmet Dalton and Tony Lawlor directed their gunfire with the professional detachment of men who had gone through the hellflames of France. Dalton was full of sadness and sorrow and remembers even today that Rory O'Connor and Liam Mellows were utterly sincere men who were ready to die for their principles.

O'Connor, a short, dark, dynamic man, won the admiration of them all. His old tweed coat seemed to be everywhere. Es-pecially, as an expert himself, he kept an eye on the explosives dump where a section under Frank Cotter manufactured bombs—"what we used to call 'wall flowers'", says O'Reilly—an alarming enough task at any time, a hazardous one indeed when 18-pounder shells were whining through windows and exploding inside the building. In the dump were thousands of sticks of gelignite, two lorry loads, seized by the Republicans soon after the occupation of the Four Courts.

The bombardment had done relatively little damage to the great labyrinth of a building, either inside or out, nor had the garrison, who had access to cellars and rooms below ground, suffered much harm.

"When it became apparent to me that the defenders were not suffering inconvenience and did not intend to surrender, I knew that a breach would have to be made and an assault mounted in order to secure the buildings," explains Dalton.

During Thursday, shells at last cracked a wall of the western wing, in Morgan Place, and Paddy Daly asked Lawlor to try to widen the crack. Firing through open sights, the gunners lowered the trajectory of each shot, but one over-enthusiastic gunner depressed the barrel of the gun too far and blew a hole in the Liffey wall on his own side of the river.

When an appeal was made to the commander of a section of National troops to allow a nurse and a woman companion

327

into the Four Courts, the officer became suspicious. Perhaps he thought there were enough nurses in the building. The nurse turned out to be Tom Barry seeking to add his formidable fighting powers to the strength of the garrison. Instead, he became the first prisoner of the action and he must have wished he had taken more notice of Moss Twomey who had suggested to him that he would "do better to get the fellows inside out, not to go in". The previous night Twomey had tried to persuade Dick Barrett to "come down to the country instead of going back", but Barrett had gone.

That night, nearly forty-eight hours after fighting began, the Provisional Government launched an assault on the Four Courts. Flurries of rain hissed along the pavements. The streets were almost deserted. Above, on roof-tops lost in darkness, snipers sent bullets cracking across the city, futile bullets for the most part, aimed at a rifle flash or just at a vague shape in the night. Along the banks of the Liffey a machine-gun clattered sporadically to little purpose. The big guns roared ponderously from time to time. Lawlor received orders from Dalton to take his guns back to Winetavern Street because men would be coming in from the Kingsbridge side. Chips of stone from the river wall, sent flying by machine-gun bullets, had lacerated Lawlor's face. Peadar MacMahon had set up more guns in Green Street.

The streets came alive suddenly. Two thousand men in several parties converged on the Four Courts. Ambulances and motor cycles sped past them. Then a fearful caterwauling of machine-guns and rifles broke out, somehow sounding a great deal worse than it was. Troops followed, racing at the double across the Liffey bridges. Commandant Joe Leonard was wounded as he led an assault party through the breach in the west wing but Commandants McGuinness and O'Connor broke through from the Church Street side into the western end of the rear buildings without casualty. More troops, Dalton among them, battered their way in. Most of the garrison withdrew into the eastern part of the rear building, but not all. At close quarters, with bomb, bayonet and bullet, men who had once stood so valiantly together now tried to rip each other apart. By midnight a large part of the Four Courts, including the Central Hall and the library, was in Government hands. A number of concealed mines was found and the wires were cut. Thirty-three Republicans were taken prisoner and large quantities of arms and explosives were captured.

MacManus, replacing the wounded Leonard at Daly's request, had taken charge of the western wing and in the darkness placed men throughout the three floors. Huddled in the black, eerie chambers, they were not very enthusiastic.

The National Army casualties, three men killed and fourteen wounded, and the Republican prisoners had been removed safely from the building, and early on Friday morning a temporary truce was arranged so that Republican wounded could be evacuated. Twenty doctors rode to the Four Courts in a coal dray. Fallen masonry littered the road and broken tramwires lay in tangles. An ambulance service was hurriedly organised and the wounded were taken to Jervis Street Hospital. Then the fighting was renewed.

The *Mutineer* charged up and down between the main building and the building at the rear, the crew discharging machine-gun fire through the windows of the main building. MacManus blazed back with a Lewis gun and ripped off both the near tyres. The armoured car backed into a doorway opposite and the crew leaped out and ran inside as bullets from the Lewis gun spurted into nearby walls. The marks of them remain.

In the basement of the western wing MacManus found a room full of explosives; there were also mines. Patrick Kelly, Director of Engineering, was summoned to dismantle them but was hit in both arms by bullets as he climbed a heap of rubble to enter the building. With leaves from law books, lathes from the ceiling and handkerchiefs, MacManus fashioned splints for Kelly's broken right arm. Before he had time to deal with the other arm an ambulance arrived and Kelly was taken to hospital, but MacManus has always been proud of the fact that the broken arm healed rapidly and well while the superficial wound which he had not treated became septic.

At 11.30 the Solicitors and Bankruptcy departments of the Four Courts were set on fire. At the time it was believed that the garrison were responsible, but Tom O'Reilly explains that heavy shelling from the Bridewell end began the blaze. An hour later occurred one of those explosions that go down in history. The city shook with sound. For a moment the great building seemed but a modest plinth for the towering columns of sombre black smoke that rose above it. Then the smoke began to spread and drift and as it slowly crumpled red flame glowed like paint beneath a dark glaze. The smoke rolled away to the east, now like thunder clouds, and from it fluttered millions of pieces of paper, some blackened, some still gleaming white. For an hour or more they tumbled, settling upon the city and far beyond, the charred remains of historical records dating back to 1170, wills, census returns, legal documents of every kind. Entire books hurtled for miles.

More fiercely the flames threaded ways through the smoke, leaping as if to reach the great dome which stood in all its invulnerable dignity above them. Fire brigades rushed to battle with the inferno. National Army troops rescued what documents they could and loaded them on to lorries. The garrison had been driven to a furthermost corner. Soon they would have to surrender.

They had been expecting the explosion and had plugged their ears with cotton wool. It was all they could do, but it was like trying to ward off machine-gun bullets with an umbrella. Ernie O'Malley had suggested that it would be a good time to make a break. National Army armoured cars and Lancias were at the gate, but there were mines beneath them and the touch of a switch would clear the way. He called for twenty-five volunteers to rush the gates when the explosion occurred and to take the Medical Mission opposite where there was a National Army post. But the shock of the explosion numbed all movement, all senses. O'Reilly remembers standing and watching huge presses full of law tomes shift from the walls. There was no rush to the outside. Incredibly, no one was killed though about forty National Army troops in the Central Hall were badly hurt.

There were more explosions in the afternoon, two beneath the Records Office at about 2.15 and another at the back of the building at about five o'clock which engulfed the western side of the two blocks in vast curtains of flame. MacManus had moved his men away from the immediate danger area but they were blackened by one of the explosions. "Blocks of masonry were flying like leaves in the wind," says MacManus, "but we hadn't a single casualty."

330

According to *War News*, Republican troops were moving to the relief of the garrison but were unable to get through because of "the accidental explosion of a mine". Oscar Traynor ordered the garrison to surrender "to help me to carry on the fight outside". He added, "I would be unable to fight my way through to you even at terrific sacrifice."

At about 3.30 that afternoon a white flag appeared amid the smoke and the flames. The little band, haggard from lack of sleep, smoke-stained and almost paralysed by fatigue, asked for terms. The National Army gave them the same terse answer that Pearse had received from the British in 1916. Unconditional surrender. Rory O'Connor and Liam Mellows led out their men, youngsters most of them, beaten but with convictions unshaken. One carried a white shirt tied to a walking stick. "They were disappointed and upset and some of them were holding on to each other," says Lawlor, who lined them up against the river wall at Ormond Quay and collected their arms. Ernie O'Malley made to offer his revolver to him, then suddenly threw it over his head into the Liffey. Lawlor produced money from his pocket and sent for cigarettes which he distributed to the prisoners. "Then Daly arrived," Lawlor goes on, "and he was furious. He wanted to shoot the lot of them. I had a stand up row with him which ended when I said, 'Look, Daly, I haven't formally taken the surrender. I only got them lined up. You'd better go and take the surrender.' Daly went over to Rory O'Connor and I hurried some press men across to witness the scene."

Ernie O'Malley signed the surrender document, a document as inevitable as that which Pearse had had to sign. With the dejected defenders was Ginger O'Connell whose capture had triggered off the assault. He was philosophical about his days as a prisoner. "I didn't like the noise," he said to the press. "The food was running very short too."

The defeat of the Four Courts garrison had been inherent in the situation from the beginning. Republicans like Twomey had never been convinced that the taking up of a defensive position would achieve their purpose. Before the attack Oscar Traynor had tried to persuade the garrison to evacuate the building. There had been a lesson in the failure of the 1916 Rising, but from that defeat had come the ultimate victory, and perhaps O'Connor and his friends believed that something

331

similar would happen again. The seizure of a large and important public building had been in the first place a demonstration that the Republic continued in being and was entitled to suitable accommodation. And there was more than a hint of symbolism in the choice of the headquarters of justice. It must be remembered, too, that the Four Courts garrison did not see themselves as an isolated outpost beyond the reach of aid. It was believed that a great ring of Republicans would close in from outside, trapping the National Forces between them, a variant on the pincer strategy. But, as was to happen so often in the coming months, somehow action that was expected never took place.

The destruction inside the Four Courts was almost indescribable. Daylight streaming through perforated walls illumined the plight of the defenders who had been forced to vacate one untenable position after another. Amid the debris, clothing, tattered bedding, stale food and broken guns lay abandoned. In the chaos of charred paper in some rooms bookcases with row upon row of legal volumes stood intact. Outside the Four Court houses lurched drunkenly together, their windows shattered, their doors blown flat.

The cause of the mighty explosion is still disputed. Did O'Connor's men deliberately blow up the Four Courts or not? Tom O'Reilly is firmly convinced that the fire caused by shelling reached the explosives dump, as it was bound to do. Emmet Dalton is sure in his own mind that a mine was detonated in an attempt to destroy as many Provisional Government troops as possible, and certainly the building was extensively mined for this purpose. National Army men in the Central Hall swore that the fire had not reached that part of the building and MacManus says that he saw under the dome a cylinder about seven feet long and two feet thick. Ernie O'Malley told Daly not only that the explosion was intended, but that he regretted there had been so few National Army casualties. But O'Malley could be pardoned for a little bitter bravado at that time.

Neither side was pulling its propaganda punches and, whether the explosion was deliberate or not, it wasn't surprising that the Provisional Government made the most of it. They were annoyed when Thomas Johnson, Secretary of the

332

Irish Labour Party, who was as nearly neutral as the times allowed, having been given permission to interview the Four Courts garrison prisoners in Mountjoy, wrote to the Minister of Defence (and sent a copy of his letter to the press) that he had been assured the explosion was accidental. Johnson was accused of abusing his trust—he had no right to discuss such matters, it was said—and the Government issued a statement to refute the garrison's vicarious denial. Johnson's reply was sharp but full of dignity. He had gone into Mountjoy to try to find a way to peace and did not believe that the "dissemination of untrue stories calculated to poison the minds of the people on either side" helped at all. Later, O'Connor himself published a statement, humorously headed: "Publicity Department, Mountjoy Jail", in which he claimed that the "munition shop" had caught fire following a bombardment. He admitted, however, that 20 lbs. of explosive had been laid in the doorway of the Lord Chancellor's court to cover the final retreat.

In the House of Commons, Winston Churchill explained that the British Government's attitude to the dilemma of the Irish was one of "interest and sympathy". British troops had orders to shoot in self-defence if fired upon; otherwise, it was "not our business at all". Asked about the loss of records accumulated through centuries, he replied, "Better a State without archives than archives without a State."

In the minds of the surrendered garrison there *was* no State. Escorted to Jameson's distillery they were confined in a room with barred windows. But the bars had mellowed like old whiskey and even fatigued hands could bend them. O'Reilly got to the street door and looked out. A group of women stood talking outside. Quietly he closed the door. It seemed that there was a chance for them all. Six men slipped out of the door, O'Malley, O'Brien, Rigney, Lemass, Griffin and Fitzpatrick. But they were too eager, in too much of a rush. The women in the street gave the alarm, National Army guards raced up and no more Republicans got away. Instead, they went to Mountjoy.

But if the Provisional Government believed that the fight was over in Dublin they were soon disillusioned. The Executive Forces already held posts in Fowler Hall, the Kildare Street Club and the Masonic Hall, all of which had been occupied on April 14th, the day the Four Courts was seized. Now, on June 30th, when the Four Courts garrison capitulated, and during the following morning, a whole block in the heart of Dublin was virtually isolated. In O'Connell Street (or Sackville Street as it still was) they took possession of a two hundred yard frontage. Armed men swarmed into the Gresham, Crown, Granville and Hammam Hotels; visitors were told to pack their belongings and get out; those who were unfortunate enough to be away at the time were stranded and their luggage was used to barricade the foyers. Windows were knocked out with rifle butts and barricaded with anything that came to hand, books and boxes, furniture and bedding. There were sandbags, but not nearly enough. In O'Connell Street traffic was impeded by the crowds rather than by the activities of Republican soldiers. The Rotunda was also occupied by the Executive Forces who thus put themselves in a position to set up a crossfire at the junction of Parnell and O'Connell Streets. More posts were set up in Gardiner Street, Lower Abbey Street and elsewhere in the city and the ruined Custom House also was in Republican hands. Snipers roamed over the roof-tops.

The Republicans did not forget that the British were the root cause of the trouble and did not overlook the possibility that they might be provoked into fighting. In this case many a Free State Irishman would swiftly shed his faith in the Treaty. But the British were cautious. Republicans in the Rotunda fired at English soldiers as they passed Rutland Square in a lorry, but there was no answering fire. One British machine-gunner indignantly directed a short burst at Moran's hotel in Talbot Street when Republicans opened fire on an armoured car and a lorry. Two British soldiers of the Border Regiment, members of a small party collecting money from a bank, were shot at and wounded. But, to the relief of the Provisional Government and the chagrin of the Executive Forces, the British continued to remain aloof from the developing struggle.

In Dame Street, Abbey Street and Westmoreland Street there were brief hand-to-hand encounters between Republicans and National troops, and snipers of both sides duelled overhead. Sometimes innocent people got in the way of bullets; a girl was· killed when Provisional Government troops fired after a
334

suspect who broke from arrest. All over the city, as the tempo of disaster quickened, suspense heightened. A landmine exploded in Earl Street; hand grenades were flung from roof-tops at National Army vehicles; more snipers rattled bullets on an armoured car; Republicans raided a market near the Custom House and seized provisions; street barricades appeared, ambulances darted everywhere; shops began to close. More Republicans stormed in from Bray and Rathfarnham (Co. Dublin), abandoning and burning the police barracks they had been holding, to reinforce their friends in the city. Everyone awaited a big attack by National Forces, but there were only outlying engagements. A house in Harcourt Street was mauled by machine-guns and thirty Republicans surrendered. For half an hour Republicans occupying workshops in Stanley Street sustained a bitter defence but finally gave in. Altogether, the Provisional Government now held some four hundred prisoners.

In Clarence Street a man threw a grenade at an armoured lorry but it bounced off and exploded in the road. The man ran and for a moment was in the sights of a machine-gun on the armoured lorry, but the gunner did not fire. "I could not bring myself to fire," he told a reproachful comrade. "Sure it would have spoiled the lovely street and all the fine shops."

"In the name of God—it's not our town," was the disgusted answer.

Vinny Byrne, the man who had saved the Bank of Ireland for the Provisional Government, having delivered stores to a Government post, was travelling back along Jervis Street in a Lancia with two other men. "I didn't know the anti-Treaty forces had taken over the Swan Hotel at the corner of York Street, and they knocked hell out of us," he says. "At the time I thought it was a street ambush and ordered my driver to go down Dick Street, round into Mercer Street, and we'd catch these fellows in York Street. We caught it again, from the houses this time." Byrne gave up and reported the incident at Portobello Barracks. An armoured car named *The Fighting Second* was sent, with Paddy Griffin in charge, to clear the Swan Hotel. The Republicans made a fight of it but eventually they slipped out the back way and disappeared.

During the day, Saturday, yet another attempt was made to find a peace formula. Dr Byrne, Archbishop of Dublin,

Lord Mayor O'Neill and Thomas Johnson, accompanied by Father Albert, so recently come from the Four Courts, drove in a Red Cross car to the Hammam Hotel where they met de Valera, Traynor, Brugha, Barton and Countess Markievicz. Only the previous day de Valera had cycled to the Gresham himself with a draft for a settlement he had drawn up—as a newly-enlisted private in the Executive Forces. Representing a number of women's organisations, Maud Gonne, once the darling of Yeats, demanded of the Provisional Government that there should be no further military operations until the new—and prorogued—Dail had met to discuss the situation. But there seemed no way now of stopping the struggle.

So far, though there had been many incidents throughout the country, there had been little sign of a general rising. With the attack on the Four Courts, Liam Lynch had finally decided upon belligerence. At the Clarence Hotel a proclamation was drawn up in picturesque and evocative terms: "At the dictation of our hereditary enemies our rightful cause is being treacherously assailed by recreant Irishmen. The crash of arms and the boom of artillery reverberate in this supreme test of the Nation's destiny." The proclamation appealed to "all citizens who have withstood unflinchingly the oppression of the enemy during the past six years to rally to the support of the Republic and recognise that the resistance now being offered is but the continuance of the struggle that was suspended by the truce with the British." A special appeal was made to the "recreant Irishmen" to return to their allegiance to the Republic.

Once that had been safely dispatched to the printers, Lynch, with Liam Deasy and Sean Culhane, left the Clarence Hotel and set out for the country. The party was seen in an outside car by Emmet Dalton, who was sitting in his staff car in Parliament Street.

Dalton's forward headquarters during the Four Courts attack was the Dolphin Hotel, quite close to the Clarence. Liam Tobin was with Dalton in the car and Pat McCrea was the driver. Dalton instructed Tobin to arrest the group and to take them to Wellington (now Griffith) Barracks, while he himself continued his direction of the artillery action at the Four Courts.

What was said at Wellington Barracks between Lynch and

O'Duffy, then the National Army's Deputy Chief of Staff, has been disputed. "At this time," says Dalton, "it was well known that the Volunteers in the South were split on the issue of the Treaty, but no definite decision or statement had been made. Collins was doing all in his power to avoid a complete break in the Volunteer movement and was, I believe, willing to go to great lengths to keep the uncommitted leaders in a neutral state."

Mulcahy's feeling was perhaps stronger than that of Collins, for he had a very great affection for Lynch, and for Deasy too, and an absolute conviction that Lynch would not take up arms against the Provisional Government, or, more accurately perhaps, that the I.R.B. tie would prove too strong for him and that he would not, in the end, dissent from the decision of the Supreme Council. Indeed, he was angry that Lynch had been arrested at all.

Dalton was with Mulcahy and Collins later when O'Duffy "made it quite clear that Lynch had given an undertaking that he would not take up arms or take any active part against the Government forces." According to O'Donoghue's account in *No Other Law*, the interview was conducted on a most informal basis and Lynch told Sean Moylan shortly afterwards that O'Duffy had merely asked his opinion of the situation and he had answered that they were all mad, or that the men in the Four Courts were mad. In view of Mulcahy's faith in Lynch, it is certain that O'Duffy was anxious not to antagonise him and did not press him very hard. He probably inferred more than Lynch intended by his casual remark and formed the impression that he was not a danger.

Lynch was released and, not without adventure, arrived at Mallow on June 29th. It appears that he was held up by Provisional Government troops at Castlecomer and again was allowed to go. Once more there were suggestions that he had given his parole, to Colonel Prout in this instance. O'Donoghue strongly refutes this but, apparently, after a convivial evening, Lynch and his friends did sign a rather ambiguous document, scarcely bothering to glance at it. From Mallow Lynch went, on the same day, to Limerick, where he set up his headquarters. He had delayed long enough in Mallow to indulge his predilection for the pen. A lengthy statement explaining that he had resumed his position as Chief of Staff, Executive Forces, "owing to attack on G.H.Q. and other posts occupied by our troops by Dail forces, and position created by draft Free State Constitution", was issued over his signature from Mallow on June 30th. The document claimed: "Latest reports from Dublin show that the Dublin Brigade have control of situation, and reinforcements and supplies have been dispatched to their assistance." The Four Courts fell the same day and it could hardly be said that the occupation of "the block" in O'Connell Street amounted to "control of situation".

However, it was not until about six o'clock on the evening of Sunday, July 2nd, that any concerted move was made to eject the Republicans from their O'Connell Street stronghold. By now they had connected all the buildings with a system of holes knocked in walls, and planks and ladders, so that they had a single large fortress.

Their headquarters was the Hammam Hotel. Executive Forces were in possession of numerous other buildings also and in one of these, the Moran Hotel, they held out for some time against machine-gun fire from an armoured car and were only dislodged when an 18-pounder was brought up. The third shell persuaded them that it was not healthy to stay and they then took shelter in Hughes's Hotel in Gardiner Street, which they were also forced to vacate. Thirty of them were taken prisoner.

The borrowed British guns which had won the battle of the Four Courts were now destined to achieve the same results in O'Connell Street. There the Provisional Government Forces had occupied buildings on the opposite side of the street from the Republicans and improvised their own fortress on similar lines. Tom Ennis, one of the best Irish soldiers of the day, master-minded the operation and a large crowd of spectators gathered to witness the battle. At the same time National Army forces were attacking smaller Republican strongholds, mainly in the Gardiner Street area, east of O'Connell Street.

At first the fighting was a matter of desultory exchanges of rifles and machine-gun fire and in this the Republicans had an advantage, their shrewd seizure of the National Bank on the corner of Parnell Street having provided them with a very effective firing point. Indeed, until the arrival of reinforcements, the National troops were rather hard pressed, and it was a relief to them when the bank was recaptured on the
338

Monday. Machine-gun fire spurting from both sides of O'Connell Street soon produced the familiar lacework of broken and tangled overhead wires. Glass and chips of masonry littered the pavements. There was a strange callousness about the destruction of so much property, a menacing irresponsibility on both sides, for Dublin belonged to them all. A city invaded by an alien foe may be nobly sacrificed but it is a melancholy state when a city's own people encompass its ruin. And strange, too, though very human no doubt, was the detachment of those who assembled to watch.

All over Dublin in that first week of July sporadic skirmishes left houses with jagged windows and blasted doors, houses that hung open like toothless mouths. Sometimes the little garrisons of these makeshift fortresses were taken prisoner and sent off to the jails; often they crept away, over fences and through alleyways, to make a stand in some other building until that, too, became untenable and was left derelict. The climax of this immolation of Dublin was to be reached in O'Connell Street.

National troops were doing all they could to contain the Republicans within the block. During Sunday night armoured cars prowled along Gardiner and Talbot Streets and from time to time bullets cracked through the walls of Republican strongholds. Throughout Monday the pressure was increased and by evening most of the posts held by the Executive Forces on the south side of the city had been captured or stealthily evacuated. National Army sappers bored through the walls of adjoining houses to explode bombs in the Y.M.C.A. building which was also held by the Republicans, although it was on the opposite side of the street from their main fortress. The building caught fire and other buildings were soon threatened. Sixteen men from a blind workshop were led outside and taken away by ambulance. Excited crowds and fusillades of shots from both sides of the street made it almost impossible for firemen to work, but bravely they tried.

Restlessly, tirelessly, Cathal Brugha patrolled the roof-tops from the Hammam to the Gresham. Armed with a Mauser automatic to which he had fitted a rifle stock, he was a fiery, self-appointed instrument of retribution. On the Monday night the garrison in the block was quietly reduced from the original seventy men and thirty women because it was realised that
339

there was no chance of holding on. Most of the leaders including Traynor and Stack went and so did de Valera, named by the newspapers as *the* leader, but no leader at all for the time being. Mysteriously they filtered through back alleys and through the not very effective National Army cordon.

Rumours that Republican troops were assembling at Blessington ready to sweep into Dublin filtered into the city and it was thought by many that Liam Lynch also would launch a rescue operation from Limerick, but no help came.

Early on Tuesday afternoon, fifteen Republicans marched out under a white flag from the Hammam Hotel but another group, still full of fight, set up a firing post in Mooney's Bar on the North Quays and opened up on the Ballast Office across the river, a Government strongpoint. The Republicans seemed able to move about the city in spite of street barriers where earnest young National Army men, many of them fresh from the country, searched passers-by for arms, never suspecting the existence of clandestine ways known to men who had used them so often during the struggle against the British.

In the meantime, the Provisional Government "had intimated that if they could be supplied with some form of gas grenades their task in clearing the rebels out of their strongholds would be greatly simplified".

The British Cabinet considered their request on Tuesday, July 4th, and decided that it would be improper to supply gas of "a lethal or permanently injurious character" but that if it were not an infringement of the Washington Resolution "ammunition containing lachrymatory or other similar gas might be supplied".[3] Much loss of valuable life and damage to property might have been saved had someone thought of tear gas earlier.

An 18-pounder was positioned at the mouth of Henry Street on Tuesday night and its fire concentrated on the Granville Hotel where the beleaguered Republicans continued to resist strongly. But the battle now was one of men against fire. Much of the block was burning with the intensity of a blast furnace and only rain slowed the spreading of the flames. The Gresham had been evacuated as early as Monday night, although part of it was in use again next day to house the wounded. Garry Houlihan and four more resumed the fight

[3] Cabinet conclusion 37/22 (6) of 4/7/22.

340

from the Gresham on Wednesday but, cut off by flames, were forced to surrender. It was surprising that the Republicans survived Tuesday night. Above the battering of machine-guns the boom of the big gun resounded, and with chilling inexorability the great blaze worked its way along the block. Throughout Wednesday the artillery blasted the block at point-blank range. Only twenty-five shells, in fact, were fired, but they did enormous damage and the smoke and flames in the buildings were ever more menacing. The courage of the firemen was surpassed by none, except perhaps by Brugha. He remained undaunted, comforting the wounded, encouraging the defenders, never allowing his own nerve to slacken for a moment, and many men on both sides must have recalled 1916 when he had fought on with wounds which, shared between half a dozen men, could have killed them all.

The Hammam disappeared in a roar of flame and a thunder of falling masonry. It was then about midday on Wednesday. A small figure appeared on the roof carrying a white flag, then he ran down a fire escape. Captain Dan Stapleton advanced to take the surrender but fell, wounded in the neck, as a volley of shots came from the Granville where the garrison had mustered for its last stand. But the flag had not been intended to betoken surrender. Realising that firemen were in danger from mines, Brugha had sent out a warning message to the Commandant of the National troops and had himself shown a flag to cover the advance of his emissary. The move had been misinterpreted, not surprisingly, for Brugha ought not to have displayed the flag on the roof but allowed the messenger to carry it himself. Nevertheless, it was an action of extraordinary thoughtfulness in a moment of awe-inspiring crisis and was characteristic of the man whom Emmet Dalton describes as "a lovable fanatic". Brugha's last sacrificial act was yet to come.

The Granville Hotel caught fire at about five o'clock on the afternoon of Wednesday, July 5th. The women members of the garrison and some medical staff were sent out. A fountain of blazing oil from a chemical store at the rear of the hotel ignited the building also and, caught between two walls of flame, the garrison could survive no longer. Brugha ordered the surrender.

Led by Art O'Connor, the remnants of the garrison emerged

341

from the fire into a lane. They did not know that Cathal Brugha did not intend to come with them. National Army officers saw that he was not among them and guessed at once that he planned a martyr's death in the flames. Firemen battered down the door and a St John Ambulance officer rushed in. Brugha shook him off, even threatened him with his gun, and ignored his last desperate warning. Brugha ran out of the building and began shooting. A Lewis gunner in Findlater's building cut him down, as Brugha knew he would. Badly wounded in the leg, he was attended to by a doctor, then taken to hospital. There the flame that was Cathal Brugha died. Some quality of that narrow, purposeful, single-minded little man, a steadfastness and a cold purity, suggested one of his own ecclesiastical candles. His death, in the tradition of Pearse, was a sublime declaration of the faith he had in his own convictions. It was also, in the opinion of some, intended to strengthen the will to resist of others, less ardent Republican leaders.

The prisoners were taken away, except for the women among them who were immediately released. One was the formidable Mary MacSwiney, another Kathleen Barry, sister of the executed Kevin, in whom was epitomised the youthful idealism that was at the heart of the Volunteer movement.

The names of Barry and MacSwiney will live long in the sad songs of Ireland, longer perhaps than the names of leaders. It was little wonder that their sisters should have been implacable enemies of those who had dared sign an agreement with England.

The cost of the siege of O'Connell Street had yet to be reckoned. Almost the whole of the eastern side of the street, from the Nelson Pillar—which was to endure for another forty-four sturdy years—to the Rotunda, lay a smoking waste. On the other side of the street about one third of the buildings had been gutted and most of the remainder damaged. The total bill was estimated at five million pounds. Much more tragic was the cost in lives. In just over a week 64 people, not all participants, had been killed and nearly three hundred wounded.

On July 6th a call to arms was issued by the Provisional Government in words as colourful as any Liam Lynch committed to paper. It began:

342

"Men of Ireland, the valour and patriotism of our National Army have broken the conspiracy to override the will of the nation and subject the people to a despotism based on brigandage, and ruthlessly regardless of the people's inalienable right to life liberty and security."

The cry for recruits, which belied the confidence expressed in the preamble, had a good response; large numbers of raw young men were enlisted. Not all the recruits joined from conviction; many saw the prospect of a career in the National Army following a short and not too dangerous war.

There was good reason for the Provisional Government's caution. The "conspiracy" was not broken, only a little bent. All over the country the attack on the Four Courts had triggered off trouble. Issues became clearer and opinion crystallised. It was as if the mysterious shadows of the night appeared in recognisable dimension with the coming of daylight.

In the South Wexford Brigade area there had been no split. At the signing of the Treaty the Brigade staff were in training camp and among the staff, as among the men, there was a crisis. The question Brigade Adjutant Frank Carty asked himself was: "Is this a surrender of the Republic, a compromise we cannot agree with?"

This same question every man, from the Brigade O.C., Thomas O'Sullivan, to the newest volunteer, put to himself. And opinions were divided. Elsewhere this divergence had led to brigades and divisions all over the country falling into two and duplicating all offices; had led, indeed to the ultimate formation of two opposing armies.

"Our feeling in the matter," Carty explains, "was that if we were an army—as we were—we should act as a unit. This meant keeping together and not taking any drastic step without being sure that the things we believed in were being sacrificed." O'Sullivan and Carty decided that this situation had not yet arisen and that they should try to keep the Brigade together as a unit of the I.R.A. Until they were asked to act in a way that was inimical to the Republic, they would not commit themselves to an independent line. In spite of the passionate conviction of some other officers that the break should be made at once, the Brigade was kept as a unit and a normal relationship with General Headquarters was main-

343

tained until Rory O'Connor, disowning all political authority, including that of de Valera, marched his men into Four Courts and took possession. It was quite obvious by then that the two sections of the Army were irreconcilable. The South Wexford Brigade declared for the Executive and severed relations with what was now the National Army headquarters. There were no breakaway groups; the Brigade remained united. A new division was formed on instructions from Executive H.Q. This, the Third Eastern Division, commanded by Paddy Fleming, consisted of the North and South Wexford Brigades and the Carlow Brigade. Frank Carty was appointed Training Officer and saw that strict training was continued until, with the attack on the Four Courts, the Brigade was geared to military operations.

Bloodshed was to be avoided if possible and the two sides in the area carried out their opening manoeuvres with something of courtesy. National troops were already occupying the old police barracks in Abbey Quay, Enniscorthy, and on Friday, June 30th, the day of the surrender of the Four Courts garrison, they took possesion of Enniscorthy Castle. The Executive forces, who had taken over the old courthouse, strengthened their defences and next day, with their numbers reinforced, occupied the Portsmouth Arms Hotel, the Technical Institute, St Mary's Protestant church and three houses near the courthouse.

The Castle garrison under Sean Gallagher mounted machineguns on the roof and the Republicans replied by fortifying the belfry of St Mary's. Having completed their preparations, they left the church so that the Sunday services should not be interrupted and returned in the evening. At 10 o'clock that night an ultimatum was sent to Gallagher, who was now virtually surrounded but not very worried about it. Gallagher later claimed that shots were fired by the Republicans before the ultimatum had expired and while he was still drafting his answer. In the next few days intermittent firing went on which to some extent disrupted business in the town but otherwise did very little harm.

Meanwhile, a Tipperary flying column of seventy or eighty men, commanded by Mick Sheehan, came by way of New Ross into Enniscorthy on their way to Blessington which was in the First Dublin Brigade area. Because he knew the country so

344

well, Carty went with them to ensure their safe arrival in Blessington, where Republican forces were assembling. Most of them had arrived on July 1st. Advance parties had already commandeered buildings and set about rustling up food for about six hundred men. They made the Ulster Bank Ltd. their headquarters and also occupied the Bank of Ireland, the courthouse and a number of strategically placed houses. Preparations were made to defend these positions and, for additional security, an observation post was established in the tower of the Protestant church. A dairy was converted into a casualty station and guards were posted on all roads leading into Blessington. The men were billeted all over the town; the people accepted the invasion in good humour and even appointed a committee to smooth away any difficulties between townsfolk and military visitors. Blessington would not be an easy place to defend, the Republican leaders knew, but it was of strategic importance because of its situation on one of the two southern approach roads to Dublin on the west of the massif formed by the Dublin Hills and the Wicklow Mountains.

In Blessington were the brothers Boland, Gerry and Harry, the latter drawn back in despair to Ireland from a mission to the United States, Andy MacDonnell, O.C. South Dublin Brigade, and the ubiquitous Father Dominic. Sean Lemass, Tom Derrig, Paddy O'Brien and Ernie O'Malley, all of whom had escaped after the fall of the Four Courts, joined them.

"There was a big gathering of men there," says Carty, "and my feeling was that this was a force that could be used to go into Dublin. I was somewhat surprised to find that this was not the intention, that I was to take back the Tipperary men— no one knew where. It was simply that they were not wanted in Blessington. There they were, tip-top fighting men, but there was nowhere for them to go, no fight to fight." Enniscorthy at least offered some prospect of action so the disgruntled column from Tipperary returned with Carty. O'Malley and O'Brien joined them.

More than a thousand Provisional Government troops from six bases began an encircling movement through the Dublin Hills and exerted pressure on Blessington. Brittas, a few miles from Dublin, fell to the Government, but surprisingly few prisoners were taken. Republicans were searched and released

345

although, a few minutes before, newspapermen had seen them with merrily crackling rifles. Not a few of them promptly made for Blessington.

More men came from Bray, on the coast south of Dublin, where they had been in possession of the police barracks, courthouse and coastguard station. On July 1st they fired the courthouse and barracks and while the majority left in commandeered cars and charabancs others remained to hinder the firemen. The courthouse was gutted. A patrol of local citizens was formed to keep order until National troops arrived to take over.

Still more men retreated into Blessington from outlying posts. Three National Army columns were now converging on the town, one under Commandant Heaslip approaching from Brittas on the road from Dublin, another, led by Commandant Bishop, marching eastwards from the Curragh, and the third, with Commandant McNulty in charge, moving in from the mountains. They were equipped with artillery.

Ballymore Eustace, three or four miles to the south-west of Blessington, was besieged by 100 men under McNulty on the evening of Wednesday, July 5th. There was a sharp exchange of fire as the first National Army group, led by Commandant (later Colonel) Dineen, crossed the bridge. Dineen was wounded in the knee. The main Republican garrison, who had been barricaded in three hotels, escaped and only eight prisoners were taken.

McNulty's force included a number of officers under training at the Curragh and one of these, Dick O'Sullivan, a Kerryman, led a group with an armoured car into Ballyknockan at the south end of the Poulaphouca Reservoir.

"They came out and ran for the hills," says O'Sullivan. "We chased after them firing but we never got one. They were firing back. You could hear the bullets plugging the ground in front of us. We were far away. Eventually we got back to Ballyknockan and had a nice lunch at Osborne's. We heard later that some of the Irregulars were enjoying their lunch upstairs—we hadn't searched the place."

In the early morning of Friday, July 7th, the National troops began their offensive and encountered heavy rifle fire outside Blessington. In the town roads were trenched, mines laid. The sound of guns was heard in the town all that

346

morning and fingers grew restless on their triggers. But there was to be no fighting that day for the Republicans in Blessington. They were, as Carty already knew, to fade quietly away.

By 7.30 p.m. the rearguard had gone, and when the National troops marched in next morning, finally closing the net, they found that their quarry had vanished. So they took Blessington bloodlessly. There was, after all, no Battle of Blessington to make an alliterative mark on the memories of future generations of school children. To the disappointed Republican troops the withdrawal was inexplicable, but against artillery and an attack from three directions they had little chance of survival. Their position had been made even less tenable by the National Army's capture of Abbeyleix, where nearly three hundred Republicans had held the old Union Hospital, and by the Provisional Government's control of most of Kilkenny. This meant that the Republicans were contained in a narrow strip between the mountains to the east and the area to the west held by strong opposing forces.

But the real reason for the withdrawal was a decision by the leaders of the Executive Forces in Dublin to fight no more pitched battles in defence of fixed positions. Even before the fighting in O'Connell Street came to its incandescent end, Oscar Traynor had sent Lisa O'Donnell to Blessington with instructions that there was to be no battle and no march into Dublin. A few days later Traynor stated that the Dublin Brigade had been "able to disengage almost intact in personnel and material" and that they would "now at once revert to the tactics which made us invincible formerly".

Carty's party reached Enniscorthy at about midnight and at about five o'clock next morning Carty, O'Malley, Thomas O'Sullivan and Paddy O'Brian from Dublin, and a Volunteer named Spillane set out to reconnoitre the Castle. Day was breaking and there was the vibrant stillness of a summer morning as they turned down the lane towards the Castle. Near the Castle, and commanding a view of the lane, was a public house, shuttered and silent.

Suddenly a first-floor window in the public house slid open and rifles cracked. The wily Gallagher had led a small party over the wall of the Castle and taken up an ambush position. The reconnaissance party, completely exposed and taken unawares, suffered immediate casualties. Spillane was killed and Paddy O'Brien fell wounded. At once the party returned the fire and gained a moment's respite. Then Carty and O'Sullivan carried O'Brien between them, back along the lane, while the dauntless O'Malley kept up a rapid protective fire. Somehow they got round the corner and out of the line of fire.

A few days later, the Castle capitulated to a Republican attack and Paddy Fleming, with what Carty feels is almost childish chivalry, returned to the National Army officers their surrendered revolvers. They were released then, and left the area, but Carty had not seen the last of Sean Gallagher.

Wexford County became a new Republican Command area with O'Sullivan as O.C. and Carty as Adjutant. Carty now held the rank of Commandant-General, though, as he says, they did not take rank very seriously. The Command established, the Tipperary column moved to Newtonbarry, ten miles to the north of Enniscorthy and a little to the north-west of Ferns. O'Malley, who went with them, left the Wexford men with instructions to blow all bridges in the north of the county.

A few hours after their departure, on July 8th, Carty was informed that a National Army column of twenty-two lorries, with armoured cars and artillery, was approaching North Wexford through Wicklow. Led by Brigadier-General Niall MacNeill, with a number of prominent officers including Tom Keogh, Paddy Slattery and Joe Vize, the column was one of the several which had moved out of Dublin on the surrender of the Four Courts. The overall command was in the hands of General Emmet Dalton who had returned from a brief mission to Dundalk. MacNeill's column had apparently travelled down the coast road from Dublin and was already in Arklow, about twenty-four miles away.

O'Malley in Newtownbarry was warned, and O'Sullivan and Carty expected to hear that they were to join forces with the Tipperary column and attack the convoy. But O'Malley, too, seemed to have been infected with the spirit of non-aggression. The Wexford men had no idea as yet of the change in tactics and were disappointed to learn that they were to continue with the destruction of the northern bridges as arranged.

To slow the Provisional Government advance towards Enniscorthy it was decided to blow up a bridge north of

348

Ferns. Carty's men were weary after several sleepless nights during the attack on the Castle and, unwilling to order them to do the job, he called for volunteers.

"Eight or nine fellows came with me and I got a chap on a motor bike to scout ahead of our lorry. We duly blew the bridge but we had not come very far on the return journey when the engine of the lorry broke down. It was the big-end gone. We clattered into Ferns, making a most unholy row, round the hill to the post office. There we stopped the lorry and I got the fellows out of it. Two of them I sent to find alternative transport.

"I also sent a man to take up an outpost position. We had seen no sign of the enemy, but it was as well to be prepared. In the post office there were some local fellows who had been knocking down trees for road blocks. They were asleep upstairs, but I didn't know this at the time."

The footpath outside the post office was warm under a high sun and most of Carty's men stretched themselves out, their heads against the wall, and fell asleep. Carty stood in the open doorway with one of his men, O'Keefe, anxiously awaiting the return of the two who had gone to search for a lorry. When they heard a heavy engine they relaxed. The vehicle came into sight round the hillside and, as machine-gun fire spurted at them, they realised their mistake. Somehow their lookout had failed to warn them of the approach of an armoured car. In fact, Carty's party had been seen as they blew the bridge and the armoured car, finding a way through the fields, set out in pursuit. The crew had not expected to find their quarry so easily.

Carty and O'Keefe dived into the post office and slammed the door; there was little else they could have done. The sleeping men came to shocked consciousness, some wakened by the sting rather than the sound of bullets. One, Fitzgerald, ran the gauntlet of machine-gun fire, raced to the back of the building and leaped to the top of the wall. He was shot down from the other side. The post office was surrounded. Outside, the men on the footpath had surrendered. Bullets splintered a way through the walls of the building. Upstairs, the local men had not been expecting trouble and had made no defensive arrangements. Even if they had done so the position would have been hopeless. Carty surrendered. The National

349

Army moved on to Enniscorthy, which the Republicans now evacuated.

The prisoners from the post office were taken to the schoolhouse across the road and Carty had a chance to assess the strength of the force which had been ranged against them. It was a quite impressive army of three or four hundred men, with officers who introduced themselves proudly as "Custom House Boys".

Carty and his friends accepted that their captors were first-class fighters. They were also well-equipped, as the Republicans had discovered, and Carty appreciated the irony of the "Official I.R.A." painted on the lorries and the armoured cars.

More local men were rounded up during the day, until between thirty and forty prisoners were held in the schoolhouse. Throughout the Black and Tan period, Carty had operated in Wexford. His captors were Dublin men and did not know him. Already he was wondering about escape and it seemed to him that his anonymity, enhanced by the civilian coat he wore over his military breeches and leggings, could be an important factor.

A National Army officer told Carty that one of his men, Paddy Brady, badly wounded in the action and now lying in a cottage down the road, was asking for him, and arranged for Carty to be taken under escort to his bedside. There he was joined by a priest and together they consoled Brady, who was disconsolately certain that he was dying. Carty thought he looked near death but, in fact, Brady survived.

Carty suggested to the priest that they went for a walk down the road, hoping that once he was out of the hands of his escort, any other National Army men he might encounter would not recognise him.

"The priest knew damn well why I wanted to take a walk down the road," Carty recalls, "but he was quite willing. We went quite a good distance and then we were stopped. They suspected me. Looking back, the ruse must have been pretty obvious. Anyway, I was stopped and returned to the schoolhouse."

That night the prisoners were to be moved to the Castle in Enniscorthy, the strongpoint which Carty and O'Sullivan had captured only a few days before. As the long light of the July day faded, the Republican prisoners were lined up in the schoolroom. It was that tense moment which every prisoner taken in war remembers, the moment when he is to be transferred from his first improvised prison, guarded by his fighting captors who are thankful that the positions are not reversed, to quarters more permament, more secure, and watched over by prison guards, unsympathetic custodians of the defeated.

A few candles lit the schoolroom and their wavering flames sent deep shadows chasing across the drawn faces of the line of prisoners. A group of National Army officers moved slowly along the line. Among them was Sean Gallagher, one of the officers who had been privileged to have his revolver returned to him at Enniscorthy. "I caught his eye, and he caught mine —you know the way it happens sometimes," says Carty. "But we said nothing and he gave no sign of recognition."

The order was given to march out to waiting lorries. There had been no count of the prisoners and Carty, a diminutive figure, moved silently into a corner where all the schoolroom benches and forms had been stacked. He crawled under and wriggled as far as he could. In his long, low tunnel he lay, hoping he had not been seen. There was a last shuffle of boots, then the lone footfalls of someone moving round the room to douse the candles. Suddenly the last glow snapped from the floor and Carty lay in claustrophobic blackness. Outside the school, feet clattered on the road and thudded on the boards of the lorries. There was officious shouting and defiant gibes were yelled back. An engine roared.

Gallagher's voice cracked through the noise like a whip-lash, "Where's Carty?" There was a sharp order. Three or four men returned to the schoolroom. Torches flashed. But none of the searchers got down on hands and knees so the beams of the torches did not reach far enough under the schoolroom benches. They returned to Gallagher and reported that Carty was not there.

"He is there. I saw him," Gallagher snapped. This time he came himself and the beam of his torch blinded Carty who crawled out "very ignominiously", "It was a very unheroic effort," Carty adds apologetically.

Gallagher made to kick him as he emerged but Carty

avoided the boot. He felt like a schoolboy caught in some misdemeanour by a senior boy. Next morning, Gallagher came to see him in Enniscorthy Castle and apologised for the kick, which he had delivered in a moment of exasperation. It was a chivalrous note which Carty appreciated.

From Enniscorthy the Republican prisoners were taken to Wexford military barracks where they remained for some days. Then they were told they were to be transferred to Dublin and at about 4.30 on July 24th they were taken to Wexford station and put in special carriages coupled to the end of a mail train. Altogether, their escort comprised about 130 men, and a National Army officer settled watchfully in each compartment.

"Now I had sent out word secretly—actually through a girl who visited me—that we would be on that train," Carty relates. "On the platform to say goodbye to me was my mother, and she slipped into my hand the key of the carriage —a pretty fine thing for a mother to do, I thought, because she knew very well the danger involved in attempting to escape from the train."

Carty did not know whether his friends had arranged to help them beyond providing the key, but he thought it likely that they would attempt to stop the train at some point early in the journey, and he was ready to make the best of any opportunity. He had not long to wait. When the train emerged from the tunnel at Killurin, the next station, it was stopped by a fusillade of shots. At once, the National Army troops leaped down to the track and took up positions below the embankment on either side. Some of them crumpled as unseen snipers shot truly. They blazed back, but the bullets flew indiscriminately, for they could not see where the ambush was placed. Some, believing that their prisoners had managed to conceal arms and were firing at them, turned their rifles on the train. Bullets from the ambushers also ripped through the carriages, but none of the prisoners was hurt. Carty learned later that Bob Lambert, who was to make quite a name for himself as the war went on, had rushed to Killurin with a handful of men to attack the train. They had found a ditch on a hillside overlooking the railway, from which vantage point they could use their fire-power sparingly but effectively.

Their effort to free the prisoners was in vain. In ranging

352

themselves on both sides of the train the guards had frustrated Carty. When he leaned through the window, hoping to use the key, he saw that they would have to jump down the embankment among their adversaries. If they tried then to run, they would be shot down.

So the brief but quite nasty battle ended in stalemate. Several of the guards had been killed and others wounded. The casualties were left in friendly hands and the train went on. Further along, an obstruction on the line was removed, then on reaching Enniscorthy the train was taken out of service and the prisoners were transferred to another. A disagreeable atmosphere now prevailed between prisoners and guards, and Carty, because he was known to be senior officer, was none too happy. Somehow the tension did not snap and there were no incidents until the train arrived at Harcourt Street station in Dublin at about ten o'clock that evening. The prisoners were lined up on the platform ready to be marched away when some of the Provisional Government officers, unable to contain their anger any longer, drew their revolvers and whipped shots around the feet of their captives to set them dancing, trying not so much to hurt as to humiliate. One Republican was hit in the foot, another suffered a leg wound and died from an aftermath of complications some months later. The driver of the train, John White, was arrested but no charge of complicity in the ambush was brought against him.

After a night at Portobello Barracks, the Republican prisoners were removed to the old Victorian jail at Maryborough (now Port Laoighise) in County Leix where, much to their resentment, they were treated as felons, not as prisoners of war, or even as political prisoners. One at a time they were examined and given a number; each man's possessions were taken from him and tied up in a small sack. Then they were marched upstairs and lodged three or four in a cell. Carty's recollection is that there were four landings and that altogether the prison held about 900 men. Special preparations had been made to receive Republican prisoners. There were new beds, new mattresses, new tables and stools, even new chamber pots. The prison was also handsomely floored with pine.

Carty and his cell-mates talked things over. Bitterly they objected to the treatment they were receiving, which was aggravated rather than ameliorated by the provision of new furniture and equipment, and they were determined not to knuckle under to it. Already, after but a few hours, they were bored with their confinement. They looked up when they heard someone at the spy-hole in the cell door. "What are you doing in there?" asked a fellow prisoner. They learned that the door of the cell was pregnable. A lever skilfully exerted would lift it off its hinges. Within three or four hours all the cell doors had been prised open and they were never put back. The National Army guards simply accepted the situation and from that day the men could wander within the prison as they wished.

While Carty and his comrades endured their first days of captivity the National forces under General Dalton strengthened their hold on the counties of the south-east. Newtownbarry and Tullow were taken, then, says Dalton, "A report came in that there was a group led by Ernie O'Malley in the village of Baltinglass. So I took Tom Ennis and his troops and we surrounded the area. Some of our men were moving in more slowly than others and we got a bit restive and went in ourselves with an armoured car and a touring car. Pat McCrea was driving the car and Ennis and I were with him.

"We took prisoners as we went in, while the others were coming down from the hills. At a bridge we had a little bit of a battle, an exchange of shots, if you like."

McCrea was wounded in the hand by a sniper and splinters of steering-wheel stung Dalton's face. More prisoners were taken, twenty-five in all and the village was soon captured.

"That cleared the area," says Dalton.

SIXTEEN

The Four Courts battle was still raging when McEoin and his wife arrived at Mrs Ramsay's Hotel in Sligo. He was returning to his headquarters in Athlone after a honeymoon in Donegal. Their wedding a few days before had been an occasion of much gaiety. Collins was there, and forgetting the troubles and uncertainties of recent months, was in playful mood. For McEoin the day was enhanced by the arrival of a present from the mother of District Inspector McGrath, for whose death he had so nearly forfeited his own life.

Like so many other towns, Sligo was garrisoned by the two parts of the broken I.R.A. Here, the thicker segment belonged to the Executive Forces. The British had handed to the I.R.A. the old military barracks, large and sturdily walled on a dominant hill top, but those members who continued their allegiance to General Headquarters had had to leave. Nos. 1 and 2 R.I.C. barracks had come into the hands of the Executive Forces in the same way. Then, as the Treaty supporters gathered strength, they took possession of the County jail and, later, of the courthouse. So Ireland's two armies inharmoniously garrisoned the town, while the townspeople passed between them on their normal business.

When the Dail Forces attacked the Four Courts their Sligo adherents took over William's garage directly opposite No. 1 R.I.C. barracks and certain office buildings, and fortified them. The Republicans also strengthened their posts. As all the signs of a drastic clash became more and more evident, tension in Sligo built up. Large crowds gathered on Friday evening, June 30th, to watch National soldiers unload vast quantities of barbed wire at the courthouse. Well aware of the strength of the Executive Forces, the townspeople appreciated the additional defensive measures taken by the National Army.

Strangely, that night the Executive Forces changed their tactics; the policy of "burn and clear out", which was to become almost general, was applied in Sligo. Stealthily, they moved out of No. 1 barracks and the very lively recreation hall nearby which they also had occupied. No one knew what was going on until flames engulfed both buildings.

At his hotel, McEoin heard explosions and dashed out with his A.D.C., Captain Louis Connolly, and his driver, Sergeant Ingram. He saw that there was no hope of putting out the fires and that, if something were not done, nearby houses also would be destroyed. The fire brigade had not put in an appearance and a young man who had tried to fetch a fire-hose from the Town Hall had been turned back by armed men. McEoin took a squad of men from Williams's garage and got the hose himself. He directed the water on to the end of the building from which danger was most likely to come and checked the spread of the flames. The fire brigade arrived at last but by 4.30 a.m. the recreation hall was burned out. Most of the Republicans had withdrawn to the military barracks; some had gone right out of the town to strengthen other posts.

Anticipating that the Executive Forces might also decide to get rid of their other small post, McEoin hastened to No. 2 R.I.C. barracks in Wine Street and happened to arrive just as eight men were pouring petrol on the floor.

"Ye're dirty birds to burn your own nests," he rasped.

"What are you here for?" asked one. "If you'd stopped out we wouldn't be burning them." They were apparently convinced that McEoin's arrival meant he had substantial forces behind him and they wanted to be sure he did not use the barracks. Wine Street barracks remained and the Republicans left, but some returned later to reoccupy them.

All next day, Saturday, there was much National Army activity in Sligo. People passing the courthouse were stopped and frisked and cars were also held up and searched for arms. A number of young men with known anti-Treaty opinions were arrested but later released. Early that afternoon a Ford van with armed guard left the military barracks and sped to Gilbride's garage in Bridge Street. The men demanded petrol, tyres and spare parts, but Gilbride refused to supply them without a proper order and one man returned to the barracks to get one. The others were waiting for him when McEoin, hearing what was afoot, hurried to the spot and covered the men with a large revolver. Troops from the courthouse arrested them. An hour later, National troops commandeered the Harp and Shamrock Hotel and a solicitor's office, which were strategically placed in relation to the barracks.

Later in the evening about forty Republicans with rifles and revolvers took up a position outside the National Bank and searched pedestrians, but there were few about now. A battle on the grand scale was expected and not many townspeople wanted to risk being caught in the middle. The last thing anyone would have guessed was that the Executive Forces, several hundred strong, would abandon their barracks-fortress, but at about midnight they dug up a mine they had planted, spread petrol around the barracks and set the
356

building on fire. Possibly the recovered mine was used in the blowing up of Ballysadare Bridge, which had been repaired only that day following an abortive attempt to destroy it the previous night. This time they succeeded in blocking the principal road into Sligo, but a two-foot sliver of the bridge remained which reckless pedestrians could use.

Now that most of the Executive troops were out of Sligo and already beginning to cause havoc elsewhere in the area—railway lines were torn up at Collooney, six or seven miles to the south, on the Saturday morning—McEoin decided that he could no longer delay his return to take up his command in Athlone and, at six o'clock that evening, July 1st, he was ready to leave. Sergeant Ingram was having trouble in starting the engine of the touring car and McEoin was standing watching him when a woman standing to his right shrieked a warning. McEoin turned to see a young man, a brother of a Republican leader, aiming a revolver at him. The man fired and the bullet scored a red line across McEoin's forehead but did not draw blood. As he sprang instantly at his attacker, he heard the hammer of the pistol click, but this time it did not fire. Seizing the gun, he threw it on the ground; then he removed two hand grenades his assailant carried, took him by the scruff of the neck and the seat of his breeches and tossed him into the river. Fished out, he was then taken to Sligo jail.

Calmly, Sergeant Ingram cranked the car and at last it started. McEoin, his wife, Captain Louis Connolly and the Rev Patrick Higgins of Ballintogher joined Ingram in the car. Two miles out of Sligo, on the road to Ballintogher, they were ambushed. Bullets whirred through the hood of the Crossley, but none of the five was hurt. Revolvers in hand, McEoin and Connolly leapt from the car. There was an immediate order to cease fire, possibly because either McEoin or the priest had been recognised, or because there was a woman in the car, and Captain Gilmartin who commanded the ambush party showed himself. McEoin called him over, put his revolver in his pocket and coolly ordered Gilmartin to surrender with his men. There was a curious half-heartedness about the Executive Forces in many parts of the country. They seemed to want to make a gesture, to show that they were against the Treaty, but to go no further. Gilmartin surrendered almost casually and McEoin let him and his men go.

Further along the road McEoin saw another car approaching and ordered his driver to stop. He got out, halted the car and questioned the three occupants. They had arms and claimed to be Free Staters. Blandly McEoin told them that he could not allow soldiers of the National Army to roam aimlessly round the country.

"God's truth, sir, but we're Republicans after all," admitted one of the men.

"That's worse," said McEoin. "Get out."

The men got out and McEoin stowed their guns in his own car. Then he made them turn their vehicles and drive in front of him. When they came to a road block he ordered them to clear it, but they baulked at this and McEoin guessed that it was probably mined. Short of shooting one of them, which he had no wish to do, there was no way of making them clear the road. So he decided to turn back. Ingram saw to it that the other car would not start and McEoin's party drove back the way they had come, leaving the men. Mrs McEoin wanted to drive the other car herself rather than abandon it, but "You'd better stay in the back where you are," was the dry answer she got from her husband. They had dinner at Ballintogher and, after several alarms on the way, reached Glassan, Athlone, where they found the road blocked. Trees had been felled across it and, rather oddly, some of the tops had been lopped. Tired now, for it was after midnight, McEoin's party disconsolately surveyed the scene, and when they discovered about twenty bicycles lying against the wall, McEoin was all for smashing them up. He refrained when his wife appealed to him to turn back without losing any more time. Perhaps she guessed that the owners of the bicycles, no doubt interrupted in their work, were not far away and she felt she had gone through enough for one day.

So they returned to a friend's house nearby where they stayed until morning. McEoin sent word to the unit in Ballymahon to clear the road block at Glassan and then he learned how much he owed to his wife's fatigue, or perhaps to her intuition, the previous night. The bicycles belonged not to the Republicans who had felled the trees but to a party of his own troops who had begun to clear the road and who had taken cover when McEoin's car approached. Had McEoin begun to break up the bicycles, the clearing party, uncertain of

358

the identity of the people in the car, would have taken them
for Republicans. McEoin would have found himself ambushed
by his own men. But there had been for him an even more
tragic potential in the situation, for the road clearing party
was commanded by Captain Seamus McEoin, his own brother.

From reports coming in McEoin soon realised that civil
war was flaring all over the country.

For some months there had been a lot of activity in County
Donegal, directed across the border, and, as we have seen,
the Treaty and anti-Treaty sections of the I.R.A. jointly had
sent men and materials to the North. McEoin, though he
did not cross the border himself, was involved in a raid, on
February 8th, to rescue Volunteers who had been captured
and were threatened with hanging. But even in the border
counties the Oath had proved in the end a stronger reagent
than Partition was a solvent, and the two elements were
separated, a process probably hastened by the presence of
those officers from southern divisions, such as Sean Lehane,
who had been transferred to the North to lend an experienced
and zestful hand. Now the Republican groups were concerned
less with their nuisance raids across the border and more with
holding their positions in the name of the Republic.

National troops under Commandant-General Sweeney began operations against the Executive Forces on Thursday,
June 29th, the day after the attack on the Four Courts was
launched. Finner Camp, south of Ballyshannon, was taken
after a brisk two-hour fight and the barracks at Ballyshannon
and Bundoran also were captured. Further north, near Letter-
kenny, twenty Republicans had ejected the owner from Bally-
macool House but were surrounded by Provisional Govern-
men troops who opened fire with rifles and machine-guns.
They held out unconcernedly enough until one or two bombs
were hurled into the house, when they surrendered. At
Buncrana National troops took possession of the railway
station, commandeered a train and set off towards Clonmany
and Cardonagh. More troops left Moville by road to complete
a pincer movement designed to gain control of the Inishowen
Peninsula. They met with stout opposition but overpowered
the Republican garrison of Cardonagh police barracks after
a twenty-minute skirmish. But Republicans were well entrenched on Inch Island in Lough Swilly and had mined all

approach roads. Commandant Sean Lehane had occupied Glenveagh Castle further west and, on July 3rd, his men swooped on a train at Church Hill and helped themselves to food and petrol. A share of the loot they conveyed to the defenders of Inch Island during the night. A British destroyer, nosing into Lough Swilly, caused excited speculation, but whatever its mission might have been it showed no interest in the belligerent activities of the Irish.

Sweeney's operations in Donegal were of much more than academic interest to McEoin, who knew very well that whatever progress was made in the north would be nullified if the Republicans controlled County Sligo and County Leitrim. The passage between the Ulster border and the sea was so narrow that Sweeney's forces would be helpless if they were contained within it. But McEoin had no post west of the Shannon except Roscommon town, a small post at Markree Castle near Collooney and the still precariously held positions in Sligo. Already, on Monday, July 3rd, news was coming in of intermittent attacks on Markree Castle, whilst in Sligo there was anything but peace. There, at 1.45 a.m. on that day, a small Ford lorry with two drivers and five other men made the short journey from the courthouse to the jail. At the jail gate they were audaciously ambushed by Republicans. Bullets came from all directions and Volunteer James Beirne was killed at once. The others leapt to the ground and tried to crawl to the jail gate using the lorry as cover. Two more were wounded, but the party got safely into the jail and bombs thrown after them caused no casualties. At the same time another body of Republicans used the ruins of the recreation hall and No. 1 barracks as cover while they attacked the courthouse. Firing went on for more than an hour and several National soldiers were wounded.

McEoin learned also that on Saturday night, while he was still in Sligo, he had lost the one small post, the markethouse, he held in Collooney. The town was the headquarters of 3rd Western Division, Executive Forces, and was strongly held. To take the post was simply a matter of their convenience and, when it suited them, the Republicans made prisoners of the garrison and burned the building.

Resolved to drive straight through to Sligo, McEoin realised that the first essential was to reduce the Republican strong-
360

hold of Boyle Barracks, which lay on the road between Roscommon and Sligo. There was no point in circumventing Boyle for that would allow the Republicans to take his forces in the rear. Provisional Government troops, under the command of Brigadier-General Michael Dockery, had already established themselves in Boyle workhouse, but shrewdly the Republicans carried out some stealthy preparations in the early hours of Sunday morning, July 2nd. Men were moved into houses overlooking the workhouse; the post office was entered and telephone and telegraph apparatus put out of action; trees were felled across roads for four miles around.

Shortly after 6 a.m. they began an attack on the workhouse but were driven back after some ferocious hand-to-hand fighting. Both sides opened fire now with rifles and machine-guns, and townsfolk on their way to Mass decided that home was safer. Snipers were busy and one sharpshooter succeeded in picking off Dockery. So yet another hero of the Tan war died at the hands of his compatriots.

All day bullets whipped across the streets and down the streets and then, at about seven in the evening, reinforcements sent by McEoin and an armoured car, *The Ballinalee*, arrived. Relentlessly the armoured car routed the Republicans from one post after another. Two hours later they abandoned the barracks, leaving them in flames. The Provisional Government Forces were able to save part of the building, but valuable stores had been lost. Driven out of the town, the Republicans regrouped and courageously returned to seize new posts. For two more days a grim game of hide and seek was played. Intermittently, storms of bullets gusted through the streets. One woman was killed as she stood in her own doorway. By Wednesday, July 5th, the Provisional Government Forces, led by Colonel-Commandant Alec McCabe, a member of the Dail, were in control of the area.

From Boyle *The Ballinalee* was driven on to Sligo where for several days it patrolled the streets. The armoured car was to become a familiar sight in the town, where business was now almost at a standstill. Republicans had raided the post office and wrecked communications. Trains were held up at Collooney; roads were blocked; the town was virtually cut off. Even food was becoming scarce and already the people were tired of the war.

361

On Thursday, July 6th, *The Ballinalee* took part in an attack on Wine Street barracks, which were still intact and occupied by Republican "police". They were an extension of the I.R.A. police who during the Tan war had done much to curb crime while the men of the R.I.C. were too busy trying to defend their own barracks against I.R.A. assaults to worry about ordinary lawbreakers. The Republicans in Wine Street barracks refused to surrender and shot back when *The Ballinalee* opened fire, but very soon they had to give in. Two men were taken prisoner and a small boy was also found in the building. But the tragic outcome of the brief action was the accidental shooting of two civilians. One, an elderly man much respected in Sligo, died and became for the townspeople a symbol of the horror and futility of civil war. There were protests, too, when on Saturday, July 8th, the home of the Mayor of Sligo was raided by National troops, who found nothing.

An attempt by the Republicans to seize *The Ballinalee* was easily beaten off on July 10th, but the Drumkeen ambush near Collooney two days later was well planned. Fifty Republicans waited for twenty-four hours and saw to it that no message was sent out of the village by Government supporters. Guards were mounted on houses where there were known sympathisers. Surprise is the essence of any ambush, but on this occasion hair-trigger timing was imperative for there to be any chance of success against the armoured car. Escorted by *The Ballinalee*, National troops left the new post at Markree Castle at 6 a.m., bound for Sligo. Captain Michael Robinson travelled in charge of the armoured car, whilst his commanding officer, Commandant Paddy Callaghan, was with the majority of the men in the lorry. As they approached Dooney Rock, they were stopped by a road block, when immediately the ambushers opened fire. Their first volley killed Callaghan and a young volunteer from Longford, Sergeant John Farrell.

"Whatever tempted Robinson, I don't know," says McEoin, "but he got out of the armoured car and the ambushers captured it. With its Vickers gun it was a formidable weapon in their hands."

The Ballinalee was not surrendered without a hard fight in which Quartermaster Sean Adair was killed and another
362

volunteer, Sweeney, fatally wounded. Ironically, Adair had taken part in the rescue of Frank Carty (namesake of the Wexford officer) from a prison van in Glasgow and it was Carty's men who killed him. Other wounded were tended by the victorious Republicans and taken by them into Dromahaire for proper medical attention.

On the same day, McEoin's troops from Boyle, under McCabe, fought a sharp two-hour engagement with Executive Forces who had occupied the barracks, courthouse and other commanding positions in Ballymote. McCabe cleared the village but could not prevent the barracks from going up in flames. This success was of some consolation to McEoin, particularly as Ballymote, desperately short of food, had appealed to him for help. But it did not solve the problem posed by the occupation of Collooney by the Republicans. From their strongly held base they were making nuisance raids throughout the area and were constantly derailing and looting trains on the line from Boyle and Enniskillen to Sligo.

McEoin decided to drive the Executive Forces out of Collooney. On the previous Monday an attack had been started and continued into Tuesday, when the Provisional Government troops had been compelled to withdraw. "It was an expensive operation," says McEoin. This time he intended to go himself.

"At this stage," he admits, "some of our forces and some of our staff were not loyal," and there is no doubting that their disloyalty hurts him still. If they wanted to be on the other side that was fair, but to pretend to be one while they helped the other was contemptible in his eyes. "Whether it was the typists who copied out the operation orders, or who it was, I don't know." He seems glad that he does not know who among those he trusted let him down.

Craftily he issued an operations order for the entrainment of 120 troops for Dublin, and at about six in the evening of July 14th the men clambered aboard the train at Athlone, anticipating no doubt a merry night or two in the capital. But at Mullingar McEoin left the train with another officer to cut the telegraph wires between Mullingar and Sligo. That done, they switched the train on to the line to Longford, Boyle and Sligo, and reached the outskirts of Collooney at six next morning. He was joined by another force led by Lawlor which

363

had come on the main road from Ballymore. McEoin sent Commandant Farrelly with half his own force to take care of the south-west side of the town and Lawlor's force to cover the Sligo road to the north. He himself assumed responsibility for the south, where the road came in from Boyle, and a contingent from Markree Castle guarded the east.

When his troops were deployed to his satisfaction, McEoin sent messages to the Catholic priest and the Protestant minister instructing them to lead their respective flocks from the town between 8 a.m. and 9 a.m. that morning.

"They were to bring nobody, only the people of Collooney, no stranger unless he was known to be a commercial traveller or a business man," says McEoin. At the stipulated time the evacuation began.

"Priest and parson came out, each under a white flag, their two flocks, Catholic and Protestant, walking after them. They were like a pair of Pied Pipers," McEoin recalls.

"Where's Sean? What are we to do?" asked Father Doyle, the parish priest, who knew McEoin. He was given directions and the whole civilian population retired to a safe distance, though many of them, unable to find billets, were to spend an uncomfortable night in ditches.

An ultimatum was sent to the Executive Forces, none of whom had attempted to leave in the guise of civilians. A volley of shots was the only reply. The Republicans had strong defensive positions. Moreover, they were expecting *The Ballinalee* to arrive. McEoin did not hope for an easy victory. Few of his men were experienced and he did not know if they were capable of sustained action over a period. He anticipated that it would take a considerable time to capture the town and everyone in it.

McEoin called up his artillery, a very ancient 18-pounder which had been fired at the attack on the Four Courts, and positioned it in a sawmill. At once a burst of machine-gun fire came from the tower of the Protestant church and, McEoin remembers, "the first man that was hit was old Sergeant Cassidy from Kenagh. The bullet made a red hot crease across the top of his scalp and he fell back shocked. He got hopping mad and took cover behind the shield of the gun while he looked around to see where the bullets had come from. I showed him and he levelled the gun at the tower. The first shell went straight in through a window in the belfry and exploded. Every bell rang and the whole of the top of the tower was blown up into the air, sandbags, machine-guns, Irregulars and all, and it landed and got jammed in its usual place just as if nothing had happened, and not a single man was injured. I know, because we immediately charged. Colonel Lawlor had under him a number of ex-British soldiers trained to bayonet fighting. He ordered them to charge and I'm damned if a man among them would cross the road. Tony was really mad. I told him to fall back. Now I had a bunch of lads, none over eighteen, that had never seen a bayonet before in their lives. And I gave them the order to charge and of course I jumped with them over the wall of the church. We dashed up into the graveyard and there were sixteen fellows, with rifles and all, lying on the flat of their backs. Not only did they put their hands up, but they put their feet up too."

Sean McEoin had spared the Auxiliaries at Clonfin and no doubt would be magnanimous again, they said.

The prisoners were taken to the rear and McEoin pushed on until he reached the burnt-out market house. For six hours bullets had whined in all directions and his men had been without food or water. Sooner or later, he was sure, the Republicans would decide to abandon the town and he thought the most likely direction of their breakout would be towards the south-west, where the reliable Farrelly was positioned. He was somewhat disconcerted when Farrelly casually walked up to find out why McEoin had not linked up with him. Farrelly was not uniformed but wore an old trench coat and a Volunteer's cap.

"What's keeping you?" he asked cheerfully.

"Get the hell back to your post. They'll be breaking any time now."

"Everything's going all right then, is it?"

"Everything's going all right. Get back to your post."

Farrelly obeyed, but he had not gone far when he encountered a group of Republicans, the first evidently to make a break. He thought he was finished but his wits were quick. He looked like one of them.

"Come on," he shouted. "You'll have me waiting for you all day. At the double." Farrelly led the way. Tramp, tramp,

365

tramp they went through the streets, doubling all the way. Suddenly, to McEoin's astonishment, they appeared in front of him.

"Halt," roared Farrelly. "Ground arms. Four paces to the rear-march." They obeyed. "Prisoners, sir," Farrelly reported smartly, and only then did his involuntary captives realise what had happened.

"Good God Almighty!" came a disbelieving voice. "We've been captured by one man."

By late afternoon McEoin had control of the town. A few shots were to be fired through the night and up to about ten o'clock next morning when the Republican Commandant O'Beirne and twenty-two men were captured in a house near the Southern Station. Altogether, more than seventy prisoners were taken but many of the Republicans, among them Commandant Breheny who shot his way through with a Lewis gun, broke out to the country and fell back towards Sligo and towards Ballaghaderreen. The only serious damage in the town was one house burned—most of the furniture from which was saved by National soldiers. Not a man on either side was killed, though McEoin himself had a narrow escape.

"I was standing at a hall door when a machine-gun opened up on me and it cut the track of myself in the hall door and cut my tunic and coat to ribbons. A young soldier from Killaloe saw where the machine-gun was placed and he jumped out into the street, went down on one knee and fired, wounding the gunner."

For McEoin the most satisfying capture of the day was some very fine salmon. "Some time the night before," he relates with relish, "the Irregulars had put the salmon, alternately heads and tails like sardines in a tin, in a huge iron pot with a close-fitting lid and left it on a wood fire. During the fighting the fire had gone out and the water had already boiled away. And there the salmon was—beautifully cooked and still piping hot—enough for us all and the sweetest meal I ever touched in my life."

The Ballinalee did not appear at Collooney, though McEoin learned later that several messages had been sent out by the Executive Forces appealing for its assistance. The armoured car was busy elsewhere that day. It had roared into Sligo early in the morning and its spectacular manoeuvres excited much admiration. The Executive Forces then commandeered the Harp and Shamrock Hotel, Mrs Ramsay's Hotel, where McEoin had stayed on his return from honeymoon, and other points which commanded the courthouse and the jail, the Provisional Government posts.

Given a second chance by McEoin after the fiasco in Boyle, Colonel-Commandant Martin Fallon was in charge of the courthouse garrison and must have cursed himself when the armoured car appeared, for he had earlier sent a substantial part of his force to deal with Republicans who, it had been reported to him, were preparing a large-scale ambush outside the town. Fallon had left himself with only ten men. Tension, growing throughout the day, was broken by a truce for the burial of Adair, killed in the Dooney Rock ambush.

At 6 p.m. a note signed by Seamus Devins, Commandant, Executive Forces, H.Q., 1st Brigade, 3rd Western Division, and addressed to O.C. Free State troops, was handed to Fallon. It read:

"You are herewith demanded to surrender unconditionally the positions held by your troops before 6.30 p.m. this evening in the name of the Republic. Please reply in writing per bearer."

Fallon paraded his men, read the ultimatum to them, told them that he had been sent by McEoin to hold the post and invited their opinions. All were determined to fight till the last, so Fallon drafted his reply. Headed H.Q. Sligo Brigade, Courthouse, and addressed to O.C. Executive Forces, it was:

"Being the National Army with a mandate from the Irish people, I, as O/C., and my men shall never surrender our barracks unconditionally. I would wish you to distinctly understand that we hold these positions for the Irish people and for the Republic when they so will it."

Nothing happened then until eight o'clock when Canon Butler and Rev Father P. J. Mulligan brought word that if Fallon would hand over his prisoners, Devins would let him know on what terms he would accept surrender, otherwise he would attack in ten minutes. Fallon answered: "Tell him he can come on; we are ready for the attack."

Instead of attacking, the Republicans sent a message to Dr Coyne, the ageing Bishop of Elphin, informing him that Fallon and all his men would be killed if they did not surrender. They were hopelessly out-numbered and had no chance of defending themselves. Though he was ill, Dr Coyne went to the courthouse and urged Fallon to surrender to save lives. The young officer faced up to the church dignitary. The G.O.C. in Athlone had entrusted to him the task of holding the barracks, he said, and if he were to surrender he would never be able to face General McEoin again. He would rather know that McEoin could say, "Good man, Martin. You held it while you were alive." Fallon concluded by saying simply that he held the post for the elected Government of Ireland.

"You are quite right," said Dr Coyne, and went to the door. "Mr Pilkington, Mr Devins," he called. "We will not surrender." He intended to stay with Fallon in the courthouse to the end. At the Bishop's request, Fallon sent out word that he was prepared to exchange prisoners, but Devins denied that any National troops were held prisoner in the area. Fallon challenged Devins to attack but it was the challenge of a small boy thumbing his nose to another in the presence of the headmaster. All through the night the two sides waited and neither made a move. Dr Coyne stayed, sharing the rather frugal fare of the troops, and enjoyed the success of his tactics. Early on Saturday morning, the Republicans gave up and left the town. Shortly afterwards, the rest of the courthouse garrison returned.

Later in the day *The Ballinalee* charged back into Sligo accompanied by a strong force on foot. A few shots echoed. The streets were thronged and there was pandemonium. Horses were whipped up, vehicles collided all over the road, shopkeepers rushed to shutter their windows and women screamed. National soldiers engaged in raiding houses were intercepted in the streets and a lorry with their supplies was seized. The gates of the courthouse were closed only just in time but *The Ballinalee* fired a few bursts at the building before making a "victory circuit" of the town. Next morning, having held the town practically on its own, *The Ballinalee* disappeared as suddenly as it had arrived. The Republicans were certainly having fun with their new toy.

Sligo remained in an unsettled state. On Sunday night two boys, brothers, were killed and a woman wounded by shots which came from no one knew where, fired by no one knew whom. One of the great tragedies of the Civil War was the
368

number of casualties among innocent non-participants. They occurred, often, when soldiers on both sides went unscathed. The loss of life and the damage to property compelled many Republican sympathisers to support the Provisional Government Forces simply because they wanted an end to strife. They were not prepared to pay the price of tearing up the Treaty. On Monday, July 17th, a curfew was introduced by Colonel-Commandant McCabe for the protection of civilians. The same night, three of McEoin's men from the new garrison of Collooney were captured by Republicans when they paid a visit to Sligo. Another incursion by Republicans resulted in the burning of the Custom House on the Quay.

McEoin, hard-pressed for men in an area where the Republicans were in some strength, was concerned about the position in Sligo which, though fairly securely held, was open to these hit-and-run attacks. His responsibilities weighed a little less heavily on the evening of Tuesday, July 18th, when people of "all creeds and classes" in Athlone presented him and his bride with a bank draft for £279.15.6d., a handsome start to their married life and an indication of the admiration the people of the district held for McEoin.

It was not till the end of that week that McEoin was able to release troops to augment those holding Sligo. They arrived on July 21st and took over all the strategically situated main buildings. At once the tension eased and the townspeople, thankful for the chance to live near-normal lives again, gave the troops a splendid welcome, though two days earlier, at a meeting of the Sligo Council, members deplored the arrest by the Government of Councillor J. Devins. "What he was arrested for nobody knows. It is a shame," commented one councillor.

There was no longer any real threat of the town changing hands and to this extent the people of Sligo enjoyed a measure of security, but there were still odd shots and occasional skirmishes, often attended by inconvenience. For some reason the Republicans seized the *Rosses*, a ferryboat which plied between Sligo and Rosses Point, and McCabe was impelled to assume a command at sea. Aboard the *Tartar* he and his troops provided an escort for another ferry and was promptly ambushed from the land. There were no casualties but gleeful bullets splintered woodwork as the Republicans enjoyed this

369

new way of catching a *Tartar*. National troops tried to cut off the Executive Forces operating in the Rosses Point area and there was a spectacular but inconclusive running battle which lasted for a couple of hours. It was said that the aim of the National troops to encircle their adversaries on the peninsula was frustrated by a woman who signalled a warning. At all events, the trap was avoided. A few days later, National troops raided a vessel at Sligo Quay and captured Vice-Brigadier Hegarty of the Mayo Brigade.

Possession of *The Ballinalee* was giving the Executive Forces a great psychological advantage and they used it well. The armoured car operated over a wide area, seeming to come from nowhere, and small garrisons were constantly apprehensive.

The Ballinalee paid one more devastating visit to Sligo, well supported by Republican troops, in the early hours of August 4th. For an hour and a half guns blazed. A mine wrecked the Ulster Bank, which was then raked with machine-gun bullets until the small garrison surrendered. Other Provisional Government posts, notably the Harp and Shamrock, received sharp reminders that *The Ballinalee* was Republican property now, then the commando-type attackers withdrew. A few days later the armoured car surprised campers at Rosses Point. Tents, clothes and food were appropriated by the Republicans, who were politely regretful that such action should be necessary. No doubt the campers were philosophical about their losses, as people are who go to see a fire and have their eyebrows singed.

SEVENTEEN

General Michael Brennan does not believe it is fully appreciated, even now, that outside Dublin "the whole Civil War really turned on Limerick". He puts it that "the Shannon was the barricade and whoever held Limerick held the south and the west." Nevertheless, the importance of holding the city was not lost on either side. Liam Lynch believed that by isolating the south, where Republicans were already well entrenched, he could frustrate the setting up of the Free
370

State. He made no effort to relieve Dublin, which he probably thought untenable, and in any case he preferred to move in his own territory. Limerick was obviously the most suitable headquarters for him.

National Army H.Q. saw the danger and Brennan was "directed to occupy Limerick with troops of the 1st Western Division and such support as the 4th South Division could provide." Commandant Donncada O'Hannigan commanded the 4th Southern. O'Hannigan was an old friend of Liam Lynch. In Black and Tan times, commanding Cork No. 2 Brigade and East Limerick Brigade respectively, they had often worked together.

Brennan was not short of men, though a large number of them were inexperienced recruits, but he could muster no more than 200 rifles. His area covered the whole of Clare and that part of Galway south of the Galway and Ballinasloe railway line for which also he was responsible. His headquarters were at Ennis, in Clare, about twenty-five miles northwest of Limerick. Liam Lynch's forces, mostly from Cork, were already in possession of the four military barracks in the city of Limerick, with the New Barracks as their headquarters, and Lynch also controlled the two Shannon bridges. He had not thought to seize the Athlunkard Bridge some way outside the city and Brennan took it. With headquarters in Cruise's Hotel, he established a line of posts covering the route to the bridge.

"Most of the men in these posts were unarmed," Brennan recalls, "but the few rifles they had were kept very much in evidence, and in some cases lengths of piping were used to simulate Lewis guns."

But he knew that Lynch was not altogether deceived; that with 800 rifles at his disposal Lynch must have realised that Brennan had little chance of holding his ground. He began to bring men by train from Ennis, fifty at a time. They left the train at Long Pavement, just across the river from Limerick, and marched over Athlunkard Bridge into the city. All carried rifles. Naturally, word of these movements quickly reached Liam Lynch, but what the Chief of Staff of the Executive Forces did not know was that the fifty rifles had been taken by lorry from Limerick to Long Pavement and there handed to the troops. The rifles were quickly collected up again in

371

Limerick and sent back to Long Pavement ready for the next detachment of men from Ennis. Brennan repeated the manoeuvre several times over two days.

In subsequent discussion arranged by an Augustinian priest, with Frank Aiken, a friend of both men and at this time considered a neutral, smoothing the way, Liam Lynch's whole attitude convinced Brennan that his stratagem had succeeded. Lynch based his proposals for an agreement on the assumption that they commanded forces of equal strength. The truth was that Brennan had only 150 rifles in the city and insufficient ammunition to feed those for more than a day or so. He had had repeated assurances from Dublin that a consignment of arms and ammunition was to be sent, but nothing arrived.

"My whole fright was that Lynch would attack me before they turned up, because we couldn't last," says Brennan. "I had to keep him talking to keep him from attacking. And we met, and we met, altogether about a dozen times. We used to meet in the presbytery of the Augustinian church, and we argued and argued."

Except for Clare, South Galway and part of Limerick, Lynch was in control of the whole of the south and west. "The importance of Limerick in this set-up was painfully clear" to Brennan. As he saw it, if the Provisional Government Forces in Limerick ceased to be an effective obstacle, "the whole of Connaught and Munster became a solid block against the Treaty Forces and Lynch was free to rush strong bodies of men to intervene in the Dublin fighting. At the worst, this could have involved the defeat of the Provisional Government; at best it would mean prolonged fighting in and around Dublin, then a fight all the way through Connaught and Munster."

Convinced that the Provisional Government Forces in Limerick were as strong as his own, though a quarter of his force could have contained them, Lynch did not dare move men to Dublin and leave Limerick at risk. From Limerick the National Army could divide the territory he controlled and base future operations against him.

His solution was to neutralise Brennan's and O'Hannigan's forces in some way, and in their discussions he kept drafting agreements the theme of which was that neither side would attack the other. This would mean that there would be no civil war in Limerick or Clare. O'Hannigan did, in fact, sign such a document on July 4th, but Brennan wanted only to keep Lynch talking. Lynch was emphatic that, except for some isolated posts, he controlled the whole of the country outside Dublin and he was confident, too, that the fighting in Dublin would end in favour of the Executive Forces despite the set-back at the Four Courts. "His whole case was that we hadn't the remotest chance of winning now and, as nothing could be gained by further bloodshed, could we not agree to stop it," says Brennan.

Although he believed that Lynch was bluffing, Brennan was not sure until Lynch claimed that the garrison of Templemore R.I.C. barracks had surrendered to the Executive Forces occupying the big military barracks just outside the town—when he knew this was not so. In fact, the position at Templemore was that on July 3rd Dr Harty, Bishop of Cashel, had persuaded both sides to agree to avert a conflict.

Very little news from Limerick was getting through to Dublin. Most of the country between was held by the Executive Forces and wireless was erratic. But some idea of the agreement signed by O'Hannigan in Limerick reached General O'Duffy at Beggar's Bush and he briefed Commandant-General Dermott MacManus, who knew the area well, to go down to Limerick. Blisteringly he apostrophised Brennan and O'Hannigan for going soft.

"O'Duffy, as he was inclined to do, had jumped to conclusions. I imagined that he had far more information than he did, because I found when I got down there that things were not as dangerous as he had led me to believe," says MacManus. "At the same time I had very definite instructions as to what I was to do."

MacManus travelled first to Athlone and returned the gun Lawlor had taken to the Four Courts. Then, in the guise of a tramp he made his way to Limerick. Arriving on July 5th, MacManus promptly cancelled O'Hannigan's agreement with Lynch. Neither Commandant-General O'Hannigan nor Commandant-General Brennan had any authority to enter into such agreement, he informed Lynch. There were to be no more meetings.

MacManus then left Limerick and went on into County

Clare to carry out another assignment. Meanwhile, Brennan explained the position to a meeting of his senior officers. He was ready to play Lynch at his own game and to gain time, not merely by stalling but by signing an agreement—provided that a loophole were left. All were agreed that Lynch's objecttive was to neutralise as large an area as possible to release men for use in other areas, that he wanted, as Brennan puts it, "a free hand to overrun the country and wreck the Treaty, in spite of the people". Observes Brennan: "Neither Hannigan nor I, nor any of our officers, believed that he had the slightest intention of ending 'this fratricidal strife' except on the basis of imposing his views on his opponents."

It was decided that Brennan and O'Hannigan should sign a new agreement, the text of which they had in front of them. It was a much less specific document than the first had been. Indeed, it was rather an odd document altogether. It provided for a meeting of "Divisional Commandants representing the 1st and 2nd Southern Divisions and the 1st Western Division of the Executive Forces, Irish Republican Army and the Divisional Commandants representing the 4th Southern Division and the 1st Western Division and the Mid-Western Command of the Dail Forces, Irish Republican Army", to be held "as soon as Sean McKeown can be got into this area."

As a guarantee of good faith towards a permanent agreement, the Divisional Council of the 1st Western Division Dail Forces were to hand in their resignations if agreement was not reached by the meeting of Divisional Commandants. The document further declared that a truce now existed, that no troops were to appear in public with arms except by arrangement and that outposts were to be withdrawn to agreed centres.

The clause requiring the resignation of the 1st Western Division Council evidently reflected some doubt in Lynch's mind of Brennan's intentions, but Brennan had no worries. So far as he was concerned, the agreement had an infallible safety catch—there was not the slightest doubt that McEoin would agree to participate in any such meeting. Brennan even asked Lynch what would happen if McEoin refused to come and Lynch answered that they would worry about that when the time came.

Though he had never thought of Lynch as shrewd—he re-
374

members him as "an innocent sort of man, very attractive, of unquestionable courage, the kind of man who gets others to follow him"—Brennan was rather surprised that Lynch was so easily hoodwinked. The point was Brennan had gained time for Limerick and possibly saved Dublin from an invasion from the west. "If Lynch had attacked us we were helpless. He had plenty of lorries and could have been in Dublin in a matter of hours," says Brennan.

In fact, Lynch was hoping for victory without blood and, whether there was a flaw in the agreement or not, the document was a propaganda goldmine and at once he publicised it. This aspect was what MacManus believed Dublin feared. Brennan's name was synonomous with honesty and sincerity and so was Lynch's. If it were thought that these two had come to an agreement, wavering National Army men might be won to the Republican cause and even the stalwart discouraged.

It was a shock to Brennan when his own leaders appeared to be first to fall for the propaganda and not only failed to appreciate his motives but "assumed that I was getting out, that I wasn't going to support the Treaty any longer." But the real difficulty was the problem of communication at a time when men everywhere were torn between logic and emotion, between conviction and loyalty to old comrades, and no man's actions surprised. Brennan's dilemma seemed likely to go on perpetuating itself; because no guns had arrived he had had to negotiate and because he had negotiated no guns were allowed to reach him.

Returning to Limerick on July 7th, the day of the new agreement, MacManus wrote again to Lynch. Though "absolutely disapproving" of the agreement he was "willing to allow this matter to go ahead on condition that there is no change in the military position here." He added, "I cannot agree to any interference with our present strong military position."

If Brennan and MacManus had got together, much heart-burning might have been saved but, resentful of Dublin's lack of faith represented by the very presence of MacManus, Brennan did not confide in him, while for his part MacManus believed that "Brennan realised fully the disaster of a civil war and was doing all he could to prevent it. I thought he was taking tremendous risks and that he was giving Liam Lynch credit for sincerity that he did not deserve." Brennan was confident that Sean McEoin would realise exactly what was happening and sent one of his chaplains, Father Dick McCarthy, to Athlone with a copy of the agreement and instructions to explain the position to him.

Leaving Limerick in its uneasy state of truce, MacManus set out to report back to O'Duffy in Dublin. Given a free hand, he would have taken a very different line but O'Duffy's briefing had been clear and limiting. At the same time MacManus was afraid that Lynch was going to seize the advantage in Limerick somehow, and this would jeopardise McEoin's position. The military car in which he was travelling was prevented by road blocks from going very far and MacManus borrowed a motorboat from a friend on the east side of Lough Derg. He also acquired a companion, a young medical student anxious to return to Dublin. This was Geoffrey Bewley who was to enjoy a distinguished medical career in days to come. They crossed Lough Derg, their boat swirling in the wind, and landed at Whitegate, where they found a jaunting car to take them into Scarriff. Here, MacManus had learned from friends, the only available car in the area was the doctor's Ford. Scarriff was in Republican hands and the doctor had hidden parts of his car so that it would not be stolen, but he agreed to lend it to MacManus and Bewley who set off without hindrance from a group of Republicans gathered rather uncertainly in the road.

A few miles from Scarriff they saw a tree-felling party at work. MacManus was all for charging through with guns blazing but Bewley preferred to turn the car and go another way. At Portumna, which they reached in the middle of the night, they had a meal with friends of MacManus, then they pushed on in another car to Athlone where they arrived at 3 a.m.

Anxious though he was to get on to Dublin, MacManus had not expected McEoin to move quite so decisively as he did. In no time he had turned fifty men out of their barracks and commandeered a train, an engine and two carriages. "The driver was an old fellow," recalls MacManus. "I went along to see him. Sean had told him to go like hell, but I said to him he had no less a person than the Blacksmith of Ballinalee

376

on board and he was to drive carefully and not to land us in a river or ditch or something." MacManus took a seat in the carriage but the eager McEoin rode on the footplate.

McEoin had wirelessed ahead and when the train pounded into Broadstone Station at about 8 a.m. an armoured car was waiting. They crammed into the armoured car but as their way led past Bewley's hospital they all got out to see him safely back. As they pushed the sleepless, blackened student through the door, the Matron saw him, and cursing the drink that was the ruin of medical students, she stalked and sniffed away.

At Portobello Barracks the two weary generals routed Collins, Mulcahy, O'Duffy, O'Murthuile and O'Sullivan from their beds, where these days they spent few hours undisturbed. Over a dishevelled breakfast it was decided that O'Duffy should take over the South-west Command. In the meantime, Seamus Hogan was on his way to Limerick with the convoy of arms for which Brennan was waiting. MacManus was to intercept him at Scarriff. Hogan had chosen to travel through his native Loughrea district, about thirty miles north of Scarriff, but the heavy vehicles had been delayed by bad roads and the journey had taken three days. Hogan went on ahead to Scarriff and sent word to Brennan to meet him there. During the Tan war Hogan had been Brennan's right-hand man in his column and the two men were good friends. They met on the morning of July 11th, Brennan unaware that Hogan was to decide whether or not he got the arms he so desperately needed. Hogan was satisfied and reported back to G.H.Q. that he thought Brennan and O'Hannigan "always realised clearly that Liam Lynch was trying to break our strength by negotiations when he could not do so by fighting."

Bluff was no longer needed as a weapon and Brennan sent Lynch a polite note ending the truce, a frail thing anyway, at the mercy of tension and brawling bullets. One victim had been Frank Teeling, the only man captured of the squad which had liquidated the British Intelligence men on Bloody Sunday. Sentenced to death, Teeling had escaped spectacularly from Kilmainham jail. It was one of the many ironies of the time that he was now laid low by an Irish bullet.

By 5 p.m. on July 11th the Provisional Government troops, reasonably well armed now, were taking up new positions. As one of their men erected a barricade he was shot in the back, but it is doubtful if that incident precipitated the conflict which began two hours later when the Provisional Government's post in William Street opened fire on the Republican garrison of the Ordnance Barracks.

Once his truce-signing flirtation with the pro-Treaty officers had ended, Lynch left Limerick and on July 11th, the day that the first shots in anger were fired, he set up his headquarters in Clonmel and was joined there by de Valera. Perhaps he was confident of victory in Limerick and felt his presence was needed further along the Limerick-Waterford line, which bounded the area in the south where Republican forces were dominant, but his preoccupation with the south is difficult to understand.

Dan Breen would have staked all on Dublin. "I thought they'd throw men into Dublin and end it there. Whichever side won, that would be the end—except that the British would have thrown in their forces on the side of the Treaty. So we couldn't have won." He told Lynch, "In order to win this war you'll need to kill three out of every five people in the country—and it isn't worth it."

But Lynch was impossible to convince. "He was an absolute dreamer and an idealist," says Dan Breen. "He wasn't a man for the world. A monastery was his place. This was true of a lot of them at the time. Dinny Lacey was the same. Lynch had a very strong Catholic upbringing and he was stuck with it. He didn't understand compromise." Four days after the move to Clonmel, Lynch transferred his headquarters again, this time to Fermoy. De Valera, who had faith in the line, soon returned to Clonmel to lend his talent to Seamus Robinson, now in command of 2nd Southern Division. The line ran roughly from Limerick to Tipperary, in a loop through Golden and Cashel down through Fethard to Clonmel and along the Suir River to Carrick-on-Suir and Waterford. Except that it followed main roads and the river, the line had little more substance than the Equator. In any case, as Brennan had seen, the key to it was Limerick.

On July 13th the Provisional Government announced the setting up of a War Council whose members were Michael

Collins, Commander-in-Chief, Richard Mulcahy, Minister of Defence and Chief of Staff, and Eoin O'Duffy, Assistant Chief of Staff and G.O.C. South-western Command. These appointments had been decided at a meeting the previous evening and it was Mulcahy who had urged that Collins "go into uniform". The move was intended to inspire confidence and it was not expected of Collins that he should take any very active part.

O'Duffy set out for Limerick. In Dublin little news had seeped through from that unhappy city. Snipers infested belfries and upper windows; barricades blocked the streets, even farm machinery being employed for the purpose; civilians huddled in their homes, listening to the heavy crossfire and the explosions of grenades, or picked up their children and sought refuge outside the city. Food was scarce, though General Brennan tried desperately to organise the distribution of what supplies there were. Each side sallied out to attack the strongholds of the other but very little was gained by either.

On Sunday, July 16th, MacManus sent out a dispatch, timed 5.30 a.m., to Commandant-General Seamus Hogan who, having delivered the consignment of arms to Brennan had stayed to help use them. MacManus explained that he had arrived in Killaloe at the toe of Lough Derg, about twelve miles to the north-east of Limerick, "with instructions to prepare the place for General O'Duffy's headquarters. I find that the mutineers are in occupation of Ballina on the left bank of the Shannon. According to the latest information their strength is about 40, and they occupy 5 or 6 houses."

To allow him to "deal with them decisively and rapidly", MacManus asked for a Lancia, a Lewis gun—not mounted on the Lancia—and about thirty men. He wanted the reinforcements by noon and could return them to Limerick before dark. He suggested that he could take ten men from O'Briensbridge, about five miles towards Limerick.

Replying, Hogan stated that he was sending Captain Kelly to Thurles to meet a convoy of troops under Commandant Galvin.

"I do not think our troops can reach Killaloe earlier than midnight," wrote Hogan, "and consequently if I send you an armoured car, Lancia and small party tonight, in conjunction

379

with the incoming troops you ought to clear Ballina." He suggested that MacManus send a priest or a girl to Nenagh to ask Brigadier Holohan to have food ready for the troops.

He went on newsily, "At the moment we are engaged on an attack on the Strand Barracks, and there is rather a serious shortage of ammunition."

Hogan also authorised MacManus to "draw in as many men from O'Briensbridge as you think fit", and later in the day he sent Captain Walsh with a Lancia car and a Lewis gun and he also advised MacManus he had heard that the Irregulars had withdrawn from Ballina.

That same day MacManus, who had about twenty men and an officer, took steps to disperse a small band of Republicans who had fortified a house on the other side of the bridge at Killaloe and commanded the crossing. His strategy was carefully worked out—but the story is one that MacManus enjoys telling against himself:

"I sent a letter to them demanding that they should surrender. I gave it to my officer and told him to send one of the men over with it. I said, 'Don't attack until you give me time to get across the river.' I got into a boat with my batman, who was a fellow sportsman, and we rowed across the river and got into a field, moving behind the bridge so that when these people retreated, about 20 of them, we could catch them and shoot them up. Unfortunately it didn't go as we hoped. It was a large field and I suddenly saw my batman turn round and take to his heels and run like hell. I knew he was a man of considerable courage and I couldn't understand what was happening, until suddenly I heard loud snorts and there was a fierce bull, leaving him and coming for me. I hadn't moved so fast for a long time as I got out of that field. We were thoroughly defeated by the bull. That delayed us a bit but we went on. Unfortunately, my officer hadn't waited for me to cross before he attacked. He went for them straight away and by the time that I got around they were 400 or 500 yards away running for the hills."

Republicans, possibly the group who had fled from Killaloe, seized O'Briensbridge and on July 17th Hogan, acknowledging MacManus's report of the incident, thought "there must be treachery in the loss of O'Briensbridge. Otherwise the morale of the men must be very low."

In Limerick, he said, "the morale of the men is good. On every occasion they fought well when tested. We are maintaining our present position here, pushing out a number of advance parties. The enemy made an attempt to develop an offensive today but were repelled with at least five killed and a large number of wounded." Hogan said that he would leave for Killaloe as soon as MacManus notified him of Galvin's arrival. Meanwhile he was sending a unit to seize a house commanding the bridge at O'Briensbridge.

Galvin arrived at Nenagh on Monday July 17th with troops, machine-guns, an 18-pounder and General O'Duffy. They were met by Brigadier Holohan. That evening they went on to Killaloe where the local hotel was glad to see them. MacManus had been enjoying the hospitality there, though salmon trout which he was given for every meal, was becoming a little wearisome. During the day a party from Killaloe under Captain O'Leary worked hard to clear felled trees from the Nenagh-Killaloe Road. O'Leary sent a plaintive dispatch to his opposite number in Nenagh asking for help from that end and for the use of some lorries as his men were fatigued.

Heavy street fighting with many casualties persisted in Limerick throughout Tuesday 18th as the Republicans tried to get control of the city before reinforcements reached Brennan and Hogan, but on the following day the Provisional Government troops set up their 18-pounder on Arthur's Quay and aimed it at the Strand barracks. The Republicans were invited to surrender but Mackey, their leader, sent girls from the Red Cross Hospital adjoining to Cruise's Hotel with a message that he would not surrender while he still had ammunition. It took several hours and thirty-three shells to break the four foot walls. The gun was then moved to assail the rear of the building. Not only did the garrison withstand the ordeal of shelling but they resisted a storming party with desperate gallantry. Colonel David Reynolds, who later took charge of Limerick, was severely wounded and there were several dead on both sides. Some of the defenders were captured, others made their escape through the hospital.

On Thursday the 18-pounder was moved to the next offensive, Castle Barracks. Flames soon sprang up from this Republican stronghold, whether from shellfire or action by

381

the Republicans is still uncertain. By nightfall, after a day's bitter fighting, the Republican cause in Limerick was lost. Flames sprang up all over the city as the Republican garrisons fired their strongpoints and the fire brigade, which had been performing miracles for more than a week, could do little now. Irate citizens, afraid for the gas works, managed to douse the fire in Frederick Street barracks before it gained a hold.

In the early hours of Friday a stream of cars and lorries whirled the Republicans out of the city to the south. They moved towards Mallow and Fermoy and entrenched themselves in Bruff, Bruree and Kilmallock where the National Army garrison had surrendered the Union Barracks on July 14th after a two-day siege. This was small comfort to Liam Lynch who had left Limerick to consolidate his position in what some called the Munster Republic.

The loss of the city certainly cramped his plans and was of inestimable value to his opponents. Provisional Government Forces cleared the Shannon estuary so that ships could again use the port of Limerick. About 600 Republican prisoners were shipped out at this time. Five or six patrol boats, some crewed by Aran Islanders who spoke nothing but Irish, and some by Dubliners, kept the estuary under surveillance. The crews also managed some peaceful fishing.

At Killaloe, O'Duffy was planning with General W. R. E. Murphy, who had fought in France as an officer of the British Army, to thwart Lynch by driving from Limerick straight down to Cork. He also published a fulsome proclamation in which he lauded the victory of the National Army in Limerick. But he still had in his mind the fact that there had been some sort of negotiations beforehand and he sent word to Brennan that he wanted to meet all the senior officers of the area in Ennis. Brennan assembled them at Ennis and O'Duffy addressed them. His audience, many of them officers who for ten days had been fighting the Executive Forces in Limerick, listened unbelievingly as O'Duffy urged them to make up their minds which side they were on. Once they had made their decision there was no going back, he warned. His harangue seemed endless but at last the men left the meeting. O'Duffy seemed pleased with himself but the officers were furious. Later, Brennan's brother, Austin, who commanded the Clare section, drew Brennan aside.

"You'd better come out to these fellows. There's going to be trouble."

Brennan hurried out to find the men, in mutinous mood, on the point of going back to their homes and refusing to have anything more to do with the fight. "Let O'Duffy do the fighting himself," was the general feeling. It was some hours before Brennan was able to smooth their ruffled feathers.

As commander of the 4th Northern Division, enjoying the support of both sides, Frank Aiken, who had intervened in the Limerick negotiations between Brennan and Lynch, was in a unique position. Officially he took his orders from Beggar's Bush and his men were on the National Army payroll, but his sympathies were undoubtedly with the Republicans. What he wanted above all else was to maintain a neutral position and until the Four Courts pushed grey-minded people either towards black or white this was not too difficult. Aiken was confident when he left his Dundalk headquarters for Limerick that he had nothing to fear from anyone. He had told Mulcahy expressly in a letter dated July 4th that he did not intend to align himself on either side. Civil war could "only ruin the country without gaining any ground for the Republic. He pointed out to Mulcahy that whatever tactical mistakes had been committed by those opposed to the Treaty the wrangling and fighting boiled down to a simple national abhorrence of swearing allegiance to an English king . . ." and he asked Mulcahy:

"Are you prepared to carry on a war with your own people to enforce that oath of allegiance to England, while you have a splendid opportunity of uniting the whole Nation to fight against it with success?"

This argument, to Mulcahy, placed Aiken firmly in the opposition camp and he sent Emmet Dalton to Dundalk to sort out any difficulties. Finding that Aiken had hared off to Limerick, Dalton put Commandant-General Dan Hogan in charge then returned to Dublin to take command of the operations in the Dublin Hills. Aiken, on his return, and Hogan hardly saw eye to eye and the Provisional Government moved to put Aiken out of business. In the early hours of July 16th he awoke to find a gun at his head. He was under arrest and Dundalk was in the hands of Provisional Government Forces. Anne Street Barracks, Bridge Street Barracks and the jail had been taken and 300 of his men were prisoners. The National Army tactics had been carefully planned. Additional troops had been brought by road from Monaghan. Dundalk had first been surrounded, then buildings in the vicinity of the jail and barracks had been occupied, finally the strongholds had been seized. There was little that Aiken's men could have done to resist in any case, for so that he could not obey orders from Beggar's Bush to attack Republican forces, Aiken had concealed the arms of his 4th Northern Division. What he had not reckoned upon was that he should be treated as an active opponent of the Provisional Government. A number of the Anne Street Barracks garrison tried to get away across open land known as the "Demesne" at the back; one was killed outright, another died later from his wounds.

After his capture Aiken went on parole to Dublin and asked Mulcahy to release his men. He also wanted it made known why 300 men had been taken without offering resistance. Mulcahy was cool. So far as he was concerned, Aiken's men were Government forces whose loyalty was now in question and he was prepared to release them only if they signed a document recognising the Government. Aiken would not accept the condition but he was told that his men would be treated as prisoners of war.

They were not prisoners for long. On July 27th, about 200 of Aiken's men who had not been taken in Dundalk filtered quietly into the town and succeeded in mining the prison wall. As the mine exploded, shattering windows and cracking walls in the town and reducing part of the prison wall to dust, street barriers suddenly appeared and Provisional Government posts were attacked. Most of the prisoners got clean away.

Aiken still hoped to end the struggle by persuading men in the National Army to his way of thinking. In a published statement he urged his men, for their country's sake, to "put your trust in God and keep your powder dry". Cessation of the Civil War depended upon the men in the National Army,

384

was the theme of appeals he made to them at this time. "While you attack the men who can never accept the oath you are in the wrong and must be met." So, in spite of himself, Aiken was now committed.

He was to prove a dangerous adversary but he never ceased to take every opportunity to seek peace by persuading the people that acceptance of the Treaty had been a mistake.

On August 14th he succeeded in recapturing the military barracks in Dundalk. His men entered the town undetected in the early hours and mined the buildings in several places. Machine-gun fire followed the explosions which killed one man and wounded many more. Several sentries were shot dead. Once the military barracks had been taken the other Provisional Government posts surrendered. Republican prisoners were released from the jail and the National Army men found themselves behind bars.

A public meeting in the Market Square was called by Aiken for the following day and a resolution was passed demanding an immediate truce and the summoning of the prorogued Dail to re-affirm Irish sovereignty and conclude peace between the parties or, alternatively, dissolution of the Dail and a new election with the Constitution as the main issue.

Aiken's troops remained in Dundalk for three days, evacuating the town as National Army columns converged on it. On Wednesday, August 10th, an aircraft made a brief sortie against the Republican held barracks, the first air attack of the war. This the Republicans found a somewhat unnerving experience.

They quitted the town finally in two columns both of which encountered Provisional Government Forces. One group eluded prowling armoured cars and escaped under cover of darkness, the other fought a hard battle before surrendering. Aiken's men, for the most part, got away to continue fighting a guerrilla campaign and many prisoners from different parts of the country, freed from Dundalk jail, made their way back to their own territory. With arms seized from the defeated National soldiers, they were ready to take up the fight again.

EIGHTEEN

There was a "dangerous area" in Dublin which needed cleaning up, Gearoid O'Sullivan explained to Tommy Ryan, who was at a loose end once the Four Courts had fallen. Ryan did not wish to return to Athlone and he had given up ideas of emigrating to Australia. O'Sullivan told him that a number of officers of the National Army had disappeared in the Gloucester Place area. A flying squad of fifty men had been sent to deal with the situation but a number of them had failed to return. Ryan was to take a squad and see what he could do. He was not sure why O'Sullivan emphasised that as "a clean country lad" he was just the man for the job and, when he surrounded the area, he was astonished that there was no opposition. The next move was to search the houses and he soon realised what O'Sullivan had meant by a "dangerous area". The enemy proved to be not the kind of "Irregular" he expected but gangs of prostitutes infuriated by the attempt to remove their customers.

"It was quite an experience," Colonel Ryan sighs. He asked for a posting back to his own area of Tipperary.

In an effort to break the hold the Republicans had on the south, the Provisional Government had begun to create new brigades to replace the old Volunteer brigades which had "gone Irregular." The Adjutant-General sent Ryan, now a Commandant, to Kilkenny to serve under General Prout.

There was no activity in Kilkenny and Ryan decided on his own initiative to reconnoitre the area between Waterford and Tipperary. Arriving in Waterford, he went to the Munster Hotel where the proprietor, who knew him, hurried him upstairs. The bar was full of Republicans. Reluctantly, he agreed that Ryan should stay for the night. Next morning, Ryan took notes of the positions held by the Republicans and tried to assess their strength.

When he reached Waterford station, intending to buy a ticket to Tipperary, a group of four Republicans seemed suspicious of him but did not challenge him. Nevertheless, he decided to buy a ticket to Cappoquin only, boarded the train
386

and saw the four Republicans enter a carriage further back. There would be trouble at Cappoquin, Ryan guessed.

As soon as the train stopped he jumped out, ran straight into the toilet and got his gun ready, expecting that he would have to try and fight his way out. But there was no sound of any siege being laid and, peeking out, he saw his adversaries at the entrance of the station. Evidently they had not seen him leave the train. There was nothing between him and the still waiting train, so he dashed back to his seat just as the train pulled out.

About two miles on, Ryan pulled the communication cord, jumped down and headed for the Blackwater River. He got a boat and rowed across, then made his way to Mount Mellary Monastery, where he was given an excellent meal. With a full belly and in a cheerful frame of mind, he set out to make his way across the mountains to Newcastle, Co. Tipperary, but after he had walked about four miles, fog enveloped him and he dared go no further. After one of the toughest nights of his experience he was able to resume his march at about five o'clock next morning. He was longing for a cigarette but had smoked his last two during the long fogbound hours.

Arriving in Newcastle, he went on to Clogheen and called at a farm where he knew he would be warmly welcomed. Fortunately for him, his friends were milking the cows and were able to tell him there were Republicans in the house. The sentry had gone fishing. The visitors were to leave that morning and Ryan remained in hiding until they went. He stayed three days, helping with the organisation of local units, and somehow the Republicans learned that he was in the area. Ryan heard that he was to be shot on sight if he were found for Lacey still resented what he regarded as Ryan's defection. Dressed as a priest, he was driven through Cahir, which was held by the Republicans, a number of whom he knew and saw in the street. He was to stay the night at Ballydavid, near Bansha, on the Tipperary road, but the lad who was driving him did not take the main road in case they encountered Republicans from Bansha. Instead, he took a roundabout route and at one point all but went over a precipice. It was late at night when they reached their destination.

Ryan planned to go on to Thurles next day and thence to Urlingford where he would spend the night before returning to Kilkenny. Urlingford lies ten miles from Thurles and fifteen from Kilkenny. As it happened, there was the prospect of a lively party in Thurles so he stayed there for the night.

During that day, July 5th, a Republican force under Dinny Lacey and Bill Quirke was moving towards Thurles on a wide front in an arc from Commons to Castleiney, a distance of a dozen miles. Lacey did not want to leave nuisance garrisons in his rear and that evening his troops took Urlingford after a sharp fight with the National Army garrison of seventeen men, who surrendered their post, the County home—or poorhouse —after exhausting their ammunition.

Some of the garrison made their escape on a Crossley tender and were congratulating themselves on their getaway until, as they backed the vehicle up the hill, they came into the Republican line of fire and could not get any further.

They were freed next day when a small National Army column under Mick Small left Thurles in a rescue bid. The main body of Republicans had left Urlingford and reached the cross-road known as Mary Willies, named for the public house which stands there invitingly. After breaking their journey of a mile or so, they were climbing aboard their lorries when Small's column approached and opened fire. Jim Dwyer, then aged 19, remembers that "there was an argument about how far we were from them. Some said 1,400 yards, others 1,800, and we settled for 1,600 and set our sights at that range. Shots were exchanged for about an hour, then they got into their lorries and moved away and the prisoners they had taken at Urlingford the previous day were re-covered."

Commandant Jerry Ryan, in charge of Thurles, had a garrison of no more that seventy men and the Republicans, including columns from Cork and Kerry, closed in. They set up road blocks, sabotaged railway lines and attacked convoys, and flour and other commodities began to run short in the town. Miss Bridget Fitzpatrick, who was later to marry Jerry Ryan, was sent to Kilkenny to see if she could get reinforcements and more ammunition. She was accustomed to this kind of mission. At great risk, she had sent in her own name one of the warning telegrams when Sean Hogan was rescued at Knocklong, and she had once travelled by train from Dublin with a heavy bag of ammunition for the
388

I.R.A. in Tipperary. She must have been breathtakingly beautiful as a girl, for she is lovely still and surely one of the most charming women in all Ireland.

"I found General Prout and Tom Carew, John Quinlan and some others," she says, and adds feelingly, "I was entertained in Kilkenny and I thought it very unfair for them all to be there not doing anything. However, they sent reinforcements to Thurles and ammunition and so on, and Quinlan and the others came back." Two hundred and eighty men, in fact, marched from Kilkenny, traversing bogland near Urlingford in heavy rain. After skirmishing for an hour with Republicans at Two Mile Borris on Thursday, July 13th, they arrived in Thurles.

In the meantime, Ryan had led out a force to try to break through the Republican cordon. Craftily, the Republicans withdrew to the north-east, through Moyne and towards Lisduff. Throughout the day they kept just ahead and the two forces did not make contact until the evening, when the Kerry column under Jerry Miles, with James Stack (brother of the better known Austin) as his adjutant, stayed to fight a rear-guard action.

"They were down behind a fence in a boggy kind of field and we were on higher ground, but to get closer to them we would have to advance down through a fairly open field," Jim Dwyer explains. "We were behind a big, high ditch, too, and it was realised that we could stay there the rest of the week and never get anywhere. Eventually we decided to hop over and rush down across the field.

"They opened fire with Lewis guns but not one man was hit. We had spread out in half-moon formation and they tried to get away to the right, but that was after the engagement had been going on for nearly two hours. In the early stages one of our fellows, Sergeant Furlong, got killed. In the end they surrendered but it was dark by the time we had them all rounded up. We marched them back to Thurles and they were imprisoned in the Confraternity Hall.

"We used to let the prisoners out for exercise on a small patch of ground at the front and a few evenings later they were out there when some National Army troops from Kerry passed through Thurles. Some of these fellows knew some of the Kerry Irregulars and they got talking through the railings.

389

Then some of the prisoners started to climb over and they were helped by the fellows on our side. An awful lot of people in Thurles supported the Irregulars at the time and they crowded round the railings, too, and started handing in parcels and things to the prisoners inside. There were only about half a dozen guards and the prisoners were getting pretty obstreperous.

"Anyway, about a dozen of us rushed up in two old T/Model Fords and we cleared the streets, but we didn't know if some of the prisoners had got away. We had a hell of a job getting them back into the hall. When we lined them up to be counted they did the old stunt of running around and getting counted twice. They were more or less accounted for in the end."

More troops arrived from Kilkenny on Sunday, July 16th. No less than twenty-five lorries were drawn up in Liberty Square. Nine of these, with two armoured cars, left Thurles on the Monday to take Templemore barracks, the third largest in the country, but the massive walls were breached instead by the wisdom of Dr Harty, Bishop of Cashel, who persuaded the Republicans under Commandant J. Leahy to withdraw, several hours before the National Army troops arrived. Leahy even left instructions to enable his opponents to find mines which had been laid during his occupation of the barracks.

On his return to Kilkenny, Tommy Ryan found that Prout was preparing a campaign against the Waterford end of the Limerick to Waterford line. The information Ryan had gleaned during his solo espionage effort was valuable. Prout's first objective was the city of Waterford.

"There was no question of a concentration of troops at Kilkenny," says Colonel Patrick Paul whose Waterford Brigade was part of General Prout's Waterford Command. "We didn't bring troops in. Each area had to find its own troops and train them." This was broadly the case all over the country, but there was in many areas a stiffening unit of the Dublin Guards.

"We were in Kilkenny and we were told we were going to take Waterford," says Tommy Doyle, speaking for his friend David Moran as much as for himself. "We were moved to a place called Kilmacow, six or seven hundred of us. We were all brought into a field and given general absolution." It must
390

have been a strangely moving sight as the men knelt among wild poppies in the sunlit grass. Civilian transport had been requisitioned. "You might have some of the cars for days, sometimes for weeks," recalls Colonel Paul, touching on one feature of the struggle which most exasperated civilians.

The estuary of the Suir River strikes inland in roughly a north-westerly direction and Waterford lies on the southern, or even western, side of it. Across the river the escarpment of Mount Misery looms over the town like a formidable school-master contemplating an erring small boy. But from its frowning crest the mountain slopes benignly to the north. Oddly, the Republicans made no attempt to prevent their opponents from securing this commanding height. Perhaps they reckoned without Prout's 18-pounder, one of the hardy pieces which, inexpertly handled though they were, contributed much to the ultimate success of the National Army in the Civil War. The cantilever bridge across the river had been raised, which was a sensible precaution. Roads had been mined and, having thus cut themselves off, the Republicans under the command of Brigadier "Pax" Whelan prepared to sit tight in selected strategic posts such as the post office and jail. The plan might have been good enough to withstand attack by infantrymen. They were welcome to Mount Misery, from which they were hardly likely to jump into Waterford, unless they parachuted with a strong wind behind them.

"We wanted as far as possible to avoid inflicting casualties or sustaining casualties ourselves," says Paul, whose first plan was to move in quickly to secure the bridge before the Republicans raised it, as Paul himself had raised it once during the Anglo-Irish war. But the three or four Whippet armoured cars needed to carry out this plan simply were not available. Paul then considered two other possibilities. The first of these, to cross the Suir up-river and to move on the city from the west, he discarded because it would invite attack from strong Republican forces at Carrick-on-Suir and Clonmel. The second alternative, to cross the river on the harbour side, was adopted, but it was decided to soften the opposition by means of the 18-pounder first.

Little happened on the first day, July 18th. "We had expected opposition to stop us taking the heights," says Paul, "but they only fired at us from the city." On the next day

391

the 18-pounder went into action. "It was a perfect day for shelling," Paul continues. "I could see where the shells landed with the naked eye." Mostly high-explosive shells were used, though a few shrapnel shells were fired for aiming. The two towers of Ballybricken prison were useful landmarks for the gunners, though except for the roof the prison was not much damaged. Meanwhile, men were preparing boats for a river crossing that night.

Moran and Doyle had gone off on their own, taking three or four boxes of ammunition with them. "We fired at everything, even birds. There were no human beings in sight on the quays."

A hundred men under Captain Ned O'Brien and Dominic Mackey crossed the river in small rowing boats and entered the city scarcely noticed. "They just caught a few fellows in a car," says Paul. "Their instructions were to seize a block of buildings to command the Quay, which was the main thoroughfare, to set up headquarters and to secure the position so that we could get the bridge down and get the main body and the transport across." O'Brien's men carried out instructions. They seized the Adelphi Hotel, the Imperial Hotel and the County Club and then sat tight. Accurate fire from the post office garrison troubled Prout next day and he signalled across the river that he would like something done about it. The reply was that reinforcements were needed. The big gun was brought down and from the Ferrybank a few shells were aimed at the post office.

Moran and Doyle, tiring of their sport and becoming impatient of the lack of action in the city, approached Commandant Heaslip and asked permission to make a sortie of their own across the river. Heaslip referred them to Prout who sanctioned it. With another youngster, whose name also was Doyle, they went right down to the harbour where merchant ships were anchored "waiting for the row to stop".

They got a rowing boat and began to cross the harbour. Bullets spattered the water but they were well out of range. The tide presented far more problems to their inexperienced oars. In spite of all their efforts, they began to drift. Seeing their plight, a sailor on an anchored vessel instructed them to pull in, then he climbed down a rope ladder, jumped into the boat and saw them safely across.

392

Finding themselves in a cul-de-sac, the way blocked by a big timber door, they shot off the lock and entered a bakery, which was stacked with fresh loaves. The aroma was tempting, but they pushed on to the Imperial Hotel, where they found Dominic Mackey sitting in a large armchair and smoking a cigar. The earlier force had taken the Imperial and adjacent buildings without much effort. Mackey was surprised to see the newcomers and explained that he was still waiting for reinforcements before attempting to advance. The trio were looking for action and told him that they were going to tackle the post office.

Mackey was not very interested and they set off themselves. First they searched the tenth century Reginald's Tower but found no one there, then they filtered through a network of streets, arresting two men with sacks full of loot from a jeweller's shop. Moran sent prisoners and loot back to the Imperial Hotel, with young Doyle as escort.

At the corner by the post office a crowd of old shawlies was screaming impartially, "Up de Valera! Up Collins!" "Their language was shocking," Moran says with awe in his voice even now. "Tommy Doyle went down by the side of the post office, reached up to the window ledge, looked in and beckoned to me. He leaned down and whispered that there were six or seven fellows inside. Next minute he fired some shots through the window and yelled, 'Hands up!' Then we marched them out and took them back to Mackey who was getting back to the post office with Tommy to collect the arms and Tommy cut every wire he could see that might be connected to a mine."

Later Moran and Doyle went down the Quay to the Grenville Hotel. In the hall was a large tea-chest which Doyle thought suspicious. He soon discovered that it concealed a mine and he cut the wires, then followed them up the stairs until he found the plunger near the head of a fire escape. Two men were outside on the escape and Doyle ordered them in and took them prisoner. Mackey's men took them away and Moran and Doyle decided that, now the post office had been silenced and the quays cleared, they had done enough, so they settled down to enjoy a drink.

Prout and Paul were now able to have the bridge lowered by hand, a long business during which a wary eye had to be kept for snipers, and at last they got their men across. Already the Republicans were leaving Waterford on lorries, having set the two barracks ablaze. The jail and the workhouse were occupied by the Provisional Government troops with no more than a shot here and there to worry them. Looting was rife in the city and Prout issued a stern warning to those who were culpable. Moran and Doyle had been away from their unit for a night and a day and Commandant Heaslip thought they had overdone it and arrested them for being A.W.O.L.

Although there were nine deaths in the action, one that of a girl of ten, Waterford had fallen far more easily than Prout and Paul had expected. The Republicans' failure to seal off Mount Misery had been a vital factor, and another was that an attack from the rear by a force commanded by Lacey, which they constantly expected, did not materialise. In the town itself opposition had been slight, except for the sharpshooters in the post office. It seemed that the Republican policy was to put up token opposition in towns, to abandon them, generally burning the barracks as they went, and to get into the country so that they could employ the old familiar guerrilla tactics which had succeeded so well against the Tans.

Apart from that, there was among many Republicans a lack, not of conviction or courage, but of heart in the fight. They wanted to make their protest as urgently as they could and to keep on making it; they wanted to stop the Provisional Government from working the Treaty and building up an administration. They did not want to take life if they could avoid it, and neither did most of the Provisional Government troops, and so flights of bullets hurtled through the air harmlessly as migrating birds. The air above Ireland was criss-crossed with busy bullets with no particular object in view.

In an attempt to stop the flames of civil war from spreading the Labour Party called for a meeting of members of the Dail at the Mansion House on July 20th. Only Labour members attended and the Provisional Government made it clear that they intended to suppress the "armed revolt" and would not compromise. They were rapidly gaining control of the country and it did not seem that the Republicans, so many of whom were half-hearted, could keep going for much longer. Even the recalcitrant south seemed to be yielding.

After Waterford Prout should have pressed on quickly to Carrick-on-Suir, which Lacey was determined to defend rather more zestfully, but he returned to Kilkenny to get on with his administration, which he enjoyed much more than fighting. Paul was left in charge of Waterford. Men who had had to lie low during the Republican occupation were now recruited and Paul began to build up his forces so that he could first secure the town and then drive out to the west.

With Limerick and Waterford now in the hands of the Provisional Government the famous "line" had curled up at the ends. But a long arc of it from Carrick-on-Suir to Clonmel, Cashel and Tipperary still held. When Prout was ready his army could be expected to roll up the line still further, through Carrick-on-Suir and on to Clonmel. The Republicans faced the further threat that troops from Thurles would strike south in an attempt to cut the line between Tipperary and Cashel. Had Thurles been taken by the Republicans, as they had hoped, this danger would have been appreciably less. They decided to move troops into Golden, where it was thought the National troops might build up their forces for an attack, either on Cashel to the east or Tipperary to the west.

Anticipating the move, Commandant Jerry Ryan sent a section of twenty men from Thurles on the evening of Wednesday, July 26th. They were joined by another section from Templemore which included Dublin Guards. One section observed three men laying a mine on Golden Bridge and opened fire. The Republicans fled and were followed by their garrison, about sixteen men, from the barracks nearby. The two sections then occupied a mansion just outside Golden and a public house at the top of the village on the road coming in from New Inn. Four hundred troops under Commandant Ryan, with Captain Connell as second-in-command, entrained on the evening of Friday, July 28th. They travelled only as far as Goold's Cross and advanced towards Golden, about seven miles to the south. A Republican force, quartered at Goold's Cross and waiting to attack Golden, were themselves forced to fall back on the village, spoiling a plan for a simultaneous attack from three directions. They had with them an armoured Lancia.

In the early hours of Saturday morning the armoured car drove past one of the National Army posts and on towards the centre of the village.

"We had a Lewis gun at the outpost," recalls James Dwyer, "and immediately they had gone past, the gunner, a chap named Sergeant-Major Lennon, took the gun into the street and opened up on the armoured car. They backed the car to turn but went into the wall of a broken-down house, their engine stalled and they couldn't move it.

"Five or six men in it got out through the back and they took their Hotchkiss gun with them. At this stage, we were coming down from the mansion we were using as a barracks and they dropped their gun and made for the fields. Meanwhile, another column was coming in, part of it along the main road from Cashel. They were about a mile out of Golden. Among the fellows in our outpost was one Paddy Ryan, known locally as Paddy Ryan Masters because of the abundance of Ryans in Tipperary. With some of the others he proceeded out along the road to look for the men from the armoured car. He got separated from the others and about a mile outside the village he found that he was quite alone. He saw a bunch of fellows down a boreen, realised they were Irregulars and waited for them to come up. They mistook him for one of their own. Ryan Masters pulled his gun on them, and marched them, all twenty of them, into the village as prisoners."

When the main column of Republicans reached Golden they were attacked by Ryan's men and retreated towards Cahir, fighting a rearguard action which lasted for two hours. Tom Kennedy of Rathgormuck and Quirke of Hollyford were killed and several men were wounded. Altogether, twenty-six prisoners were taken and escorted into Thurles.

Jerry Ryan next turned his attention to Tipperary, and by 5 p.m. on the Saturday afternoon his troops were attacking. There was little fighting, though firing went on through the night and there was loss of life on both sides. Roads had been trenched and mines laid, which made progress slow. One Republican ran towards a house, to which went the leads from several mines, and was shot down. In the morn-
396

ing the Republicans began to withdraw from the town, setting Cleeves' condensed milk factory ablaze as they went. There seemed little sense to this kind of scorched earth policy but Cleeves' was held by 400 workers who had set themselves up as a soviet and had been not a little troublesome.

As if the Irish problem was not complicated enough, in Tipperary and some other counties groups of workers had seized creameries and run up the red flag. Some co-operative creameries were burned and an attempt was made to compel farmers to deal with the Red creameries. It is doubtful whether there was any direct Russian influence behind the trend; Russia did make some attempt to implant her communist philosophy in Ireland but was singularly unsuccessful. The seizure of the creameries stemmed from avarice rather than politics.

The burning of Cleeves' had the desirable result of causing the collapse of the soviet and so enabling anti-soviet farmers to resume supplying their milk to the co-operative creameries.

By midday Sunday, Tipperary was in Provisional Government hands. Only twelve prisoners had been taken, for most of the Republicans had got clear of the town and were making for Bansha en route to Cahir and Clonmel. Three lost their lives when a mine they were laying to delay pursuit blew up.

The garrisons withdrawn from Tipperary and Waterford provided the Republicans with strong reinforcements for the region in between—rugged country from which it would be difficult to prise them. During the respite given them by Prout after Waterford they made preparations to defend Carrick-on-Suir, which lies roughly half way between Waterford and Clonmel. Two bridges, one dating from the fourteenth century, were largely destroyed and, as usual, roads were mined and railways torn up. De Valera, who had been wandering in the south like a plaintive itinerant troubadour, arrived in the town and set up a temporary headquarters. Provisional Government propaganda still painted him as a dangerous military adversary, just as it cast Childers in the rôle of a demon king devilishly blowing up bridges and tearing up railway lines with his bare hands. But de Valera was preoccupied with keeping his political movement alive, appreciating that when the strife was done the people would

397

look for their government, not to military men, however distinguished and however ruthless, but to civilian leaders. His humble rank of private was, in a way, the stamp of his civilian authority.

Childers, too, visited Carrick, not to blow up bridges but in his rôle of Republican Director of Propaganda, and Constance Markievicz also bustled in. Carrick seemed likely to become a Republican redoubt protecting Clonmel and threatening Waterford and Kilkenny. The townspeople sourly saw the arrival of Lacey, Robinson and Breen. Lack of communications disrupted their lives and threatened their businesses; cars and stores were commandeered and food was running short. Receipts for goods taken for the Republican commissariat were given in most cases and Lacey, always a steely disciplinarian, took stern action when he discovered instances of the unofficial appropriation of goods. The goodwill of the people was vital to the Republican cause and it was difficult enough to prevent its slipping away. Even receipts were precarious compensation for actual loss.

Lacey established his headquarters in the workhouse, from which eighty inmates were removed to Clonmel. He had at his disposal perhaps 500 men drawn from Waterford, Cork and Tipperary, including the column led by Sheehan which Carty had escorted from Enniscorthy to Blessington, only to find that they were not wanted. Men from Templemore, persuaded by Dr Harty to refrain from battle there, also had joined Lacey at Carrick-on-Suir. Lacey deployed his men in an arc a couple of miles from the town to block attacks either from Kilkenny to the north or Waterford to the southeast. Five miles or so further out was an outer ring of defensive positions in difficult country. To deal with these, Provisional Government columns under Commandant Liam McCarthy and Tommy Ryan began to make sweeps from Callan and Kilkenny.

At Ninemilehouse, Dan Breen held a seemingly impregnable position in a group of buildings surrounded by earthen fences and ditches. His men, from Cork, Kerry and Tipperary, were reliable. Many of the Provisional Government troops, on the other hand, were youngsters who had never been under fire. Ryan, with 150 men, had been assigned the right flank. He had among his troops a young farmer's son from the area who knew the mountains as well as he knew his father's farm.

"A second column under Joe Byrne was to attack on the left flank and Liam McCarthy with 200 men was to make a frontal attack, but neither came into the picture," Ryan explains. "McCarthy delayed removing mines from the roads and Byrne got lost in the mountains at Windgap. We went from Kilkenny to Mullinahone, where we waited till nightfall before we headed into the mountains. I marched through most of the night and got my men in position, fifty yards from Breen's post, at about four in the morning. I would never have succeeded without the young farmer fellow. My trouble then was to extend men along 200 yards when they had little idea of what was wanted. I had hardly got them deployed when a machine-gun opened up. My chaps started belting off and I saw all the ammunition being gone in a couple of hours and the column captured and disgraced on top of that." Ryan had to walk out in the open under machine-gun fire, chivvying his men and showing them that it was possible to remain alive in spite of the bullets whirring about. Some of his men "were sticking their heads in bushes and praying for their lives." He steadied them and cautioned them to make sure what they were firing at.

"Anyway, we got to scrapping," Ryan goes on, "guns going on both sides in spells with a lull in between. I'd got such a good position on the bank that although they were firing at us from 5 a.m. to 3 p.m., no one was injured."

Ryan himself was luckier than he knew. "I could have shot you forty times or more when you were out in the open," Dan Breen told him some years later. Perhaps his generosity towards an old comrade cost him the post, though it was not overwhelmed; Breen simply decided that there was no purpose in staying to be captured and he and his men faded away.

Between them, McCarthy, Ryan and Byrne broke up the Republican outer ring from Mullinahone, through Ninemile-house and Windgap, to Kilmaganny. Ryan's instructions were to join Prout's main body on the road from Waterford into Carrick but he was not needed. On July 31st an advance party from Mullinavat made their way across rough ground and made contact with Republicans in a woodland near the river, east of Carrick. There they were held until joined the next day by the main force. Exchange of rifle and machine-gun fire made little impression on either side and it was not until Prout's faithful 18-pounder was brought into action the following day, August 2nd, that the Republicans retreated from swathing shrapnel. They counter-attacked fiercely across the river at one point, but once that assault was blunted, the fight was all but done. Carrick was abandoned and, in the usual way, the R.I.C. barracks and the courthouse were burned. The Executive Forces fell back on Clonmel.

Again, Prout did not follow up the attack immediately. "We spent several monotonous days in Carrick, just kicking our heels," Ryan remembers. A few snipers took potshots in the streets, otherwise the days were peaceful. Becoming impatient, he suggested to Prout that he should try to take Clonmel with his own column. Prout elected to do the job himself. Avoiding the direct route, which was strongly defended, on August 8th he swept his 1200 men in a northerly arc. Two companies formed an advance guard and the main body followed. Prout was not expecting Clonmel to fall easily, for Robinson and Lacey had had plenty of time to prepare strongpoints both inside and outside the town. They were not the men to let shamrocks grow under their feet.

At Kilcash a couple of shells from Prout's 18-pounder were fired into the castle in case it was occupied, then a party under Lieutenant Moran reconnoitred some fields. A few shots were loosed. Signals were exchanged with an unidentified group about four hundred yards away in another field, but neither side gave anything away. Captain Ned Reilly, who was dressed in civilian clothes, climbed the fence and moved out into the centre of the field, where he was met by his opposite number from the group of Republicans—as they turned out to be. The two men chatted for a moment or two then returned to their own sides. When each man had safely climbed the fence on his side of the field, firing began. But it soon died away as the Republicans moved out of range through the cornfield.

As the Provisional Government troops advanced along the picturesque Slievenamon Valley, opposition was more tenacious.

"Prout came along a hollow of a road with his advance guard and his main force," says Colonel Ryan, "and machine-guns opened fire from the hillside on the advance guard. It caused quite a commotion, and the main body came to a halt. While they just went on waiting Frank Thornton, who was down from Dublin with us, saw the danger that three or four machine-guns could cut them to pieces. The firing was spasmodic and he had an idea that they might bring more machine-guns round on the other side to set up a cross-fire. He sent someone back for me because I knew the country so well. When I came up with my company he told me he didn't like the delay and ordered me to go and see what was happening. A Captain Foster, who had been trained in the British Army, was in charge of one of the advance guard companies, and I found him with his watch, a compass and a map all laid out. He was sending back dispatches every few minutes advising that he had moved six yards this way or six yards that way."

Ryan told Foster to tear up his dispatches and he would see what he could do to eliminate the machine-gun emplacement. Taking a few men, he worked his way round the hillside and within an hour located the gun. There was only one, not the several which Thornton had feared. The Republicans took their gun and moved elsewhere.

Fighting a delaying action, though firing few shots, the Republicans made the most of well-concealed strongpoints and Prout made slow progress. Towards nightfall, he brought up his one big gun and propelled a few shells into woods where his elusive adversaries had taken cover. Then both sides settled down for the night, Prout's forces at Ballyglasheen House and Stoke's Farm, the Republicans moving closer to Clonmel.

Next day, the advance continued on a fairly broad front. Ryan had 130 men spread over half a mile, with scouts ahead. They moved cautiously but swiftly, crossing each field as the scouts signalled all clear. On his left, Dominic Mackey also had extended his men at fifteen-yard intervals. As they approached the railway line at Redmondstown, they came under heavy fire from a Kerry column established in a hillside position. One man, Corporal Kelly, who had gone over a fence ahead of his companions, was killed and Tommy Doyle

401

had a narrow escape when he went out to bring Kelly back. This engagement lasted about thirty minutes, then there was no more firing.

"When we came to the railway line," says Colonel Ryan, "I halted because I expected there would be a fight between here and the town. I got my section commanders up and gave them instructions, but we got the whole company across the railway and out on to the main road without a shot being fired. After that, it was a gallop into Clonmel."

The main body of Republicans had, in fact, abandoned the town and burned the barracks. One column had been left as a rearguard and, augmented by forces pushed back into the town, made the National troops unwelcome. But their object was only to allow their men time to get clear. Their armoured car, which had harried the invading columns, came to grief in the Waterford Road. Prout's men appeared suddenly from a side road in front of them and the crew, trying to turn too quickly, slewed the car and overturned it. The crew escaped with their lives, and their liberty too, for they took to their heels and, satisfied with their capture of the vehicle, Prout's men did not pursue them. The last shots were fired in Clonmel by Jim Nugent at the Gashouse Bridge, where his machine-gun ensured that the last of the Republicans got safely out of the town.

The Limerick-Waterford line, always something of a joke, had crumbled, but the Republicans' redoubt in the south, protected by roads and railways made impassable, still seemed formidable.

The National Army, which had seemed to be carrying all before it, had found itself engaged in a slugging match in the Kilmallock-Bruree-Bruff triangle into which area the Limerick Republicans had retreated. O'Duffy and Murphy had worked hard on their plans and Murphy, whose mind was still conditioned by his experience of trench warfare, issued elaborate orders for an attack on the ancient town of Kilmallock, now the main Republican stronghold in the area of south Limerick and west Tipperary. "We had never seen the like of them," says Jack Byrne, who still looks astonished as he recalls them.

For once there was a fairly well defined front line each side having a string of outposts at crossroads, or upon commanding hillocks, or in the villages and towns. A "no-man's

402

land", varying in width from a few hundred yards to a mile, separated the two sides and Murphy, to general contempt, actually gave orders to dig trenches.

Fighting began on Sunday, July 23rd, when National Army troops, trying to turn the Republican withdrawal from Limerick into a rout where checked at Kilmallock, to which they had driven, through heavy rain, over roads made treacherous by mud and slime. A Republican armoured car from Cork took one National Army group by surprise and captured men and arms.

Frank O'Connor tells in *An Only Child* how he and two companions were captured by Provisional Government troops on that Sunday while carrying dispatches from Liam Deasy, the Republican divisional O.C., whose headquarters were in Buttevant, to Kilmallock. Escorted as a prisoner to a nearby farmhouse where the National Army had set up a temporary post, O'Connor was soon dodging Republican bullets as his own friends besieged the farmhouse. His captors had been ready to leave on lorries when the Republicans appeared and had dashed back into the farmhouse, leaving the engines running.

One of the defenders, Sergeant O'Mahoney, was killed, and the National Army commander, a man named O'Brien, was wounded in the mouth. The garrison wanted to surrender but their signal went unobserved, so O'Connor obtained permission to run to his friends waving a white handkerchief. An officer of the National Army opened the door for him and closed it after him. Surrender was accepted and O'Connor was put in charge of the prisoners who were taken back to Buttevant. Later, the wounded leader O'Brien changed sides, a not uncommon action in times when men were sure of what they were fighting for but uncertain as to the method of its achievement.

On the same Sunday, Republicans captured Bruff in a counter attack, and two days later they ambushed National Army troops of the Dublin Guards under Commandant Tom Flood who had taken command of field operations in the area. Flood's troops were caught in a narrow, hollowed out road with thick hedges pressing up to it, but received some warning from an outrider. Bullets ripped through the hedges as hidden men probed for hidden men. Finally the National

Army men withdrew with the loss of three killed and another man fatally wounded.

Throughout the week the battle endured, with Republicans getting the better of it though Bruff was recaptured by the National Forces, then on Sunday, July 30th, the National Army attacked Bruree in strength. Containing Republican forces with a series of diversionary attacks, they approached from two directions. Murphy, with the artillery which had turned the scale in Limerick, came in from Bruff to the north-east, while Flood aimed a sharp blow from the south-east. After some hours of stout resistance the Republicans were compelled to withdraw, but they were unwilling to leave Kilmallock exposed, as it was now, to attack from Bruff and Bruree, the one five miles to the north, the other about four miles to the north-west. Kilmallock, meeting point of half a dozen roads and within sabotage distance of the Dublin-Cork railway, was too valuable to lose.

Three days after quitting Bruree they were back, with two improvised armoured cars. Surrounding the town, they concentrated their fire on Flood's headquarters. Craftily Flood had moved to another building and his attackers, who had already overrun one of his posts, a school-house, and taken nine prisoners, were caught in a cross-fire. Nevertheless, he was hard pressed until reinforcements under Hogan came from Limerick with a Whippet armoured car, *The Custom House*, which chased its homemade counterparts to within a mile of Kilmallock.

Earlier in the day, Republican forces had struck further north and taken Patrickswell, less than ten miles from Limerick, on the road leading to Newcastle and on in to Kerry. The Republicans were anxious to screen Kerry and to block the southward penetration of O'Duffy's forces to Cork. In this they were succeeding and O'Duffy admitted, "The best fighting material the Irregulars can muster is ranged against us." The National Army included large numbers of untried troops but they were bolstered by men of the Dublin Guards, an élite unit compounded of those men of the Dublin Brigade who had followed Collins. The policy of sending small groups of Dublin Guards to stiffen the fighting qualities of their troops in various parts of the country was to pay off handsomely for the Provisional Government.

On August 3rd, after a mere twenty-four hours in occupation, the Republicans withdrew from Patrickswell and next day National Army columns under Brigadier Keane and Colonel-Commandant Tom Keogh converged on Adare. Several artillery shells were fired at the Republican headquarters, the Dunraven Arms Hotel, and it was abandoned. Michael Hartney, one of the Republican leaders, was badly wounded.

Other National Army forces went for Kilmallock and Kilmallock Hill, dominating the town, was taken. But already the Republicans were filtering away quietly, leaving a tenacious rearguard to mislead the National commanders into expecting grim resistance in Kilmallock. Murphy paused to martial his forces before crashing into Kilmallock on Saturday, August 5th. Some prisoners were taken but most of the Republicans were well on their way south-east to Charleville, before Flood's column could position itself to cut them off.

The experience and dash of the Dublin Guards had contributed much to ultimate success in the long wearing-down process round Kilmallock, but the main reason for the Republicans allowing their front door to give so easily was the news that intruders had burst in the back.

The Kerry Republicans had stormed into Tipperary and elsewhere to help stave off the contenders for the Free State, confident that, if needs be, they could fall back into their stronghold of Kerry and Cork. But they may have been a little complacent about the strength of the Republican grip on this area. On Friday, June 30th, the day of the surrender of the Four Courts, there had been fighting in Listowel. This ended with the surrender of the main National Army post, which happened to be the workhouse, and the signing of an agreement by Commandant T. J. Kennelly and the Republican Brigadier Humphrey Murphy. They saw that "Ireland's interest cannot be served by civil war", and their solution was: "As patriotic Irishmen we have decided to unite in face of the common enemy." Murphy could safely assume that he had little to fear from the National Army in north Kerry. On July 5th he asserted his dominance by proclaiming that no cars, motor bikes or lorries in his Brigade area were to be used without a permit from the Republican police. Petrol was to be controlled; garages could sell only when the necessary permit was produced.

Shortly afterwards, Murphy attended a peace meeting at Tralee called by Kerry Farmers' Union at which he claimed "I have done more to bring about peace than anyone else," and that he was "instrumental in bringing about the pact." He was alluding to the part which, after the tussles with McEoin in which Collins had intervened, he had played in the negotiations leading to the Collins-de Valera Pact, the lapse of which was still a sore point with Republicans, as was also the postponement of the opening of the new Dail. Murphy explained to the meeting that Collins had been convinced that differences of opinion between Republicans in the south and those in the Four Courts would ensure that the Civil War did not develop. But, said Murphy, "We will defend every town to the last, and then you know what the result will be. You will have towns in ruins and Ireland in ruins, and famine finishing what has escaped the bullets. The Provisional Government started this fight without any authority from an Irish Government. We are fighting on the defensive, and we will stop at nothing in that defensive fight, and we are going to win even if it takes years to win."

Many of Murphy's listeners left the meeting protesting that this was no way to peace but the claustral fervour of the believers in death before dishonour carried them beyond even acknowledgement of protest, whether logical or not. Sooner or later, the Republican ideal would burst through the envelope of acquiescence and ignorance that stultified it and all Irishmen would acclaim the justice of the fight. That was their faith.

So many in the south adhered to this blind faith that the Provisional Government leaders, already dashed by the stubborn resistance of Kilmallock, were daunted by the prospect of a war of attrition through the fastnesses of Cork and Kerry, of grim battles for the towns and the perilous rooting out of guerrilla bands from their familiar mountains.

General Emmet Dalton suggested that instead of the laborious campaign through the countryside, a series of attacks be launched from the sea. Thankfully, the National Army staff fell upon the idea. Dalton was put in charge of sea-borne operations and told to go ahead.

On August 2nd, three days before Kilmallock was cleared, Dublin Guards under the command of General Patrick Daly landed at Fenit on the north side of Tralee Bay. Claimed by some to have been the birthplace of St Brendan, Fenit, with its good harbour and beaches, was a convenient set-down point. Under tough leaders, Daly himself, and Commandants McGuinness and Dempsey, the National troops took Tralee with verve and panache, conduced to by the sporadic but spirited resistance they encountered. From the surprise landing on the Kerry coast the National Army derived the dual advantage of meeting little opposition, because of the absence of large numbers of the Kerry fighting men in Kilmallock, and of shortening the struggle of Kilmallock as the Kerry men there turned, too late, for home. Humphrey Murphy, commanding Kerry No. 1 Brigade, did manage with a few companions to reach Tralee ahead of the invaders and to burn the barracks.

On the day of the Fenit landing, General Brennan was asked by Collins to second Michael Hogan and two or three hundred men from his forces in Clare to help in Kerry. In Limerick MacManus arranged for three small vessels to collect the group at Kilrush at 3 a.m. on August 3rd and to ferry them across the Shannon estuary to Tarbert on the north coast of Kerry. Hogan and 140 men sailed on the *Corona* and the remaining 100 men of his force were carried by the smaller boats. Hogan moved quickly to secure first Ballylongford, then Listowel.

As Hogan pushed southward again, Daly's main force moved to the east and south-east towards Castleisland and Farranfore. The two towns fell to their combined attack. Meanwhile, yet another National Army force, under Brigadier James Slattery, was driving into the heart of Kerry. With armoured cars and artillery this group started from Adare, quickly overran Rathkeale, was held for a time at Newcastle and finally completed the link-up. The fertile, undulating lands of north Kerry were relatively easy country through which to campaign once the initial breaks had come, but the craggy terrain of south Kerry was altogether different. Here, too, assault from the sea was to provide the answer.

In an effort to regain the initiative for the Republicans and to restore fading morale, Ernie O'Malley conceived a plan to isolate Dublin by destroying roads, bridges and

407

railway lines around the city. O'Malley was officer commanding the Republican Northern and Eastern Command, one of the commands instituted by Liam Lynch—the others were the Western under Michael Kilroy and the Southern under Liam Deasy. Cork Republicans were sent to Liverpool then crossed back to Dublin for the coup.

On 5th August groups of Republicans moved to their places but, unfortunately for them, plans for the whole operation had been captured and the National Army was ready. About two hundred prisoners were taken. Some of these were among those released by Aiken in Dundalk a few days later. There was little fear now of any major operation taking place in the capital but the hard beating heart of Republican intransigence lay in Cork, and in Dublin General Dalton was preparing an attempt to penetrate to it.

NINETEEN

Searchlights blazed through the night and isolated the *Arvonia* on the dark breadth of the sea. Staccato British naval voices challenged her with an assurance bred of the Navy tradition of gunboat diplomacy. On the deck of the *Arvonia* General Emmet Dalton stood with the captain.

"I authorised him to signal who I was and my purpose, and to request at all cost no interference," recalls Dalton, whose purpose was, in fact, to sail up the Lee into the heart of Cork and to capture the city. From there he would seek to gain control of the whole region.

The plan, worked out by Collins, Mulcahy and Dalton, had been put to General Staff only twelve hours before the *Arvonia* and the *Lady Wicklow*, Irish Sea packets, were commandeered by the Provisional Government on Monday, August 7th. Collins had been receiving reports from his sister, Mrs Powell, for some time and knew that he could count on a force of between 300 and 500 men in Cork city who, for lack of arms, were lying low. In spite of virtual military occupation by the Executive Forces, a civil administration had been established and, although there were many Republican sympathisers among the people, the majority were
408

ready to accept the Treaty, if only for the chance it gave them to rebuild their cruelly violated city. In the June election they had rejected the anti-Treaty candidate.

Civil and military leaderships stubbornly contended for power. The Executive Forces set up their own Inland Revenue office but when they made demands on the local taxpayers outraged fingers snapped purses and pockets firmly shut. Instead, Customs and Excise monies were confiscated. Goods and, as usual, cars were seized but no one had much faith in the requisition orders which were given in exchange. Unemployment was growing. The *Cork Examiner* was censored. Nowhere was there more horror of the Civil War than in Cork and many of the peace moves in the next months originated from that city. Father Duggan, especially, was a tireless intermediary. A People's Rights Association was formed and promoted an indirect exchange of views between Lynch and Collins. Both were intransigent. Lynch simply said that "when the Provisional Government cease their attack on us, defensive action on our part can cease." He saw no difficulty as to the allegiance of the Army "to any elected assembly—provided that it was a government of the Republic". Collins asserted in reply that when the Irregulars saw fit "to obey the wishes of the people, expressed through their elected representatives", there would be no need to prolong the war. He pointed out that prisoners held by the Provisional Government were refusing to sign a form promising not to use arms against the elected Parliament or the Government responsible to it and not to interfere with other persons or their property. If Liam Lynch were animated by the same spirit there was little point in trying to talk terms.

Confident of support in Cork, Collins determined to take the city. Dalton thought an attack by land was impracticable. Roads, railways and bridges had been torn up or blown up so that the transport problem was almost insuperable, while to the north of Cork, Republican troops, falling back after the long tussle round Kilmallock, were a danger. A surprise attack from the sea was the answer. Dalton was given command of the operation and was, in fact, in overall charge of combined operations in the south.

From the outset, the captain of the *Arvonia* had told Dalton his plan was impossible and neither he nor his crew,

409

mostly Welshmen, were in the least anxious to become involved in the Irish quarrel. Advised by the British Navy that he would need a deep-sea pilot to proceed into the outer harbour, Dalton sent for him. After a time, the man came aboard. The 456 officers and men under Dalton's command were concealed below decks and, says Dalton, "the only give-away was my uniform." The pilot was puzzled until Dalton told him exactly what he intended to do. He told the National Army leader that he was mad, that he needed a river pilot and that none was available, that the Executive Forces had sunk a vessel to block the channel and that any still-accessible berths were mined. Dalton came to the conclusion that the pilot was involved with the Republicans; he knew too much for a disinterested pilot.

"There always comes a time when a commander must take an all out risk, and I felt that for me this was it." So he drew his revolver and ordered the pilot to take the ship as far up the river as he safely could. "I don't believe you've been a pilot here for years and don't know the river." If he refused, he would be shot, Dalton told him.

"If I make a mistake it's your fault," said the pilot after a pause.

"So be it," snapped Dalton.

The pilot steered them to a landing stage at Passage West, the only safe landing on the river, Dalton learned later. Because of the blocking of the river and the necessity to land further out, Dalton had to revise his plans. Speed was essential, and he decided to advance at daybreak in "spread out screens of troops towards Douglas and Cork City". He was expecting hard opposition and was very conscious of the fact that 200 of his forces were novices—some had had to be taught how to load their guns during the voyage from Dublin. On the other hand he had some very experienced officers, among them Tom Ennis, Liam Tobin, Ben Byrne, Tom Kilcoyne and Frank O'Friel. There was also Peadar Conlon.

Collins had asked Sean McEoin to send him 300 troops and nine officers, or, for preference, 100 men and Conlon. A native of the Ballinalee district from which McEoin himself hailed, Conlon had served in the British Army during the 1914/18 war and became secretary of the local branch of the

British Legion in Longford. When he joined the Volunteers at the end of 1919, Conlon was given testing assignments by McEoin, who always took time before deciding whether or not to trust a man. Nothing seemed impossible to him. Suspected by the British, he was badly beaten up, and as a result even more determined with a machine-gun. After the Clonfin ambush he had become McEoin's regular machine-gunner. He was one of the toughest and bravest fighters produced by the I.R.A., a hard and bitter man to some, but to his friends a great character whose many malapropisms are still recalled with infinite delight. He liked using words that were new to him and on one occasion, having drilled a squad of officers to his liking, he announced with a flourish, "Now gentlemen, we'll syncopate our watches."

As the *Arvonia* neared the landing, Dalton sent a reconnaissance party ashore. Twenty men climbed into a boat. O'Friel, who had been orderly officer for the voyage because of his war-time experience at sea, led the party, but the more senior Liam Tobin accompanied them in his capacity of Intelligence Officer.

It was two o'clock in the morning on Tuesday, August 8th when the boat was tied up and O'Friel and his men jumped ashore, each step an act of faith in the unrelenting darkness. Almost at once they came up against a wall and there seemed no way to the street. O'Friel used the butt of his rifle to smash a back window of a house fronting Dock Terrace.

"A poor old man came downstairs in his nightshirt," O'Friel remembers. "He was terrified and didn't know what was happening at all."

The house was on a corner and jutted out a little beyond the neighbouring building so that, with eyes becoming accustomed to the darkness, O'Friel could see the mill, believed to be occupied by Republicans, down the road and he led his men from the old man's house.

The men in the mill must have heard the landing. None remained when O'Friel entered but there was evidence of a hurried evacuation. The telephone rang and Liam Tobin picked up the receiver. Blandly he assured the inquirer at the other end that all was well at the mill. Quickly O'Friel divided his men into patrols and they made a round of the village.

411

Furtive shadows, sounds not quite suppressed, betrayed Republicans seeking shelter and a few prisoners were taken. O'Friel led the way to the boat and the party returned to the ship.

At daylight an armoured car and an 18-pounder gun were put ashore from the *Lady Wicklow* and Dalton sent 150 men in three parties, under Kilcoyne, Conlon and Tom Ennis, to form a protection screen half a mile inland. Then the rest of the force landed.

The Republicans, alerted now, at about seven o'clock blew up the road bridge into Rochestown, startling people from their beds for miles around. They also took possession of the railway station.

As soon as the Executive Forces received reports of National Army troops advancing towards Rochestown, they took up commanding positions on the hills overlooking the road. Local units had been reinforced by men from as far as Limerick and Kerry who had been sent by special trains to Cork and directed from there to Rochestown. One small party hastening into position suddenly encountered a National Army patrol. Both sides recovered quickly from their surprise and opened fire at close range. One man from each side was killed and there were several wounded. Peadar Conlon had the tops of three fingers blown off but this did not concern him very much and they were not properly dressed until two days later. That evening, the National Army took twenty prisoners. They also took Rochestown, driving the Republicans into Old Court Wood. One man, badly wounded in the surprise encounter, was left at the Mills. He was attended there later by Dr Jim Lynch.

The doctor and his family had had a trying day. They had learned of the landing at about ten that morning and, shortly afterwards, heard two loud explosions which were probably shells from the 18-pounder. Dr Lynch tried to persuade his wife and two daughters to go to his mother's home in Cork but they would not go without him. That he would be needed he knew. Indeed, for some time past he had been storing bandages and surgical equipment for just such an occasion. Now the girls helped him set up a dressing station. Bandages, lint, cotton-wool, antiseptics and splints were got ready; surgical needles were threaded, hypodermics charged with

412

morphia. In the kitchen Mrs Lynch set to work to bake food enough for half an army. Gunfire sounded ever closer as they worked and, early in the afternoon, the house trembled as the railway bridge was blown.

Dr Lynch went outside and helped his neighbour to round up his cattle. He could see a line of men climbing the hill on the opposite side of the glen; they appeared to be under fire from a wood lower down on his side. Once a stray bullet flicked past his head. Soon after he got home he was called to Douglas where, he was told, a Republican soldier urgently needed his attention. Fastening a Red Cross band on his arm, he set off on his bicycle. Again and again he was stopped by a shout of "Hands up", but each time cheery voices bade him go his way and wished him luck. The condition of the patient had been exaggerated and both he and the doctor were soon on their way home.

Sitting down to a late lunch, Dr Lynch was soon called out again, this time to a Republican soldier sheltering in a cottage near the Monastery. He was suffering from shock, though his own diagnosis was that he had run so hard from Passage that his heart was in his throat and he wanted it back in its rightful place. On the way home again, Dr Lynch watched the two sides taking up positions on either side of the glen and the tragedy of so many fine young men preparing to slaughter their fellow countrymen on their native soil ineffably saddened him.

Once more, Mrs Lynch patiently put her husband's meal in front of him. Volleys of shots sounded from the Old Court Wood and resounded along the hillsides. A man in Dr Lynch's employ rushed in, followed by his wife and family, and the doctor settled them in safety in a dark passage outside the coal cellar. Two little girls arrived and told him that a Republican soldier was bleeding to death in Rochestown Mills. Nonchalantly they had come through the hazardous wood. When Dr Lynch agreed to see the man, they went as imperturbably as they had come.

Mrs Lynch and her two daughters saw him off though stray bullets burred past them. In the nearby field were Republican soldiers. The doctor told them where he was going and asked for a hand over the wall. A big man whisked him across but demanded his promise not to betray their presence to the

413

approaching Free Staters. After some parley, his assurance that he was not interested in politics but only in helping the wounded was accepted. In return, he asked them not to frighten his family more than they could help. At once the order was given that no one was to go near his house and, though National troops were in the house later and for an hour there was firing all around it, the Republicans kept their word.

It was growing dark as Dr Lynch, carrying a heavy midwifery bag of equipment, floundered across fields to the road. Warily he climbed two barricades across the road, expecting each moment to feel the impact of a bullet in his back.

"Come along, Doctor. We'll show you the way." The two little emissaries had waited for him. They led him to his patient whom he found lying in a pool of blood from wounds under his right collar-bone and through his left arm. This was the man wounded in the encounter with Conlon's patrol. The young soldier was surrounded by women who were wailing and helpless. Dr Lynch dressed his wounds and arranged for him to be taken to hospital.

When he reached the first road barricade on his return journey he almost leaped into the arms of two priests from the Monastery who were on their way to see the patient he had just left. They were as startled as he. Passing Old Court Wood, he heard intense firing still going on, but he doubted its effectiveness in the darkness. Crossing a cornfield he was in fear lest the silhouette of his head attract a sniper's bullet, then, near his own home, he encountered a Republican soldier who had lost touch with his company and was hungry and fatigued almost to dropping. The kindly doctor took him in, fed him and sent him on his way again. The Lynch family went to bed at last with the dissonant chords of rifle music and the percussive clump of the big guns still sounding distantly.

Both sides snatched a brief respite for sleep but, shortly after daybreak, the guns began again. Following Dalton's plan Conlon and O'Friel, who had slept at Ford's public house, parted here and led their companions in different directions. Kilcoyne went in yet another direction. They were to meet again in Douglas. Fire was intense in Old Court Wood; there were shots in Rochestown and near Ballyorban

House to the south. Lorry-loads of Republicans drove up Maryborough Hill during the morning while the National Army troops advanced steadily on a four-mile front searching every house and bush. What worried Dr Lynch, who was watching, was that both sides were only about a quarter of a mile apart and his home was right in the middle.

Returning from a call into Douglas, he found his family and that of his man huddled underground. Firing all around the house was a continuing staccato. Once the doctor found a fire in his bookcase; a bullet had set alight a roll of cotton-wool he had left there. The firing came so close that the doctor, telling his wife they would have no milk for their tea, went out and herded his cows into their byre for safety. There seemed to be a battle going on in McCarthy's field across the lane. He had no sooner got back when he heard a hammering at the door. When he opened it Peadar Conlon burst in, while about twenty-five of his men searched the stables and outhouses. Conlon interrogated the doctor, and when he saw the preparation in Dr Lynch's study decided that this was a Republican hospital and arrested him. Outside, his men, now hidden in the doctor's shrubberies, kept up a constant exchange of fire with Republicans on a hill opposite. Conlon took the doctor upstairs while he decided at which window to place a machine-gun and when they got down-stairs again, they found Mrs Lynch and the two small girls watching the fighting from a window. Already they had seen one man shot dead on the path about twenty yards away. Dr Lynch, valuing those three precious, vulnerable heads, promptly sent his family back to the underground shelter. Conlon rushed outside to give orders to his men and Dr Lynch went upstairs to watch the fighting in and around the turnip field opposite. Other National soldiers he could see moving as if to surround Belmonte Hill. O'Friel had come up from Rochestown by way of the Monastery and had decided to search the turnip field.

"We got into the middle of it, and, by God, did we catch it. A machine-gun opened up from somewhere. I shouted to the men to get down and I dropped flat myself. A moment later a turnip near my head was split open and another bullet put a hole in my cap. There was not much we could do so I told the men to stay put and made for the ditch. I was lucky.

I got to the ditch then worked my way round to the back of the field where we had a machine-gun post. I asked the lads did they know where the firing was coming from. They pointed to a cottage on the left. I watched for a moment or two then, sure enough, I saw a burst come from one of the windows."

O'Friel took over the machine-gun and opened fire. His first burst hit the roof of the cottage but at a second attempt he hit the window. Satisfied with his aim, he shouted to the men still in the field to retreat when he began firing again. The Republicans in the cottage withdrew hastily from the window as O'Friel resumed firing and the men in the field were able to return without casualty. O'Friel and his men then repaired to a house which he learned later was that of Dr Lynch, who opened the door himself to O'Friel's none-too-gentle knocking. Lynch has described his visitor as "so plastered with mud and blood from the top of his head to his feet that his features were quite indiscernible." The doctor took him to the bathroom and left him to detach some of the mud from himself while he went for refreshments for him. O'Friel gratefully drank a glass of malt.

Mrs Lynch was making tea for O'Friel and his weary men when Conlon raced back to the house.

"Come on, Frank! We've got to take this hill. They're strong up there. I've just lost six men." Turning to Lynch, he said, "You'd better come too, Doc, and bring your bag." The two officers took twelve men with them and Dr Lynch saved them time by leading them across his fields to the road. He also secured the release of three of his neighbours who had been arrested by National troops but had, in fact, taken no part in the fighting. Entrenched in Cronin's cottage, with machine-gun posts commanding the road from high banks, the Republicans made their last stand. There were 200 of them altogether, with nine machine-guns. So intense was their fire that the bullets cut a grey line across the road, but the National Army men, keeping close to the banks and urged on by Conlon and O'Friel, both of whom took enormous risks, did not falter. Dr Lynch took shelter for a few minutes in a drain by a wall, yet bullets still cracked stones near his head and brought down showers of berries. Then the soldiers advanced again and he went with them. He attended a Re-

publican the muscles of whose back had been ripped to
ribbons. The man, Donoghue, told him grimly that when he
was wounded he had been about to open fire on the doctor with
a Lewis gun. Having dispersed the outlying posts, Conlon and
O'Friel attacked the cottage itself. The two officers, whom
Dr Lynch regarded as the bravest men he had met, called on
the beleaguered garrison of Cronin's cottage to surrender and
themselves rushed the door. A shotgun applied to the door-
latch socket was fired from inside and shot hit Conlon in the
face at a distance of two yards. Luckily for him, most of the
discharge was absorbed by the door.

Then bombs were thrown into the cottage and machine-
guns riddled it. Resistance ceased. Neither side had realised
that the National Army attackers were heavily outnumbered.
Had they done so, the Republican tactics would have been
very different, though it is doubtful whether Conlon and
O'Friel would have mounted an attack at all if they had
known the odds against them. The National Army men were
fortunate, too, that the Republican's armoured car, *The
River Lee*, did not arrive a few minutes earlier. O'Friel
saw it in the distance and had time to barricade the road.
Thwarted, *The River Lee*, a huge, armour plated lorry
home-built in Cork, lumbered away. Dalton's armoured car
was engaged elsewhere.

Dr Lynch was still dressing the back muscle wounds of the
man who had so nearly shot him when Conlon approached.
"Doc, you'd better have a look at my face when you've
finished with him." Lynch turned and was horrified by what
he saw.

"I thought he was done for but he only laughed. When I
washed his face, I found that the wound was not serious but
his face was grained with shot marks. He was lucky his head
wasn't blown off." Dr Lynch sent Conlon to the house while
O'Friel ordered his men to collect the dead of both sides.
"We had sixteen laid out at the side of the road, nine of
our own, including six Conlon had lost in Morgan's cornfield, and seven of the boys," recalls O'Friel.

Dr Lynch helped, and he it was who found the bodies of
Kennedy and Murray, two of the Republican leaders, lying
across the road near Cronin's.

When the doctor got home he found Conlon lounging in a

chair enjoying a cigarette and the attention of the small girls. O'Friel was still busy blocking roads, posting sentries and sending prisoners with escorts back to the Lynch house. Many were wounded and all were exhausted. Men came in, not only from the Cronin's cottage battle, but from some distance around. Rifles and machine-guns were left in the hall while the men were served in the doctor's dining-room with tea, bread and butter, and bacon and eggs as fast as Mrs Lynch, her two servants and two small daughters could prepare the food. Between eighty and a hundred famished men were fed that night. What those women and girls did is best described in Doctor Lynch's own proud words:

"None of them had ever been near a dead person, or seen a real wound, or even heard a shot fired except at a distance. Yet, among the dead and badly wounded, in a veritable shambles, where their feet were wet with human blood, where the breath they drew was thick with the steam of it, and where for hours their ears were tortured with the cries of agony and the groans of the dying, they stood at my side on and off for hours, holding a wounded leg or a dressing, while strong men turned sick at the sights and had to leave the room." During the evening wounded men continued to be brought to the house. Dr Lynch was called into the yard where he found a dying man on a stretcher outside the coach house. He gave him morphia and had him carried into the house. Back in his study he extracted a bullet from a man's arm and attended a youngster who had had the whole calf of a leg shot away. He was told that there was another case in the lane outside. On a lorry he found three men dead and another in great pain with a knee splintered by a bullet. After giving him morphia he returned to see the dying man in the hall and found his younger daughter sitting on the stairs beside him. Her face was resting on her hands. She was beaten at last. Dr Lynch sent her to bed and as he kissed her goodnight he heard the man give his last gasp. Only then did he realise he had not sent for a priest and he was relieved to find that his wife had done so. The priest had been while he was ministering to the man in the lorry.

Dr Lynch took stock. In the hall near the dead man three men were slumped asleep on chairs. Around them were rifles and machine-guns, greatcoats and webbing. In the study twelve wounded men lay on the floor. Blood was everywhere. Ten men were asleep in the drawing-room, eight more in the dining-room, and there were even two more in the pantry. More accommodation was essential. He explained the position to Conlon who sent Lieutenant Leonard with ten men to occupy a house, any house.

Three of the wounded were loaded on to a hand-cart. Outside, soldiers were lying asleep on both sides of the road with sentries pacing up and down between them. None of the sleeping men awoke as Dr Lynch and his party made their way to the neighbouring home of Pearson Clarke. There, once they had identified themselves, they found ready admittance. Dr Lynch returned home, attended to some minor wounds, took a rough supper standing up between the two sleeping men in the pantry and went to bed at last at two o'clock. Still exhausted, he was awakened at daylight by a hammering at the front door and went with an angry swish of his dressing-gown to open it.

"What the hell-fire blazes do you mean by this?" he roared at the men on his doorstep. A gentle voice answered him. "I'm very sorry to disturb you, Doctor, but I must see the officers in your house. I'm General Dalton and this is General Ennis."

Full of apologies, Dr Lynch led them to Conlon who was asleep on a sofa in the drawing-room. Even the two young generals, whose experience had encompassed so much that was melancholy and macabre were astounded by the strange scene in the dawn light, the shrunken dead as yet uncovered, the wounded writhing in pain, men sprawled asleep in the abandonment of exhaustion, the sentry nodding on a chair, his rifle between his knees, the litter of weapons and clothing and accoutrements, the harsh patches of coalgulated blood.

Shortly after six, Mrs Lynch and her servants started getting breakfast ready. The men were full of bleary oaths as they were awakened but then, as they saw the food, the pleasure in their faces was almost comical. One hundred and twenty men were fed that morning.

Conlon and O'Friel got their men together and Conlon invited Dr Lynch to accompany them on their drive into Cork. So the doctor got out his bag and his bicycle; the two companies fell in and went down the hill. Dr Lynch, wheeling his cycle, walked with Conlon. When they reached Hegarty's

Wood, Conlon sent his men through it in extended order and the whole force got to Maryborough gate without incident. Near the Windsor gate machine-guns placed on Maryborough Hill began to sear the road and Republican guns also opened fire from across the water near Ravenscourt.

At Windsor Dr Lynch got ready a room in the Lodge in case of casualties. *The River Lee* was reported to be prowling in the vicinity. But although machine-gun fire was incessant, little of consequence happened and the National Army troops went on towards Douglas. They were joined by their armoured car, *The Manager*, and a truck carrying the 18-pounder gun. A few shells were sent across towards Ravenscourt and the Republicans there replied with machine-gun fire. More Republican guns opened up from a hill behind the rectory, catching the National Army troops in a cross-fire and compelling them to take refuge in some cottages. Dr Lynch found himself in a room with two machine-gunners who were directing a constant stream of bullets at the hill. But the Republicans seemed to have worked out exactly where the gun was placed and bullets kept thudding into the wall behind the window. Immediately opposite the window a statuette of the Blessed Virgin stood on a bracket in the middle of the wall. Bullet holes surrounded it but not a single bullet had hit the statuette. Outside, a huge white sow patrolled backwards and forwards, ignoring the bullets that flicked the dust around and sometimes underneath her. When at last the firing had ceased and *The Manager* had gone on into Douglas, Dr Lynch went out to the road and saw that not a pane of glass remained in the row of cottages. As he put it, "Their walls were indented like a face with small-pox."

The arrival of *The Manager* in Douglas was the first intimation there of the National Army advance. The armoured car was stopped opposite Driscoll's public house, which was on a corner. A lorry of Republican troops came round the corner and, perceiving *The Manager*, the driver promptly turned and made for Cork by the back road. *The Manager*'s crew rushed back to their vehicle and set out in pursuit, but the Republicans had time to blow the bridge near O'Brien's Mill and the armoured car got no further. More Republicans waited in ambush in houses on both sides of the street, and only the warning of a woman who spotted them saved Conlon and eight men. Quickly he turned the tables and took ten prisoners. Altogether, thirty-two prisoners, with arms and ammunition, were taken that day.

All three companies had now arrived in Douglas. They had been fighting hard for three days and Dalton, unwilling to push them further, thought to spend the night there. But the men, elated with success, were anxious to push on to Cork. Dalton readily agreed.

"I was more concerned with occupying the whole County of Cork than I was with getting into the city, though of course it was essential to take it," he says. "I didn't know what I was going to encounter, but I thought we should have to fight for it."

Again the three companies were to take different ways. Before they set out, Dalton promoted Captains Conlon and O'Friel to the rank of Commandant. Promotion in the field was a rare distinction. Conlon's fighting qualities are remembered with awe but it is sometimes forgotten that he needed the deeper thinking leadership of Emmet Dalton as once he had needed McEoin's. Though still only twenty-four, Dalton was an experienced military officer, whereas the skill of most other Irish leaders on both sides had been tested in guerrilla warfare only. Already he had carried through the Four Courts artillery operation, led the round-up in the Dublin hills, temporarily relieved the situation in Dundalk and planned the coast invasion strategy.

Sean Hendrick was asleep and Michael O'Donovan (writer Frank O'Connor) had just got their mimeographed paper on to the street when O'Connor saw a car with National soldiers roar down the road. Surprised, for the latest reports were that Dalton's forces were being held in the Passage area, he woke his friend and together they hurried to Headquarters at Union Quay Barracks, where a senior officer was gesticulating to a nonplussed crowd of Republicans and shouting that it was "every man for himself".

The men were astonished, puzzled, resentful. In Dublin the Executive Forces were counting on Cork to throw the lever which would switch Ireland from the Free State back to the Republican track. This they knew. They knew, too, that the capture of the *Upnor* had provided them with plenty of weapons, that the money appropriated from the banks was ample to finance a long struggle, that they had a strong force imbued with the Republican ideal and stout hearts. Yet they were to evacuate Cork. It didn't make sense to them. To the leaders perhaps it did. Their access to shipping had enabled the Provisional Government to sail round the flimsy Limerick-to-Waterford line and it seemed that they could fragment the Republicans at will. However resolutely the Republicans fought for Cork, they could not prevent their containment in the city and, in the long run, their resistance was bound to prove futile.

From Union Quay a huge convoy of cars, lorries and guns set out for the country, the barracks were set alight and Cork was left to the Free State. Sean Hendrick and Frank O'Connor decided to call on their writer friend, Daniel Corkery, who had a cottage at Inishcarra, and they walked the five miles, enjoying brilliant sunshine and the summer hum of the fields. Ballincollig was evacuated and the barracks set on fire as they marched through.

After lunching with Corkery they decided to press on to Macroom. They had walked far enough so they sat by the roadside and waited for a lift. Cars and lorries whizzed past them. Erskine Childers they saw crouched on a running board. Nowhere was there room for them. They had almost given up hope when they saw an open lorry approaching very slowly with no one aboard but the driver. He stopped for them and they clambered into the cabin. At a careful ten miles an hour the lorry lumbered along, the driver taciturn with concentration. "In the name of God, can't you make it go any faster!" Hendrick exploded at last. "At this rate we won't be in Macroom until tomorrow."

"Sure, it's the devil of a hurry you're in to meet your Maker," the driver expostulated. His lorry, one of the last to leave Union Quay, had been loaded very hurriedly. Bombs, detonators and explosives had been bundled in loose. "He was in the horrors, poor devil," says Hendrick, "especially if we were going up a bit of an incline and he had to change gear." Then they would hear their hazardous cargo slithering towards the tailboard of the lorry and, when they went downhill, clattering towards the front again.

At dusk they came to a temporary bridge. They approached it downhill. The bridge was a foot below the level of the road. Down crashed the front wheels. Hendrick and O'Connor waited for long moment for the rear wheels to follow. Again came a tremendous bump, but still the lorry went serenely on. At midnight they reached Macroom and put up at Williams's Hotel. Childers was there already.

Next day the Republican force as such was disbanded and many of the men returned to their homes some eighty miles and more away. From now on it was to be a war of flying columns, ambush and harassment—the tactics they knew so well.

On August 9th, as Dalton was making his assured way into Cork, Michael Collins set out on an inspection tour of the west. The Commander-in-Chief was still driving himself and all about him. His major task was to build up a state in spite of the shambles that Ireland had become, but he knew that the chaos would have to stop or the building could not continue. More and more of the administration he was leaving to able lieutenants like Cosgrave and O'Higgins who still had Arthur Griffith to lean on, though Griffith was ailing now, his great fire burning low. He had become cantankerous but was still wise.

Collins was concerned now with the efficiency of the National Army, only a proportion of whom were the old I.R.A. men whose ways he knew and upon whom he could rely. There were callow youths from the country and knowing Dublin gutties, some zealous and some on the make, and there were discharged Irish soldiers from the British Army, some anxious to restore order in their homeland and some who had been away so long that they knew little of the trouble. Recently I met one old sweat who was a cousin of a renowned I.R.A. fighter in the National Army. Old Patrick had served from boyhood in the British Army and, having received an honourable discharge, thought to continue his military career in the National Army of his own land. He was astounded to find himself fighting in a civil war and, as soon as he decently could, discharged himself and returned to live among his old cronies in England.

To make of this motley crowd an army which would bring

423

order to Ireland, and then maintain it, was a responsibility which Collins, as Commander-in-Chief, saw as primarily his. He was even planning at this time to send a delegation to Switzerland to study the pattern of that country's army. Of his own future he was less certain. His moods thundered in and out like a loose sail in a wind and in his bleaker moments he would hint to his intimates of presentiments of death. The loss in the Civil War of men dear to him weighed heavily on him. As recently as July 31st, Harry Boland, his close friend from days when the cause of Irish freedom had been at its nadir, had been shot dead in the Grand Hotel, Skerries, where he had been trapped by a party of National soldiers and given no quarter when, it was said, he attempted to escape. And in London Collins's protégés, Dunne and Sullivan, were waiting to die on the scaffold. Both had made brave speeches from the dock in the Casement tradition. Their grim deed had been done for Ireland's sake but Collins must have wondered if the end was worth the sacrifice.

On his way to Limerick Collins inspected the prison at Maryborough, with a meticulously unsympathetic eye Frank Carty remembers:

"He was clever enough to see that the grey colour of the top of the wall would help prisoners trying to get over it. After he had gone a strip at the top of the wall was whitewashed.

"When he was walking through the ground floor of the prison a number of prisoners fired utensils at him. He was not hit and it was probably only a demonstration."

From Limerick Collins went on to Tralee. He was anxious for the campaign against the south to succeed, so that he could offer to negotiate from a strong position. On August 10th, two small ships, *Margaret* and *Mermaid*, the latter only a pleasure vessel, sailed from Limerick under the command of General MacManus to take Kenmare from the sea. The landing was to be in charge of Commandant Tom (Scarteen) O'Connor. The two vessels slogged round the sprawling ruggedness of the Kerry coast and at dawn on Friday 11th arrived in Kenmare River estuary.

A party went ashore and returned for reinforcements to take the Lackeen coastguard station which was held by the Republicans, but the small garrison promptly abandoned the
424

station after setting it alight. O'Connor sent a dispatch, still extant, to MacManus:

"I am to proceed to Kenmare across the mountains so I think it would be the best plan if you run up the bay to the end and wait to land until I board the vessel."

Later, he sent word to MacManus to meet him at Templenoe pier. Kenmare was taken almost without incident, the Republicans—too few in number to make a fight of it—marching away before the enemy arrived. MacManus is somewhat sceptical of the whole operation.

"I was merely in charge of bringing them down from Limerick and putting them ashore. I told them to take up defensive positions round the outside of the town, garrison the barracks properly and patrol the town itself; instead of which they occupied a few houses and the old police barracks, then went out drinking and visiting their friends. There was no discipline. Even on the ship I had a good deal of friction with these young fellows." MacManus had told Collins it was a mistake to use local men in these circumstances.

It was this kind of bumbling soldiering that Collins was anxious to be rid of, but his tour of inspection was halted when news of Arthur Griffith's death was brought to him. Collins returned at once to Dublin.

Griffith, barely fifty but aged by the intolerable strains of so many years, died of a cerebral haemorrhage as he rose on the morning of August 12th. The Cabinet in London were informed of his death by Lloyd George the same day[1]. He told them that the King was waiting to know whether he should send a message of regret to the Provisional Government. They were reminded of "the firm and loyal attitude towards the Treaty displayed throughout by Mr Griffith". He would probably have been a Minister of the Crown had the Constitution been passed and was indeed connected with a Government which was fighting a loyal battle so far as the Crown was concerned. The point was, however, that at the time of his death he was "merely President of the Dail". This little problem of protocol was solved in characteristic style by the Cabinet. The King should send a personal message to the widow and the Prime Minister and other signatories of the Treaty would send one to Collins.

[1] Cabinet conclusion 45/22 (1) of 12/8/22.

In Ireland no shot was withheld for the sake of Griffith's death but grief struck across the boundaries of dissension nevertheless. De Valera, hunted in the country, lamented that he could not be at the funeral. At the head of the procession marched Collins, blankfaced, his sorrow secret beneath the fine new uniform of the Commander-in-Chief.

The newsreels of those days seem filled with black horses and black hats, and the ebony professionalism of funeral processions continually rolling towards Glasnevin, but the stillness of the dark, tearful crowds almost stops the heart.

Sir Nevil Macready in his autobiography[2] described Griffith at the truce talk of July 1921: "A square, squat figure, rather huddled up in his chair, hardly uttering a word, and then only a monosyllable, in whose eyes one could read nothing of what might be passing through his mind. During that hour I understood how it was that Arthur Griffith became a great leader of the Irish."

"Griffith sacrificed his life—a life of great ability—for the Irish people," says Sean McEoin. "He was the poorest man in Ireland when he died."

A few days before Griffith's death, Winston Churchill had summed up for the British Cabinet[3] what had recently been taking place in Ireland. He himself was "not discouraged but rather encouraged." He suggested that "had the Cabinet been told three months ago that the Free State Government would be waging war against the rebels, as they were now doing, they would have been surprised. There were a great many difficulties in the relations of His Majesty's Government and the Free State Government but these were being dealt with by the Cabinet Committee. The Committee proposed to continue to give all reasonable assistance to the Free State Government and, in particular, to give them up to 30,000 rifles."

Churchill said that the Loyalists in the South were probably suffering no more inconvenience than the Irish Catholics but that "the exasperation of the people with the Republicans was daily increasing". He thought it might be some weeks before the rebels were subdued.

In the North murders and incendiarism had almost entirely

[2] Annals of An Active Life Sir Nevil Macready.
[3] Cabinet conclusion 43/22 (7) of 3/8/22.

ceased. "This might be due to the fact that the gunmen were engaged in the South, and that with their return there might be a recrudescence of outrage, but at the moment life in Belfast had almost become normal." He noted "increasing signs that justice was being meted out to Protestants and Catholics equally."

Unlike Churchill, Collins derived no satisfaction from the situation. Always he kept open his lines of communication with his fighting friends on the other side, hopeful that they would see reason and accept the Provisional Government's terms, while at the same time he planned with all his energy and flair to compel them to submit. He loved to wrestle with his friends and was playful as a big cat, but sometimes he could not resist using his crushing strength. Something of the dichotomy persisted in his handling of the Civil War dilemma. Before he set out again for the west he sent his trusted lieutenant, Colonel Frank Thornton, to try to contact Republican leaders in the hope that a conference could be arranged at Clonmel, from which all troops but members of the old I.R.A. should be sent away. But Thornton was ambushed on the journey and badly wounded.

When he left Dublin in the early morning of August 20th, Collins was unwell and still fogged with the gloom of Griffith's death. O'Duffy met him at Limerick the same day and there was a meeting of officers from a wide area. Among them was Jerry Ryan, who was asked to provide fifty of his tough Tipperary fighting men to strengthen Dalton's forces in Cork. The Tipperary reinforcements were taken to Limerick by car and shipped to Bantry.

Once he had driven a wedge into the city of Cork, Dalton had lost little time in opening up cracks through the country and columns under his command were soon probing deep. Conlon led one force in a greedy march to Macroom; Tom Ennis, much admired as a soldier by Dalton, took Skibbereen and Clonakilty. Brandon was taken and John L. O'Sullivan made a river crossing under fire "with bits of boat flying" to get into Kinsale. Neilis O'Driscoll marched his unit of largely inexperienced troops to Bantry and managed to cling on to half the town. From the Kilmallock area Tom Flood travelled south to take charge of Mallow. In Cork city Dalton began to reorganise, tackling the desperate problem of

427

unemployment, doing what he could to meet immediate needs, getting trade flowing and the banks, closed on orders from their head offices, open again.

If the National Army troops had settled like watchful pigeons in the towns of County Cork, the Republicans swarmed like flocks of disturbed starlings through the hilly countryside which Michael Collins, who belonged there, was now approaching.

TWENTY

Glasnevin is full of enshrined heroes, among them Michael Collins, brought there from the chill valley where he was taken by surprise and killed. Collins died in fair fight according to the code of the time, in a trap, but one which was always to be expected and of which, in any case, he appears to have received a warning which he ignored. Whether the men who lay in wait that day knew that their quarry was the legendary Collins is still argued. Sean Hendrick, a totally honest man, says that only some hours later did the returning ambushers hear rumours of the identity of their victim. Tom Barry, who escaped from Gormanstown Prison immediately afterwards, describes in *Guerilla Days in Ireland* how he questioned the men who took part and was told that they did not know.

Quite likely they were unaware that they had caused any death, but they must have known that it was the Collins convoy they had attacked. Few convoys which included an armoured car were travelling round West Cork at the time and, as he moved through his native countryside his progress had hardly gone unnoticed.

Eoin Neeson says[1] that the ambush was "planned, laid and manned by senior officers, including the Brigade staff of Cork No. 3 Brigade, officers from the five brigades battalions and some divisional officers" who had assembled for a meeting in Beal na mBlath. There was some degree of improvisation since it was not known that Collins was to come through Beal na mBlath. When he did travel through on that morning of

[1] *The Civil War in Ireland*, by Eoin Neeson.

August 22nd, 1922, it was realised that it was very much on the cards that he would return by the same route later in the day.

If Collins was counting on sentiment to preserve his safety, then he was foolish at a time when the separate loyalties of brothers had blasted through even family affections, when so soon after the death of Arthur Griffith the leaders of the Executive Forces might well have felt that the removal of the Commander-in-Chief and Chairman of the Provisional Government would leave the Treaty Forces leaderless and allow the great ideal of the Republic to prevail. His adversaries did not think like that, it is true; if they had done, they could have killed him in Dublin or in Cork without the trappings of an ambush. But he ought to have considered the possibility. Instead, they offered him a fight on equal terms.

John O'Connell was, when I met him (he has since died), a short, ruddy, spry man, with an active memory, a proud survivor of the Collins convoy, which he joined at Mallow on Sunday, August 20th, two days before Collins's death. The convoy had travelled from Limerick, through mainly Republican territory, and was bound for Cork. Roads had been blocked or mined and bridges blown, so they had to travel by back roads. A man with local knowledge was needed and O'Connell volunteered. At the Royal Hotel, then a military post, Collins listened to the troubles of the people of Mallow which were put to him by the Bishop of Cloyne, Dr Roche, and Archdeacon Corbett.

The big stone bridge which carried the railway to Cork across the Blackwater River was down, and the townspeople were also concerned lest the road bridge lower down were also destroyed. Erskine Childers was blamed for blowing up the railway bridge. For some strange reason poor Childers, who was no more than a propagandist, was held responsible for every railway torn up and every bridge destroyed.

The Archdeacon wanted to know when the bridge would be repaired. Collins protested, "Give me a chance," but promised to have workmen there within a month. When Archdeacon Corbett asked for news of the struggle in the country, Collins answered briefly that things were going well enough and that he hoped reconciliation would soon come. O'Connell recalls that as Collins strode away Archdeacon

Corbett said prophetically, "The poor man is in a hurry to meet his death."

The party travelled by mountain road to Whitechurch, making little speed on the rudimentary road. *Slievenamon*, a formidable but ponderous armoured car thundered along behind the yellow Leyland tourer in which Collins sat with Commandant Sean O'Connell (not to be confused with John O'Connell, the guide). Most of the escort travelled in a Crossley tender ahead of the Leyland. Lieutenant Jack Smith on a motor cycle acted as the convoy's scout.

At Whitechurch an open-air dance was in lively swing and the convoy stopped to search for arms. When they reached Cork it was almost dark. "Cork city police, with bands on their arms but no uniform, cleared a way for us," John O'Connell recalls. "As Collins stepped from his Leyland car to go into the Imperial Hotel, a few distant shots were fired, probably a warning that he'd arrived." The escort, O'Connell among them, went off to quarters in the Victoria Hotel.

Next day, August 21st, was the last calendar day that Collins was to live through. Painted slogans all over the city asked why he marched through Cork rather than Belfast, wishful thinking this, for the Republicans, looking for any factor which would reunite the I.R.A., had hoped that the Orangemen might provide it. The escort, having spent the morning warily exploring the city, reported in the early afternoon to the Imperial Hotel, General Dalton's H.Q., where they were joined by Collins and Dalton, who had been inspecting military posts and interviewing various prominent citizens, including several bank managers. The convoy formed up. On this occasion the armoured car *Dublin Liz* was taken instead of *Slievenamon*. An inspection was made of the National Army post at Macroom, which was commanded by the redoubtable Conlon.

Almost every night, anti-Treaty forces attacked the post, once the workhouse, and Conlon warned Collins that he needed more arms and ammunition to hold it. The Collins party gave him a Lewis gun and some pans of ammunition then, as *Dublin Liz* was behaving badly, returned to Cork. Collins decided that he would devote the whole of the following day to an inspection of the Command Area, travelling as far as Bantry.

Collins and his officers spent the night at the Imperial. During the evening they were joined by Frank O'Friel, to whom Collins mentioned that he had hopes of meeting certain Republican leaders and of bringing the Civil War to an end. Though probably no more than a pleasantry to a junior officer, it confirms a statement from Mr P. Moylett, quoted in Rex Taylor's *Michael Collins*, that before leaving Dublin Collins had confided in him that he was going "to try to bring the boys round", but that if he failed, he proposed to "get rough with them". Dan Breen, for one, was on his way to meet Collins in Cork.

"Father Dick McCarthy in Limerick got in touch with me that Collins would like to see me," says Breen, "and I said I'd go on to Hickey's of Glenville. It was an old meeting place of ours and he was to contact me there."

Emmet Dalton says that while Collins hoped that the Republicans would throw in their hand, he had no intention of offering any concession. He was bitter and disappointed to the verge of illness by de Valera's adamantine insistence on the dogma of republicanism and his ungenerous refusal to recognise the achievement of Irish freedom. Michael Brennan supports Dalton's view. He talked with Collins in Limerick and "did not have the impression that he was on a peaceful mission. At the same time he was very attached to Cork men like Lynch and Deasy and didn't want to fight them. He was miserable."

When he talked to Jerry Ryan in Limerick and asked him to send fifty of his best fighters to West Cork, Collins told Ryan that he doubted if peace moves would come to anything and he was determined to end the conflict. According to General McEoin, Collins was hoping to appeal to the loyalties of Cork members of the I.R.B., believing that they had followed Liam Lynch misguidedly and that they could be persuaded to resume their allegiance. He intended this not merely as a step to end the Civil War but to repair the break in the great revolutionary instrument which meant so much to him. In McEoin's view, the hope that he could achieve this was one of the main factors in deciding Collins to make the journey to the south.

It was important, too, for Collins that he should have long discussions with Dalton, the man on the spot and a man whose judgment he respected. In the past, Dalton had carried out many secret and unusual tasks for him and the two men were firm friends. Collins wanted a full understanding of the military position to take back to G.H.Q. and, as Chairman of the Provisional Government and Minister of Finance, he was anxious to recover money belonging to the Customs and Excise Department which the Executive Forces had obtained by compelling the Official Collector to sign cheques which subsequently were paid by the banks. Childers's banking transactions also interested him. Both points he covered in a letter to Mr Cosgrave dated August 21st, 1922, and timed 3.30 p.m. It ran:

"The Bank position here is slightly obscure. It will require a full investigation and combined with that investigation there must be an examination of the Customs and Excise position—all monies paid in and out must come under this. We shall require three first class independent men. Unfortunately Brennan has gone to London.

(2) It would be very desirable to make an examination of the destination of certain drafts on the London County, Westminster & Paris, London. Childers (Mr and Mrs) kept and keep an account or several accounts at the Holborn (I think) Branch of this Bank. I am sure the Bank will give details of any recent transactions.

(3) I wired today re Moor Park and Kilworth—see Hogan and let him send down whatever man was dealing with this matter. It is urgent that we must collect back-rent even though it may already have been paid to the Irregulars. The people here want no compromise with the Irregulars.

(4) It is wise to postpone the Dail meeting as already suggested.

(5) You might get before mind's eye three persons under Part I but don't announce anything until I return.

(6) It would be a good thing to get Civil Guards both here and in Limerick. Civil administration urgent everywhere in the South. The people are splendid."

Nothing in this document suggests that Collins was seeking any compromise with the Executive Forces, but there is an optimistic emphasis on the aspect of civil administration which suggests that he did not believe the Civil War had long to run. Collins was interested in the Childers' bank accounts because
432

he had an idea that the Republicans might be planning to buy arms abroad and to pay for them through this channel. The fact that Collins favoured the postponement of the first session of the new Dail suggests that his attitude towards the Republicans was hardening.

From O'Friel, Collins wanted information about wounded National soldiers and asked the names of those still in hospital. He was especially concerned to hear of another Mick Collins, a lad who had rushed a machine-gun post at Rochestown and had been fatally wounded. Beaslai tells us that "the startling words—Michael Collins shot dead" which evidently related to this boy, were entered in Collins's note-book. Was he perhaps recording a presentiment of his own fate?

On the eve of Collins's death four men billeted themselves at "Gurranreigh", the farmhouse of Mr Joseph O'Sullivan, about four miles from Beal na mBlath. Three of the visitors were officers of the Executive Forces, Liam Deasy, Sean Lehane, and Gibbs Ross; the fourth was a man of very humble rank, Eamon de Valera. The four were not particularly welcome since Joseph O'Sullivan was a staunch supporter of Collins and the Treaty. Although the Republicans had come uninvited, they had a soft spot for the O'Sullivans, who had courageously sheltered many an I.R.A. man on the run in Black and Tan days. Tom Barry affectionately recalls[2] the old man: "Joe was over seventy years of age, a dignified and patriarchal old gentleman. He always received us with an old-fashioned courtesy, but never sought to hide his opinion that our generation was only a poor second to the one which peopled the land in the days of his youth."

During the evening, the old Fenian, Joseph O'Sullivan, argued fiercely with Eamon de Valera about Document No. 2, and the quarrel was resumed in the morning. The irate farmer eventually stamped out of the house declaring to his wife that he would not spend another five minutes under the same roof as "that man".

Other officers of the Executive Forces, according to Neeson, stayed that night at the home of Mr John Long at Beal na mBlath and, since there was to be a conference next day, no doubt more were billeted in the area.

On the Tuesday morning, General Collins and Major-

2 *Guerilla Days in Ireland*, by Tom Barry.

General Emmet Dalton left the Imperial Hotel at ten minutes past six. "I remember very well looking at the hall clock in the hotel," says John O'Connell, who had been waiting outside in the Crossley tender. O'Connell's services as a guide were no longer needed but he managed to stay with the escort.

The party travelled first to Macroom, then, because of the destruction of bridges and the obstruction of roads, south by a roundabout route through Beal na mBlath, so apparently firing the idea of a later ambush. Joe Dolan remembers that they actually stopped and asked for directions.

"We dropped into Bandon town," O'Connell goes on. "In fact, it was out through Lord Bandon's demesne we had to go because the main road into Bandon was blocked.

"From Bandon we went on to Clonakilty, but on the way we came to a lot of felled trees there across the road. General Collins said we'd get out and try to shift the trees because it was fair-day in Clonakilty the next day and a lot of people would never get by.

"We had hatchets and saws on the floor of the Crossley tender and we cut up one or two trees and pulled them to one side, into the dike of the road, with the aid of a wire rope and the armoured car. I remember well trying to cut through a heavy limb with a felling axe. General Collins came up to me and said, 'Show me that axe, boy. It's not the first time I've used one.' I handed him the axe and he wasn't long cutting through the limb.

"After about an hour he said we were taking up too much time. There were plenty of idle soldiers in Clonakilty who could come out and clear the road. We had to go back a bit, and up through the fields, and came out exactly at Clonakilty workhouse. It had been blown up, I suppose by the Irregulars. We were then just a mile from Clonakilty. Anyway, we ran into Clonakilty and, while we looked round the town, General Collins and his party went into a hotel. It was a Free State post then."

O'Connell had never been in West Cork before and was puzzled by the country dress of the women. He mistook their long, buttoned-down-the-front dark cloaks and hoods for nuns' habits.

"What sort of order of nuns are these?" he asked a soldier.

434

"They seem to be plentiful about the place. Or what do they represent at all?"

"Take care," answered the soldier, laughing. "It's the women that do the work down here and they wouldn't be long in pulling a revolver from under their cloaks and leaving you low."

Collins and Dalton had lunch at the home of friends, then set out for Roscarbery and Skibbereen. It was perhaps pardonable pride which took Collins then to Sam's Cross where he was born. The house of his youth no longer remained; it had been razed by Black and Tans. But he met members of his family, and drank at the public house owned by his kinsman, Jeremiah. Near it now stands the memorial which Tom Barry unveiled in 1964. Collins called his escort in to the pub and bought them a couple of pints of Clonakilty "Wrestler".

At Roscarbery and Skibbereen Collins made a normal military inspection. "He conferred with the garrison officers, listening to their complaints, giving them advice and assuring them of effective co-operation from the Army authorities," says Emmet Dalton. Everywhere crowds turned out to greet him. As it was getting late, it was decided not to go on as far west as Bantry but to return the way they had come. The road outside Clonakilty was still blocked by trees. Collins's orders for their removal had been disregarded, the excuse being that the working party had been attacked by Republicans. Again the convoy took to the fields, *Slievenamon* rumbling reluctantly behind the other vehicles.

The armoured car had lagged from time to time all day. Once, after the convoy had left Bandon in the morning, *Slievenamon* failed to appear for so long that the rest of the convoy returned to search for her. According to O'Connell the armoured car was stationary outside a public house and her crew were enjoying a drink. Collins took the lapse lightly. "Sure, the cars need a drink, so why not the men?"

At Bandon, Major-General Sean Hales, a member of the Dail, was in command. His brother Tom was a column leader on the Republican side, a situation tragic for the Hales family and bewildering to many simple people in the district who were accustomed to follow their lead. Sean Hales expressed anxiety for Collins's safety. His escort was small and the country he was to travel through was rife with bands of

Republicans. Hales wanted to escort him by way of Innish-annon until he had seen him safely over a precariously improvised bridge but Collins, still convinced that no harm would befall him in his home county, insisted on travelling back the longer, but probably quicker way to Cork through Beal na mBlath and Crookstown towards the Macroom-Cork road. The convoy left Bandon soon after seven that misty evening and took the serpentine road. Perhaps recalling Hales's warning, Collins remarked to Dalton, "If we run into an ambush along the way, we will stand and fight them." But it is unlikely that the thought of an ambush occurred to many members of the convoy. Commandant Joe Dolan, sitting in the open at the back of the armoured car, was leaning drowsily on his rifle. A number of the men were Dubliners, familiar with the tactics of street fighting but lacking experience of surprise attacks on country roads.

As they entered the bleak valley of Beal na mBlath, Collins picked up his rifle from the floor of the car and placed it alertly across his knees. Perhaps it was a premonition, perhaps a precaution. Men hidden on the hillsides could see the winding road for miles and watch any travellers appear and reappear from one curve to another.

Neeson's information is that the first warning the ambushers had of the approach of the convoy was the arrival of Lieutenant Smith on his motor cycle, but even if they were tired of scanning the road they must surely have heard the sound of engines.

On this occasion, Lieutenant Smith was a short fifty yards ahead of the convoy, and before he could turn back to report that an overturned dray lay round the bend in the road, the rest of the convoy had caught up with him. There was a burst of fire; the windscreen of the Leyland was shattered and another shot passed behind the legs of the two drivers of the Crossley tender. Dalton shouted, "Drive like hell," but Collins countermanded this very sensible order and sprang out of the car ready to fight. A section of the ambush party had removed part, if not all, of the obstruction when they were interrupted by the arrival of Smith and had to take cover in a hurry. The ambush had broken up in the belief that it was now too late to expect the Collins convoy and that it had gone another way. The main body was already some distance down the

436

road, but a few men had been left in the ambush position, Neeson says, "to cover the removal of the barricade".

As bullets crackled from the hillside, Commandant O'Connell ran back to join Collins, Dalton and the now wideawake Joe Dolan who had leapt off the armoured car. If *Slievenamon* could have been driven off the main road and on to the track which led away to the left, curved and climbed and finally ran level along the ambushers' ridge and parallel to the road below, the story might have ended differently. The half dozen men still ensconced behind the thick shrubbery several hundreds of yards distant would have been driven back along their escape road. But the manoeuvre would have been difficult for the armoured car and, in any case, standing square on the road as it was, *Slievenamon's* machine-gun should have put paid to the ambush. But the gun was firing only spasmodic single shots and the armoured car served little purpose other than to ensure the safety of her own crew. MacPeake, the machine-gunner, a Scottish mercenary, later sold *Slievenamon* to the Republicans. It can be wondered, therefore, whether he made any very serious effort to keep his guns going.

At first, the Republicans concentrated their fire on the men in the Crossley tender. O'Connell did not see any of the ambushers and is sceptical of those of his companions who thought they did. "They would yell, 'See that fellow,' and they fired and fired. But I don't believe they were used to ambushes at all. I honestly think that any fellow on top of the hill wasn't so foolish as to expose himself to our fire."

Probably because the officers, Collins himself, Dalton, Commandant O'Connell and Captain Joe Dolan, were firing more dangerously from prone positions on the road some distance behind *Slievenamon*, the fire switched to them. The Provisional Government men were vulnerable. To the right of the twisting road, the east side if one considers that its general direction was north and south, the ground climbed steeply, offering no sanctuary; to the left was open marshland and a stream, behind which lay the ambush ridge. It was, in O'Connell's words, "a desperate, deadly looking place."

Warned by the first shots, the departing ambush party apparently tried to work their way round the eastern slope above the road with the idea of setting up a cross-fire.

437

"The firing was going on for the most part of half an hour," O'Connell relates, "and we could see the road being split up with bullets. In fact, I'm sure if they'd wanted to, they could have killed us all." Dalton doubts it.

There was a lull in the firing and Collins got to his feet and, as O'Connell puts it, "had a gaze around him." Dalton recalls that Collins used the armoured car for cover and fired from relative safety until he saw some of the ambushers break cover and begin to retreat up the road behind them. He moved further back then and again began firing from a prone position. Dalton, Dolan and O'Connell were not far away. "I heard someone say the C.-in-C. was hit," says Dolan. "I didn't know how bad it was until I saw Sean O'Connell whisper an Act of Contrition close to his head." That head, behind the ear, had been slashed open. General Michael Collins was dead.

For a shocked moment the Provisional Government soldiers stopped shooting and the ambushers, realising that they had won some kind of advantage, intensified their fire. Then Dalton ordered his men to keep up a heavy fire while Commandant Sean O'Connell dragged the body back to the shelter of the armoured car. With Dalton's help, he rested the burly frame on the right front mudguard. At last the firing slackened. Dalton and O'Connell bandaged the frightful head wound and, aided by Lieutenant Smith, who had been wounded in the neck during the last flurry of shots, lifted him into the Leyland.

The soldiers removed the last cases and broken bottles which had spilled from the dray, and the melancholy cortege set out for Crookstown three miles away. Dalton sat with the head of the dead Collins resting against his shoulder. With Smith wounded, and no one else capable of riding a motor cycle, his machine was abandoned.

It was now almost dark, and at a crossroads the party took the wrong turning and headed down a narrow road towards a bridge crossing the Cork-Macroom railway. Nervous now, the men grabbed their guns when a warning shout sounded in the lingering twilight. A man sitting, smoking a cigarette, just below the bridge, calmly pointed to the railway line forty feet below the broken bridge.

Unable to turn the cars in the narrow road, the Provisional
438

Government soldiers took them into the fields. The going was slightly uphill and a haze of rain had made the grass greasy. Engines roared; wheels spun but did not grip. Then greatcoats were spread to give the wheels a holding surface and full tins of petrol were used to prevent them from slipping back. Some of the tins burst and the men's clothing was saturated with petrol. The Crossley tender and *Slievenamon* were got to the road, three fields away, with the troops shouldering them along to supplement the engine power. When they returned for the Leyland in which Collins's body lay, the engine would not start. So they hoisted the great frame of their lost leader on to their shoulders and carried him to the road. He was laid on the seat of the Crossley tender and Dalton still supported his head, almost as if he found it impossible to believe that he who had seemed indestructible had been destroyed. Around them in the tender the men stood hunched in grief, an unintended guard of honour.

"We went astray many a by-road," says O'Connell, as he ends the story he has told so often. "We got into a farmer's yard one time. It was only like an old boreen and it was an awful job to turn and get out."

"At long last we reached the city of Cork," wrote General Dalton. "It was midnight now, still and silent, and very dark as the dead Chief's escort passed through the city." Collins was taken to the Shanakiel hospital, which was still a hospital for Irish soldiers wounded in World War I, and a room was specially prepared for him.

At 1 a.m. the news reached General Richard Mulcahy. In the next two hours he drafted and telephoned to the newspapers a message which will always have its place in Irish history:

"Stand by your posts. Bend bravely and undaunted to your work. Let no cruel act of reprisal blemish your bright honour. Every dark hour that Michael Collins met since 1916 seemed but to steel that bright strength of his and temper his gay bravery. You are left each inheritors of that strength and of that bravery. To each of you falls his unfinished work. No darkness in the hour—no loss of comrades will daunt you at it. Ireland! The Army serves—strengthened by its sorrow."

When news of Collins's death became generally known in Cork on the following day, the National troops were bent on

439

the kind of revenge that Mulcahy was trying to prevent. O'Friel and other officers spread the story that Sean McEoin had been captured by Executive Forces in Sligo and that if there were any trouble McEoin would surely be shot. Dalton, at gun point, prevented some of the local officers from setting out on a mission of revenge. Although there were isolated incidents and at the Red Cow inn in Clondalkin three Republican soldiers were shot in cold blood, Mulcahy's admonition was heeded in most places. Nevertheless, from the time of Collins's death there seemed little chance of reconciliation—"Everyone looked on him as a sort of bridge," says Moss Twomey—and a new element of bitterness permeated the struggle. And, in time, there *were* "cruel acts of reprisal".

At "Gurranreigh" the O'Sullivan family heard the rifle fire in the valley of Beal na mBlath, but did not know what had happened until Sean Lehane called next morning and said, "We've got your friend Mickeen at last—shot last evening at Beal na mBlath." There was a note of sadness, and a touch of bravado perhaps, in his tone and in his use of the affectionate diminutive. Men on both sides mourned the death of Michael Collins, but it was undoubtedly a victory for the Republicans, and triumph and regret were mingled in many hearts. Sean Collins, Michael's brother, captured by Republicans a few days later and then released, reported them jubilant.

Frank O'Connor records in *An Only Child* that the men who brought the news were rejoicing and that he and Sean Hendrick rejoiced too. But Hendrick and he paused when Erskine Childers, who was with them, quietly took himself off and wrote a tribute to Collins for publication in *War News*. Later, Hendrick began to ask himself questions. It has always seemed inconceivable to him that the Commander-in-Chief of the Provisional Government Army should spend several days at the height of the Civil War "fooling about in the south"—as Sean O'Casey put it—carrying out inspections of small posts like Bandon, unless he had another purpose in mind. "I am convinced," says Hendrick, "that Collins came down to contact the leaders down here and to wipe out the Civil War. There were even rumours of it at the time."

There was a day when, Hendrick relates, "we came up

440

through the pass of Keamaneigh from around Ballylickey. We had an outpost in the area of Keamaneigh and if that were not held the Free State, who had Bantry, would have had access to all that area where our people were. So there was supposed to be a column guarding the pass. As we came through, Childers was looking for sentries and was aghast to see none.

"When we got into the village of Ballingeary we met an officer whom we knew and Childers complained to him that there did not seem to be anyone guarding the pass. 'I'm not going to have any of my men killed and there'll be a bit of peace tomorrow,' replied the officer.

"You see, there was a thing in the air about the two sides coming together and the thing that ties up in my mind with it was the visit of Collins."

It must be remembered that to his contemporaries Collins was not the saint he has since become, but one of themselves. a man with failings as well as great abilities and rare personal magnetism, whose tongue could be sharp, who had wrestled with them and sometimes delighted overmuch in his superior size and strength, whose very exploits they had shared. If to some he was a national hero, to others he had become next door to a traitor; while to the Republican leaders, who themselves occupy niches little below his own in the frieze of Irish history, he was as intractable, as tenacious a believer in his point of view as they were in theirs. Their affection for him was not dead but it was transcended by their conviction that their cause was right for Ireland—and his wrong.

About his death there are still questions as yet unanswered and this is perhaps a good thing. The mystery contributes not a little to the legend, and every Irishman can believe what he wishes and upon none can blame, if it is a matter for blame, be laid with any certainty. For those—and there are many— who love to speculate, the field is open.

Elizabeth Lazenby, an American journalist, writes[3] that as far back as May, Mrs Erskine Childers told her of plans "for dealing with Michael Collins" which had been discussed at the Childers' home. The first plan was to persuade him to turn against the Treaty and to make him the hero of the ultimate victory. If this failed, two courses were open—to discredit

[3] *Ireland—a Catspaw*, by Elizabeth Lazenby.

Collins or to shoot him. Attempts to discredit him had been made before, notably in the Dail debates on the Treaty, those sad occasions when Irish eloquence plummeted to the depths of the mundane and deeply felt passions exploded into fragments of trite backbiting. Against Collins, Brugha alleged with relentless bitterness that during the struggle against England he had been no more than a disloyal and ineffectual underling with a craving for notoriety; and Countess Markievicz taunted him with the suggestion that he might marry Princess Mary.

At the time of the discussions in the Childers' drawing-room some hope remained that Collins would hoodwink the English by palming off on to them a Republican constitution. Collins could hardly have believed the English so naïve, but he may have had hopes of their generosity. But the English had insisted upon a Constitution in strict conformance with the Articles of Agreement and Collins had recognised that there were to be no more concessions. He had already accepted the position and, realist that he was, was prepared to use the power conferred to create more power.

Now, as Chairman of the Provisional Government, he was succeeding in establishing a workable administration. Was it time then "to shoot him"? In Dublin he was under heavy guard but in the south he seemed almost to be inviting attack—unless he was merely too confident of the immunity afforded him in the precincts of his boyhood. But it is extremely unlikely that the purpose of the ambush was to kill Collins. As I have said, it would have been easier by far to pick him off in Cork. Surely there was nothing reprehensible in the leaders of one side planning an act of war against the others. Collins would simply have to take his chance with the others. "Let's scare the pants off Mick" might well have been the motto of the ambushers; and there would have been laughs all round. One wonders, in any case, what would have been de Valera's ultimate fate if he had been taken at this point.

It is easy to see that, in later years, de Valera would not have wished particularly to be associated with Collins's death, whether or not he was a party to it. He was always rather reticent about the event, but in a speech at Donegal in September, 1927, he was stung to reply to a letter from Father Treacy which had appeared in the *Southern Star* and

442

the *Cork Examiner*. Alluding to de Valera's stay with the O'Sullivans, Father Treacy virtually accused him of conspiring to bring about the death of Collins. De Valera explained that he had happened to pass through Beal na mBlath on the fateful day, on his way to Dublin "to be at the postponed meeting of the elected representatives, which I thought might be held in accordance with the pact".

In an editorial the *Cork Examiner* accepted de Valera's denial, adding censoriously, "But it strikes us that there is something cold and callous about his disclaimer. He has not uttered therein one word in condemnation of the abominable assassination. Indeed, he refers to Michael Collins as 'Mr Collins' as if he had never known him." The newspaper was right to rebuke de Valera for the unforgiving tone of his words, utterly wrong, surely, in propagating the contentious myth of assassination.

It was coincidence that the Republican leaders met at Beal na mBlath on that day, and by the same coincidence, no doubt, de Valera was present. De Valera's statement is but a half truth. Certainly if he expected to attend the "postponed meeting of the elected representatives", it was a pretty pious hope. He does not deny staying the previous night with the O'Sullivans. The occasion is remembered too vividly for there to be any doubt that he was there. In any case, it is unlikely that he would have passed through without making contact with so many Republican officers. The probability is that they were charged with seeing him safely through the area, that he spent the previous night with some of them and was on his way before Collins reappeared in the evening. Dalton heard next day that de Valera had reached Fermoy and ordered a search for him but he was not discovered.

Some believe that de Valera was in the area in the hope of opening negotiations with Collins. Others are convinced that he knew Collins was in danger of his life. The attitude of Liam Lynch is interesting. Acknowledging a report of the ambush from Deasy, he sent a curious memorandum in which, having complimented "the very small number of men engaged" on making such a success of the operation "under such heavy fire and against such odds", he added a reproach—"Considering you were aware of the fact that the convoy contained an armoured car, it is surprising you had not mines laid to get

443

this,"—and concluded with a patronising tribute to Collins "who rendered such splendid service in the late war against England", and the rather sanctimonious underlining of what he hoped was the lesson to be learned. "It is to be hoped," wrote Lynch, "our present enemies will realise the folly of trying to crush the Republic before it is too late." Lynch is remembered with great admiration and affection by many who were his "present enemies", but this document, a copy of which is in General McEoin's possession, does give the impression that Lynch was succumbing to the lure of power. His cavalier treatment of de Valera shortly afterwards and later his refusal to convene a meeting of the Executive tend to confirm this impression. The document also makes it clear that the ambush of Collins was planned.

Collins was hit in the back of the head, and this, together with the fact that there was no post-mortem, excited speculation. But men, even leaders, who died of bullet wounds in battle are not generally subjects of post-mortems. Dr Leo Aherne did examine the body in Cork and, like Dr Gogarty later, was sure that the wound was caused either by a richochet or a spent bullet. Emmet Dalton, who was lying on the road near his chief and who bandaged his wound, is absolutely certain that the fatal bullet ricocheted from the road, that in that sense at least, Collins's death was accidental. Commandant O'Connell considered that the bullet ricocheted from the armoured car. Joe Dolan has another theory, that the bullet was fired, not from directly opposite Collins, but from much further along the valley so that it hit the back of his head at an angle.

This is credible, especially if Collins involuntarily contributed to his own death by turning at that very moment, perhaps to reload, perhaps to make sure that his comrades were still unscathed. In that case the fatal bullet may have come not from the ridge in front of Collins but from the slope behind. General Dalton agrees that a few shots did come from that slope along which the main body of the Republicans were slowly working their way back. But whatever quirk it was that traced the distorted path of that bullet, the paramount thing was that Collins, so soon after Griffith, was dead.

As the *Innisfallen* carrying Collins back to Dublin passed a British gunboat off Cobh (then still Queenstown), the British sailors lined the deck and presented arms. British bugles sounded *The Last Post*. In Dublin silent crowds waited at North Wall. As the *Innisfallen* edged in, Emmet Dalton stood on her bridge, alone in the moonless night. A procession formed behind the coffin as it was brought ashore and Michael Collins was carried through the streets of Dublin where once he had seemed invulnerable. Oliver St John Gogarty embalmed the body at the Royal College of Surgeons and Sir John Lavery made a death mask. He also painted the dead leader as he lay in state at the City Hall. The funeral was a massive affair and, ironically, Collins was borne to his place in Glasnevin Cemetery on one of the gun-carriages borrowed from the British for the attack on the Four Courts. It was drawn by four black artillery horses purchased by the Provisional Government from the British for the occasion. General Richard Mulcahy, finding yet fresh inspiration, delivered a historical oration.

Mulcahy replaced Collins as Commander-in-Chief and it was not long before walls in Dublin bore the slogan:

MOVE OVER MICK. MAKE ROOM FOR DICK.

TWENTY-ONE

The press in England and America searched out their richest phrases to pay tribute to Ireland's great dead leader and in America sympathy for the Free State cause quickened. Lord Birkenhead grieved for the death of the man who had in a strange way become his friend, "a complex and a very remarkable personality," he said, "daring, resourceful, volatile and merry." In his official message to Cosgrave, Lloyd George talked of "personal sorrow", and writing to Collins's sister, George Bernard Shaw urged: "Don't let them make you miserable about it: how could a born soldier die better than at the victorious end of a good fight, falling to the shot of another Irishman—a damned fool, but all the same an Irishman who thought he was fighting for Ireland—'A Roman to a Roman'?"

Collins was lamented not least among Republican prisoners.

445

In Kilmainham, says Tomy Barry[1] "There was a heavy silence throughout the jail, and ten minutes later from the corridor outside the top tier of cells I looked down on the extraordinary spectacle of about a thousand kneeling Republican prisoners spontaneously reciting the Rosary aloud for the repose of the soul of the dead Michael Collins, President of the Free State Executive Council and Commander-in-Chief of the Free State Forces." Barry adds that there was "little logic in such an action" though it was a just tribute from men who remembered that Collins was once "an inspiration and driving force in their struggle with the alien army of occupation."

As a body the Republican prisoners had little to be grateful for and at Maryborough Collins had had scant sympathy for them. Because the Executive Forces had nowhere to keep prisoners, particularly since Liam Lynch had directed on August 19th that the troops should be formed into small active service units and operate in the open, they had to release captives, usually having exacted from them a tongue-in-cheek promise not to carry arms again. Controlling the towns, and so the jails, the Provisional Government had accumulated some thousands of prisoners and their treatment of them was one of the most contentious issues of the times.

Like the British before them, the Provisional Government insisted that they were not fighting a war but suppressing a rebellion and, especially in jails as distinct from prison camps, they treated their captives as felons not as prisoners of war. This attitude provoked intense resentment among Republicans. On the other side of the coin, again like the British before them, the Provisional Government troops wore uniform and often fell victims to the guns of apparently harmless bystanders who disappeared into innocent crowds, or, having used their unsuspected guns, promptly gave themselves up claiming to be prisoners of war.

"In a village towards dark you would see all the women leaving, then the men would come in firing," says Joe McGuinness of the Dublin Brigade who fought under General Daly in his pitiless Kerry campaigns.

In Maryborough Prison where Frank Carty and his Wexford comrades were incarcerated a drastic bid for recognition of their status as prisoners of war was planned.

[1] *Guerilla Days in Ireland.*

A list of complaints was sent to the officer commanding the prison and the men threatened to refuse food from 3 p.m. next day (which would allow them to indulge in a satisfying lunch) if their demands were not met. The guards grinned knowingly whenever they encountered conspiratorial groups of prisoners and had no suspicion that anything more dangerous than a hunger strike was the subject of their whispered conversations. But the complaints and threats were all a red herring. The prisoners' intention was to set fire to the prison.

At three o'clock the next afternoon, August 29th, the gates to the exercise yard were opened for the recreation hour and the prisoners pushed their way in, making a little more noise than usual to make up for the absence of nearly a third of their numbers. Lots had been drawn and in each cell one man stayed behind. Carty, in a cell on the top landing, waited. The new furniture, the mattresses, even a few dollops of butter, were piled into a highly inflammable pyramid. A whistle blew. It was the signal to light the fire. Carty struck a match. So did all the other prisoners who had been allotted the task. Making sure that the pile of furniture was well alight, Carty made his way out on to the landing. Already the smoke was thick, issuing from all the cell doors on his landing and rising in dense, choking clouds from below. At once Carty realised that separate signals should have been given for each landing. Instead, the fires had been lit simultaneously on all landings and it was quite likely that he would suffocate as he tried to make his way through the smoke. He patted his pocket into which he had dropped a turkey egg. This had been sent to him by his father who, presumably, thought a turkey's egg would provide more nourishment than a chicken's. It had seemed a pity to leave it behind. Taking a deep breath where the smoke seemed thinnest, he felt for the stairs and, having found them, raced down them with the instinctive sure-footedness of an alarmed mountain goat.

He reached the exercise compound safely. The prisoners were in a state of jubilant excitement and, understandably enough, the guards began to fear an attempt to rush the fence. As Carty says, "If the prisoner thinks a guard with a gun looks frightening, nine hundred prisoners on the verge of a stampede must seem just as alarming to the guard."

There was a crackle of rifle shots and the prisoners threw

447

themselves flat. Five were wounded but most of the bullets were aimed high simply to deter any concerted move towards the wire. As they lay, the men could hear the gale of flames now sweeping the prison. Slowly they got to their feet. Carty's turkey egg was unbroken in his pocket. Came the rain. "A soft, a lovely soft Irish mist fell on our cheeks." Carty can almost feel the gentle touch of it still.

All through the night the rain drifted steadily down but the prisoners in the compound scarcely noticed it. Heedless of the efforts of the local fire brigade, the fire burned on, feeding on all it could find yet contained by the massive stone walls. The rain stopped about ten o'clock next morning and a couple of hours later the fire finally succumbed to the Dublin Fire Brigade which had been called to assist.

The prisoners agreed to return to their cells but declined to give an undertaking that they would not destroy any new furniture and equipment if it were issued to them. Heat had sunk deep into the huge granite blocks of the old prison, and, as the men made their way up the stairs and along the echoing landings, it seemed to them that they had entered a vast kiln. Back in their charred cells they stripped off their wet clothing and the heat from the walls dried it within an hour.

Their stubborn refusal to sign the undertaking meant that they were given no new bedding, no utensils, and a bizarre existence began. The men began to improvise their own comforts. With pieces of wood which had not been burned through some built bunks for themselves, and were not concerned that each time they clambered into them they blackened their hands. Others contrived to suspend themselves from the ceilings in hammocks. Carty merely wrapped himself in newspapers and slept on the floor. Ingenious fireplaces were made by breaking open the ventilator shafts which ran through the cells and fixing biscuit tins into them. Twisted, blackened receptacles were salvaged and used for a variety of purposes. For some four or five months they lived under these conditions.

The Provisional Government staff contented themselves with guarding the outside walls of the prison, from which it was said only one man had ever escaped. They allowed the prisoners the run of the building and to govern themselves.

448

It was a strange kind of autonomy, rather like that of the French prisoners in Dartmoor in Napoleonic times.

It was, in a sense, a victory for the prisoners, for they had broken the regime under which they had been treated as convicts and had established within the jail a prisoner-of-war camp. And, as in any prisoner-of-war camp, they began to organise dramatic societies and educational classes. Consistent attempts to build tunnels from cells on the ground floor were begun.

Prisoner-engineers estimated that it was necessary to sink the initial shaft at least twelve feet because of the depth of the foundations of the building, but invariably they met water. In spite of constant propping, walls and roofs crumbled. Once Carty was astonished to find that above him was no earth at all, only the exposed underside of a cell floor. Obstinate wills forced progress but none of the tunnels ever got very far. Free State troops would make midnight raids, searching the cells while the inmates were held under guard outside. When tunnels were discovered, the prisoners were punished by the age old method of stopping mail and parcels for a time.

The traditional battle of wits between prisoners and guards was unceasing. Prisoners seek out the venal or the sympathetic guard and usually there is one, sometimes more than one, but they know that they are as likely to be betrayed as helped. It is a chance that has to be taken. In Maryborough there was always the hope that one Irishman would help another, for there were waverers on both sides during the Civil War. The hope was never realised; the proffered friendship was unfailingly spurious.

In Limerick Jail, too, conditions were grim. Eight hundred prisoners were herded in a building meant for a hundred and twenty and General MacManus, Command Provost Marshal, was moved to write to the Civil Governor[2]:

"I cannot credit that such amazing ignorance exists at your headquarters with regard to the conditions at the County Jail partly under their jurisdiction.

"In view of the fact that at the moment an average of 12 prisoners sleep in each single cell, if conditions do not improve before the end of this week, I will have every cell

[2] Letter dated 6/11/22.

door taken down, in the interest of elementary sanitation and, indeed, of humanity."

But the interest of sanitation and humanity worked against the interests of security and the prisoners in Limerick Jail, among whom MacManus reported were "some of the most dangerous Irregulars in this command and in Kerry Command", had little to do but plan escape. Doubtful of the reliability of some of the guards—he had found from intercepted letters that some were taking bribes—MacManus put in his own men to gain the prisoners' confidence. Numerous smuggled letters passed through his hands but, though he took copies of them, they were delivered without delay. It was soon apparent that, while the Republican men were absent in roving guerrilla bands, the staunch women of the Cumann na mBan were exceedingly active. In Limerick the skeins of escape plots were in the energetic hands of Miss Madge Daly and Nurse Guthrie of the County Infirmary.

None were more irreconcilable Republicans than the party's women. This had been evident in the Dail debates when Countess Markievicz, Mrs Tom Clarke and Miss Mary MacSwiney had spoken with icy intransigence. These women had not settled back to become supporters on the touchline but were playing active, largely unhampered parts. In Cork, the brilliant and dominating young Miss MacSwiney, until her arrest in October, ran what was virtually Republican headquarters in Dalton's territory.

Once, when information was received that Erskine Childers had been seen at her home, Frank O'Friel went to the house and, without formality, entered by the open drawing-room window. There was a man there and O'Friel, in no doubt that it was Childers, arrested him. The man proved to be a journalist who remarkably resembled Childers but that was little consolation to O'Friel. Mary MacSwiney lashed him with such vituperation that her words ring in his ears yet.

Another visitor to Miss MacSwiney was Sean Hendrick who, with Frank O'Connor, was helping Erskine Childers to produce his newspaper under insuperable conditions. Constantly on the move, they were forever dismantling and reassembling their printing machine. Paper was a problem too, difficult to obtain and heavy to hump round the country.

When a small but vital part of the printing machine broke,
450

Hendrick took it to Cork to have it repaired. The job was soon done.

"I called up to Miss MacSwiney's before I left Cork to see if she had any messages," Hendrick remembers. "A mountain of documents she wanted me to take. I don't know if they were secret documents or what, but all I had was a raincoat and a bicycle and I had to point out that I hadn't a hope in hell of getting through with a whole lot of stuff like that. But I did take some military dispatches, hiding them in my sleeve. I had all sorts of forged stuff with me to explain who I was and what I was doing in that area."

Hendrick put his bicycle on a train and travelled to Coachford. Arrived safely, he was wheeling his bicycle along the main street when he almost ran into a sentry outside a National Army post. As he began a last minute rehearsal of his cover story, a car came from the opposite direction and stopped. An officer came from the post and walked to the car. To avoid the sentry, Hendrick approached him and asked the way to Macroom. He was given vague directions and went on his way, the sentry not bothering to stop a man who had passed muster with his superior officer.

Carrigadrohid was the next stage and there Hendrick hoped to hire a car. He cycled as far as a pub on the outskirts of the town and went in, making sure that he had a good view of the road. The man behind the bar told him that because a funeral was in progress there was not a car to be had.

"Then I saw a pony and trap coming down the road in the direction of Macroom and I went out and stopped the driver. He said he could give me a lift to Macroom. So I sat up on the high seat with him and we drove off. We had an edgy sort of conversation all the way, and when we were coming towards Macroom, he said, 'I suppose there'll be a guard on the bridge as usual.' The chap was giving me a hint, but anyway there was no guard on the bridge and he drove me right into the heart of Macroom and stopped outside the old Victoria Hotel, which was a Free State post. There were armoured cars there, troops, everything.

"I went into Williams's bar and there were Free State officers talking and drinking, many of them from Dublin like the fellow I'd asked the way in Coachford. I'd brought in the

451

man who had given me a lift for a drink, and I wasn't at all comfortable. An officer saw the *Cork Examiner* I had tucked under my arm and asked me if it was that day's paper. He just made off with it.

"So I finished up my drink and told Williams, who was behind the counter, that I had to get to Inchigeelagh on urgent business and could I hire a car. After a lot of humming and hawing finally he agreed to hire me a side-car. Before I went I located the officer who had taken my *Cork Examiner*, which I hadn't read myself, and asked for it back.

"Then I went out to a battered old side-car, put my bike in and set off. I got a great kick out of going from one Free State post to another. If there'd been even a perfunctory search, I'd have had it. I'm sure the driver of the side-car suspected who I was and where I was going, and he stopped a couple of miles short of Inchigeelagh and refused to go one inch further. I got a lift the rest of the way in a cart. The people I was looking for had gone on to Ballingeary. I carried on and found they'd gone from there too and were away over near Ballyvourney. I caught up with them there early in the morning having been on the road from Cork nearly twenty-four hours."

The Executive Forces were strongly entrenched in the region of Ballyvourney and Ballymakeery, on the Cork side of the Derrynassagart Mountains along the Cork-Kerry border, and it was from here that, early in September, they initiated an attack against Macroom. An armoured car, home-built in Cork, was to have helped in the attack but Sean Hendrick remembers that it failed to arrive in time because it had no reverse gear and, driven by a man from Galway who had to rely on a guide who stuttered, it kept missing turnings.

Attacks like that on Macroom were infinitely more costly to the Provisional Government than the effort to take the towns in the first place. Now the initiative lay with the Executive Forces and Lynch and his staff intended to use it. Lynch had burned his Fermoy headquarters on August 11th and taken to the hills where he worked out plans for small, highly mobile columns to operate in their own areas. In the end, they were bound to fail, for many doors once open to men on the run now were closed and, unlike the British, their opponents knew the terrain and the people, and they

452

knew the ways of guerrilla fighters. But the Republican effort, though it could achieve little, was far from spent.

As Dalton had occupied most of Cork, so Colonel Paul moved westward from Waterford to Dungarvan. Prout's men had pushed on from Clonmel to Cahir. The valley lands of Kerry were largely in Provisional Government hands. But it was a tenuous control. In the Knockmealdown Mountains and the Galtees men of the calibre of Dinny Lacey and Seamus Robinson organised one ambush after another. The road from Clonmel to Cahir was especially hazardous. On August 19th three lorries came under heavy machine-gun fire from a farm near the road.

"They stripped the leaves from the trees above us," says David Moran, but they had the range of the second lorry just right. Several men were killed. His friend Tommy Doyle commandeered a hire car from Cahir which the terrified driver had stopped in a gateway and drove into Clonmel for reinforcements. When Moran led a group to investigate the farmhouse, they found the family saying the Rosary. They had heard the firing at the back, they said, but had seen nothing. The ground was littered with bullet cases.

Sometimes the Republicans fired from the hills at the barracks in Clonmel and were amused when some of the National Army officers from Dublin rushed into the street and fired back at the mountains, which seemed deceptively close to their eyes.

An attempt to form a Neutral I.R.A. Association in Clonmel was broken up by National troops. Neither they nor the Republicans had much time for those who would not take sides. The men came from Bansha, Tipperary and Clonmel and their idea of acting as mediators had much to commend it, but they were not listened to and the fight went on.

In the Mullaghareirk Mountains across the border of Limerick and Cork, and the Ballyhoura Mountains further east of the same border, in the Derrynassagart Mountains and through the rugged heart of Kerry to the Slieve Mish Mountains and the Dingle Peninsula, the Republicans lived rough, hunted, sometimes merry lives. They were hard to find and though many of them kept away from trouble others were relentless setters of snares for their enemies. The west coast of Kerry was still mainly controlled by the Executive Forces.

With about a hundred men, as many as he could spare from Kenmare, Scarteen O'Connor sailed for Valentia Island on a boat carrying flour and meal. His aim was to take Cahirciveen, Waterville and Sneem to create several more National Army pockets in the Republican lining of Kerry. If he succeeded, he would control the four main towns along the coast road skirting the wild mountain hinterland. His troops, among whom was a Cork contingent, were well received in Valentia, then important for its Atlantic cable station. O'Conner crossed to Reenard Point, and as the troops landed they came under fire. Commandant Dick O'Sullivan (a captain at that time), Scarteen O'Connor's close friend and his second-in-command, says that they "were extended across the road from Reenard Point, advancing towards the main Waterville-Cahirciveen road. A few fellows were wounded—there may have been one or two killed. We were at it all day. The Irregulars were retreating as we were advancing, and they were keeping quite a safe distance between us—which suited us well."

Progress was slow and the National troops halted for the night. There were a few houses along the road one of which belonged to an elderly and very enthusiastic Republican. Food had been got for the troops, including fish brought up from Reenard's Point.

"I was in charge of the bit of commissariat that we had and the poor old devil was giving us buck, grumbling away, calling us traitors, 'Green and Tans' and so on, but we didn't take much notice. Eventually someone threatened to put him under arrest and he went upstairs to change and shave, full of himself." The old man was disappointed to learn that they were not moving on that night.

In the morning, following both road and railway, O'Connor's men renewed their advance into Cahirciveen, two miles away.

"Next thing," recalls Dick O'Sullivan, "the old chap caught us up, dressed in his Sunday best. I asked him where the hell he was going. 'I'm arrested,' he says. I had to send him home."

The National troops were anticipating a battle for

Cahirciveen which, with the hill behind it, lent itself to effective defence. But there was no fight. O'Connor's men took over the several posts, commandeered four or five cars and, that night, part of the force set out for Waterville, eight miles to the south-east on Ballinskelligs Bay.

"We had men hanging on to the cars at all angles," says O'Sullivan, who was driving the second car, O'Connor himself leading the way. The weight was too much for the front axle of O'Sullivan's car and he and his men had to find a foothold on the other vehicles. It was an improbable invasion force, but Waterville was taken without a shot fired. The landlady of the Butler Arms had hysterics when the National troops burst in, but O'Sullivan was able to pacify her. Several posts were established and sparsely garrisoned, but O'Connor had insufficient men to attempt to go on to Sneem on the Kenmare estuary, and in any case he was anxious to return to Kenmare.

Next day, he instructed O'Sullivan to return to Cahirciveen and to get hold of a boat. He was to sail to Waterville and there pick up O'Connor. It was not easy to persuade the owner of the nobby to make the trip. "A very decent little fellow, but he had the wind up," was O'Sullivan's verdict. By pretending to be irresponsibly drunk and brandishing his revolver he got his way. Some twenty Republican prisoners were loaded in the hold of the boat and they put to sea. The weather was rough and the prisoners were soon sea-sick. Packed in the hold as they were, they were probably also frightened, and with reason. So were the few National Army men O'Sullivan had with him. A good sailor himself, O'Sullivan still found it necessary to strap himself to the mast with his Sam Browne belt. Finally, they anchored in the lee of a church about four miles from Waterville and O'Sullivan sent a man into the town to let Scarteen O'Connor know they had arrived. He gave the messenger his revolver, the only one on board, and described the lie of the land to him.

As the messenger approached the bridge leading into Waterville, he was halted by a sentry, one of his own comrades. There was a misunderstanding and the sentry was shot dead. It was an angry commander who accompanied the emissary back to the nobby.

Kenmare was reached without further incident, the prisoners were removed and O'Connor ordered the boat to be held ready for him as he proposed to visit Cork, presumably to seek reinforcements from General Dalton. He had expected help from Killarney to the north, but a party of Dublin Guards under Brigadier-General Fionan Lynch had been ambushed at Robbers' Glen on the way and turned back. This was Lynch's own constituency and it was reported that Commandant Bishop, who was with him, commented ironically that his constituents did not seem to think much of him.

O'Connor was left in a precarious position. His men were now widely scattered; Kenmare was none too strongly held and the garrisons he had left in Cahirciveen and Waterville were isolated from Kenmare and from each other. Fortunately for him, they had been augmented by men from Cahirciveen who until now, like Brer Rabbit, had lain low and said nothing. The widely admired Fionan Lynch had a strong following in the Cahirciveen area from which he came.

The one National Army leader in South Kerry capable of rallying his men to his standard, Scarteen O'Connor was in himself a threat to the Republicans. During the Anglo-Irish war he had proved his courage many times. On one legendary occasion he had entered Kenmare alone, set himself up in the Library, a matter of fifty yards or so from the Black and Tan barracks, dispensed accurate bullets for several hours, then run in bare feet out of the town and finally got clean away on horseback. Laughingly, men had told him, "Scarteen, you'll never die with your boots on."

There was no doubt that if Scarteen O'Connor could be got rid of, Republican domination of the area would be much more secure.

On their return to Kenmare, on the evening of September 8th, O'Connor and O'Sullivan went to a party at Dr McCarthy's home, but the weary O'Sullivan left early, hoping to snatch some sleep before going out in the early hours of the morning to set a trap for Republican marauders who, night after night, had been harassing the O'Connor farm at Scarteen —from which the family's sobriquet had come. The plan was to travel in a noisy party of cars which would return to

Kenmare after O'Connor and O'Sullivan had been left behind to set up an ambush in the Scarteens' haggard.

When he left Dr McCarthy's, O'Sullivan made his way to the Scarteens' house in Kenmare, No. 5 Main Street, where the family had a bakery. A number of National troops were billeted here and in the adjoining houses. Their main post was the National Bank on the corner of the opposite side of the street. O'Sullivan got into a large bed beside John O'Connor, younger brother of Tom, who had been sleeping upstairs but had moved back to his own room and was determined to stay there because he had a cold which he blamed on upstairs draughts.

O'Sullivan woke at about dawn on Saturday, September 9th, to find Tom Scarteen O'Connor in the bedroom. He was telling someone standing behind him that Dick O'Sullivan was worn out and that they would go without him. "I jumped out of bed, full of youthful loyalty and told him not at all—I was going with him," says O'Sullivan. He got out his motor cycle and set off ahead of the cars. O'Connor's orderly travelled on the pillion. Arriving at the Scarteens', they decided to raid some of the local houses where the people were known to be unfriendly. "And the result was that we got the fellows we were looking for and took them in as prisoners to Kenmare. There was no need now to lay an ambush." The change of plan was to prove fateful.

First back into the town was O'Sullivan, with his pillion passenger. They had left the convoy two miles out, considering that scouts were no longer needed. It was well after 6 a.m. when they got back to Main Street. The orderly pitched himself down on a camp bed and went to sleep; John O'Connor was still in the big bed. O'Sullivan and Tom Scarteen, who had just come in, also got into the bed. Shortly afterwards, another Tom O'Connor, a cousin of the Scarteens and better known as Tom Thady, arrived and O'Sullivan invited him to "lie in here for a couple of hours".

"There's no bloody room there," answered Tom Thady and decided to go down to the Halls' public house, which opened early, and have a glass of porter. They were close friends and O'Sullivan elected to go with him. On the way out they met Scarteen O'Connor senior who was on his way back to the farm but was also intending to have a glass of porter at Halls' before he set out. There was no picquet; Scarteen O'Connor had sent them off to get some rest.

They had not been gone more than a few minutes when a group of Republicans entered the house, probably through the bakery at the rear, and climbed the stairs to the room on the first floor occupied by Brigadier-General Tom Scarteen O'Connor, his brother John, and his orderly. Upstairs on the second floor were quartered some National soldiers, and in another room were two girls. One, Nora O'Sullivan, aged twelve, had already known tragedy. Her father had died some years before and lately she had left her home in Valentia to help nurse an elderly relative in the Kerry-Cork mountains. Now, after his death, she was trying to make her own way home. Alone she had walked across the mountains and reached the farm of her distant relatives, the Scarteen O'Connors. Pat, the fourteen-year-old brother of the Brigadier-General, had cycled with her into Kenmare and left her at No. 5 Main Street where she was waiting for Tom to arrange a passage to Valentia for her. Her cousin, Kathleen Moriarty, a spirited girl of nineteen, shared the room with her. She had been adopted by the O'Connors.

When they heard the bell for Mass, Kathleen got up and dressed to go, but Nora decided not to attend that morning. Every detail of the next hours remains engraven in the memory of Nora O'Sullivan:

"I heard shooting, about two shots I think, and I got up and slipped into a black frock. As I was racing for the door, I heard Tom O'Connor's voice shouting, 'Great God, John is shot!' Then I looked over the landing and saw a thin cloud of smoke and the body of John lying on the landing, feet out over the stairs, head to the back of the wall, right arm, left arm to the doors; and Tom, not clothed, being dragged down the stairs by three or four men.

"I couldn't hear what they were saying but I heard Tom pleading, 'Would you not give a man a chance?' Then he was dragged down the turn of the stairs and I was looking over the top banister, and I heard him say to something they said, 'You don't shoot an unarmed man.'"

Almost half a century later she can still hear his voice utter

458

that last reproach to those who once had fought with him, whose own cause had been his cause and, the tragedy of it, was so still. Every inflection is as new in her mind as the sound of bells on the wind a moment since.

"I didn't hear any more clearly," she goes on. "There was an altercation then two or three more shots and smoke coming up all the way. Then Kathleen Moriarty was chased up the stairs by several men. They caught her and put her with her back to the wall and a gun to her breast and told her they would shoot her if she spoke one word.

"And she called the men by name, called three of them by name and shouted 'Murderers' at them."

They are dead, all three, and there is no point in branding them here. Their methods had, unhappily, become the norm of the times. They had been Collins's methods, the methods of Bloody Sunday, the methods of the British when, for instance, they killed Tomas MacCurtain, Lord Mayor of Cork. The nature of the struggle with England had made ambush and assassination necessary. But the methods and the weapons of war soon brutalise, horrify at first then become familiar. In 1940 an R.A.F. officer was reprimanded for not untying a bundle of propaganda leaflets before dropping them over Germany—he might have endangered the life of a German civilian. In 1945 there was Dresden and then Hiroshima and Nagasaki.

The Republicans, who seemed to have been drinking, searched the house for "the other bastards", presumably more of the Scarteen O'Connors for they did not bother about the National troops. This suggests that there may have been an element of personal vendetta. Of the National soldiers Miss O'Sullivan says, "They would be half dressed as they would also have heard the shooting." There is no reproach in her voice but the behaviour of those men surely fell short of courage. Perhaps they did not realise what was happening, or where the shots had come from, for the whole incident took less than five minutes.

Kathleen and Nora were locked in the back bedroom and from the window they saw the Republicans go. Some of them Miss O'Sullivan remembers vividly, especially one "who wore a navy jacket and had golden yellow hair". Two of the men wore National Army jackets. Oddly, there was a lull in the noise from the bakery as they went and their footfalls sounded to the girls upstairs.

"About the time they got past the outside wall and in amongst the sycamore trees, firing started in the town from two sides," Miss O'Sullivan continues. "Bullets began to rain in the window where we were, so we lay flat on the floor of the bedroom. The men from the front rooms joined us, then we crawled on our tummies to one of the other rooms."

They saw several National Army men run from neighbouring houses to join the garrison in the National Bank, which now came under concentrated fire diagonally from houses further along the street.

"I heard the men calling for Scarteen, and they were calling for quite a time. It was quite pitiful. They must have been calling for the most of an hour. Later, men tunnelled down from a shop called Maybury's, down through Meighan's, through half a dozen houses and right into the sitting-room of our house. They had fought their way through. There must have been some Free State soldiers still in the other houses."

As the Republicans battered their way through into Murphy's next door, which would bring them almost directly opposite the Bank, "there was shooting going on between our sitting-room and the room next door. While this was happening, we two girls and two Free State soldiers—Tom O'Connor's orderly was one of them—crawled downstairs over the dead bodies and into the kitchen." One of the Republicans who had tunnelled into the house was Seamus Robinson from Tipperary, another was Tom McEllistrim, now a member of the Dail, who was upset by what had happened in the house that morning and went out of his way to express his sympathy to the girls. He was very concerned that young girls should have been subjected to such an ordeal.

When, late in the afternoon, the battle was done and the girls had watched the defeated garrison of the Bank lined up as prisoners in the street, they set to work to clear up after the shooting. Both Tom and John O'Connor had been shot between the eyebrows and the backs of their heads had been blown off. Blood and brains had spattered the walls. "It was

460

part of my job, being young and agile," says Nora O'Sullivan simply, "to clean that part of it up." That was what civil war meant to a girl of twelve.

Dick O'Sullivan and Tom Thady O'Connor knew nothing of the assassination of their leader. After leaving Main Street, they had given up the idea of a drink, and instead walked down Henry Street to O'Sullivan's own home.

"It was a small hotel, our place," O'Sullivan explains, "and we went round the back and over the gate. There were birds in the trees and on the roofs of the sheds. Tom Thady fired a shot—he wouldn't hit a haystack, but the noise roused my father, who shouted at us from a back window."

They were admitted to the house and a maid got them breakfast. Then came a warning that "some Irregulars were coming up the next backway to ours. We looked out and saw five or six lads coming up. They knew we were there. We came out to our hall door to see if we could get down to the Bank, but when we put our noses out the door was licked with bullets from the Bank, from our own fellows. The bloody place was a turmoil of shots."

O'Sullivan's father thought they were going and tried to shut the door, but they pushed their way back and climbed up through a skylight into an attic, which was not easy to find and which during the Tan war had been used to hide "whatever bits of I.R.A. arms" O'Sullivan had in his possession. Republicans searched the house but did not investigate the attic; nor did they return when a girl in the street shouted to them that O'Sullivan and O'Connor were still there.

"They could have made a much more thorough search, but they were in the charge of a local lad and he may have been a bit half-hearted about it," says O'Sullivan.

The fugitives in the attic were given distorted reports of the fighting as the hours went on, but eventually it was clear that the Republicans had taken the town. Brigadier Rice had achieved this with about seventy men. Each of the three main Government posts, the National Bank, the Library and the workhouse, had succumbed to his tactics of moving men down through a line of houses and attacking unexpectedly from a position directly opposite. Throughout the Civil War, as in the 1916 Rising, it was the defenders of buildings besieged by men with more freedom of action who usually

461

came off worst. Neither the lesson of the Four Courts, nor the earlier lesson of the G.P.O. in Dublin had been learned.

"I said to Thady, 'Begod, you know, now things have quietened down, they'll remember this hideout,'" continues O'Sullivan. "We'd always had an escape route from the attic, out on to the roof and over a big cement water-tank. So we took it and got down to a hayshed at the bottom of the yard. We stayed there until dusk, then we got out into the country."

For two or three days they stayed in hiding and were joined by three others, Seamus Cooper, Mickey Connolly and Swayne—who had been the National Army commander of Kenmare under Tom Scarteen O'Connor, who was in charge of South Kerry. They stole a boat, though Tom Thady and Swayne were reluctant to join in this venture, and at night rowed several miles in rough water down the Kenmare estuary to Blackwater. Near collapse, they were picked up by a British patrol boat, the *Seawolf*. Their clothes were dried and they were given a meal, then in the early morning they were transferred to the *Gaelic*, a coaster which had slipped out of Kenmare and was now anchored twelve miles down river. On board the *Gaelic*, O'Sullivan and his friends went on to Cork. There he sought advice at the Mercy Hospital as he had tonsilitis badly, but he refused to be admitted, preferring to stay with Tom Thady at the Imperial Hotel. As they left the hospital they saw the body of Tom Keogh carried in.

Colonel-Commandant Keogh had spent the previous night at Macroom and was leading a sweep to Killarney where he was to link up with General Daly. At Carrigaphooca they found the road had been mined on the bridge. The mine had been booby-trapped so that it exploded when lifted and Keogh and several of his men were killed. Keogh was another of the men who had been closest to Collins and he was one of those who had taken part in the McEoin rescue attempt. His death by such a means reflected the increasing nastiness of the war. The booby-trap device became common in Cork and Kerry. It led to prisoners being made to remove mines and from that it was but one more step to destroying prisoners deliberately.

TWENTY-TWO

The aims of the two sides in the Civil War were identical in the long term. What separated them was the difference of approach. It was rather like two people meeting on the International Dateline at midnight and arguing whether it was Tuesday or Wednesday. Some held strong views and others had only to meet an old friend with a plausible tongue to switch sides. Both groups had sympathisers among the civilian population. The ultimate loyalty of all was to Ireland. Lesser loyalties were frailer. Friends became foes overnight and there was no telling who among non-participants was ready to betray one side to the other. Secrets were vulnerable and information received suspect. It all made life very difficult for the military leaders.

General McEoin was planning the final clearance of Sligo. He was desperately keen to recover the lost armoured car, *The Ballinalee*, which the Executive Forces were putting to clever use. On September 9th, they attempted to recapture Tobercurry which, on July 28th, they had abandoned without a fight to McCabe who had marched a strong force eleven miles across country from Ballymote. *The Ballinalee* attacked the several Provisional Government posts, including the R.I.C. barracks, but the garrisons fought sturdily as the armoured car passed one way and then the other with machine-gun crackling busily. For a time the car disappeared; when it returned, it carried a mine on a hastily rigged shelf at the rear. *The Ballinalee* was backed close to the barrack doors and attempts were then made to drop the mine. The idea just did not work out, and at about 9 p.m., after a five hour engagement involving one death on either side, the Republicans retired.

Ballina was their next objective and they swooped on the town on September 12th, disarming the garrison and taking them prisoner. McEoin sent Lawlor to take the town back. The main body of Republicans had already left, some taking the coast road to the north and west, the remainder disappearing into the Ox Mountains. There was no fight and Lawlor,

463

having quickly restored National Government control of the town, set out to rejoin McEoin at Tobercurry.

"Kilroy was waiting for us in the Ox Mountains," says Lawlor. "The road made a series of S-bends round low, bumpy hills. We had a number of vehicles and we couldn't see more than one car's length in front of us. They ambushed us, got us badly. Colonel Joe Ring was with us, a great old fighter, and I said for him to take one side of the road and I'd take the other."

With another man, Lawlor took up a position behind a low bank. To his astonishment, bullets appeared to be coming through. He was hit in the arm himself and his companion was seriously wounded. Then he saw that behind them a man lying flat on the ground was shooting at them with a revolver. Once discovered, the man did not stay to argue. Lawlor, who was not wearing a shirt, slung his comrade over his shoulders and staggered to a shed. There he found two or three armed Republicans who took one look at him and ran. Lawlor realised that with the wounded man's blood all over his head and shoulders he must have seemed like a devil.

McEoin now had another armoured car and this he sent to meet Lawlor in case of trouble. When it arrived, the ambushers had been fought off and ten had been taken prisoner, but Colonel Joe Ring, who was to have taken up an appointment as a commissioner of the new *Garda Siochana*, was dead. "The armoured car had joined us," resumes Lawlor, "and next thing *The Ballinalee* shot out from a side road and bullets flew everywhere. I was in a touring car and we jumped out and sheltered behind the armoured car. But the gunner in their car and the driver in ours were dead."

Says McEoin: "The driver of my armoured car was drilled through the head, a bullet whipping through the visor. In his dying motions he knocked the gear lever and the car stopped. The second driver pushed him aside, took his place and they drove off *The Ballinalee*."

The prisoners were brought to McEoin in Tobercurry. "I ordered a court-martial and they were sentenced to death, the whole lot," says McEoin. "There was a mission in the town and some of the missioners came down and asked mercy for them. I told them they'd had none for Joe Ring and those fellows on the road, so it was hard for them to expect me to
464

have it. Then I said, 'Very well. Here they are for you. Take them yourselves and be accountable for them.' They swore, both to me and to the missioners, that they would stop all their activities.

"I had no intention of shooting them. I didn't want prisoners and I knew anyway that they'd be in trouble, because no one would believe they'd got their freedom without giving something away."

The Republicans had hotted up their action throughout the area. On September 13th a large group, arriving in cars and on bicycles, surprised the National garrison in Ballymote and seized one post. A second post they attempted to capture by a ruse. One of their number acted the roysterer going home and tried to stagger close enough to the barbed wire round the post to hurl a bomb into it. The sentry ordered him back and at once his companions opened fire. Shots were exchanged for an hour before Provisional Government troops reasserted their control of the town.

Ten days earlier, Republicans in stockinged feet overpowered the sentry of a Provisional Government post in Dromahair and helped themselves to guns. They took the commanding officer prisoner but ignored the rest of the garrison. Four National soldiers were killed in a surprise attack on Seskin on September 15th. Among their seventeen prisoners was General Neary who, shortly afterwards, shot two guards dead and escaped.

In the same week, the old *Tartar*, McEoin's one-vessel naval squadron, had a twenty-minute battle with Republican troops who came from their "Rahelly" headquarters to ambush her at Raughley Head, but so often had she been machine-gunned from old hookers or currachs from Donegal, that McCabe had covered her with a patchwork of old iron shutters and mounted a swivel Lewis gun in her bow, and she came to no harm. More Republicans waiting for her at Rosses Point were thwarted, for the *Tartar* missed the tide.

Since McCabe had first requisitioned her in July, the *Tartar* had done sterling service. Once she had sailed with a consignment of petrol for Lawlor at Ballina with Matt Farrelly in command. Lawlor describes Farrelly as "about six feet tall and six feet wide. A bullet head with a shock of red hair. Revolver on each leg, Thompson machine-gun under the arm

465

and a bottle of whiskey in the hip pocket. A good soldier and a hard one."

The pilot boarded the vessel at Enniscrone and explained to Farrelly that as Ballina was a shallow port he would have to wait for the tide. Farrelly was furious, blamed the pilot and called him a Bolshie and, finally, with a great roar of mirth, had him hoisted by the ship's derrick.

On September 16th the Republicans attacked Boyle in force during the night and the next day made two attacks on Castlebar county jail. On each occasion they were driven off, or they left having accomplished all they set out to do. It was not their policy to set up defensive positions but to cut and thrust their way across the country, striking unexpectedly.

Meanwhile, McEoin's own plans had been maturing and he had brought in reinforcements, war-hardened men, to mount a large-scale operation against the Executive Forces to the north of Sligo.

His aim was to encircle the very active Republicans who were operating in large numbers in the north of counties Leitrim and Sligo under the command of Generals Liam Pilkington and Seamus Devins. He hoped, too, that at last he might recapture *The Ballinalee*, so expunging the humiliation of Dooney Rock. At the courthouse in Sligo were concentrated troops, armoured cars, motor lorries, machine-guns and the old 18-pounder gun on the barrel of which was chalked "McEoin's Peacemaker".

Columns were to be led by McEoin himself, Lawlor (who had an arm wound) and Farrelly, whilst General Simons, based in Sligo, as to be controller of operations. General Joe Sweeney was to bring a force south from Bundoran, another column was to come in from the coast near Benbulbin and yet another, under Colonel Seamus Connell, was to march in from near Drumbodmean just across the border in Fermanagh. More men were to come from Collooney, Kiltyclogher and Manorhamilton. On Sunday, September 17th, McEoin led his forces from Sligo. Precise as always, he signalled his order to march by a blast on a whistle. They were given an enthusiastic send-off by the townspeople, then McEoin sealed off the town. He was genuinely sorry that he was forced to put people to inconvenience but this was his solution to the problem of security. The farmer driving home from town, the
466

beguiling girl on a bicycle, the young man going fishing might easily carry a message to the enemy forces.

The first encounter of McEoin's drive was at Drumcliffe Bridge at about ten o'clock next morning. On the other side of the bridge, which had been blown up, *The Ballinalee* waited impertinently. "We had an armoured car with us and an old 18-pounder with three shells, all that remained of nine," recalls McEoin. "But, of course, we were held up there until we could bridge the gap and get across. I ordered up the 18-pounder and to my pleasant surprise *The Ballinalee* withdrew."

McEoin's force made the crossing but met with strong resistance. They pushed the Executive Forces back, only to be held fiercely for twenty minutes at Rathcormach. Six prisoners were taken. *The Ballinalee* was still prowling and when the National troops advanced towards the home of Mr Warren Henry at Milltown the armoured car produced a blizzard of shots which drove farmers into the creamery for safety. Outside, there was turmoil as horses panicked, carts collided and cream threatened to turn itself into cheese at any moment. The farmers had to stay under shelter for some time as bullets skeltered in all directions, splattering windows and walls and skidding off roof-tops. At length, the stronger fire power of the National troops began to drive the Republicans back and a well-placed shell from the 18-pounder hastened their departure.

The encircling National troops closed in relentlessly. To the north in Co. Leitrim Sweeney captured the villages of Kinlough on Lough Melvin and Tullaghan on the coast near Bundoran. Eastwards, Kiltyclogher was captured and thirty prisoners taken. Fourteen more prisoners were taken at Manorhamilton, four of whom were in possession of a hundred-weight bomb. One of the main objectives of the pincer movement was the Executive Forces Headquarters at "Rahelly", a mansion on the Gore-Booth estate between Sligo and Bundoran, but it was deserted when the National Forces reached it. They made a haul of bicycles and bedding but little else. Some of the National troops who raced to join in the encirclement had left Dromahair the previous Sunday night after compelling a strong detachment of Republicans to quit. But on the Monday the Republicans

467

returned and wrecked the railway line to Enniskillen across the border.

Monday was a big day in Collooney, where life had resumed its normal tenor; it was the day of the annual Harvest Fair. In the evening a special train loaded with cattle and cattle dealers left the town. As it rattled down a steep slope half-way between Collooney and Dromahair, the driver saw a signal at red and, beyond the signal, closed crossing gates. This was all very unexpected and the driver could not stop the train. As it crashed through the gates, a dozen Republicans signalled frantically to the driver to stop. A few shots were fired. Slowly the brakes began to hold and the ambushers, racing after the train, reached the engine.

Apologetically they explained to the driver that they intended to derail his train in order to stop the National troops from using the line. The driver saw the point but asked them to allow him to go as far as Dromahair. This was agreed and a number of the Republicans joined the train. At Dromahair the driver asked what was going to happen to the cattle when the train was derailed. The problem was appreciated and it was solved quite ingeniously. Some empty waggons were coupled to the rear of the train which then proceeded to a convenient point a few hundred yards outside Dromahair where it stopped. The empties were uncoupled, the Republicans tore up the line behind the train and the engine-driver shunted the unwanted waggons into the gap. That satisfied the Republicans and satisfied the train driver, too, for he was able to continue with his cargo of cattle to Enniskillen.

Contained though they were in McEoin's iron circle, the Executive Forces, in some strength, fought stubbornly as the week went on. Those driven from Rahelly made for the Glencar Mountains but were headed off by "McKeon's Peace Maker" and turned eastwards towards Manorhamilton where, subsequently, there was hard fighting.

In the mountainous region round Grange, Ballintrillick and Cashelgarran the sporadic but relentless struggle endured. Wary as wrestlers reaching for each other's fingers, each side probed the other. It was the National Army which exerted the pressure. For a time it would be resisted, the advance held, then their Republican adversaries would melt elusively away. Nevertheless, about a hundred prisoners were taken in three days. One was a young fellow flushed out of a field like a frightened bird as McEoin's men deployed across it. He was out of breath and McEoin, suspecting at once that he carried dispatches, had him arrested. But all he had in his possession were three or four rounds of ammunition. He admitted that he belonged to the other side, gave his name and asked to be allowed to see his mother and sister before he was taken away. His sister, he said, was leaving for Australia next day to be a nun. This story McEoin later verified.

The young man pointed out a neat thatched cottage on a nearby corner and McEoin told him to walk beside him. "I'll come in with you," said McEoin and almost wished he had not, for the mother and sister of his captive at once started to cry and the mother begged him not to take her boy away and leave her alone in the house.

"How can I agree to that when he is behaving like this? He'll just rejoin the Irregulars if I let him go."

The mother promised that he would not; she would see to it herself, and McEoin gave in.

"Take him and keep him," he said.

Often cautious, sometimes weighing up and testing a man for days before forming a judgment, McEoin yet had a remarkable faith in human nature. Simple country folk like these he could sum up rapidly. "When you got that kind of assurance it was usually honoured," he says. "Anyway, I found that this was much better than taking prisoners."

On Wednesday, September 20th, McEoin, who was at Grange almost on the coast, had news of *The Ballinalee*. She had turned right, down along the Benbulbin Mountains. The trail was still warm and to his astonishment McEoin discovered that "the armoured car had taken a road which runs along in a horseshoe, up then down, going nowhere."

"We immediately blocked the two ends of the road," continued McEoin. If we lost the armoured car in a slipshod manner, they lost it even more reprehensibly, because they knew the operation was on. Anyway, the five men in *The Ballinalee* left the car, dismantled the Vickers gun and took it with them. They went up the face of the mountain and reached the top but by this time a party of National Government troops under my command had come up from the back of Benbulbin."

Lawlor, acting within the framework of McEoin's overall plan, had sent three men in a T Model Ford to cut off any stragglers who found their way across the Benbulbin Mountains. "One of the fellows told me that there was no way out for them unless they came down the waterfall," says Lawlor. "I sent my men up the mountain and what happened then no one really knows."

McEoin believes that "when the crew of the armoured car appeared over the crest, my men opened fire and killed them all." And that, he says, "was in accordance with my orders. We had had most of the funerals up till then and I felt that when they were under arms and on the alert they couldn't complain if they were shot at."

McEoin's view that the death of the five men was ruthless but fair may well be the right one. If it is not, then only those who survive of the National Army party know the truth. Being the man that he is, whatever happened, McEoin will insist that his was the responsibility. Among the dead was Brigadier-General Seamus Devins and his Divisional Adjutant, Bryan MacNeill, son of Eoin, now Minister of Education in the Provisional Government. Bryan MacNeill's death was the more poignant because his brother was a captain in the National Army. "Fratricidal strife" was not a mere figure of speech when brothers such as the Hales and the MacNeills were on opposite sides. That they should have been so makes nonsense of the propaganda of both sides, which insisted that friends and brothers had become monsters overnight, traitors to their country and capable of any atrocity.

It is true that good men on both sides became embittered and brutalised as the Civil War dragged on, that there were atrocities which will never be forgiven by those who suffered. But they are an aging and mellowing generation and the time to forget must soon come. The great majority have nothing of which to feel ashamed.

The killing of MacNeill, Devins, and their comrades may or may not have been above board but the theft of a watch from one of the bodies certainly wasn't. Years later, General

470

McEoin learned of it from the man's bitter widow and did not rest until he had recovered the watch for her.

For Tony Lawlor, who sent the troops up the mountain, the grief of the day still lingers, for Bryan MacNeill had fought with him in the 6th Dublin Brigade during the Tan War and when, after the split, Lawlor had been sent to Athlone whilst MacNeill had joined Pilkington in Sligo, the two men remained fast friends and corresponded with each other throughout the struggle.

"That was the end of the war in Sligo," says McEoin, and adds dryly, "They had their funerals three days later and after that we had none and neither did they."

TWENTY-THREE

By the end of August, de Valera saw that the Republican cause in the field was lost. He had never had much heart in the fight and now it seemed to him that stubborn anger, rather than idealism, excited fingers on triggers, that the military leaders were going their own way impatient of the political objectives which in the beginning had been the justification for the bullets. He saw that the people were unlikely to separate military and political aspects and that they were unaware he was no longer in effective control.

Provisional Government propaganda relentlessly insisted that he and Childers were the "Irregular" leaders and the people, Republican supporters among them, who were fed up with the fighting and destruction, had little reason to disbelieve it. The simple fact was that "Dev", the former President, was the recognised leader of the opposition to the Treaty and he had made a mistake in joining the Executive Forces in any capacity. If he had hoped to link the political and military functions, then he had failed. In Professor Michael Hayes's view, "The Civil War would have been no more than a riot only for Dev's political cloak over it."

De Valera was anxious for more cohesion between the military and political leaders and he urged abandonment of the struggle. Failing that, he wanted it made clear that its continuation was the responsibility of the Executive. He was

471

glad to learn from a letter smuggled from Mountjoy Prison that Liam Mellows was thinking upon similar lines. Other Dublin supporters who were outside the military circle also were pressing de Valera to reorganise the political front of the anti-Treaty party.

But Liam Lynch was politely unco-operative. When de Valera wrote that he wished to interview the individual members of the Executive before their next meeting, at the end of August, Lynch answered that because of the risks to the officers involved, and as the military situation had improved, he had not thought a meeting necessary. Loftily he told his chief that he would be "only too pleased to have your views at any time on the general situation, and matters arising out of it, and they will receive my earnest consideration."

However, this letter did not reach de Valera until the middle of September and by then he had taken action on his own initiative. Filtering unostentatiously through Tipperary he got to Dublin where secretly he met Mulcahy on September 6th. The encounter was arranged by an American priest, who convinced a doubtful Mulcahy that it might end the Civil War. Mulcahy was in a dilemma as members of the Cabinet had agreed to eschew lone wolf peace moves and consulted his colleague, MacNeill, before going ahead.

Mulcahy and de Valera stood throughout their brief interview. Mulcahy insisted that the Treaty should stand and the army should be subject to Parliament. De Valera's reply, he reported to the Cabinet next day, left "no room for discussion." Some men were led by faith, some by reason, de Valera said. While men of faith, like Rory O'Connor, were taking the stand they were, he was a humble soldier following them. This was no more than the truth. De Valera had chosen his lowly rank himself and, in what had become an essentially military situation, leadership of the Republican movement had devolved upon Lynch.

Almost three months after the election the new Dail met at last, on September 9th, the day that the Scarteen O'Connors died so dubiously in Kenmare. The Republican deputies were hardly in a position to attend, even if they had been prepared to do so, and Mr Laurence Ginell was quickly expelled on his refusing to sign the roll because he could not get a satisfactory answer to his question: "Is it Dail Eireann for the whole of Ireland, or is it a Partition Parliament?"

The Dail was not sure itself exactly what it was. Pointing out that they had been working as an "interlocking directorate", Gavan Duffy wanted to know whether the President to be elected in the Dail would be Chairman of the Provisional Government, whether the Ministers would be the Provisional Government, Mulcahy proposed Cosgrave, who had been Acting President, as President of the Dail, Michael Hayes had earlier been elected Speaker.

If he were elected Cosgrave said, he would "implement the Treaty, enact the Constitution, support and assist the National Army and ask Parliament if necessary for any powers thought necessary to restore order, to expedite a return to normal conditions and to speed reconstruction and reparation."

He made it clear, in answer to Gavan Duffy's question as to whether "the present system of dual government would be unified", that the old dichotomy of Dail and Provisional Government would come to an end. Cosgrave was elected. Thomas Johnson, leader of the Labour Party "with great regret" voted against him. Earlier, in a well reasoned speech which stamped him at once as a potentially effective Opposition leader, he reminded the Dail that the public had never been told why the conferences of a few months earlier had broken down; they knew only "the eventuality of civil war". He allowed that "perhaps it was necessary in a revolutionary period that the Government should take on itself responsibilities and not be accountable at that period to any Assembly for their acts", but he insisted that the Government was the servant of the Dail and asked that the country be given "some kind of hope that something less than grinding in the dust is going to satisfy the Powers that be and the Powers that hope to be."

As he saw it, "the situation that faces the country arises from a different interpretation of the promises, the undertakings, the pledges that men gave, and of the temperaments of those men", and he asked that instead of trying to flatten opposition it could be made clear that it was recognised the country was accepting "something very definitely short of its rightful demands". He urged that a solution of the unemployment problem would in itself ease the war situation and wanted an assurance that the new Ireland "would mean a country in which cash relations would be minimised and human relations magnified."

Johnson was right to pinpoint unemployment as an aggravation of the war, for many young men in search of a career were eager to join the colours of the National Army, and innumerable stalwarts of the Republican I.R.A., leaders among them, accustomed from boyhood to the freedom and adventure of the guerrilla fighter's life, to the camaraderie of men on the run and to the frugal but wholesome living off the countryside, were little tempted by the prospect of becoming hungry nonentities on street corners.

Cosgrave nominated his Ministers. Richard Mulcahy remained as Minister of Defence, Kevin O'Higgins was given Home Affairs and Desmond Fitzgerald Foreign Affairs, Ernest Blythe was to take charge of Local Government, Patrick Hogan Agriculture, Joseph McGrath Industry and Commerce and Eoin MacNeill Education. The new Postmaster General was J. J. Walsh and Cosgrave himself was to be responsible for Finance. E. J. Duggan and Fionan Lynch were Ministers without portfolio. Of the Treaty delegation Duggan alone remained in the Government. Griffith and Collins were dead. Robert Barton had thrown in his lot with the Republicans and was a prisoner and Gavan Duffy, though he supported the Treaty still, had resigned from the Cabinet because the old English Judiciary had been adopted by the Provisional Government whereas he believed that the new Judiciary should have evolved from the Republican courts established during the war with England. He was to become a remorseless critic of the new Government.

In a long statement Cosgrave summarised the course of events. He declared that the enemies of the Treaty could have maintained "an attitude of opposition on constitutional lines to the Government policy". Instead, it had become evident "that neither peace, order nor security could possibly be maintained if the Government did not take strong and definite action" and he adduced evidence to show that the Republicans had sought to provoke the return of English troops and English administration in the hopes of securing unity.

474

"There must not, and will not, be an armed body in the community without the sanction of Parliament," said Cosgrave.

On September 18th, President Cosgrave introduced the Constitution Bill but it was Kevin O'Higgins, whose political star was rising fast, who was charged with the task of piloting the Bill through the Dail. From the signing of the Treaty O'Higgins had spent much time in London helping to unravel the problems which arose from the handing over of power and the withdrawal of English troops, and later taking part in the negotiations which followed the submission of the draft Constitution.

O'Higgins, son of a doctor, was thirty. Expulsion from Maynooth had ended a not very fervent ambition to be a priest and when he joined the Volunteers in 1914 he was an almost equally unenthusiastic law student. He had always used words with wit and style, often financing a round of drinks at Mooney's by scribbling some piece which he could sell to a newspaper for a few shillings cash on the spot. As he interested himself more profoundly in the nationalist ideal he soon made himself an effective speaker, and in 1918 he served a five months' jail sentence for his views. One of his fellow prisoners was Ernest Blythe, now his Cabinet colleague. Elected to Parliament in the Sinn Fein landslide, O'Higgins became Assistant Minister of Local Government to Cosgrave in the clandestine Dail Government which did so much to undermine English administration. In the Dail Cabinet which Griffith formed, and in the Provisional Government under Collins, O'Higgins had been Minister of Economic Affairs.

Though he respected the qualities of the steady Cosgrave, a veteran of the Easter Rising whose death sentence had been commuted, temperamentally O'Higgins was often at odds with him and would have preferred Mulcahy as leader at this juncture. But Mulcahy was essentially a military man, as O'Higgins and Cosgrave were political beings, and temperaments began to clash. O'Higgins always spoke light-heartedly of his military career. At this time he was Assistant Adjutant-General to Gearoid O'Sullivan, and Patrick McGilligan, who was then at the very beginning of what was to prove a distinguished political career, remembers O'Sullivan's good-humoured resignation as his rather untidy desk received constant attention from O'Higgins's orderly fingers.

It was inevitable that a revolutionary army, that is men fighting for a political ideal, should throw up some leaders who had a flair for soldiering rather than politics and some whose bent was for politics rather than for military leadership, and it followed that in the post-revolution period there would be an element of conflict as each sought to preserve positions of leadership. This rivalry between the military orientated and the politically minded developed in both pro-Treaty and anti-Treaty parties but as yet it was impossible to separate out the functions.

By September, 1922, the National Army had established its superiority and it was obvious that the Republicans could not win. What they could do, and showed every sign of doing, was to keep guerrilla activities going for years. In essence, and ironically, the Provisional Government found themselves in much the same position as the British had been, but with the added disadvantage of having, not to maintain an administrative system made effective through centuries of experience, but to build up a system, to learn the functions of government and to govern. Meanwhile, for the sake of their ideals, the Republicans seemed bent on creating a pauperised people in a charred land. Bombs and fire were eating at the heart of the country's new and insecure economy. Unemployment was reaching a dangerous level. Moreover, every effort was made to frustrate the new administration and even to set up rival administrative organs. The courts particularly were hindered. Again the Republicans were following the pattern which had been so effective against England.

"The life of this nation is menaced," said Kevin O'Higgins in the Dail. "It is menaced politically, it is menaced economically, it is menaced morally." He saw that the country must collapse if the corrosion of Government power were not halted quickly. Impatient of the Army's inability to settle the issue, he sought more control by the Cabinet. Army leaders, on the other hand, thought he was meddling in their affairs already and that he should give more attention to his own Department. Mulcahy, holding the dual appointment of Minister of Defence and Commander-in-Chief, thought there was sufficient liaison between the Army and the Cabinet.
476

There was no friction between the Ministry of Defence and the Commander-in-Chief," Mulcahy says humorously, but between him and O'Higgins a tension grew which Cosgrave was compelled to try to check.

It was difficult to maintain army discipline in the face of attacks, often by seemingly innocent civilians who either disappeared into a crowd or, having achieved their object, then surrendered as prisoners of war. O'Higgins was critical of lapses by the National Army, and some of these lapses were inexcusable. Mulcahy, as high-principled as O'Higgins, deplored them too, but better understood the provocation and supported his officers. In the Dail, Mulcahy frankly admitted some of the accusations against men of the National Army.

He asked the Government, on behalf of the Army, for special powers, powers to hold military courts and to inflict severe penalties, including death, on men convicted of the possession "without proper authority" of firearms, ammunition or explosives; of arson, looting or the destruction of private or public property; of taking part in, or aiding and abetting, attacks on the National Forces; or of the breach of any general order or regulation made by the Army Council.

The proposals were considered at arduous length and with the utmost anxiety by the Cabinet, and finally were accepted unanimously. The decision was emphatically that of the Cabinet, the responsibility of every member being precisely that of every other. If the instigator were Mulcahy, the advocate in the Dail, ironically, was O'Higgins. As usual, he spoke concisely, logically and well. "I don't think any of us hold human life cheap; but when, and if, a situation arises in the country when you must balance the human life against the life of the nation, that presents a very different problem." This situation now existed in Ireland, he argued, and they could see the country "steering straight for anarchy, futility and chaos."

By forty-eight votes to eighteen, on September 27th, the Dail gave the Army the powers it sought. To Republicans it was a pro-Treaty party decision, and it is true that in the absence of the elected Republican members, the Dail would scarcely have had a whiff of democracy had it not been for the Labour party who, admirably led by Thomas Johnson, were to develop into a sturdy and efficient Opposition. These

477

men allowed the processes of democracy to work and to them, in no small measure, Ireland owes her democratic being.

On October 10th, the granting of Special Emergency Powers to the Army of the Provisional Government was announced. They were to apply from October 15th. A week earlier, an offer of amnesty, open also until October 15th, was made to all those "engaged in insurrection and rebellion against the State" who handed in their arms and ceased to play any part in the struggle against the Provisional Government forces.

At this point it would be well to reiterate the issue, in terms of black and white, omitting the subtler greys, because the Civil War in Ireland was not a struggle between a long-established government and a coterie of rebels. Each side claimed, and could argue its claim vehemently and not illogically, that it was the legitimate Government. The Republican argument was simple: "Ireland was proclaimed a republic in 1916; in 1919 the First Dail, elected by the people, confirmed it, and we all took an oath of allegiance to it. The Irish delegates had no right to sign a treaty that disestablished the Republic. We know they had a tough assignment but they were wrong. The damage ought to have been undone in the Dail but it was not. The majority voted for the Treaty, but they were wrong too. They were wrong because they agreed to accept an oath of allegiance to the King of England when they were already bound by their sacred oath to the Republic. We know the people voted for peace and, aware of all they have suffered, we can understand their desire. But the fact of the Republic is inescapable. It exists and none of us has the right to destroy it. Votes, whether wise or misguided, are not relevant to the issue. We shall fight on, whatever the cost, because not to do so would be to betray those who gave their lives for the Republic which they believed would, whether openly in freedom or clandestinely under tyranny, live on after them."

Equally unambiguously the Provisional Government argued; "We have not forgotten our oath to the Republic. But at the time we took the oath we could not operate any kind of government properly. The Republic was a reality that we fought for too, and the ideal of the Republic is as firmly rooted in our hearts as it is in yours. But if we are to have a living country in which the Republic can develop, can become
478

re-established, not this time as an underground movement, but as something which all the world can see and recognise, we must call a halt to death and destruction. Freedom and democratic ways come first, because without them we shall never get the Republic we want. The Treaty gives us the chance to live in freedom and practise democracy. We deplore that England would not give way altogether, but the fact is she did not. Nevertheless, we have made a tremendous stride forward. The alternative was to step back into the burnt out shell of our Republic. Our delegates did well, and the majority in the Dail, and an even larger majority of the people, were for sanity and preservation rather than for madness and ruin. If democracy is to mean anything in this country that verdict must be respected."

Even in these skeleton terms it is evident that the impolarity of viewpoints was not so pronounced as events made it seem. The conflict turned upon the interpretation of words and phrases. One of the great stumbling blocks, as Professor Hayes says, was vocabulary. The place to settle polemical issues was in the Dail. Instead, men were using bullets because they had come to believe that these were the only arguments that mattered and because, as so many incoherent, unimaginative and repetitive speeches during the Dail debate had proved, tongues were not easy weapons to use in expressing feelings, but rifles were.

Well, rifles were being used; so were bombs, armoured cars, artillery, machine-guns, stealthy pistols and blazing petrol. Chaos and destruction had to be brought to an end and in time the end came. It can be assumed, but never proved, that the special powers given to the Army hastened that end. It has to be conceded, I think, that Mr Cosgrave's Government took the only logical decision in the circumstances, a courageous and conscience-searing decision, but one which brought new horror into what was already a situation of tragic and growing bitterness. It was a terrible price to pay for the peace for which the majority of the people had voted and the time would soon come when the people would react against that horror and cast their votes away from the men they held responsible for it.

Drastic action had to be taken by one side or the other to end something that was ineffably wrong, and it could be taken

479

only by the stronger group, the group in power. In a sense, once the battle had begun the question of which side was right and which wrong was transcended by the paramount need to save the nation from destruction. In spite of the thunder of Republican propaganda, the never-ending gibe that the Government were British hirelings carrying on the British cause and using British methods, O'Higgins's words, "I don't think any of us hold human life cheap," have the stamp of sincerity. One can read into them that only after the most stringent questioning of consciences was the fateful decision reached.

On October 16th, when the new Special Emergency Powers had been in operation for twenty-four hours, the Army Executive, which had not met since June, assembled at Ballybacon close to the Glen of Aherlow in the fastness of which many Republicans found sanctuary. Lynch himself had joined other members of his headquarters staff at Rossadrehid in the Glen late in September. Of the sixteen members of the Executive present at the last meeting ten were able to attend These were Lynch, Deasy, O'Malley, Tom Derrig, Seamus Robinson, Sean Moylan, Joe O'Connor, Frank Barrett, Pax Whelan and Tom Barry. Barry, captured when he had attempted to join the Four Courts garrison during the attack, had escaped from Gormanstown camp in August. Two members, Kilroy and Ruttledge were unable to reach the meeting in time and four, Rory O'Connor, Liam Mellows, Joe McKelvey and Peadar O'Donnell were in Mountjoy. These four were replaced by Aiken, Lehane, Sean MacSwiney and Con Moloney.

The Executive met to consider, among other ˙things, a memorandum put forward to Lynch by de Valera, who had been vexed by the earlier brush-off from the Republican Chief of Staff.

"This is too good a thing and won't do," he had exclaimed, and later threatened to resign publicly if he did not get the position clarified. If party policy was to leave everything to the Army he saw no point in party members continuing as public representatives. In his memorandum he put three alternatives to the Executives. The party, Cumann na Poblachta, could set up a Government, but unless they were in effective control and had the allegiance of the Army this
480

would be futile. Or the Army Executive itself could become a military dictatorship, a course which in de Valera's view was undesirable. Finally, some kind of joint committee might be set up. This did not seem a practical solution to him. Above all, he wanted the Army Executive publicly to accept responsibility for the military campaign if this was to continue. "This pretence from the pro-Treaty party that we (Cumann na Poblachta) are inciting the Army must be ended by a declaration from the Army itself that this is not so."

Because "there is no doubt as to whether the Army would give its whole-hearted allegiance to any other than its own Executive, or the creation of that Executive," de Valera thought "the proper course would be for the Army Executive to call on the Republican members of the Dail to set up the Government."

There were three points upon which de Valera felt a frank understanding should be reached. These were:

"1. The right of the People to determine freely their own Government, and the relations of the State with foreign States.

"2. The terms on which the present armed opposition to the Free State (if it continued to have a majority) might be desisted from, and

"3. The terms, short of a simple recognition of the Republic, on which, if we succeed in establishing ourselves in Nationalist Ireland, we might make peace with England and the Northern Unionists."

On point 3 de Valera adverted to his old contention that his Document No. 2 represented a solution which Britain might be persuaded to accept but beyond which there was no hope of concession.

The Executive were reluctant to relinquish to a civil body the power to decide whether and upon what terms the fight should be given up. And so, before considering this question they first sought to define the minimum acceptable terms. They decided that the Executive should instruct the Army Council, which was set up at this same meeting and comprised Lynch, O'Malley, Aiken, Derrig and Deasy, to negotiate terms of peace "such as will not bring this country within the British Empire". The final decision was to remain with the Executive.

De Valera's proposal of a Republican Government was then dealt with. He wanted the Republican deputies elected in June to form their own Parliament and their own Republican Government. It would be a one-party minority government, an underground movement, but it would be, in de Valera's view the true successor to the First Dail. This, in Republican eyes, the hireling Dail in Dublin was not and never could be.

On the whole the Executive were not averse to the idea. While the Republican cause was seen to be entirely in military hands it was in danger of being discredited. It needed to be set in some kind of constitutional framework. Already the Irish Hierarchy of the Roman Catholic Church had dealt them a damaging blow. The Hierarchy had first made its sentiments known very forthrightly in their April pronouncement. Whether their admonition won votes for the Treaty party in June is debatable, but the elections were certainly not free from violence and the gun more than ever had come between friends. A joint Pastoral was issued by the aged Cardinal Logue and the Archbishops and Bishops of Ireland on October 10th, the day the Provisional Government announced thé Special Emergency Powers. The coincidence seemed to the Republicans full of malice. In the Pastoral the Hierarchy charged that, "A section of the community, refusing to acknowledge the Government set up by the Nation, have chosen to attack their own country as if she were a foreign power." They had forgotten that "a dead nation cannot be free" and had "wrecked Ireland from end to end".

"They carry on what they call a war, but which in the absence of any legitimate authority to justify it, is morally only a system of murder and assassination of the National Forces," pronounced the Bishops. No Republican could evade the teaching of the Church "by asserting that the legitimate authority in Ireland is not the present Dail or Provisional Government. There is no other and cannot be, outside the body of the people. A Republic without popular recognition behind it is a contradiction in terms. Such being Division Law, the guerrilla warfare now being carried on by the Irregulars is without moral sanction, and, therefore, the killing of National soldiers in the course of it is murder before God, the seizing of public and private property is robbery, the breaking of roads, bridges and railways a criminal destruction, the invasion of homes and the molestation of citizens a grievous crime."

There could be no doubting which side the Hierarchy were on but the Republicans were incensed that God was being hailed as a supporter of the Treaty. The Hierarchy protested carefully that "in all this there is no question of mere politics, but of what is morally right or wrong according to the Divine Law", but they did not convince the dissenters who, good Catholics too, looked to the Hierarchy to console all their Irish sons without taking sides. Instead, the Pastoral warned them that they would not be absolved in confession and they would be denied the Sacraments.

A sharp weapon this, but it did not deter the young Republican soldiers and their leaders. They did not believe that the edict reflected God's will but the very earthy opinions of a reactionary group of Church leaders and they were soured too by a conspicuous lack of Christian charity among many of the Chaplains in the prisons and prison camps. This they had never forgotten.

"The Civil War was bad, but it saved us this much—it saved us from the government of Maynooth," says Dan Breen forthrightly. "The people were split on the issue of the Treaty but the Hierarchy went out and attacked the Republic, threw bell, book and candle at it in nearly every pulpit in the country. And they drove one half of the people against them with the result that they never regained the power they once had."

The Army Executive decided to provide the constitutional framework that de Valera wanted, but to retain power of veto on peace terms. They resolved:

"That this Executive calls upon the former President of Dail Eireann to form a Government which will preserve the continuity of the Republic. We pledge this Government our wholehearted support and allegiance while it functions as the Government of the Republic, and we empower it to make an arrangement with the Free State Government, or with the British Government provided such arrangement does not bring the country into the British Empire. Final decision on this question to be submitted for ratification to Executive."

Accordingly, on October 26th, *War News* announced that there had been a secret session of Dail Eireann, the

Parliament and Government of the Republic, secret because the "traitorous conspiracy and armed revolt" of the Provisional Government and its army had the upper hand. It had been resolved "to call upon the former President, Eamon de Valera to resume the Presidency and to nominate a Council of State and Executive Ministers to assist him in carrying on the government until such time as the Parliament of the Republic is allowed freely to assemble or the people are allowed by a free election to decide how they shall be governed."

So Eamon de Valera again was the leader of an underground government and the Provisional Government was compelled to parallel the role England had once had. In November a proclamation was published over the signature of de Valera as President and P. J. Ruttledge as Minister for Home Affairs rescinding the Dail's resolution on January 7th, 1922 which approved the Treaty.

But de Valera's nebulous Government failed to halt the progress of Ireland towards the status provided for by the Treaty. On October 25th, 1922, the Dail passed the Free State Constitution Bill. The Treaty was put in as a schedule to the Bill and the oath of allegiance was obligatory. Provision was made for the representation and protection of Southern Unionists. On December 6th, the anniversary of the signing of the Treaty, the House of Commons passed the corresponding bill. The Irish Free State, the translation of *Saorstat Eireann* which de Valera had put to Lloyd George in their discussions of July, 1921, was born.

Wars are remembered for their spectacular episodes. Long uneventful days are forgotten, small incidents matter only to those who took part in them. But some aspects catch the wider imagination, create atmosphere, arouse passions and engender myths. In the same way the inspired goal, the determined try, the punch-up, a referee's decision, are remembered in isolation and not just as incidents in the course of a game. The true perspective is lost.

Three episodes of the Civil War in Ireland proved the focus of most memories. These are the death of Michael Collins, the excesses of National Army soldiers in Kerry, and the executions. Vital factors though they were, the importance of all have been inflated. Some writers have it that the seventy-
484

seven executions carried out by Mr Cosgrave's Government scarred Ireland forever. There is no doubt that they have left an ugly mark, but history will set them back in the context of the Civil War as a whole, indeed, as a not very significant factor in the growth of a nation, for whatever passions were fired by the executions and blaze still in the minds of individual men and women, the Civil War, every murderous shot of it, every bridge blown and train derailed, every building shattered, every life destroyed, every heart grieved and every lie snarled by one side or the other, was the real trauma that Ireland suffered.

It was to be a month from the passing of the Emergency Regulations before there were any executions. On November 17th four young men were shot. They had been caught in Dublin with loaded guns in their possession and were apparently preparing a street ambush, a form of attack which Mulcahy despised.

Mulcahy's explanation in the Dail placated Johnson, who shared his loathing of street corner traps but who, following the brief announcement of the executions, had voiced shocked questions.

"The nation's life is worth the life of many individuals," O'Higgins contributed unarguably, but somehow one suspects that he was no longer questioning his conscience. Disarmingly, he explained that the first to suffer death under the new emergency powers had been nonentities. If they had chosen to execute first "some man who was outstandingly active and outstandingly wicked in his activities, the unfortunate dupes throughout the country might say that he was killed because he was a leader, because he was an Englishman, or because he combined with others to commit rape."

This was rather an odd assortment. One would have thought the execution of a leader a more effective deterrent than the rushed shooting of four unknown boys. Moreover, the announcement of their execution was so uninformative that its value as a deterrent was doubtful. As for the rapist in company, he was a rare bird anyway, and no one believed that the emergency powers had been introduced to exterminate his kind. It sounds almost as if O'Higgins, lost for a third alternative, said the first thing that came into his head. The significant words were "because he is an Englishman".

485

Only one supposed Englishman counted at the time and he, Erskine Childers, that same day had stood trial for his life. O'Higgins, like Arthur Griffith before him, hated him. Childers had been arrested a week before, on November 10th, at the house of his cousin, Robert Barton, the home of his own boyhood. In his possession was a tiny revolver, given him by Michael Collins, which customarily he wore fastened to his shirt with a safety pin.

It was in the Coole Mountains, between Dunmanway and Macroom, that Childers produced the last issue of his paper. He had worked at it conscientiously and, if not impartially, at least with an occasional nod in his opponents' direction, rather in the manner of a boxer sportingly acknowledging a telling blow. Because of the difficulties of producing it, especially when part of his printing machine was lost in a bog, and that the fact that he kept finding unopened parcels of the paper in cobwebby corners of local hideaways, Childers decided to give up.

At Headquarters he informed his superiors of his decision and offered his services in any other capacity. One of the officers threw up his hands in horror and said something like, "That wouldn't do at all. My God, if the Free State troops down in Dunmanway heard you were with us they wouldn't give us any peace, night or day." That at least was the sense of the expostulation as Childers gave it to Sean Hendrick. It revealed two things: that there was a good deal of half-heartedness among many of the Republicans, and that they knew very well the Free State men were gunning for Childers and were not particularly concerned for his safety. The pejorative tag of "Englishman" clung to Childers, though he deserved it no more and no less than Pearce and Brugha. He was certainly as Irish as de Valera. In the Dail Griffith had rancorously refused to talk to this "damned Englishman". Perhaps Childers tried too hard to be Irish. He once asked Professor Hayes the Gaelic for Childers. "It was like asking what is the English for *Figaro*," says Hayes dryly. The orphaned Childers was brought up with his cousin, Robert Barton, at Glendalaugh, County Wicklow, but educated in England, at Haileybury and Trinity College, Cambridge. In the Boer War he fought in the Honourable Artillery Company: in the First World War he served first in naval aircraft then as an Intelligence officer. Later he joined the Royal Flying Corps. For a time he was a clerk in the House of Commons. His background marked him out from his fellows and, except for those who were close to him and came to appreciate him, few had any affection for him. Converted to Home Rule in 1908, he produced, three years later, a complex and thorough treatise on the subject. Without him there is little likelihood that the Howth gun-running episode would ever have taken place; without his coolness in a crisis it would have failed anyway. Yet after that incident he fought again for England. The Irish got an odd answer when they put that two and two together.

As a secretary to the Irish delegation he fought with bitter intensity against the signing of the Treaty, made his own reports by telephone to de Valera and hopelessly antagonised Griffith. Strangely, though much has been made of the failure of the plenipotentiaries to telephone Dublin for authority to sign the Treaty, few have noted that Childers also did not think of it.

None of the Irish leaders understood British constitutionalism better than he, yet he was wildly inaccurate in assessing the powers which the Treaty conferred. He was convinced that Britain would never allow Ireland the same status as Canada enjoyed, holding that her very proximity precluded this. A strong influence on de Valera, he convinced his chief of that, too, and helped him formulate his alternative of an externally associated republic. Childers, probably blinded by his hatred of British imperialism—though he did not hate the English people—allowed his judgment to be affected. When ultimately de Valera found himself once more at the head of affairs of State in Ireland, he was surprised to discover how much power was, in fact, allowed under the Treaty.

How much, one wonders, did Mary Childers, née Mary Osgood of Boston, the highly intelligent, partly crippled anglophobe wife of this strange man, influence his thinking. We are told by Basil Williams that "they felt and thought for the rest of their lives almost as one being".[1] There are some who were convinced that she did all the thinking, was his evil genius. In *Ireland—A Catspaw* Elizabeth Lazenby reported

[1] *Erskine Childers 1870-1922—A Sketch*, by Basil Williams (privately printed).

487

that Mrs Childers told her Ireland was merely "the keystone in the arch of the predatory system" of British imperialism. Snapping her fingers, she declaimed, "I do not care that for the independence of Ireland; it is simply that if Ireland goes the whole structure will fall."

Was it to start the Empire crumbling rather than to secure Irish independence that Childers rowed so angrily with Griffith at Hans Place? If the Irish had any inkling that Childers had other and secret motives, that for him Ireland was but a pawn in his own personal game, it is little wonder that he was mistrusted, that there are today distinguished and perceptive Irishmen who still believe that he was a British agent to the end. In the Dail, Griffith hinted strongly that this is what he believed. So far as I know, there is no evidence, even of the flimsiest, that Childers was a traitor to Ireland, though there is some that, disillusioned with England, he sought her downfall rather than Irish independence for its own sake. But his Civil War record suggests that he was no more than he claimed to be, a staff-captain employed on propaganda and doing it as well as he knew how. Sean Hendrick paints a delightful picture of him standing on a five-barred gate half-way between opposing forces firing hectically at each other, oblivious to the bullets hissing past him from either direction and carefully taking notes for an article he would write later.

On one occasion he used a story about a pro-Treaty officer, which was vouched for by a responsible officer on his own side. Furious when he discovered the story was not true, he printed a handsome apology.

When Headquarters declined to use Childers's services, Hendrick asked him what his plans were. Childers answered that he would make his way back to Dublin, collect his papers, particularly those relating to the Treaty negotiations, and prepare them for publication. For some time friends had written to warn him that his life would be in danger if he came to Dublin. They claimed they had definite information that if he came into the hands of the Free State Government he would be executed, but Childers merely joked about the warnings.

Erskine Childers refused to recognise the military court

that tried him but, in cool language, he put his position to them:

"The collapse of the whole Convention[2] and the attempt to force conscription convinced me that Home Rule was dead, and that a revolution, founded on the rising of 1916, was inevitable and necessary, and I only waited till the end of the war, when I had faithfully fulfilled my contract with the British, to join in the movement myself. With the formal establishment of the Republic in 1919, it became necessary for people like myself, of mixed birth, to choose our citizenship once and for all. I chose that of the Irish Republican Army . . ."

It was typical of the man that he should have desired to fulfil his contract with the British before engaging in a revolutionary movement against them.

Childers was persuaded to apply for a writ of *habeas corpus*, not for his own sake but in the hope that the finding of the court would protect eight prisoners whose names the Government would not divulge. The Master of the Rolls found that he was unable to deal with the application because a state of war existed. This was embarrassing for the Government whose case was that they were dealing with a revolt and that captured insurgents were therefore not prisoners of war.

It was late evening on November 23rd when the Master of the Rolls gave his decision and at 8 a.m. next morning Childers was executed. On the day of his trial he had said, "Whether I am to live or die, it must help Ireland." It is difficult to see how his death helped Ireland, for although in his last months he had become querulous and obstinate, he was a man of great ability and would have served Ireland well. He was granted an hour's postponement of his execution so that he could see the sun once more, and shook hands with each member of the firing squad.

There were many who admired his fine qualities and mourned him. "A man of immense charity," Sean Hendrick says of him. Dermott MacManus remembers his modesty. He was with him once when he was looking for a book for his wife. The assistant in the bookshop suggested *Riddle of the*

2 The Convention of 1917-18 of which Erskine Childers was one of the secretaries.

Sands, his own famous novel. Quietly Childers told her that his wife had read it.

In an emotional speech in the Dail on November 29th, Gavan Duffy described Childers as "one of the noblest men I have ever known". He acknowledged that the task of Ministers was "a difficult and terrible one", and claimed that often their actions were tolerated when they were deserving of censure but, he cried, "Silence is not possible when an Irish Government executes Erskine Childers for possessing a pistol in a dwelling house without the authority of the Provisional Government, which is his political opponent." Childers, he said, had been the victim of propaganda to the degree that people sincerely believed that he was "a monster of wickedness" and "an *agent provocateur* of the British Government and no fate was too bad for him." Scrupulous precautions against doing an injustice should have been taken but there had been instead "this unnecessary secrecy which seems to pervade the dealings of the authorities with these strange tribunals."

Cosgrave defended his Government. It was right that if anyone were to be executed it should be leaders, not followers, he argued. Harsh words came from O'Higgins. Childers was an Englishman who had come into the national struggle "on the last emotional wave", and O'Higgins vowed that "anyone coming in here for adventure will get it."

The Government's cold demonstrations of its intention to act under its new measure against all ranks of the Executive Forces shocked the Republican leaders and appalled the families of young men whose lives had seemed in jeopardy enough.

On the day that Childers went to his death Michael Kilroy was captured. That night, a weary Tony Lawlor stayed with the Catholic curate of Newport. With mostly untrained troops Lawlor had wrested the town from the Republicans. At one point he had ordered a charge from behind a wall into "a tarbarazzle of fire" across the road, and led the way, only to find himself alone, with his own men, and his opponents too, gazing at him in silent astonishment.

During the evening, Lawlor was called to the door by his host and confronted by a very beautiful woman holding the hand of a small girl. She was demeaning herself she told him by coming to ask for the life of her husband, General Kilroy.

"Kilroy's quite safe. We don't do those kind of things." Mrs Kilroy was sceptical and Lawlor gave her his word of honour.

"*Your* word of honour," she answered scathingly.

"That is all I have to offer you," said Lawlor.

Later, he heard that Kilroy had been moved from Athlone to Dublin and was being held as a hostage. "The Irregulars had got the idea of bumping off T.D.'s," Lawlor explains. He was most concerned, for he admired Kilroy and was miserably aware that his word of honour might go for nothing. Appreciating the position, McEoin interceded with Mulcahy and no harm came to Kilroy.

The first threat to members of the Dail came in a letter from Lynch, who had moved his headquarters to Dublin, to the Speaker on November 27th.

"The illegal body over which you preside has declared war on the soldiers of the Republic and suppressed the legitimate parliament of the Irish Nation," wrote Lynch who went on to claim that his side had always adhered to the recognised rules of warfare. "Many of your soldiers have been released by us—three times although captured by arms on each occasion," he said, whereas "the prisoners you have taken have been treated barbarously . . ."

He warned the Speaker: "Next to the members of your 'Provisional Government,' every member of your body who voted for this resolution by which you pretend to make legal the murder of soldiers, is equally guilty. We therefore give you and each member of your body due notice that unless your army recognises the rules of warfare in future we shall adopt very drastic measures to protect our forces."

Lynch followed this up three days later with instructions to commanding officers of all battalions of the Executive Forces that people of fourteen named categories were to be shot at sight. These *Orders of Frightfulness*, as they were sometimes called, also required the destruction of their homes and offices. Included were all members of the Dail who had voted for the Army Emergency Powers Resolution, hostile newspaper men, High Court Judges and, for good measure, "aggressive Free State supporters". Senators also were listed, and as these included representatives of the Unionists and other minority groups, many of them men of wealth and influence, they suffered a good deal in the next months.

The Senate came into being on December 7th. Lloyd George had made it clear that whether the Irish Free State had a unicameral or a bicameral system was for the Irish to decide for themselves. Arthur Griffith earnestly believed that there must be a place in the new nation for all people of Irish birth whatever their antecedents, that differences and feuds could be eliminated by men of goodwill. He saw that among the Unionists, those who had favoured the continuance of legislative union with Britain, there was a wealth of experience and ability which could be of ineffable value. They were mostly Protestant, of British descent, and enjoyed wealth and privilege far beyond the reach of the majority. But they came of generations of Irish born families, were a unique breed, and the excesses of the Black and Tans had soured the British affections of many of them. They knew that the Unionist cause in the South was dead, that they had to choose, as Erskine Childers had had to choose, between Irish and British citizenship.

But men do not easily relinquish possessions, privilege and power, and the Unionist representatives in their London discussions with Griffith and O'Higgins in June had striven hard to secure an effective voice in the legislature of the new state. They were not entirely satisfied with the Heads of Agreement signed on June 14th. Although they acknowledged the concessions made, they did not believe that a Senate which ultimately, though not at first, would be elected by popular vote, and the powers of which were strictly rationed, would afford the minorities real protection.

The other side to the question is expounded by Donal O'Sullivan,[3]

"It is inconceivable that, in the circumstances then existing, Griffith and O'Higgins could have advanced further than they did in the way of concessions to the minority's point of view without jeopardy to the whole Treaty position—the upsetting of which would have been at least as bad for the Southern Unionists as for anyone else."

On December 6th the new Constitution came into force. The veteran Nationalist, Timothy Healy, was sworn in as

[3] *The Irish Free State and its Senate* by Donal O'Sullivan.

Governor-General and the Vice-Regal Lodge soon came to be called "Uncle Tim's Cabin". Cosgrave was elected President of the Council and on the same day nominated thirty Senators, among them W. B. Yeats and Oliver St John Gogarty, the Earls of Mayo, Granard, Kerry and Wicklow, Sir Horace Plunkett and two women, Mrs Wyse Power and the Dowager Countess of Desart. Cosgrave's brief was to have special regard to seniority groups. Another thirty Senators were elected by the Dail. Colonel Maurice Moore, who had been so concerned with the seizure of lands by Republicans, was one; another was Mrs Alice Stopford Green in whose drawing-room the Howth gun-running episode had been planned. The sixty senators were to retire in groups of fifteen after three, six, nine and twelve years, so that gradually triennial elections—by an electorate of the over-thirty age group—could be introduced.

As expected, the Six Counties of the North-East exercised their right to opt out, so opening their borders to the inquiries of a Boundary Commission, a gamble of which, perhaps with good reason, they were unafraid.

The same day, December 7th, Dail Deputy Sean Hales was shot dead in the street. His companion Padraic O'Maille, the Deputy Speaker, was seriously wounded. The assassination was carried out as a military operation in exactly the way that the Squad had once operated.

Swiftly and ruthlessly, the Free State Government acted. After a long, grim session, the Cabinet decided to execute Rory O'Connor, Liam Mellows, Joseph McKelvey and Richard Barrett all of whom had been in prison since the surrender of the Four Courts. They were summarily shot in Mountjoy next morning.

These men, one from each of the Provinces, Leinster, Connaught, Ulster and Munster, were among the finest of their remarkable generation. In Mellows, before 1916, Connolly had discerned the qualities of a great leader. O'Connor had been best man at Kevin O'Higgins's wedding only twelve months before. Much of the odium of the occasion was fastened upon O'Higgins, though his was the last vote won in that fateful Cabinet meeting and he was shaken when the Army announced the execution as a reprisal as well as a solemn warning. To apply their new measure retrospectively

493

was illegal on any count, but it was an act of courage and the very enormity of the deed showed that without a hint of doubt the Government was not going to stand for the piece-meal decimation of the Dail. No more deputies were assassinated.

Later in the day, Thomas Johnson belaboured the Government in the Dail and Mulcahy replied without apology that they were "shouldering responsibilities that are very heavy and great." The most telling speech came from Deputy Fitzgibbon. In his opinion the men had been treated leniently after their capture, but he deplored their execution for what they had done months previously and appealed to the Executive Council "not to continue the policy that appears to have been commenced today."

This was not an act of revenge, said Kevin O'Higgins, adding sombrely, "I think that somehow we must have gone long past anger and past the mere emotional wave of temptation." In realistic terms he put it that "all government is based on force, must meet force with greater force if it is to survive", and he promised that "we will not acquiesce in gun-bullying, and we will take very stern and drastic measures to stop it." He broke down as he denied accusations of personal animosity. "Personal spite, great heavens!" he cried. "Vindictiveness! One of these men was a friend of mine." Two months later, his father, Dr T. F. O'Higgins, was murdered in the presence of his wife and daughter, and the motive for that crime could have been nothing but vindictiveness. Property rather than lives now became the principal target of those who sought to carry out Lynch's orders. On December 10th, the house of Deputy Sean McGarry was destroyed by fire and his seven year old son died later of burns.

On the same day bombs were thrown into premises belonging to Senator Mrs Wyse Power and a great deal of damage was done. This was the beginning of a campaign of arson and terror, but in the south, Tom Barry, with the flair that had made him perhaps the most feared guerrilla leader of the war against Britain, was demonstrating that the Executive Forces, given the right leadership, were capable of military action that still held menace.

With tried veterans like Bill Quirke, Dinny Lacey and Mick Sheehan to support him, Barry led a strong attack on

Carrick-on-Suir on December 9th and took the town. Within four days his troops had forced the surrender of Callan, Mullinavat and Thomastown. Prisoners were contemptuously set free but Barry took possession of valuable quantities of arms and ammunition. The Free State commander at Callan, Ned Somers, switched sides, a move that was to cost him his life.

Barry planned to strike northward through Tipperary to Templemore, then eastwards to the Curragh from where he reckoned to have Dublin in his sights, but he could not sustain the brilliant blaze. The increasing strength of the Free State forces, the day by day capture of Republicans, the threat of execution for those caught carrying arms and the apparent futility of the fight had taken a heavy toll of enthusiasm. From Cork and Kerry came desperate cries, as from men clinging by their fingertips to a narrow ledge, that they could not hold on much longer.

In Kerry, John Joe Rice still had dreams of victory, but there the Free State troops had snatched back Kenmare, and everywhere in the county the harshness of the occupation was bearing heavily. From the outset, Daly's forces had been free with gun and boot. Daly once said to Michael Hayes, "No one told me to bring kid gloves, so I didn't."

Men in uniform away from home are seldom angels and there is always an element in all armies who go too far. In Ireland violence and death had been a commonplace for years and the hearts of few young men bumped more rapidly in the presence of horror. Yet, humanity was not a lost property of the Irish soul and even in those bitter days it was in evidence.

Few on the Free State side deny that "things got out of hand in Kerry." Eventually, the authorities were impelled to hold an inquiry and Daly was relieved of his command. Like many others, Daly had been fighting for years. Close to Collins, he had undergone more strain perhaps than most, and he seems to have developed a puritanical streak the obverse of which, as happens so often, was harshness.

But it has to be conceded that men under his command were in Kerry subject to unusual provocation. The rugged terrain lent itself to ambush and Free State troops—as they can now be correctly called—could scarcely move without

495

being shot at by men they could not see, or being blown up by mines. Sometimes they detected the mines only to succumb, as Keogh did in Cork, to the trigger-mine beneath it. The Free State men were angry too because they believed that in Kerry many who had not fired a shot at the British were now earnestly shooting down their compatriots. Some even remembered how Roger Casement had been captured without an attempt being made to rescue him. For them Casement's ghost did indeed haunt Kerry.

In a Christmas message de Valera humbly sought God's enlightenment and direction so that peace and happiness could be achieved by the harassed Irish people. But in the next days a 74 year old Senator was pushed out of his car at midnight and the vehicle burned, Senator John Bagwell's home with its remarkable library and art collections was destroyed and Senator Gogarty was kidnapped. Gogarty escaped by diving into the flooded Liffey.

Sir Horace Plunkett's home was blown up by a mine on January 29th and on the same day petrol was sprinkled through the Earl of Mayo's home in County Kildare and it was completely destroyed. Historic Moore Hall, home of Colonel Maurice Moore, and Sir Bryan Mahon's mansion at Ballymore Eustace were burned; Castle Forbes, Irish seat of the Earl of Granard was blown up by mines and Ballynastragh, Sir Thomas Esmonde's home, part of which dated from 1300, was gutted. All over the country the insensate destruction went on, not only of lovely houses and priceless treasures, but of railways, public buildings and public services. In Athlone the waterworks were blown up, in Tralee the gas-works were put out of commission with sledge-hammers and in Sligo the railway station was destroyed. Behind the ruinous campaign lay the Republicans' last glimmer of hope, that by reducing the Free State administration to impotence they might finally prevail.

But the new Government was growing stronger. The pitiless system of executions continued. By the end of January more than fifty men had faced the firing squads. The people became hardened to it and in a curious way respected the Government for its determination to win complete control at any cost. They longed for the deadlock to be resolved and saw that the only way was to crush the resistance of the
496

Republican guerrilla fighters. At the same time a reservoir of sympathy slowly filled upon which one day the Republican Party would be able to draw.

Cosgrave's Government were not only fighting the war, and trying to rebuild as they went, but planning and putting into operation the country's administrative system. In eight months forty-seven acts, most of them temporary, were put through. A number of them were passed during the Civil War. Local government was organised, a civil service set up, a magistracy instituted. In September 1922 a new police force, the Civic Guard or *Garda Siochana*, had been instituted under the command of General O'Duffy. Mulcahy felt that he could ill-afford to lose him but the appointment was amply justified. The unarmed Garda could not intervene in the war but their advent began the restoration of law and order throughout the country. Crime was rife and was usually disguised as the work of the military forces of one side or the other. Who could tell whether a man had been murdered for his political sympathies or for his money, whether a mansion was burned under the Republican reprisal policy or by thieves making it appear so? There were bad hats among the rival armies; both sides employed "trucers" or "trucileers", men who had taken no part in the war of independence but had swarmed into the I.R.A. during the long Truce for reasons often, though not always, reprehensible. Some were youngsters only now of age to join and full of idealism, others were opportunists and some were criminals. In any event, their entry into the I.R.A. had been unfortunate for it is doubtful if the old I.R.A. however divided, could have fought each other to the death if the influx of strangers had not thinned their comradeship.

TWENTY-FOUR

The capture of Liam Deasy, member of the Executive and Officer Commanding Lynch's Southern Command, resulted from an odd mischance. Tom Ryan tells the story of that day, January 18th, 1923.

"A young lieutenant in Clonmel went home for a couple of days leave. His people lived on the mountainside. His father mentioned there were some of 'the boys' at another house and one of them seemed 'a prominent kind of fellow'. He came back and informed me and I went to Cahir and told them to get out and get the man. It was Deasy. He was brought back to Clonmel, tried by court-martial and sentenced to death. The firing squad was told off and so was the officer to take charge. A couple of bottles of brandy were set aside for them. At 4 a.m., Deasy was ready for death, calm and courageous.

"Then a message from Mulcahy to Prout came through by wireless. Mulcahy instructed Prout to send Deasy by armoured car to Dublin immediately. Wireless was pretty erratic at the time and he had a close shave."

Before his capture Deasy had been trying to work out a way to end the war without surrendering the Republican ideal. He was now in a difficult position but he agreed, as the only means open to him, to sign this document:

"I accept and I will aid in immediate and unconditional surrender of arms and men as required by General Mulcahy. In pursuance of this undertaking I am asked to appeal for a similar undertaking and acceptance from the following: E. de Valera. P. Ruttledge, A. Stack, M. Colivet, Domhnal O'Callaghan, Liam Lynch, Con Moloney, T. Derrig, F. Aiken, F. Barrett, T. Barry, S. MacSwiney, Seamus Robinson, Humphrey Murphy, Seamus O'Donovan, Frank Carty, and for the immediate and unconditional surrender of themselves after the issue by them of an order of surrender on the part of all those associated with them, together with their arms and equipment."

With a covering letter, which he was permitted to frame as he wished, copies of the document were conveyed by Father Duggan, who had several times acted as a go-between during the past months in efforts to secure peace, were delivered to Lynch and de Valera.

Lynch's answer was a brusque refusal but the plea, from a man so admired by his fellows, was an important factor in bringing the devastating conflict to an overdue ending. "So many people thought he had acted to buy his life," says General Brennan, "but I knew, and anybody who knew Deasy knew, that nothing on earth that was dishonourable would be done by him to save his life. Physical courage is

498

probably the commonest quality in this country but moral courage is rare. Liam Deasy's action after his capture was the greatest act of moral courage I have known in my life."

The document was sent out on January 29th, but to suit their own purposes the Free State Government did not publish it until February 9th. An amnesty was promised to all who surrendered with their arms before February 18th. On the same date Lynch sent a special message to all ranks urging them not to be deluded by the enemy's wiles into "surrendering the strong position you have so dearly won. The war will go on until the independence of our country is recognised by our enemies, foreign and domestic."

Among Republicans the conviction still persisted that England was dictating the Free State campaign, but whatever else might be said against Lloyd George, there is no doubting that once the Treaty had been signed he had every intention of observing scrupulously the dominion status his Government had conferred. Partly because of his commerce with the Irish leaders, partly because of his Greek policy, Lloyd George and his hybrid Cabinet had been ousted by the restive Tories in October, 1922. Already ailing, his successor, Bonar Law, had no wish to embroil England in the Irish struggle. The Executive had plans for operations in England but the organisation there was closely watched and numerous arrests aborted the plan.

Lynch now seemed blinded to realities and his determination and optimism were not reflected in the minds of other leaders. It was not that they faltered. Ireland's inclusion in the Commonwealth and the truncation of the Six Counties were anathema to them, but men like Barry saw there was no longer any possibility of reversing what had been done, at least not at this stage. For some time Lynch had resisted requests for a meeting of the Executive. Barry, accompanied by Tom Crofts, saw Lynch in Dublin on February 6th and put it to him that a meeting was imperative.

On February 10th, a meeting of the council of the 1st Southern Division was held at Cronins' at Gouganebarra, the lovely, land-locked water into which the River Lee flows. "You could believe in the fairies there," says Dan Breen. The meeting decided to send Lynch a further request for a meeting of the Executive. On February 13th, before the letter reached

499

him, Lynch left Dublin and, after a long journey through the south, arrived at Ballingeary on February 26th. Discussions with his officers convinced him at last that a meeting of the Executive was necessary.

De Valera, too, had been trying to contact his elusive Chief of Staff. On February 22nd he wrote to the Adjutant-General, Con Moloney, that he was anxious to hear from Lynch about the situation in the south. He made it clear that the Government's peace terms requiring the surrender of arms were unacceptable. "It would simply amount to letting the Free State function, and if we are ever driven to that stage a simple 'quit' would be the best."[1]

Again, on March 5th, he wrote: "It is strange that the c/s has sent no report. His silence seems ominous to me."[2] He was afraid that, having lost most of its senior officers, the south would probably be a "fruitful hunting ground for peace moves". Certainly there were peace moves afoot and Dinny Cronin told me of an occasion when General Tom Ennis accompanied Canon Duggan to Gouganebarra with a proposal. Cronin was ready to run when he saw Ennis's uniform. Duggan was associated with an approach made to Tom Barry by a number of churchmen and other dignitaries, and in the middle of March he talked with Lynch and later with Cosgrave and Mulcahy.

It was with relief that de Valera received an invitation to attend the Executive meeting, which was held in the region of the Monavullagh Mountains in County Waterford. Bearded, he travelled in a large car with Frank Aiken and Austin Stack as supposed American tourists.

De Valera was anxious to stop the war but he stated that Irish sovereignty and the abolition of the Oath were pre-requisite. Tom Barry proposed that the Executive recognise that continued resistance would not further the cause of independence. His motion was defeated by 6 votes to 5, and after a meeting which had lasted from March 23rd to 26th it was decided to reassemble on April 10th.

The Executive Forces were dwindling rapidly. Perhaps 8,000 remained in the field. Some 13,000 were prisoners. Among these was Ernie O'Malley, Assistant Chief of Staff, who was badly wounded when he covered de Valera's retreat

[1] From captured document quoted in *Irish Times* of 11/4/23. [2] Ibid.
500

from a house in Dublin one night in November. Another was Con Moloney, taken as recently as March 7th in the Glen of Aherlow. Dinny Lacey had been killed in the Glen on February 18th. Trapped in a house at Ballydavid, he fought his way out and was shot dead as, ignoring a call to surrender, he tried to help a wounded comrade over a fence. Dan Breen and his friend, Jerry Kiely, were trapped in a house at Lisvarnane, again in the Glen of Aherlow, and killed a Free State officer at the cost of Kiely's life. Breen escaped.

In Kerry, little quarter was given on either side. At Knocknagoshal, a woman inveigled some Free State troops to investigate a field where she said there was a Republican arms dump. There officers and two men were killed by a trapmine. On March 7th, fearful reprisals were taken. The worst of these was at Ballyseedy where nine men were roped to a log and a mine exploded. The remains were distributed between nine coffins but one man had been blown some distance into a wood and lived. One of the men who died had in his possession a safe-conduct pass signed by General Michael Brennan. There were similar incidents at Killarney where four died and one survived, and Cahirciveen where five men were killed.

As the time for the adjourned meeting of the Executive approached, Lynch lost two more of his staff. Thomas Derrig, who had succeeded Moloney as Adjutant-General, and Maurice Twomey were captured in Dublin on April 6th. Derrig was wounded.

Lynch spent the time between the meetings in pensive hiding, moving from place to place. His dilemma was acute. He was as determined as ever to go on, his main hope lying with the men in the west, but he knew that with every passing day more of the men who meant so much to him would be lost. For a few days he stayed near Callan in a very ingenious hideout known as "Katmandu" then, with Frank Aiken and Sean Hyde, he set out for Araglin in County Cork. Three days later they were joined by Quirke, Sean O'Meara and Sean Hayes, and on April 8th the party arrived in the Goatenbridge area.

Lynch's men were billeted in farmhouses at Croagh, between

the River Tar and the Knockmealdown Mountains. They knew the area well and were with friends. Guards were provided by the 3rd Tipperary Brigade and Lynch was satisfied that he could fend off any Free State raiding party. Such raids were commonplace and when he was warned by scouts in the early hours of Tuesday, April 10th, that a Free State party had been sighted, he took the report calmly, settled down to a cup of tea and awaited developments.

What he did not know was that information of the presence of Republican leaders in the area had reached Prout as early as Sunday and that sweeps were being carried out by more than a thousand Free State troops. Commandant Tommy Ryan knew the farmhouses where the Republicans were quartered. He had slept in them many times during the Tan war, and he knew as well as they that there were only two passes through the Knockmealdown Mountains that Lynch could use as escape routes.

He devised a plan which he hoped would "have the G.H.Q. staff back in Clonmel by evening and end the Civil War".

Ryan sent one column from Clonmel to cover the east and west sides of Lynch's billeting area and himself led two columns from the north, one the other side of the Tar river "in case they slipped back". Lynch would have no alternative but to make for the passes through the Knockmealdown Mountains. The vital part of the plan was the positioning of men on the further side of the passes to spring the trap. He entrusted this mission to Captain Tom Taylor who was to leave Clogheen at midnight with 50 men.

The plan went awry because over difficult terrain Taylor made slower progress than had been anticipated and, far from being in a position to close the gaps, was still at Goatenbridge when Ryan arrived. Ryan knew that Lynch's scouts would by now have reported movements of troops and, indeed, they had done so before dawn. He guessed that Lynch and his staff were safely on their way through the gaps, but it was not until scouts brought in news of the approach of the column from Clonmel that Lynch realised that this was no mere small-scale raid but a carefully planned trap, and that he was in danger of being encircled.

Many of the Free State troops had now ceased to take the plan very seriously themselves and were pot-shotting at rabbits
502

among the gorse on the mountainside, but Ryan, in an attempt to save the day, sent Lieutenant Clancy with half the Clogheen force to seal off the gaps as planned. They were too late, for the Executive G.H.Q. staff were already making their way along the bed of a dry stream up the mountain, but they glimpsed Lynch's party and opened fire. For the moment the Republicans were in no real danger, but once they had to leave the stream and make their way over a bleak hump of mountain they were exposed to the rifle fire of their Free State pursuers. However, the range was several hundred yards and Lynch's party struggled on unscathed, though bullets picked at their heels. Their own revolvers were useless at the distance.

And then, just as Michael Collins had fallen to a single long-range shot, so did Liam Lynch. A bullet passed right through his body just above the hip. He was still alive, though in great pain, and his companions, Aiken, Quirke and Hyde carried him for a time. Finally, at his insistence, they left him. He knew he was dying and realised that they had little hope of escape so long as they had to carry him.

Clancy's men thought they had captured de Valera, whom the tall, bespectacled Lynch did resemble superficially, but Clancy soon established the captive's identity. He dressed Lynch's wounds and then the party carried him downhill on a litter improvised from rifles and coats. For the wounded leader it was an agonising journey to the foot of the mountains, and little better when he was transferred to a hay cart and borne into Newcastle four and a half hours from the moment when he had fallen. Clancy telephoned Clonmel and Prout himself returned with an ambulance and a doctor.

After two priests had attended him, Lynch was carried across the broken bridge at Newcastle and placed in the ambulance. He was taken to the military ward of St Joseph's Hospital in Clonmel. Tommy Doyle was convalescing in the same ward.

"He would ask me to turn him in the bed," he recalls. "He would put his arms round my neck and draw himself up."

Before he died that evening, Liam Lynch called Prout to his bedside and asked to be buried beside his friend Michael Fitzgerald who had died on hunger strike in Cork jail in 1920.

503

At the Inquest, held in the Clonmel Union boardroom, it was stated by witnesses, Free State soldiers, that Lynch's party had fired first and that shots had been exchanged for twenty to thirty minutes. The jury found that "death was due to shock and haemorrhage following bullet wounds caused by a party of the National Army in the execution of their duty." It was the formula of the day. But they added "a vote of sympathy with the relatives of Liam Lynch", and one juror asked for an assurance that Lynch's last wish would be carried out.

Throughout the night of Wednesday, April 11th, girls of Cumann na mBan guarded Lynch's body, which lay in the small church belonging to the workhouse, and among the many who came to kneel there were soldiers of the National Army.

Like that of Collins, Lynch's death was half-accidental, another bizarre incident in this strange war. When Collins died, the first phase of the Civil War ended; with Lynch's passing all the sting went out of the resistance to the Free State Government. Rumours were rife that Lynch and his party—among whom it was then believed were de Valera, Breen and Stack—had actually been interrupted in the course of a conference and that they were discussing peace problems. They were not far from the truth, but de Valera was not there. He was waiting in Dublin to hear the outcome of the conference.

Dan Breen had been with Lynch the previous night and was still in the area, within the Free State cordon. So were Austin Stack, Frank Barrett and a number of others. Prout's men were scouring the countryside, probing the Knockmealdowns and the Comeragh and Monavullagh Mountains. Whippet cars patrolled the roads and boats were removed from the rivers; an aircraft lingered above. Breen's party reached Mt Melleray at midnight of the day following Lynch's capture. Before daybreak they were on their way again, but shortly afterwards they were seen and came under fire. The party divided then, and Breen, with Andy Kennedy and Maurice Walshe, struck out almost due north towards Newcastle. For two days they were forced to lie low in the hills with nothing but snow to eat or drink. But they got through and headed for the hospitable Glen of Aherlow. Breen had a dugout in the Glen and there he fell into an exhausted sleep. When he wakened he heard movements outside and went out to find himself in the hands of Free State soldiers. What he did not know was that they had been there for several hours, calling to him from time to time but not firing a shot.

From Mt Melleray Austin Stack had worked his way northeastwards towards Ballymacarbry. When a party of Free State troops under Lieutenant Moran searched a farmyard on Saturday, April 14th, Moran "went poking round in the sheds" and took no notice of a man who was splitting firewood with a hatchet. But a Limerick man who had known Stack challenged him. Stack, who was wearing a beard, tried to bluff, but it was of no avail. He said no more, but threw down his hatchet, picked up his coat and was marched morosely away. Commandant Tommy Ryan saw him and greeted him, but Stack stared stonily back.

In a notebook found on his person was the draft of a memorandum to be put to the Executive had their adjourned meeting been possible. It read:

"Realising the gravity of the situation of the Army of the Republic, owing to the great odds now facing them, and the losses lately sustained; and being of opinion that further military efforts would be futile, and would cause only injury to our country, without obtaining any advantage; and being convinced that the defensive war which has been waged by our Army the last nine or ten months has made it impossible that the Irish people will ever accept less than their full national rights; and fearing it would cause too much delay to await the summoning and holding of a full meeting of the Army Council or Executive:

"We the undersigned members of the Army Council and of the Executive, and other officers of the Army, do hereby call upon and authorise the President of the Republic to order an immediate cessation of hostilities.

"Volunteers are required to hand in their arms to . . . pending the election of a government, the free choice of the people."

The Free State officers and men did not know how close was the end of the struggle but they realised that the Republicans were segmented and disorganised, and the hunt went on.

"In the Cashel area our troops had been continually ambushed," Colonel Ryan explains. "We knew the area well and we knew the local people. Somewhere there was a secret dugout but we couldn't locate it and we couldn't get any information about it.

"One night—there was a concert on in the barracks, I remember—three columns went out in my charge. Until 2 a.m., when I roused them out of bed, the fellows knew nothing of the plan. The three columns were to do separate sweeps and were to meet at a certain time. One column was not at the rendezvous on time. It was led by Lieutenant Patrick Kennedy—Kennedy Cashin he was usually called—at twenty years of age one of our best officers. Lieutenant Moran was with him. I was pretty fed up because I always insisted on good time-keeping. Anyway, we went to look for them."

Kennedy had been given information by a youngster he had interrogated which he thought doubtful but worth investigation. He led his party towards the old ruin of Castle Blake, which had been searched many times before, always fruitlessly.

"Just before we got there," David Moran relates, "I noticed a fox crossing a field and let fly at it—two shots—and missed. We thought then that anyone in the castle would have taken warning and cleared out after that. Anyway, we carried on over a fence and went on down to the castle. Inside we found ourselves in what had been probably some sort of pantry, and there was fresh meat in a bag on an old table in the corner."

Kennedy was scouting round outside the building while Moran and some others entered another small room, which was adjacent to the pantry. There was wooden wainscotting here about which Moran thought there was something odd. It did not seem to belong. The table was brought in from the pantry and a lad named O'Neill, from Cahir, stood on it and began to probe with his bayonet. He found a small trapdoor. Moran told O'Neill to get down, then shouted a warning to anyone in the dugout to come out. Theo English, with whom Moran had been at school in Tipperary, emerged. Asked whether there was anyone with him, he asserted that he was alone. Then he bolted through the door, into the pantry, and out into the yard. Kennedy's men saw him, yelled to him to
506

stop, then fired shots, but English hared across the yard and made for the fence. A bullet hit him as he leaped for almost certain safety, and he rolled back, dead.

A second man, Sean Cleary, came through the trapdoor and also maintained that there was no one else in the dugout. Like English, he ran for the door, but when he saw what had happened to his friend, he stopped and was taken prisoner.

Still another man appeared. This was Ned Somers, a former National Army officer, who had been with Moran and some of the other Free State men at Kilkenny and later changed sides.

"He had a bomb in his hand," resumes Moran. "I saw him throw it and the next thing he fired at me point-blank and got me in the arm. The bomb had gone right over my head and through the doorway and it landed on the stone floor of the pantry. That's where the crowd was.

"As it exploded, I dived under the table and fired a couple of shots, but I don't know if I hit him. Just then, he leaped down on to the table and from there to the floor on the other side. Then one of the lads turned his gun on him and emptied the whole magazine."

At that moment Commandant Tommy Ryan arrived to find a grim scene. Kennedy Cashin had been fatally wounded and other dead and wounded lay grotesquely where the exploding bomb had hurled them. Ned Somers was dead.

Lieutenant Moran, scarcely aware of his own wound, hastened to the road. "I wanted to get medical and spiritual aid and by an act of Providence a man on a white horse had just gone past. I whistled him to stop and asked him to fetch a doctor and a priest."

Because of Liam Lynch's death, the Executive, with several new members, did not meet until April 20th. Frank Aiken succeeded Lynch as Chief of Staff and he, Tom Barry and Liam Pilkington, Sean McEoin's old adversary, were appointed as an Army Council. The Executive decided to call on de Valera, as head of the Republican Government, and the Army Council to make peace with the Free State authorities.

De Valera presided at a joint meeting of his Government-in-exile and the Army Council, and on the next day, April 27th, issued a wordy proclamation announcing readiness to

507

negotiate an immediate cease fire. Simultaneously, Aiken ordered a suspension of all operations as from April 30th. It was apparent, even now, that negotiations would not be easy.

De Valera approached Senators Jameson and Douglas who, with Cosgrave's sanction, agreed to act as intermediaries. The conditions upon which any agreement would have to be based were submitted to de Valera. These were simple. Political issues, present and future, were to be decided by majority vote of the elected representatives of the people and the Government was to have effective control of lethal weapons. A preliminary condition to the release of prisoners was the surrender of arms, and prisoners would be required individually to accept the first two conditions.

Military action would cease when the Executive Forces delivered up their arms and every consideration would be shown for the feelings of those concerned. Finally, "the Free State Government would keep a clear field for Mr de Valera and his followers to enable them to canvass for the votes of the people at the next election, provided they undertook to adhere strictly to constitutional action."

After several days of argument with Jameson and Douglas, de Valera put counter proposals on May 7th. The draft was, according to Cosgrave, "a long and wordy document, inviting debate where none is possible." De Valera's insistence upon Irish sovereignty was superfluous in Cosgrave's view, for the principle was already embodied in the Constitution. Another condition was that no citizen should be excluded by "any political oath, test or other device" from taking his place in Parliament. As to the control of arms, pending an election he wanted the strict supervision of those in Free State hands and the assignment to the Republican forces of "at least one suitable building in each province, to be used by them as barracks and arsenals, where Republican arms shall be stored, sealed up, and defended by a specially pledged Republican guard . . ." a suggestion which drew from O'Higgins the caustic comment, "This is not going to be a draw, with a replay in the autumn."

The Oath was the kernel of the quarrel, as it had been the stumbling block of the plenipotentiaries in London, and de Valera could hardly have expected the Free State Government to scrap the Constitution and the Treaty and

508

to go back to the beginning—after a war which had cost countless lives and some thirty million pounds.

Cosgrave refused the proposals and on May 24th de Valera issued yet another proclamation to all ranks of the Republican forces.

"Soldiers of liberty! Legion of the rearguard! The Republic can no longer be defended successfully by your arms. Further sacrifices on your part would now be in vain, and continuance of the struggle in arms unwise in the national interest. Military victory must be allowed to rest for the moment with those who have destroyed the Republic."

Aiken ordered that "the arms with which we have fought the enemies of our country are to be dumped. The foreign and domestic enemies of the Republic have for the moment prevailed."

So the thing was ended, neither on de Valera's terms nor Cosgrave's; the Executive Forces simply hid their arms and stopped fighting.

Like a house wrecked during a wild party, Ireland had to be cleaned through and restored. The process took a long time.

More bitterness was engendered after the cease fire by the continued detention of prisoners, whose numbers increased as Republican combatants were rounded up. Most were not released until well into 1924.

The Free State leaders dared not set their captives free lest they went at once to their hidden arsenals. They knew the prisoners were already occupying their minds with plots to renew the struggle. An intercepted letter from Frank Aiken, dated June 27th and later quoted by O'Higgins, expressed the opinion that the rifle and revolver were out of date and it was better to concentrate on fire and explosives. "If we have to fight another war with the Staters, it will have to be short and sweet," he wrote.

Writs of *habeas corpus* were applied for in June on the grounds that a state of war no longer existed, but the Master of the Rolls held that the Republican cease fire did not specifically declare the end of hostilities and "meant nothing more than that a rest stage had been reached." But, sooner or later, the Judges were bound to decide that the war had ended. Prisoners would have to be produced for trial or released. The Free State Government hastened to introduce the Public Safety (Emergency Powers) Bill and it became law on August 1st, the day after the Appeal Court granted an application of *habeas corpus*.

In Cosgrave's Cabinet political and military attitudes still clashed. O'Higgins had long been critical both of the Army's inability to restore order quickly and of its own lapses from discipline. This angered General Mulcahy who contended that politicians like O'Higgins did not comprehend the difficulties and provocations the Army faced. An Army inquiry into the Ballyseedy affair had whitewashed those responsible, and while Mulcahy accepted the report without question, O'Higgins was inclined to take the matter further.

In June, officers of the Dublin Brigade in Kerry seized two daughters of a local doctor, a friend of O'Higgins, stripped them and plastered them with axle-grease. An inquiry was held but no action of any consequence was taken. O'Higgins quarrelled with Mulcahy, demanding courts martial. The Cabinet decided to refer the case to the Attorney-General, but no criminal proceedings were taken and O'Higgins was persuaded only with difficulty to remain starchily in office.

The Dail had nearly run the course of the year it had been given to create the Free State, but before the session ended Patrick Hogan, Cosgrave's brilliant Minister of Agriculture, managed to pilot the momentous Land Act of 1923 through the Dail. Improved by the Senate, as Hogan gladly acknowledged, the Bill completed a system of land ownership reform initiated by the British Government in earlier years. The measure did much to lessen menacing unrest in rural areas in the south.

De Valera and his party contested the election of August 27th under the old Sinn Fein banner, which must have caused a slight disturbance in the vicinity of Griffith's grave. Daring to address his constituents in Ennis, de Valera was arrested. Shots were fired and a girl was wounded. Whether harm was intended de Valera is uncertain. It is said that one man was to have assassinated the Republican leader but lost his nerve. Almost anything was possible at the time. Life was still held cheap and Civil War vendettas flared frequently.

510

Winning 63 of the 153 seats, Cosgrave was returned to power, but he had a clear majority in the Dail only because the 44 members of de Valera's party who had been elected refused to take the Oath and—those of them who were not in prison—were not allowed to take their seats.

"Those who talk about democracy cannot say, I think, that democracy in the 1923 election got very much of a chance," was de Valera's caustic comment. He himself was a prisoner at Arbour Hill.

The Republican prisoners now began hunger strikes as a protest against their continued incarceration.

"You can't lose a hunger strike provided you are prepared to die and provided your cause justifies death," says Frank Carty, who fasted for twenty-eight days. "But to say, 'If you don't let us out, we'll go on hunger strike,' was not enough. The Free State leaders knew from experience that it was not. We all knew." The strike was called off after some had fasted for as much as fifty-five days.

One very good reason for holding the prisoners long after the bullets, or most of them, had stopped flying was the dissatisfaction spreading through the National Army as the process of reducing its strength from nearly 60,000 to about 20,000 went on. Many Free State soldiers had followed Collins at the split but belonged in spirit and in temperament with their Republican opponents and expected the Government to take the same kind of action against the Six Counties as Collins had done. And although they had accepted his "stepping stones to the Republic" argument, they wanted not a cautious edging towards their objective but uninhibited leaps.

There were personal grievances too. Resentment against Trucers ran high, particularly those, including former British Army men, who had been promoted and were being retained while old Volunteers were pushed into civilian life, for which many were untrained and in which little employment offered. Gratuities were not generous.

An ultimatum, signed by Major-General Liam Tobin and Colonel Charles Dalton, was read to the Dail by Cosgrave on March 11th. It alleged that the Government were not moving towards a republican form of government and demanded the removal of the Army Council and the suspension of army

511

demobilisation and reorganisation. On the same day, Joseph McGrath resigned as Minister of Agriculture and Commerce.

The Army Mutiny of 1924 almost ended in bloodshed and could have resulted in yet another war of brothers, with an entirely new alignment of forces. There was even an abortive attempt to bring England back into the fight. Unarmed British soldiers on leave and their civilian companions were machine-gunned at Cobh. One soldier was killed and a score of people wounded.

With deputies of the Dail involved, the crisis simmered on until October. Strong measures by O'Higgins in March, sensible words behind the scenes later, and perhaps more generous gratuities in some cases brought it to a peaceful conclusion. The casualties included Mulcahy, who resigned as Minister of Defence in March, and three senior officers of the Army Council.

As Cosgrave was ill, O'Higgins, Vice-President of the Executive Council, handled the affair and emerged as the strong man of the Cabinet. He cut through both factions of the Army, removing officers involved in the mutiny and their rivals as well. In June, Mulcahy, now an ordinary deputy, moved a vote of censure on the Executive Council for "ill-considered" dismissals. O'Higgins lashed back venomously, and alluding to an attempt to revive the influence of the I.R.B., charged that "two groups or factions, or secret, or semi-secret societies" had been "lining up" in the Army. The Cabinet could not allow "the national position to be bedevilled by a faction fight between two letters of the alphabet . . ."

What had at last been established was that the Army was an instrument of the Government, the Government not a weapon of the Army, that the revolution was complete and power belonged in the hands of the people.

EPILOGUE

Perhaps it was at this point that Ireland's Civil War could be said to have ended. She had not seen the last of bombs and bullets but the gun had ceased to be a god.

It is easy to follow the historical thread of events which led to the Civil War, less easy to determine why it traced the course it did, to distinguish the causes of the conflict.

The background responsibility at least was Great Britain's. The Treaty negotiations gave Lloyd George's Government a chance to redeem themselves for the shabby war they had fought to deny Ireland the independence which was her right, an opportunity to atone for Britain's blunders and delays of past years. But, steeped in the imperialist tradition, they could not conceive of relinquishing any part of the Empire, by whatever means it had been acquired and whether or not England was held in affection by the indigenous people. It was beyond their imagination to reduce the prestige of the Crown by permitting any withdrawal of even the most unwilling allegiance to it.

It is strange that some of England's most astute statesmen of the twentieth century hadn't the vision to realise that Ireland's "external association" plan was not only feasible but would, within relatively few years, provide the pattern for colonial states such as India when they achieved independence in their turn. They failed to see, too, that the concept of the Commonwealth was already changing, that even the old Dominions like Canada were determined to have a freer hand in working out their international relations.

The Oath suggested by de Valera, recognising the King as head of the associated states of the Commonwealth, really met the British demand that the Crown be retained as a symbol, and at the same time it assured the Irish, who had no experience of the Crown as a symbol but only as the source of omnipresent power, that they would have genuine control of their own affairs.

The shadow of Britain's past record lay across the Treaty and darkened the bright promise of British signatures. Distrust set many an Irish heart against it, but Collins and Griffith rightly believed that Great Britain intended that Ireland should have the status of Canada or Australia. Having offered dominion status the British Government had no intention of belittling it and the assertion that Britain promoted civil war in order to reoccupy Ireland is nonsense. Anxious for the peaceful development of the Free State, she was extraordinarily tolerant of murderous attacks on her withdrawing forces. But every ounce of Treaty flesh she demanded, even to an obdurate refusal to modify the wording of the Oath during the Constitution crisis of June, 1922. The British Government knew that the change might well brake the gathering momentum of civil war, and although in the previous December they had expected to have to yield a little more on that point, they declined adamantly to do so now.

The problem of Partition was even more complex. Having long since given in to the vociferous Orange minority, and then created a Parliament for them that they did not want, the British Government was not in a position to do much more than try to promote harmony between the two parts of Ireland and, failing this, to fall back on a special solution —such as the Boundary Commission. It was enough for the day.

Strangely, the Partition question sparked off less surface emotion than the issue of allegiance to the King, and it was the latter that set the guns blazing. Had this not been so, war might easily have developed on a north-south axis and it would have been difficult for Britain not to become involved. The Civil War had been in progress for months before the Six Counties exercised their option to be no part of the newly created Free State, but their intentions had been in no doubt from the beginning. Of the two issues which divided the I.R.A. the second was the less acute, but only because there was no real disagreement. Those who fought the Treaty wanted to secure a Republic at once and to unite the country within it. Their opponents fought for the Treaty only because they expected to accomplish the same ends by peaceful means, though it would take longer. The persecution of Catholics in the Six Counties was met by joint action and came close to sabotaging the Treaty. It certainly led Collins into duplicity.

The signatories of the Treaty, Irish and British, knew that the Agreement would provoke fierce opposition in Ireland. Lloyd George's Cabinet were prepared to resume the war if their conditions were not met; what the Irish plenipotentiaries took back with them was a Treaty plus an ultimatum. Though they had agreed to recommend acceptance to the Dail, they had the comfort of knowing that the final decision rested with all the deputies and not with them alone. A democratic vote would decide the issue.

Chosen for their revolutionary views, the members of the Dail, most of whom were also I.R.A. men, were not representatives of moderate opinion but were the sharp end of the Republican wedge. A majority approved the Treaty, a majority of men whose views were more extreme than the people's as a whole. Once the vote had been taken, what should have been asked was whether the Dail was a democratic assembly. De Valera insisted that a constitutional solution was possible and so it was. His course and that of his followers should have been to form a constitutional opposition. That meant taking the hated Oath, but if England insisted upon forcing it down palpably reluctant throats she could hardly expect it to be swallowed without a grimace.

"One of the difficulties which led to the Civil War was the vocabulary," says Professor Michael Hayes. Many Irish folk did not really understand the difference between a republic and an autonomous government which recognised the King as its head in name. A direct cause was the Dail's proclamation of a Republic in 1919. For the more sophisticated minds it was "a national thing, a resistance device," to repeat Professor Hayes, and a "strait-jacket," to quote de Valera. But for many young idealists it was the Holy Grail. It led to the long and dogged correspondence prior to negotiations, and tied the hands of the plenipotentiaries in London and of de Valera in Dublin. And it meant that when the plenipotentiaries settled for less the cry of "traitor" went up. Furthermore, because of the long preliminaries of the Treaty, the Truce dragged through many months when not only were the original I.R.A. men girded for action when frustratingly there was none, but the enrolment books were opened to numerous young men, the Trucers, some of whose motives were less than patriotic and all of whom were an aggravating factor in the deteriorating situation.

De Valera's concept of a republic within the Commonwealth seemed a contradiction in terms not only to the British but to most of the Dail deputies, whether they supported or opposed the Treaty, but it ingeniously included both Crown and Republic as symbols. Given safeguards for the Unionist majority, the British Government could reasonably have accepted it; it provided the people of the Six Counties with a Commonwealth link and "die-hard" Republicans might have

515

been persuaded that it did not compromise their principles. But no one understood the "vocabulary" and de Valera joined the ardent Republicans rather than step across the Treaty line.

He was the one man who might have prevented civil war, for his prestige and influence were unrivalled. But he, who should have been the most forceful advocate of a democratic settlement, insisted that the minority was right and entitled, therefore, to enforce its views on the benighted majority. His speeches, whether meant to incite or simply to warn of the consequences of bloodshed, were certainly inimical to peace in a country which had now to decide whether bullets or votes counted. It is understandable that young men who had fought for freedom should want to achieve their object totally before handing over the country to civilian rule. They regarded themselves, as Peadar O'Donnell puts it, as "custodians for the people of the sovereignty of the Nation". They saw the Dail's decision as an abdication and were convinced that the I.R.A. should resume responsibility.

De Valera could not have prevented the seizure of the Four Courts, or dislodged the garrison, for Rory O'Connor and his comrades were determined to resist interference from politicians of any ilk. At that time they did not want de Valera. But if de Valera had stuck to his constitutional guns, the Four Courts garrison would have become bored with their occupation in time and the guns of the Provisional Government might never have been raised against them. De Valera should have known then, as he realised later, that armies should be answerable to governments.

Totally unyielding, his contribution to a settlement, the pact with Collins, could only work—if it worked at all—to his advantage. The Panel arrangement ensured that no follower of his was defeated at the polls by a candidate of the pro-Treaty Party, which he admitted had the support of the electorate, and he was assured also of a proportion of places in the Cabinet. But neither he nor any of his followers had any intention of taking the Oath of allegiance to the Crown. The pact could only be effective, therefore, if the British Government accepted the "republican" Constitution submitted to them or if Griffith and Collins tore up the Treaty. There was no possibility of perpetuating the pre-election dichotomy with the Dail remaining as the Government of the

Republic and the Provisional Government working to establish
the Free State. While it is true that the electorate had had no
time to study the Constitution, there was no suggestion that
they did not vote for the Treaty in terms of which the
Constitution was ultimately framed. Peadar O'Donnell attri-
butes the comparative lack of support for the Republicans to
a middle class element "concealed within the independence
movement." Lamenting that when Connolly died no leader
appeared from the Trade Unions to secure the place he had
purchased for the working class, he says, "We paid the price
for immaturity." What cannot be forgotten, however, is that
without the middle classes the revolution could not have
succeeded. Roused by the events of 1916-18, they joined in
the fight for independence rather than for the ideal of the
Republic and wished to take up their disrupted lives once
there was an end to suppression.

"All idealists are pitiless," Daniel Corkney once said; and
the middle class element were not idealists in this sense.

The attack on the Four Courts became inevitable once the
Provisional Government had been given a clear mandate by
the people. If they were to govern they had to eliminate acts
of violence throughout the country, armed opposition to the
functions of Government and the illegal occupation of public
buildings. The capture of General O'Connell was the spark, or
perhaps the opportunity. Pressure from the British Government
following Wilson's assassination was not a direct factor but
possibly created tension which demanded release.

De Valera had been turned away from the Four Courts by
the garrison and thereafter played an enigmatic role. Whether
he willed it or not, he seemed always to side-step responsibility
at times of crisis, to emerge when it had passed and resume
his unquestioned leadership. By joining the Executive Forces
he condoned military action, but he remained ostensibly a
humble private, neither accepting the rank and responsibility
that the hero of Boland's Mill might have been expected to
take nor becoming involved in the fighting. He was content
to leave the Republican cause in the hands of the military
leaders until he began to lose touch and realised that, unless he
re-established some kind of formal political organisation,
political power would pass into the hands of the Executive.

His lesson was Ireland's lesson of the Civil War and it is

517

mete that her soldiers are among the most valuable of United Nations peace-keeping contingents. She has had an important impact on world affairs, and on the shaping of the Commonwealth, and the pattern of her fight for independence has been constantly followed, with Britain stoutly resisting the guerrilla warheads of independence campaigns, only to treat with the leaders in the end. But Great Britain has a saving grace, a capacity to wipe the slate clean, to bear no grudges, and this is something which some at least of the Irish leaders of the war of independence admire. Ireland had much to remember with bitterness, numerous dead heroes to adulate, but there were those who saw that necrophilia and an obsession with the past could only stultify developments in a world accelerating into the future. From the end of the Civil War to the present day they have accomplished much.

In Cosgrave and O'Higgins, the one able and steady, the other brilliant and imaginative, Ireland had found the men of the hour. They made mistakes but they ensured that the foundation of a democratic state with a fine police force, an honest judiciary and a competent civil service was good. Ireland joined the League of Nations in 1923, and two years later, O'Higgins attended the Disarmament Conference at Geneva, learning much from Commonwealth and international statesmen.

Britain did not like Dominion participation in foreign affairs, preferring the role of mother making decisions for the family. But she could not forever keep the brood in short trousers and, at the Imperial Conference of 1926, O'Higgins took the lead in suing for recognition of maturity. The Statute of Westminster of 1931 owed much to his spadework but he did not live to see it. On July 19th, 1927, at the age of 35, he was shot down by assassins on his way to Mass. Today, the Commonwealth matches almost exactly his concept of separate autonomous states making their own international arrangements, each acknowledging the Monarch as head of their state.

Since 1948 Ireland has not belonged to the Commonwealth. John A. Costello's mixed-bag Government, which had only recently taken office after de Valera's sixteen year tenure, introduced the Republic of Ireland Act, a surprising move
518

from the dominant party of the coalition, *Fine Gael*, direct descendant of the pro-Treaty party. Ironically, the Republican party *Fianna Fail* at first opposed the Bill, arguing that it would make it more difficult to end Partition and secure a Republic for all thirty-two counties. In the House of Lords, Viscount Samuel thought that Eire had "now taken the one step most calculated to defeat that purpose."

Costello's action attracted accusations of spite or pique. "The most likely explanation, however," says Timothy Patrick Coogan[1], "is that Costello—who, as a lawyer, had been involved in a number of I.R.A. trials—was appalled at the suffering caused by this sterile republicanism, and sought to take the gun out of Irish politics once and for all by giving the Republicans their Republic."

The "New I.R.A." which had risen from the ruins of the Executive Forces withdrew its support from de Valera and the political wing of the Republican movement in 1925. Their aims were the old ones, a Republic and the end of Partition, and they proposed to achieve them by force of arms. A well-organised underground army led by men of high quality such as Tom Barry, Maurice Twomey and Peadar O'Donnell, it became as the Old Man of the Sea to successive Free State Governments.

De Valera resigned from Sinn Fein and founded Fianna Fail, leaving behind him those still steeped in the philosophy of 1919. At the elections on June, 1927, they won 44 seats, the same number Sinn Fein had won in 1923. The Labour Party, Farmers Party and National League won seats from Cosgrave, whose party was reduced to 47. Declining to take the Oath, the successful Fianna Fail candidates were not permitted to take their seats either and Cosgrave introduced a Bill to invalidate the election and to make it obligatory upon candidates to accept the Oath.

Dan Breen, an independent Republican now, and one of the men who had triggered off the war against England at Soloheadbeg, was first to take the Oath—and his seat.

"I didn't know why de Valera waited so long," he says. "You can't leave a country to rot. You must come out and

---

[1] *Ireland Since the Rising*, by Timothy Patrick Coogan, as vividly written as it is comprehensively researched, is strongly recommended to readers.

take responsibility and act." Breen held no grudge. Of O'Higgins he says, "He believed he was there as the lawful Government and as such he was out to do his duty. He did it. He hurt a lot of people, but any man in Government who will govern will hurt; if he won't hurt, he won't govern."

Finally de Valera thought of a way out of his dilemma. Pushing aside the Bible, he simply signed his name beneath the Oath and ignored its existence. He had come to see the truth of Shaw's assertion that oaths belonged in "the dustbin of history" and that "any practical statesman will, under duress, swallow a dozen oaths to get his hand on the driving wheel."[2]

Within a few days de Valera almost had the wheel in his hands, but a proposed alliance with Labour and the National League fell through. Cosgrave swiftly called another election, which increased his seats to 62 and de Valera's to 57. With the onset of the great Depression, Cosgrave's Government, already stale, caught a backlash of unpopularity. Unemployment was a grievous problem and extremist groups readily attracted recruits. On February 16th, 1932, Fianna Fail won 72 seats, Cosgrave's *Cumann na nGaedhael* (eventually *Fine Gael*) only 57. De Valera formed a Government, including among his Ministers, Frank Aiken, Thomas Derrig and Sean Lemass.

At once he made use of the Statute of Westminster and, quite legitimately, legislated to remove the Oath from the Constitution. In 1936 he abolished the Senate and seized on the abdication of Edward VIII to legislate the Crown out of the Constitution also. In its place he introduced his dear old war-horse, "external association", but he did not actually declare a Republic. A new Constitution was approved by the Dail in June, 1937. The Irish Free State became Eire, or simply Ireland, and both name and Constitution allowed for the ultimate inclusion in the State of the Six Counties. Dr Douglas Hyde was elected President and de Valera became the first *Taoiseach* or Prime Minister. The Constitution also provided for a new second chamber, the *Seanad*, to be elected on quite a different system from the old Senate and having very limited powers.

Throughout the thirties de Valera skirmished with the

2 *Manchester Guardian* of 27/12/21.

British Government and from 1932 to 1938 an economic war raged, spiteful on both sides and doing neither any good. It began with de Valera's refusal to pay land annuities, amounting to £5 million annually, which Cosgrave had assigned to Great Britain in 1923, a transaction not made public at the time. Britain retaliated with higher duties on Irish imports, the Free State replied in kind, and the doleful years passed.

Internally, also, Ireland had her difficulties. True to an election promise, de Valera released all I.R.A. prisoners. The I.R.A. relentlessly harried their old enemies in Cosgrave's party and ceaseless violence at political meetings led to the formation of a rival organisation, the Army Comrades Association, later the famous Blueshirts. General O'Duffy, who had lost his job as Chief of Police, was invited to lead the new movement. He was meant to be a figurehead only but was soon running the ship. The rival bodies, in essence stemming from the two sides of the Civil War, clashed frequently and embarrassed the Government equally. But by 1935, when O'Duffy led an Irish Brigade into the Spanish Civil War, the Blueshirt movement was breaking up and the I.R.A., too, split and splintered.

A reciprocal trade agreement ended the economic war with England in 1938. Ireland paid a lump sum of £10 million to resolve the annuities squabble and England handed back the Treaty ports, an act which Churchill rued bitterly in World War Two when de Valera preserved a slightly less than meticulous neutrality. By refraining from conscripting men in the Six Counties Britain won appreciation and a flood of volunteers both from the North and from Eire. The neutral Irish won no less than seven Victoria Crosses.

For the I.R.A. Britain's difficulty was, as ever, Ireland's opportunity. Early in 1939 extremists began a bombing campaign in England, and an explosion which killed five people in Coventry on August 25th shocked both England and Ireland. New legislation in Ireland enabled the internment of prisoners without trial and brought in the death penalty for acts of treason. In December, 1939, an I.R.A. raiding party seized a staggering million rounds of ammunition from the Magazine Fort in Phoenix Park, Dublin. Most of it was soon recovered and there were numerous arrests.

Throughout the war, the I.R.A. and Germany were in

mutually ineffectual contact. There was activity on the border too, but the I.R.A. lost valuable men in gun battles with the police, by execution and as a result of hunger strikes, and internecine quarrels reduced the movement to near impotence.

Hopes that with the hoisting of the Republican flag in 1949 the I.R.A. would pack up altogether were not realised. The Partition issue remained and they gathered strength again.

When the Northern Parliament opted out of the all-Ireland Dominion provided for by the Treaty of 1921, the Boundary Commission clause applied. The North refused to appoint a Commissioner and in 1925 the British Government nominated one for them. Professor Eoin MacNeill, the Free State representative, resigned before the findings were published, convinced that the report would not comply with the terms of reference. Only by a plebiscite would it have been possible "to determine in accordance with the wishes of the inhabitants, so far as may be compatible with economic and geographic conditions, the boundaries between Northern Ireland and the rest of Ireland." The British Government refrained from passing legislation required for a plebiscite, afraid that the Orangemen would be provoked into fighting to hold the territory which inevitably would have been voted to the South.

General McEoin's concise explanation of the position is worth recording here: "The principle involved was supposed to be similar to that applied under the Treaty of Versailles with regard to boundaries in Central Europe—they would be settled by the wishes of the inhabitants *taken by arrondissements*, parishes if you like. The Treaty lawyers left it simply as 'the wishes of the inhabitants'. The question was the inhabitants of where? The only two areas mentioned were the Six Counties and the Twenty-six. No wonder Collins said of the lawyers, 'The result of their labours make mine seem damn cheap.' "

Once more, bloodshed seemed probable, but it was prevented by a tripartite agreement signed in London on December 3rd, 1925. The boundary was to remain unaltered, the Irish Free State was relieved of that responsibility for part of the National Debt which the Treaty had imposed, and the Council of Ireland, meant as a link between the two parts of
522

Ireland, was abolished in favour of conferences between their two Governments. They, and the British Government, were "resolved mutually to aid one another in a spirit of neighbourly comradeship". Cordial and sincere the words, but they soon were lost.

From 1956 until 1962 I.R.A. extremists conducted a bloody campaign along the border, aggravating the situation, but when calm prevailed once more, there seemed to be a new hope. Early in 1965, there was an historic meeting between the *Taoiseach*, Mr Sean Lemass, and the Northern Premier, Captain Terence O'Neill. Later, O'Neill met Mr Jack Lynch, successor to Lemass. There was a trend towards co-operation, but O'Neill, who had embarked on a programme of reform, alienated the hard-liners of his own Unionist Party. As he sought to introduce "enduring standards" (as he put it) of justice, equality and generosity, which had been conspicuously lacking in the Six Counties of Northern Ireland, he gave the Catholic-Nationalist minority new heart, gave a little substance to their dream of a United Ireland. At the same time, he raised the hackles of those for whom the border had "hardened into permanence", as Lloyd George had predicted in 1921.

Encouraged by the signs of change in the harsh social and political climate, the Northern Ireland Civil Rights Association came into being.

On August 24th, 1968, the Association organized a protest march from Coalisland to Dungannon in County Tyrone, a peaceful demonstration which enraged Protestant extremists. A second march, which went ahead despite an official ban on October 5th, set alight the border fuse. The 1969 headlines read like those of fifty years before as paroxysms of violence shook Northern Ireland. The British Army marched gamely in to restore order. No one envisaged the seemingly endless task that lay ahead, a task they have undertaken with tact and skill.

There has been a decade of murder and waste, catalogued each day in the newspapers and needing no repetition here. The I.R.A. renewed itself, as it always does, by the splitting off from the main body of a militant splinter group; the Provisionals became the dominant faction and the urban guerilla campaign they have since waged has taken a grim toll of lives and limbs. Innocent people from as far away as New Zealand have been killed or crippled.

The I.R.A.'s equivalent, the Protestant extremist Ulster Volunteer Force, has participated in clandestine destruction matching the I.R.A. in a brutal tit-for-tat campaign of assassination to which journalists have attached the generic term "sectarian murders". In this age of politically motivated terrorism life has become cheap indeed, and anyone is likely to be caught in the crossfire of other people's quarrels.

Violence is at the heart of history and it is an unhappy truth that change, desirable or otherwise, is almost always achieved by violent means. The I.R.A. is not a gang of unprincipled thugs. Its members believe fervently in the legality of their cause and the justice of their actions. They declared war on a nation which seized their country long ago and still occupies part of it. Twenty-six of Ireland's thirty-two counties were liberated by their grandfather's generation. Now it is their turn to finish the job.

But they are tragically wrong. A united Ireland is the ideal of the people of the Republic and of the minority in the North, and it is, I am convinced, the logical and inevitable solution. The division of Ireland is unnatural, the border a bad border. There is in the Republic a measure of sympathy for the I.R.A., but the Republic is an increasingly prosperous country. With large injections of capital from the European Economic Community, industrial development is growing rapidly. The drain of emigration—400,000 quitted the country in the 1950s—has slowed to a trickle. Her government is respected, her troops have kept the peace in some of the trouble spots of the world. The future of the Republic is full of promise and her people are in no hurry to incorporate a recalcitrant minority, or to shoulder the economic burden of the North's unemployment and housing problems. One day, the border must go—but not yet. Without their unstinted support the I.R.A. will not achieve their aims. The last ten years have not brought a united Ireland any closer but may well have postponed it for a generation at least.

The Republic of Ireland now has a unique position on the periphery of the Commonwealth. There is "external association" but of a kind that even de Valera never envisaged. Her citizens and those of the United Kingdom enjoy reciprocal privileges which are more significant by far than the symbolic links between Britain and the old countries of the Commonwealth. These have weakened perceptibly since Britain entered the European Economic Community, in which the Republic is a partner.

In 1972 I wrote in *A State of Disunion*: "It is probable that if a solution is not reached by negotiation in which all concerned eschew recrimination, put partisanship aside and consider only the future good of all the people of Ireland, it will be produced from the exhaustion of tragic and long drawn out internecine battle." There was at that time, perhaps, an opportunity for a political settlement based on a declaration from the British Government that the principle of a United Ireland was accepted (a declaration offered in 1940 to buy Eire's entry into the War) and that by a definite date the Government of Ireland Act of 1920, under which the Northern Ireland Parliament was constituted, would be repealed. Instead, the Conservative Government imposed direct rule from Westminster.

Negotiation on a political level holds little promise now; guns and bombs will achieve nothing. The solution of Northern Ireland's problems will have to spring from the people themselves. That the potential for community action is there has already been demonstrated.

For many years brave people have cut through religious and political barriers to work in the community, particularly with youth. Others seek to perpetuate in their children the hatred which has warped their own lives and brought misery and ruin to the community. "We could have enriched our politics with our christianity; but far too often we have debased our christianity with our politics," said Captain Terence O'Neill when he made his farewell appearance on television on April 29th, 1969. Sooner or later, the truth of his words will be recognized by today's young people. Their generation has no time for hypocrisy.

As the futile strife has debilitated Northern Ireland through the years, changes have been taking place which may well create the climate for a peaceful solution. The Commonwealth is waning and the future of Great Britain and the Republic of Ireland mutually lies with the European Economic Community. Scotland and Wales should soon have parliaments of their own. A federation of states within Europe or within the British Isles would seem to be a logical outcome and might well provide a framework for a new Ireland. In the last decade, too, there has been, if not a wind, at least a zephyr of change in the Roman Catholic Church. A more liberal Catholic church in Ireland would mean a less militant brand of Protestantism and would obviate some of the practical difficulties inherent in the Constitution of the Republic

525

of Ireland, which embodies the moral law of the Catholic Church.

The Crown remains a stumbling block. The majority in the Six Counties will not remit their allegiance, while for the Republic there can be no going back. An act of faith is required on both sides of the border. One wonders whether monarchy will survive in Britain for many more decades, but it will be a sad thing if abolition of the border must wait upon its demise.

SELECT BIBLIOGRAPHY

Barry, Tom: *Guerilla Days in Ireland*, Mercier Press (Cork), 1949.

Beaslai, Piaras: *Michael Collins and the Making of a New Ireland*, Phoenix Publishing Co. (Dublin), 1926.

Beaverbrook, Lord: *The Decline and Fall of Lloyd George*, Collins, 1963.

Bennett, Richard: *The Black and Tans*, Hulton, 1959.

Birkenhead, Frederick, 2nd Earl of: *F. E. Smith, first Earl of Birkenhead*, Eyre & Spottiswoode, 1959.

Birrell, Augustine: *Things Past Redress*, Faber, 1937.

Blake, Robert: *The Unknown Prime Minister*, Eyre & Spottiswoode, 1955.

Breen, Dan: *My Fight for Irish Freedom*, Revised edition Anvil Book. Tralee, 1964. (First published Talbot Press, Dublin, 1921.)

Brennan, Nial: *Dr. Mannix*, Angus & Robertson (Sydney), 1965.

Bromage, Mary C.: *De Valera and the March of a Nation*, Hutchinson, 1956.

Caulfield, Max: *The Easter Rebellion*, Muller, 1964.

Chavasse, Moirin: *Terence MacSwiney*, Clonmore & Reynolds (Dublin), 1961.

Clark, Wallace: *Guns in Ulster*, Constabulary Gazette, Belfast, 1967.

Collier, Basil: *Brasshat: A Biography of Field Marshal Sir Henry Wilson 1864-1922*, Secker & Warburg, 1961.

Collins, Michael: *The Path to Freedom*, Talbot Press (Dublin), 1922.

Coogan, Timothy Patrick: *Ireland Since the Rising*, Pall Mall, 1966.

Crozier, Brigadier-General F. P.: *Ireland for Ever*, Cape, 1932.

Curtis, Edmund: *A History of Ireland*, Methuen, 1936, and U.P., 1964.

Dalton, Charles: *With the Dublin Brigade 1917-1921*, Davies, 1929.

Fergusson, Sir James: *The Curragh Incident*, Faber, 1964.

Gallagher, Frank: *The Anglo-Irish Treaty*, Hutchinson, 1965.

Gleeson, James: *Bloody Sunday*, Davies, 1962.

Greaves, C. Desmond: *The Life and Times of James Connolly*, Lawrence & Wishart, 1961.

Gwynn, Denis: *The History of Partition (1912-1925)*, Browne & Nolan (Dublin), 1950.

Hammond, J. L.: *C. P. Scott of the Manchester Guardian*, Bell, 1934.

527

Holt, Edgar: *Protest in Arms*, Putnam, 1960.

Hone, Joseph: *W. B. Yeats*, Macmillan, 1962.

Inglis, Brian: *West Briton*, Faber, 1962.

King, Clifford: *The Orange and the Green*, MacDonald, 1965.

Lavery, Sir John: *The Life of a Painter*, Cassell, 1940.

Lazenby, Elizabeth: *Ireland—a Catspaw*, Boswell, 1928.

Leslie, Shane: *The Irish Tangle*, MacDonald, 1946.

Lloyd George, David: *War Memoirs*, Odhams, 1933-6.

Lloyd George, Richard: *Lloyd George*, Muller, 1960.

Macardle, Dorothy: *The Irish Republic*, Irish Press (Dublin), 1951.

Macardle, Dorothy: *Tragedies of Kerry*, Irish Book Bureau.

MacBride, Maud Gonne: *A Servant of the Queen*, Gollancz, 1938.

Macready, General Sir Nevil: *Annals of an Active Life*, Hutchinson, 1942.

Martin, F. X.: *The Howth Gun-Running 1914*, Browne & Nolan (Dublin), 1964.

Neeson, Eoin: *The Civil War in Ireland*, Mercier Press (Cork), 1966.

Nicolson, Harold: *King George the Fifth*, Constable, 1952.

O'Brien, William and Ryan, Desmond: *Devoy's Postbag, 1871-1928*, C. J. Fallon (Dublin), 1953.

O'Casey, Sean: *Drums under the Windows*, Macmillan, 1945; *Innishfallen Fare Thee Well*, Macmillan, 1949.

O'Connor, Frank: *An Only Child*, Macmillan, 1961.

O'Connor, Frank: *The Big Fellow, Michael Collins and the Irish Revolution*, Clonmore & Reynolds (Dublin), Revised edition, 1965.

O'Connor, Ulick: *Oliver St. John Gogarty*, Cape, 1964.

O'Donnell, Peadar: *The Gates Flew Open*, Cape, 1932, Mercier, 1965.

O'Donoghue, Florence: *No Other Law*, Irish Press (Dublin), 1954.

O'Dubhghaill M.: *Insurrection Fires at Eastertide*, Mercier (Cork), 1966.

O'Faolain, Sean: *Life of Constance Markievicz*, Cape, 1934.

O'Hegarty, P. S.: *The Victory of Sinn Fein*, Talbot Press (Dublin), 1924.

O'Kelly, Seamus G.: *The Glorious Seven*, Irish News Service and Publicity, 1966.

O'Malley, Ernie: *On Another Man's Wound*, Four Square, 1961 (First published Rich & Cowan, 1936).

O'Sullivan, Donal: *The Irish Free State and its Senate*, Faber, 1940.

Owen, Frank: *Tempestuous Journey: Lloyd George, his life and Times*, Hutchinson, 1954.

Pakenham, Frank: *Peace by Ordeal*, Geoffrey Chapman, 1962 (First published Cape, 1935).

Phillips, W. Alison: *The Revolution in Ireland 1906-23*, Longmans Green, 1923.

Riddell, Lord: *Intimate Diary of the Peace Conference* and *After*, Gollancz, 1933.
Robinson, Sir Henry: *Memories Wise and Otherwise*, Cassell, 1923.
Ryan, Desmond: *Sean Treacy and the Third Tipperary Brigade IRA*, Kerryman (Tralee), 1945.
Shakespeare, Sir Geoffrey: *Let Candles be Brought In*, MacDonald, 1949.
Smuts, J. C.: *Jan Christian Smuts*, Cassell, 1952.
Taylor, Rex: *Michael Collins*, Hutchinson, 1958.
Taylor, Rex: *Assassination*, Hutchinson, 1961.
Tery, Simone: *En Irlande*, Flammarion (Paris), 1923.
Thomson, Malcolm: *Life and Times of Winston Churchill*, Odhams, 1965.
White, Terence de Vere: *Kevin O'Higgins*, Methuen, 1948.
Williams, Basil: *Erskine Childers*, Private printing, 1926.
Williams, Desmond, Ed.: *The Irish Struggle 1916-1926*, Routledge and Kegan Paul, 1966.

American Commission on Conditions in Ireland—Interim Report: London, 1921.
Ghosts of Kilmainham: The Kilmainham Jail Restoration Society, 1963.
Songs of the Irish Republic: National Publications Committee (Cork), 1965.
With the IRA in the Fight for Freedom: The Kerryman, (Tralee).

Newspapers, periodicals etc.

Belfast Telegraph
Blackwood's Magazine
Bray and South Dublin Herald
Cork Examiner
Daily Mail
Daily News
Dundalk Democrat
Freeman's journal
Irish Bulletin
Irish Independent
Irish News
Irish Times
Irish Weekly Independent
The Kerryman
Kerry People
Kilkenny People
Leader
Limerick Chronicle

Limerick Echo
Manchester Guardian
Mayo News
Munster Express
Nation
New Statesman
Northern Whig
Sligo Independent
Sunday Dispatch
The Times
Tipperary Star
War News

British Cabinet Documents at Public Record Office, London
CAB 41 Letters from Prime Minister to King. (These were the
        only records of Cabinet meetings up to November, 1916.)
CAB 23 War Cabinet and Cabinet Minutes (called Conclusions
        from August, 1919).
CAB 2 Cabinet papers and memoranda, G.T. and C.P. Series.
CAB 43 Conferences on Ireland: record of Treaty negotiations
        (22N143) and documents (SF series).
CAB 27 Committees concerned with Provisional Government and
        legislation dealing with Irish affairs.

Dail Eireann

Official Report for periods August 16th to 26th, 1921 and
    February 28th to June 8th, 1922.
Official Report of Debate on the Treaty.
Dail Reports from September 9th, 1922.

Miscellaneous contemporary documents, many in private hands,
were also consulted, among them a manuscript essay by Dr James
Lynch of Douglas, lent kindly by General Sean McEoin, General
Dalton's report on the Collins ambush and General Brennan's
report of the Limerick agreement, copies of which were lent
by their authors.

INDEX

536

539

540

Fontana Paperbacks

Fontana is a leading paperback publisher of fiction and non-fiction, with authors ranging from Alistair MacLean, Agatha Christie and Desmond Bagley to Solzhenitsyn and Pasternak, from Gerald Durrell and Joy Adamson to the famous Modern Masters series.

In addition to a wide-ranging collection of internationally popular writers of fiction, Fontana also has an outstanding reputation for history, natural history, military history, psychology, psychiatry, politics, economics, religion and the social sciences.

All Fontana books are available at your bookshop or newsagent; or can be ordered direct. Just fill in the form and list the titles you want.

FONTANA BOOKS, Cash Sales Department, G.P.O. Box 29, Douglas, Isle of Man, British Isles. Please send purchase price, plus 8p per book. Customers outside the U.K. send purchase price, plus 10p per book. Cheque, postal or money order. No currency.

NAME (Block letters)

ADDRESS

While every effort is made to keep prices low, it is sometimes necessary to increase prices on short notice. Fontana Books reserve the right to show new retail prices on covers which may differ from those previously advertised in the text or elsewhere.